This book is dedicated to daydreamers, berry pickers, bird watchers, tree climbers, grass dancers, valentine senders, wind storm screamers, night sky gazers and my mom.

— SHELLEY NIRO

co-curated by
Melissa Bennett
Art Gallery of Hamilton
Greg Hill
National Gallery of Canada
David W. Penney
Smithsonian's National Museum
of the American Indian

organized and circulated by the
Art Gallery of Hamilton
with the
**Smithsonian's National Museum
of the American Indian**
and with curatorial support from the
National Gallery of Canada

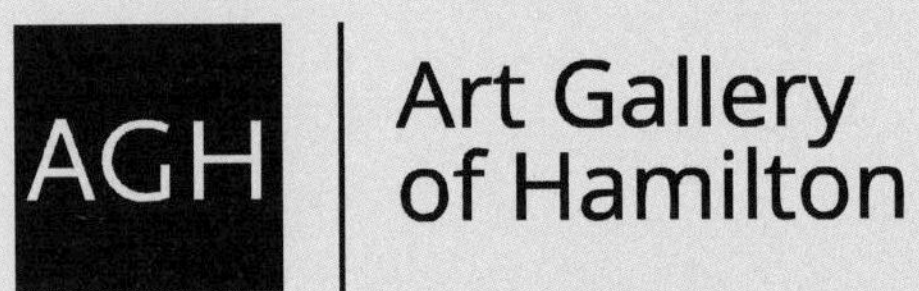

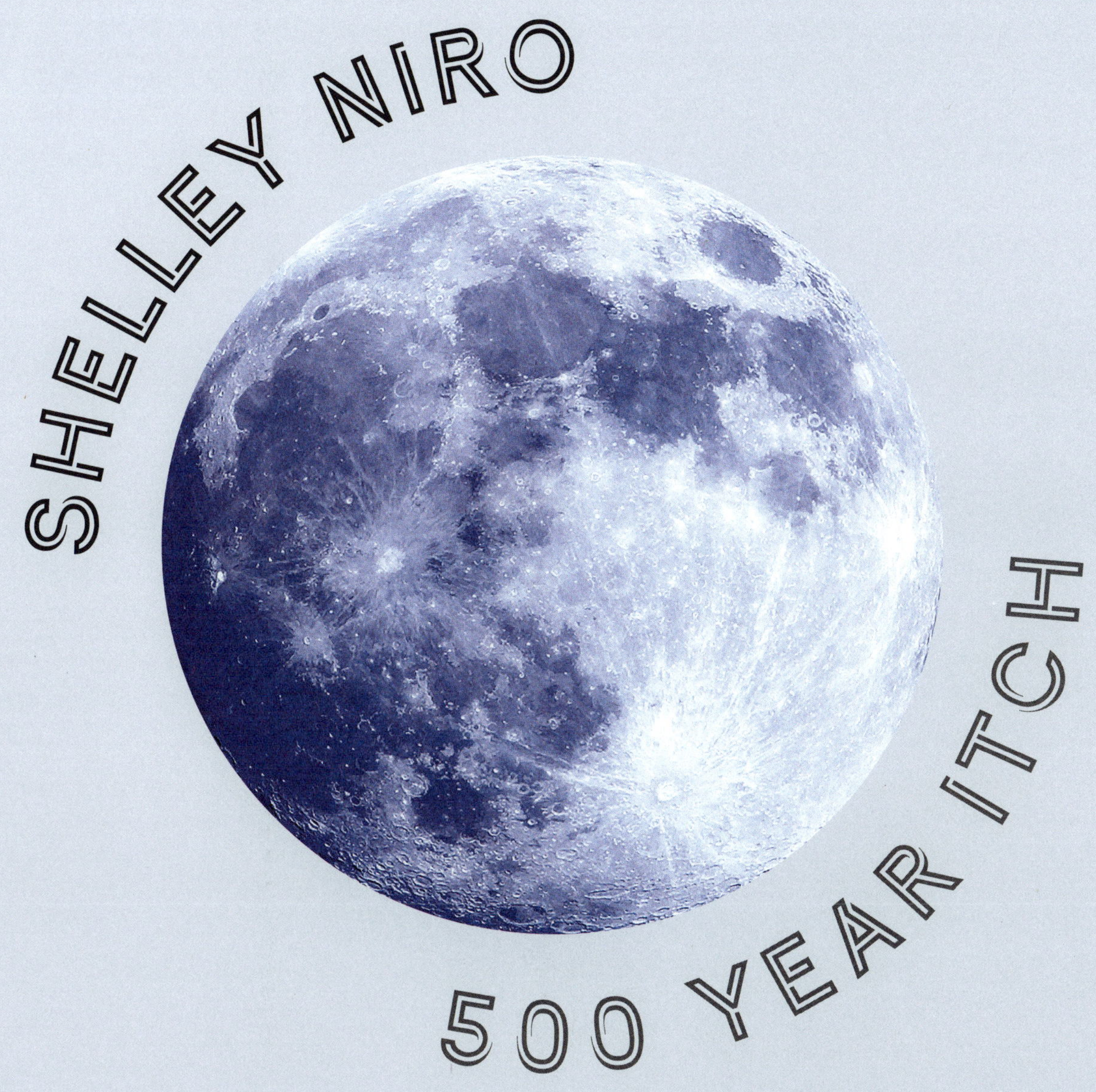

SHELLEY NIRO
500 YEAR ITCH

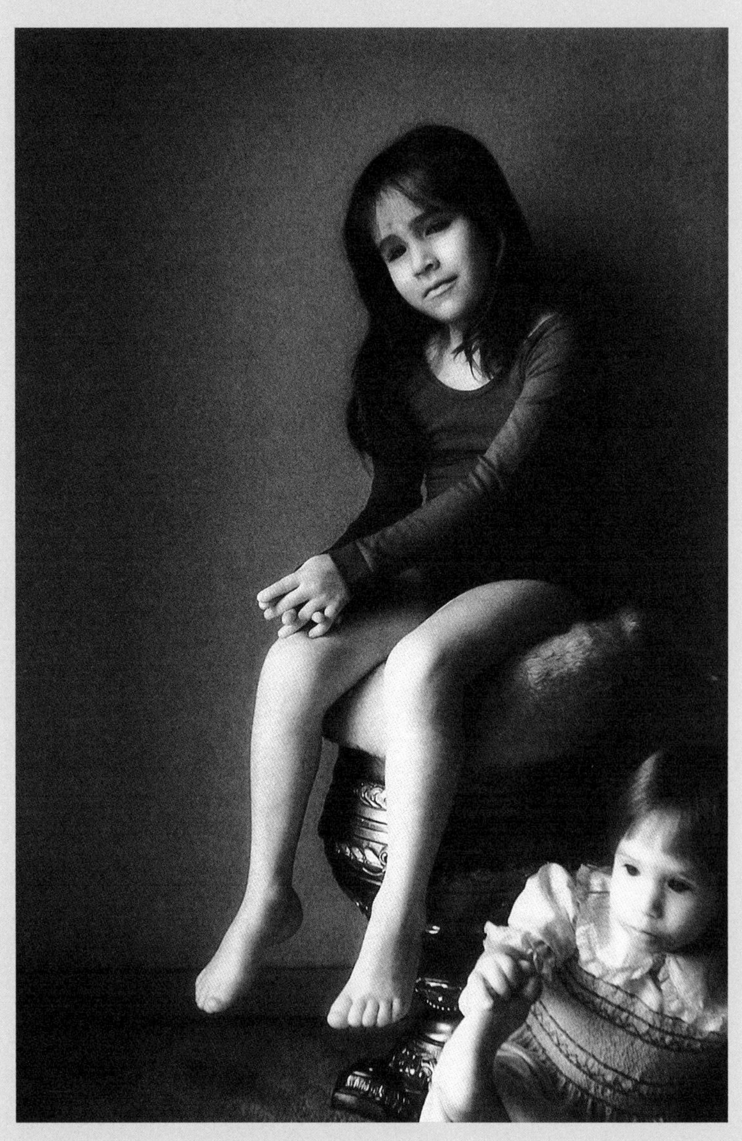

 Sisters, 1982 / 1987

SHELLEY FALCONER PRESIDENT + CEO, ART GALLERY OF HAMILTON

That summer a black bear's muzzle was coated in shellac from the aerosol can she bit through on my mother's porch. A half-century after my grandmother's mother said, don't ever shoot a black bear, they are my people. So I continue to speak more than this mortuary sunrise where I am only just alive.

Boozhoo, today is over.

— Liz Howard, "Euro – Anishinaabekwe – Noli Turbare"

Shelley Niro has played an increasingly prominent and catalytic role on the visual stage in Canada for more than four decades, with work encompassing painting, photography, printmaking, mixed media, beadwork, video, and film.

I was introduced to Niro's work in 1995, five years after the 1990 Kanesatake Resistance,[1] when her work *The Rebel* (1987, pp. 20–21) played a pivotal role in the group exhibition *AlterNative: Contemporary Photo Compositions* at the McMichael Canadian Art Collection. Tapping into deep feminine archetypes with an amused, radiant intelligence, Niro's portrait of her mother draped provocatively on the hood of the family car told me a new, exciting story about the lives of First Nations mothers and daughters.

Fast forward to 2015, when Shelley Niro's work dramatically came to my attention again in an article written by Jon Wells in the *Hamilton Spectator* entitled "'Warrior' Art Not Wanted Anymore at Hamilton Golf Club."[2] The article outlined the controversy surrounding Niro's *Resting With Warriors* (2001, pp. 212–213) four regal woodblock prints representing her matriarchal

Iroquois Ancestors and symbolizing four important cultural characteristics: emotion, strength, intellect, and spirit. Wells reported that although the golf club had purchased the works, the board had made a decision to sell the prints and replace them with trophies and golf memorabilia. Niro had invested "integrity" into her work, according to the article, and declared that witnessing the journey of the prints from the gallery to the prestigious golf club—and then having them removed—was "difficult to take."

Justice Sinclair's Truth and Reconciliation Commission Report[3] had been released only a few months previously, rendering the article all the more disturbing and unsettling. However, for me, as the Art Gallery of Hamilton's newly appointed Director, Wells's exposé catalyzed the immediate decision to acquire *Resting With Warriors*, our first Niro work, and cemented our decision to support and prioritize a meaningful Indigenous collection.

The Art Gallery of Hamilton (AGH) and the Smithsonian's National Museum of the American Indian (NMAI) are proud to collaborate with Shelley Niro in bringing the first complete retrospective of her work to North America. Throughout her forty-year career, Niro has continued to push the boundaries of multiple mediums while exploring Indigenous identity and history with complexity, nuance, and her signature wit. The AGH and the NMAI wish to thank Shelley Niro for her extensive practice and for her advocacy, unique voice, and enthusiasm for this project. Both institutions are also deeply indebted to the collectors and institutions that have agreed to lend works by Shelley Niro from their collections for the exhibition and tour.

The exhibition was developed by a team of curators led by the AGH's Senior Curator of Contemporary Art, Melissa Bennett, NMAI's Associate Director of Museum Scholarship, David W. Penney, and the National Gallery of Canada's Greg Hill, the Audain Chair and Senior Curator of Indigenous Art, who combined their respective expertise and cultural sensitivities. Together they have produced a comprehensive survey of Niro's visual practice. We would also like to acknowledge the commitment of the professional teams at the AGH and NMAI who contributed to the success of this project: in Hamilton, Tobi Bruce, Melissa Neil, Christine Braun, Greg Dawe, Paula Esteves Mauro, and Bo Shin; and in Washington and New York, Cynthia Chavez Lamar (San Felipe Pueblo, Hopi, Tewa, Navajo), Gerry Breen, Nicholas Fonseca, John George, Betsy Gordon, Adrien Mooney, Susanna Stieff, Barbara Suhr, and Jennifer Wood.

The publication takes an intentionally fragmented approach to the essays and images and was edited by Laurel Saint Pierre and designed by Barr Gilmore. We are grateful to authors Melissa Bennett, Greg Hill, David W. Penney, Lori Beavis, Sally Frater, Adriana Greci Green, Bryce Kanbara, Madeline Lennon, Nancy Mithlo, and Hulleah J. Tsinhnahjinnie for providing such thoughtful and insightful texts.

We are especially indebted to the Canada Council for the Arts for major funding of this project, a contribution that made the touring and production of this exhibition and publication possible, and acknowledge the continuing support of the Ontario Arts Council, the Canada Council for the Arts and the City of Hamilton as well as the championing of our Board of Directors, Governors, donors, and members.

Finally, we are grateful for the opportunity that Shelley Niro has provided for these two North American institutions to collaborate and produce this extraordinary project. Her work profoundly teaches us about the past while looking boldly into the future.

NOTES

1. The Oka Crisis, also known as the Kanesatake Resistance or the Mohawk Resistance at Kanesatake, was a seventy-eight-day standoff (July 11 – September 26, 1990) between Mohawk protesters, Quebec police, and the Canadian Army.
2. John Wells. "'Warrior' art not wanted anymore at Hamilton golf club," *Hamilton Spectator*, November 25, 2015, https://www.thespec.com/news/hamilton-region/2015/11/25/warrior-art-not-wanted-anymore-at-hamilton-golf-club.html.
3. Truth and Reconciliation Commission of Canada, *Canada's Residential Schools: The Final Report of the Truth and Reconciliation Commission of Canada*, 2015.

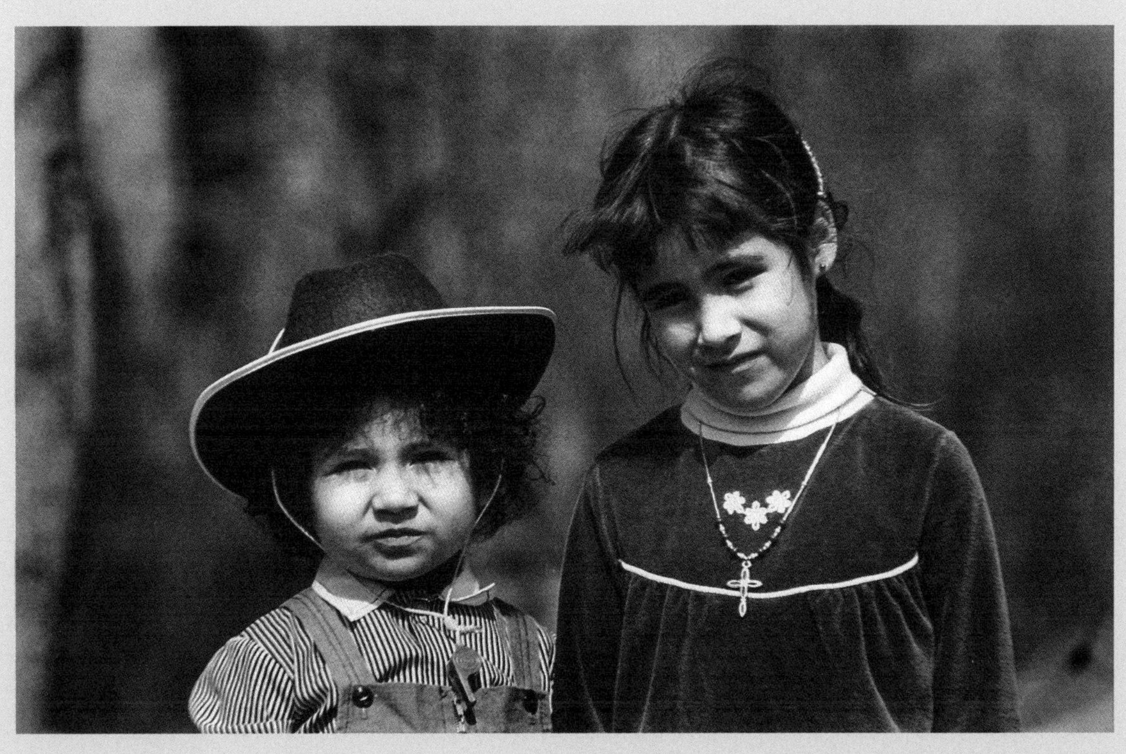

9

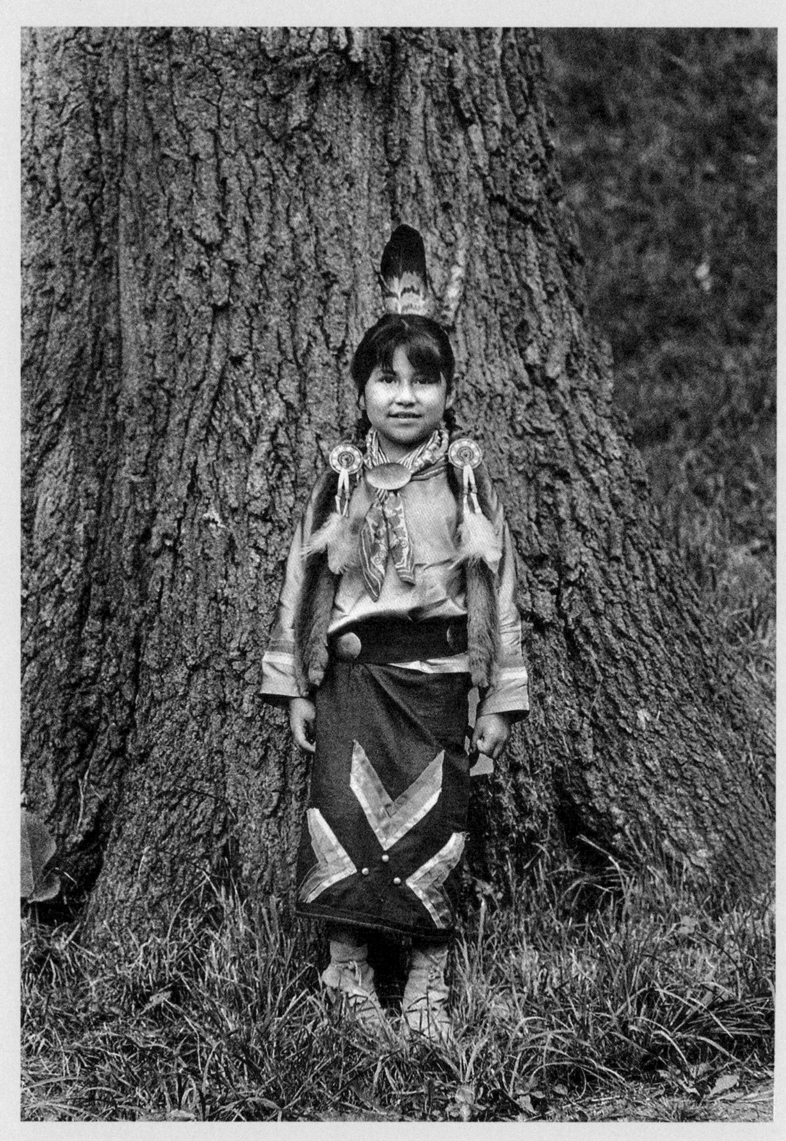

   Crystal, 1987

SHELLEY NIRO SURRENDERS NOTHING ALWAYS

TOBI BRUCE DIRECTOR, EXHIBITIONS + COLLECTIONS, ART GALLERY OF HAMILTON

When Melissa Bennett and I met with Shelley Niro one morning in October 2017 and asked her if she would be interested in working with us and the Art Gallery of Hamilton to mount her first-ever major retrospective, she leaned forward in her chair, smiled, and said, "Let's do it!" The fact that a retrospective wasn't already in the works, following four decades of ground-breaking work, was a bit confounding, but it was also not surprising given the relative lack of major solo exhibitions accorded senior women artists in Canada.

Shelley Niro's retrospective was long overdue.

We were clear from the beginning that we envisioned a project that was highly collaborative, and that Shelley would invite many of the curators, historians, friends, and colleagues who had been part of her journey to participate in some way. After all, community is central to how Shelley lives her life. Greg Hill, the National Gallery of Canada's Audain Chair and Senior Curator of Indigenous Art, who has been a steadfast and committed champion of her work for three decades, was the first name she mentioned. David W. Penney from the Smithsonian's National Museum of the American Indian, who Shelley has known for several years, also soon came on board. The past four years have seen Melissa and Shelley develop a shared sense of trust through studio visits, interviews, and always a shared meal. The three co-curators also met regularly during this period to think about Shelley, her work, and what defines her practice. The result is *Shelley Niro: 500 Year Itch*.

This accompanying publication also includes the insights of others who have worked closely with Shelley over the years, and who have come to know her in personal and nuanced ways. Lori Beavis, Bryce Kanbara, Sally Frater, Adriana Greci Green, Madeline Lennon, Nancy Marie Mithlo, and Hulleah J. Tsinhnahjinnie all jumped at the chance to participate, each seemingly waiting for the invitation, aware that Shelley's time was nigh. They each explore facets of Shelley's extraordinarily varied and complex practice, suffusing their intellectual contributions with a deep-seated understanding of the artist herself. Our deepest acknowledgment and thanks to each of them.

This introduction is a modest attempt to encapsulate something which really cannot be encapsulated. I've been thinking about how to articulate what it is about Shelley and her practice that is so unique, and that sets her so apart. There is the multifaceted intersectionality of her identities: Mohawk, woman, daughter, mother, aunt, artist, poet, and music-lover. There is the sheer extent of her artistic vocabularies: photography, painting, beading, printmaking, filmmaking, video, and sculpture. And then, critically, there are her bearing and the viewpoint and attitude she chooses to inhabit and advance in this world. It is the conflation of all of these elements that makes Shelley such an undeniable force.

Given the depth and breadth of her practice, Shelley has made relatively few straightforward self-portraits. Yet I would argue that her life's work thus far functions as an intricate, multidimensional and complex form of self-representation. In discussing with Greg Hill what elements of Rotinonhsyonni (Iroquian) culture define her thinking, Shelley replied, "you start with yourself." Hill further foregrounds Niro's "resolute assuredness in her entitlement to define herself" as central to her worldview and artistic practice.

In discussing Shelley's work, in fact, all of the authors either directly or indirectly tease out elements that reflect equally on the artist herself and on her practice. Madeline Lennon writes how she "cannot help but think of [the Canadian Museum of History's] *Sky Woman* (2001, p. 76) as a self-portrait." Lori Beavis ruminates about how the aviator cap, a repeated pictorial device for Shelley, "can be viewed as a symbol of preparedness, strength, and speed, moral goodness and adaptability" that also "symbolically represents the advantage of seeing things from a new point of view or having an expanded worldview." Nancy Marie Mithlo argues that "there is an agency at play fuelled not by a reactionary impulse, but by a deeply engaged observational perspective," and that Niro's "stoic approach... results in a clarity of perception that is at once familiar and yet oddly fresh." Bryce Kanbara observes that Niro's film scripts are "less plot-driven than... vehicles for character study" and notes the autobiographical elements in her film protagonists Mavis Dogblood and Mitzi Bearclaw. "Through the range of personalities and behaviours of her characters," he continues, "she divulges aspects of herself and what she knows of Indigenous identity and perspective." And Sally Frater beautifully concludes that the warriors in Niro's *Resting With Warriors* (2001, pp. 208, 211–213) are "resolute in their quiet determination" and that they "convey that we can move forward in love while simultaneously opening up multiple spaces for imagining," not unlike Niro herself.

Shelley consistently folds her understanding of past, her observance of present, and her dreams of future into an organic whole that is both forthcoming and fearless. She recognizes and occupies her place on the continuum. Her fury at past (and present) injustices does not preclude joy in the present nor hope for the future. "As an artist, I have no solutions," she has said, "but (my work) is something creative that can bring some joy into the lives of people. It's my contribution." [1] Crucially, this contribution is also grounded in love. In discussing her most recent film, *The Incredible 25th Year of Mitzi Bearclaw* (2019, p. 132), with Hulleah J. Tsinhnahjinnie, she says that "above all, it's about community and how we have to hang in there, making love the strongest emotion."

I recently sent Shelley an email asking her if she could identify three words that rise to the fore when she is in the act of creating, when she's in "the zone." Her response was immediate: focus, joy, temporality. These words go a long way in helping us understand not only Shelley's practice but also how she chooses to position herself in the world. She's also very funny. Humour and irony hover in and around everything she does. In that email exchange, she started by saying: "Thank you for this quirky question, Tobi. The three words I think about when I'm in my heightened sense of creativity are: WHAT'S FOR LUNCH? Just kidding." But don't be fooled. Her disarming, generous, patient, and caring disposition belies a profound wisdom and commitment to communicate stories that are urgent and life affirming. Shelley Niro is the Warrior, the Rebel, the Flying Woman, the Thinking Cap, and the Sky Woman of her creations. She begins from a place of reflection, proceeds to a place of knowing, and projects to a place of promise.

NOTES

1. Aruna Dutt, "The Incredible 25th Year of Mitzi Bearclaw: New film takes a comedic look at life on an Indigenous reserve," CBC Comedy, October 16, 2019, https://www.cbc.ca/comedy/the-incredible-25th-year-of-mitzi-bearclaw-new-film-takes-a-comedic-look-at-life-on-an-indigenous-reserve-1.5323390.

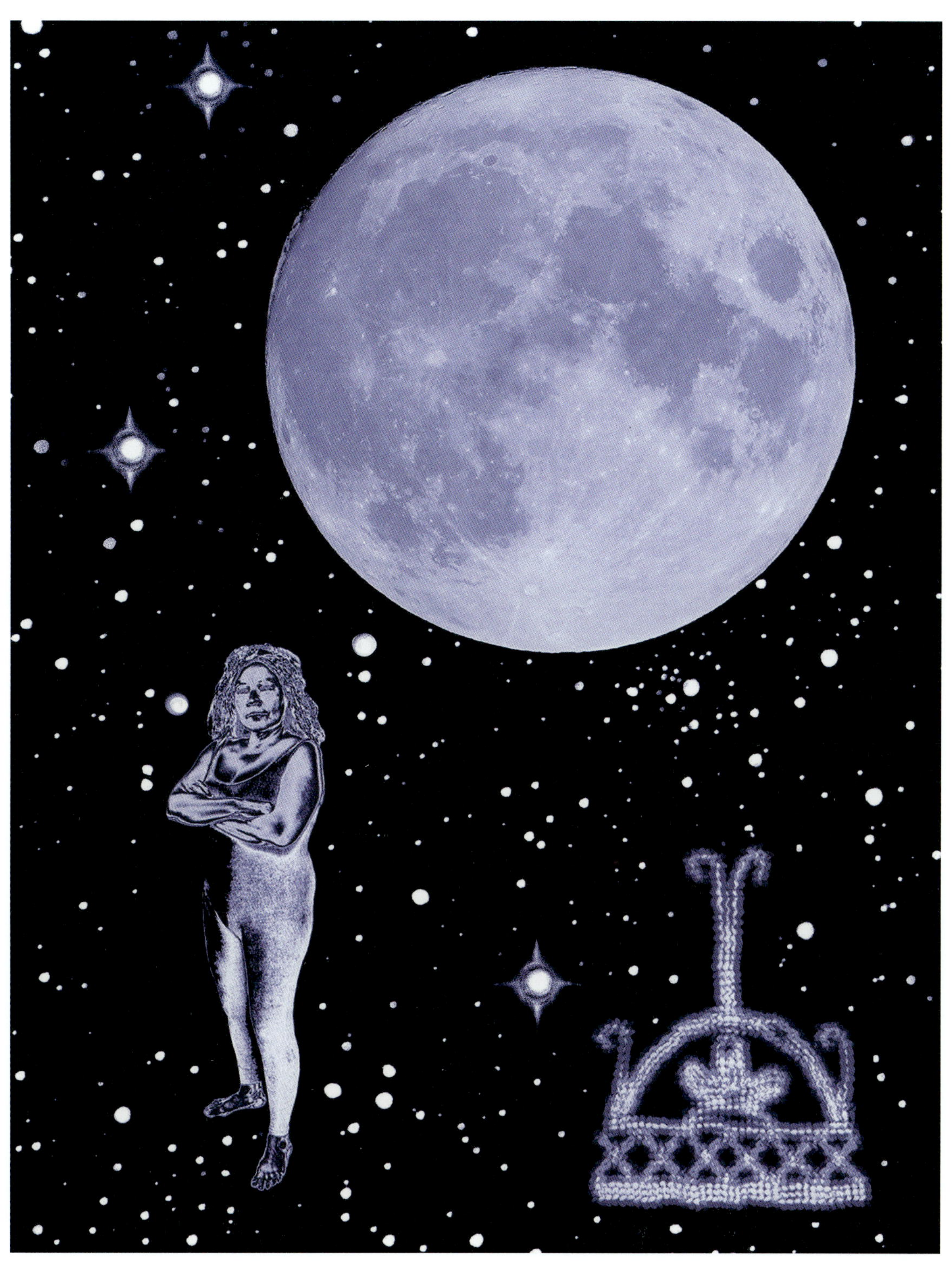

The Moon and Me and A Celestial Tree, 2010 / 2022

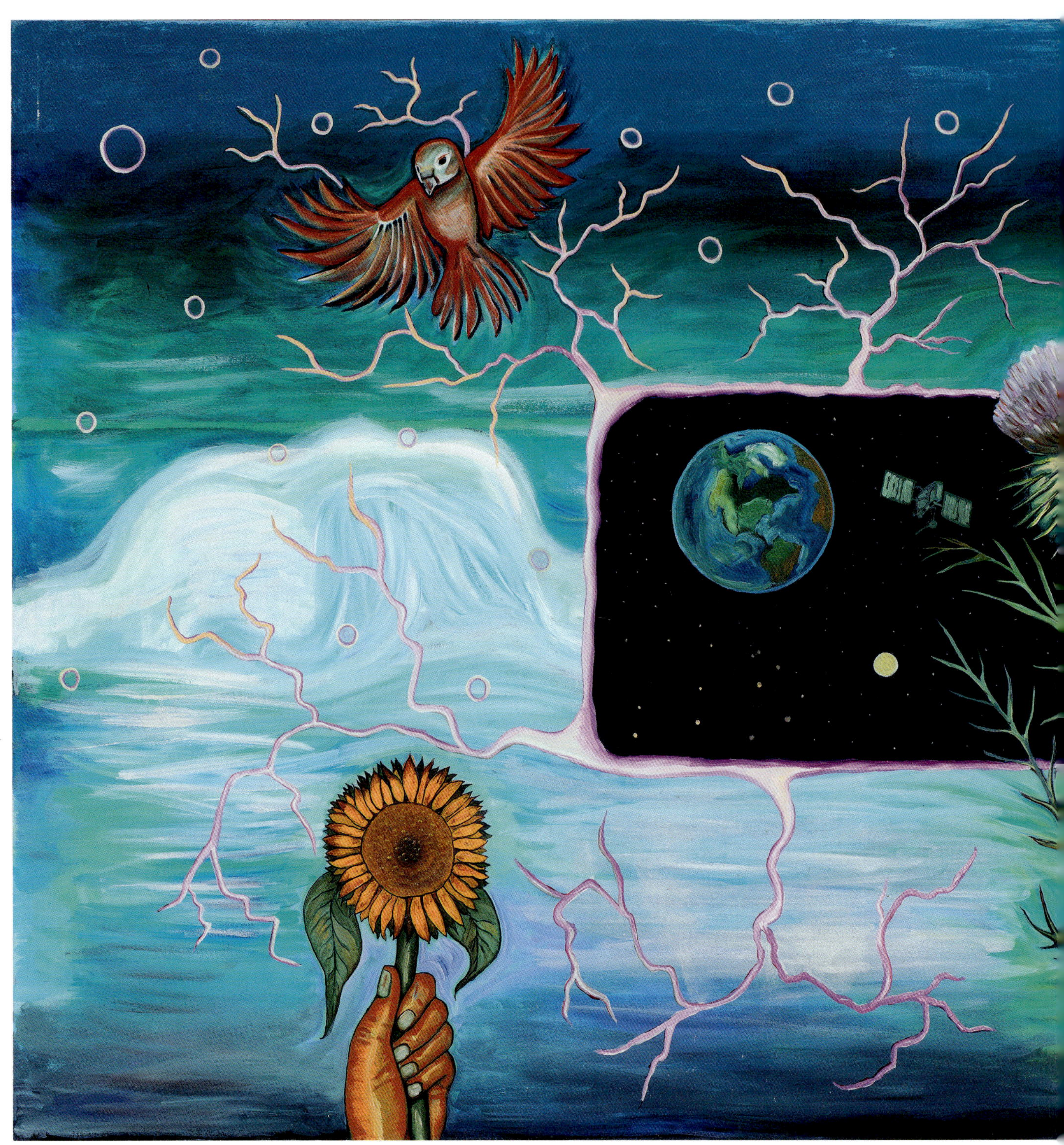

 Black Whole, 2021

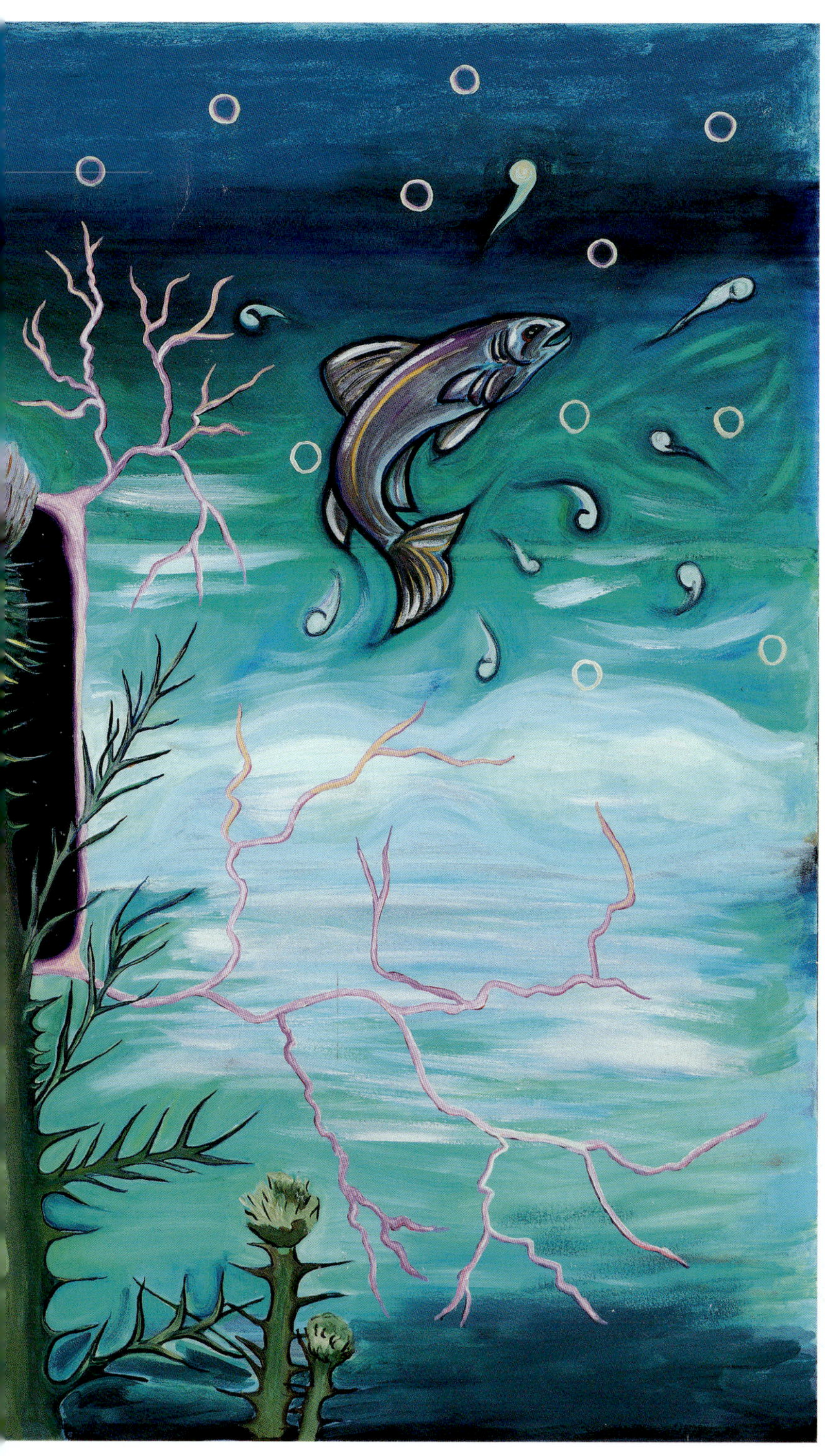

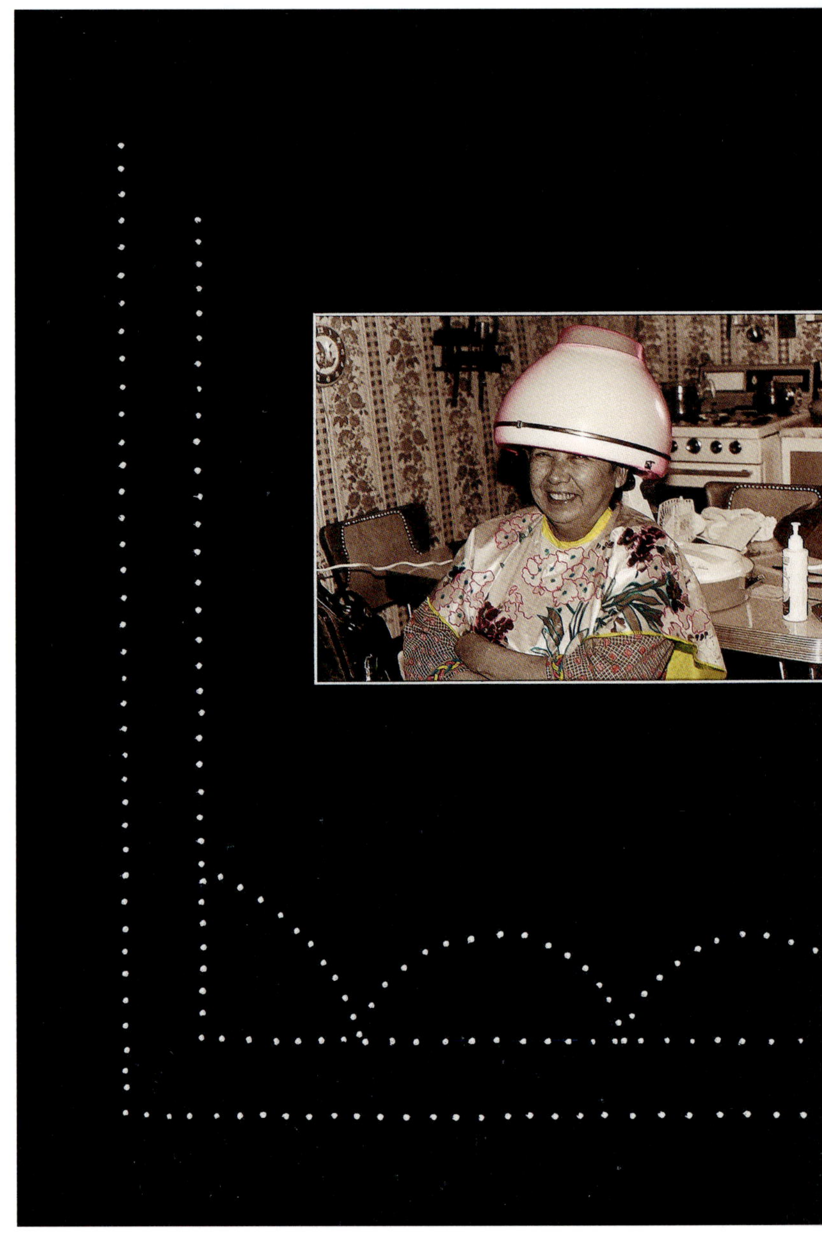

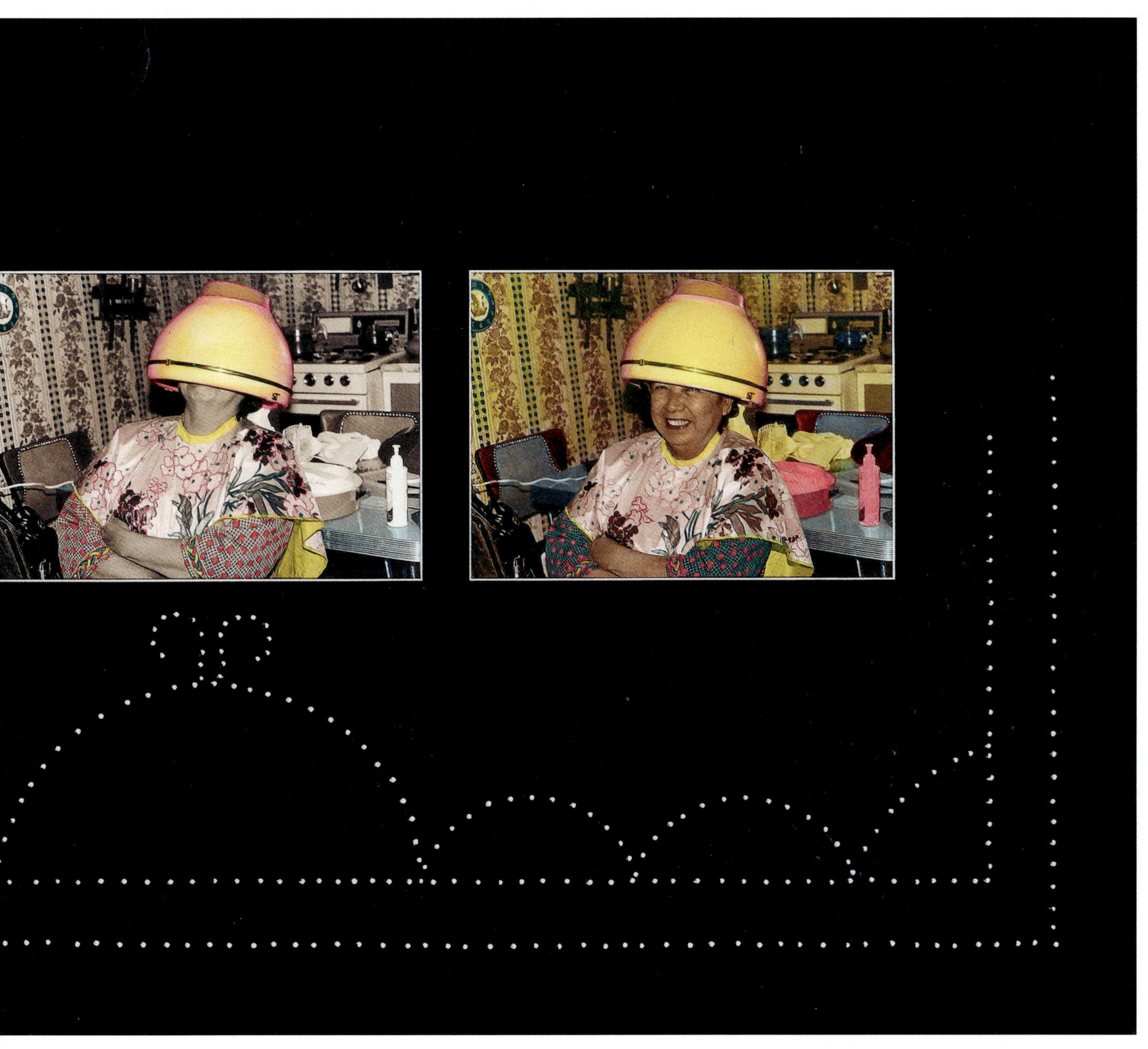

The Iroquois is a Highly Developed Matriarchal Society, 1989   17

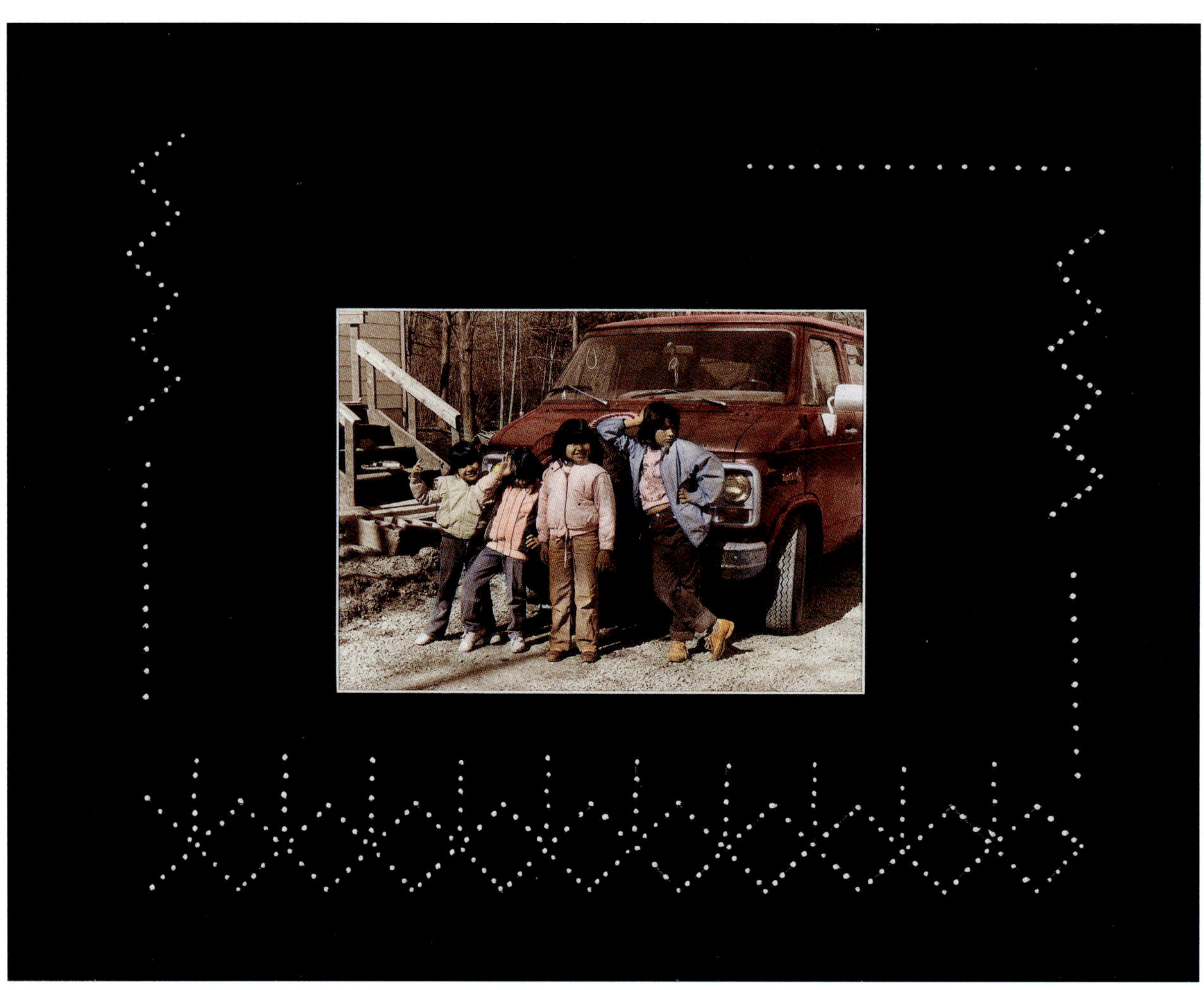

Bush Kids, 1982

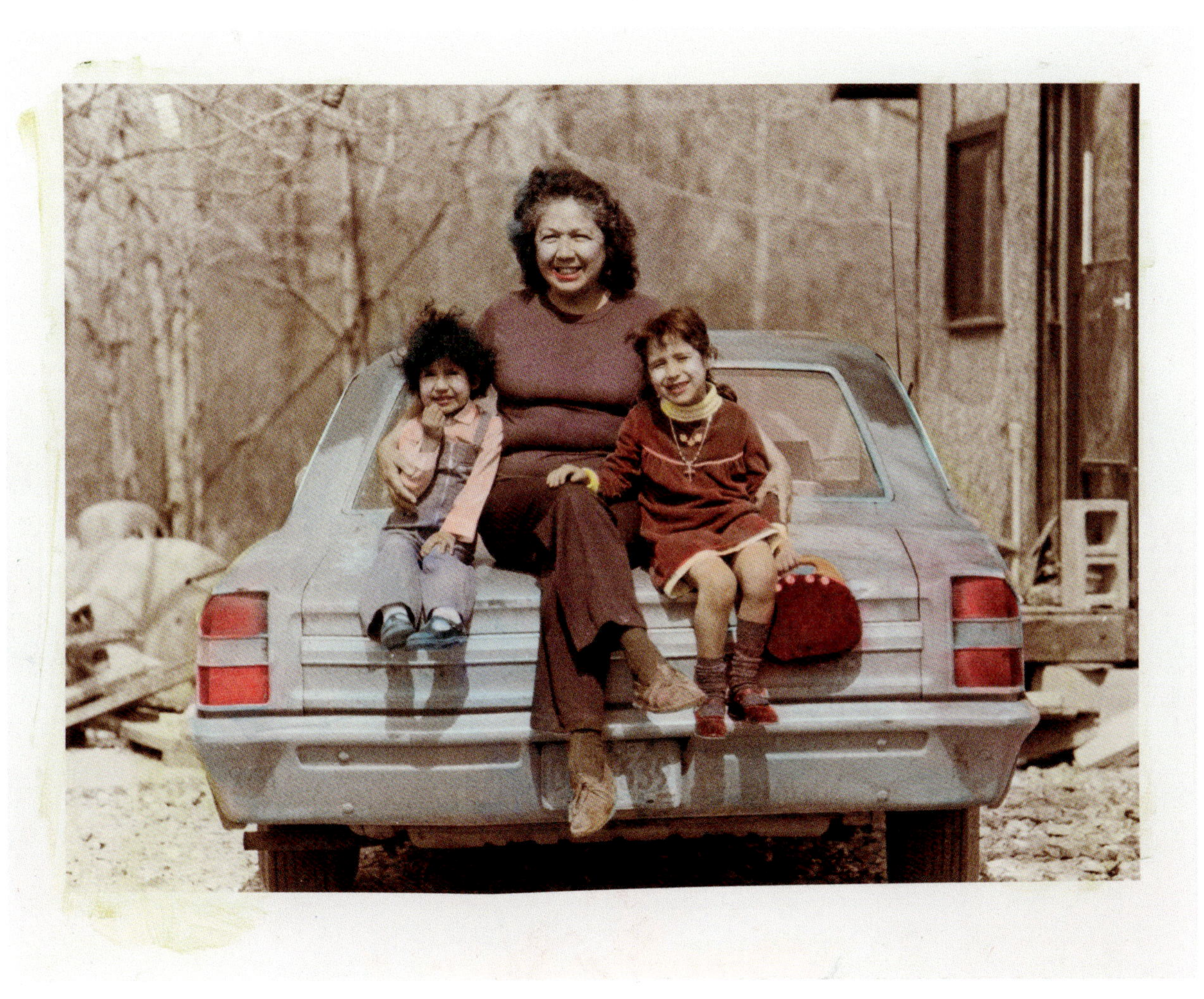

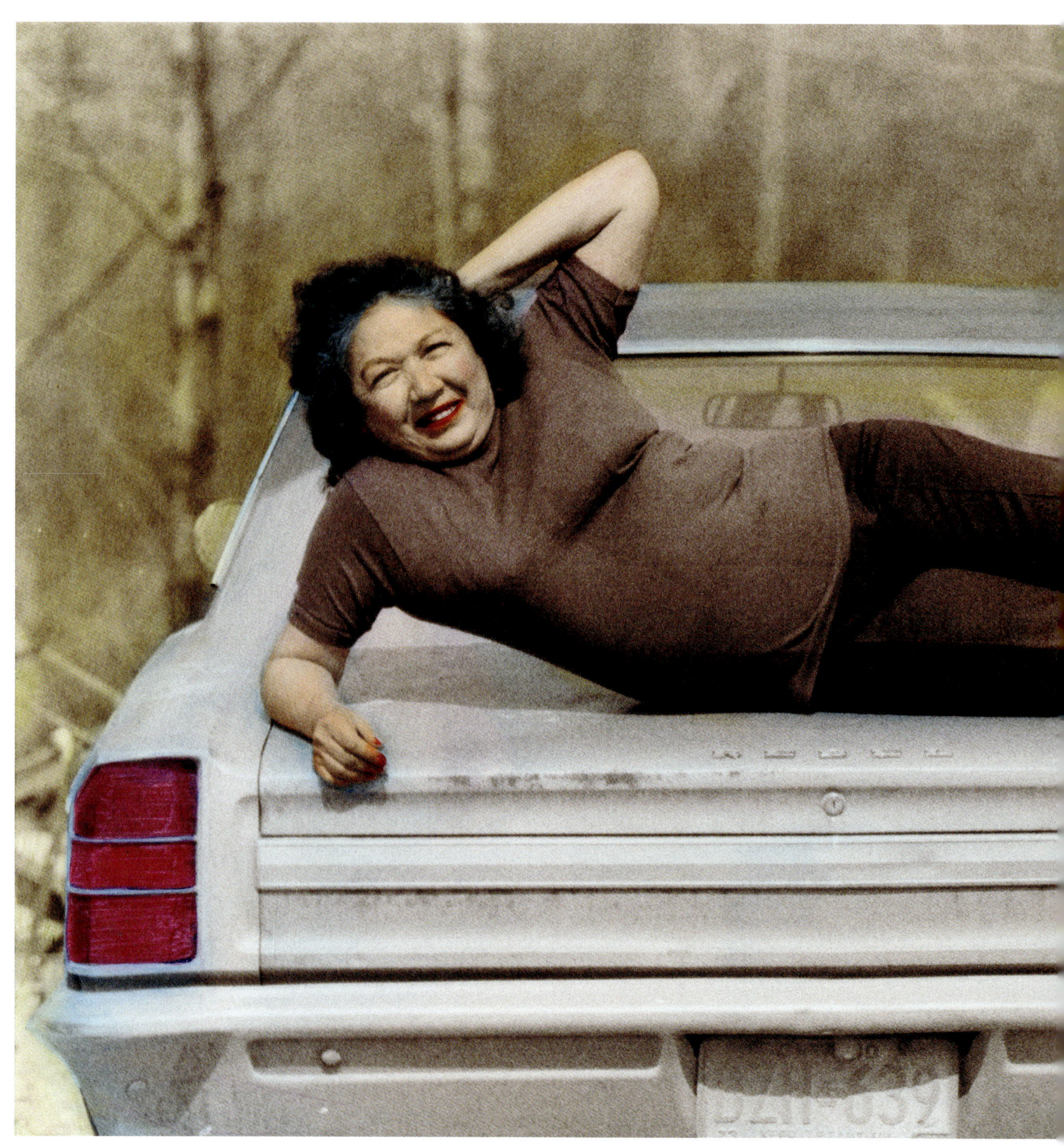

20 **The Rebel,** 1982 / 1987

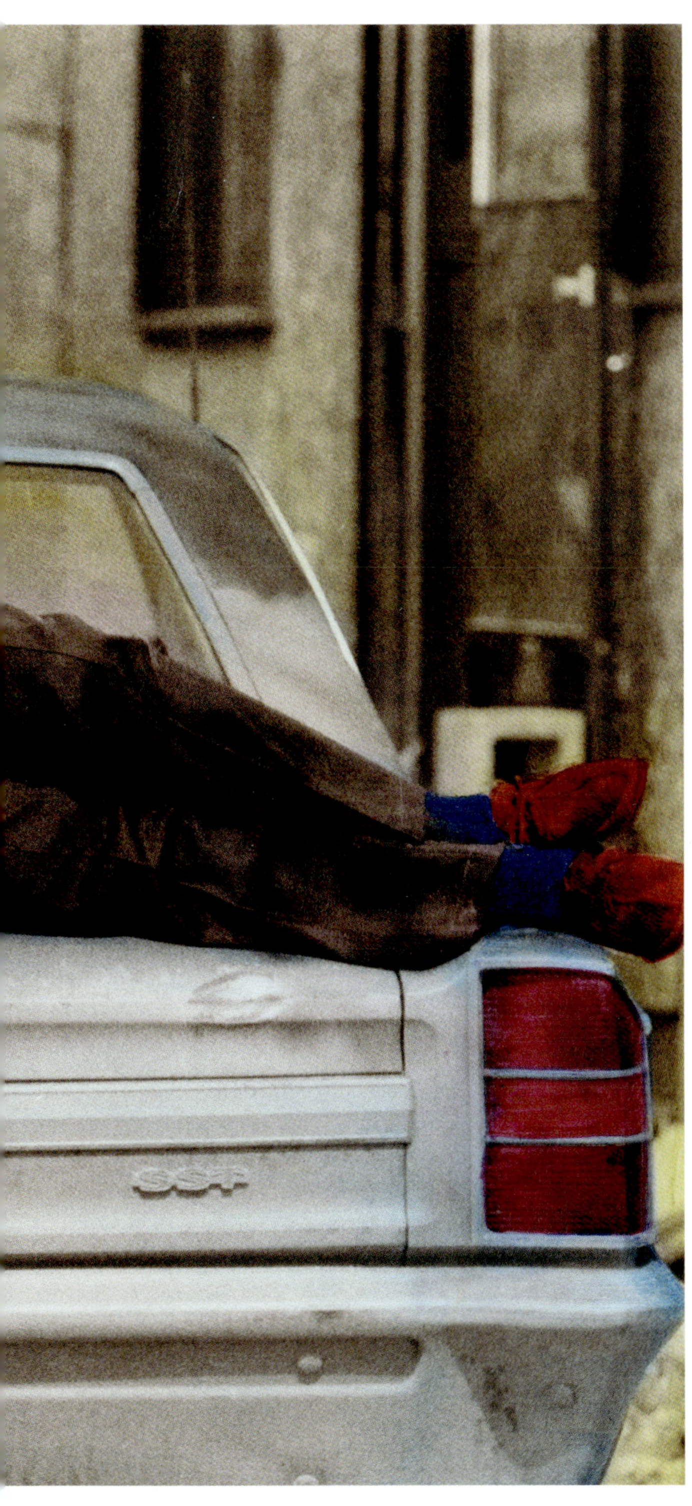

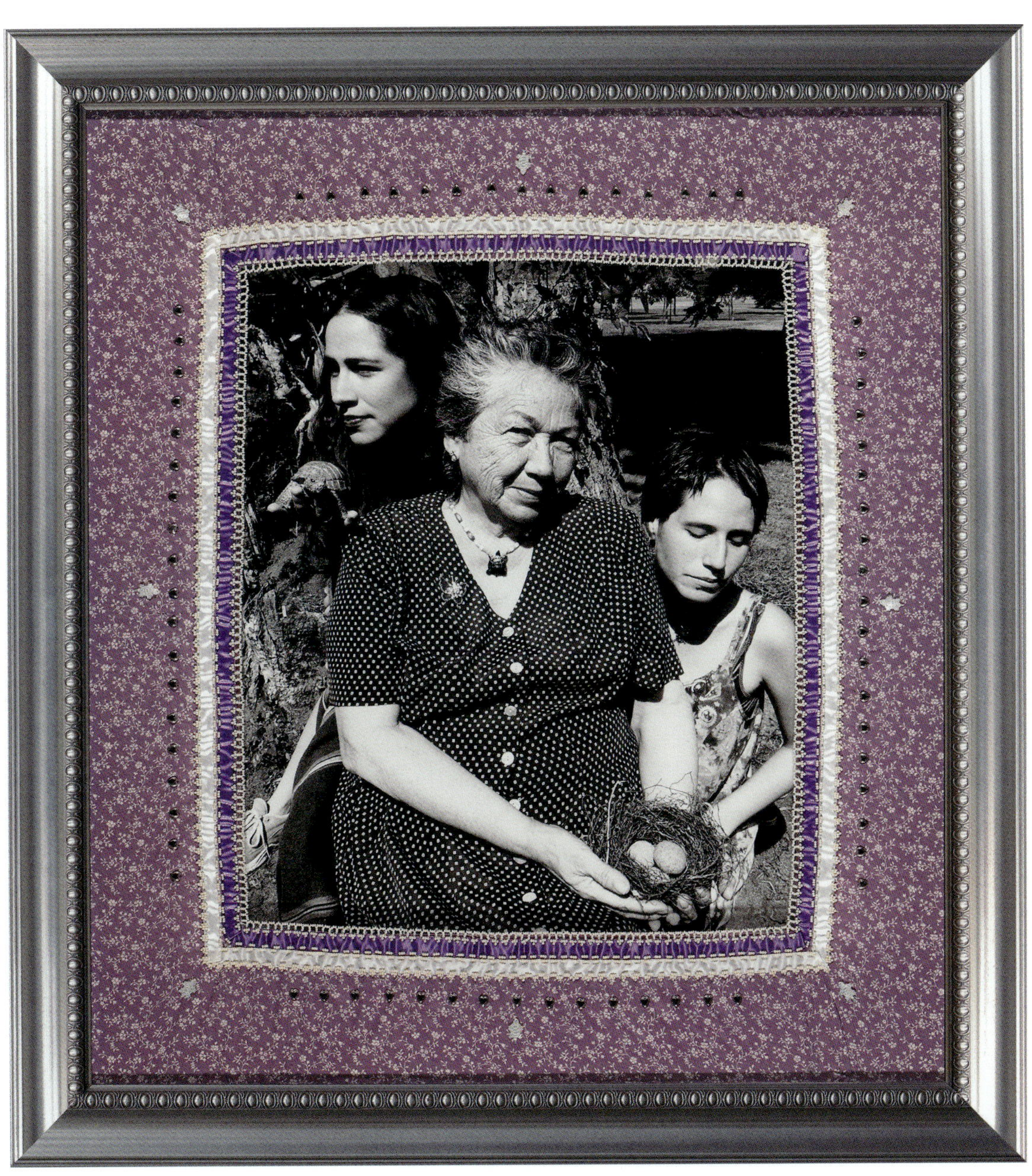

Time Travels Through Us, 1999

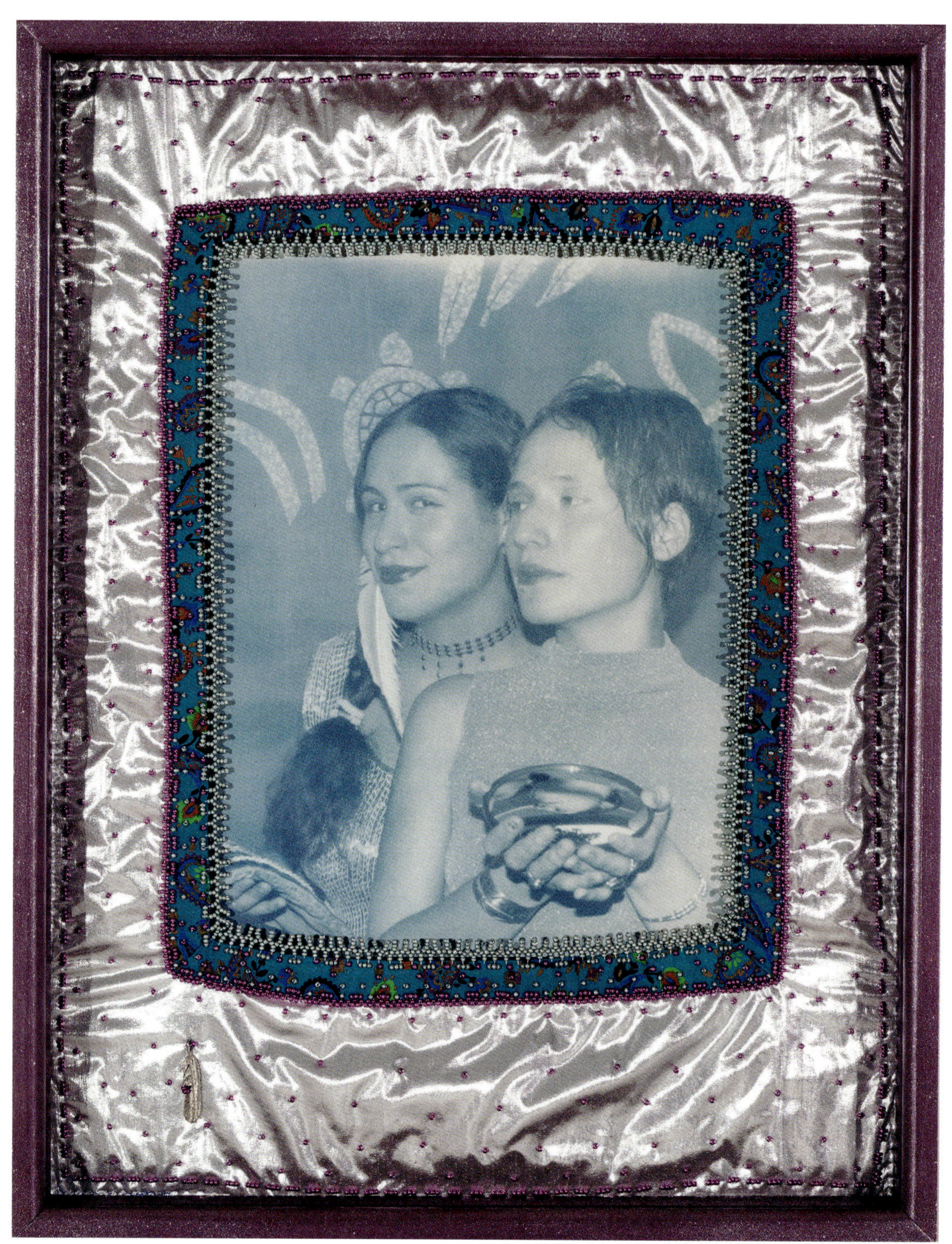

  My Girls, 2002

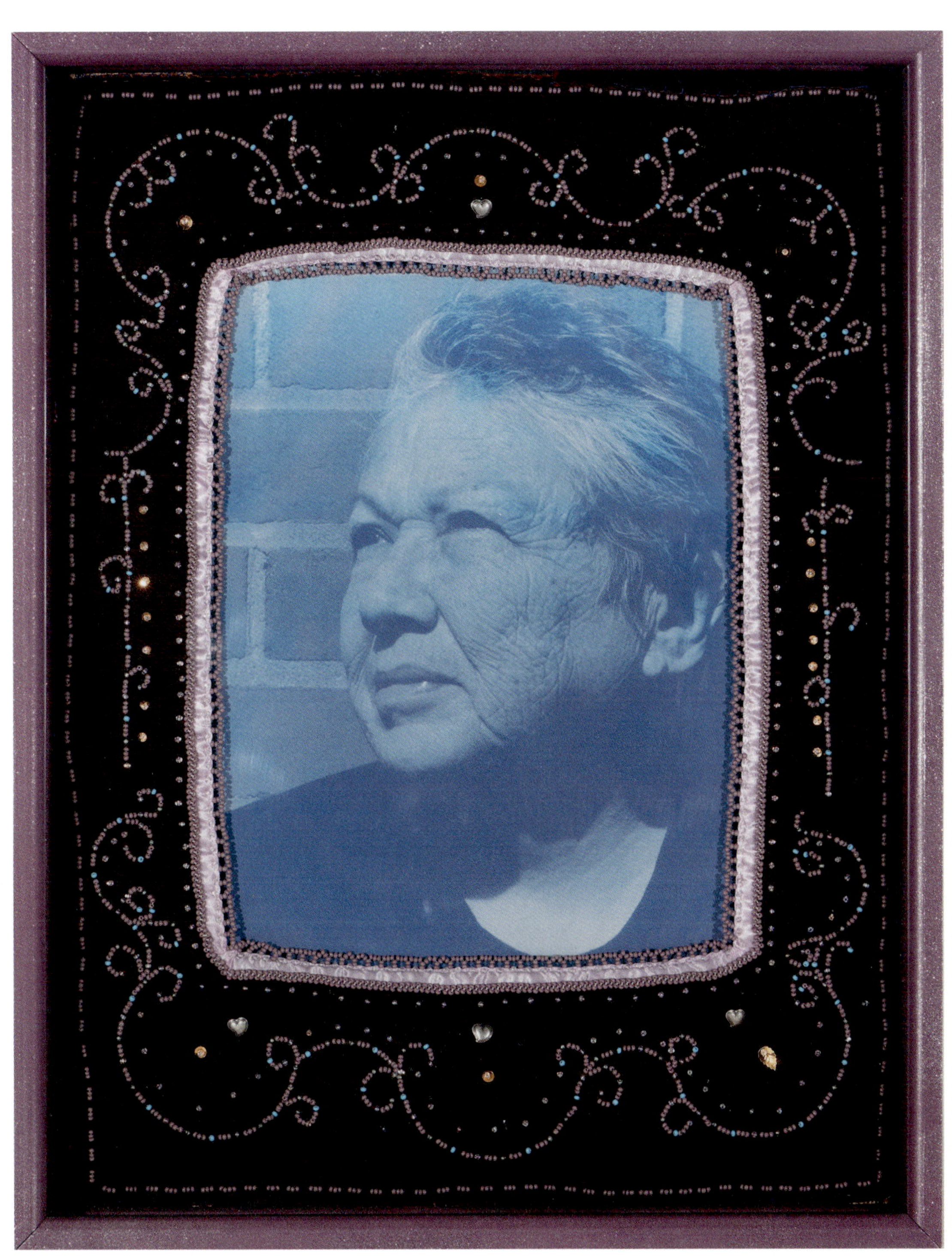

Chiquita, 2002

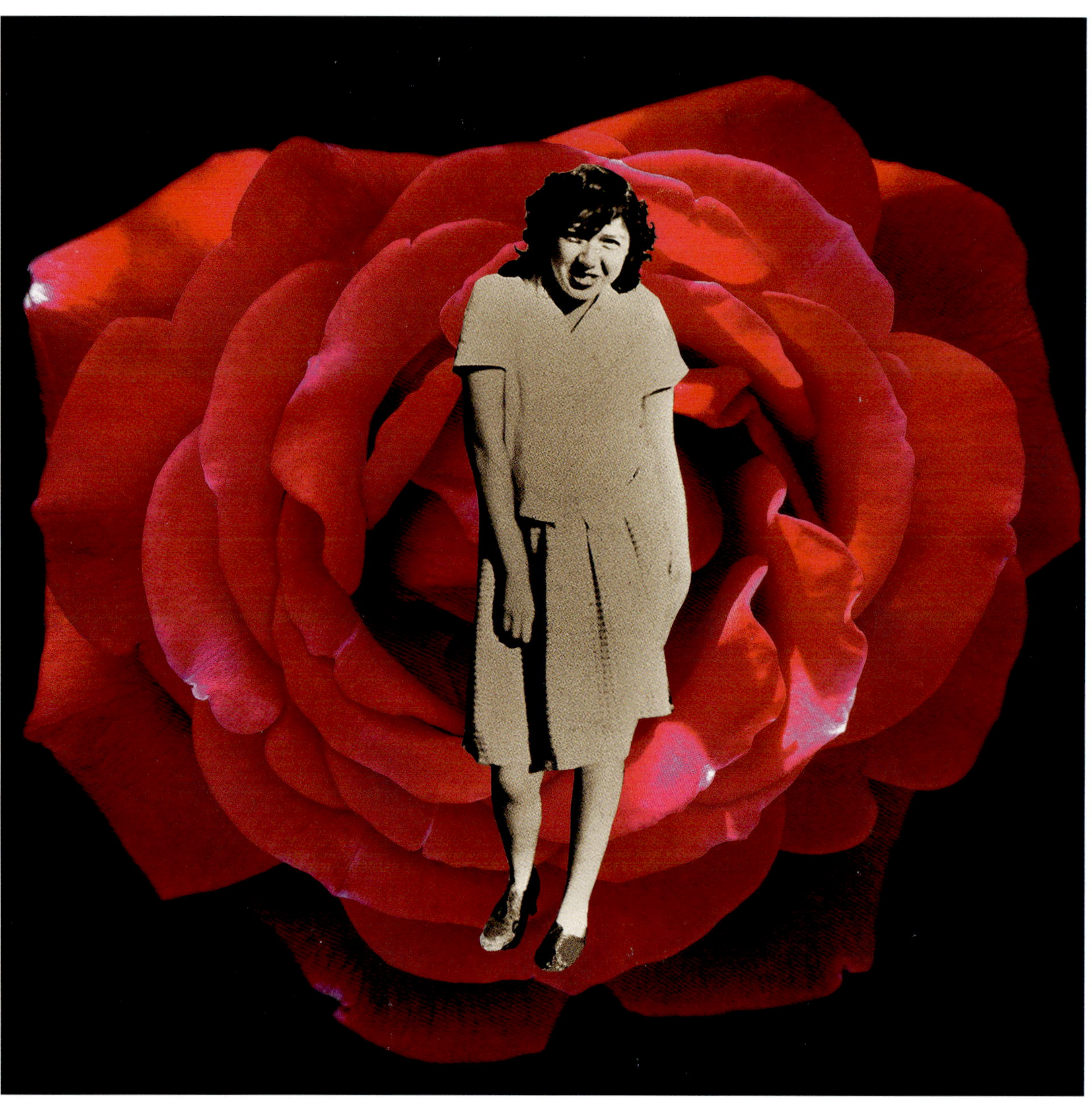

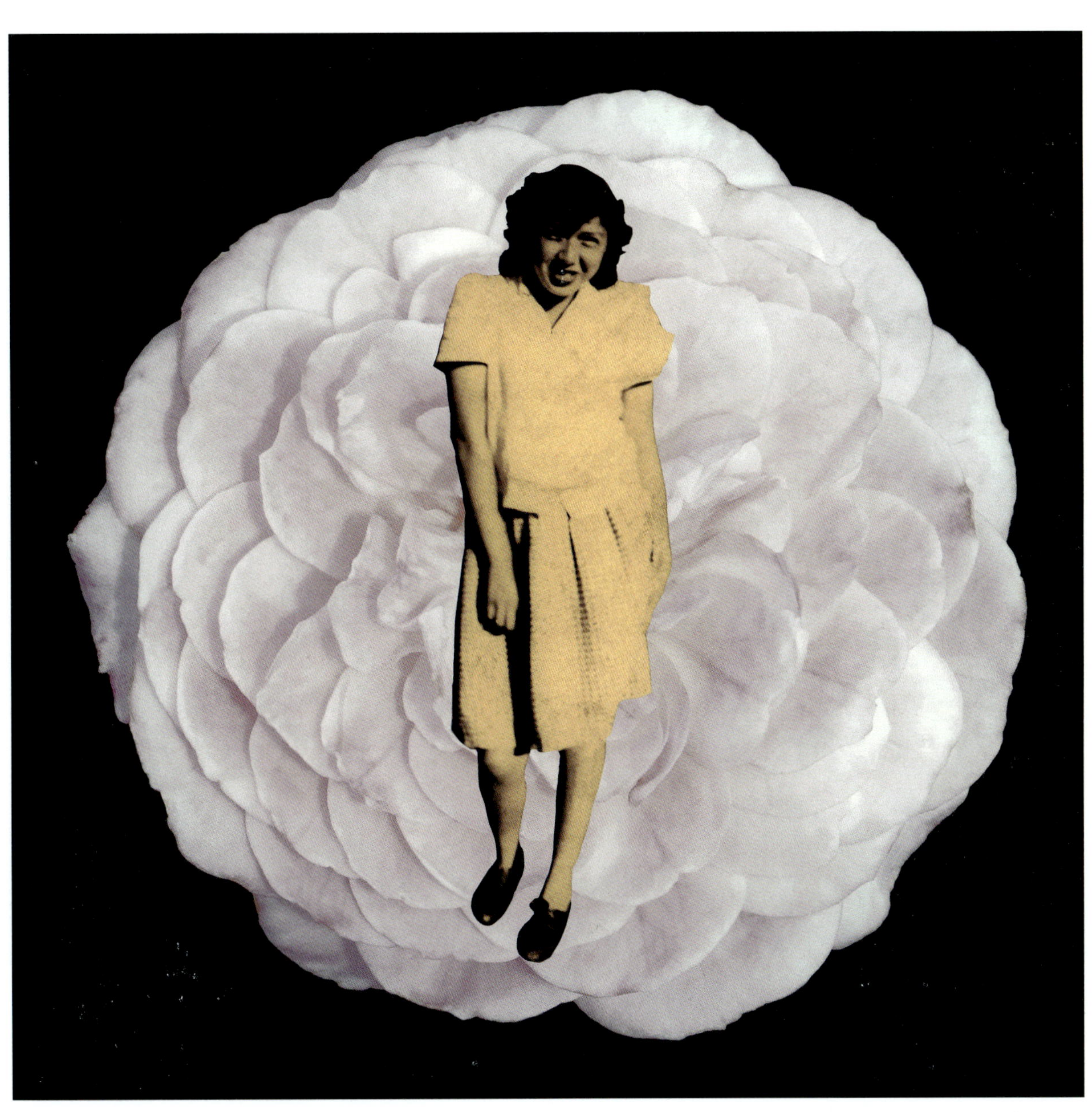

Chiquita (details), 2021

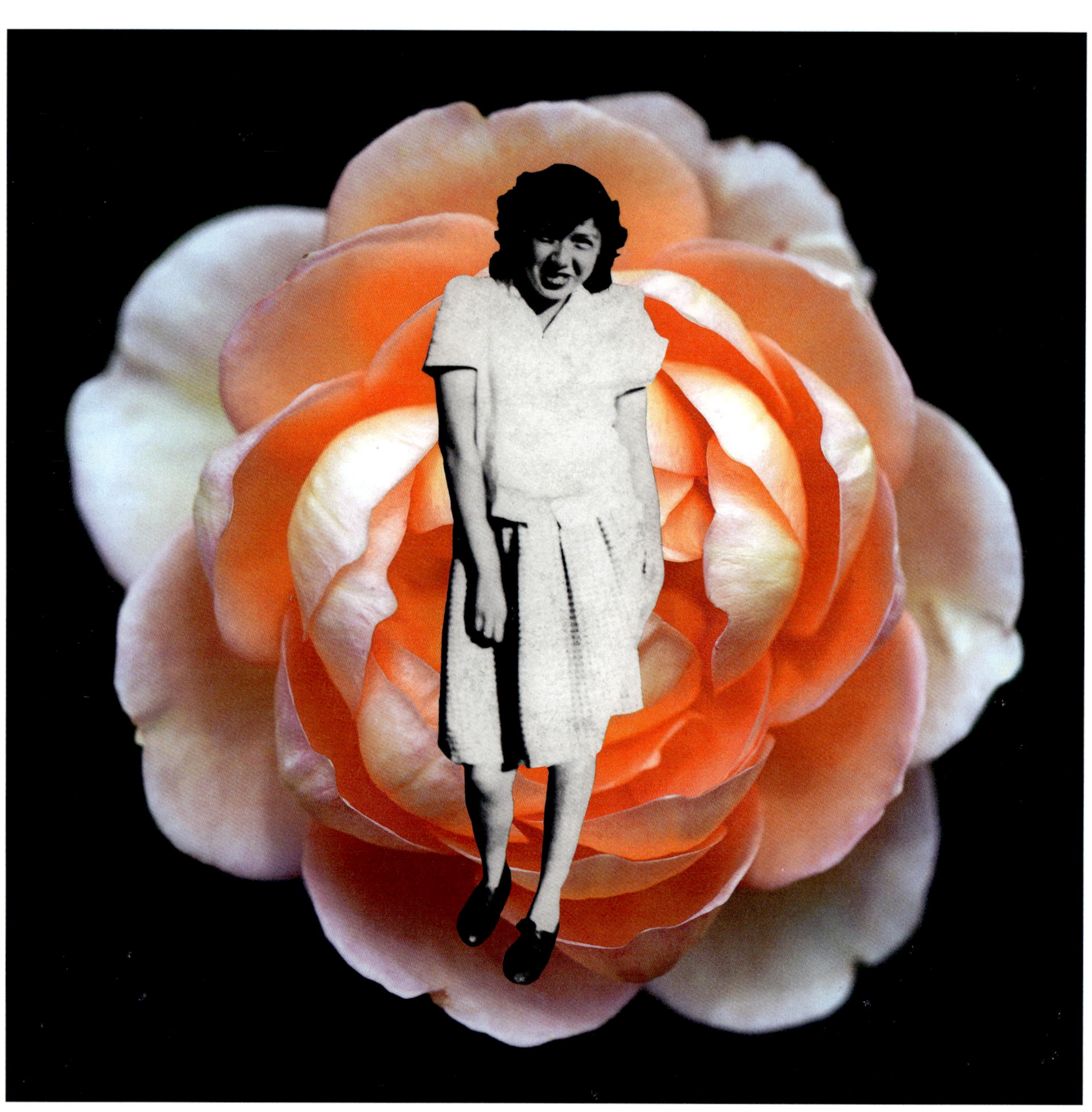

28 **Chiquita** (detail), 2021

*Chiquita was my mother's first name. It's a different kind of name.
However, it kept her distinct and gave us a different perspective of her.*

*Chiquita had a weak immune system and often ended up in the hospital
for weeks at a time. She was a chronic asthma sufferer. Late in life, it was
found that she was allergic to roses and probably other plant life she was
surrounded by.*

*Using a photograph of my mother that was taken when she was fifteen
years of age, I've placed her in the centre of a rose. She can no longer be
in danger from them. She happily stands and I feel she is conquering the
demons that have plagued her for most of her time on earth.*

Looking at the installation, I experience her youth and wonderment.

— SHELLEY NIRO

Little one... don't be afraid.
The voices of the past are calling you
The voices of the present urge you on
The voices of the dead tell you their sorrow
The sorrow inside you and beyond you.[1]

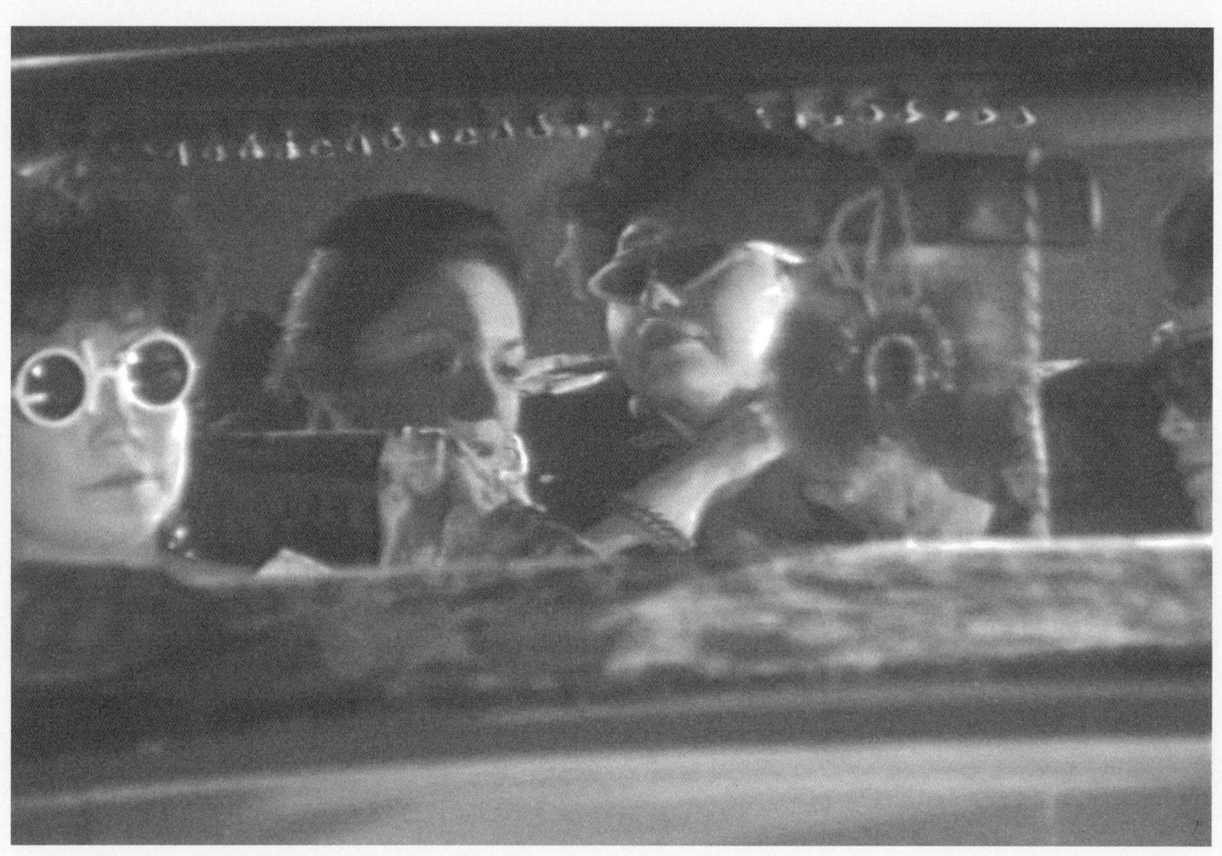

Still from **It Starts With a Whisper**, 1993

IT STARTS WITH A WHISPER

MELISSA BENNETT

It Starts With a Whisper (1993, pp. 30, 115) is Shelley Niro's first moving image work. Made with Toronto-based filmmaker Anna Gronau, it is a film (later transfered to video) that is perfectly emblematic of everything the artist would take up in the decades to follow. It is a satirical story about family, history, and the importance of remembrance. Its actors are Niro's sisters, who drive languidly through a dreamlike space, seemingly engaged in eternal banter. They are in cahoots with a young woman, Shauna, who is trying desperately to navigate the contemporary world, with all its expectations for the modern woman—let alone an Indigenous one. Niro's sisters are Shauna's aunties, and they greet Shauna as "matriarchal clowns," challenging her in absurdist ways, amid ghostly messages of survivance, voices that come from their centuries-old ancestors. The aunties model survival through mischief. They are obnoxious as an act of protest, but also as a way of encouraging the younger woman to find her own path. Theirs is a fight against patriarchy and colonialism. A fight that is humble yet determined, a fight that starts with a whisper, suggesting that perhaps sovereignty itself is a long battle best fought with measure and care. Niro operates here with optimism, persistence, humour, and as always, from the heart.

Niro is most known for her work in staged photography and film, and she regularly draws her sisters into narratives that reveal complex and often conflicting versions of history. In her signature style, she cleverly plays with cinematic tropes to challenge stereotypes of Indigenous identity. These techniques are already well-developed in *It Starts With a Whisper*, which serves as her breakout piece, paving the way for a prolific career now four decades long.

Niro's practice is one of art and advocacy for Indigenous visibility. Her extensive oeuvre includes photography (both analog and digital), painting, printmaking, collage, mixed media, sculpture, beadwork, video art, feature films, and other media. This internationally touring retrospective, *Shelley Niro: 500 Year Itch*, is the largest presentation of the artist's work to date. The exhibition centres around four key themes: Matriarchy, Memory, Relations, and Actors (supplemented by a fifth, emergent theme, The Cosmos, in the Art Gallery of Hamilton installation). Each one reveals a different facet of Niro's poetic perspective, and all of them reflect her main concern: that Indigenous Peoples be seen and heard.[2]

Born in Niagara Falls, New York, in 1954, Shelley (Doxtater) Niro is a member of the Turtle Clan of the Kanyen'kehaka (Mohawk) Nation. She grew up first in Niagara Falls, then on the Six Nations of the Grand River reserve. Niro is the second oldest of five children, with an older brother Michael and three younger sisters: Elizabeth (Bets), Beverley, and Debra (Bunny). Her mother, Chiquita June (Swain) Doxtater (1930–2004), was born in Longlac, Ontario, at the residential school, but was adopted into a Six Nations family who belonged to the Turtle Clan. Chiquita was a poet and artist who cleaned hospitals to make ends meet. Niro's father, George Oliver Doxtater (1921–1995), was a WWII veteran. He served from the ages of 18 to 23, then met and married Chiquita. He was from the Mohawk Wolf Clan family of Orenhrekowa, and was an important member of the community, as a flag carrier and an Elder. It was noted in his obituary that he was a "spiritual counsellor to countless families in times of need at the Grand River Territory (Osaken)."[3] Niro remembers that her father loved to tell stories about their ancestors, recalling in particular the beautiful Mohawk Valley in present-day New York state—a place neither he nor Niro's other immediate relatives ever visited, despite its close proximity. As a pivotal site in the decimation of Iroquois People forced to move north, perhaps it was better remembered as an idyllic landscape.[4]

Niro's childhood, through the late 1950s and early 1960s, was full of competing forces. At home, she was the one in charge when her parents worked long hours. As the oldest girl, she bore the weight of responsibility for the younger children. Her understanding of gender inequality was thus established at a young age. She noticed, too, how the men would come home from work and sit down, while the women came home and did all the housework. This didn't seem fair to her. Consequently, disparity is a topic that is prevalent in her work to this day.

Also in the 1960s, both on Niro's reserve and across Canada, government-hired social workers were entering Indigenous communities and homes without consent, under the guise of child "welfare," assessing families for their ability to feed and clothe their children, in what is now largely understood as a Eurocentric "cleansing." Later termed the Sixties Scoop, the government was intentionally removing Indigenous children to be raised in white families (an action that is now widely understood as the intentional destruction of culture). At the same time, residential schools—which had begun in the seventeenth century and lasted until 1996—were operating across Canada. Although Niro was not separated from her family, and did not attend a residential school, it would be inaccurate to say she was unaffected by these abusive systems. This was the Canada of her upbringing, and anti-Indigenous racism was a strongly felt part of her everyday experience.

It was in her childhood that her artistic practice began. Her father would encourage all his children to draw what they saw. Niro remembers it feeling a bit competitive, but in a way that was good for her. She recalls that everyone on the reserve was creative in one way or another. Beadwork was a popular pursuit. People would sit and do it together, in community. Her father revered the craft, and would buy beadwork from an older woman on the reserve in order to support and honour her. But beadwork is "hard on the eyes," according to Niro, and she wasn't sure she liked that it was often made for sale. It was a good way to contribute to their cash-strapped household, but she didn't find it inspiring in her youth. She would, however, go on to incorporate beadwork in her visual arts practice in thrilling and provocative ways. The preservation of tradition and cultural practice is important to Niro, and this is manifest in her art in material, aesthetic, and conceptual ways.

After some tumultuous years at high school, Niro couldn't wait to move away from home. She attended Cambrian College in Sudbury from 1972 to 1975, with financial support from Indian Affairs.[5] Her tuition was covered and she had just enough to eat. She first rented a room in a house owned by a woman who let rooms to Indigenous students. Later, she got her own apartment, which she thoroughly enjoyed because of the independence it finally afforded her. It was small with a little bathroom and kitchen. The curtains were mismatched and her mattress sat on the floor because the box spring had fallen apart, but she was happy to be living on her own. Her room was always full of music. The record player she purchased from Woolworth's played Joni Mitchell's *Blue*, she remembers, as well as *Tumbleweed Connection* and *Madman Across the Water* by Elton John. Niro loved her new, independent, minimalist life. During those college years, she also delved into learning the cello, and her love of classical music blossomed. She later likened the meditative feeling of being in the space of musical performance to the creative process of making an artwork.

In Sudbury, she met Celestino (Chel) Niro, who would become her husband and the father of her two children. Shelley changed her last name from Doxtater to Niro upon their marriage. She was twenty-two when she had her first child, Anastasia Naoga Niro, in 1976. She kept up her college studies and decided to study visual arts further. She took photography and art history classes during the day while the baby was in daycare, then a drawing course at night. In 1978, they moved to Oshawa, and Niro took a graphic arts class at Durham College. Her second child, Stella Michelle Niro, was born in 1980. For Niro, these years in school, when her children were young, are a blur. She frequently photographed her daughters, resulting in some very heartfelt and well-known works. The portraits *Sisters* and *Cousins* (pp. 6, 9) were both made in 1982 using infrared film, which Niro loved for the depth it added.

In 1984, at the age of thirty, Niro and family moved to Brantford. She enrolled in the Ontario College of Art, studying painting, drawing, and sculpture. Her practice also expanded as a result of her proximity to Hamilton, with its lively art scene and sense of artistic kinship. Two years later, she began working at the newly founded Native Indian/Inuit Photographers' Association (NIIPA), the longest-running Indigenous arts-service organization in Canada, where she found great community.[6] By always listening to CBC radio, she kept abreast of Canadian politics, the vagaries of which fuelled her artistic imagination.

Around this time, Niro painted one of her most critically recognized works, *Waitress* (1987, p. 112). Using parody, wit, and unrelenting nerve, she deftly captivates viewers in a narrative that both entertains and provokes. Niro pictures herself as a fumbling server, providing plated food to a white customer, on whom she's "accidentally" spilled red wine. Behind them Brian Mulroney (then Prime Minister of Canada) and his wife, Mila, dance and laugh, seemingly oblivious to the suffering and plight of Indigenous Peoples, who are represented by a conglomeration of mask-like, haunting faces in the background. At the time of its painting, Niro was thinking about how Indigenous Peoples were being ignored by those in power. Looking back at this work now, it reminds her of a sea of faces belonging to murdered and missing Indigenous women.[7] Like another of Niro's paintings from this period, *The Guest* (1987, p. 285), which also has a crowd of melancholic, peering faces, *Waitress* represents Indigenous lives lost, forgotten, and continually traumatized by the effects of Canada's colonial systems. Niro remembers constantly thinking about the past and the present when she made these works. "Here we are living in the present," she has said, "but these spirits are still hovering around. I wanted to acknowledge the past that's always there."[8]

With *Waitress*, Niro positions herself as a powerful player in a carefully constructed scene. She is an irrevocably present protagonist with the power to effect change. After making it, she found herself wanting to tell the stories of other women, who, like the waitress character, felt marginalized and invisible despite their crucial role in society. Niro's irritation with social injustices increased and a growing passion for making Indigenous women visible took root in her practice. She would go on to foreground women's stories in numerous important works.

In many ways, the hardships Niro experienced growing up motivated her to act out against injustices. This approach prevails in another early photographic work, *Red Heels Hard* (1991, pp. 46–53). For this work, as is typical in her creative process, she had an idea first and then pursued the media she found to be best suited to it. In this case, she used photography to document a politically charged public performance. Just as she did for *It Starts With a Whisper*, the artist enlisted her three sisters to act out a scene to be captured on camera. Niro then hand-painted the photographic prints to emphasize her sisters' garments and makeup. To present the images, she frames them with intricately patterned, hand-drilled mats. In the photographs, the sisters are dressed up for a day out on the town (in Brantford). Overdone in bright lipstick and bold hairdos, they parade in front of the city's monument to Joseph Brant.[9] Clicking their red heels, the young women follow a yellow brick road. They mockingly pretend to be convinced that if they follow the path suggested to them by the dominant culture, they will find the gold standards of success (according to settler values, of course). As in many of her works, Niro is articulating injustice here, both pointing out its absurdity and rebelling against it. Looking at the images in *Red Heels Hard* now, roughly thirty years after they were made, one wonders about the longevity of this battle for equality. What exactly has changed since Niro began her practice decades ago? Really, what? And yet the artist persists.

Niro is a fighter—a humble, wise, and tenacious one. Her strong spirit and wry sense of humour have helped her persevere. She fights injustice through her work, though the work itself is not always pointedly rebellious. A solid portion of Niro's practice is simply the artist making her people visible—and there is much power in that. *Red Heels Hard* is political, but it is also a very tender photograph of her and her sisters having a rollicking good time. And many of her photographs are direct and caring portraits of her mother, her sisters, or her daughters. Niro's photographic gaze gives place to those women. In a sense, this gesture gives voice to silenced Indigenous women in general (Niro would not disagree), but, at the same time, Niro is simply operating from her heart. She is bolstered and inspired by her close relationships with family members, and holds them dear, whether they are present or not. She enacts her support for her people but also her wider community, and their histories and traditions, through her artwork, in all media.

Leading up to 1992, the 500th anniversary of Christopher Columbus' arrival in the Americas, there was both a palpable hunger for critical perspectives in North America and a great wave of action by Indigenous artists and curators. That year saw a plethora of exhibitions, such as *Land, Spirit, Power: First Nations at the National Gallery of Canada* and *INDIGENA: Perspectives of Indigenous Peoples on 500 Years* at the Canadian Museum of Civilization (now the Canadian Museum of History), which toured across the country and internationally. These came on the heels of other influential exhibitions, such as *Beyond History* at the Vancouver Art Gallery (1989), *Revisions* at the Walter Phillips Gallery in Banff (1988), and others throughout the United States. *Revisions* is a great example of the goals set by Indigenous artists and arts professionals at the time. The exhibition "asserted the significance of contemporary Indigenous culture and arts practices," wrote Lee-Ann Martin, an Indigenous arts professional and the coordinator for the Task Force on Museums and First Peoples, a Canadian federal initiative that produced a landmark report in 1992 entitled *Turning the Page: Forging New Partnerships Between Museums and First Peoples*. "The artists sabotaged ethnographic stereotypes in order to redress their present and future cultural identities," Martin asserted. "They were concerned with 'deconstructing Eurocentric versions of native history and proposing their own counternarratives.'"[10]

Niro was an emerging player in this scene. She held her first solo exhibition in Toronto in 1992 at Mercer Union, a prominent artist-run centre. The central body of work she presented, *Mohawks in Beehives* (1982–1991, pp. 45–63), comprises fourteen hand-coloured gelatin silver print photographs (including *Red Heels Hard*) surrounded by mats that are hand-drilled in the style of traditional beadwork patterns. All of the images are staged, with family members dressed for certain roles. Each serves as a critique of the dominant colonial culture, overturning stereotypes of Indigeneity and also of women, who are too often represented as passive creatures or sexual objects.

In the exhibition text, guest curator Carol Podedworny wrote that the works "are about revealing the fallacy of the 'white man's Indian,' and ultimately, about taking control." Her text continues: "Through the presentation of privately and communally determined images of the Self, Niro reminds the viewer that the process of documentation or history making is comprised of a variety of remembered events recorded as both visual and literary representations. The present moment provides the opportunity for correction, and this act of correction or rewriting exerts an influence on how information from the past, present, and future is/will be perceived and understood."[11]

Niro remembers the moment well: "I took the *Mohawks in Beehives* photographs at the end of March 1991. It was after Oka and the invasion of Kuwait, and all those terrible, depressing things happening in the world. I find when I get depressed, I work the best because I'm trying to fight off the depression or be sucked more and more into it. So I talked to my three sisters and I said, 'Let's get rid of our kids and just have a fun day of it. Let's put on makeup and do up our hair. Let's go downtown [Brantford, again] and have lunch and be really loud and obnoxious.' It was just kind of a day of letting go. I felt at the time that it was really risqué—we didn't care what anybody thought of us. We went downtown and we were in the park and we were just being rude. I think that in a way we were sort of taking control."[12]

The Rebel (1982/1987, pp. 20–21) is a particularly memorable image within the suite of photographs that make up *Mohawks in Beehives + Other Works*. Arguably Niro's most iconic work, it was made in collaboration with her mother, who she asked to pose near a car. Niro thought of creating a satirical image of a woman on a vehicle, making fun of the sexualized trope of the woman as hood ornament, which was prevalent in magazine ads of the time. Up for a bit of fun, Chiquita decided to hop on the trunk of the car and lay across it, with her hand behind her head. With her hilarious uptake, Niro's aging Indigenous mother confounds the stereotypical pose. Objectifying herself for the camera, with a big, lipsticked smile, she knowingly mocks the expectations of women's bodies, especially those of Indigenous women. Enacted as a quick joke between mother and daughter, this image lives on as a banner call for both women's rights and Indigenous self-determination.

Mohawks in Beehives is a critique of outdated and troubling gender expectations, hitting every note in Niro's trademark brand of satire. Niro created this type of work with great fervor in the early 1990s, when she was in her late thirties and early forties. The Mercer Union show was well-received. People understood and acknowledged the work and Niro felt greatly encouraged. In 1992, she also created the photographic series *This Land is Mime Land* (1992, pp. 266–277), which illustrates her gregarious and intelligent manner of playing with stereotypical images. A highlight of the series is her self-portrait as Marilyn Monroe, *500 Year Itch* (p. 265)—a cheeky jab that again explores the idea of women's bodies as available for public consumption.

Niro continued to photograph her family, acknowledging and strengthening Matriarchy by celebrating the women in her life. *Time Travels Through Us* (1999, p. 23) is a gelatin silver print with cotton and beaded mat work in a silver-painted wooden frame. It shows Chiquita with Niro's daughters, Anastasia and Stella, arranged in a tender pose. The Matriarch holds a bird's nest with eggs, symbolizing life, generational connection, and fragility all at once.

By the early 2000s, Niro's practice was increasingly recognized by international scholars and curators, and her exhibitions steadily increased, on a national scale. *Unbury My Heart* was a 2001 solo exhibition at the McMaster Museum of Art in Hamilton. The central work (pp. 238–239) was an installation of four large oil paintings expressively depicting earth, air, fire, and water, alongside four red carpets, upon which 500 stuffed velvet hearts laid tied together with thin nylon ropes, signifying Indigenous unity. Niro also presented an impressive fifty-foot-long tarpaper drawing of anatomical-looking hearts—each one inscribed with the name of an Indigenous Clan, either present or past. The exhibition was accompanied by a catalogue essay by Gerald McMaster, who was then the deputy director of the Cultural Resources Centre at the National Museum of the American Indian in Washington, D.C.

In the text, McMaster wrote: "Five hundred hearts carry subtle messages of sovereignty, spirit, community and struggle. Beginning with the untroubled reference to 'five hundred,' as the timeframe for Indian-White relations…[for Niro] the heart signifies spirit and courage of the living, the vitality and capacity for contemporary Indian peoples to freely express themselves." McMaster further explains: "The reflexive part of the title, 'unbury,' is in line with Niro's centralizing focus on culture as the dynamic force rekindling the Indian spirit."[13]

If we consider Niro's modus operandi as action that begins from the heart and works toward the things that bother her politically, the concept of Matriarchy comes to the fore. Niro's Iroquois ancestors were a matrilineal society, with descent passed through mothers rather than fathers, and men and women had differing, though equally powerful roles in the community. But after repeated contact with European settlers who wanted only to speak to the males in the group, an unfortunate rearrangement of power began. In celebration of Matriarchy—and in lament for that historical loss—Niro created *Resting With Warriors* (2001, pp. 208, 211–213), honouring her Iroquois ancestors.

Consisting of four large and labour-intensive woodcut prints, *Resting With Warriors* depicts the characteristics women would have needed in order to lead their peoples north after the conflicts that ensued around 1779. As they walked the long journey, these warriors took care of families, Elders, and children, they gathered sustenance, and they provided community support. Niro wrote that: "To keep a community, a place of heart and soul, together, the women had to remain level-headed and aware of detrimental possibilities in these vulnerable times. Intellect, emotion, spirit and strength were four characteristics needed in these times of challenge."[14] Niro chose to depict strong women embodying these characteristics, surrounded by culturally significant symbols, such as strawberries and corn.

Thinking more broadly about the place of Indigenous Peoples across North America, Niro collaborated with Hulleah J. Tsinhnahjinnie and Veronica Passalacqua in 2003 to create *The Shirt* (pp. 196–207) which, like many of her works, originates from a performance for the camera—this time in a desolate grassy landscape near where the collaborators resided on the west coast of the United States. The work consists of a series of nine lightboxes; Niro also made a separate work in the form of a video. The opening scene in the video shows an empty landscape with low mountains in the distance. The next scene depicts a woman (Tsinhnahjinnie) wearing an American flag bandanna and a white T-shirt emblazoned with "The Shirt." In subsequent scenes, she appears in a succession of similar T-shirts, with changing messages that quickly reveal political unrest. "My ancestors were annihilated exterminated murdered and massacred," one reads, then "They were lied to cheated tricked and deceived." In between, Niro cuts to moving imagery of Niagara Falls, a reference to the historically sacred nature of this site for Indigenous Peoples. The messages continue in that tone and style, the content too urgent to warrant punctuation. "Attempts were made to assimilate colonize enslave and displace them," builds towards the punchline: "And all's I get is this shirt." *The Shirt* is one of Niro's most succinct and overtly political works. The final statement—and those that lead-up to it—leave very little room for viewer apathy.

In *The Shirt*, Niro employs photography for its image-making power. Tsinhnahjinnie, an artist herself, has written about the power of taking the camera into one's own hands as a political act of self-determination. The very long history of white people documenting "others" as an act of colonization is a tired history—for Niro and many other artists alike. On self-portraiture, and on Indigenous Peoples photographing one another, Tsinhnahjinnie wrote: "No longer is the camera held by an outsider looking in, the camera is held with brown hands opening familiar worlds. We document ourselves with a humanizing eye."[15] Through this work, Niro expands the scope of her subject and also her artist community, collaborating across North America with artist friends in landscapes not her own to reflect on shared obstacles.

In 2004, the Niro and Doxtater families experienced two profound losses. In March, Stella passed away suddenly at the age of twenty-three. Then, in October, Chiquita passed away as well. Their close-knit family and community were devastated. Niro remembers a spiral of emotional shock. That year, she made the photographic series *Ghosts, Girls, Grandmas* (pp. 156–161). It was something that kept her going. The photographs include close-ups of people—Jody Hill, a young man from her community; Anastasia, her oldest daughter; and Chiquita—as well as contemplative imagery of rocks and trees. They are wondrous meditations on the material and immaterial moments of Niro's world, as she grieved.

Working through such momentous personal loss, Niro continued to make intimate works, but also increasingly expanded her subjects to include more global issues, exploring political unrest and reconciliation through dialogue. The series entitled *Borders* (2008, pp. 224–231) is a key example. In each of four digitally collaged photographs, Niro depicts two arms reaching for each other from outside the frame. In two of the images (*Treaties* and *Unity*), the arms connect and hold each other, and in the other two (*Boundless* and *Borders*) they don't. Describing *Boundless*, Niro writes about a "potential union" that "results in the world spinning…continuing the procreation for the world."[16] With *Borders*, in which the hands make fists and don't meet, she expresses the discordance of race, economics, and religion. *Treaties*, conversely, which shows the hands joined, explores how such agreements are often arrived at after years of struggle. "Because we have thinking minds," Niro writes, "we try to resolve conflicts through language. This language is seen as barriers coming down. However, over the course of time, this language is seen as no longer viable and new interpretations of that language result."[17] In *Unity*, the two hands grip each other tightly, and Niro also includes small images that reference community and memory. There is a small portrait of her father in traditional clothing, an image of a young female relative, a bird, and a mound of earth that may symbolize Turtle Island and the story of Creation. The background in *Unity* appears to be a starry galaxy, and Niro may be contemplating the place of people in the world.

In her mid-fifties, Niro refined a theme she'd long been developing, and began to depict her subjects (including herself) as characters in the world, positioning them as powerful agents who respond to the events and circumstances that surround them. *The Moon and Me and A Celestial Tree* (2010, p. 13) is exemplary of this work. It is a rare self-portrait, and one of the most stark. In a single photograph, Niro demonstrates the power of a person on the land, in relationship with their ancestors. She depicts the particular significance of a middle-aged woman in a society that devalues and stigmatizes the aging female body. Situated on a starry, black background, similar to that in *Unity*, the figure here is shown in relationship with the moon and a Celestial Tree, or the Tree of Life, which is a central part of the Iroquois Creation Story. Niro pictures herself as grounded and secure.

Niro has depicted the strength of Indigenous women and girls in both photography and painting. *Raven's World* (2015, p. 97) is a large, lush oil painting that features Raven, Niro's only grandchild, who was seven years old at the time the painting was made. The child is settled on a stool, yet is perched in anticipation. Niro wanted to depict her ready for action, as though poised to take on the world. Raven shields her eyes with her hand, looking to the future in a deliberate way. She wears an aviator's cap, a subtle reference to the Traditional Stories of Sky Woman, the mother of Haudenosaunee life.

Niro includes several rich symbols around the figure, including the moon, which can symbolize Grandmother Moon, a protector and guardian of Turtle Island in Haudenosaunee culture. The moon is set against a starry night sky, evoking a macro view of the cosmos, which hints at the interconnectedness of humans in this galaxy. At Raven's feet are rows of corn, a staple of her Iroquois ancestors and a symbol of sustenance.

Raven's World, like many of Niro's works, makes reference to the ongoing traumas of colonization endured by Indigenous Peoples. She persistently positions her works as the starting point of a dialogue. They are sites of optimism, and they represent the artist's extraordinary effort to reconcile trauma and colonization through a lens of hopefulness. In *Raven's World*, for example, the implication is that the child will have everything she needs if she lives in relationship to the earth and its offerings. Raven is depicted as resilient and monumental. She appears to look to the future, suggesting that there is hope for her generation.

Niro represents Raven as a steadfast changemaker, not acting out, but simply being. This is in contrast to the early-1990s photographs of Niro's sisters (Raven's aunties), and is an alternate approach to the representation of the female figure. Viewers have long revelled in the fun and feisty aspects of Niro's earlier work. This sensibility has not evaporated as the artist has gotten older (and she has always seemed wise beyond her years), but rather, her wisdom seems to have deepened. She continues to cut through societal nonsense in her work, but with more poetic statements referring to the many versions of history.

Like *It Starts With a Whisper*, a much later work titled *1779* (2017, pp. 153–155) also contains many key elements of Niro's practice, such as humour, as a strategy for an important dialogue about history, tradition, commemoration, and the importance of place. The mixed-media sculpture *1779* is comprised of a cylindrical plinth housing a video monitor that viewers look down onto. The video shows the Niagara Whirlpool, downstream from Niagara Falls, which Niro shot from the cable car above. The screen is surrounded by a circular mat made of velvet, commemorative in style and intricately beaded with the date "1779." Placed upon the screen is a pair of stilettos covered in blue satin and velvet, with long strands of beads emerging from the tops, as if they are tiny waterfalls themselves. It is a powerful piece that was made over a period of sixteen years. Niro's meditative process resulted in an extremely poignant work, in which she makes rigorous use of symbolism. The beaded "1779" refers to the year of the Sullivan-Clinton campaign[18] and the American Confederation period. Widespread violent conflicts led the Iroquois People to embark on a journey north to what became the Six Nations reserve and the Haldimand Tract in Canada. Currently, the reserve spans more than 190 square kilometres, which represents approximately five per cent of the original 3,800 square kilometres of land granted to the Six Nations by the 1784 Haldimand Treaty.[19]

In *1779*, Niro commemorates the women warriors of this period—strong females who led their families and fed and clothed the men and children. The work is also a commentary on the Canada–US border and the power of this geopolitical boundary. Niro has crossed it many times since childhood when visiting family in New York state, and feels its rigid bureaucratic effect to this day. Niagara Falls was once a spiritual mecca, and Niro critiques the glitzy tourist trap it has become. The "glamorous" stilettos sitting within the circular commemorative mat refer to the frivolity of present-day tourism, as well as to the way women are often represented, both historically and in contemporary media, as frail and as anything but warriors. The whirlpool swirling below the shoes is a menacing and mesmerizing counterpoint, implying eternal movement and—if one were to use a positive lens, as Niro so frequently does—the potential for political and emotional renewal.

It is worth recognizing here another of Niro's regular characters: the moon. Earth's natural satellite has long sustained her interest, both aesthetically and spiritually. Niro herself says she isn't quite sure why she is so drawn to its imagery. Moons, however, feature largely in a number of notable pieces: her *Borders* series (2008), *Ancestors, M: Stories of Women* (2011, pp. 79–89), *Raven's World* (2015), *My Heart is in the Forest* (2017, pp. 42, 131), where it appears in the first shot of the video, the feature film *The Incredible 25th Year of Mitzi Bearclaw* (2019, p. 132), and her latest large-scale oil painting, *Black Whole* (2021, pp. 14–15). A photographic series begun in 2021 has her photographing the moon with a powerful lens.

As a glowing pale rock tracing circles around us, the moon can lead us to question our place in the world. A theme emerges here, though it is somewhat elusive and hard to describe, but it has to do with the cosmos. In a 2015 artist's statement, Niro wrote: "Our galaxy is a tiny part of a much larger mass in the universe. It gives me comfort in knowing I am a small particle as we move through our galaxy. Our sustenance comes from the beginning of time."[20]

The term cosmos is defined as: "the universe as seen as a well-ordered whole."[21] Niro can certainly be described as hopeful in her advocacy, and perhaps she is asserting that one day society, too, can be a well-ordered whole. Although our world is fraught with injustice, the artist's message over time seems to be one of optimism—that relationships can be fostered and that people can work together, and that reconciliation may indeed be possible. Coming from someone who has experienced so much, positivity and openness of this calibre is more than inspiring and warrants wide attention.

Gerald McMaster commented similarly in his essay for Niro's solo exhibition *Unbury My Heart* in 2001. "Not a literal but rather a figural use of the heart, the exhibition's title is about the spiritual core of our humanity: our ability to face adversity, our sense of identity and our fight for ideals that gives meaning to our core being. The heart is more than an organ; it is a powerful metaphor describing the state of aboriginality today…[Niro] continues to hold fast in her belief of a resilient future in which aboriginal peoples will continue surviving by steadfastly maintaining their cultural values and traditions."[22]

My Heart is in the Forest is a short video work that, like so many other pieces, is emblematic of the main concerns of Niro's practice over time. It begins with a quiet shot of the moon, then moves through gorgeous views of forests and fields shot around her home in Brantford and on the Six Nations reserve. Meditative landscape imagery is overlaid with the sounds of an evocative Kanyen'keha (Mohawk language) song, composed and performed by ElizaBeth Hill. A very charming section of the video follows five children (Raven and her second cousins Abigail, Athena, Howie, and Ella) dressed in traditional clothing while playfully walking and singing their way through trees, brush, and cornfields. Again, the artist warmly calls forth the importance of intergenerational knowledge sharing.

If it starts with a whisper, how does it end? Four decades into her practice, Niro continues to confront stereotypes of Indigenous identity head-on. She makes her point strongly through subtle visual ironies, rather than spelling it out in an obvious way. To say there is or was a peak in Niro's practice would be incorrect. At the time of writing, she is 67 years old and she is as prolific as ever. In the last year alone, she has produced some incredibly poignant works hinging on concerns that have occupied her throughout her career. Her most recent work, *Black Whole*, is a large oil on canvas that offers a surrealistic view of the universe. In it, an owl, a trout, a sunflower, and a thistle seem to be hovering in outer space around a black hole. Niro wanted to depict "an aftermath and what might survive," she says. "It looks like they are exploding in the process. I wanted to create an affirmation of life and with it, energy, commotion and just general joyful mayhem." She started the painting years earlier, around 2004. "I suppose nuclear holocaust was on my mind at the time," she remembers. "Stella had passed away. I don't make art to reflect my emotional state, but I think I was trying to create a new world. A desperate try."[23]

The Architect (2021, p. 287) is another highly self-reflective painting that the artist recently found the time and motivation to complete after starting it a year or two earlier. "I made the painting as a memory to my mom about the house we lived in on the reserve," she writes. "It was a small house. She would plant daffodils around it. Of course being a small kid, I didn't really appreciate the idea of trying to make the house look better. Now I do. *The Architect* title comes from the idea of where ideas do come from and how they are fostered. From there an intellectual growth begins. And who knows where ideas take you."[24] Her recent moon photographs, made with a 600-millimetre telephoto lens, continue to spark her curiosity. Not entirely sure yet where the pursuit will lead, Niro is reveling in the peculiar and highly detailed ways in which she can examine and depict the moon's surface.

The Weapon (2021, p. 150), a black-and-white oil painting, shows a hand holding a needle upright, with a bead representing a tiny drop of blood. Beadwork, Niro suggests here, is a weapon in itself. That is, the persistent enactment of cultural tradition is a force for social change as effective as any other. Beadwork, like the continuation of any aspect of Indigenous culture that has been lost or stolen, she seems to say, is a tool for the future. In the background of *The Weapon*, behind the hand holding the bloody needle, are a cast of haunting faces similar in scale and style to the ones in *Waitress* and *The Guest*. This time, however, the faces are sourced from pictures Niro found online. Each is the face of a missing or murdered Indigenous woman.

Shelley Niro is not haunted by the past. Rather, she brings her politics and personal history together in conversation to communicate what matters most to her. Her beliefs and passions are inextricably linked in a language that is uniquely hers. Because of her fundamental sense of justice, she is consistently driven to address social inequities, which makes her work both responsive and highly generative. Niro may indeed be the humble warrior, fighting the good, long fight, as described at the outset of this essay. But she is so much more still. Shelley Niro succeeds at weaving the personal and political threads of her life into a poetic and moving practice. We experience her insight, consider her vision, and are left to ponder the whole.

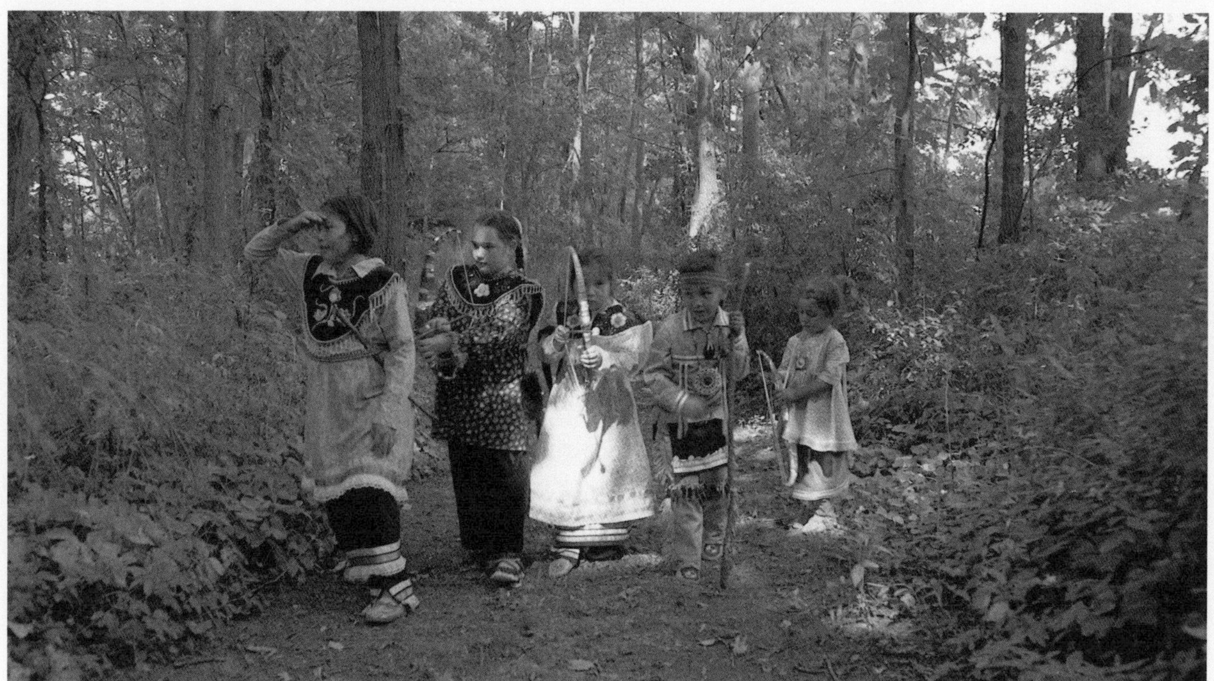

 Still from **My Heart is in the Forest**, 2017

1. Shelley Niro and Anna Gronau, *It Starts With a Whisper*, 1993, digital video, 27:29 min, National Gallery of Canada, Ottawa, https://www.gallery.ca/collection/artwork/it-starts-with-a-whisper.

2. These themes were created in collaboration with David W. Penney (National Museum of the American Indian) and Greg Hill (National Gallery of Canada), my co-curators of the retrospective.

3. Obituary, George Oliver Doxtater, *Tekawennake News* (Ohsweken, Ontario), April 19, 1995, https://vitacollections.ca/sixnationsarchive/details.asp?ID=3286709.

4. Madeline Lennon, *Shelley Niro: Seeing Through Memory* (London, ON: Blue Medium Press, 2014), 1. I thank Madeline Lennon for this thought from her biography of Niro.

5. The Canadian governmental department now known as Indigenous and Northern Affairs Canada.

6. As chronicled on the Building Cultural Legacies website (a history of Hamilton's art scene): "In 1985, a group of Indigenous image-makers came together to establish the Native Indian/Inuit Photographers' Association (NIIPA) shortly after the first-ever Conference of Native Indian Photography in Canada, VISIONS. Held from March 8–10 at the Photo Union Gallery located at 210 Napier Street in downtown Hamilton." Niro was working in the heart of this community. See Rhéanne Chartrand, "Why Not Hamilton? Shining light on the creation of the Native Indian/Inuit Photographers' Association," Building Cultural Legacies, n.d., https://buildingculturallegacies.ca/artist/native-indian-inuit-photographers-association-niipa/.

7. According to one report, 1,017 women and girls identified as Indigenous were murdered between 1980 and 2012—a homicide rate roughly four-and-a-half times higher than that of all other women in Canada during the same period. (I chose to refer to this particular report, with those dates, because of the period when Niro painted *Waitress*.) See "Missing and murdered Indigenous women and girls: Understanding the numbers," Amnesty International (blog), January 29, 2021, https://www.amnesty.ca/blog/missing-and-murdered-indigenous-women-and-girls-understanding-the-numbers/.

8. Shelley Niro, interview with the author, November 1, 2021.

9. Joseph Brant (1742/1743–1807) was a Kanyen'kehaka (Mohawk) leader of Six Nations, a Loyalist, and influential military captain. See The Canadian Encyclopedia Online, "Joseph Brandt (Thayendanegea)," by Robert S. Allen and Heather Conn, September 4, 2019, https://www.thecanadianencyclopedia.ca/en/article/joseph-brant.

10. Lee-Ann Martin, "Anger and Reconciliation: A Very Brief History of Exhibiting Contemporary Indigenous Art in Canada," *Afterall* 43 (Spring/Summer 2017). https://www.afterall.org/article/anger-and-reconciliation-a-very-brief-history-of-exhibiting-contemporary-indigenous-art-in-canada.

11. Carol Podedworny, "Shelley Niro: Mohawks in Beehives + Other Works" (Toronto: Mercer Union, 1992), https://www.mercerunion.org/exhibitions/mohawks-in-beehives-other-work/.

12. Podedworny, "Shelley Niro: Mohawks in Beehives + Other Works."

13. Gerald McMaster, "Rebuilding the Spirit," in *Shelley Niro: Unbury My Heart* (Hamilton, ON: McMaster Museum of Art, 2001), 11.

14. Shelley Niro, *Resting With Warriors* (artist statement), 2001.

15. Hulleah J. Tsinhnahjinnie, "Compensating Imbalances," *Exposure* 29, no. 1 (1993): 30.

16. Shelley Niro, *Borders* (unpublished artist statement), 2008.

17. Niro, *Borders*.

18. A military campaign ordered by George Washington, then Commander-in-Chief of the Continental Army, that destroyed more than forty Iroquois villages and their stores of winter crops, breaking the power of the Six Nations in New York all the way to the Great Lakes.

19. "History of Six Nations," Six Nations of the Grand River Economic Development Corporation, accessed January 2, 2022, https://sndevcorp.ca/history-of-six-nations/.

20. Shelley Niro and Bryce Kanbara, *Indian Summer* (Glenhyrst, ON: Glenhyrst Art Gallery of Brant, 2015), 10.

21. "Cosmos," *Oxford Reference*, accessed November 20, 2021, https://www.oxfordreference.com/view/10.1093/oi/authority.20110803095641467.

22. McMaster, "Rebuilding the Spirit," 10–11.

23. Shelley Niro, email message to the author, January 5 and 6, 2022.

24. Shelley Niro, email message to the author, January 6, 2022.

Some people think that to be Indian, you have to do certain things, but I'm saying that you're Indian no matter what you do, but you have to decide what you want to do and you have to ask questions, like, am I doing something because it's expected of me, or am I doing it because I really believe this and it's really a part of me. So I'm always questioning that, saying, "Am I being truthful to myself?"

— SHELLEY NIRO

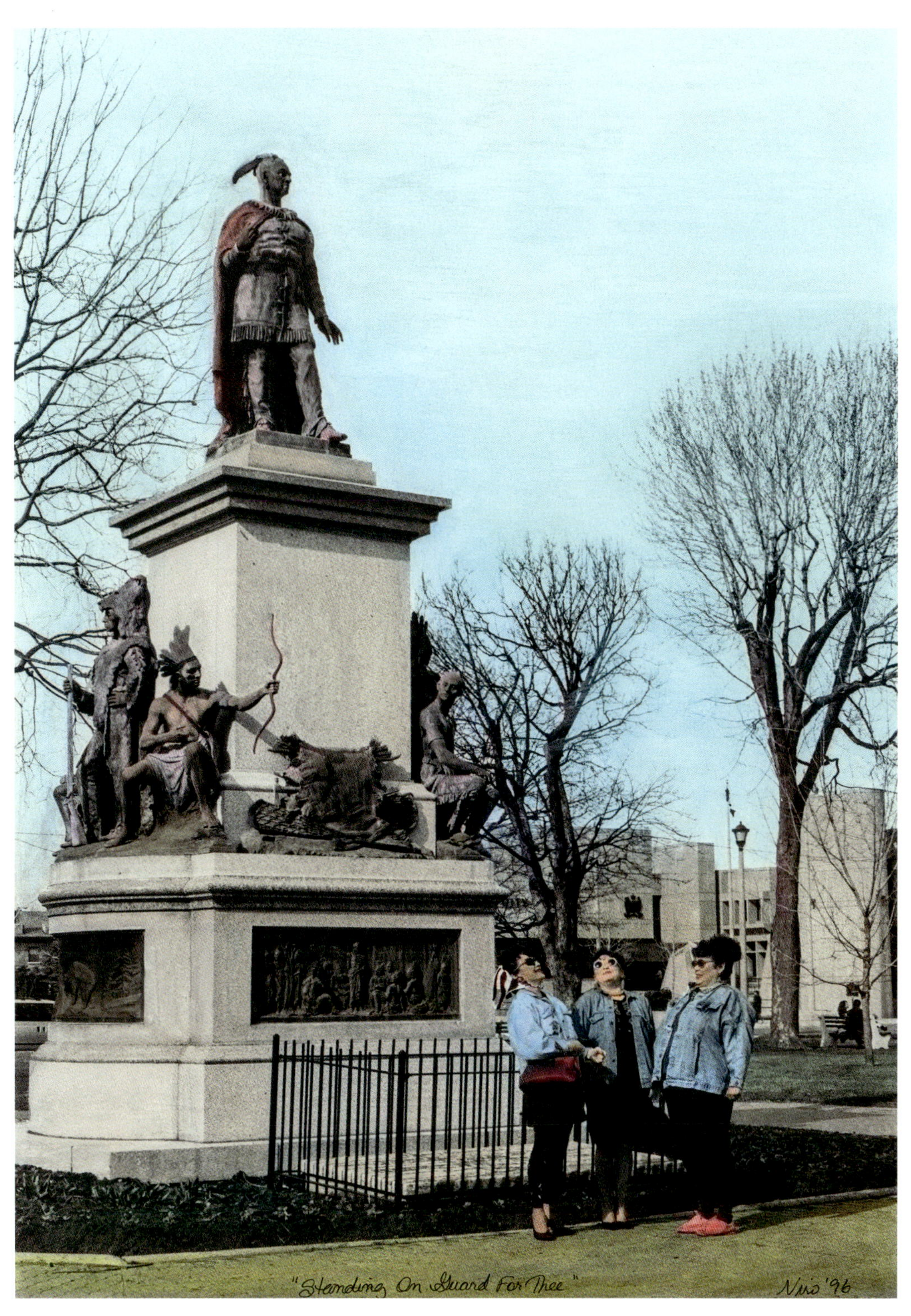

Standing on Guard for Thee, 1991

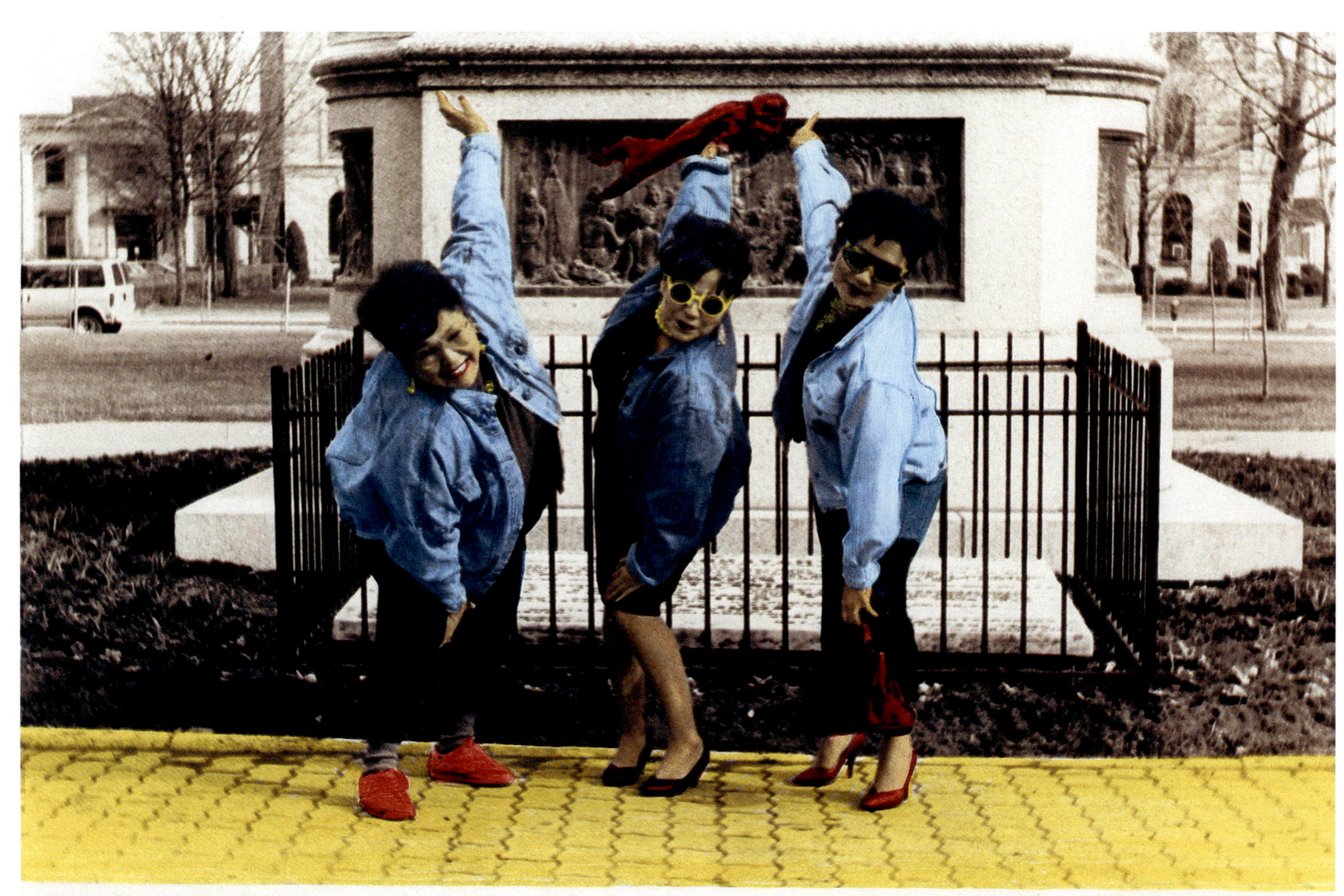

Behind us stands a monument to the late great chief J.B.

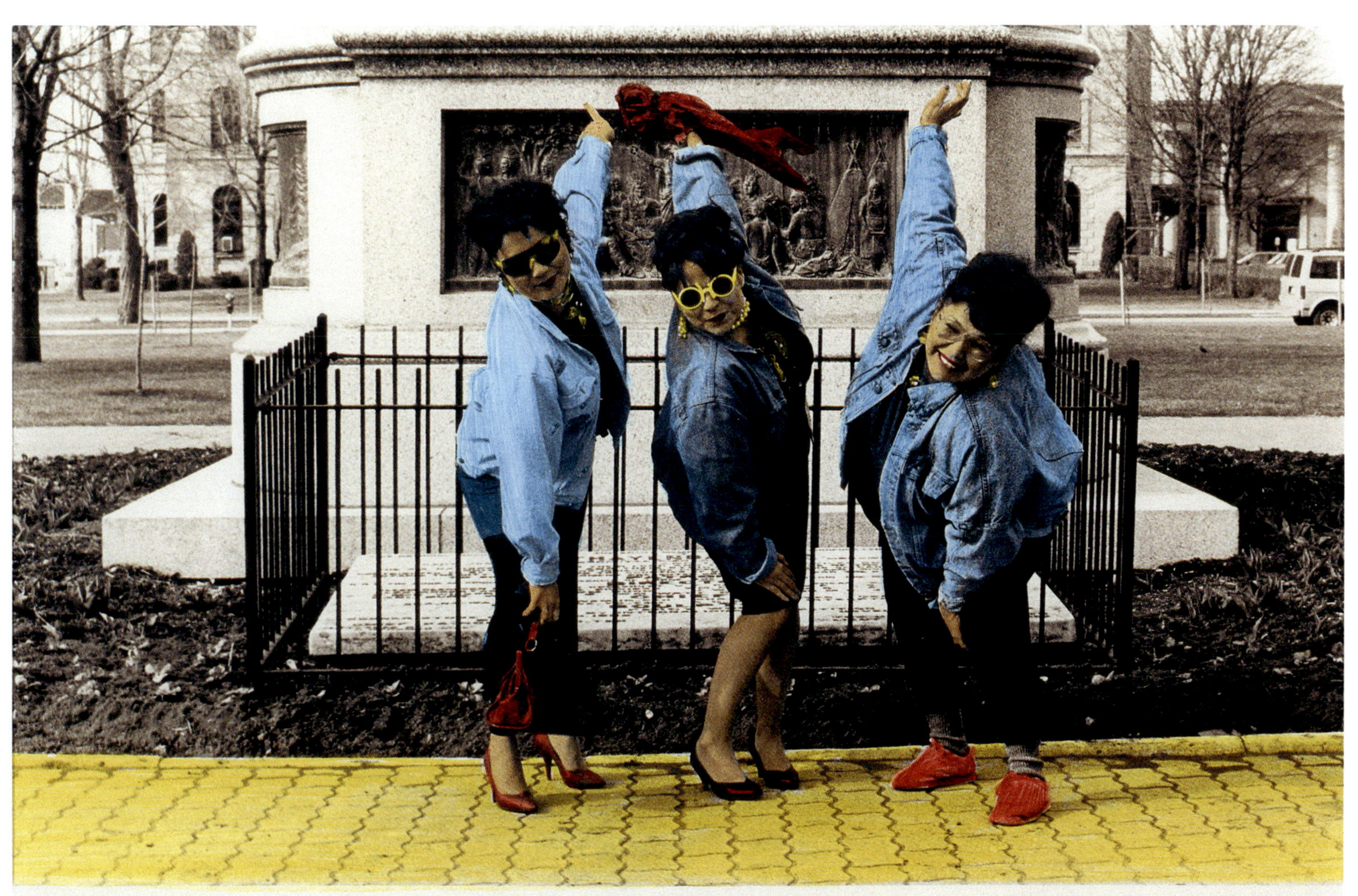

Red Heels Hard (details), 1991 47

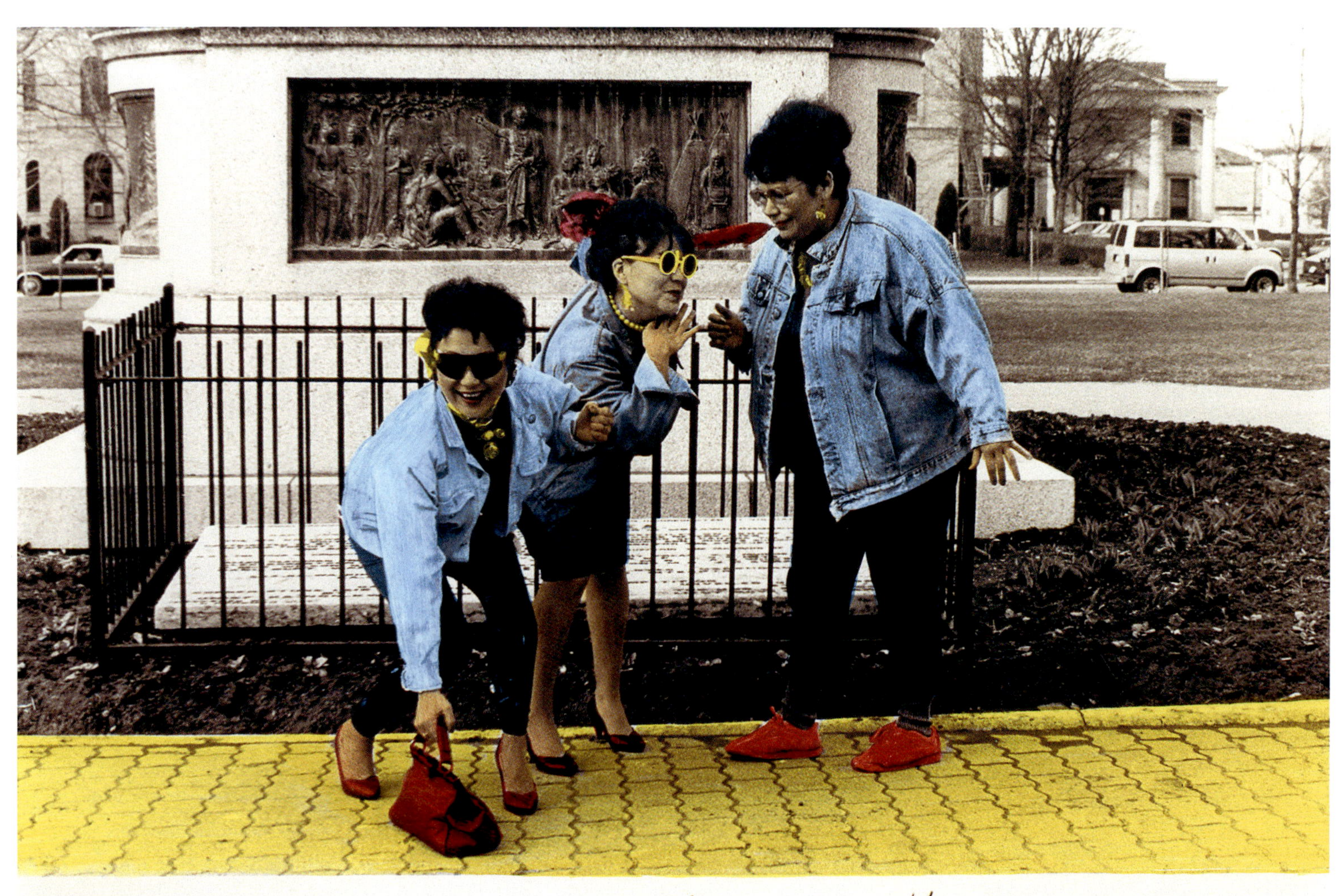

Carried in his jewelled bag and blown into the wind...

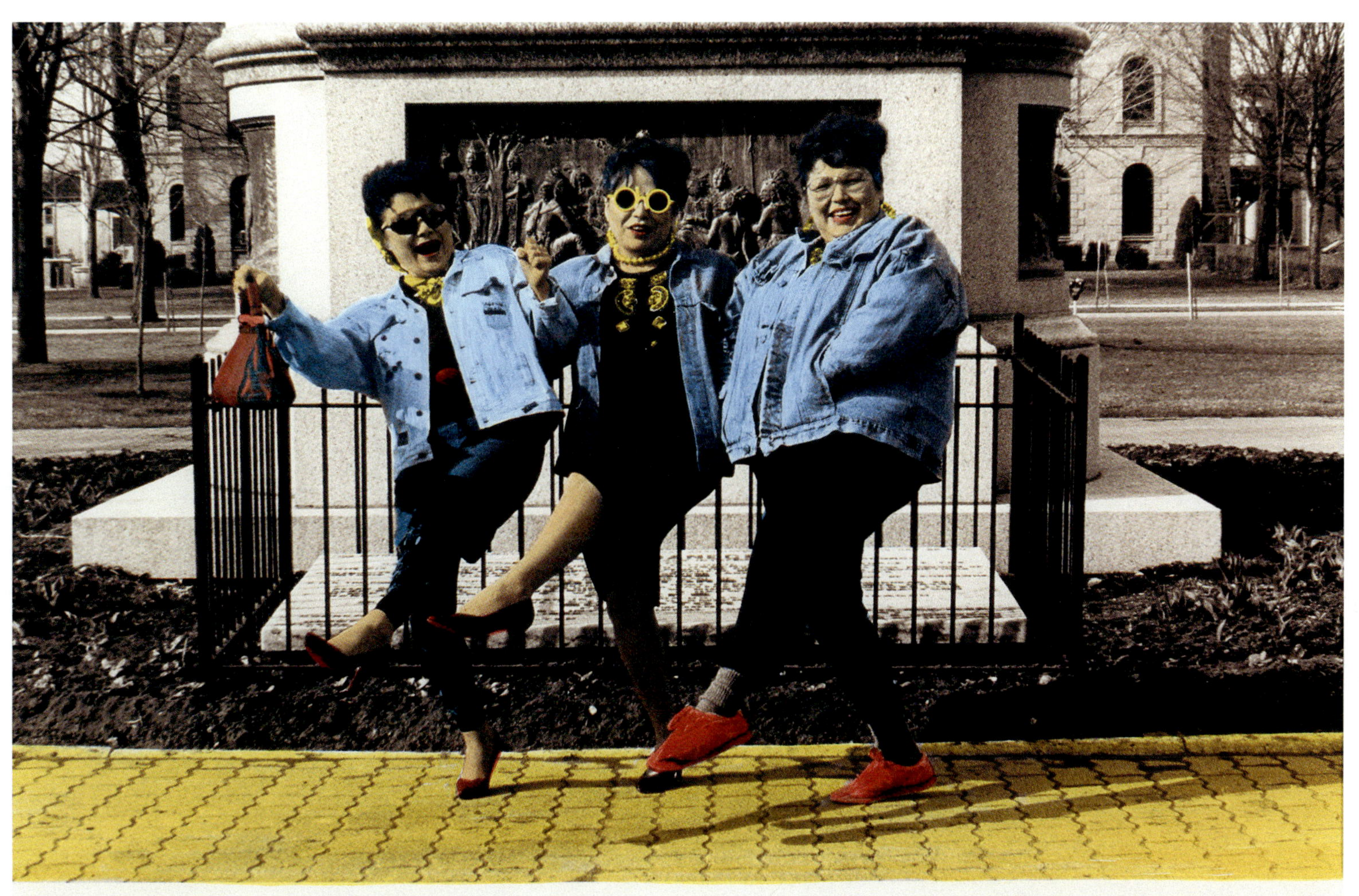

we grew as Maples, Oaks & Pines along the banks of the Grand

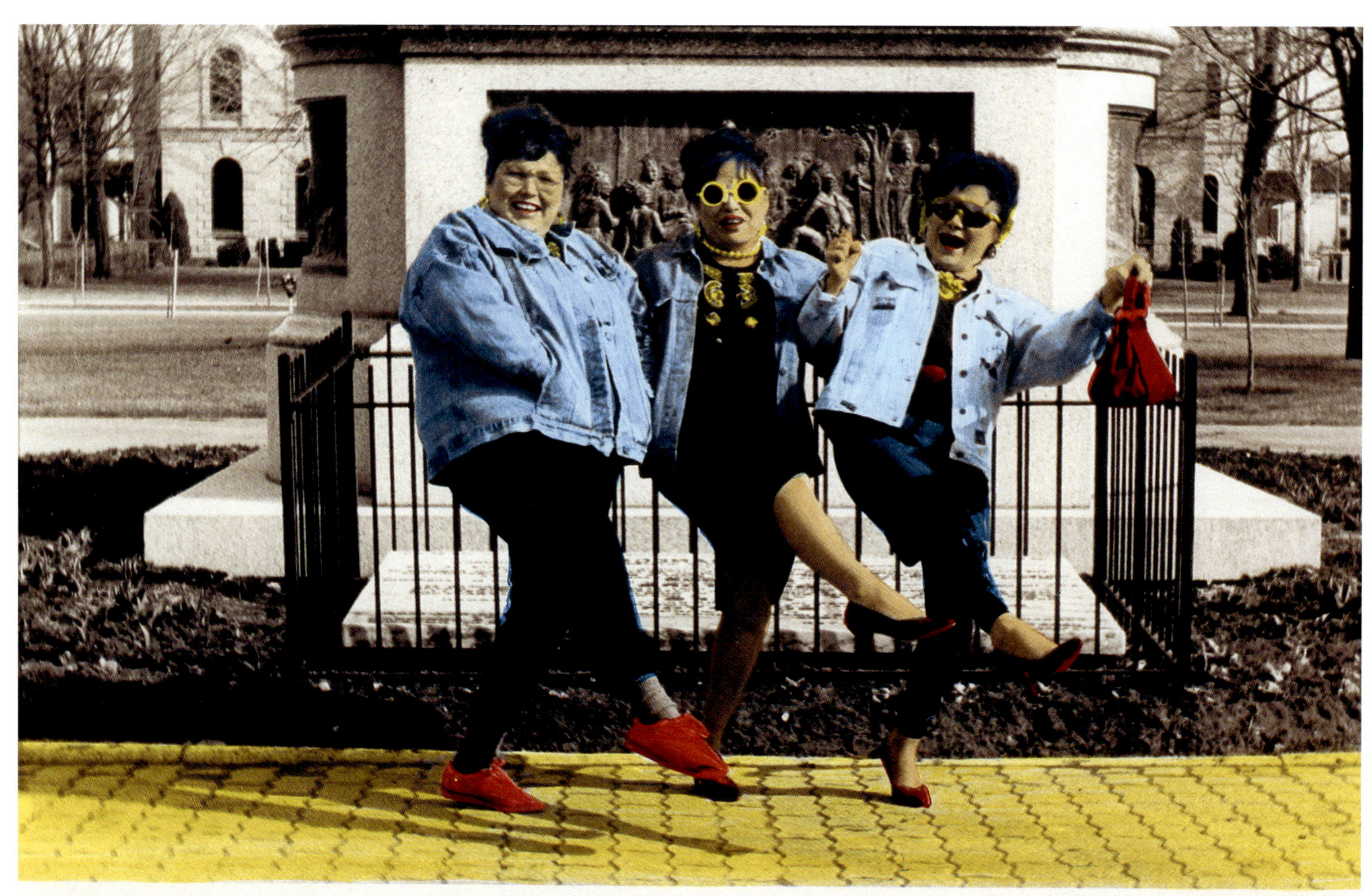

We followed that yellow-bricked road and clicked our red heels hard!

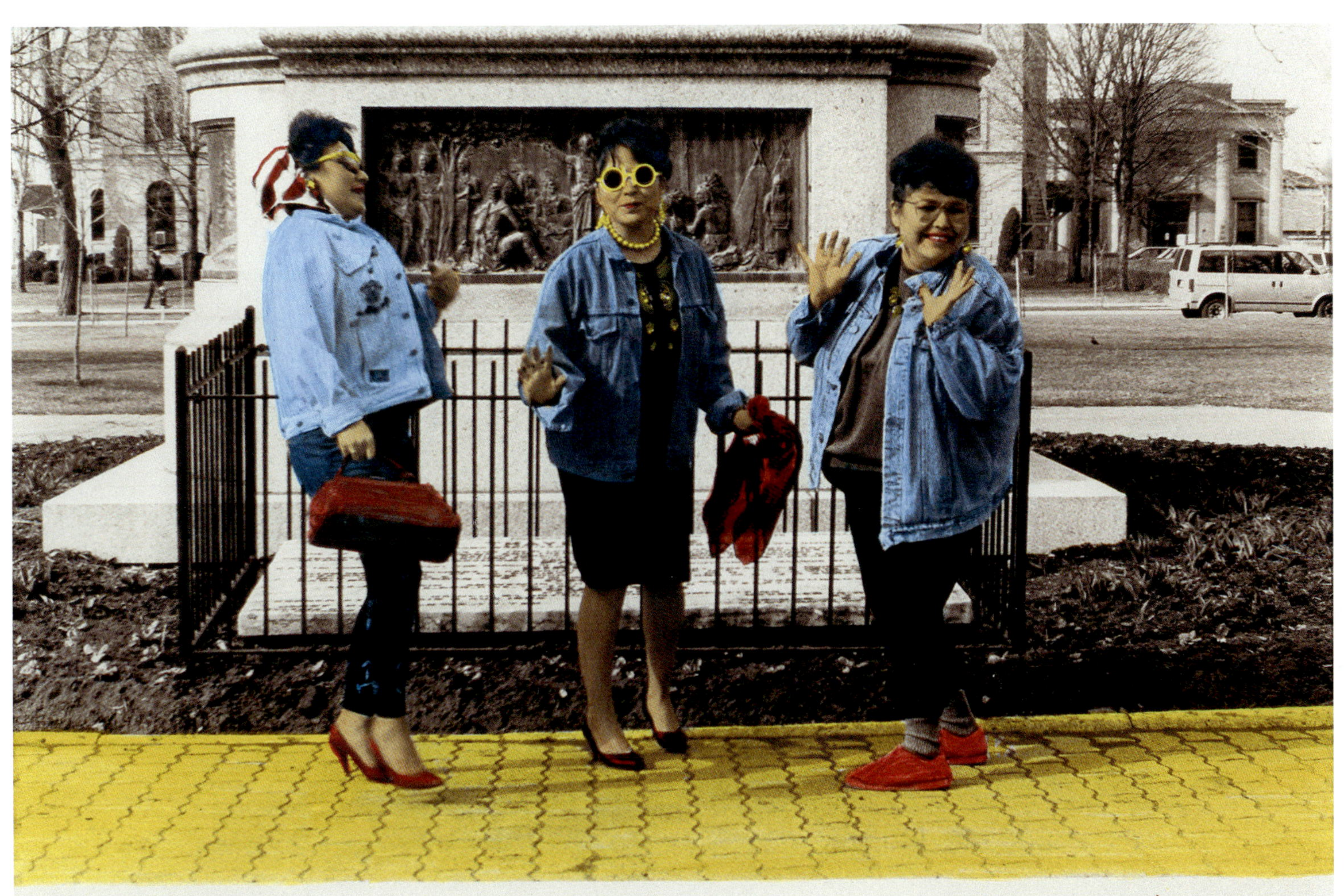

Red Heels Hard (details), 1991

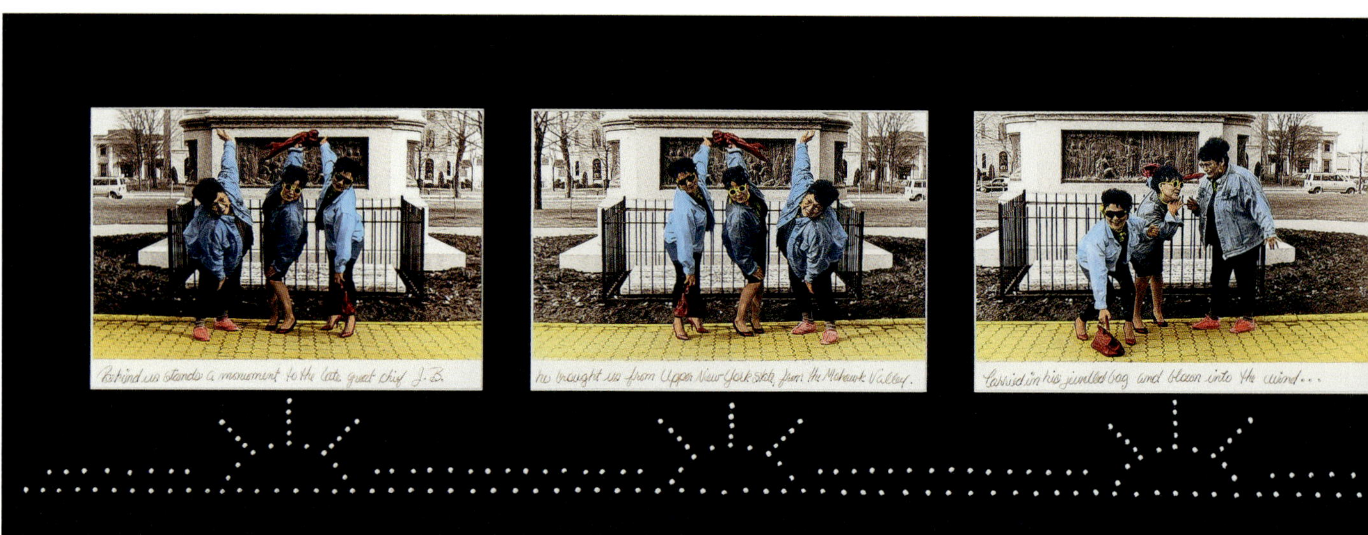

Behind us stands a monument to the late great chief J.B.
he brought us from Upper New York state, from the Mohawk Valley.
carried in his jewelled bag and blown into the wind...

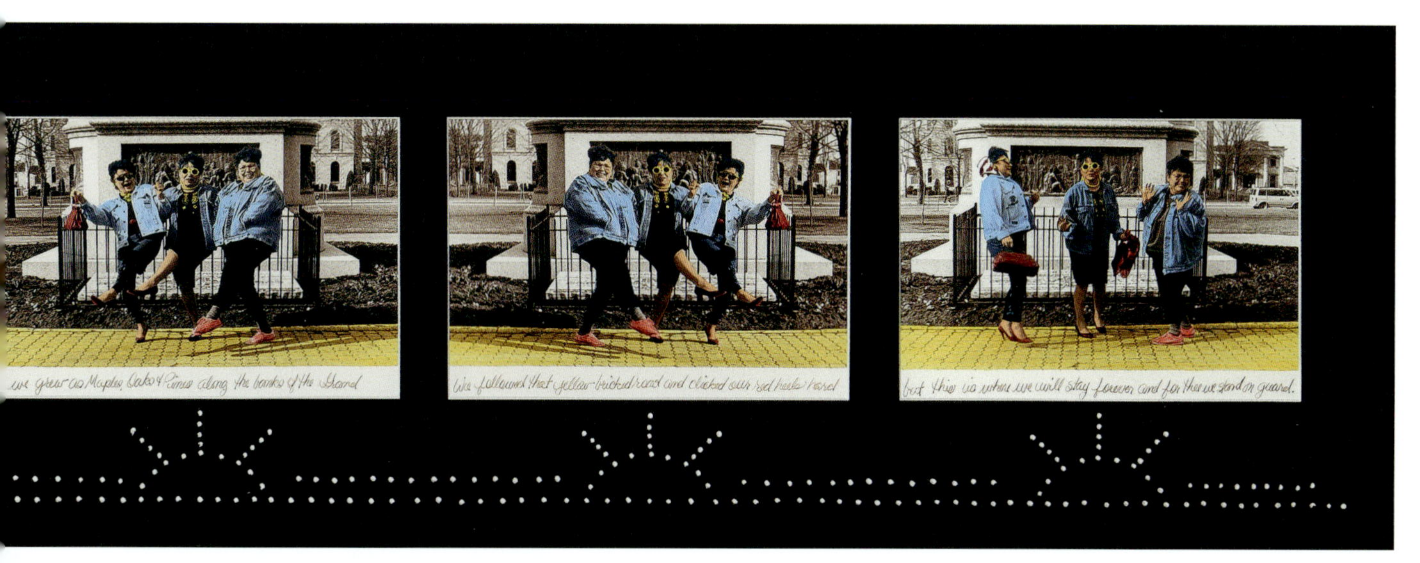

Red Heels Hard, 1991

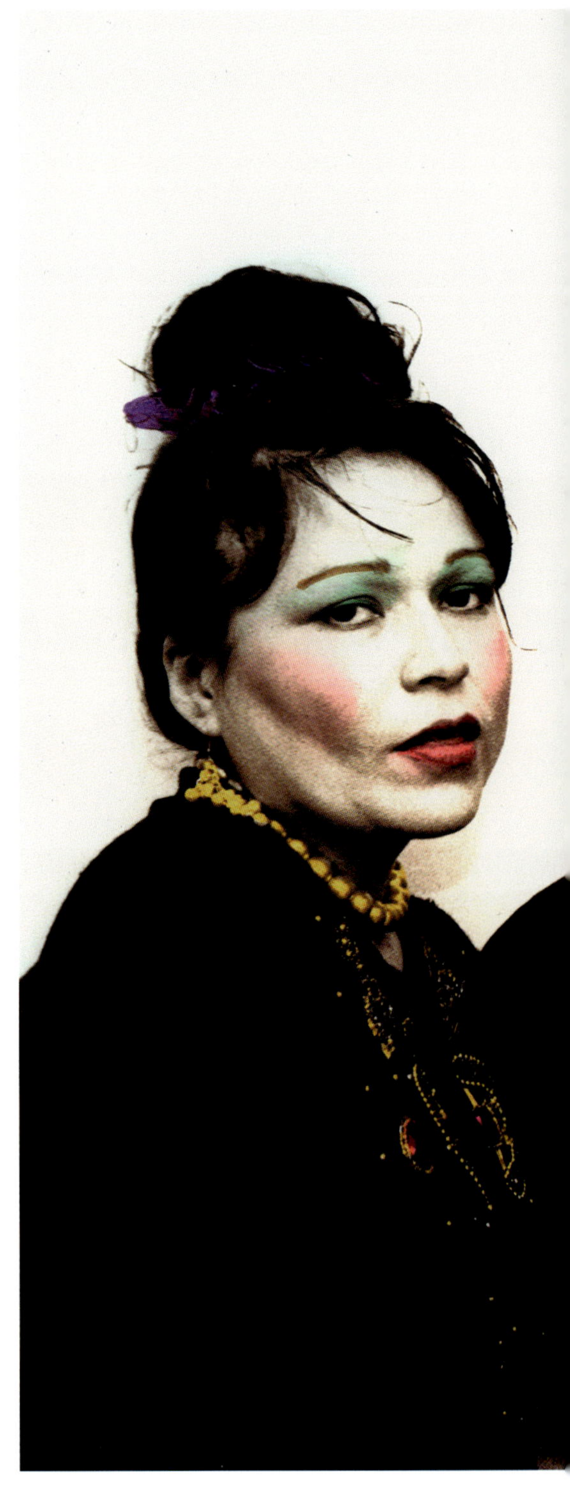

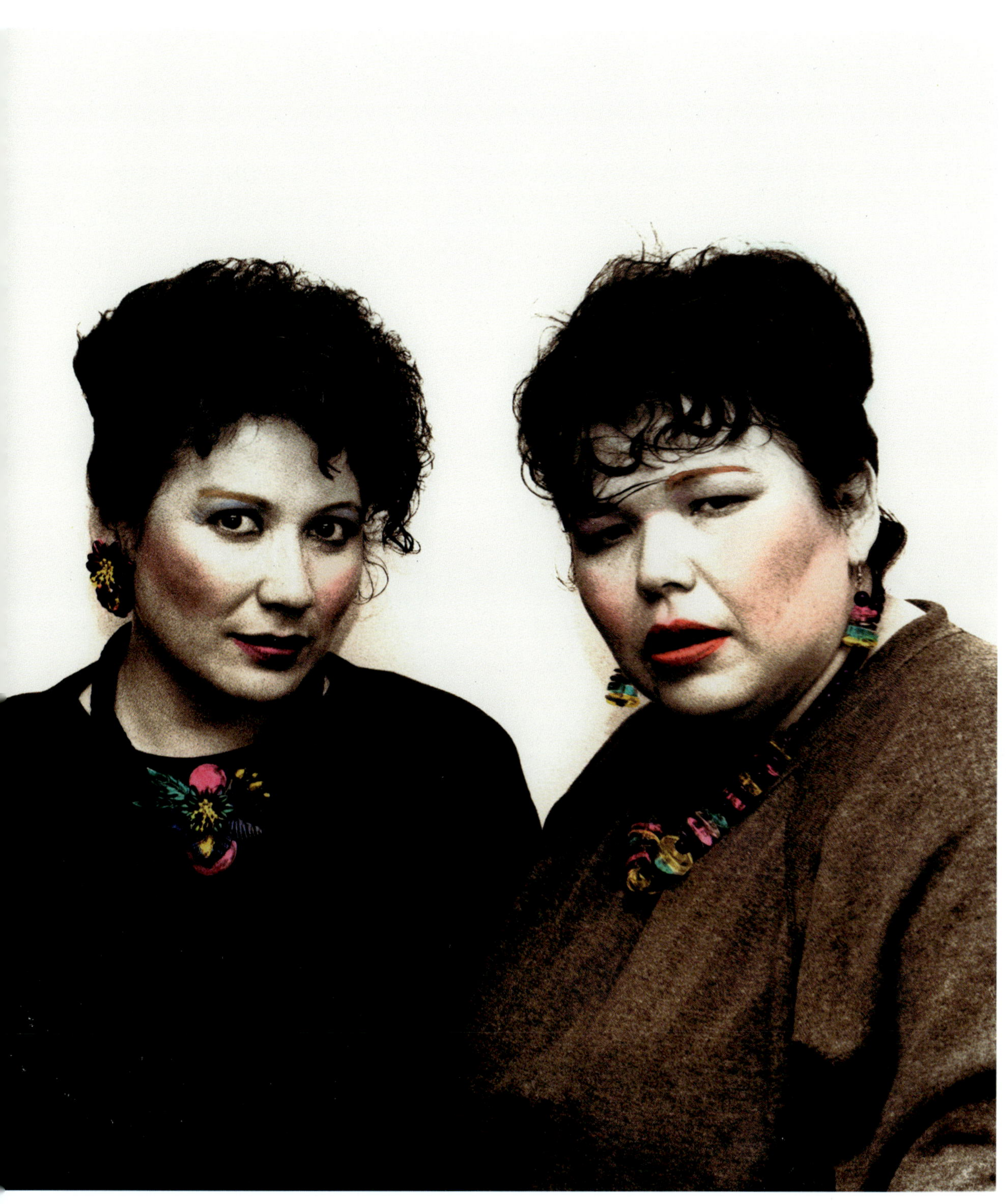

Mohawks in Beehives, 1991

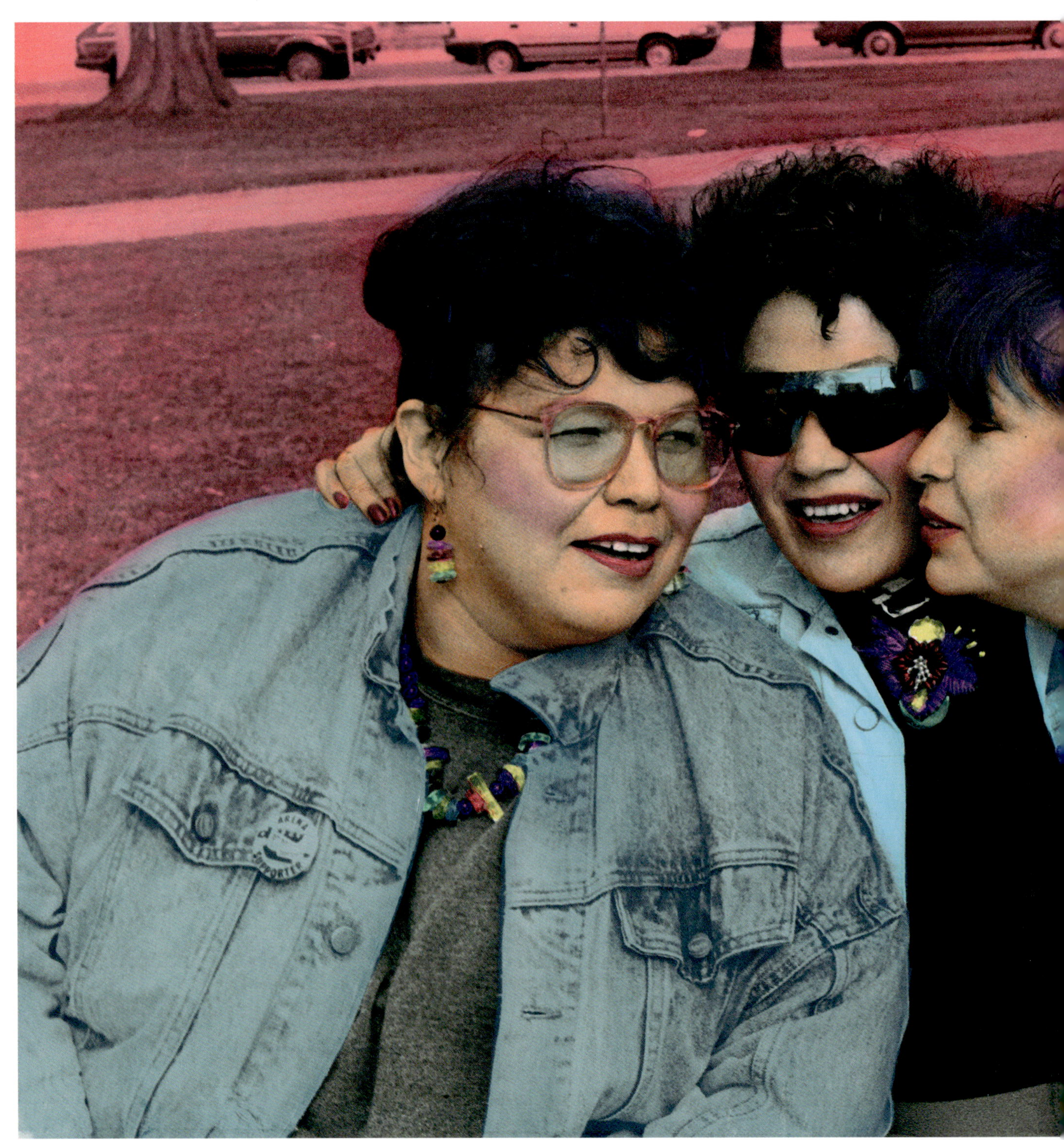

 Queen Bees, 1991

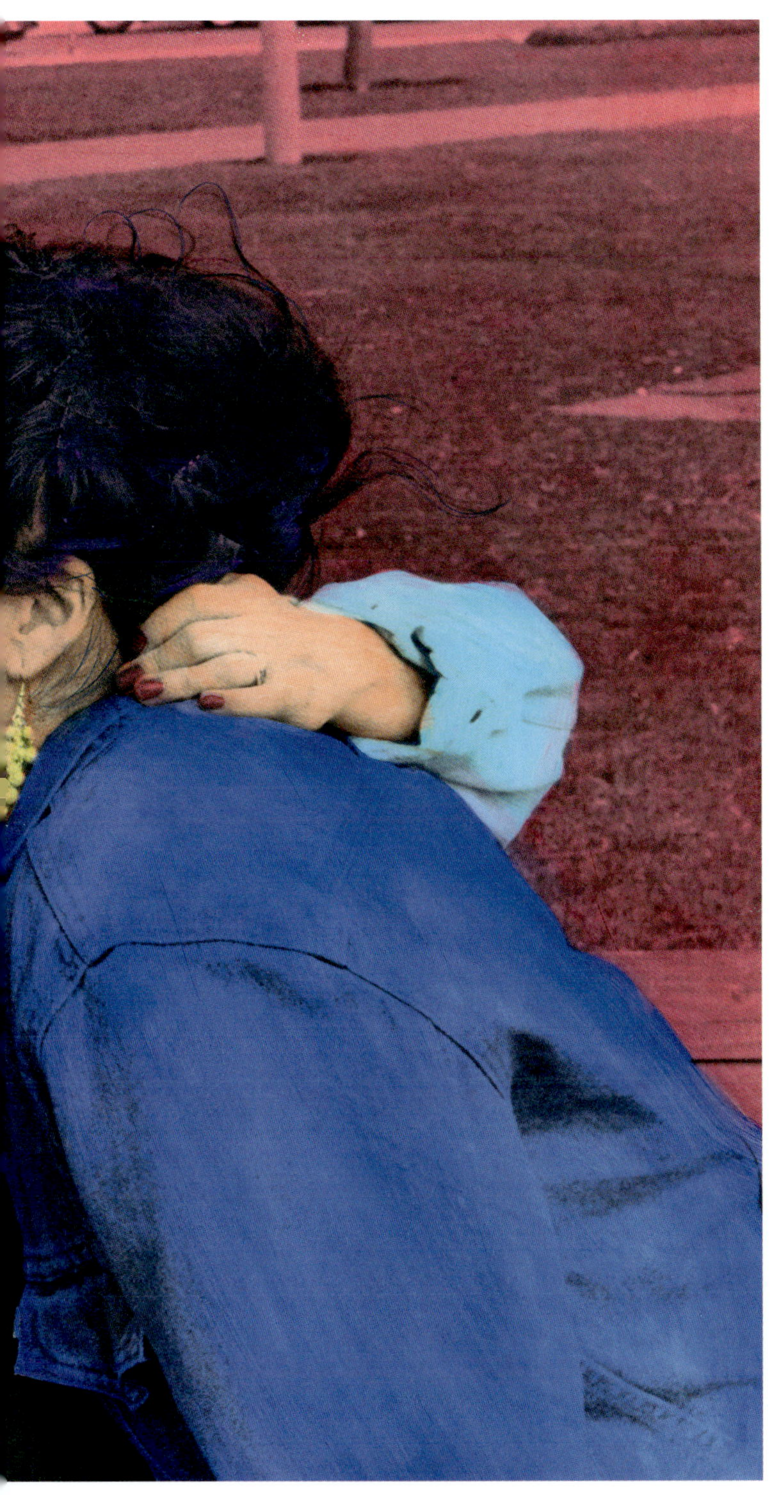

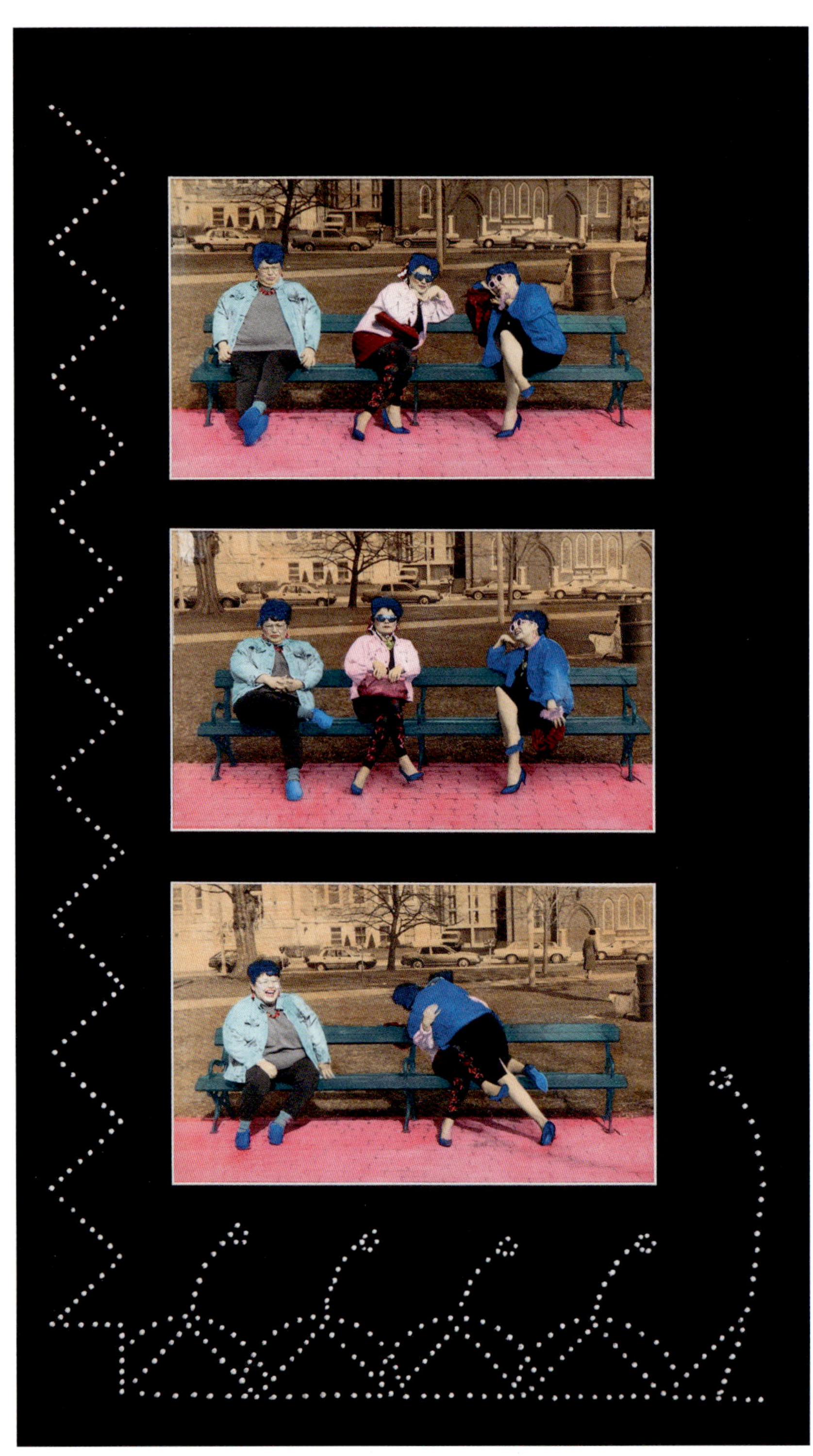

58   **Spring Fever**, 1991

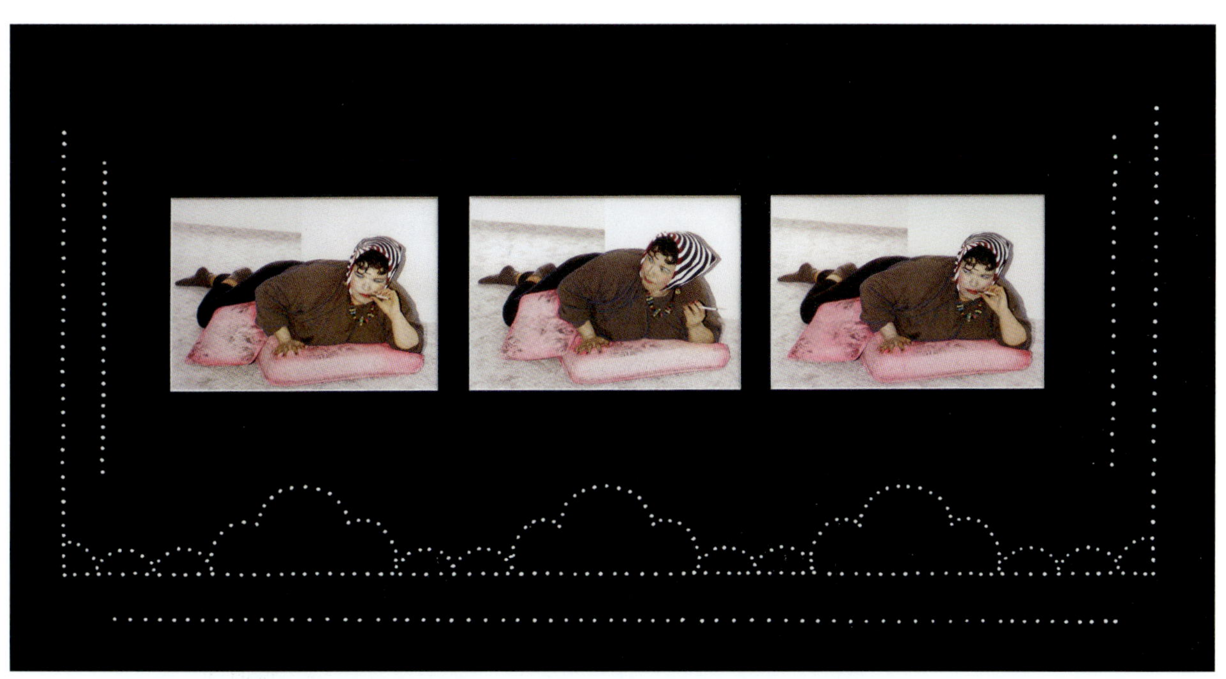

Mohawk Sitting on a Cloud, 1991

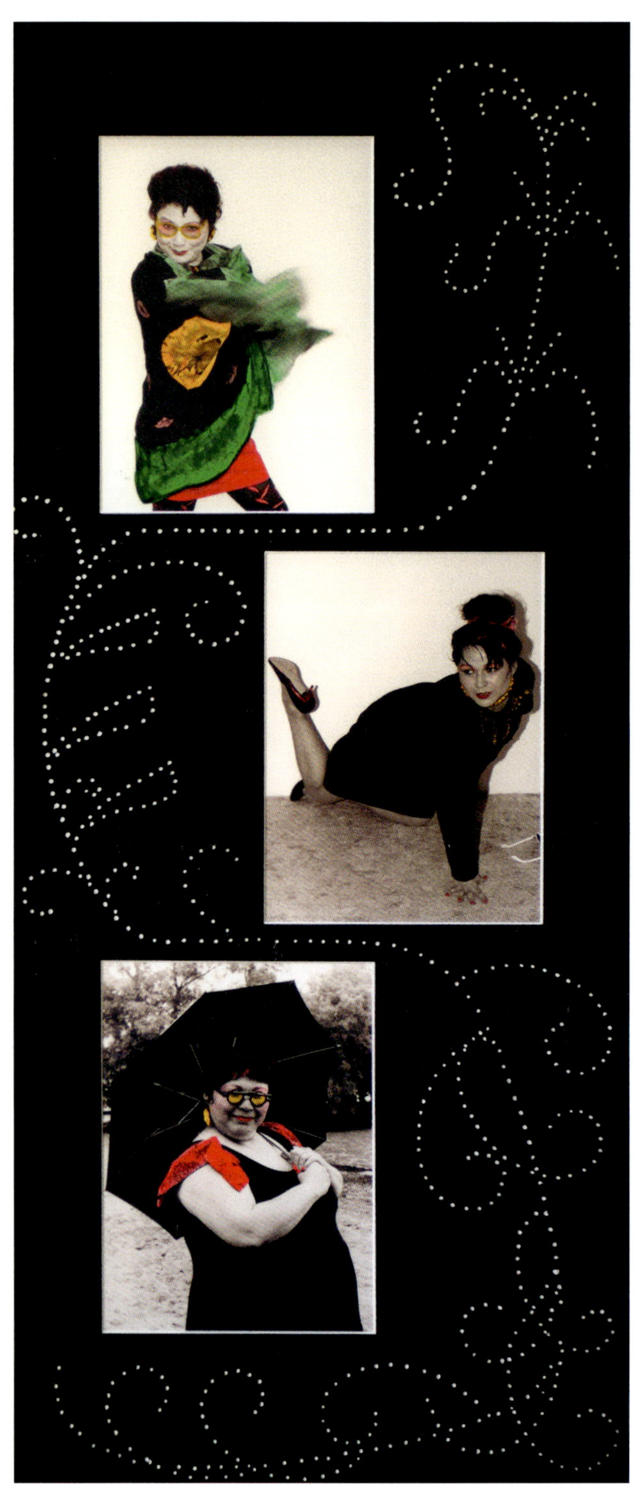

  I Enjoy Being a Mohawk Girl, 1991

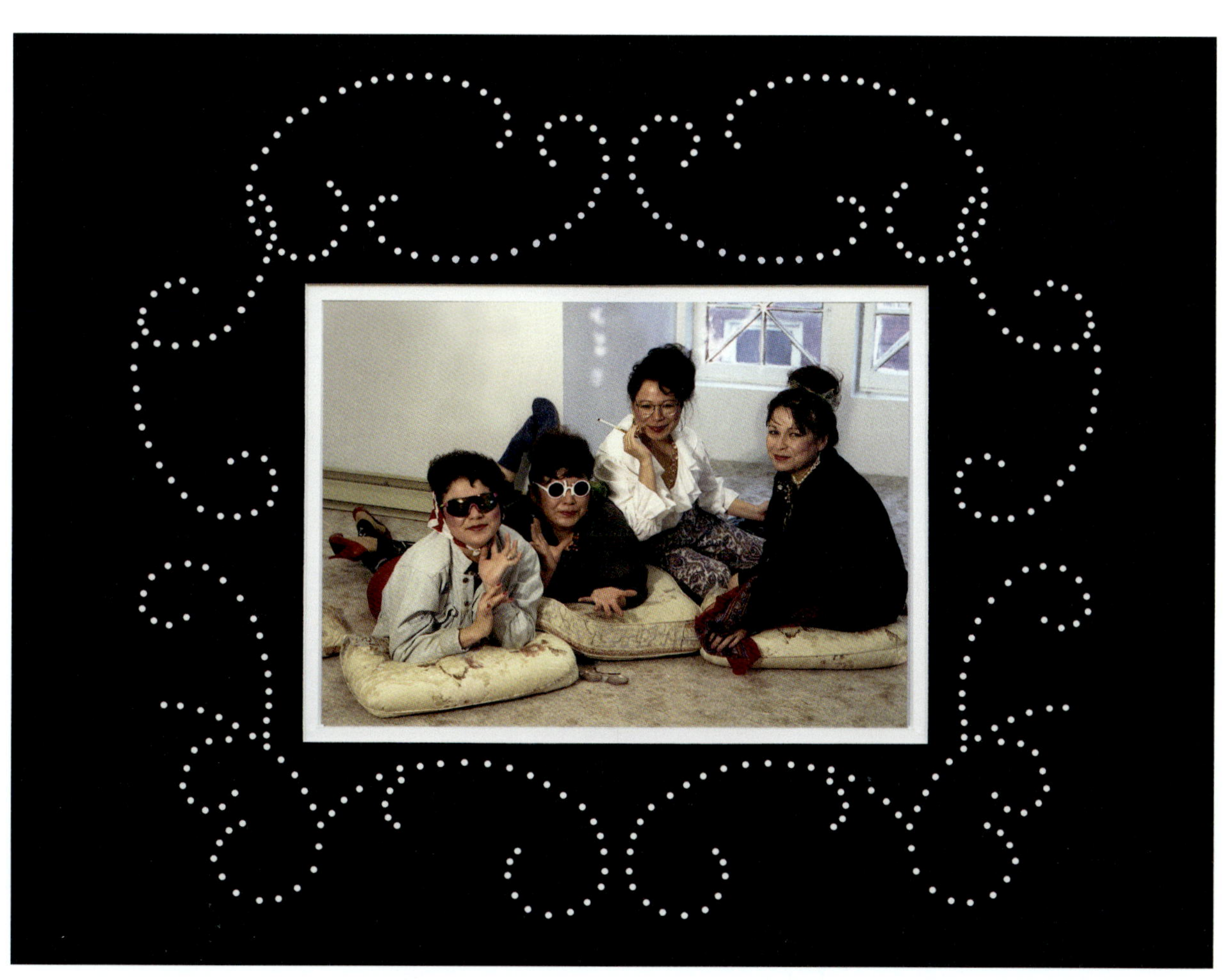

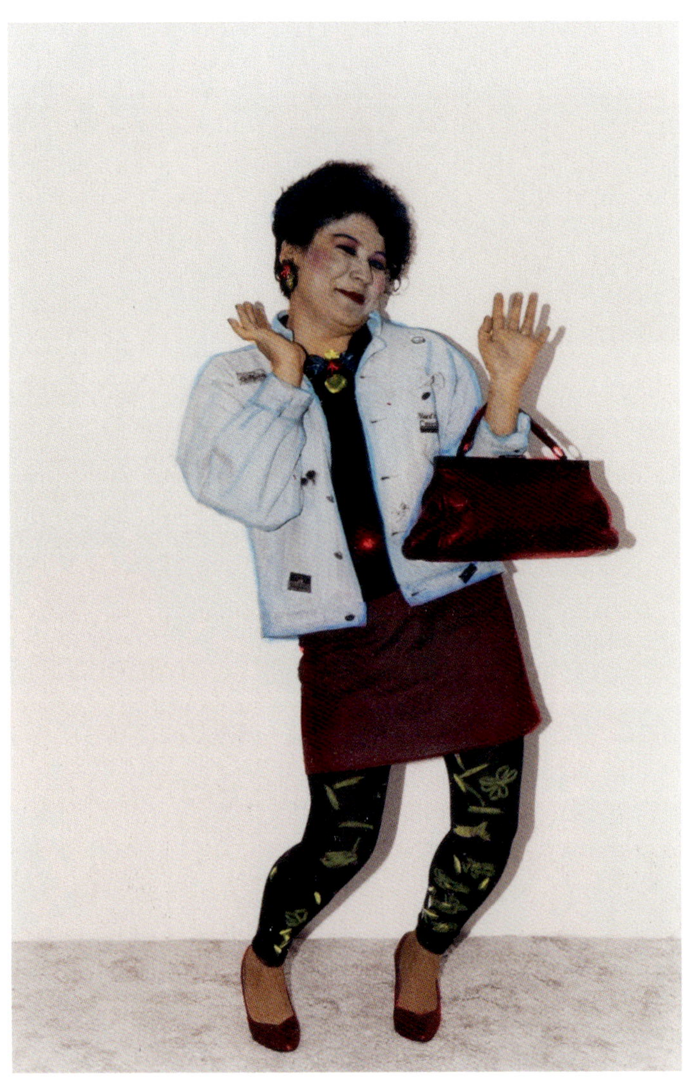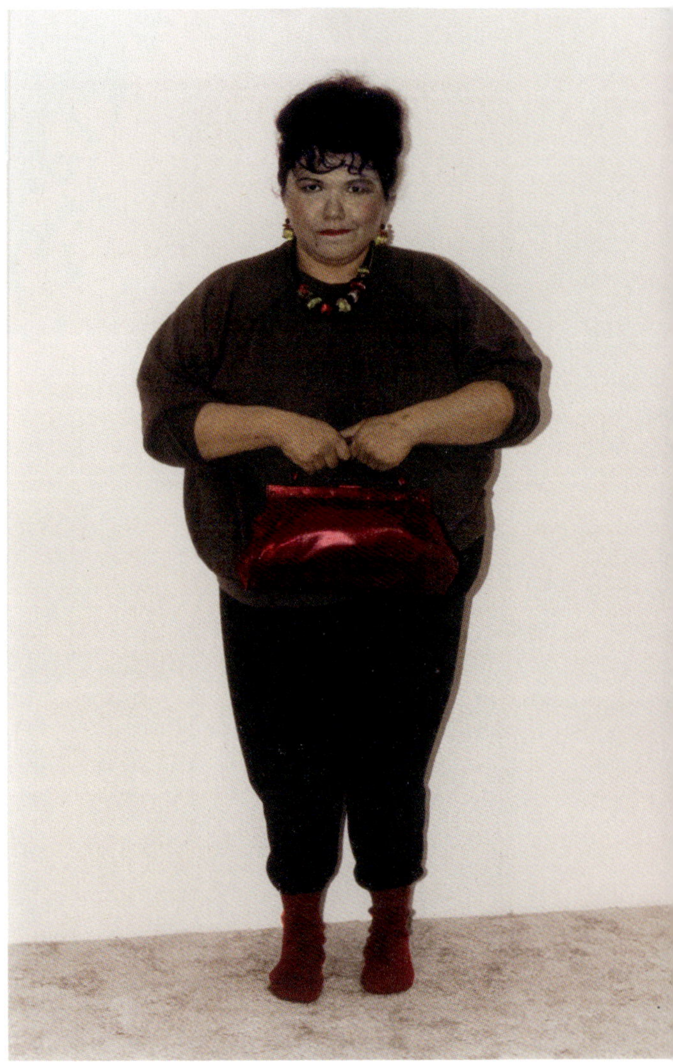

   Mohawks in Beehives II, 1991

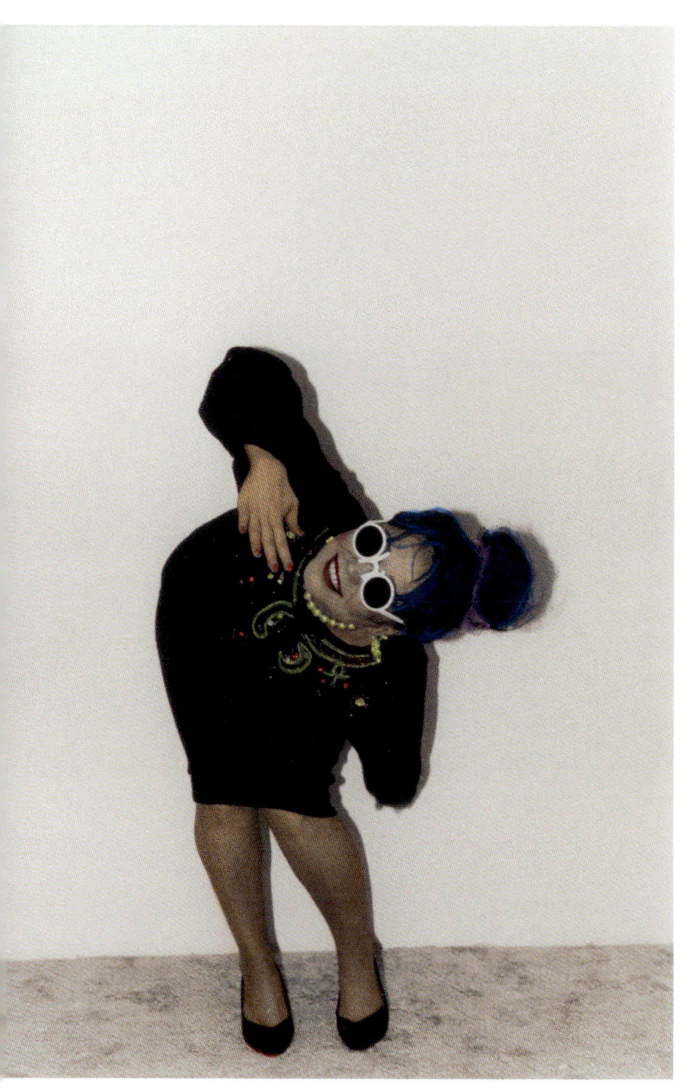

 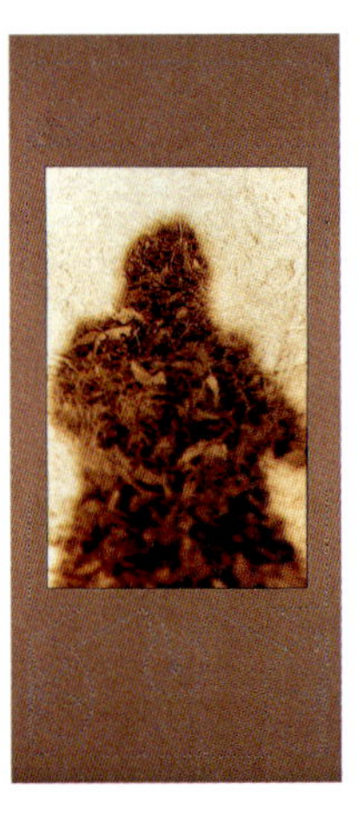 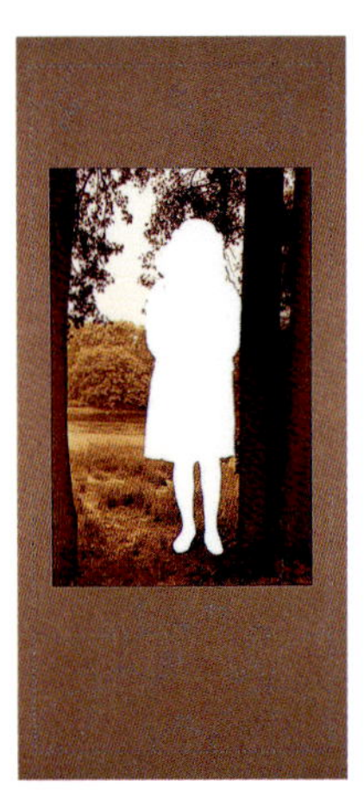 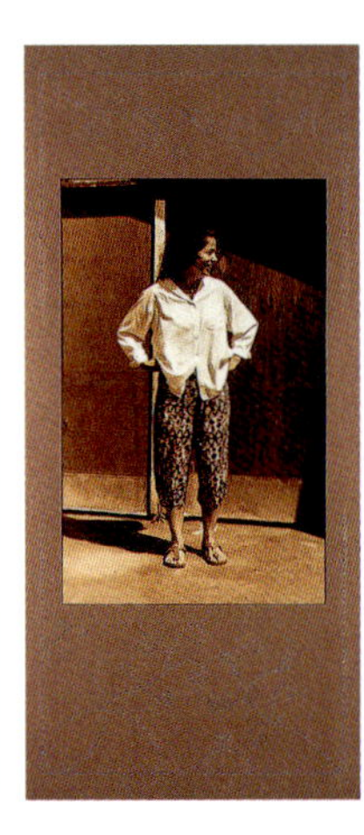 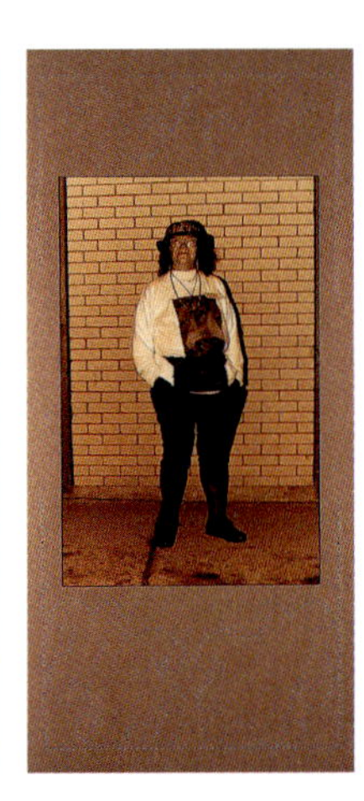 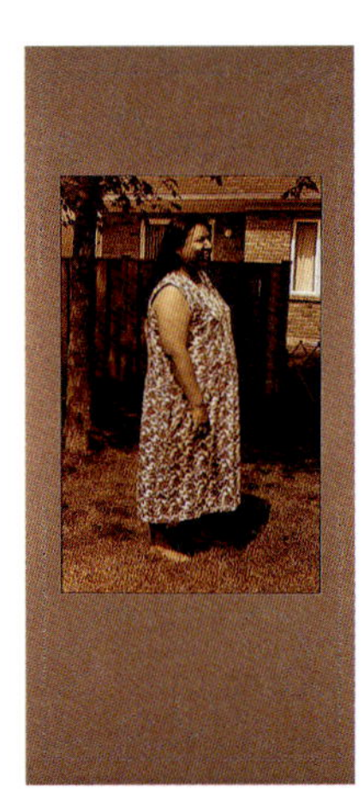 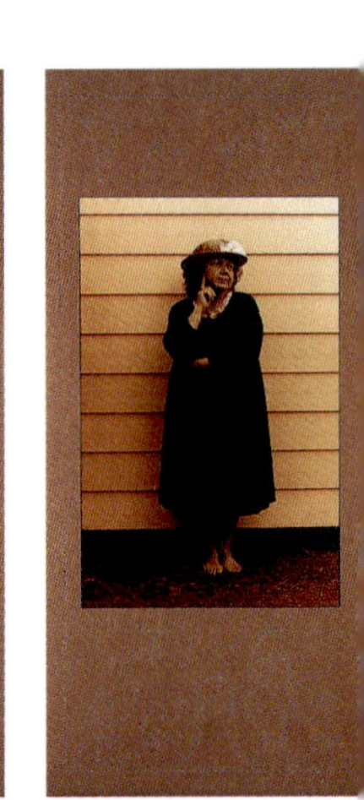

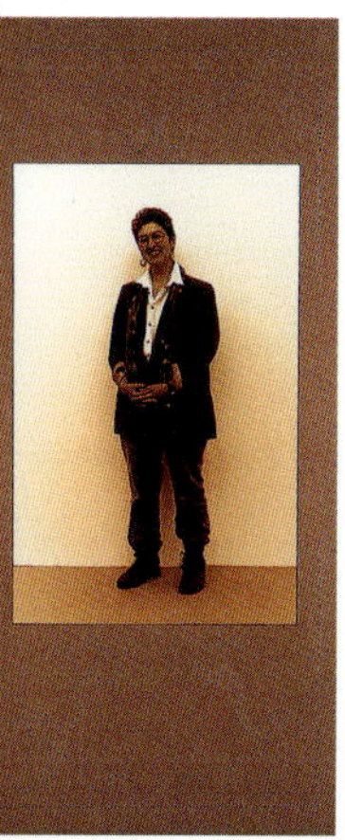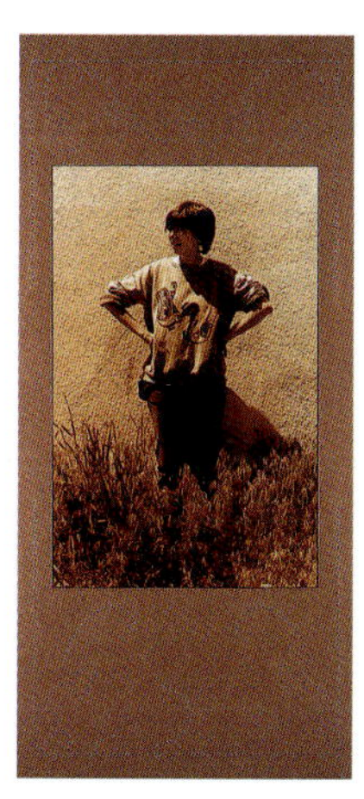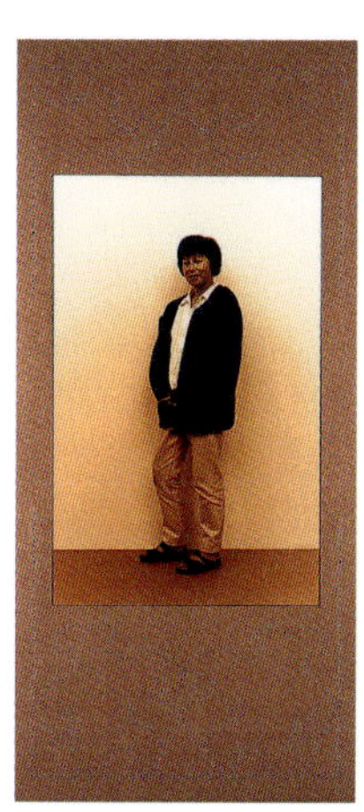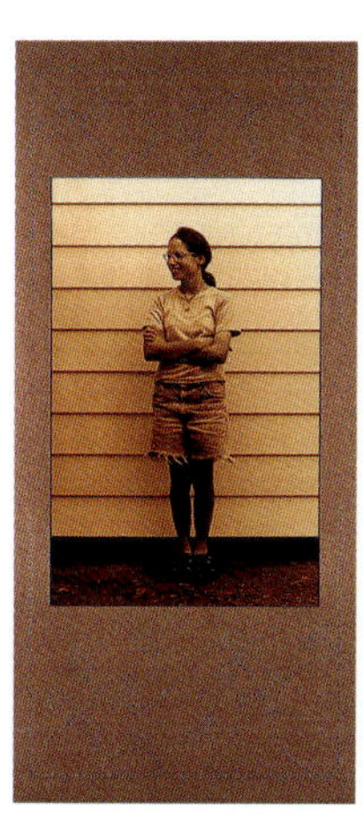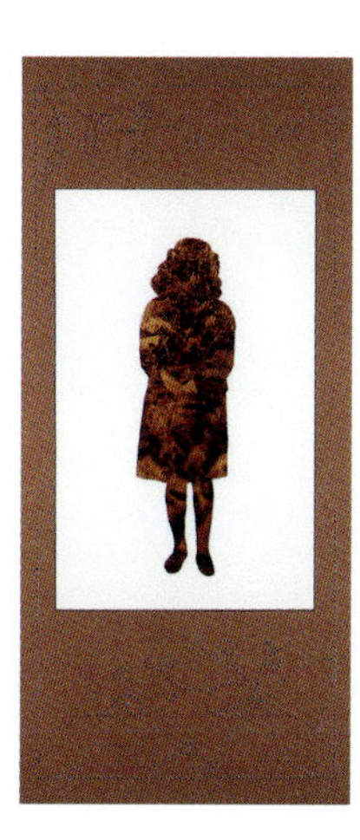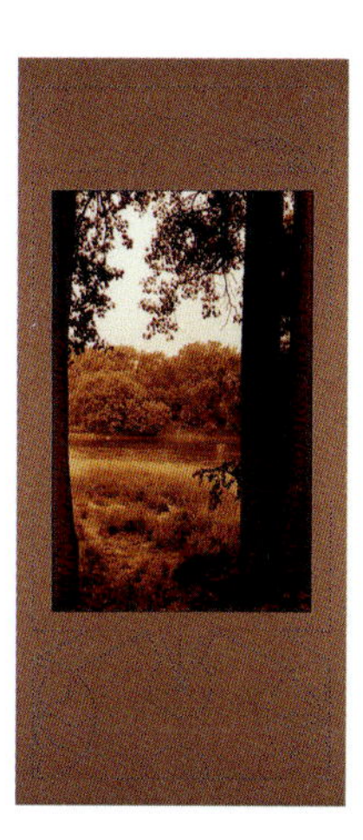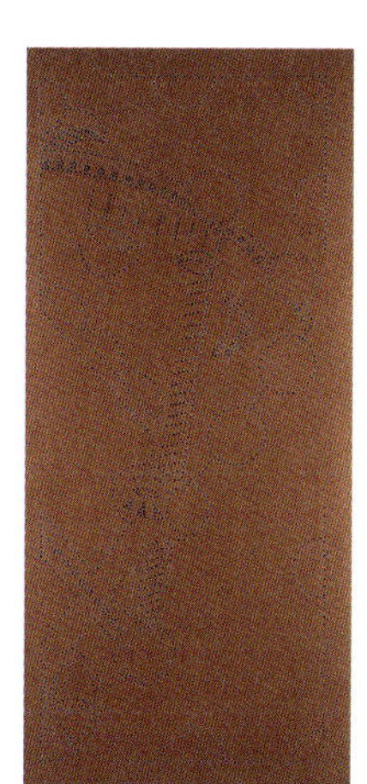

Are You My Sister?, 1994

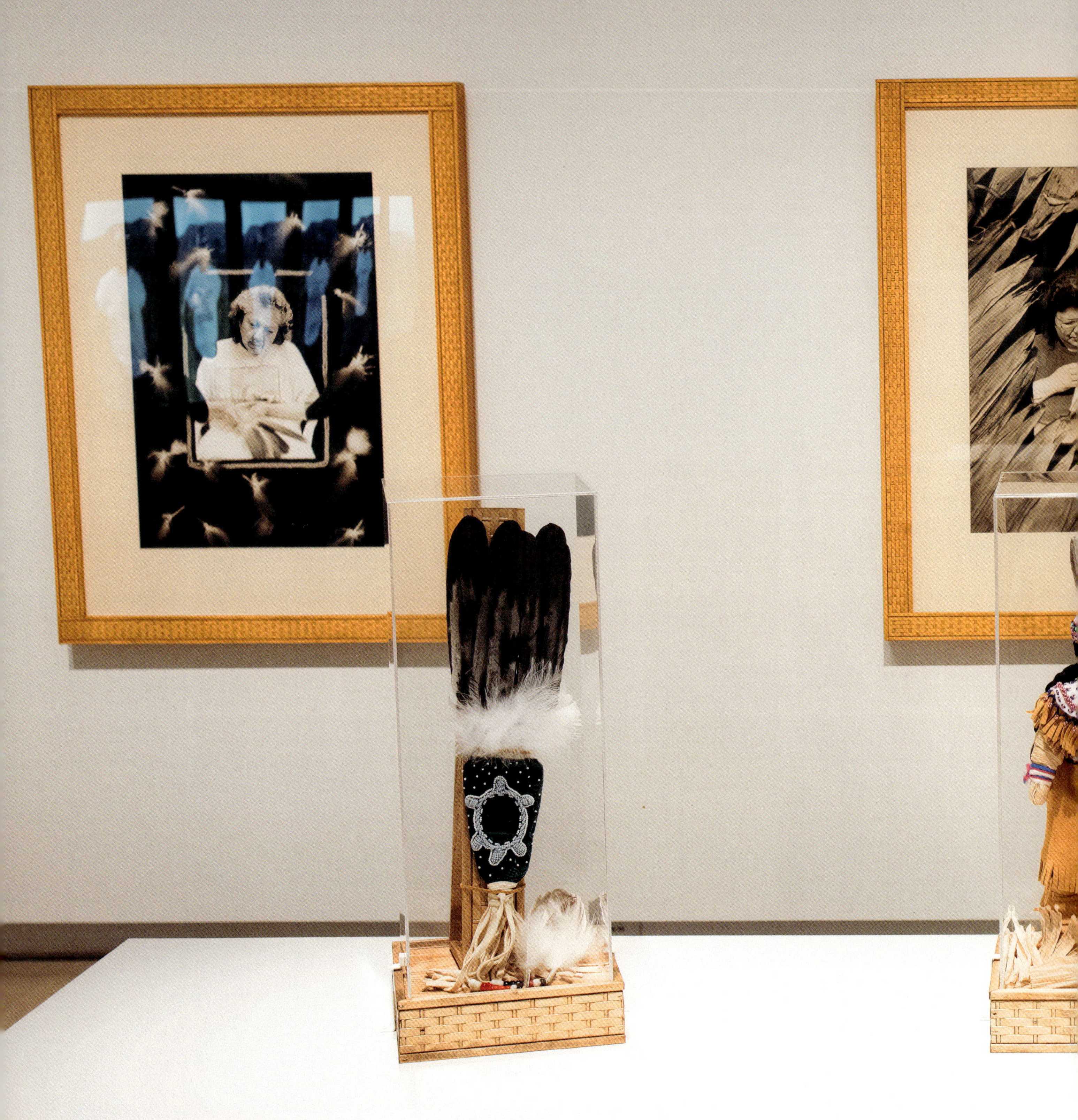

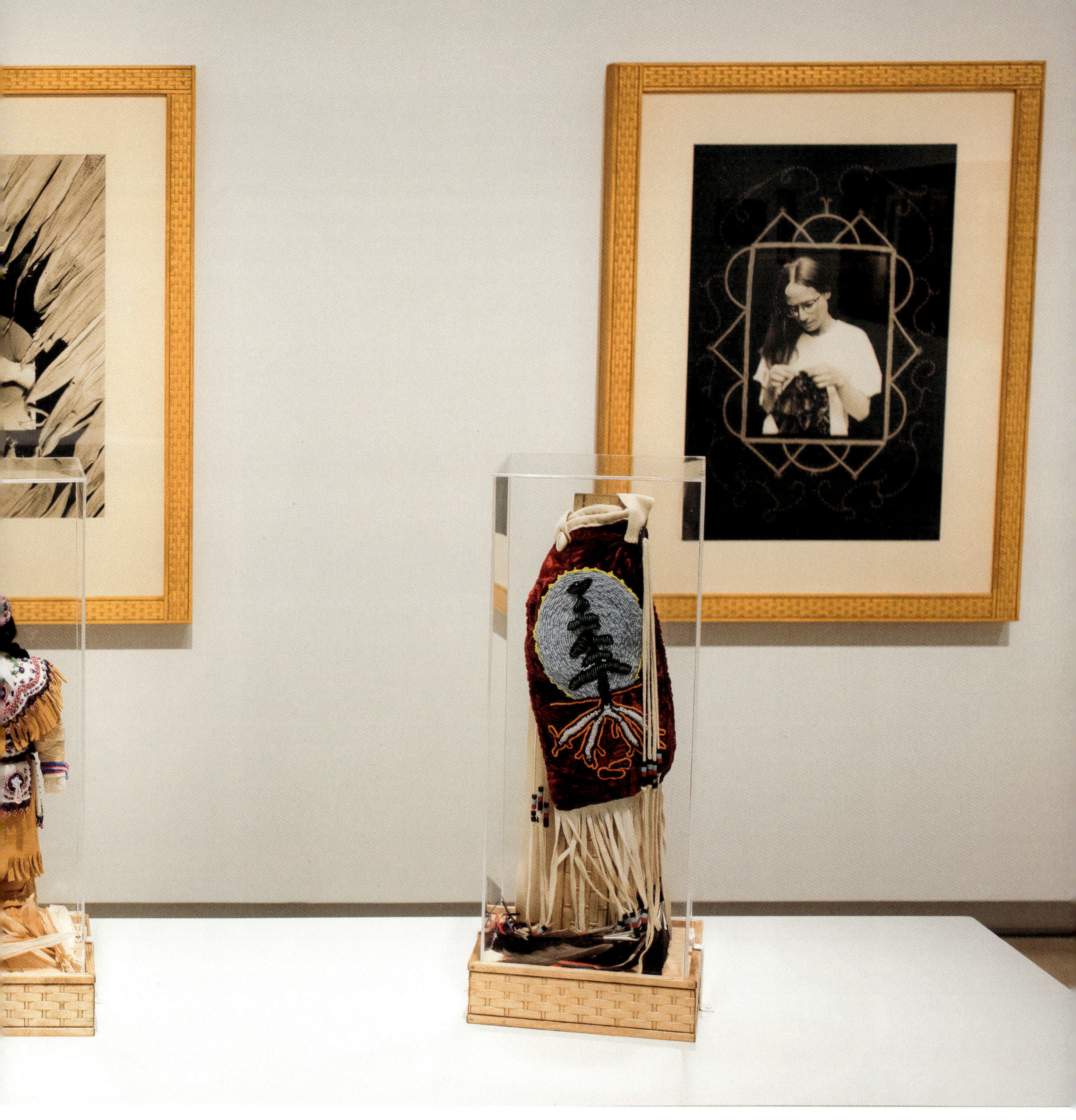

Installation view of **Chiquita, Bunny, Stella**, 1995
Shelley Niro: Scotiabank Photography Award at The Image Centre, Toronto Metropolitan University, 2018
Photograph by Larissa Issler

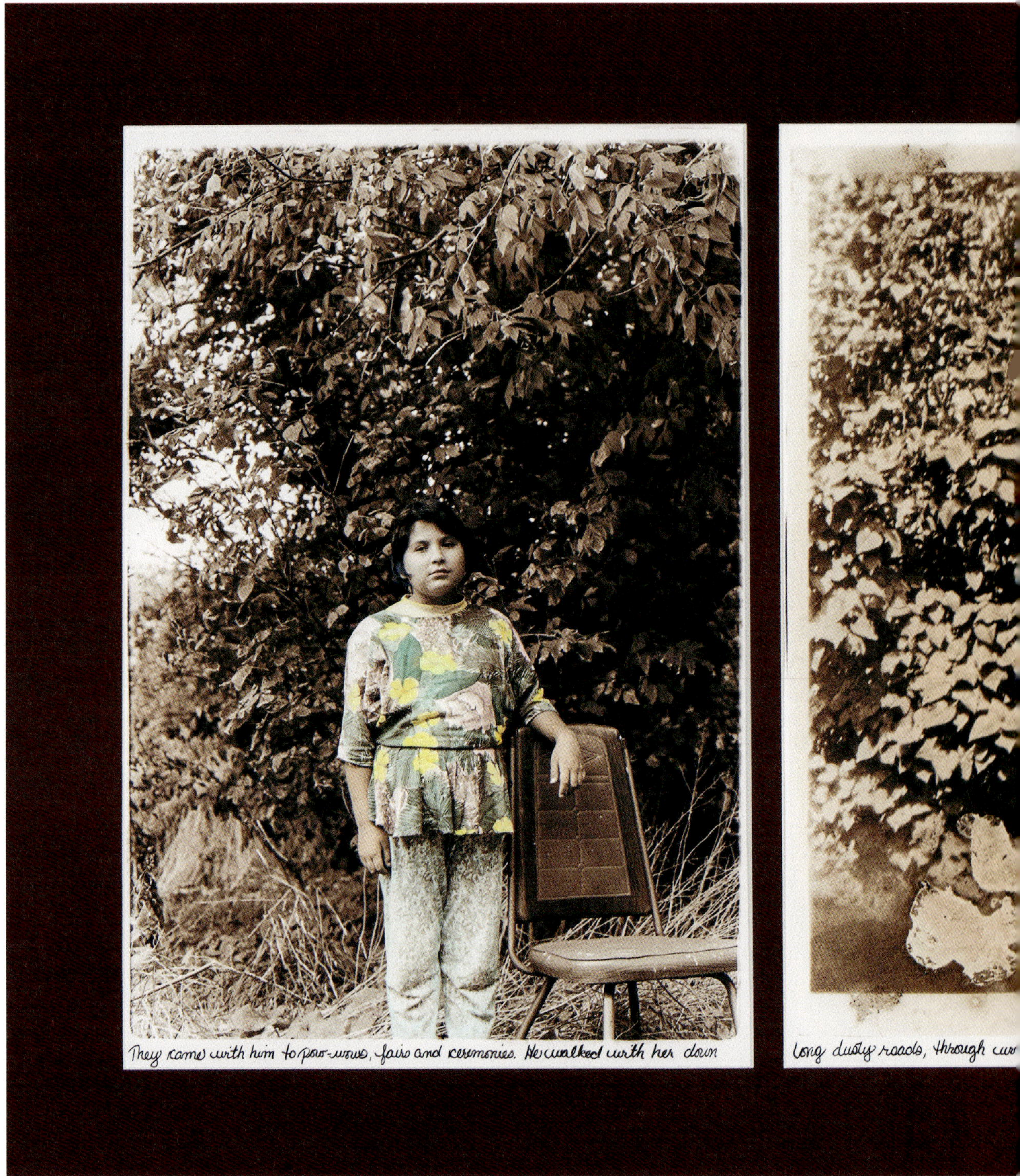
They came with him to pow-wows, fairs and ceremonies. He walked with her down
long dusty roads, through cur

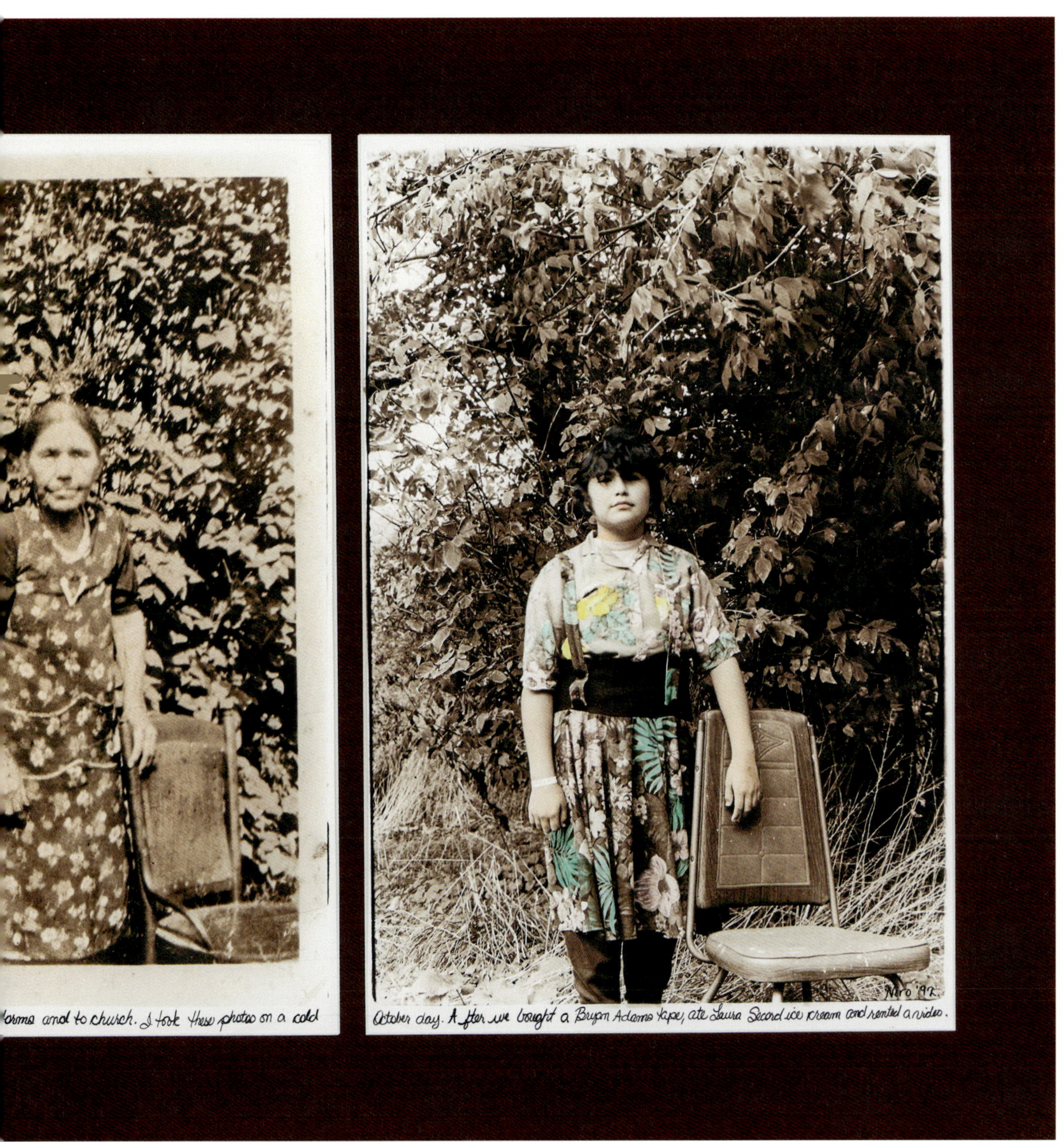
Morma and to church. I took these photos on a cold
October day. After we bought a Bryan Adams tape, ate Laura Secord ice cream and rented a video.
Niro '92.

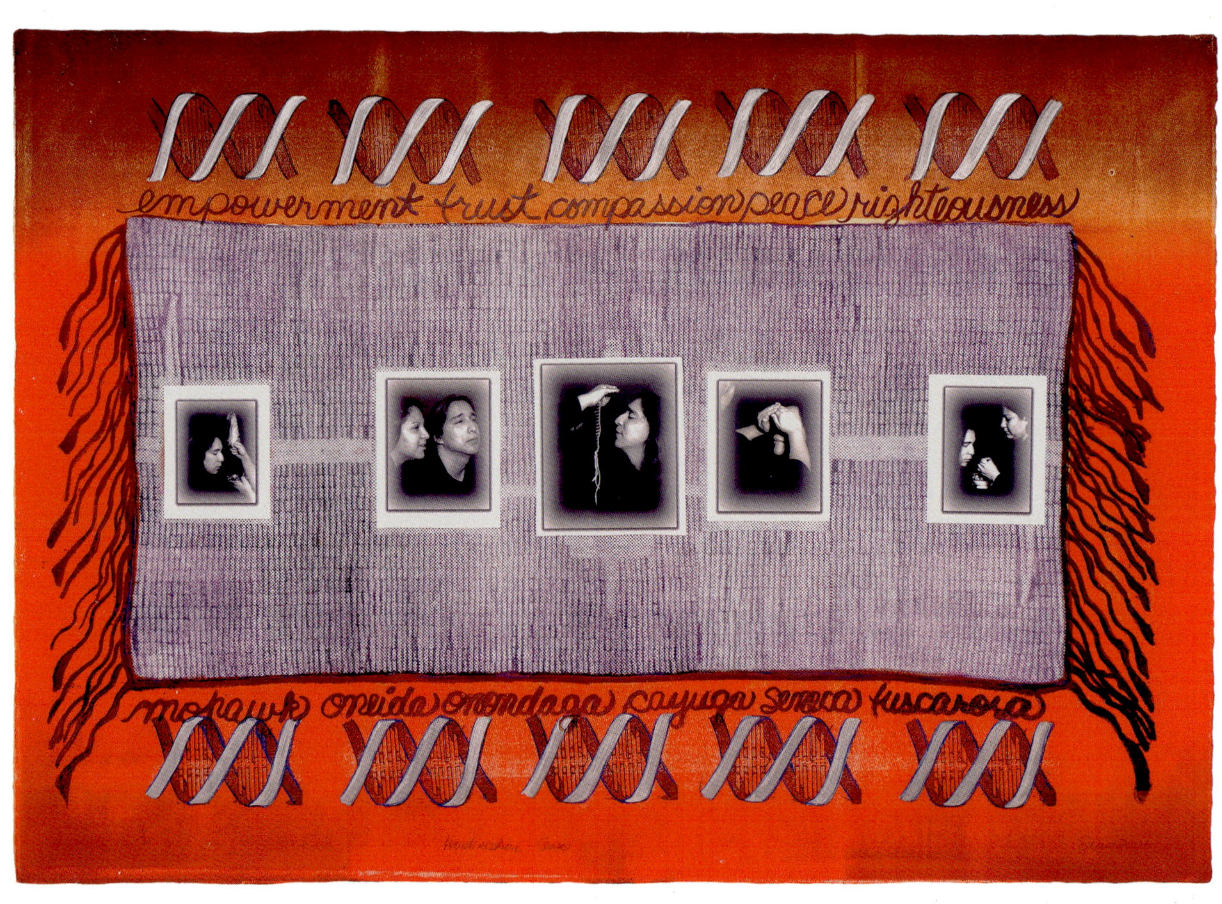

 Haudenosaunee Senses, 2001   The Essential Sensuality of Ceremony, 2002 >

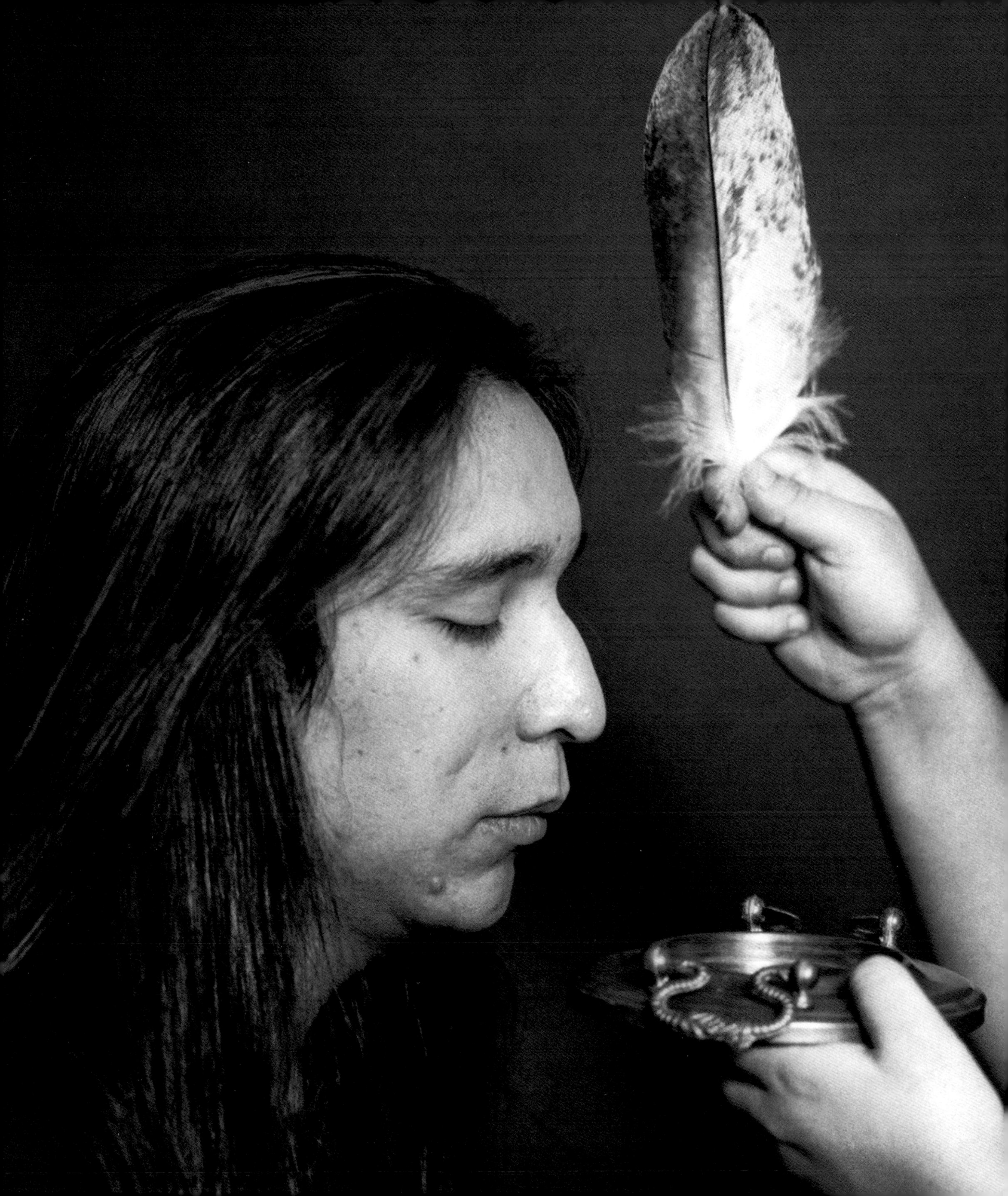

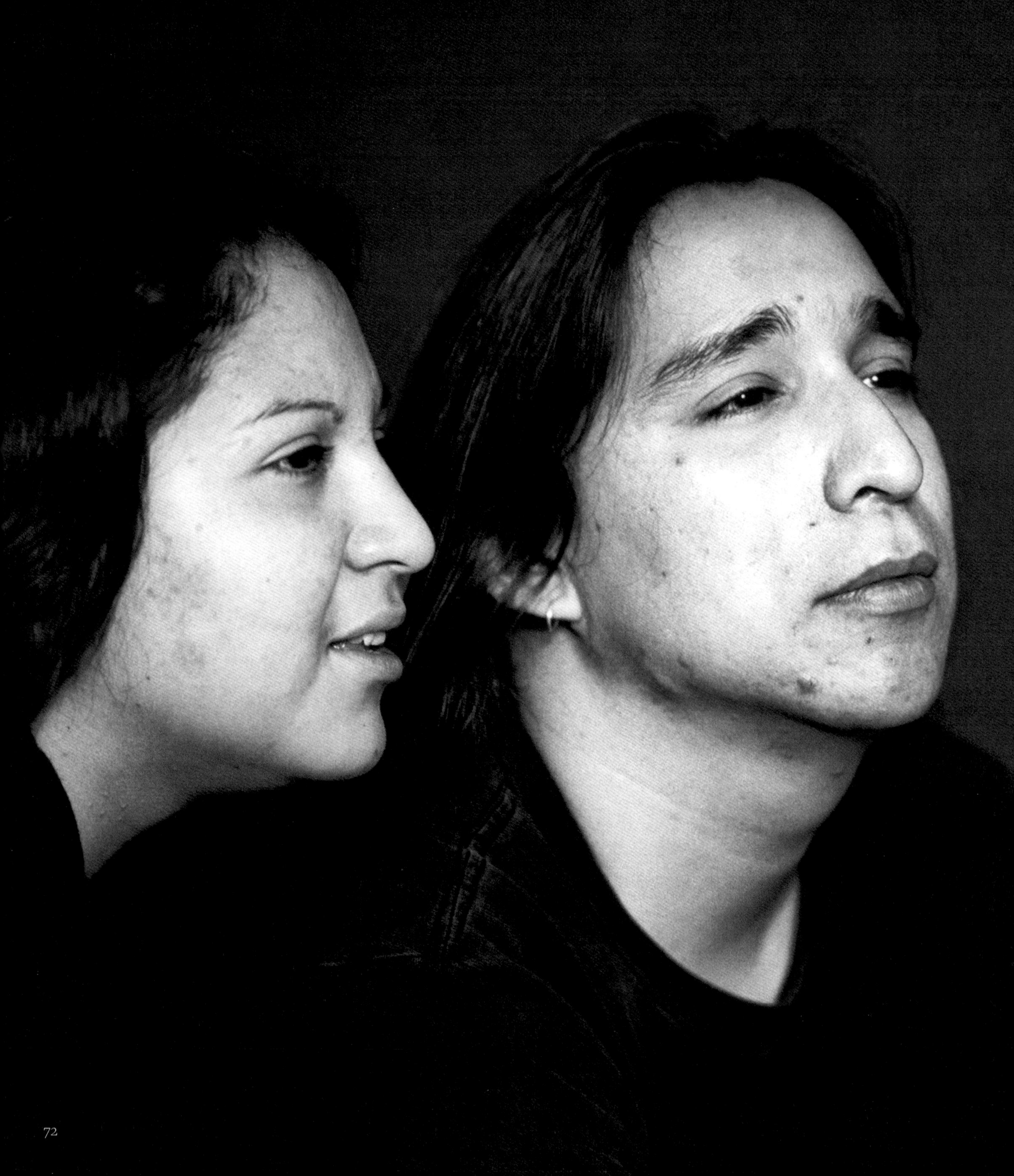

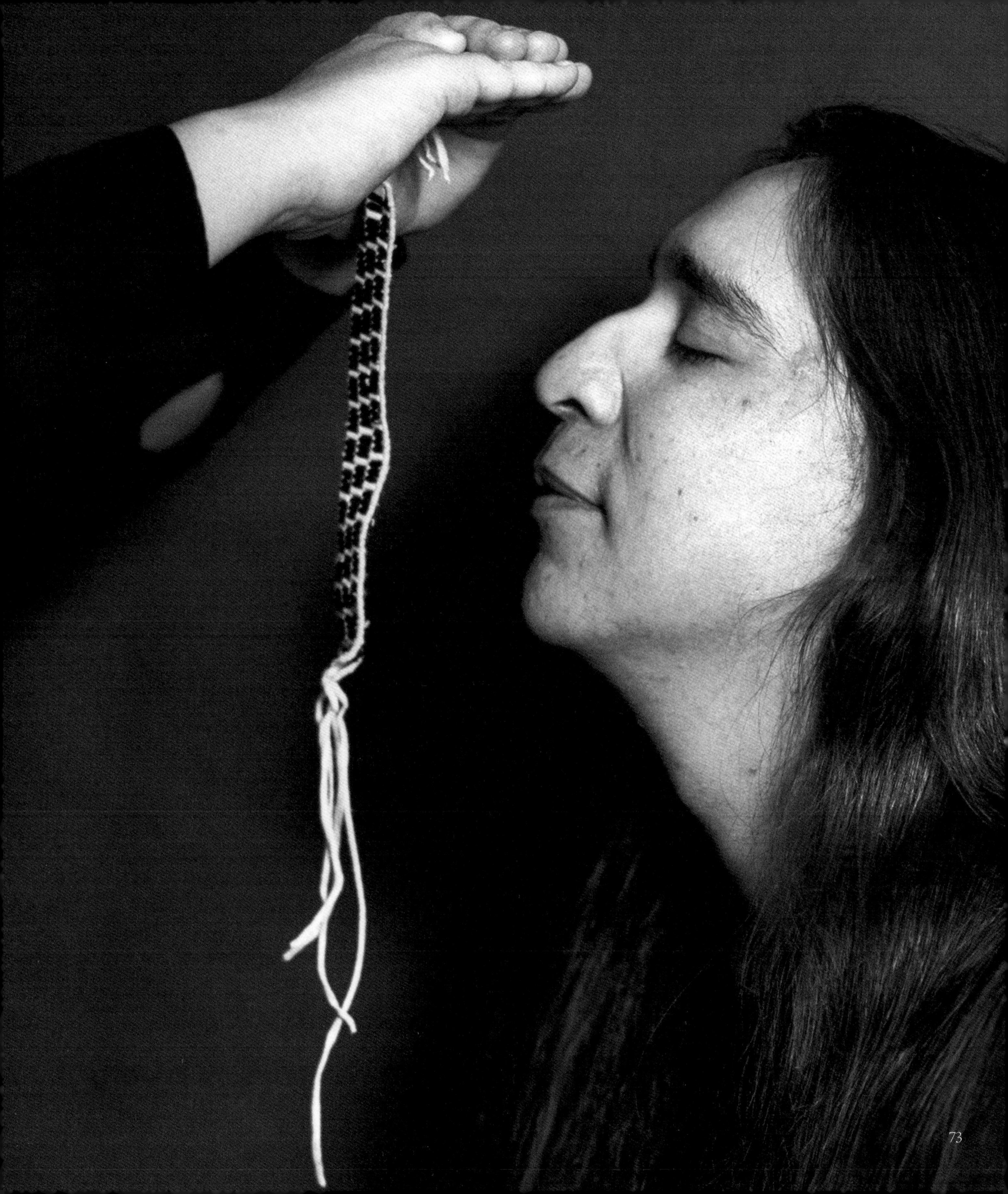

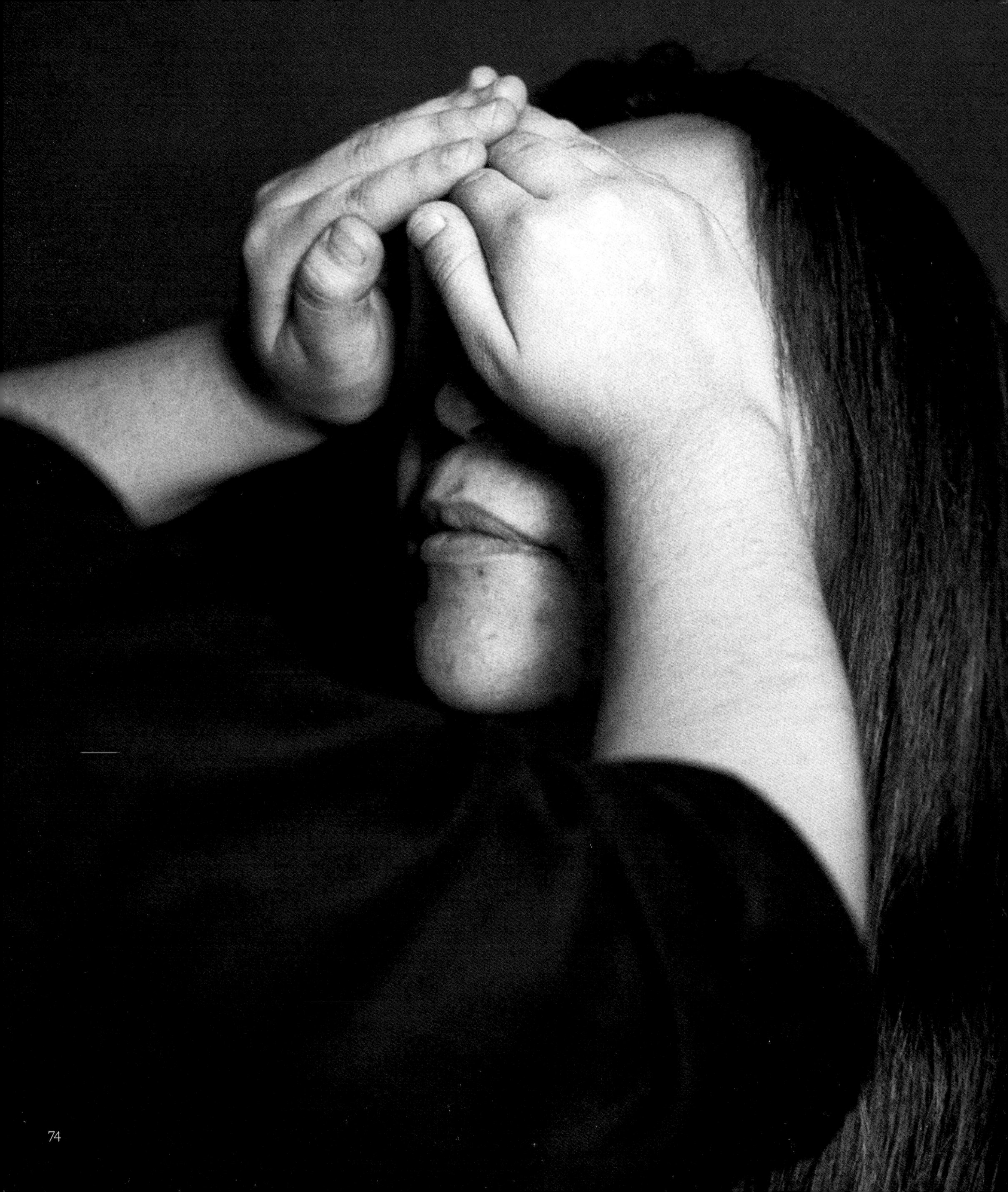

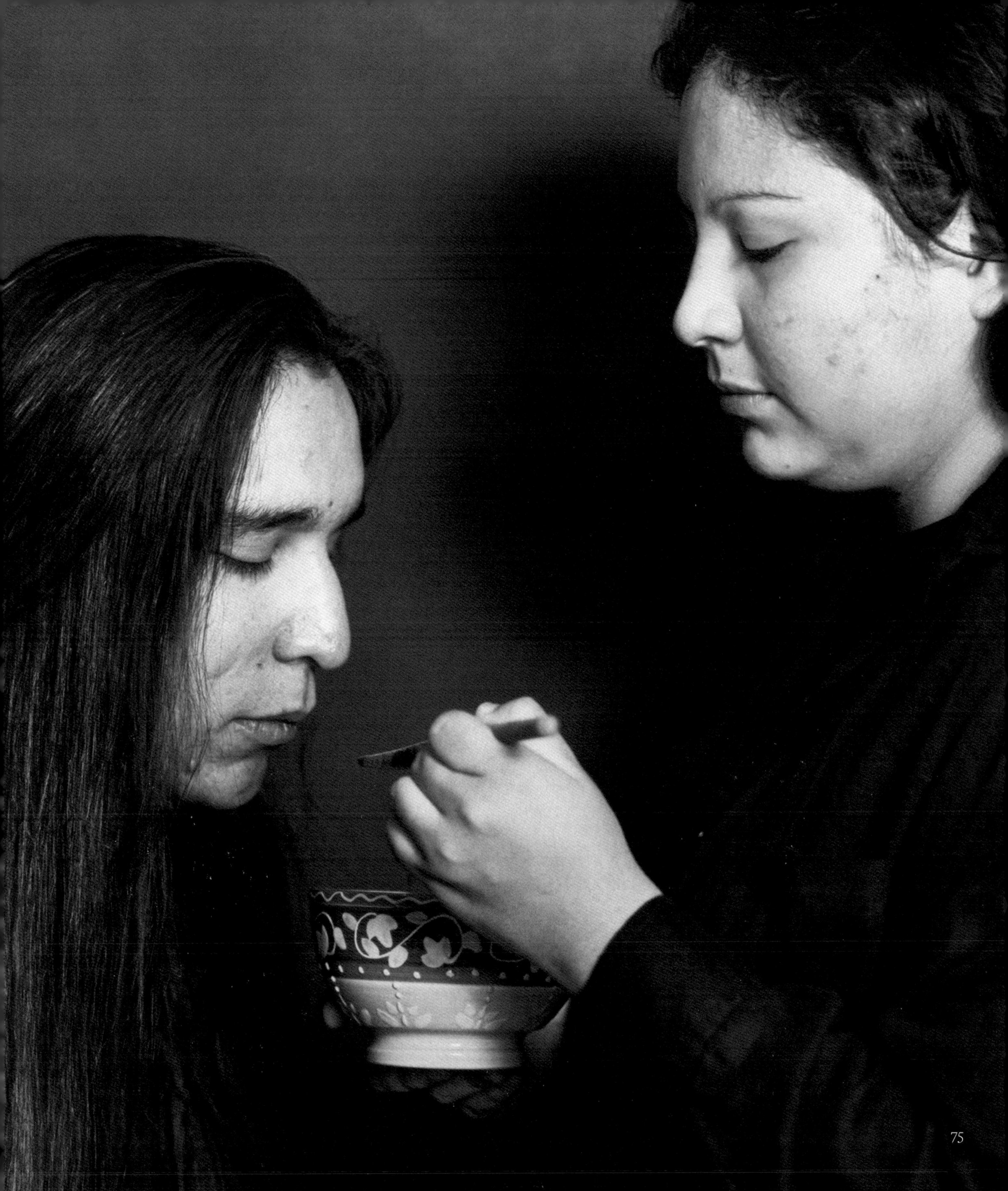

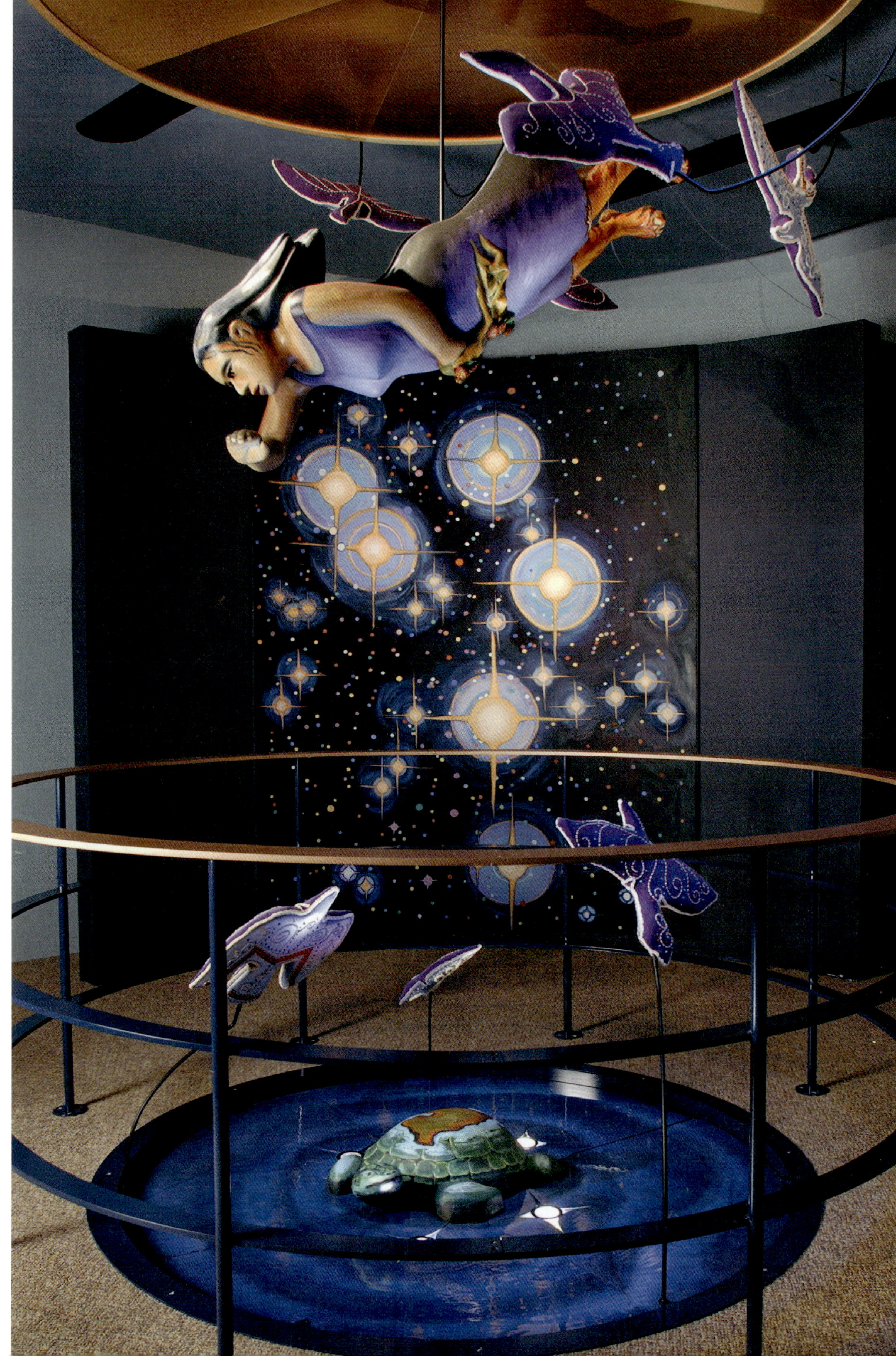

WHO IS SKY WOMAN?

MADELINE LENNON

In the Iroquoian narrative, she was the one responsible for Creation. A member of the Sky World, she tried to assist her ailing husband by fetching water from the Tree of Life, a forbidden act. But she found the tree uprooted, leaving a hole through which she slipped. As she fell toward the waters far below, she attracted the attention of birds and animals who joined forces to help her. Birds guided her to land on the back of the Great Turtle floating on the water, while Muskrat and Beaver brought earth to cover the dome of the Turtle. Sky Woman was pregnant, and gave birth to a daughter. Thus began our world.[1]

For Shelley Niro, Sky Woman evokes the image of "a woman being flung into so many dimensions, she has to figure out her life from so many angles."[2] Niro has written that she uses the emotions experienced by Sky Woman in her art. "I realize now that Sky Woman's displacement is about conditioning us to be ready for the unexpected. Through her, we prepare ourselves for the unknown and deal in the present with what we have."[3] It is not surprising, then, to find this theme recurring in her work, in a variety of media.

Niro's installation in the First People's Hall of the Canadian Museum of History brings the explicit narrative to life. *Sky Woman*, is a sculptural representation. Floating above us, Sky Woman is falling, clutching to her obvious pregnancy the strands of strawberry and tobacco plants she grabbed as she fell past the uprooted tree. She has lost a shoe and looks concerned and uncertain, as birds gather around to help her. Set behind her is a painting of glowing stars in the heavens. Below her the Great Turtle awaits, already partly covered with earth, resting in a pool of water suggesting the seas. When I look at this *Sky Woman*, I see some of Niro in her face and cannot help but think of her as an emotional self-portrait.

This *Sky Woman* is a far cry from the digital print *The Moon, Me, and A Celestial Tree* (p. 13). Here, the moon looms large, a reference to the final phase in the story of Sky Woman, where according to some versions of the tale, after her death she, or her head, became the moon.[4] Brilliant stars glow in the sky, and there on the left stands the artist herself, arms crossed and feet planted firmly in the heavens in a pose of strength and determination. In the right corner is the glowing iconic image of the Great Turtle combined with the Celestial Tree that appears in many of Niro's works, often referencing beaded work as it does here. With this image, Niro declares her strength as a Haudenosaunee woman, with all the history and experiences of her people that feed her imagination and guide her choices of stories to tell.

Early evidence of Niro's interest in Sky Woman is the series *Flying Woman* (1994, pp. 102–111). At the time, she was experimenting with photo collage and the idea of a floating woman. Using photographs of her friend Teresa Marshall, Niro worked with negatives (in this pre-Photoshop era) using different techniques (cutting, duplicating, pasting, drawing) to create ten images, some of them kaleidoscopic. She included references to the Celestial Tree and to beadwork, using light dots to form the iconic shapes we recognize. We can see these elements in *Flying Woman #10* (p. 111) where the figure seems to float serenely through a series of lighted Turtle and Tree references. This is a modern woman in the modern world. "It is as though Sky Woman observes the contemporary world and all that is possible as she 'falls/flies' from the past into the present."[5]

This theme of a modern woman in the guise of Sky Woman comes into play again in 2001 with a series of four paintings in oil and chalk pastel. The titles are revealing: *Preparing for the Fall, Losing My Stuff,*

Dreaming, Loving It (pp. 98–101). Niro approaches this narrative from the perspective of a woman who is preparing herself for change. Here the fall seems less accidental. In the first painting we see Sky Woman framed by a billowing, brilliant red cloak that she holds at its edges. She seems to look down with some concern but her pose, with arms spread and feet planted, conveys strength. It is interesting that Niro takes her through the process of losing everything she has and then "falling" into a dream-like state, only to come out of it all, still in free fall, but Loving It. We can imagine this woman as someone who sheds her past, considers her future, and delights in it. In this last painting in the series we finally see her full face very close to us and not at all fearful—in fact, looking quite serene. Her arms are spread wide as though ready to embrace her future.

This is a Sky Woman who figures out what her life can be and how to work with the conditions that are imposed on her. Applying these ideas to the women in her life, people she knows and respects, Niro created the series of ten digital prints, *M: Stories of Women* (2011, pp. 79–89). These are portraits of strength and determination in the face of what Indigenous women have had to cope with for too long, including terrible, dismissive treatment by the Canadian government and the press.

Finding Her Helpers (p. 79) is a powerful image in the series depicting Niro's daughter (Anastasia) Naoga as Sky Woman: pregnant, in jeans and high heels, blowing a glowing fire from her mouth. In contrast, in the first image of the series, titled *Beginnings* (pp. 88–89), Naoga looks at us confidently, wearing an old-fashioned aviator hat with sunglasses perched on top. The Celestial Tree icon hovers nearby, the background filled with a watery earth. In the frame are birds and strands of DNA: life begins.

NOTES

1. Janet C. Berlo and Ruth B. Philips, *Native North American Art* (Oxford: Oxford University Press, 1998), 71.
2. Shelley Niro, email message to the author, July 14, 2021.
3. Shelley Niro, "An Essential Personal Journey Through Iroquois Myths, Legends, Icons and History" (master's thesis, University of Western Ontario, 1999), 5.
4. Bruce Elliot Johansen and Barbara Alice Mann, eds., *Encyclopedia of the Haudenosaunee (Iroquois Confederacy)* (Westport, CT: Greenwood Publishing Group, 2000), 53.
5. Madeline Lennon, *Shelley Niro: Seeing Through Memory* (London, ON: Blue Medium Press, 2014), 42.

M: Stories of Women, 2011 >

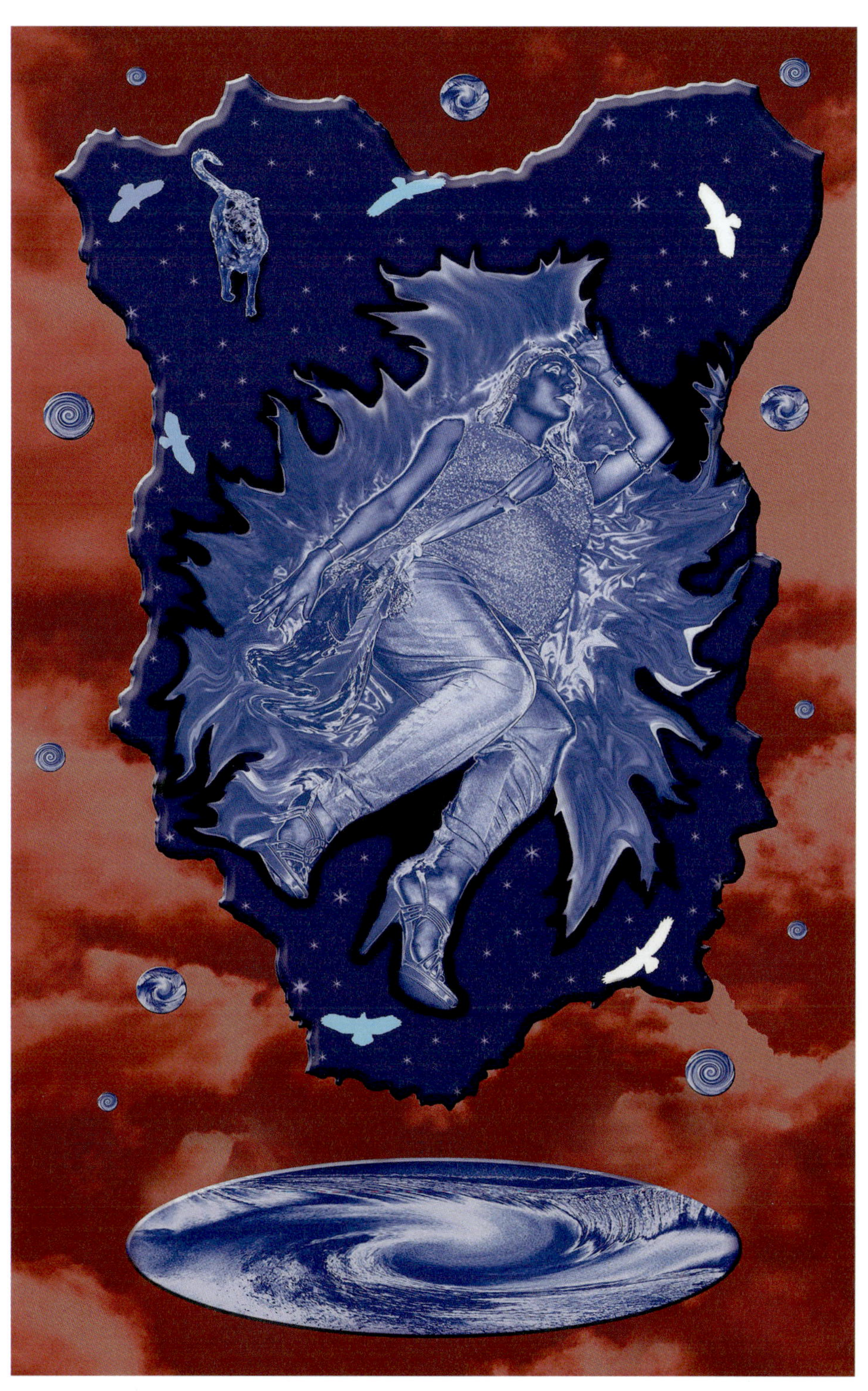

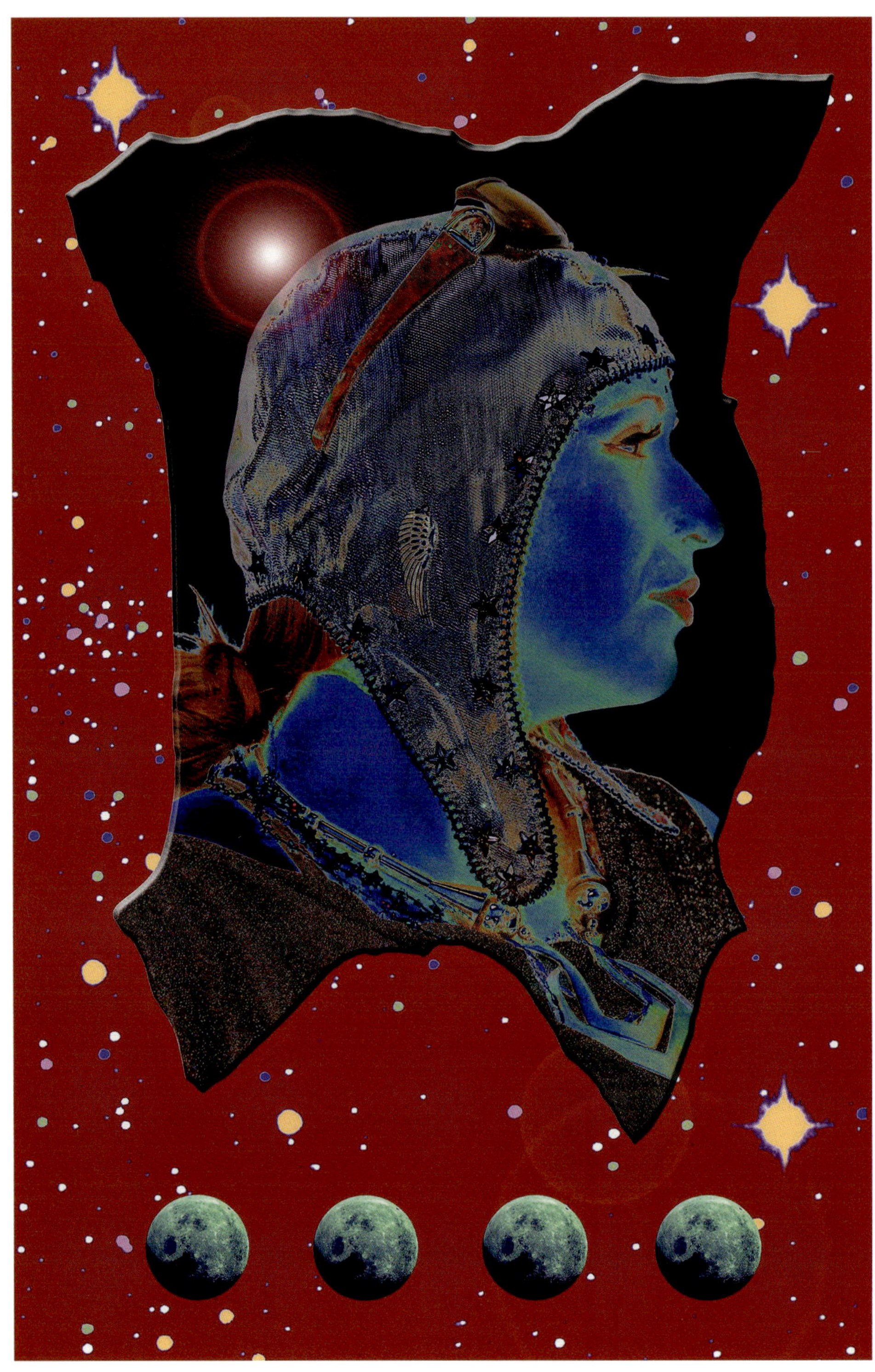

     Ancestors

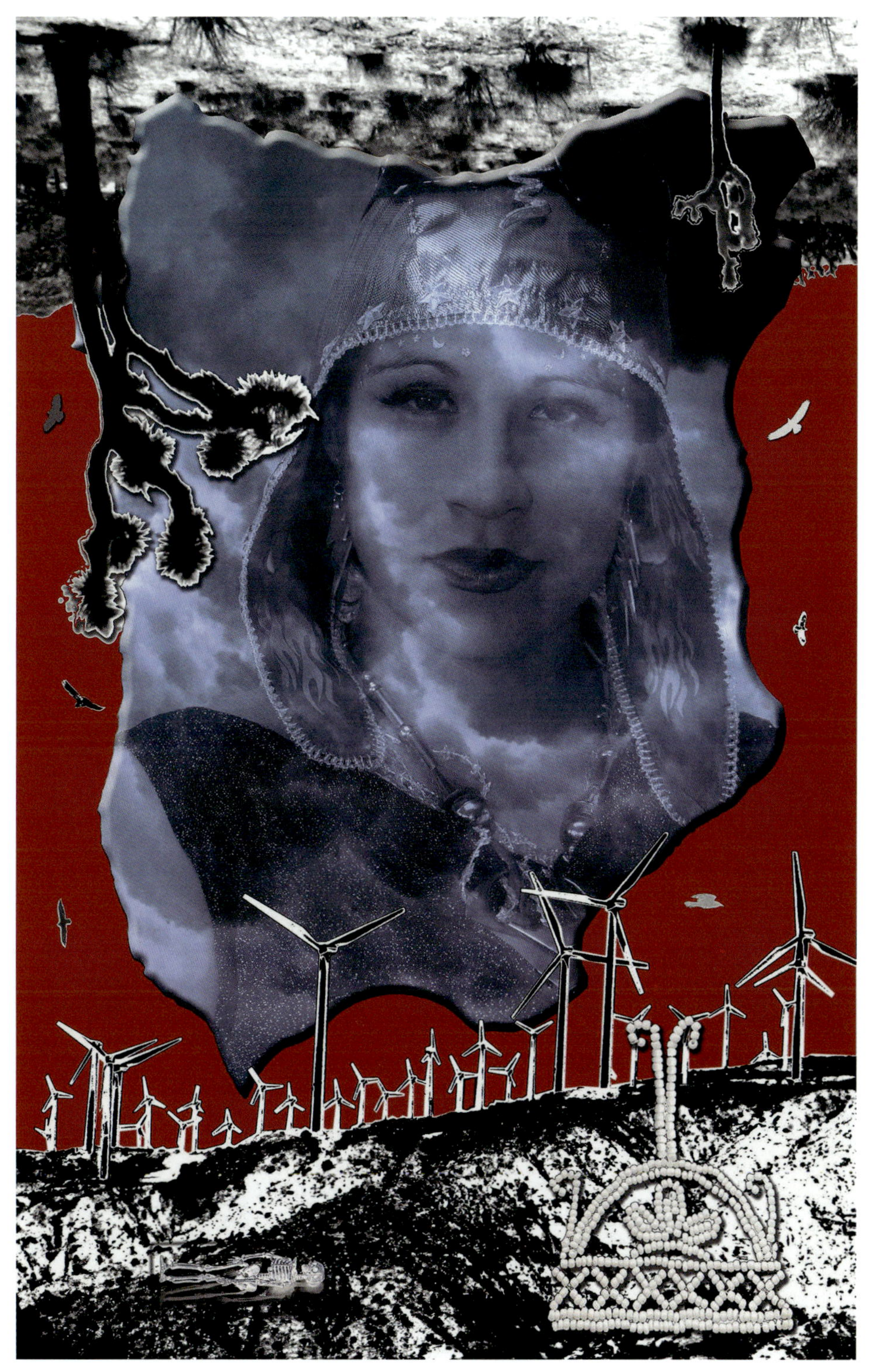

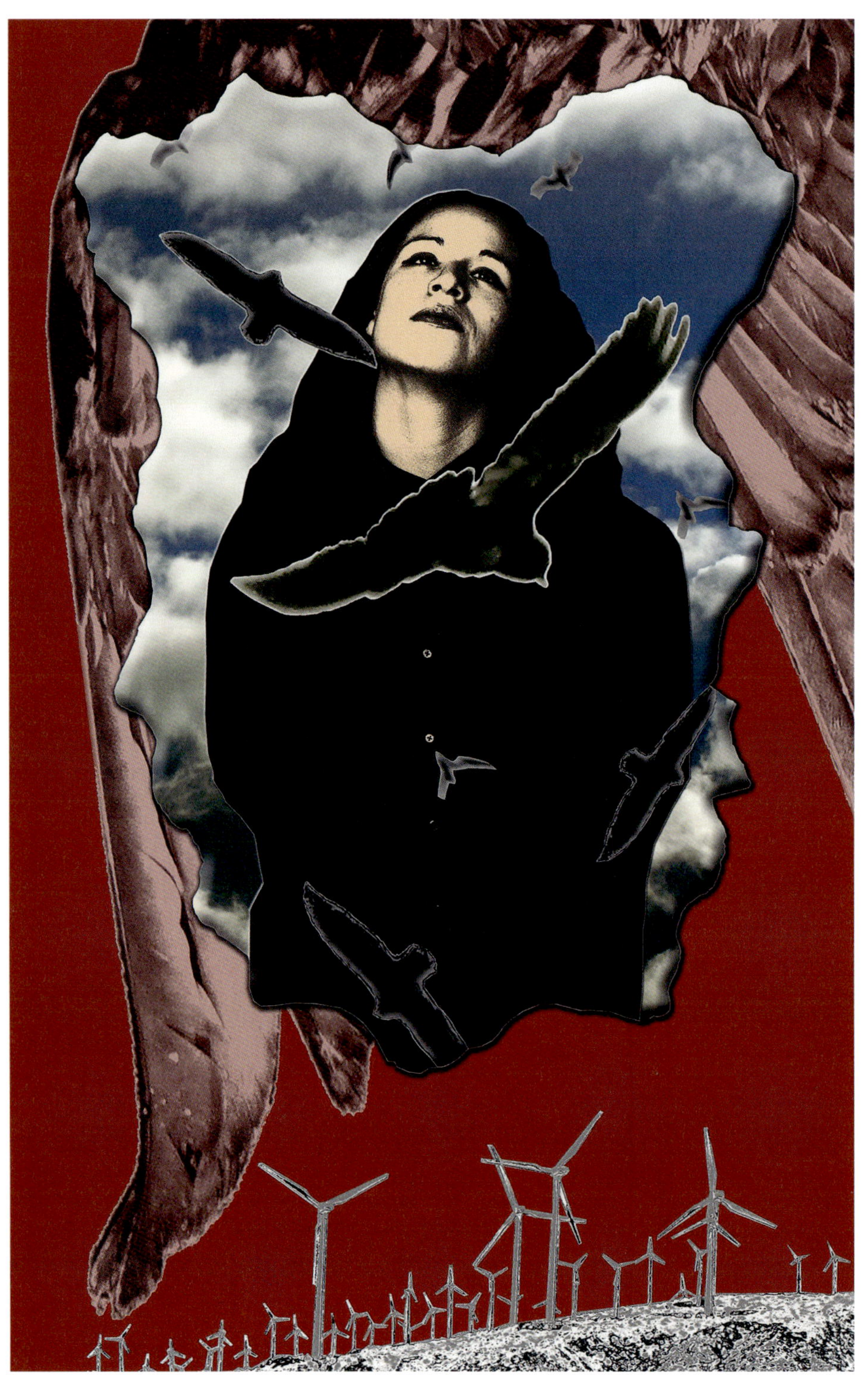

   **Memories of Flight

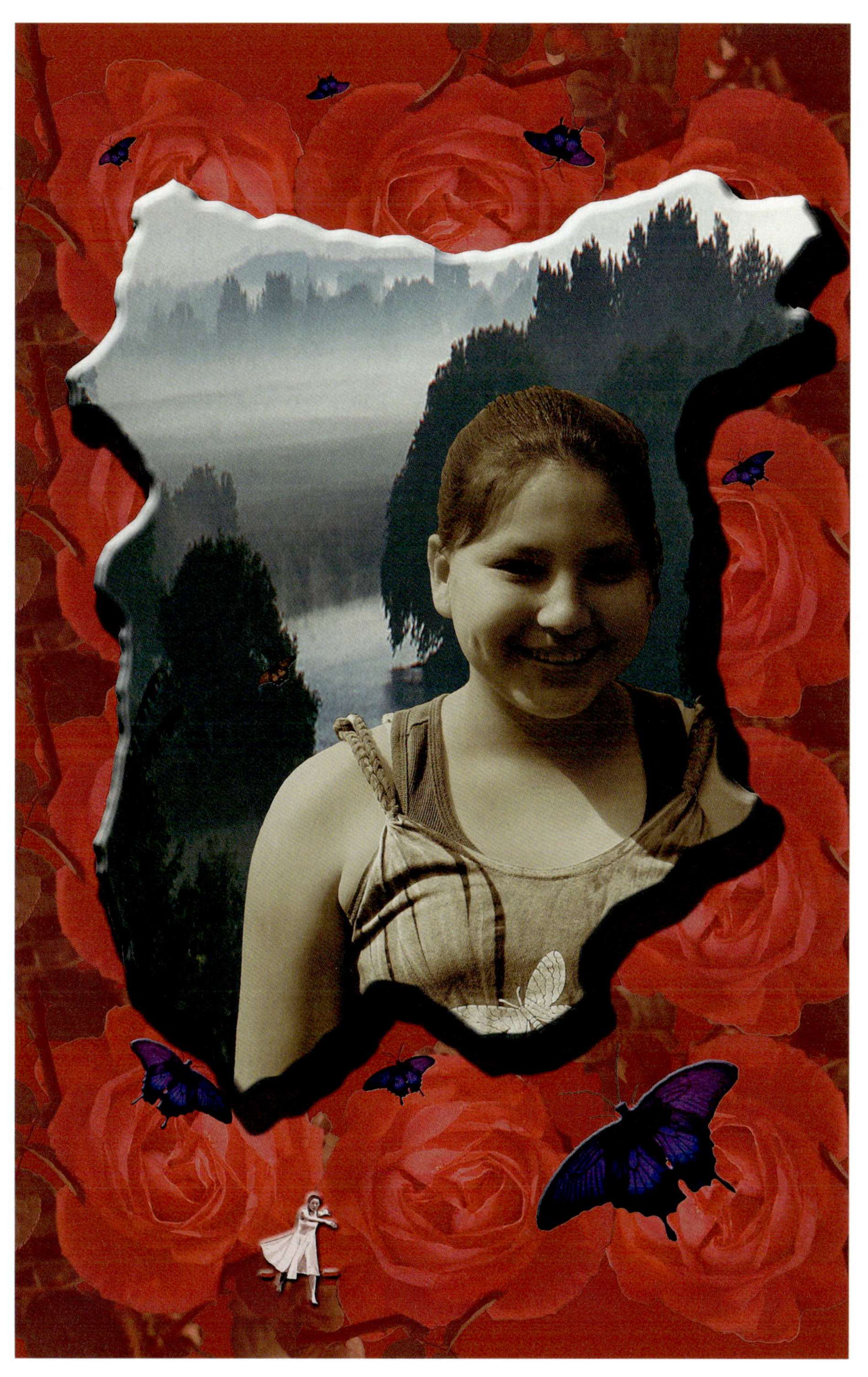

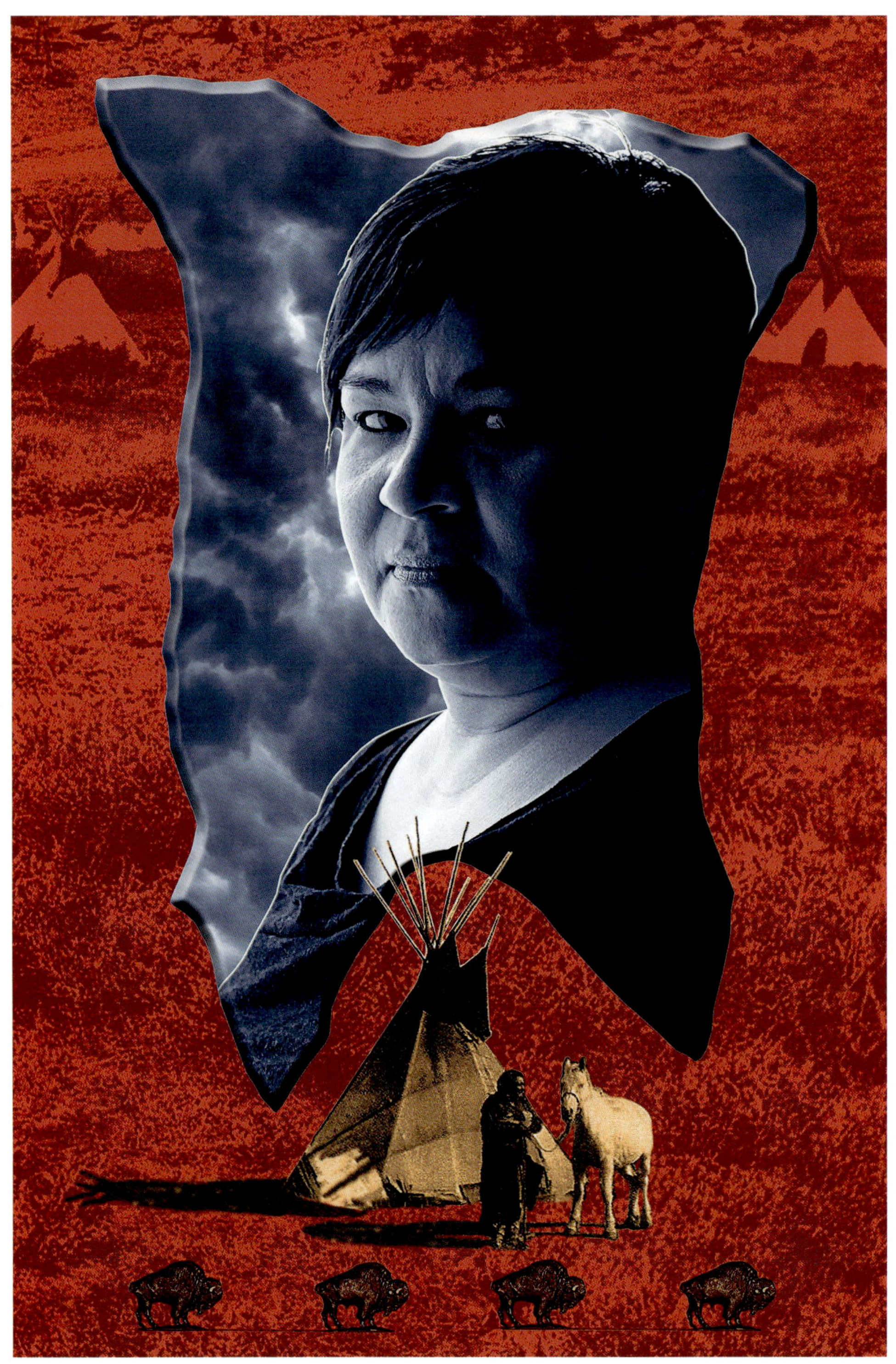

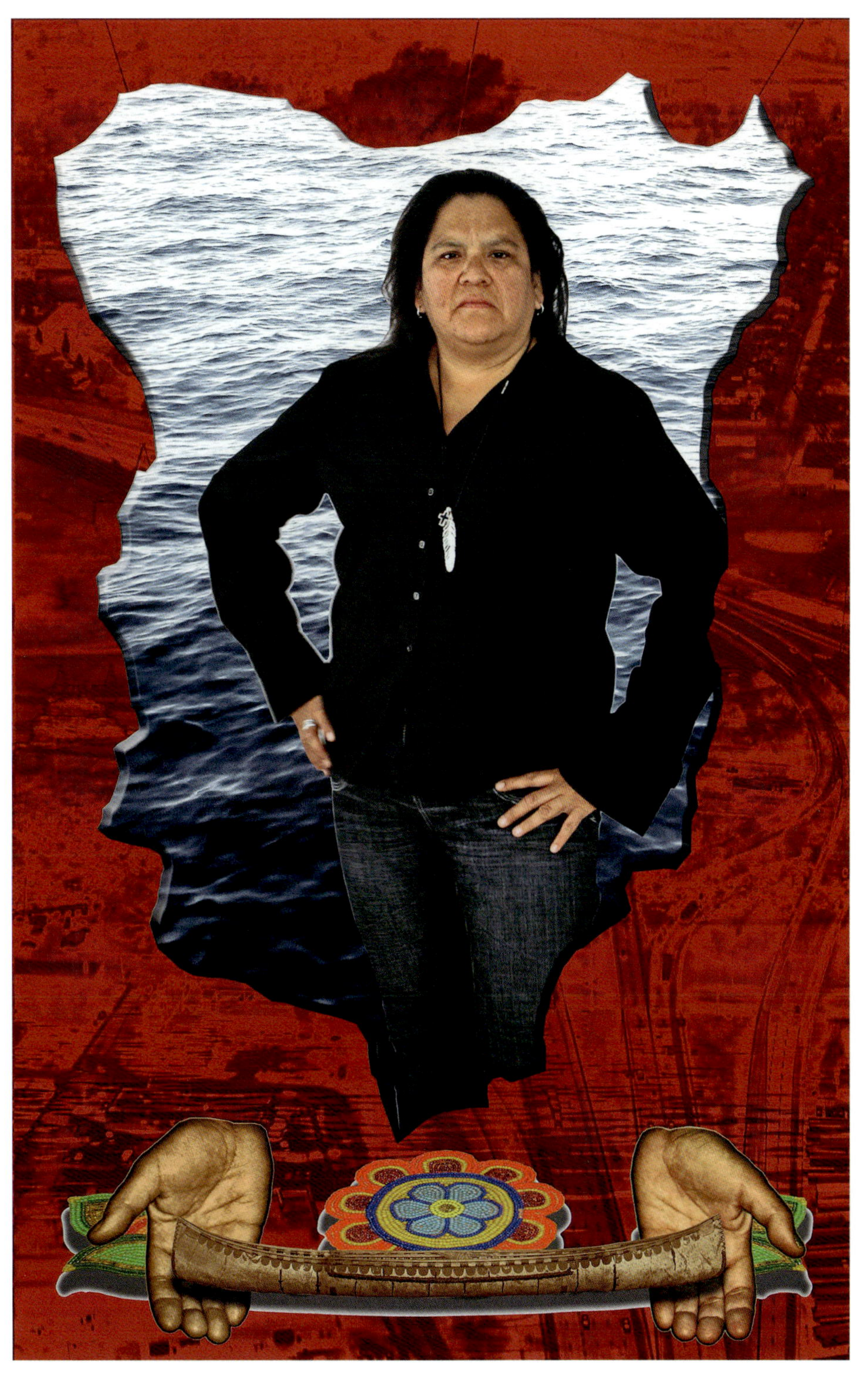

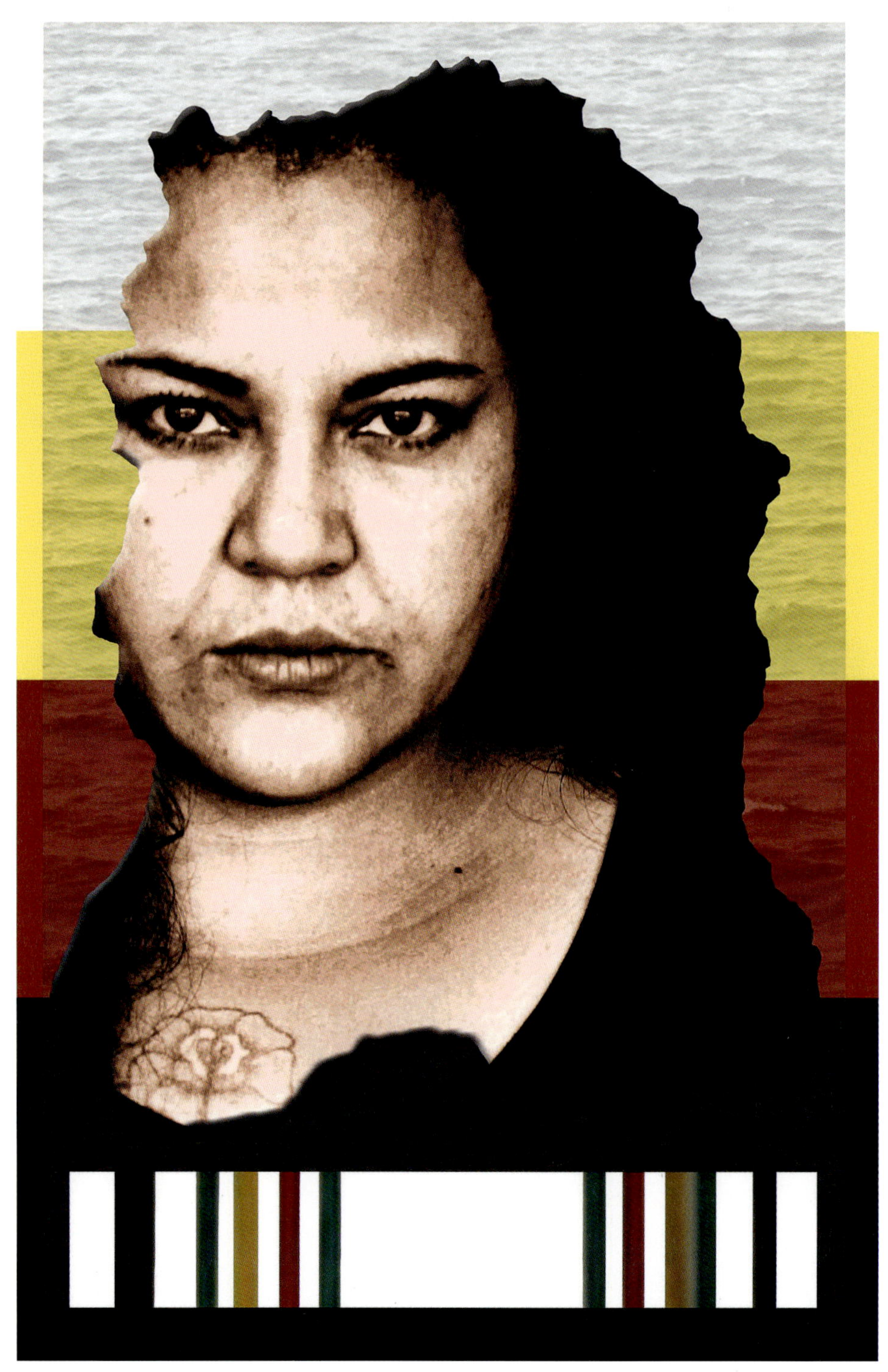

    Blanket

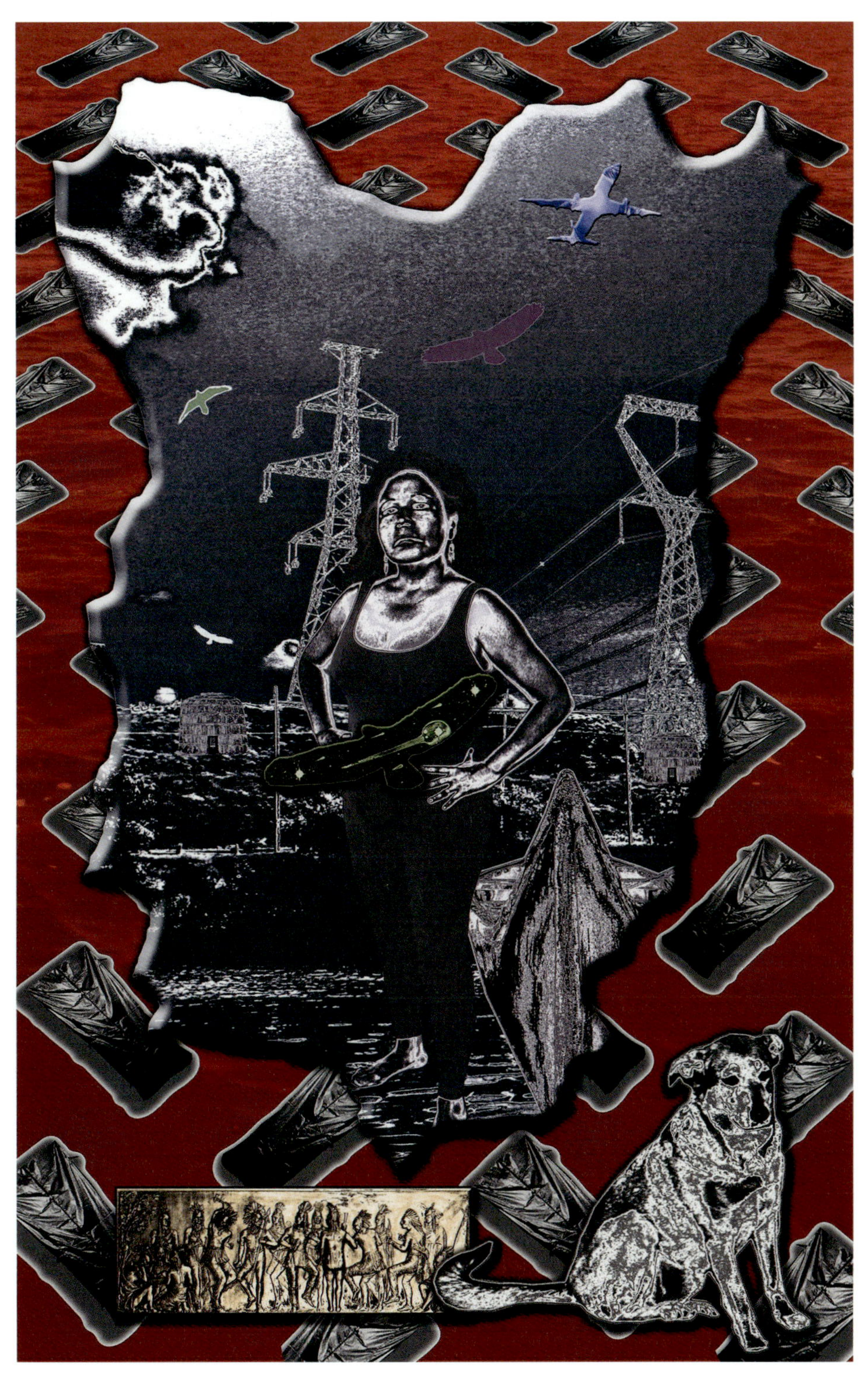

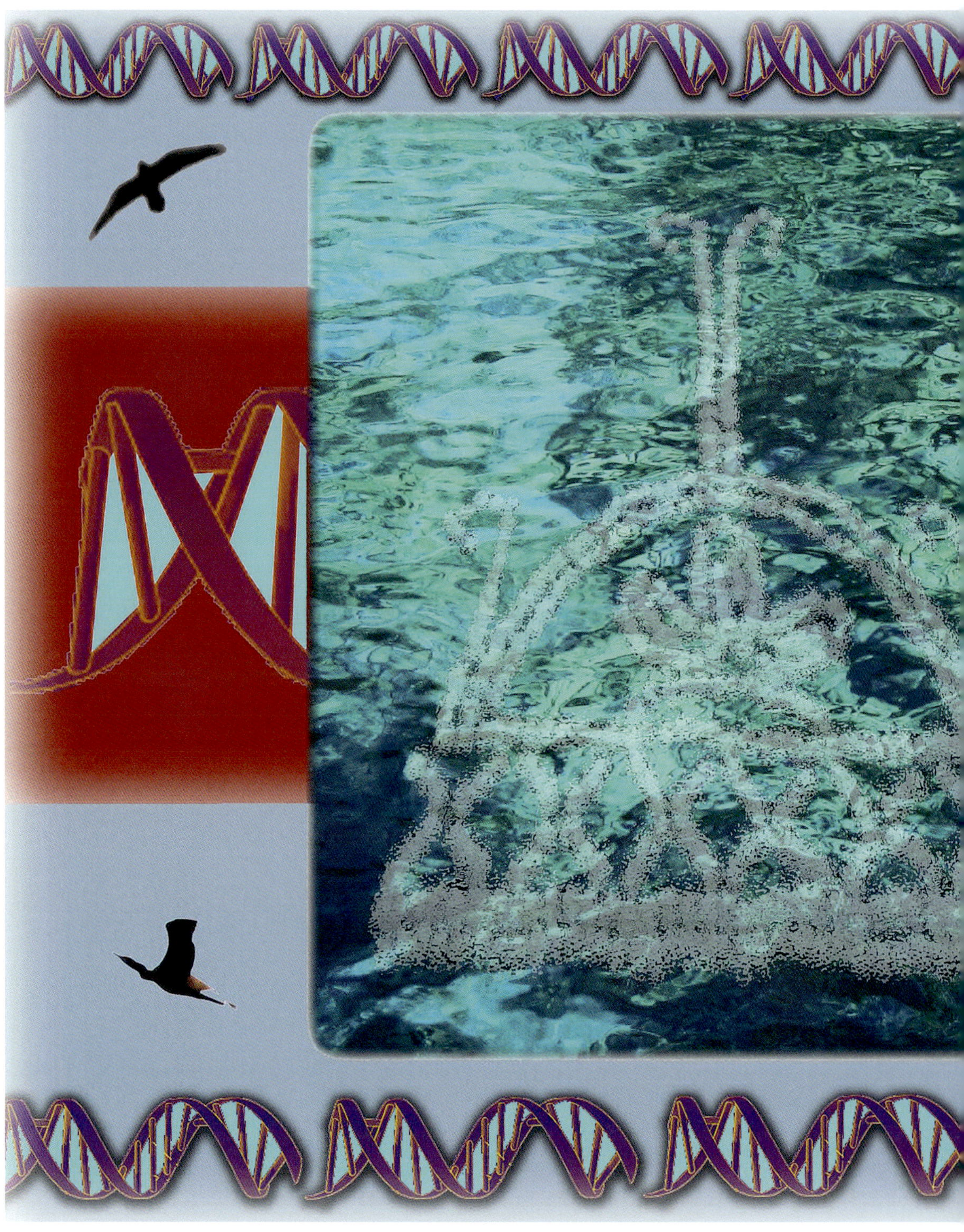

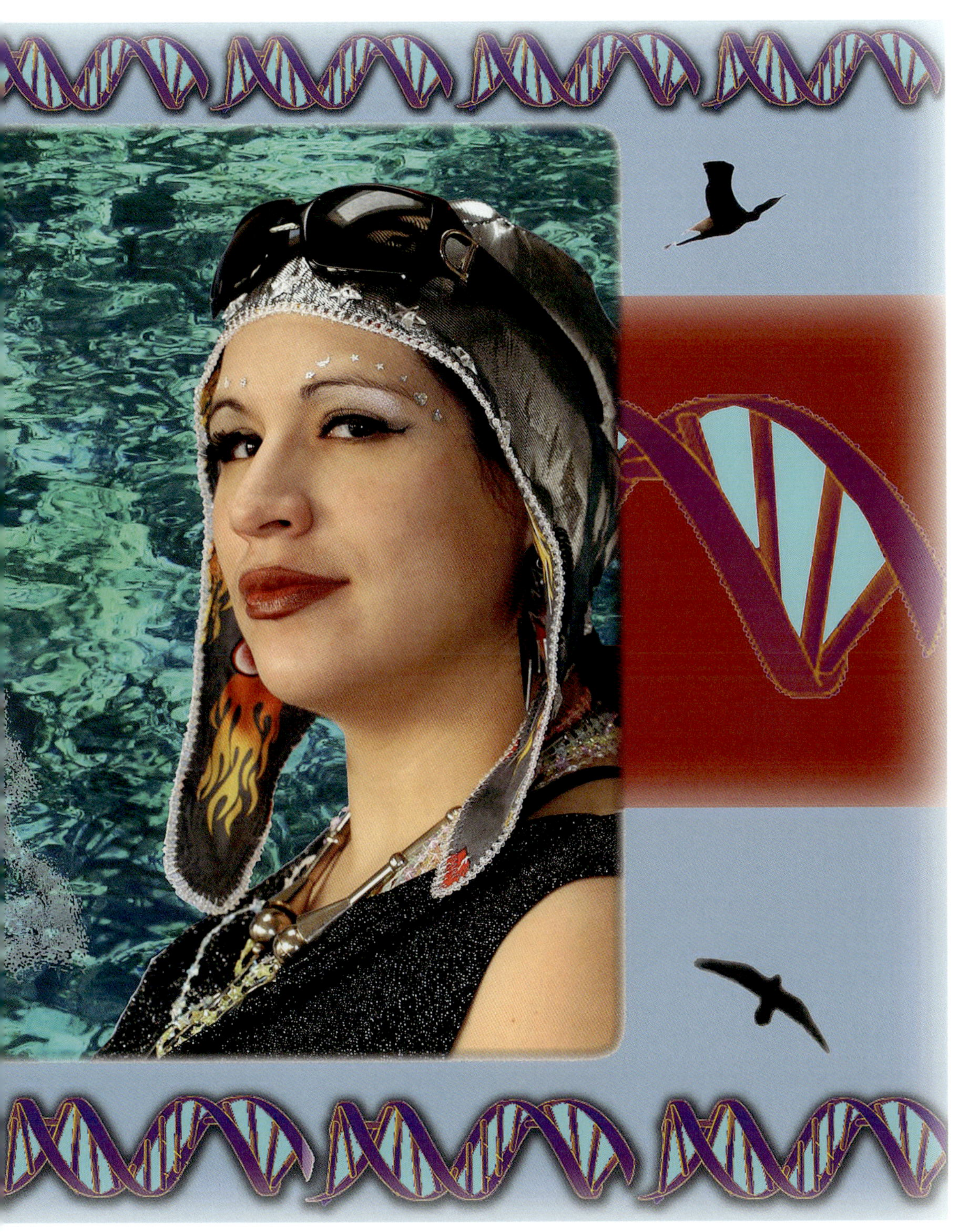

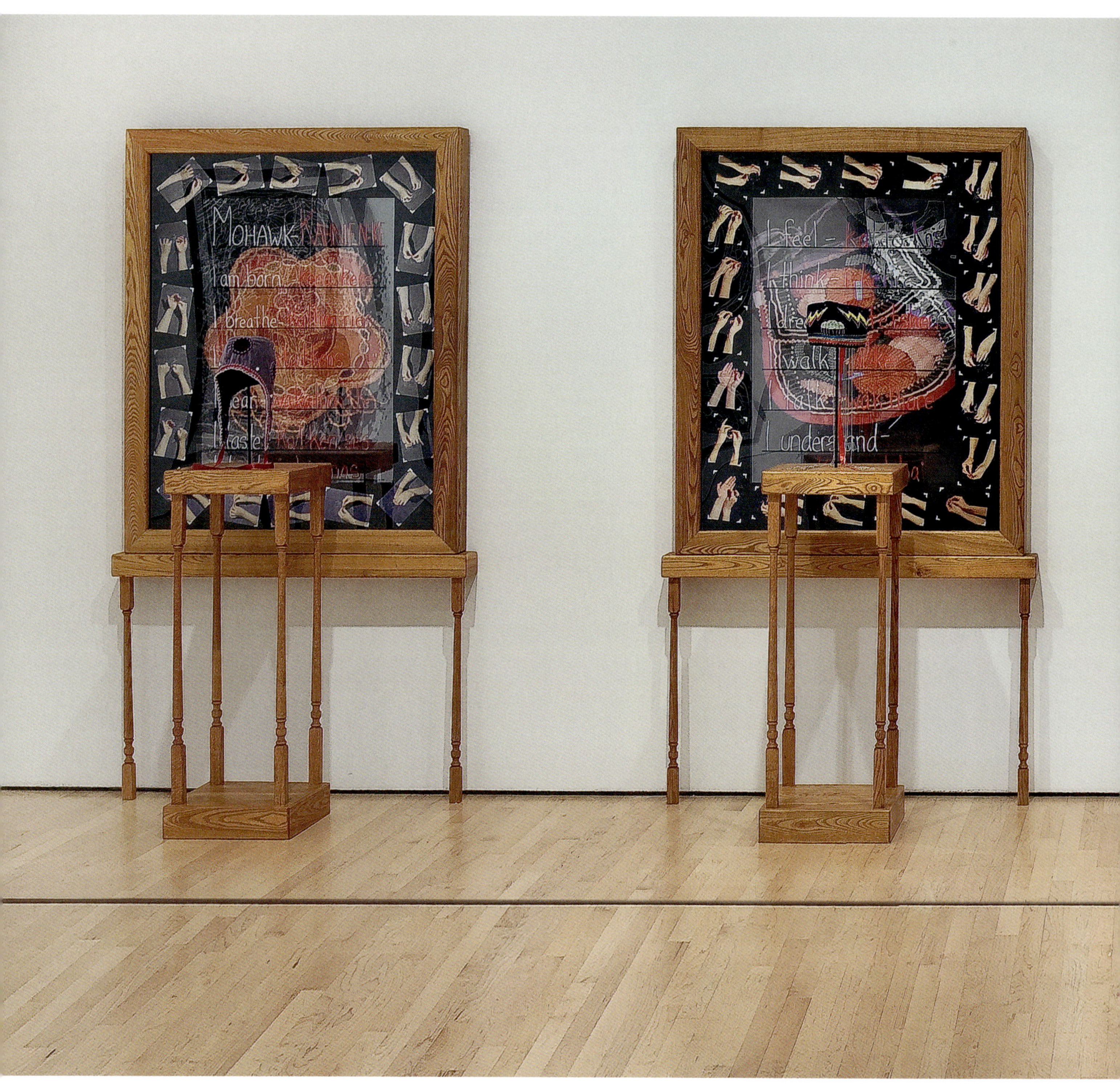

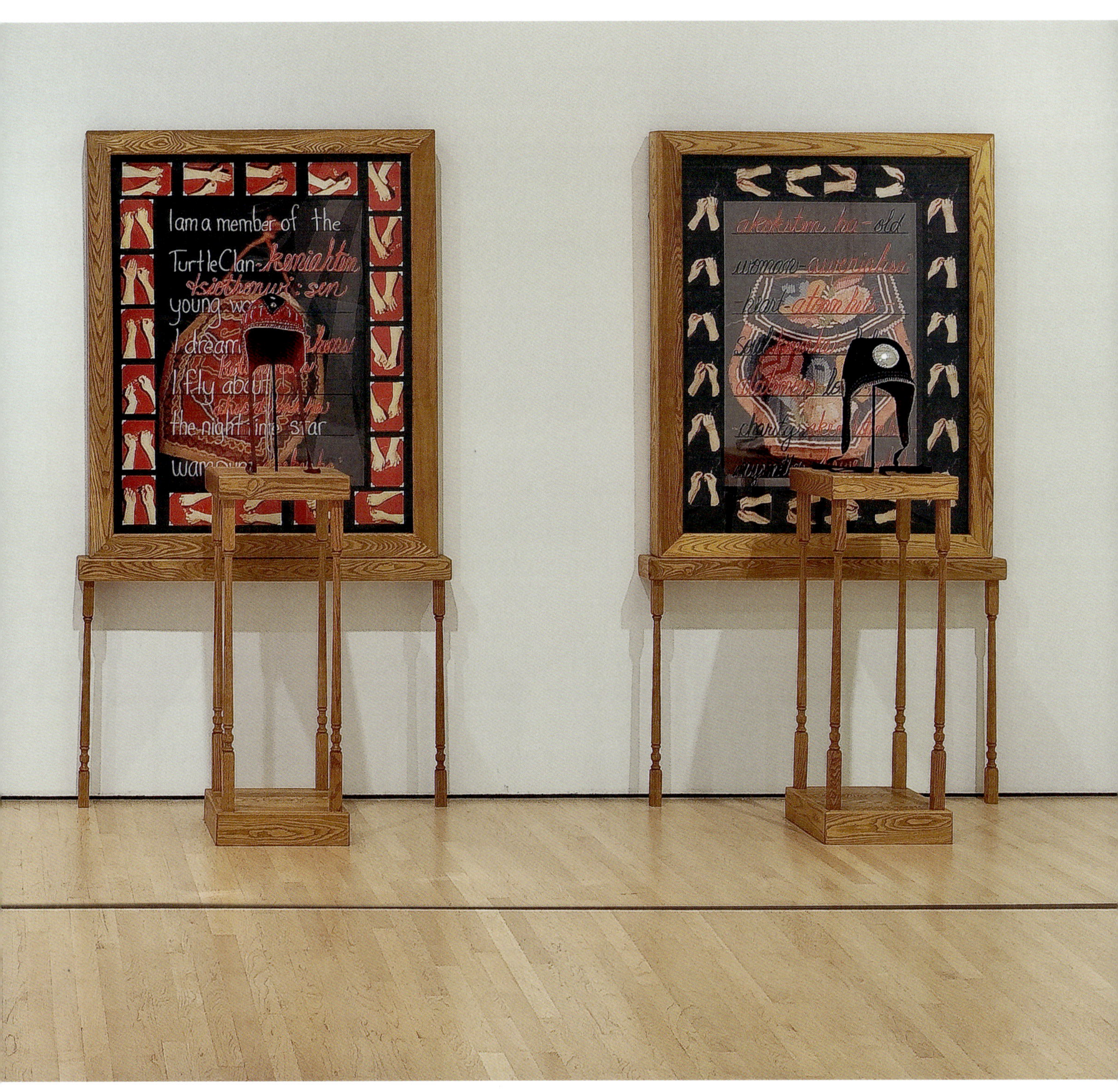

Installation views of **Thinking Caps** (1999) at the National Gallery of Canada, Ottawa, 2008
Photographs on pp. 90–94 courtesy the National Gallery of Canada

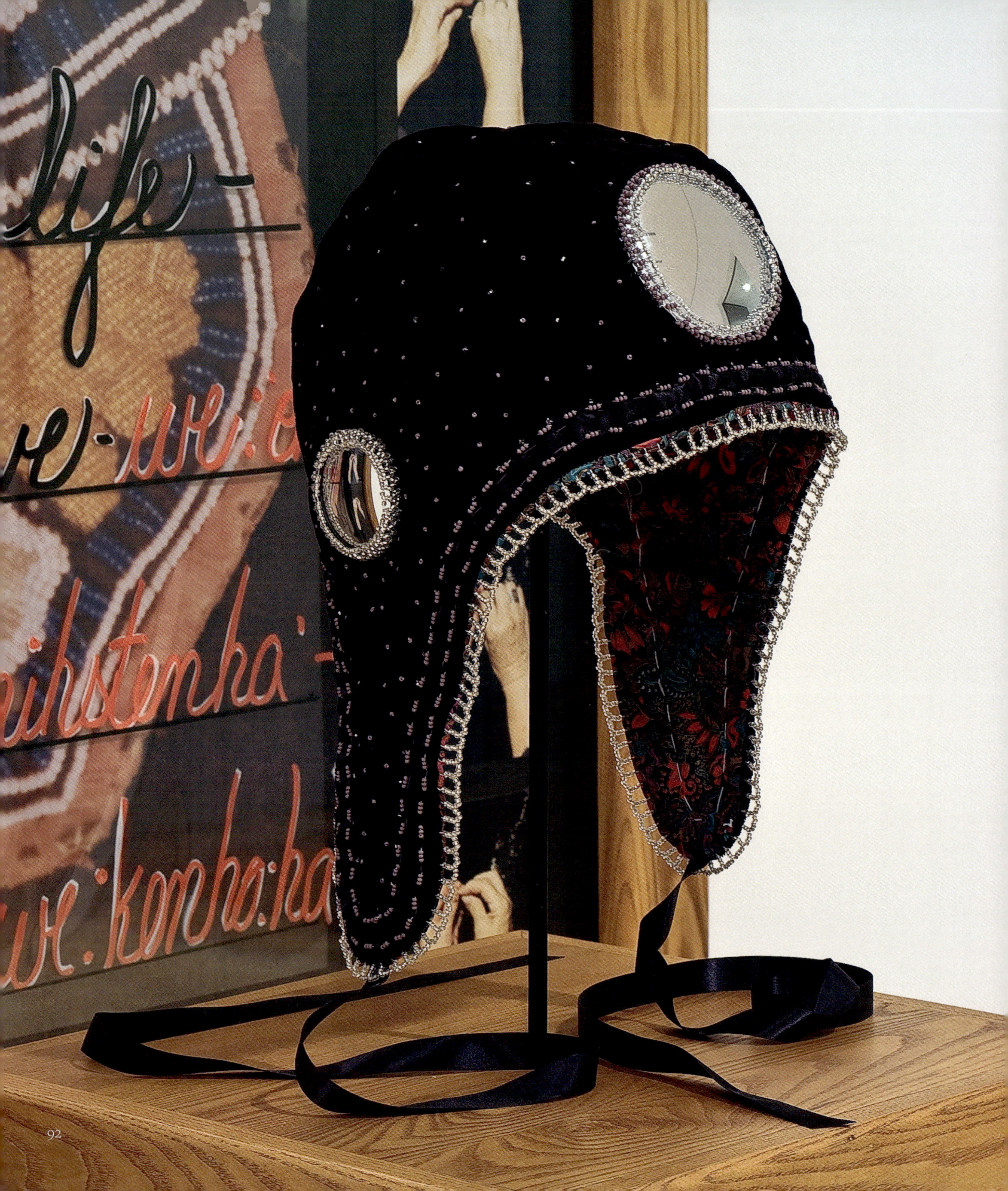

life—
we·we·c
ihstenha·-
we·kenho·ha

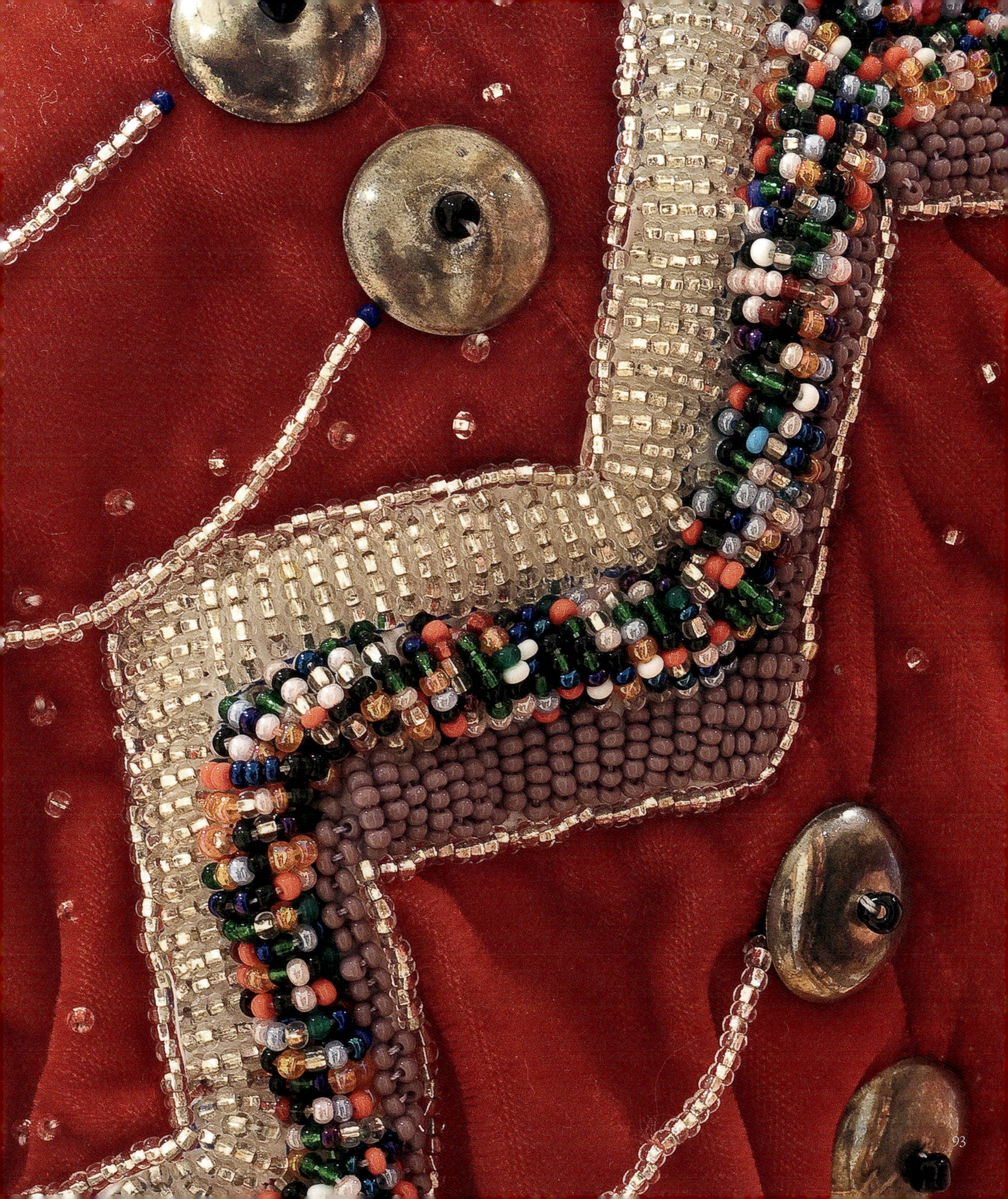

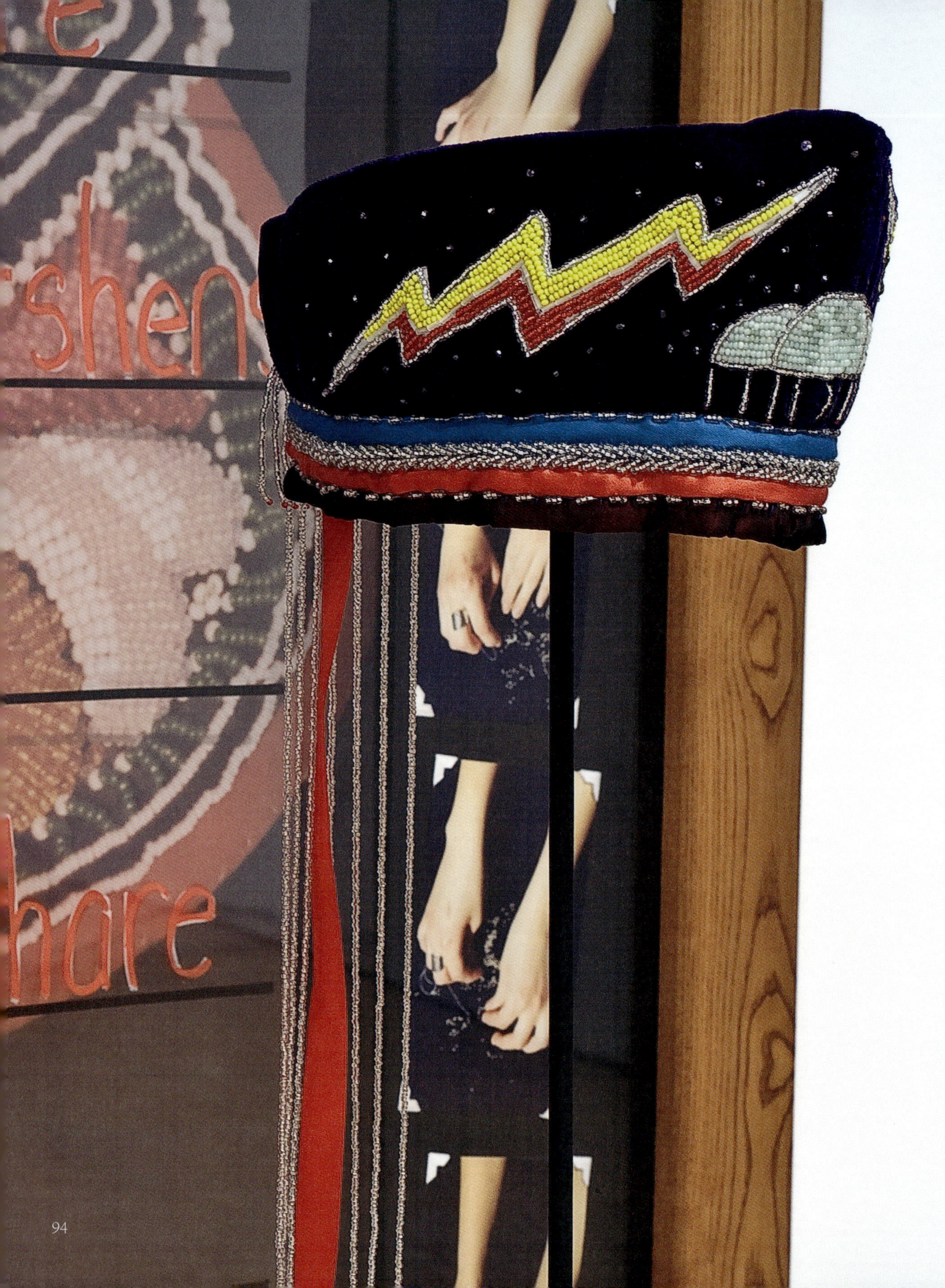

CALMLY AND FEARLESSLY

LORI BEAVIS

A few years ago, sitting at her kitchen table, Shelley Niro described how her parents and others at Six Nations were committed to making objects to keep traditions alive as well as for economic reasons. She remembers her father creating objects reflecting his own sensibility, as a Haudenosaunee man making connections across time; and she recalls the childhood memory of standing beside her mother's chair watching as she stitched floral beadwork patterns. She defined herself as an art-maker based on these early experiences.[1] In her forty-year career Niro has worked in many media and we often see threads of her production drawn through different works.

Those early experiences have also impelled Niro to tell stories, and she has often turned to the story of Sky Woman's fall from Sky World to create new narratives of Haudenosaunee women's lives or to reinscribe stories of contemporary women. The women in Niro's work are often her friends, artist colleagues, her mother, sisters, nieces, daughter, or granddaughter. These women are portrayed at different stages of life and are introduced across time and place to reinforce the notion that they are sustaining themselves, one another, and other women. Niro references women's legacies and care to work against practices and images that reinforce colonial violence, trauma, and destruction of Indigenous women. But through her work, Niro is also cherishing these relationships and the knowledge that the women hold and pass on.

In 1999, Niro was commissioned to create work that responded to the long history of Haudenosaunee women's beadwork from pre-contact through market-driven nineteenth century production to work by contemporary beadwork artists.[2] For this exhibition, Niro created *Thinking Caps* (1999, pp. 90–94). The four caps represent girlhood, young womanhood, maturity, and old age. The girlhood cap is a lavender velvet with riveted stars across the brow and down the sides and with round magenta patches over the ears and above the forehead. A dark purple hat, in the style of a glengarry cap, identifies the young woman, with two lightning bolts and a storm cloud raining strings of beads above the forehead. Adulthood is signified by the mature woman's cap in a rich red to symbolize life and medicine. This cap is heavily beaded with vertical lines that encircle the head and cascade across the brow and around the sides. The final cap, for old age, is a deep purple aviator hat. Like the child's cap, this one also bears stars that cross the forehead and run down the straps. However, rather than velvet discs, this hat incorporates mirrors to convey the notion of one looking back on a well-lived life and the knowledges that have been gained.

Each thinking cap is placed in front of a framed image of nineteenth-century beadwork covered with words in Kanien'kéha and English. Surrounding each were images of women's hands working with beads. The hats and the panels that frame them represent each period of life. From childhood's phase of awakening senses and exploration of the wonder of a new world, to youth with the gifts of imagination and intellect that articulate the world, then on to adulthood and the recognition of the strength of community and expanding creativity, and finally old age as a time of wisdom, generosity, and spirituality. The caps in this work draw a line for Niro from the practice of beading to the different stages of a Haudenosaunee woman's life as her mind, body, and spirit evolve across time.[3]

Niro is also telling the viewer of the fortitude of these women. She is paying her respect to the knowledge instilled in her through early family and community-based experiences. She is telling us that we can take strength from the things we have within to be prepared to think, dream, and articulate the world. It is for these reasons that Niro often looks to Sky Woman as a woman who clutched at the roots of the tree to stop herself but when the fall became inevitable she held on to the seeds, roots, and fruits she carries and calmly and fearlessly acknowledges that she has the strength to meet whatever comes her way.[4]

The story of Sky Woman and the *Thinking Caps* come together in the later series *M: Stories of Women* (2011, pp. 79–89), where the figure in *Ancestors*, *Legacy*, and *Beginnings*, can be read as a personification of Sky Woman. The woman in each of these images also wears a silver, star-riveted aviator hat. As Niro has written, "Sometimes the small details are the most important and their inclusion enriches and emboldens central characters."[5]

The aviator hat can be viewed as a symbol of preparedness, strength and speed, moral goodness and adaptability. It also symbolically represents the advantage of seeing things from a new point of view or having an expanded worldview.[6] While her flight through space was unexpected, both aviator hat and sunglass-goggles suggest that this woman was prepared and capable of controlling her destiny. These are images of a strong woman who will thrive as she situates herself in place and history. When Sky Woman falls from the sky, with the help of animals and birds, she creates land and territory. She has agency as the woman who will prepare and equip the next generation, pass on the traditions, and teach the histories, skills, and knowledge of womanhood.

The legacy of Sky Woman continues when the silver-starred aviator hat makes another appearance in *Raven's World* (p. 97). In this large-scale painting, Niro's granddaughter, Raven, wears the cap as she sits amid growing corn. The corn, galaxy, and hat all indicate that she will be well taken care of by those who have gone before. Raven surveys the land with the galaxy at her back. The moon is a reference to Grandmother Moon and Sky Woman and the juxtaposition with Raven references the circle of life. The star-studded aviator hat is an indication that she has been instilled with all that she will need and that she is well prepared to move into the future.

NOTES

1. Lori Beavis, "to know dibaajimowin: a narrative of knowing: art, art education and cultural identity in the life experiences of four contemporary Indigenous women artists" (PhD thesis, Concordia University, 2016), 75.
2. *Across Borders: Beadwork in Iroquois Life* (1999–2002) was a travelling exhibition organized and circulated by the McCord Museum, Montreal, and the Castellani Art Museum of Niagara University, New York, in collaboration with the Kanien'kehaka Onkwawén:na Raotitióhkwa Language and Cultural Center, Kahnawà:ke, the Tuscarora Nation community beadworkers within New York state, and the Royal Ontario Museum, Toronto. The exhibition was on view at the McCord Museum from June 18, 1999, to January 9, 2000, and it displayed more than 300 Iroquois objects dating from the mid-nineteenth century to the present. Jeffrey Thomas was another artist who was commissioned to make work that responded to the long history of Haudenosaunee women's beadwork.
3. Ruth B. Phillips, "In Focus: Shelley Niro: Thinking Caps," in *Hearts of Our People: Native Women Artists*, eds. Jill Ahlberg Yohe and Teri Greeves (Seattle: University of Washington Press, 2019), 126–127.
4. The Sky Woman Creation Story has many versions. The one I refer to here is "Creation Story, as told by Kay Olan," Learning Longhouse, accessed October 17, 2021, https://i36466.wixsite.com/learninglonghouse/creation---kay-olan. See also, Joanne Shenandoah and Douglas M. George-Kanentiio, *Skywoman: Legends of the Iroqouis* (Santa Fe, NM: Clear Light Books, 1995); Robin Wall Kimmerer, *Braiding Sweetgrass: Indigenous Wisdom, Scientific Knowledge, and the Teachings of Plants* (Minneapolis, MN: Milkweed Editions, 2015); and Thomas King, *The Truth About Stories* (Toronto: House of Anansi Press, 2003).
5. Shelley Niro, "An Essential Personal Journey Through Iroquois Myths, Legends, Icons and History" (master's thesis, University of Western Ontario, 1999), 5–6.
6. Fernando Esposito, *Fascism, Aviation and Mythical Modernity* (London: Palgrave Macmillan, 2015), 310.

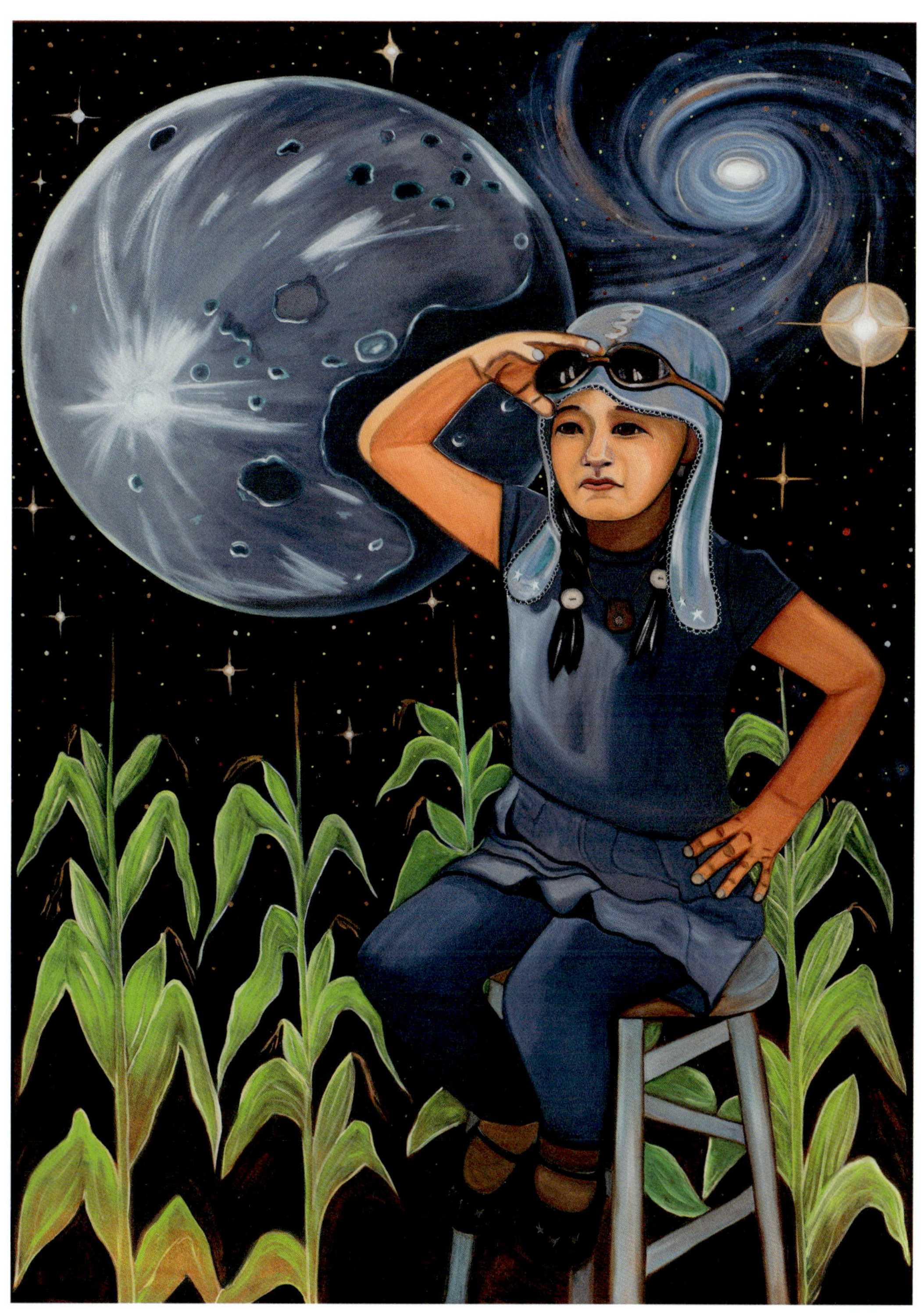

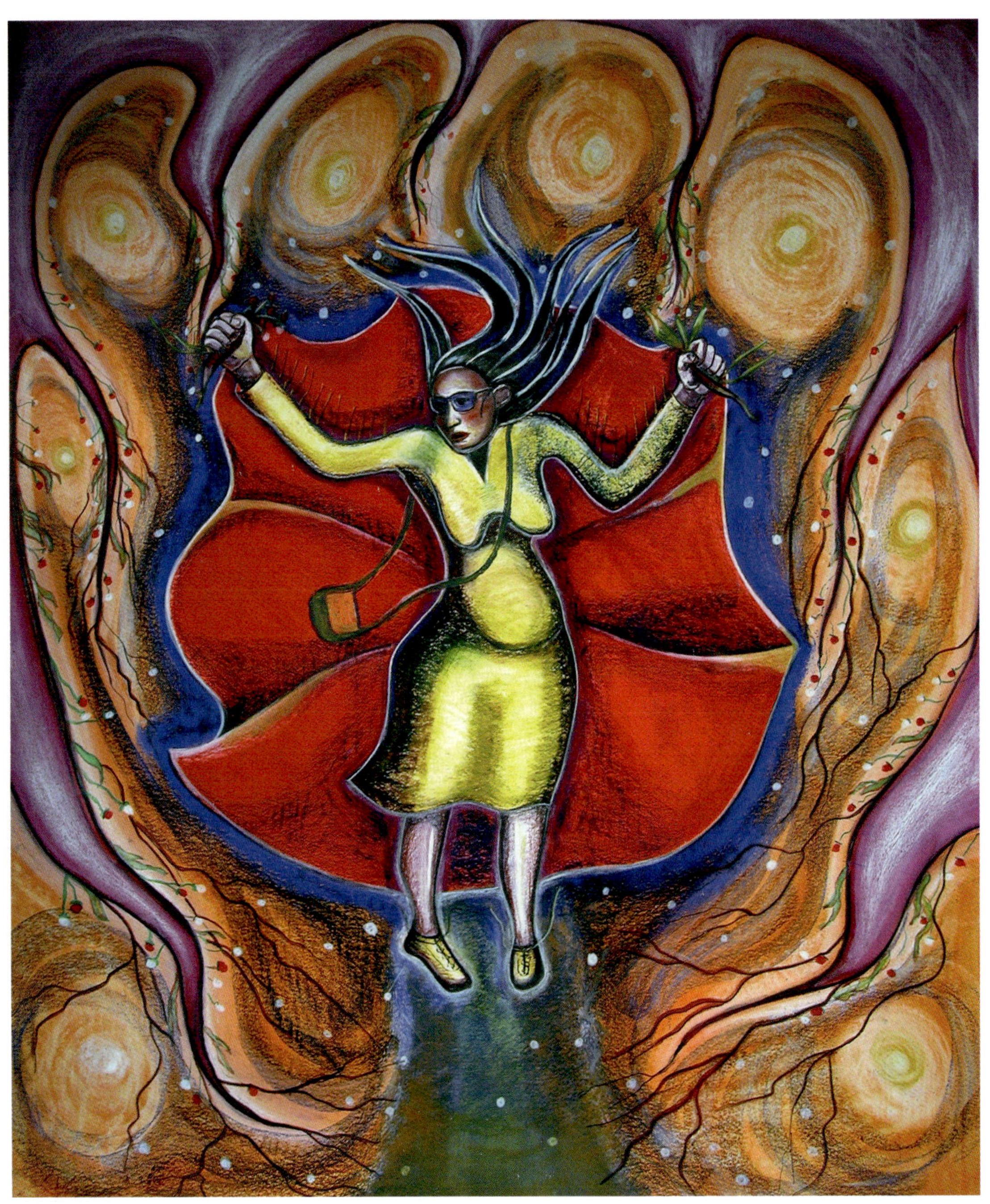

   Preparing for the Fall, 2001

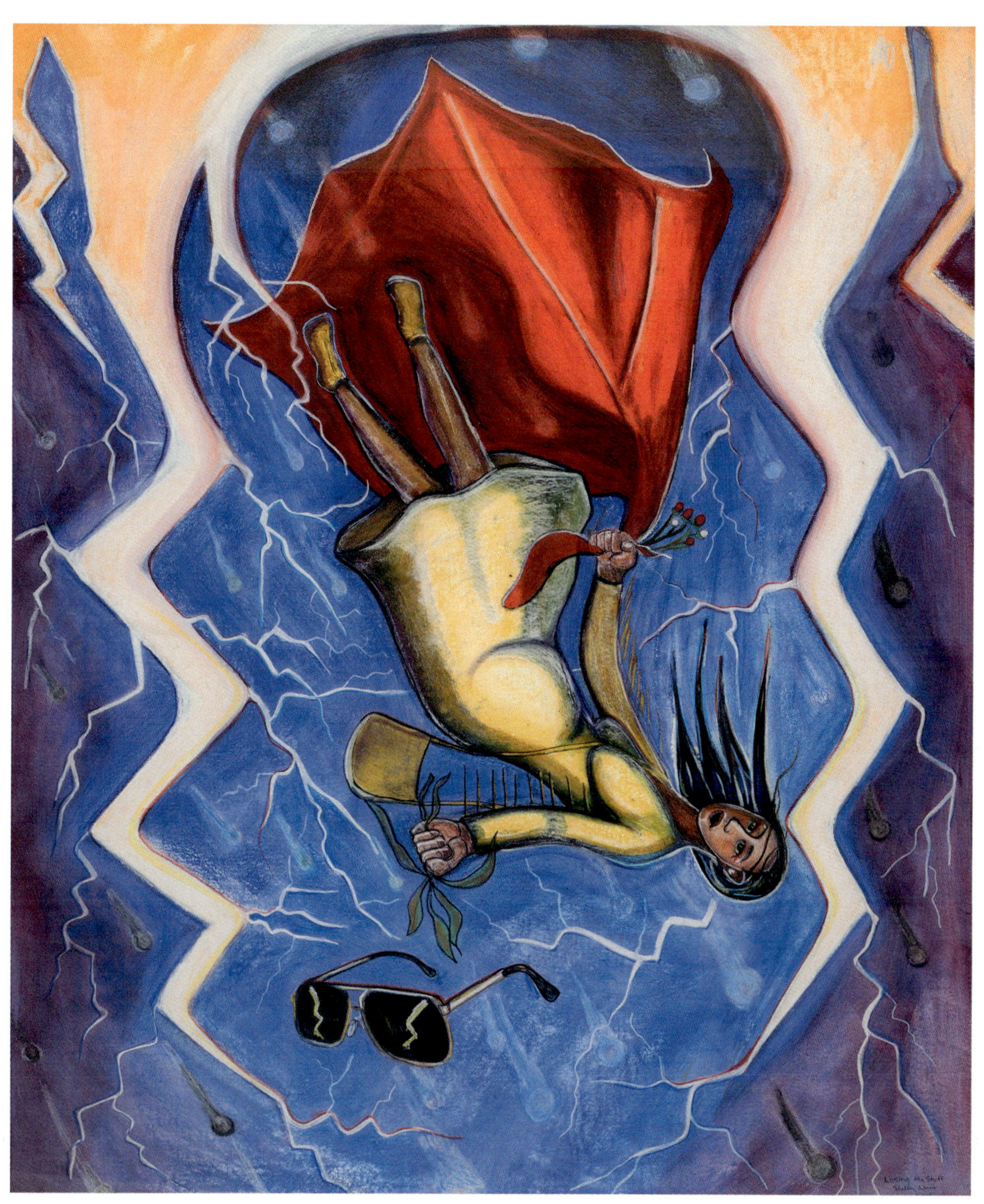

Losing My Stuff, 2001

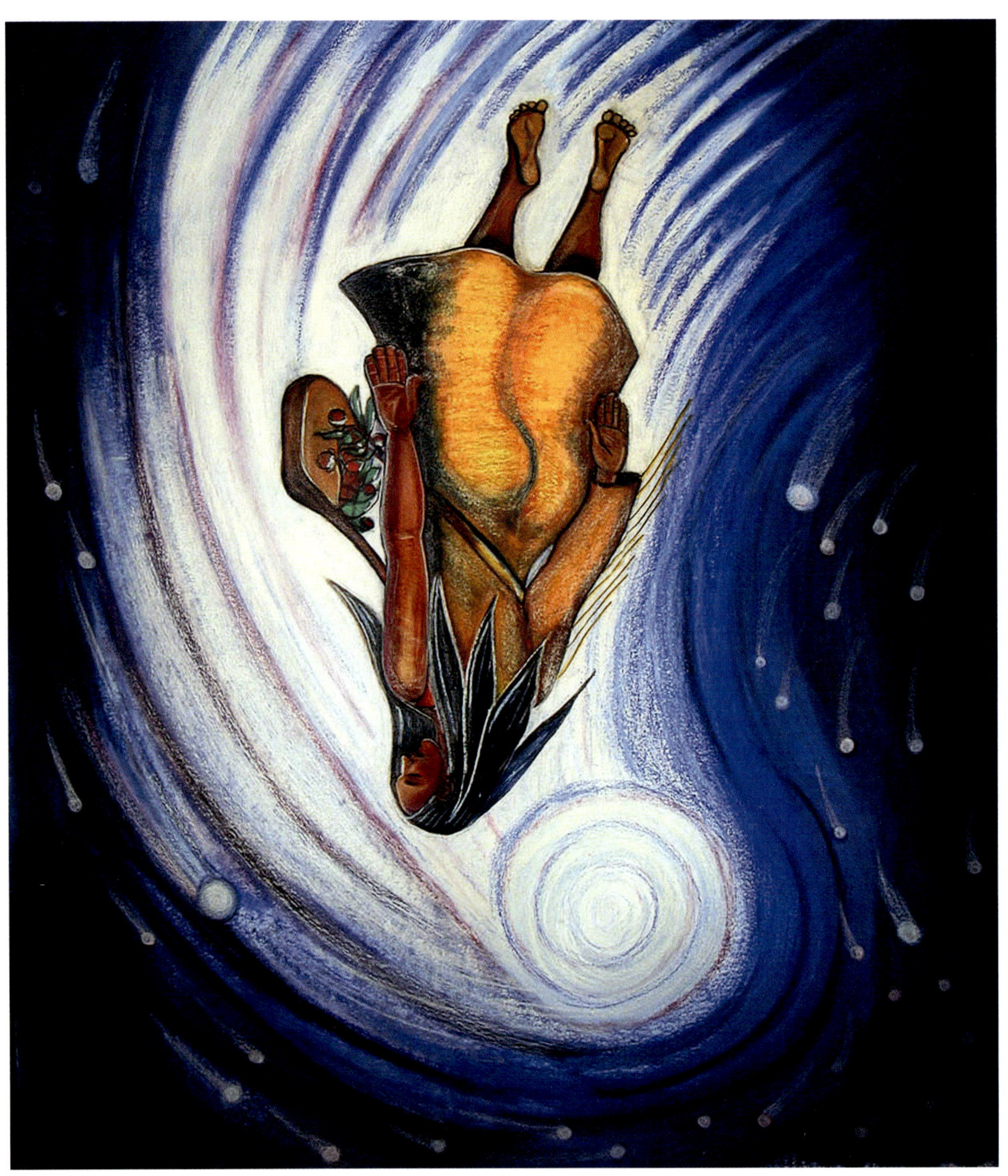

100   **Dreaming**, 2001

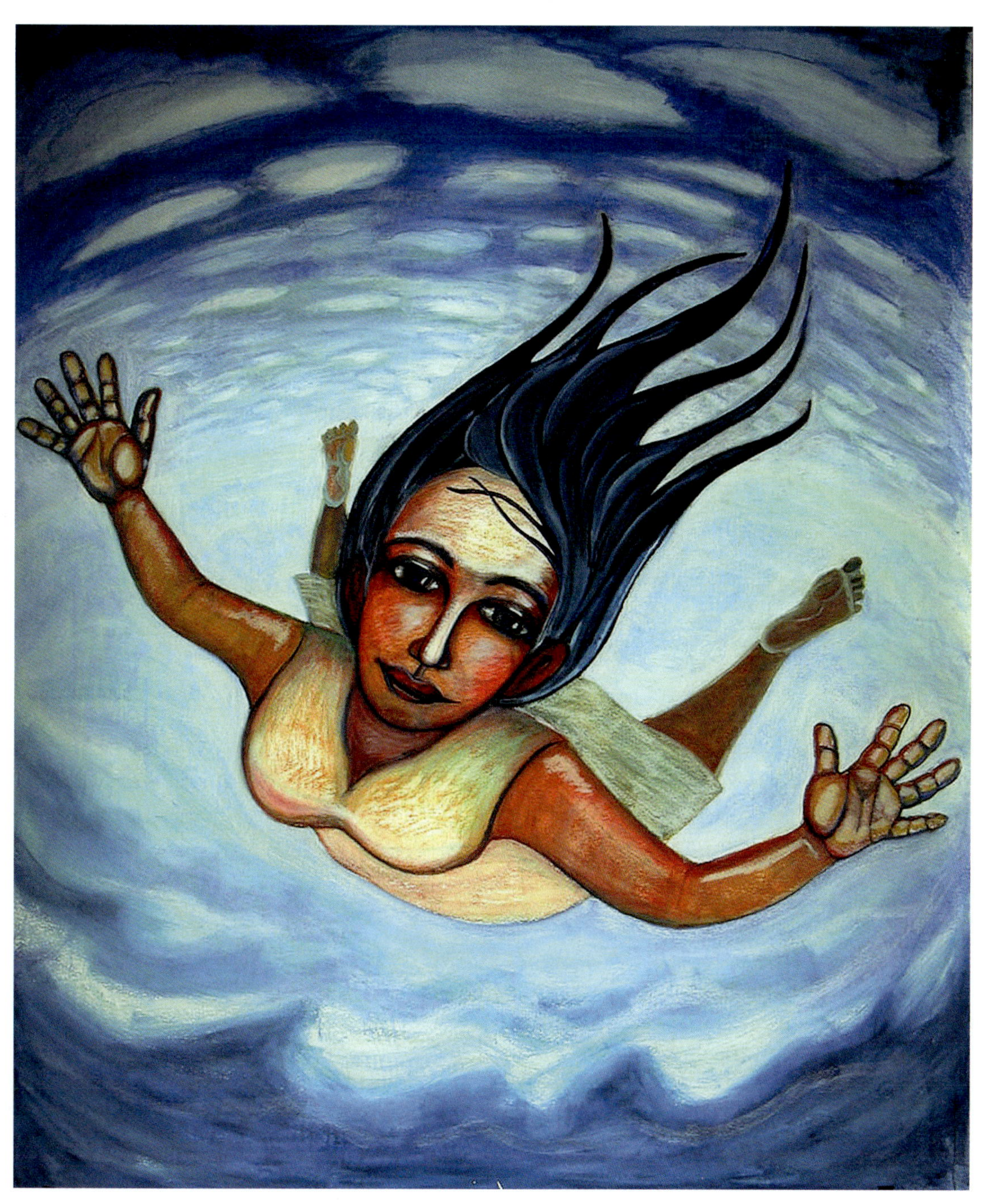

Loving It, 2001

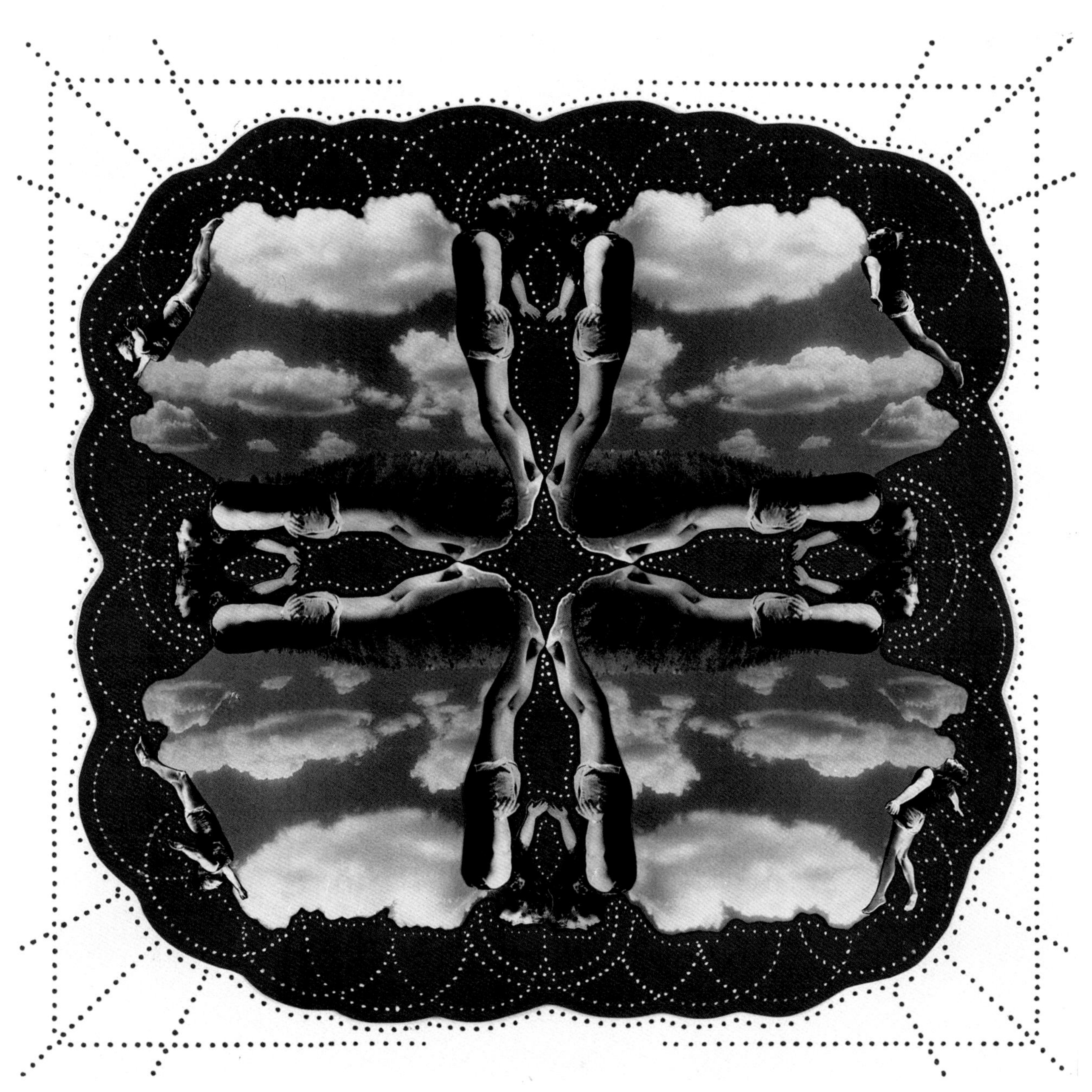

     Flying Woman #1, 1994

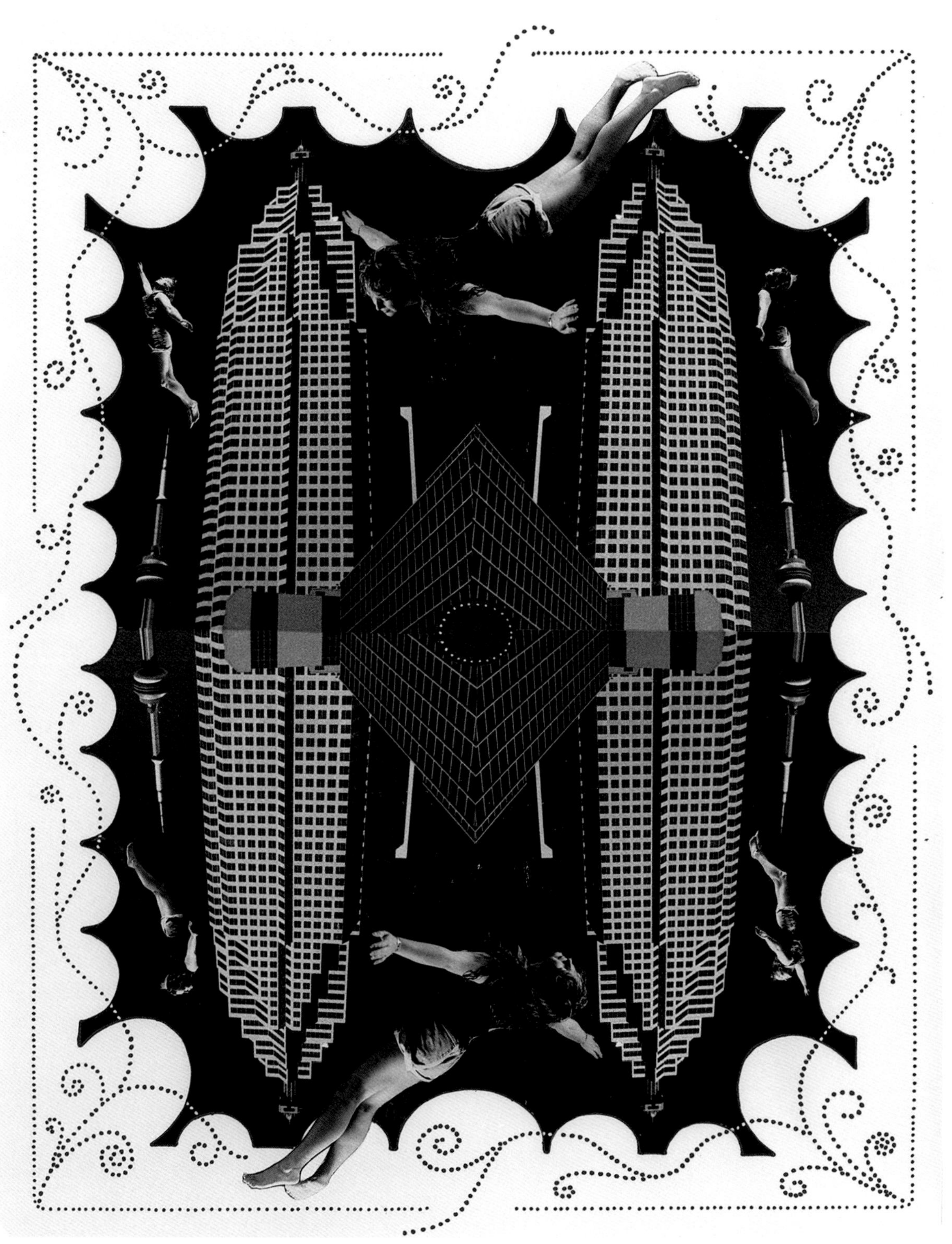

Flying Woman #2, 1994

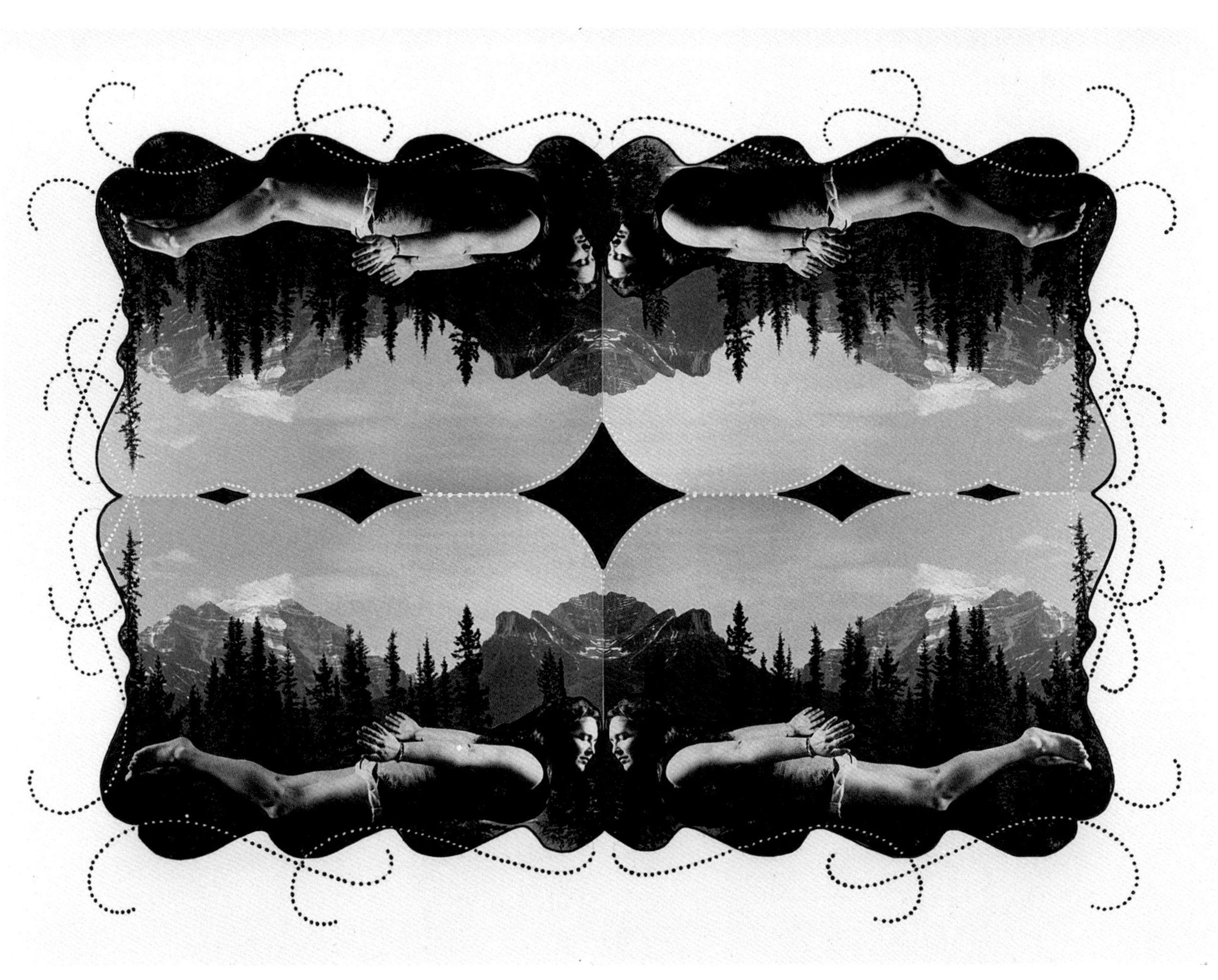

104   **Flying Woman #3**, 1994

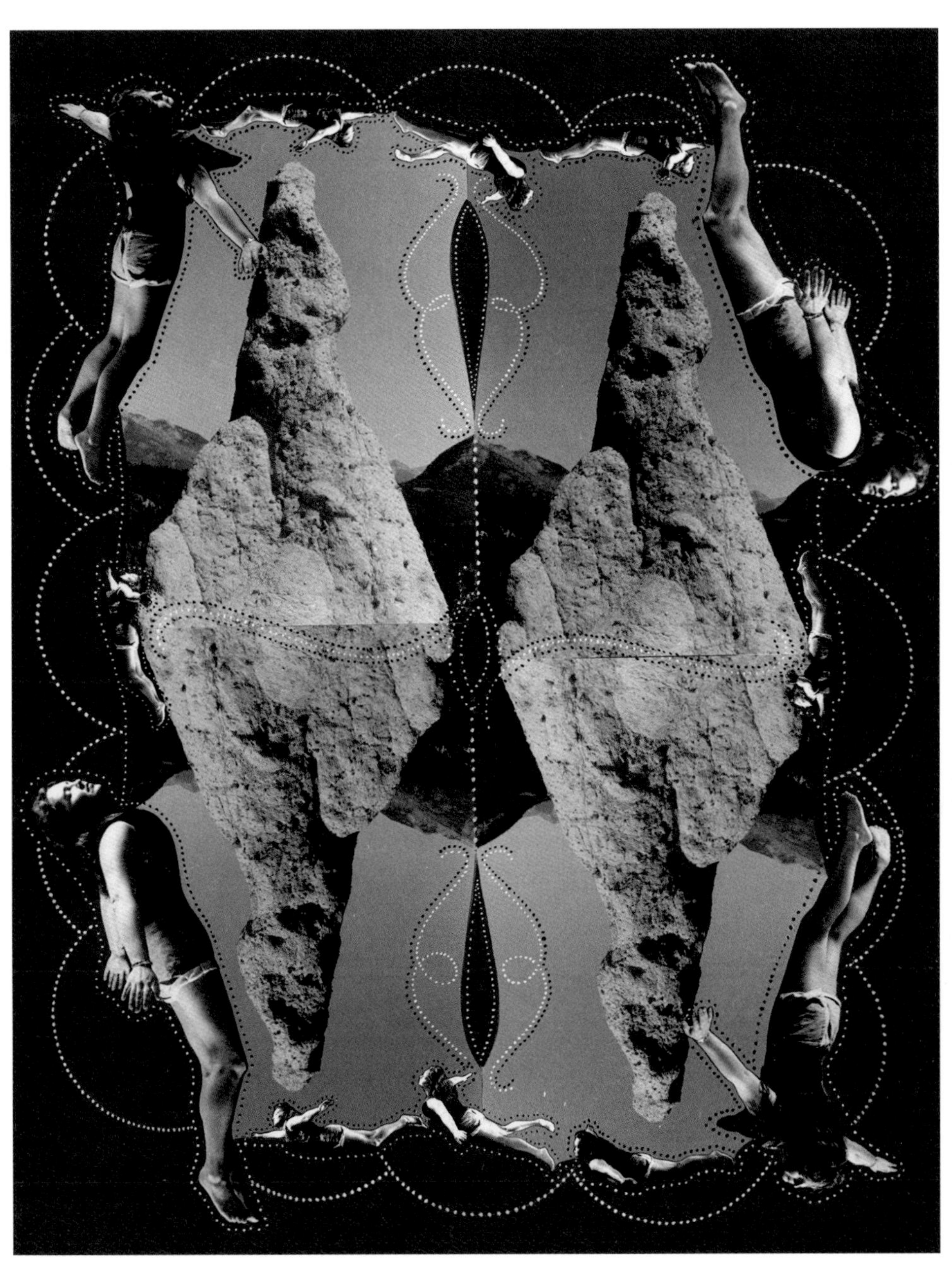

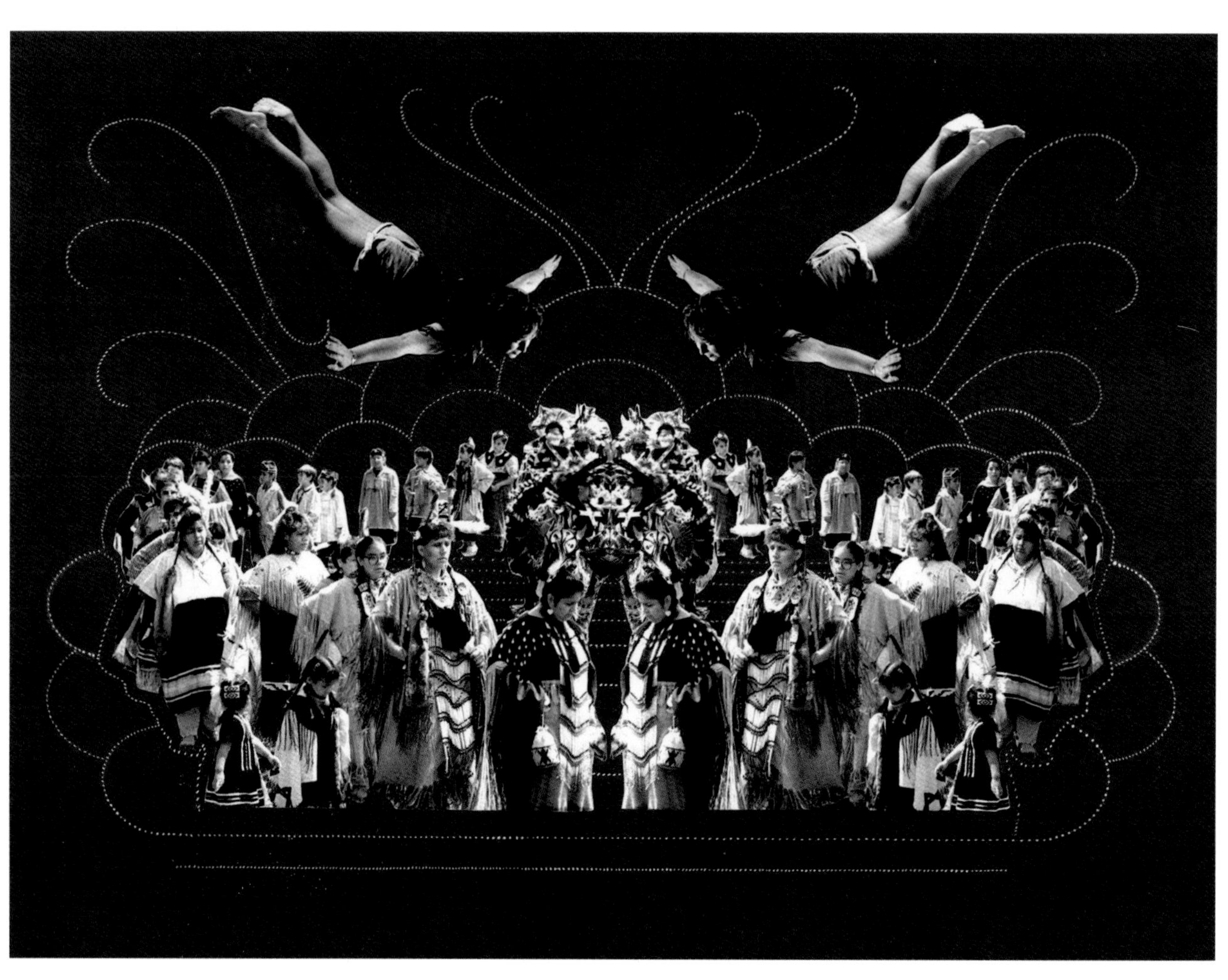

     Flying Woman #5, 1994

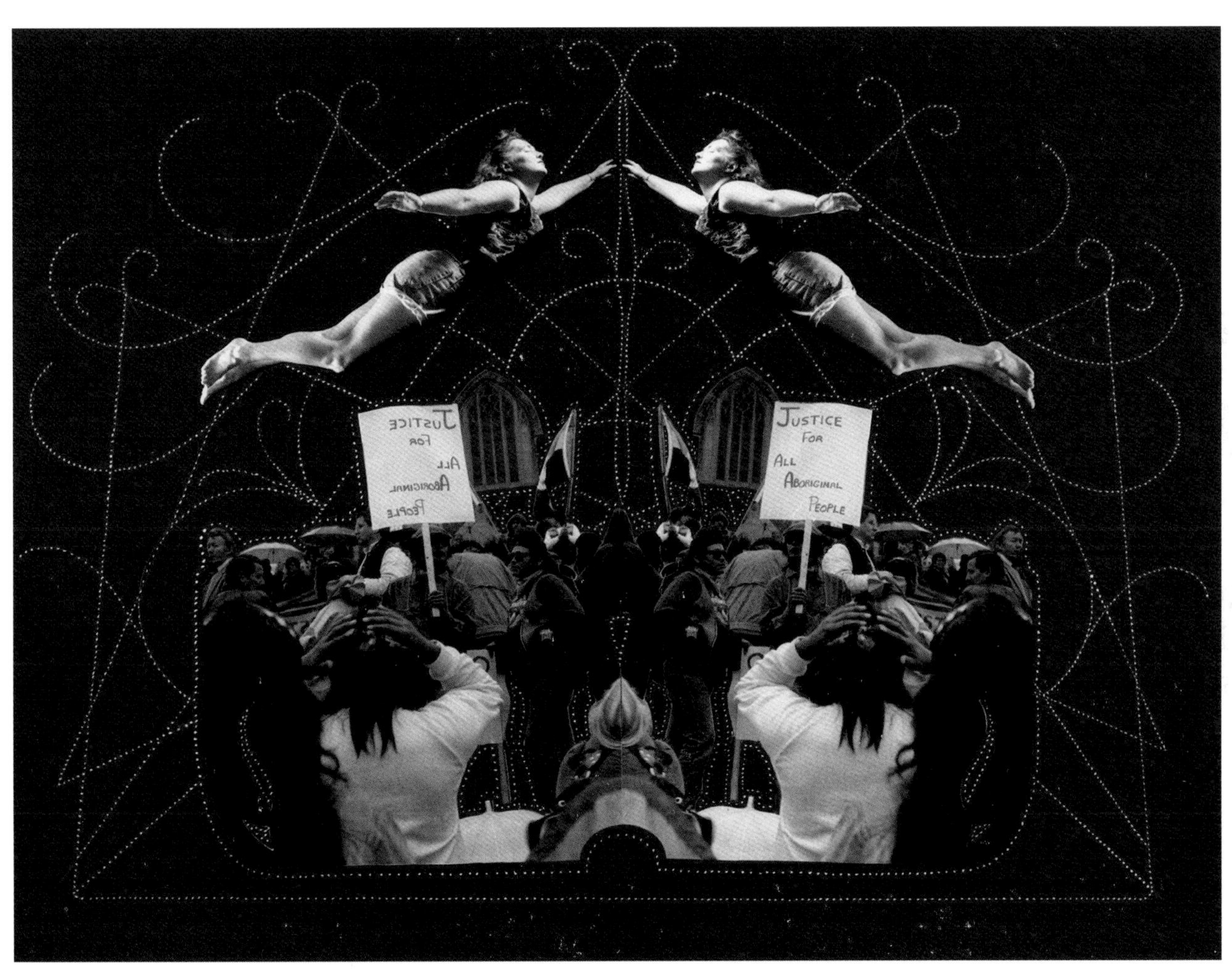

Flying Woman #6, 1994

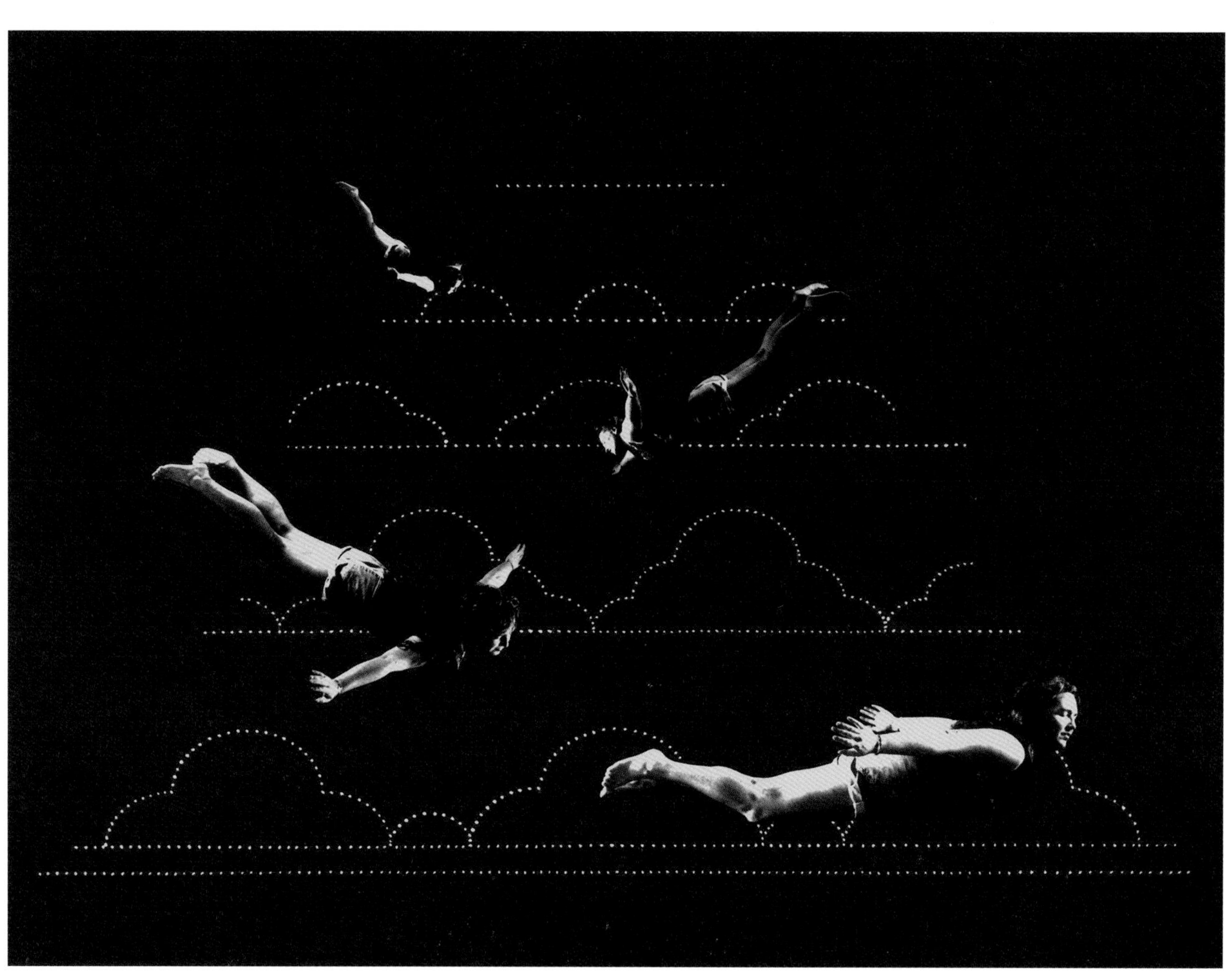

Flying Woman #7, 1994

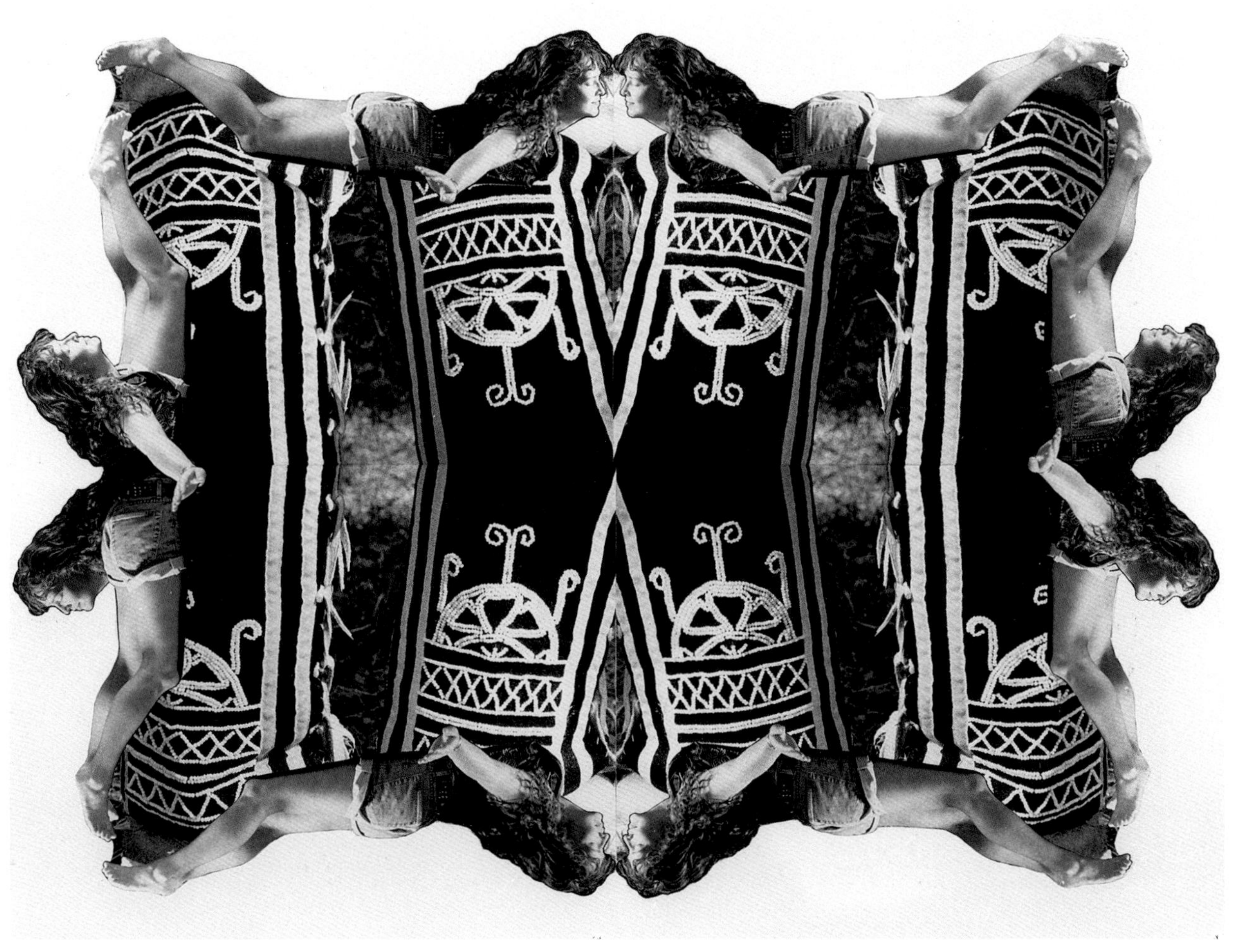

Flying Woman #8, 1994   109

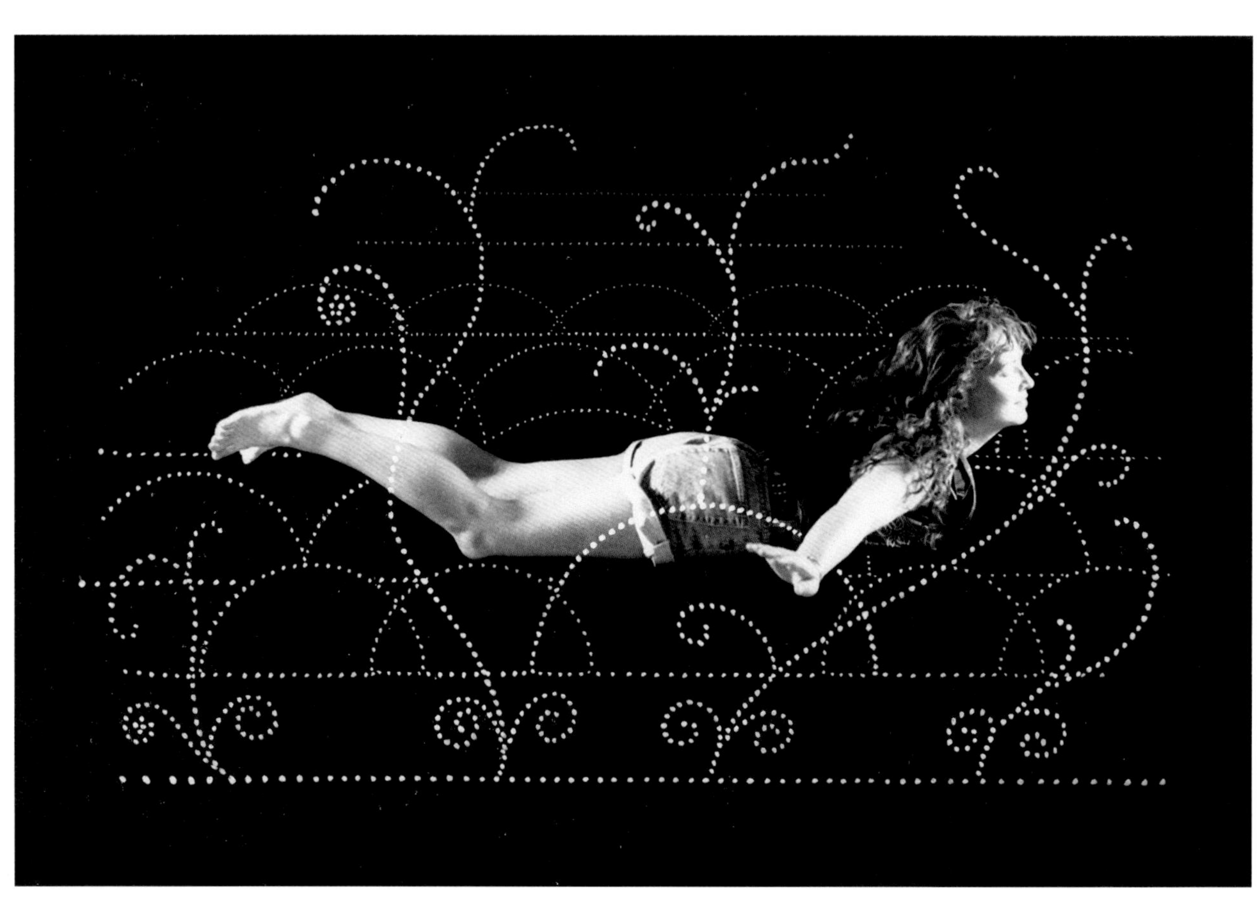

 Flying Woman #9, 1994

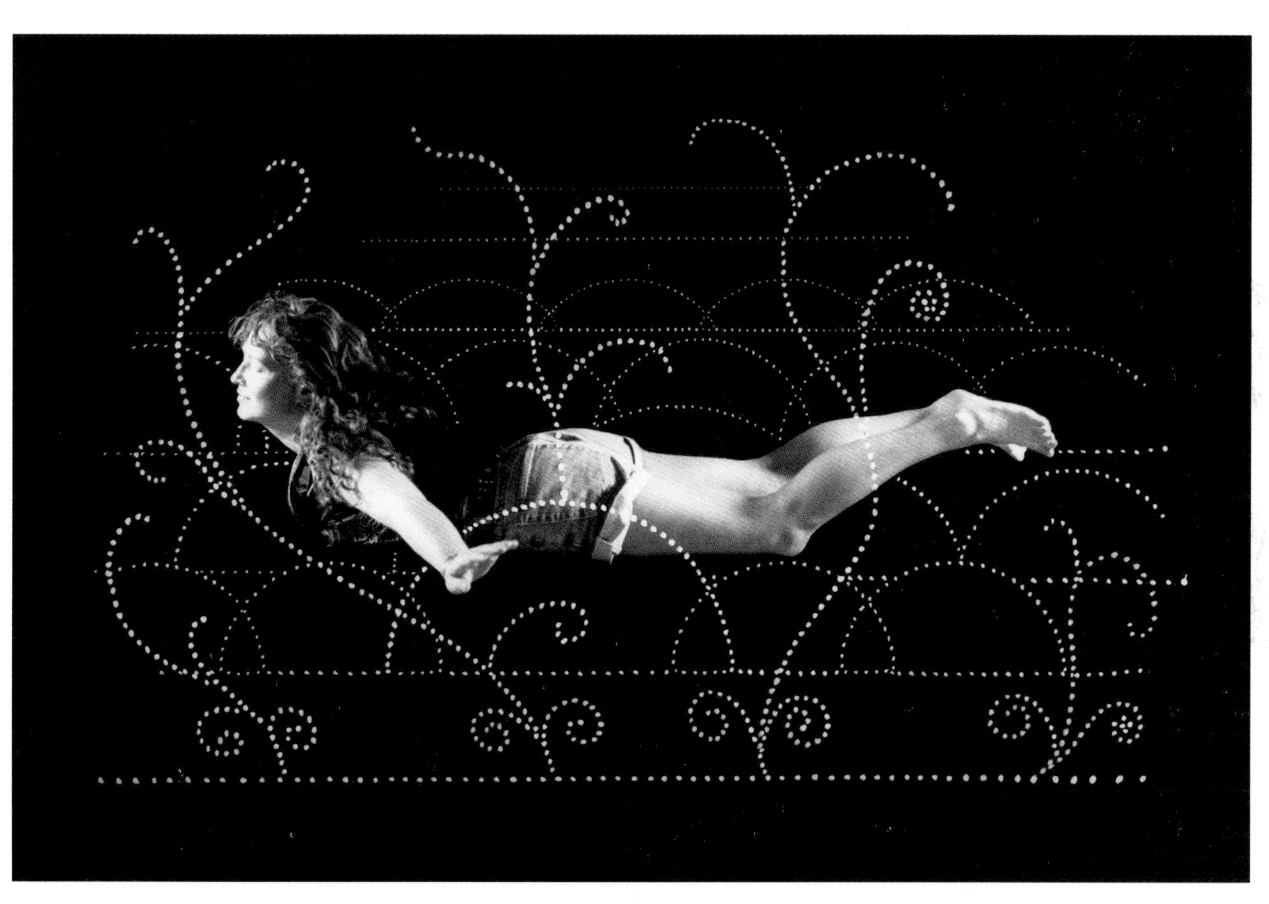

Flying Woman #10, 1994

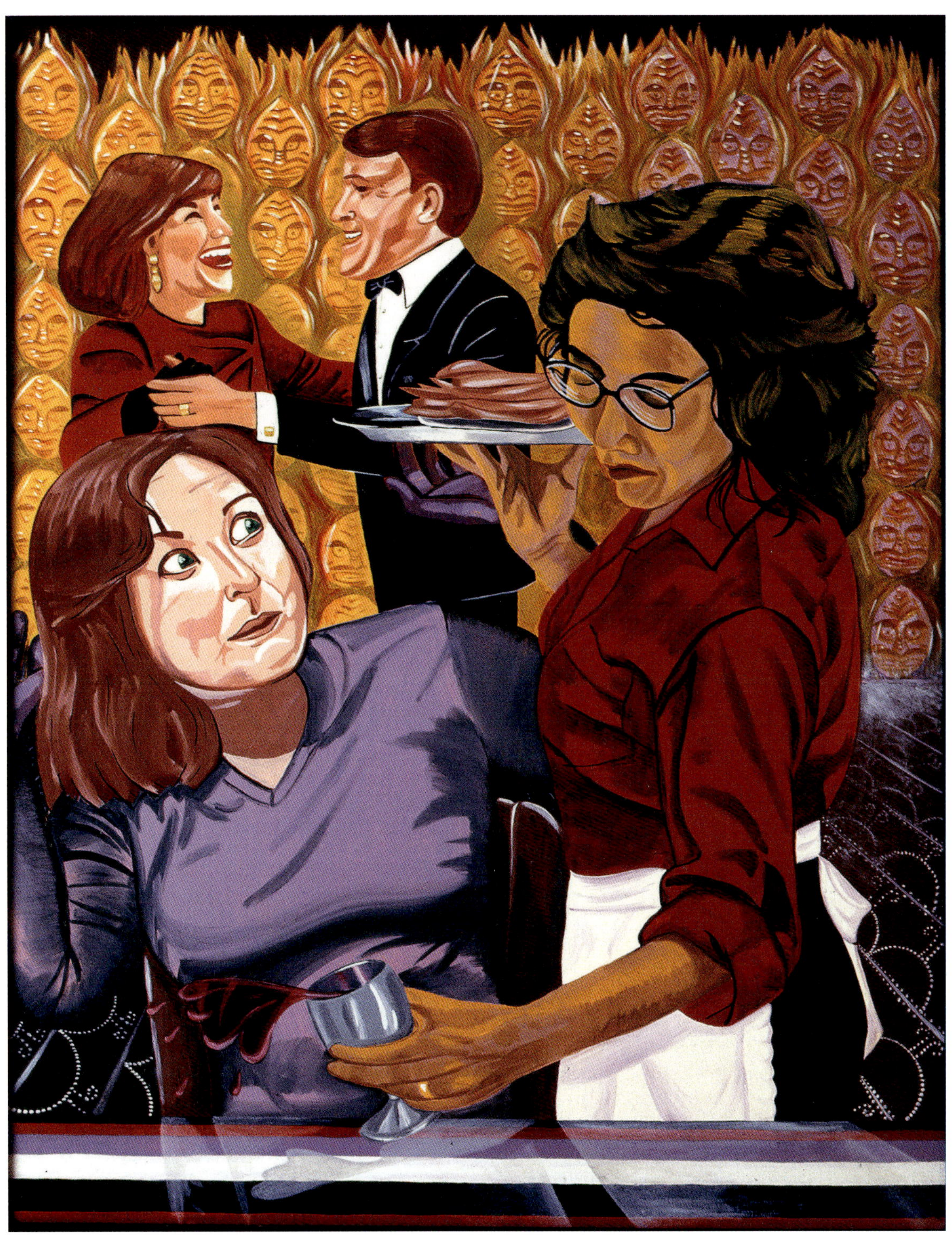

    Waitress, 1987

Do the Indian thing, man.[1]

BRYCE KANBARA

In 2018, on an exhibition label beside one of her works, Shelley Niro disclosed that as a high schooler she had played saxophone in the rez's marching band. The girls wore headbands, had feathers in their hair, and were uniformed in fringed felt skirts sewn by their mothers, making summer parades and concerts extremely uncomfortable.

This revelation was characteristic of the careful way Niro has examined what makes her who she is, and how and when she elects to tell us. Travel to other parts of Canada with the marching band provided her with not only a vantage point from which she could see her home as the vital source of every cultural and familial richness in her life, but also as a limiting tether.

With assistance from the Department of Indian Affairs she enrolled in a music performance program at Cambrian College, which took her to faraway Sudbury. Her initial saxophone studies shifted venturously to cello, whose sound she has had a continuing affinity for and uses in her film work. Niro's middle name is Patrice, and she credits her taste for music to her mother, who was a fan of the Metropolitan Opera singer and 1950s TV variety show host, Patrice Munsel. Sudbury was also the backdrop for another important turn: it's where she met her husband-to-be, Celestino (Chel) Niro.

Although music was her early focus, Niro says she was always attracted to artmaking. She has said she grew up on the Six Nations reserve "surrounded by people who did delicate watercolour paintings of men and women in their traditional Iroquois/ Haudenosaunee clothing, people who made drums and rattles from traditional materials, bark and seeds… and those who continued to do beadwork."

In 1984, after the birth of two daughters and relocations to Pembroke, Oshawa (where she took graphic art courses at Durham College), and Kincardine, the family finally settled in Brantford to be near Niro's heartland. During these itinerant years, she was finding her way as an artist. Chel poured liquid clay into pottery moulds and she painted the fired ceramic cups with Indigenous patterns. Hamilton artist Cees van Gemerden remembers seeing them at an outdoor art fair selling their wares from a rented table. Indigenous art was becoming popular and "people were hungry for native stuff," Niro says.

From Brantford, with Chel in charge at home, Niro made the long haul back and forth by train each day to the Ontario College of Art in Toronto. At a time when OCA was fervently promoting experimentation, Niro "wanted to learn to draw a face."

She says she lacked confidence and struggled to improve. Aware of the growing influence of ethnic diversity in contemporary art, she pondered how to reflect the experiences of family, community, and her people; by doing "the Indian thing," as Jimi Hendrix had called it,[1] on her own terms.

In 1987, she painted *Waitress* (p. 112), which depicts a server in an upscale restaurant (Niro herself?) spilling a glass of wine (accidentally?) on a female patron, while Brian and Mila Mulroney dance in front of a wall of false-face masks, merrily oblivious. It's a declarative work that exudes self-satisfaction in its breakthrough achievement. *Waitress* is a combination of Niro's assiduously acquired painting ability, her growing sophistication with Indigenous themes, and a percolating sense of humour. Positive public response to *Waitress* was a validation for her and gave her confidence in her method.

From here, Niro launched into a period of profuse productivity, generating images and ideas that have come to define her work and career. Increasingly, she embraced photography and film as mediums, a shift that was readily appreciated by viewers who were more attuned to looking at these media than at paintings.

Film critic Roger Ebert pointed out that the movies are about emotions, not facts, and Niro's film scripts are less plot-driven than they are vehicles for character study. Through the range of personalities and behaviours of her characters, she divulges aspects of herself and what she knows of Indigenous identity and perspective. She does this vicariously at times, and sometimes confessionally. Occasionally, she cannot resist punctuating her script with a director's authorial voice. "His droll academic dialogue bores me," she says, in *The Incredible 25th Year of Mitzi Bearclaw* (2019, p. 132). Niro's films provide her with the scope to express her affection for her people, and help the rest of us understand it.

Niro releases surges of information through her thinly disguised (and vividly named) alter egos in her two feature films *Kissed by Lightning* (2009, pp. 128–129) and *The Incredible 25th Year of Mitzi Bearclaw*. The heroine Mavis Dogblood in *Kissed by Lightning* is a painter who lives on a reserve and is working towards a New York City exhibition. She is recovering from the tragic loss of her soulmate who, apart from possessing a deep knowledge of Traditional Stories (which runs as an undercurrent throughout the film), was, incidentally, a classical violinist. In *The Incredible 25th Year of Mitzi Bearclaw*, the title character returns to the rez to tend to her ailing mother and support her beleaguered father. But Mitzi is foremost an artist who intends to storm the fashion scene with fascinator-type hats made of twigs and branches. Mavis and Mitzi both have

their feet planted in two worlds. Niro's aim is not to simplistically pit the merits of one world against the other; in life, she values both. Her focus is on how her characters behave and relate to one another in these contrasting settings and circumstances.

Niro has a natural demeanour which she is able to impart to the people in her paintings and films. Several times, in the series of vignettes that make up that make up her video *Suite: INDIAN* (2005, pp. 120–121), she dissolves the imagined barrier separating the movie and the audience (commonly known as the "fourth wall"). At the end of a studious segment showing the crafting of a corn-husk doll, the doll maker hesitantly holds up her creation and stifles a split-second chuckle. It's obvious that her self-conscious action is in mock response to an off-camera instruction from Niro. We suddenly feel we are in the same room, sharing a laugh—a typically inclusive tendency in Niro's work. In the segment *Kory and Mercedes*, we share Mercedes' delight when, walking away on Kory's arm, she glances back at the camera and flashes us a victorious grin. In choosing to include frames that could easily have become outtakes, Niro is guileless and totally disarming.

Niro's paintings, photography, and films are known and lauded around the world. Her work is in the collections of corporations and public institutions. In an educational TV spot that has aired frequently these days, Indigenous educator and spokesperson Pamela Palmeter curtly comments, "I NEVER TALK ABOUT RECONCILIATION WITHOUT TALKING ABOUT TRUTH, JUSTICE, AND RECONCILIATION. YOU WON'T GET THAT FROM HANGING ARTWORK IN AN OFFICE."[2] We know what she means, but it's a mistake to underestimate the persuasive impact that art can make on hearts, minds, and political will.

NOTES

1. Jimi Hendrix's advice to the band Redbone in the documentary film *Rumble: The Indians Who Rocked the World*, directed by Catherine Bainbridge, co-directed by Alfonso Maiorana (Montreal: Rezolution Pictures, 2017).

2. "What Is Reconciliation? Indigenous Educators Have Their Say," accessed October 7, 2022, in First Things First, produced by Michelle-Andrea Girouard, web series, 3 min, https://www.tvo.org/video/what-is-reconciliation-indigenous-educators-have-their-say. Palmeter references the Truth and Reconciliation Commission of Canada, which was established as part of the Indian Residential Schools Settlement Agreement to facilitate reconciliation among former students, their families, their communities, and all Canadians.

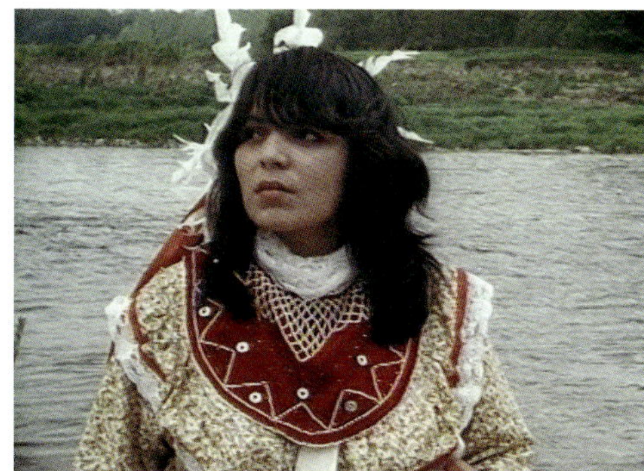
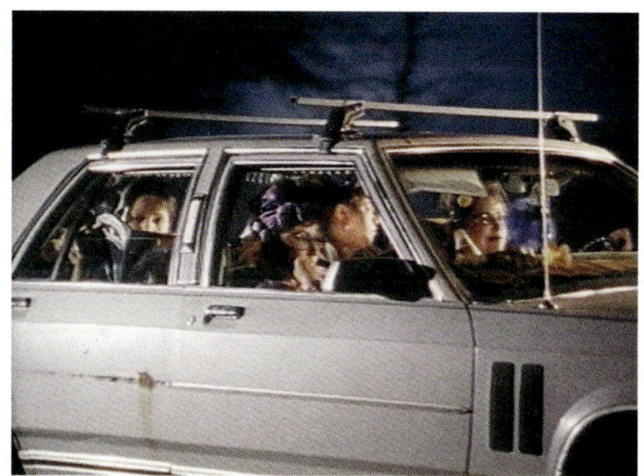
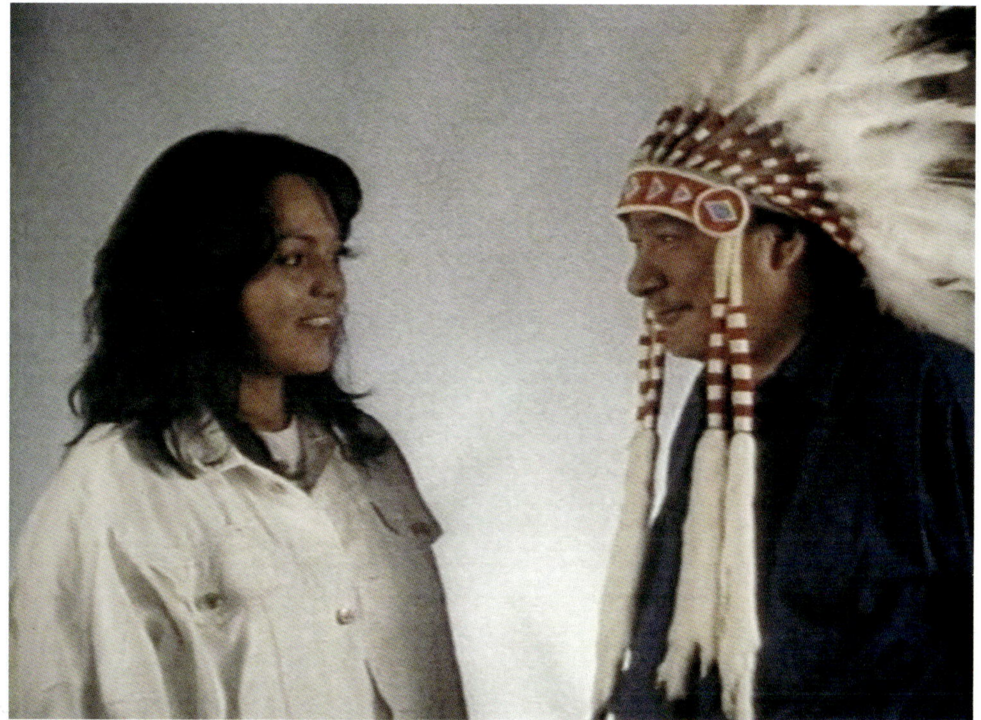
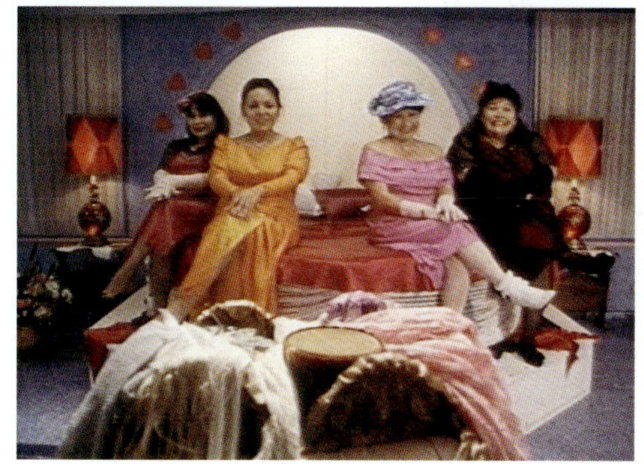

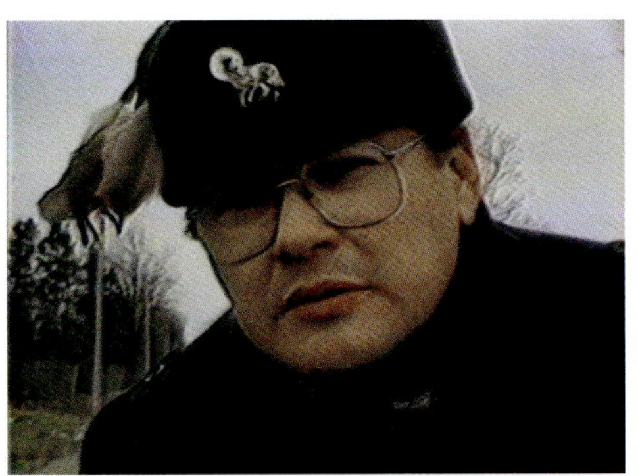

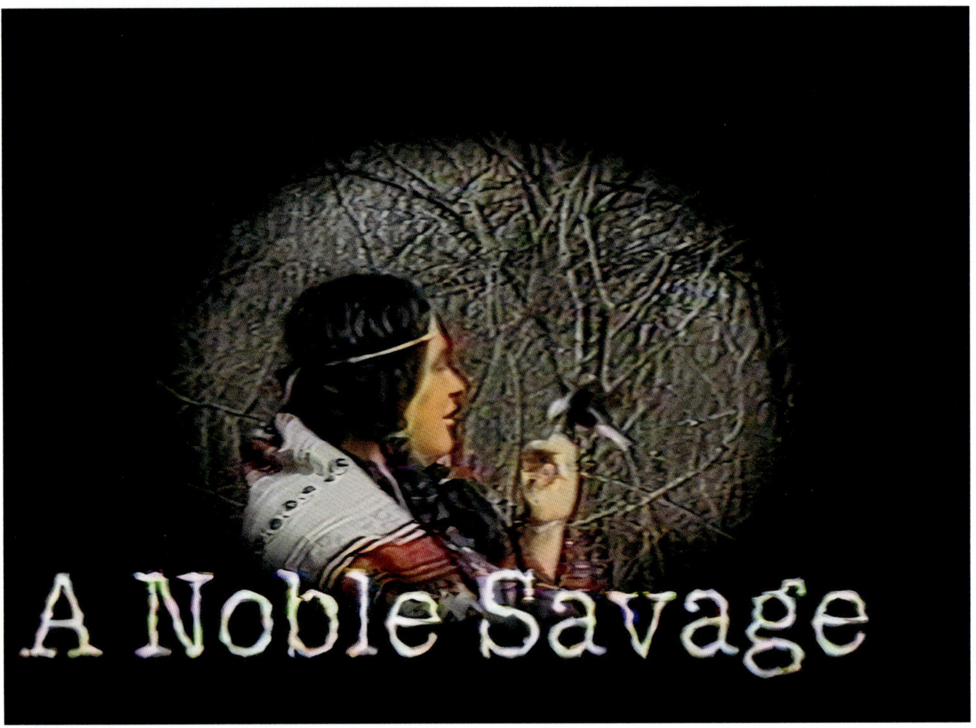

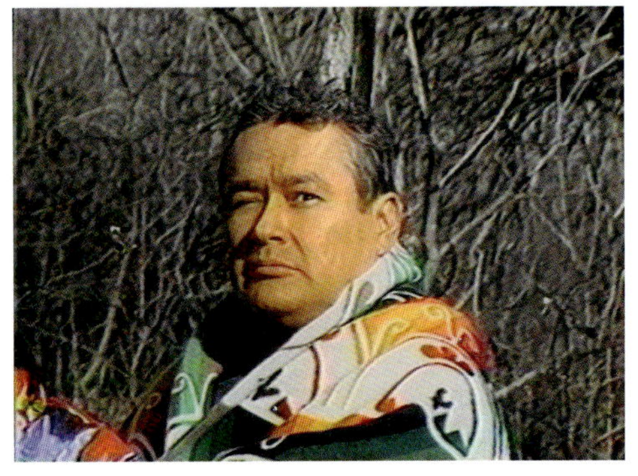

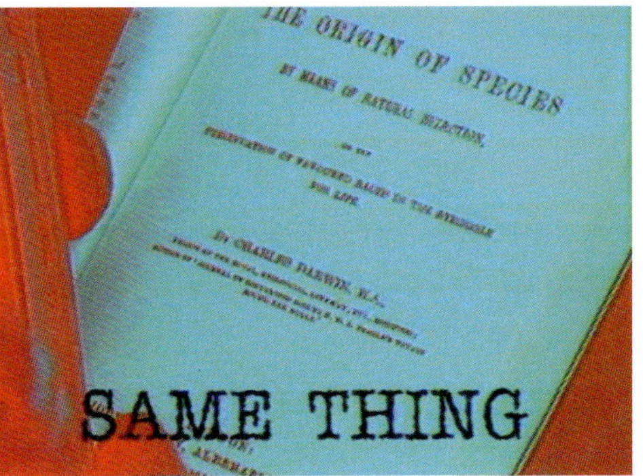

Stills from **Overweight With Crooked Teeth**, 1997

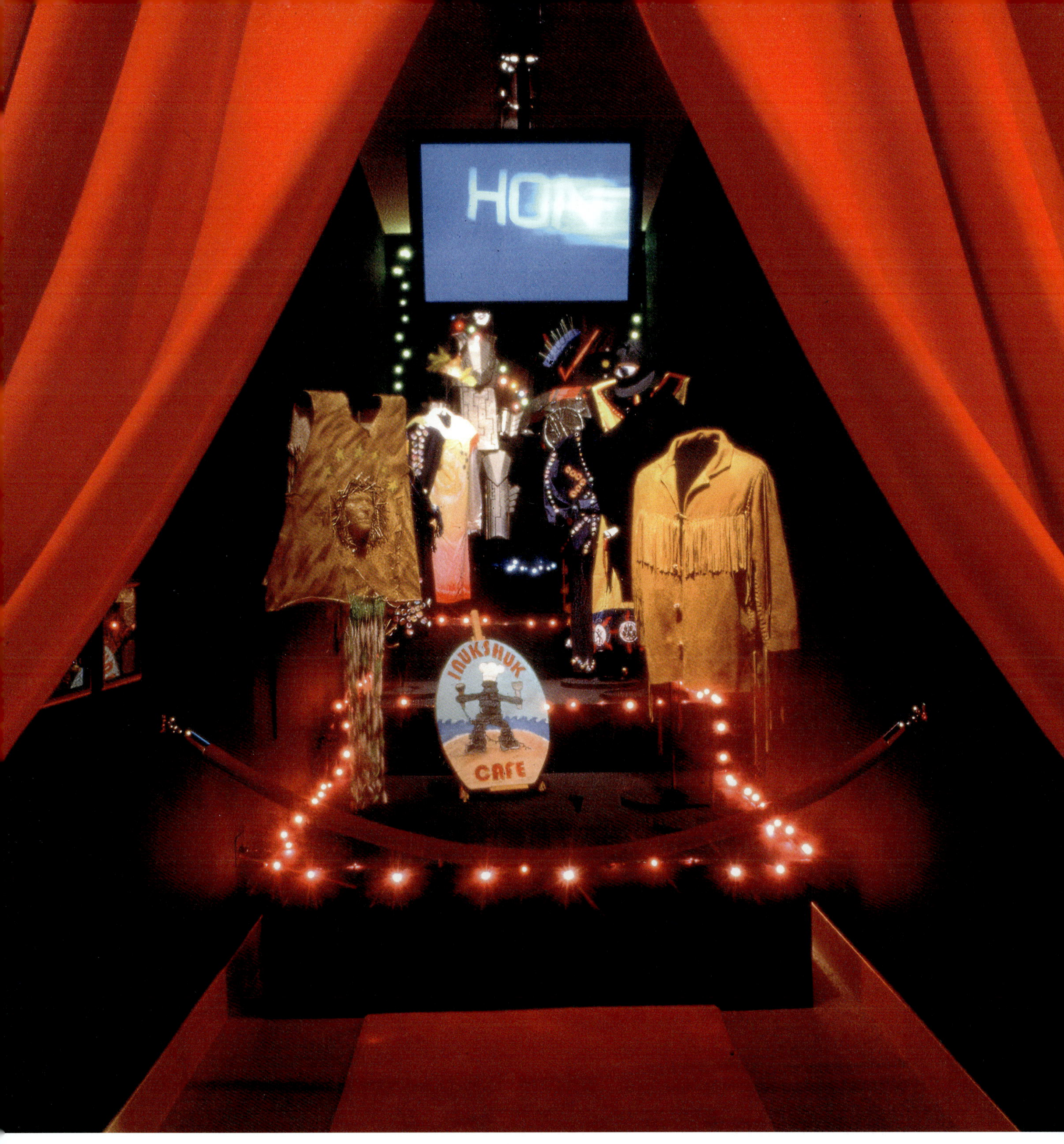

Installation view of **Honey Moccasin**, 1998
Reservation X: The Power of Place at the National Museum of the American Indian, New York, New York, 2000
Photograph courtesy the artist

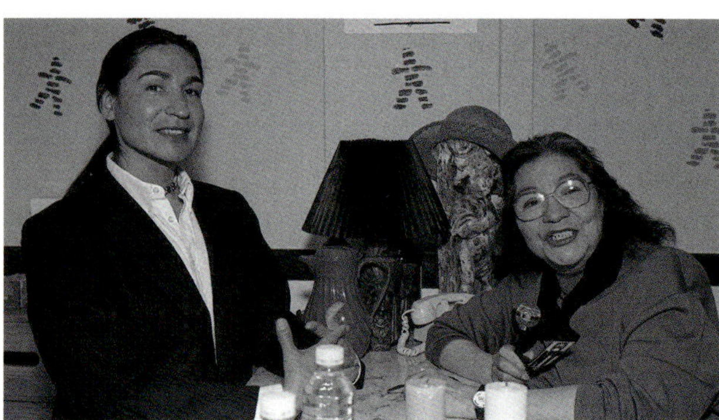

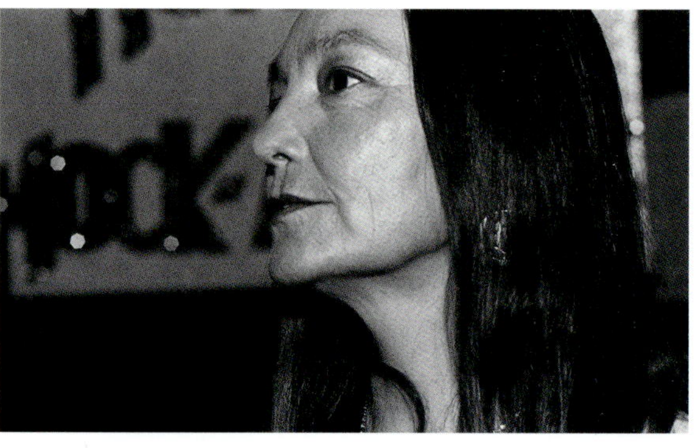

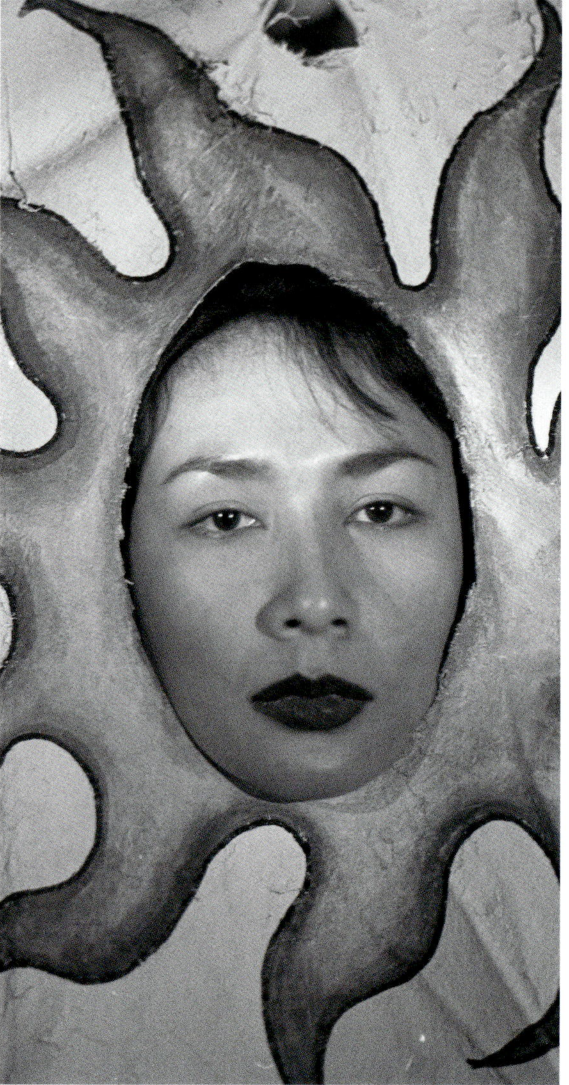

Beaded poster and production stills from **Honey Moccasin**, 1998

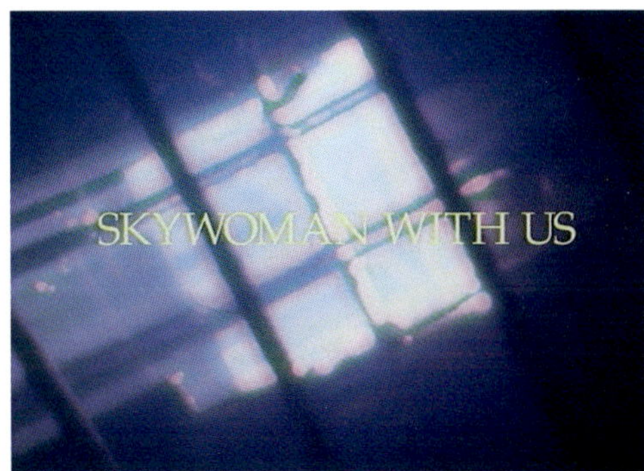

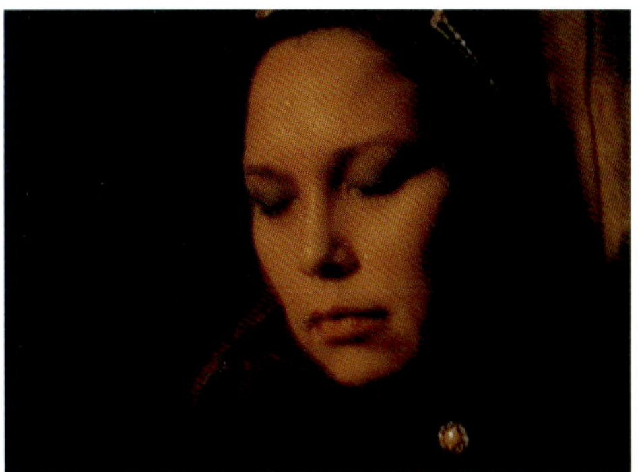

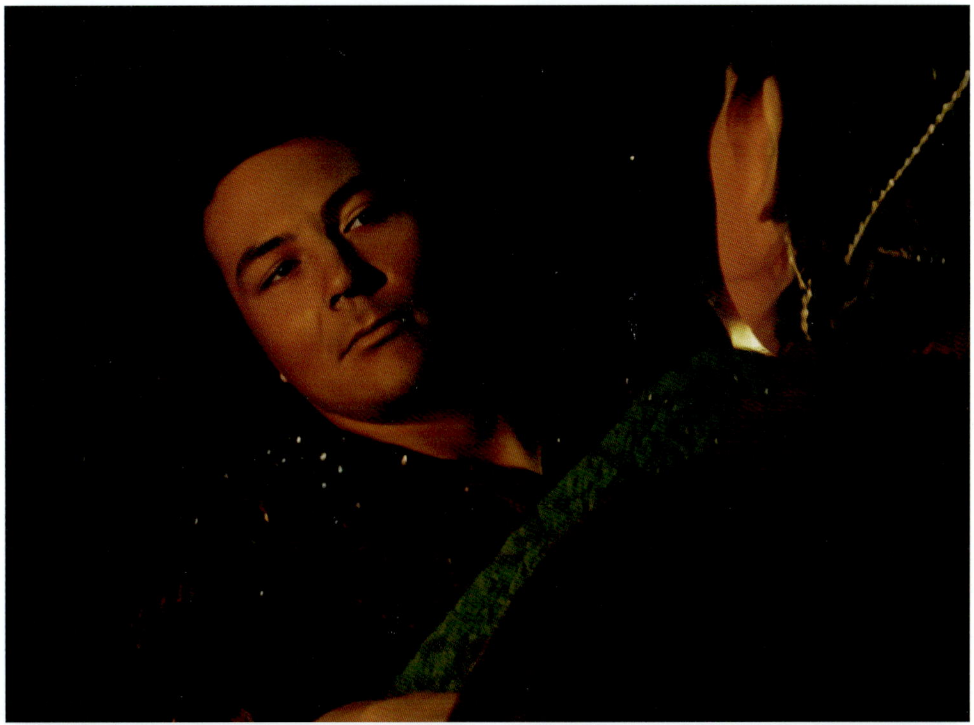

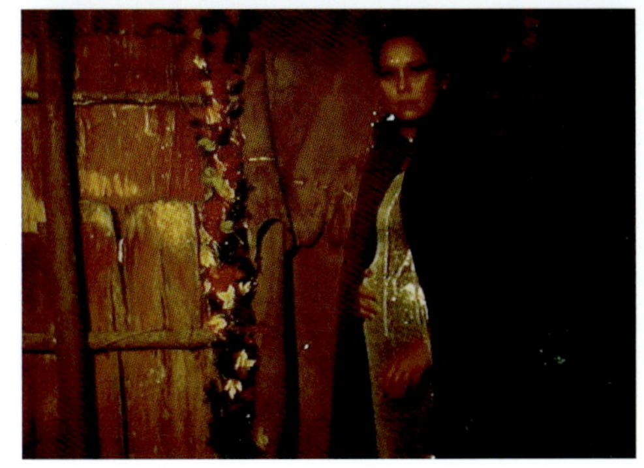

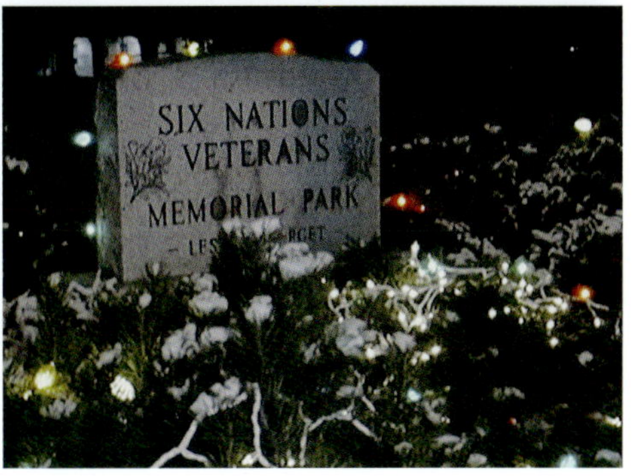

Stills from **Sky Woman With Us**, 2002

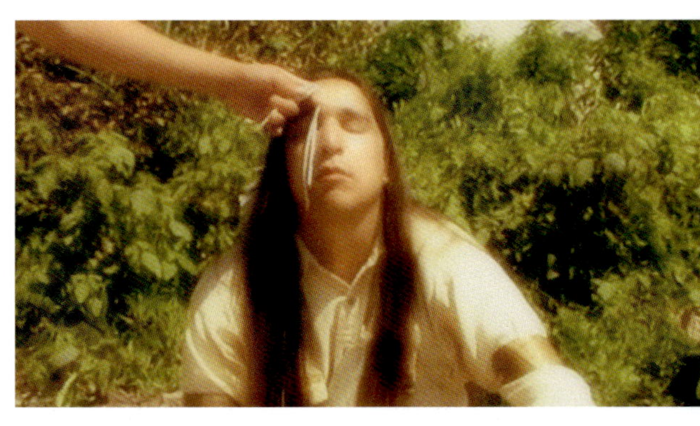
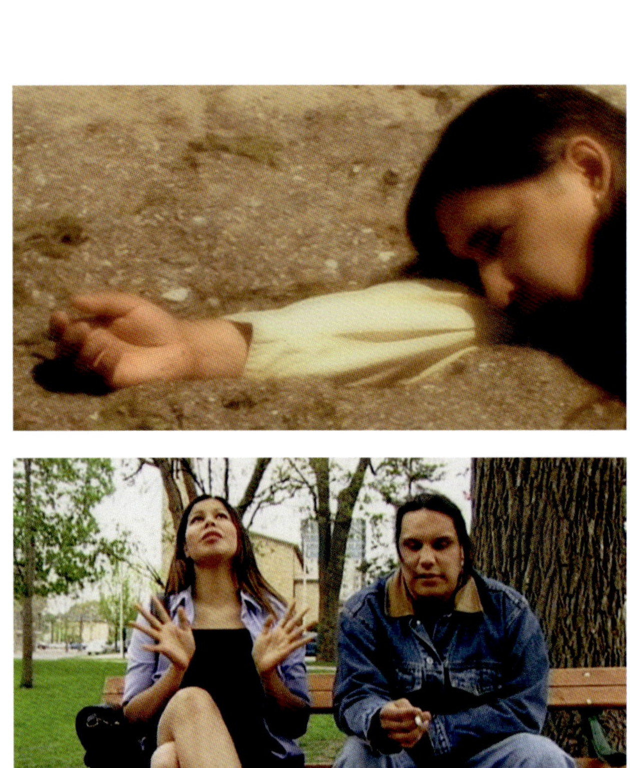
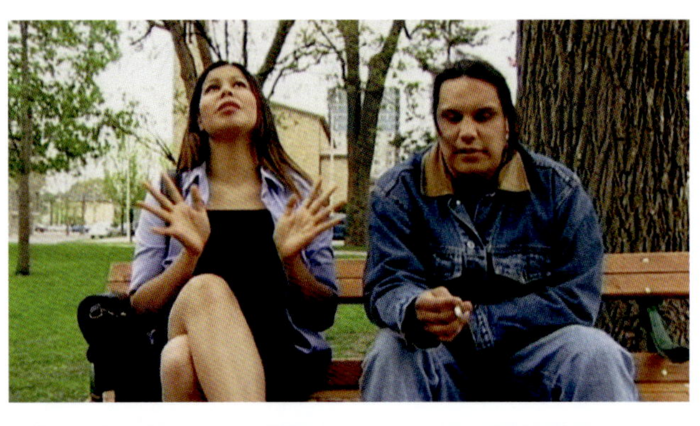
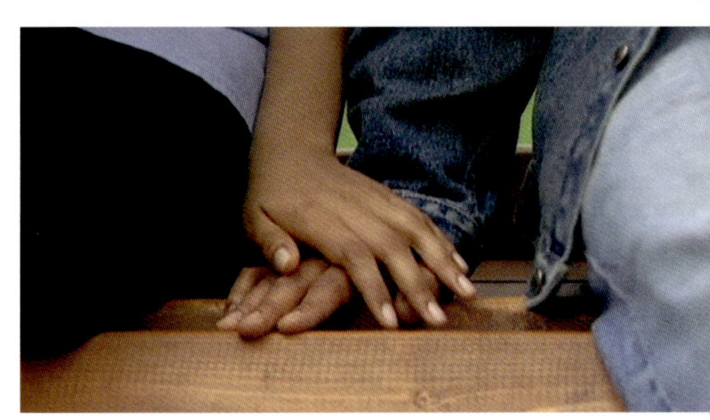
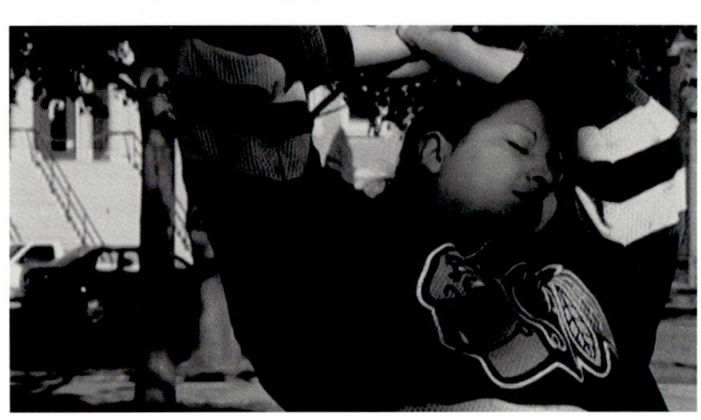
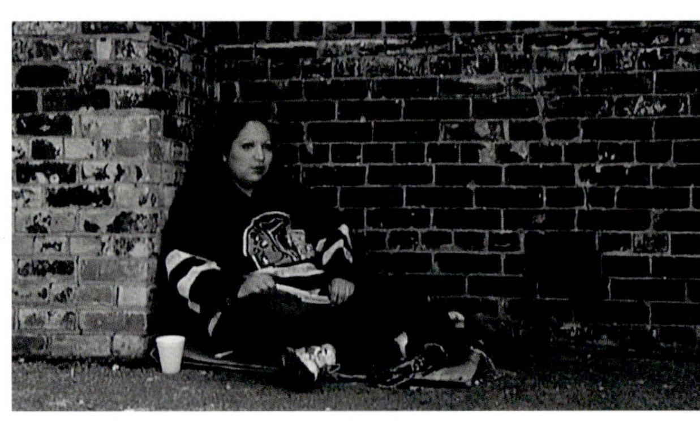
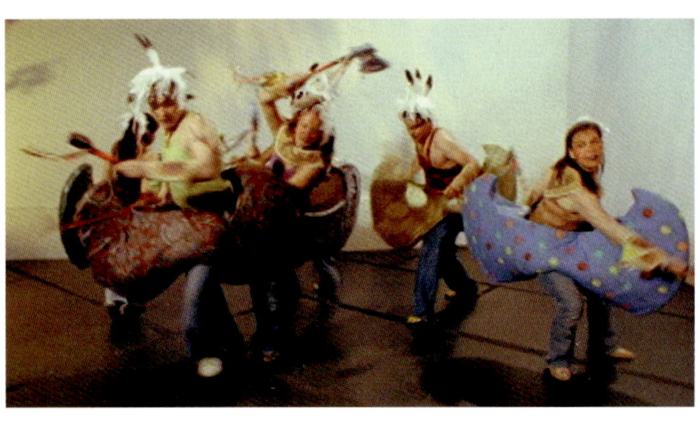
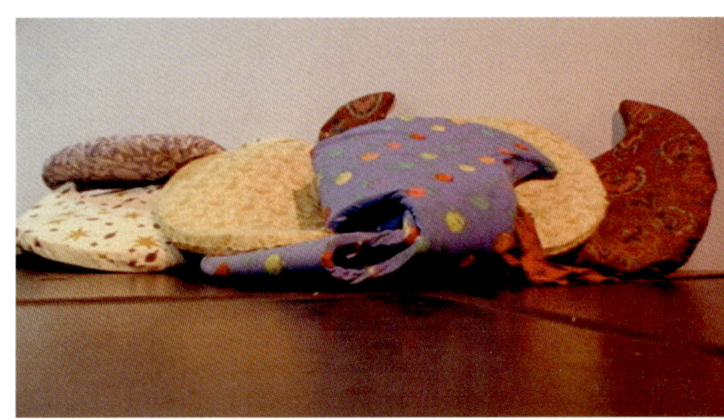

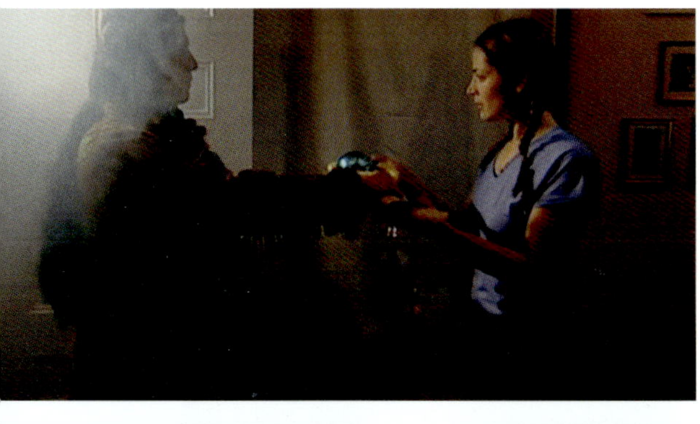
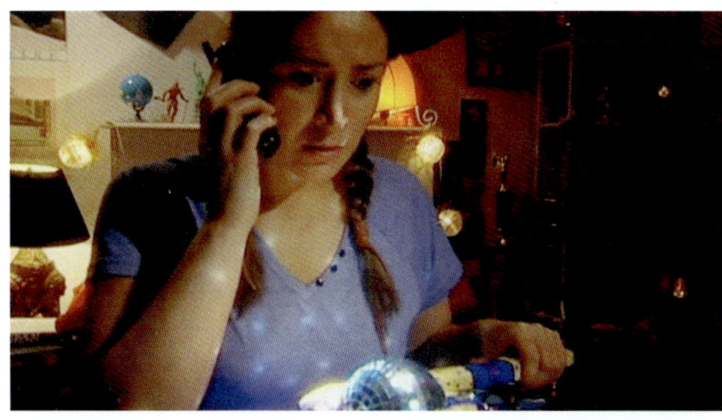
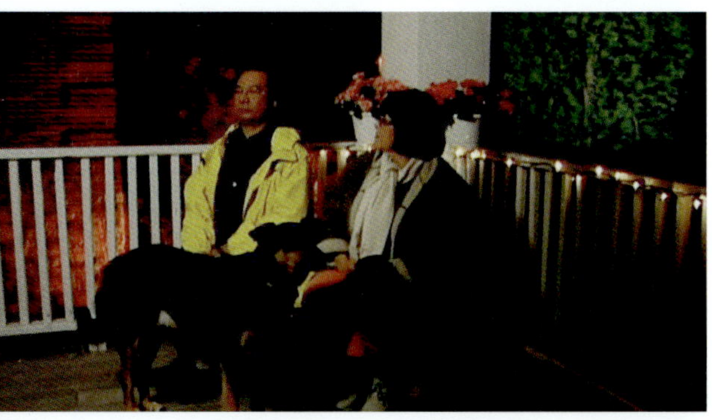
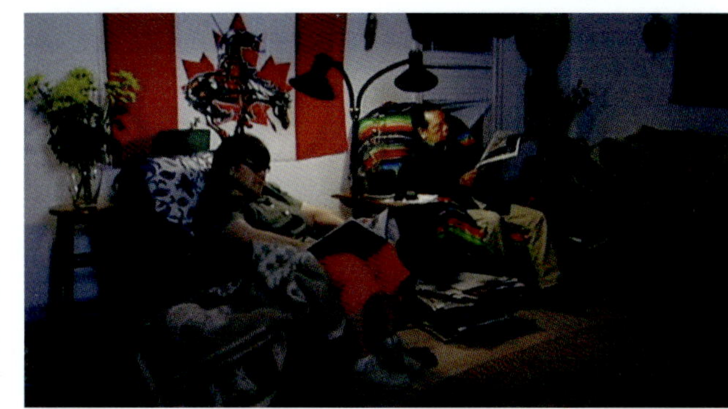
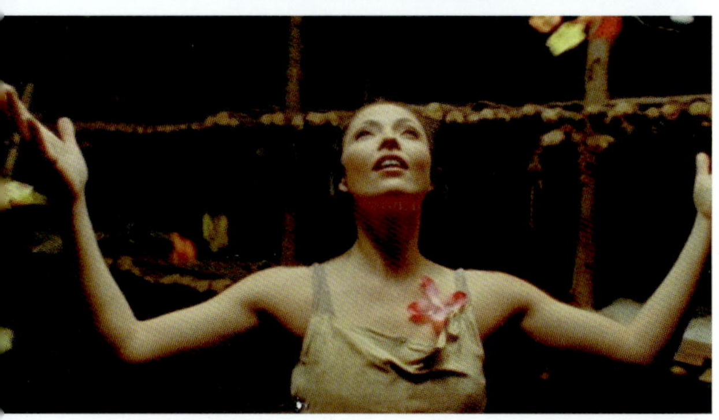
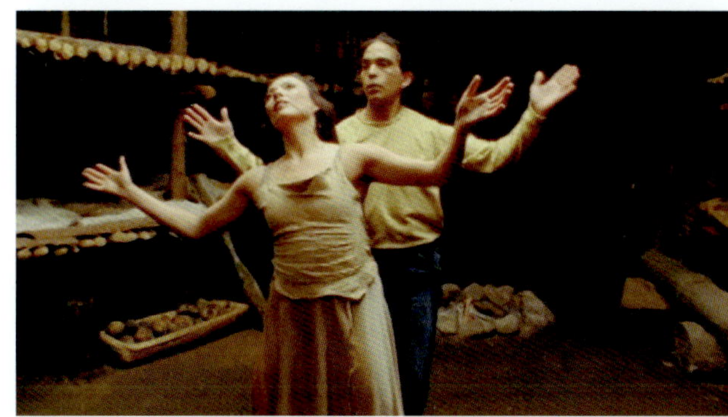
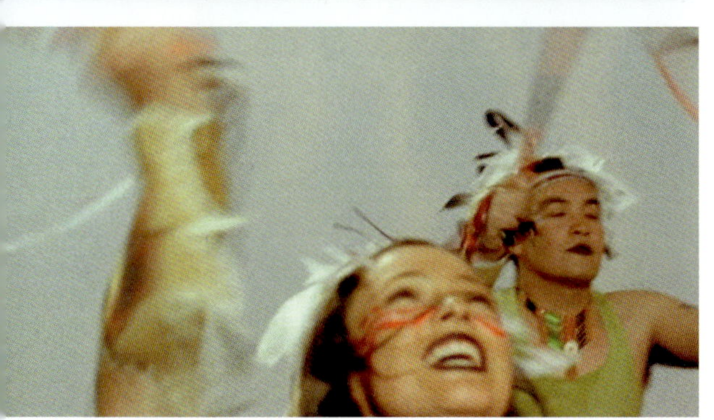
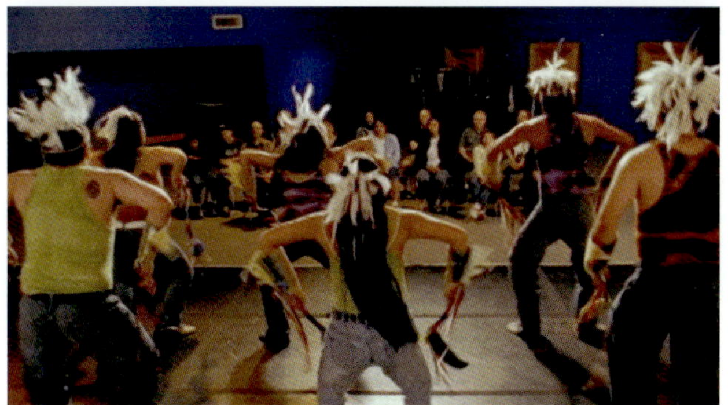

Stills from **Suite: INDIAN**, 2005

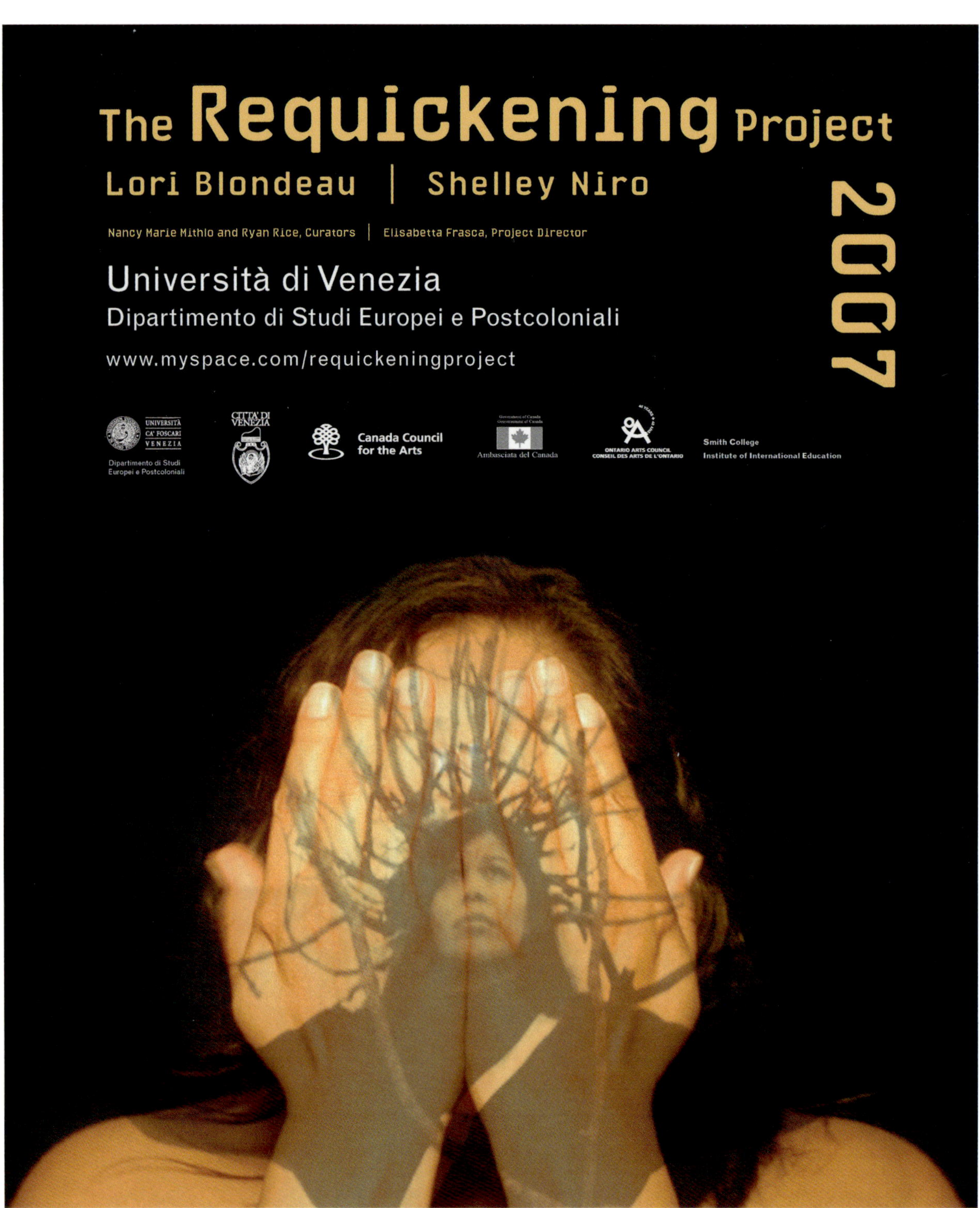

Poster design and illustration by Maureen Scanlon for **The Requickening Project: Lori Blondeau and Shelley Niro**, 2007

YOU'RE COMING WITH ME

NANCY MARIE MITHLO

The way someone looks through a camera lens tells you something about that person, what they like, how they see the world. It is like hearing a familiar voice; if you know someone for long enough, it's instantly recognizable. The film arts of Shelley Niro are something like that. You almost feel or sense the photo before you process it visually. There's a quiet curiosity, the confidence of someone who is from a long line of observers. It's instinct, but it's craft. That certain "knowing" is enhanced by a consistent palette—black and white and muted colors like a favorite shirt looks when faded from the wash. There's the subversive looking—the subtle irony and wit evident in the posing and placement. But most importantly, there is the sense of place that infuses the photo with a certain personality. For Niro, it feels like a deep wood, with a wild river running through it.

For this essay, I want to explore what this certain kind of knowing in photography and film looks like when considering Niro's adept use of reappropriation. I'll be exploring two examples—Niro's short film *Tree* (2006, p. 125) that I co-curated in 2007 at the Venice Biennale and her recent exploration of the classic film *One Flew Over the Cuckoo's Nest*. In both examples, Niro's observational positioning—what I am calling her stoic approach—results in a clarity of perception that is at once familiar and yet oddly fresh. Her honesty is as disarming as it is revelatory.

TREE

The Venice Biennale is an institution largely known for its embrace of the colonial project, with national pavilions showcasing their selected representatives under the banner of global arts. The 2007 iteration of La Biennale di Venezia's visual arts sector was the platform for *The Requickening Project*, an exhibit featuring the work of Shelley Niro and Lori Blondeau, co-curated by myself and Ryan Rice.[1] Niro's film *Tree* was projected on the public Zattere walkway along the Giudecca Canal nightly accompanying Blondeau's performance *GRACE* at dawn and dusk. Our curatorial mandate stated:

Requickening is an aspect of traditional Iroquois condolence ceremonies where human relationships are negotiated and brought back into balance after death or trauma. This cycle of grief and restoration speaks to larger concerns of global warfare and peace, colonial histories, memory, and importantly, healing. The Requickening Project *agenda calls upon indigenous knowledge to contribute to the conversation initiated by the Biennale curator Robert Storr. In response to Storr's curatorial reference "the fragility of culture in violent times," our statement speaks to indigenous concepts of resilience; acknowledging spirituality, memory and the essence of life.*[2]

Niro's *Tree* features a young Indigenous woman facing the travesties of Western capitalism, consumerism, warfare, and spiritual trauma. Viewers experience her loss, grief, and in the closing, her ability to manifest life. The complicated tableau of conventional narratives in *Tree*—the "crying Indian," "the lost Indian," "the forgotten Indian," and "the environmental Indian"—draw heavily on appropriation of Western culture. Niro's expert manipulation of these tired and over-used references subsumes and negates their referential power. Through irony, Niro avoids direct critique, preferring instead to inhabit the position of an ostensibly stoic observer, with only a hint of being in on the game.

I'M NOT GOING WITHOUT YOU, MAC

They said you escaped.
I knew you wouldn't leave without me.
I was waiting for you.
Now we can make it, Mac.
I feel big as a damn mountain.
Oh, no!
I'm not going without you, Mac.
I wouldn't leave you here this way.
You're coming with me.
Let's go![3]

At the 2021 Pocahontas Reframed Film Festival, Niro screened select cuts from the 1975 film *One Flew Over the Cuckoo's Nest*, focusing on scenes featuring Muscogee actor Will Sampson as Chief Bromden. In the film, Sampson's Indian character is portrayed as a simple and mute insane asylum patient. Watching Niro's curated selections of tape decades after the initial film's release, viewers are instantly aware of the overtly racist script of the period and the demeaning interpretations of the silent and stoic Indian character. As viewers to this condensed version of this narrative, we know that Shelley knows this depiction is problematic.

Viewers familiar with the classic *Cuckoo's Nest* will remember that the "Chief" character is ultimately revealed as totally capable of speech and critical thinking. In the film's conclusion, the "mute Indian" inhabits a heroic saviour role. After the main character Mac (played by Jack Nicholson) is cruelly lobotomized, the Chief suffocates him with a pillow and escapes alone, metaphorically taking Nicholson's character along with him, saving his friend from a distorted and literally mindless state.

Niro is a patient educator. In this evocative screening of Will Sampson's character, she has inserted yet another reminder, as in *Tree*, of our collective struggle to free ourselves from oppressive and colonial depictions of "Nativeness." The "crying Indian" featured in the Venice Biennale film *Tree* is freed by becoming one with the figure of a tree.[4] Will Sampson's Chief likewise breaks free of confinement by actively killing the brainless subject, then escaping. In both cases, there is an agency at play fuelled not by a reactionary impulse but by a deeply engaged observational perspective. Niro directs us to seeing the flawed image in a new way—redeemed anew for fresh inquiry.

In the field of "Native creatives" of the past generation, Niro's work stands out as a completely honest engagement with the excesses of decorative and trite depictions of Indigeneity. Her work pulls us closer to centre, where we collectively reside—to question and maybe even to laugh at ourselves. It is a generous endeavor, infused with heart.

She's not going without us, Mac.

NOTES

1. *The Requickening Project* was supported by the Canada Council for the Arts Aboriginal Peoples Collaborative Exchange, the Institute of International Education New York and Smith College, Northampton, MA. Our curatorial partners included Mario Di Martino (Studio Antonio dal Ponte) and Italian anthropologist Elisabetta Frasca.
2. "Venice Biennale 2007 - THE REQUICKENING PROJECT," Nancy Marie Mithlo, accessed October 11, 2022, https://nancy-mariemithlo.com/Radical_Curating_Indigenous_Art_at_the_Venice_Biennale/Venice_Biennale_2007/index.html.
3. "One Flew Over the Cuckoo's Nest - Dialogue Transcript," Drew's Script-O-Rama, accessed October 11, 2022, http://www.script-o-rama.com/movie_scripts/o/one-flew-over-the-cuckoos-nest-script.html.
4. Nancy Marie Mithlo, "'Silly Little Things': Framing Global Self-Appropriations in Native Arts," in *No Deal!: Indigenous Arts and the Politics of Possession*, ed. Tressa Berman (Santa Fe: School For Advanced Research Press, 2012), 188–205.

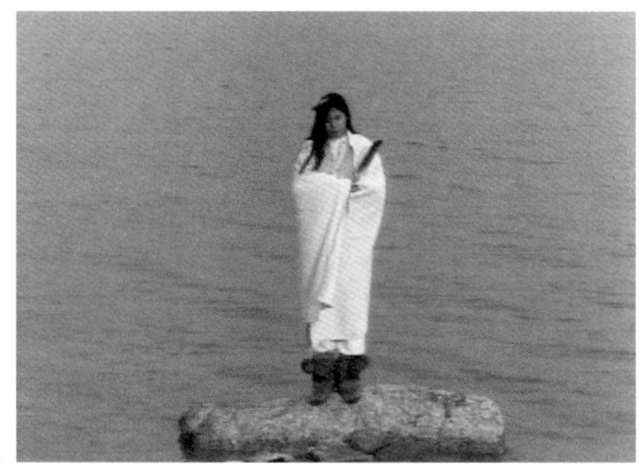
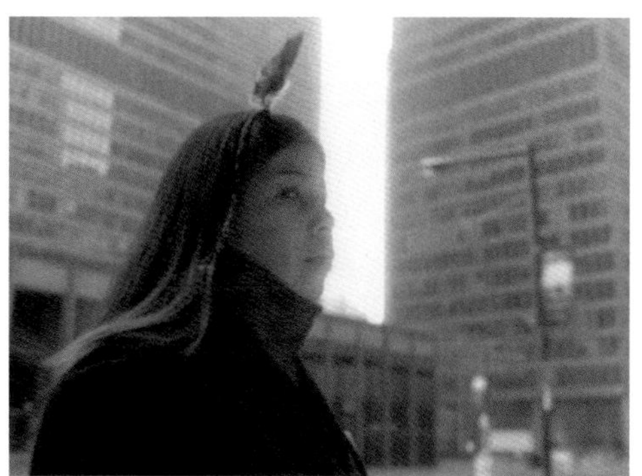
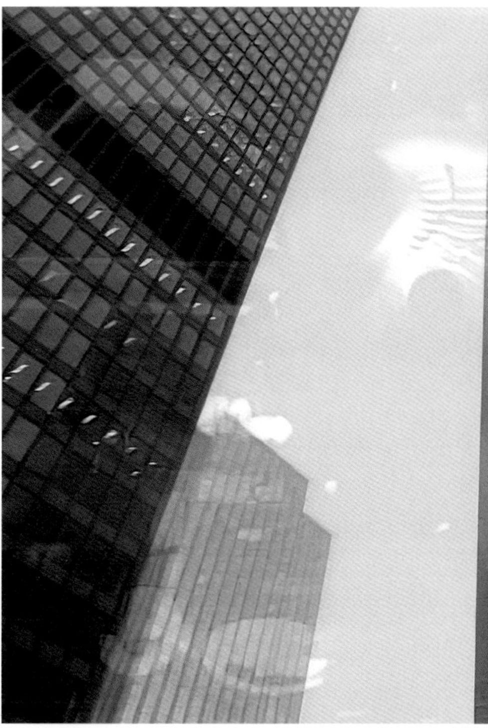
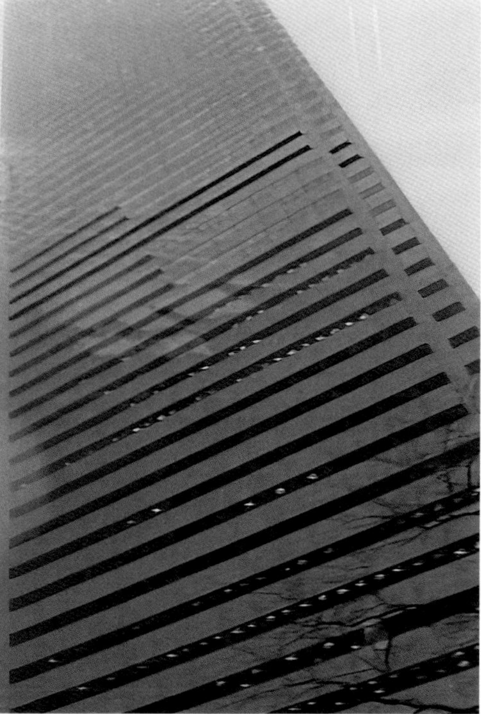
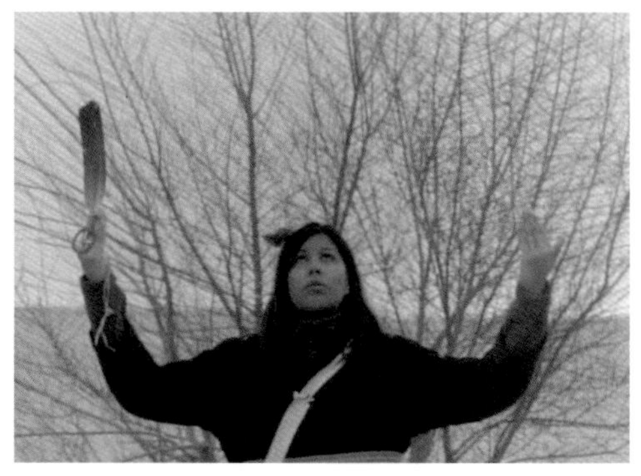
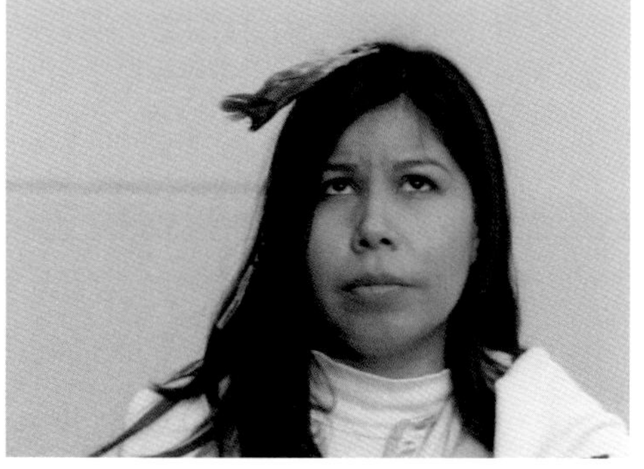

Stills from **Tree**, 2006

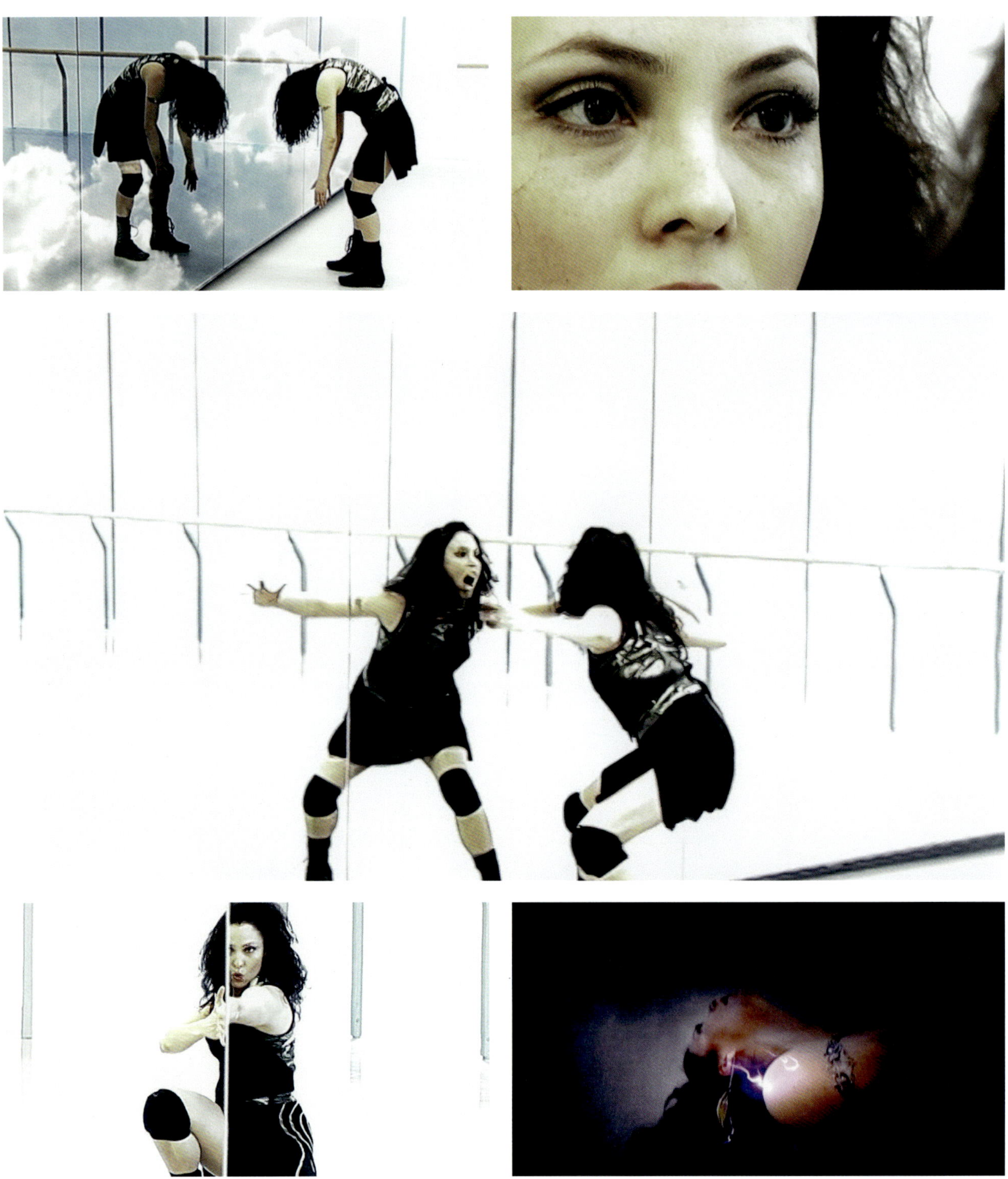

Stills from **rechargin'**, 2007

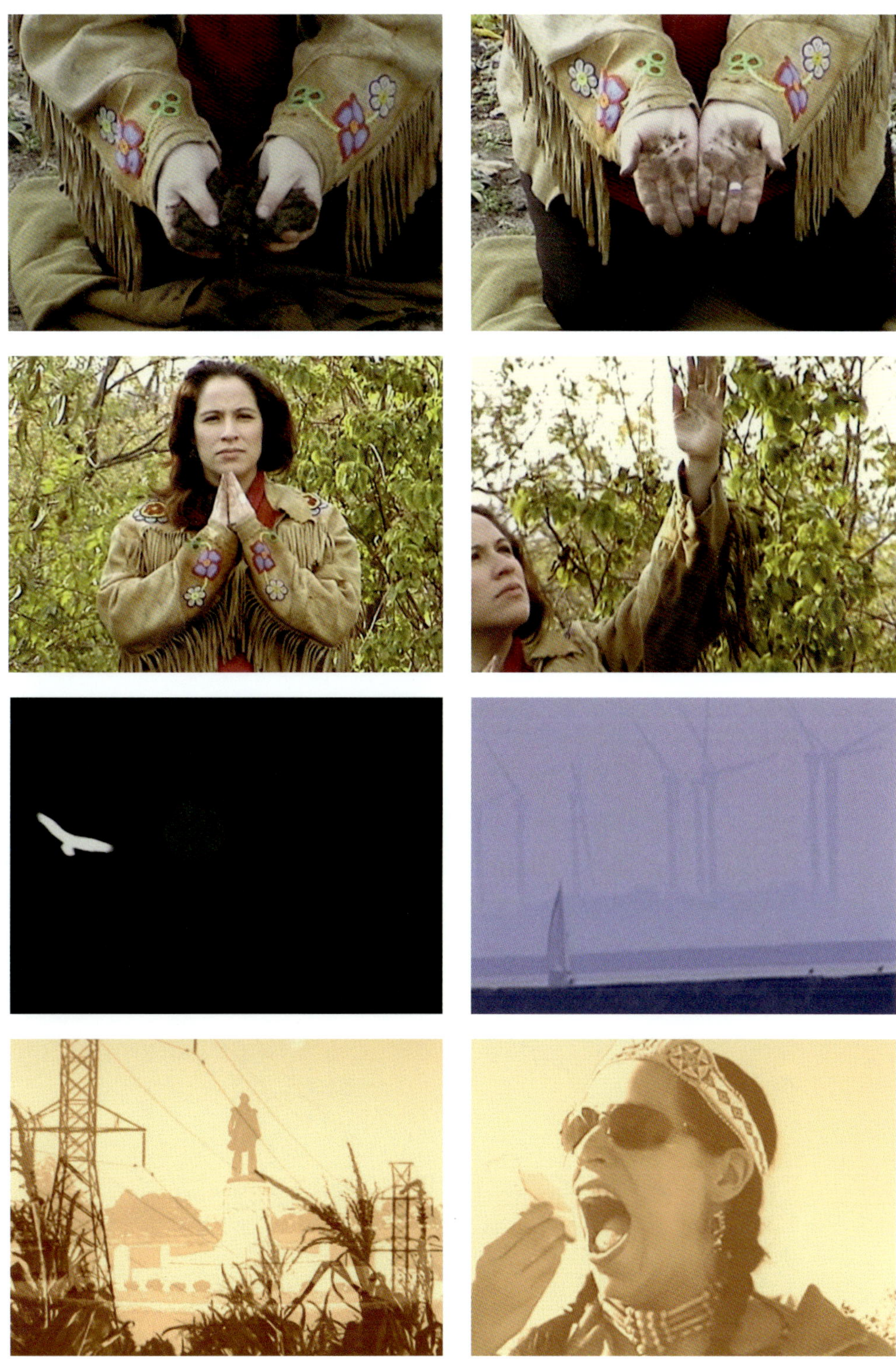

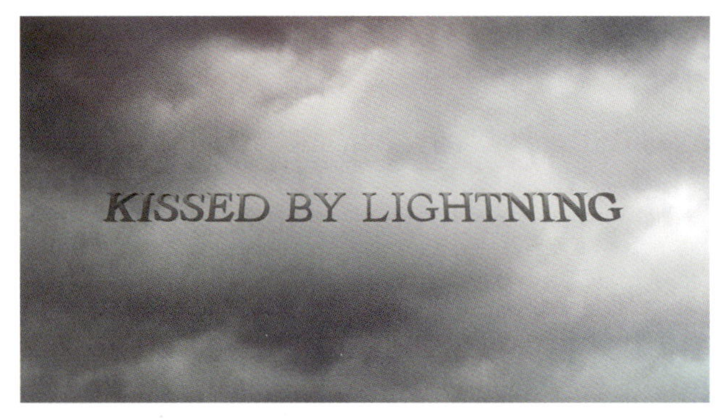
KISSED BY LIGHTNING

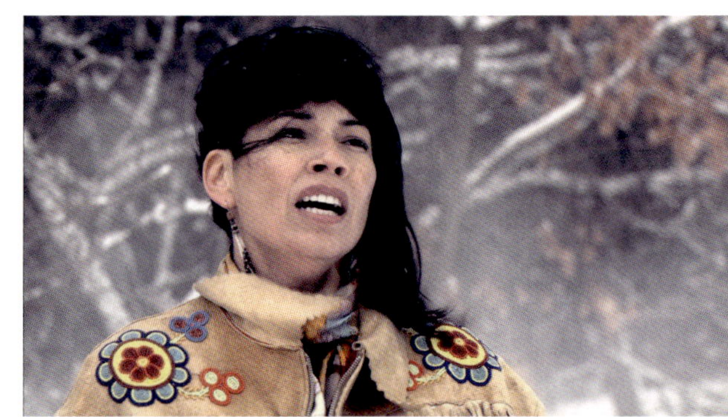

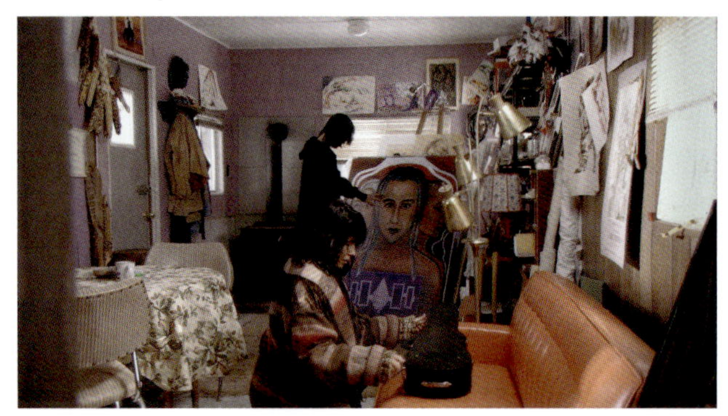

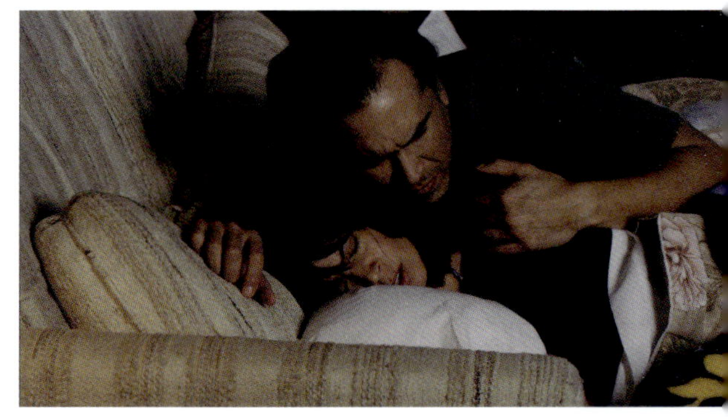

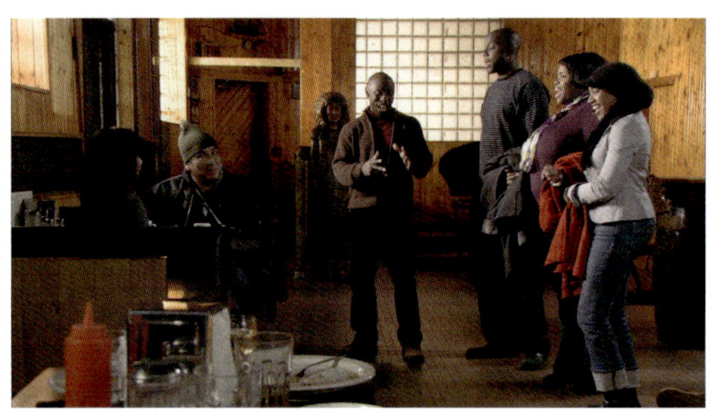

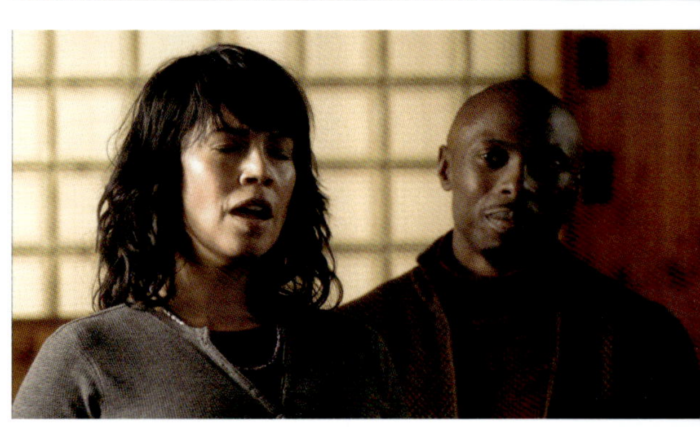

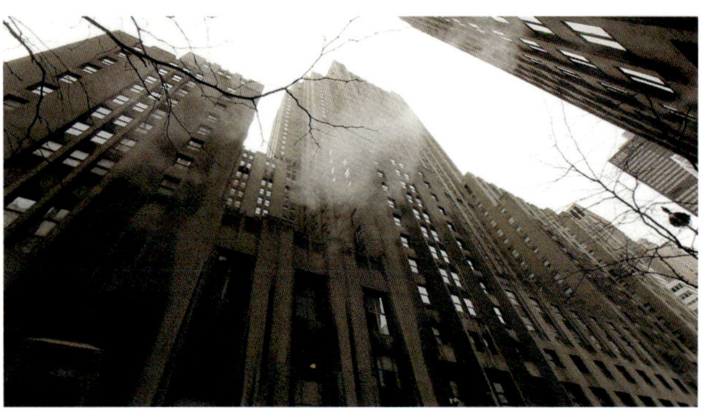

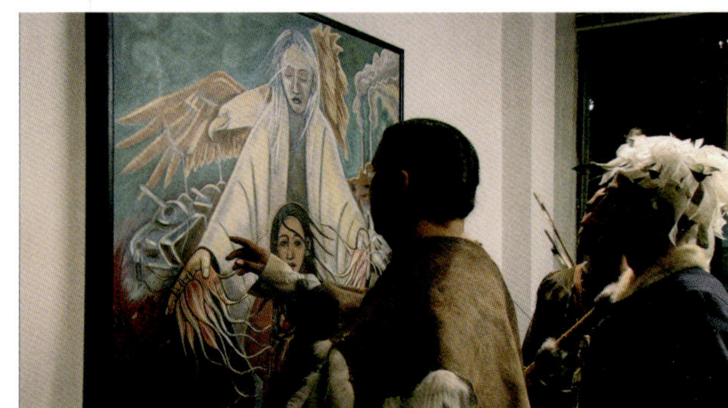

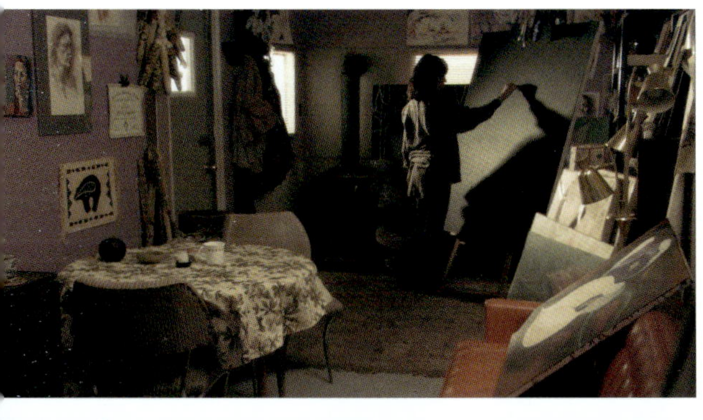
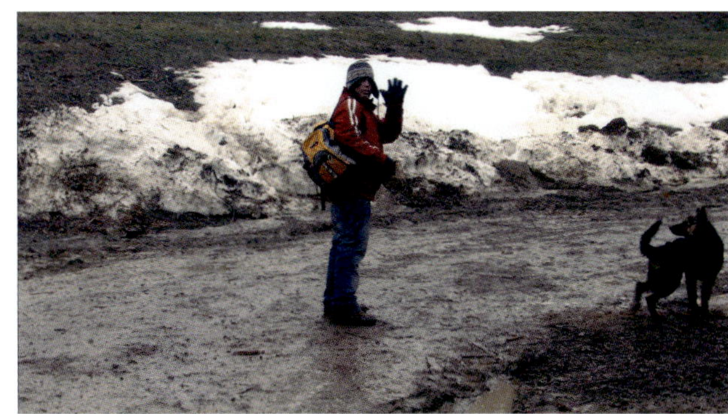
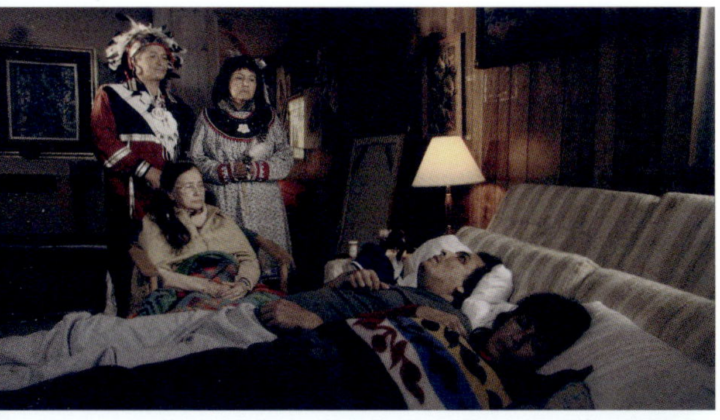
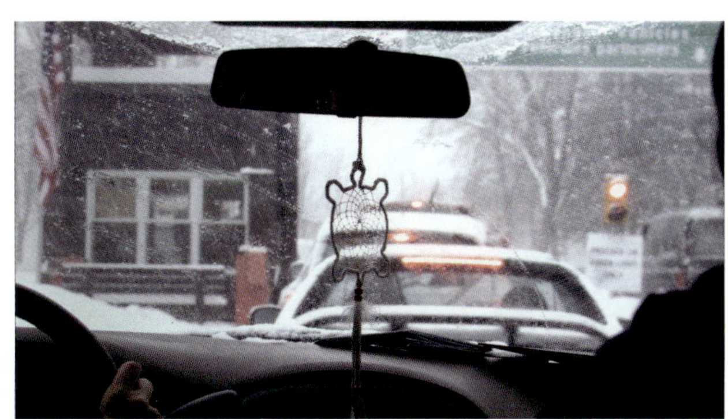
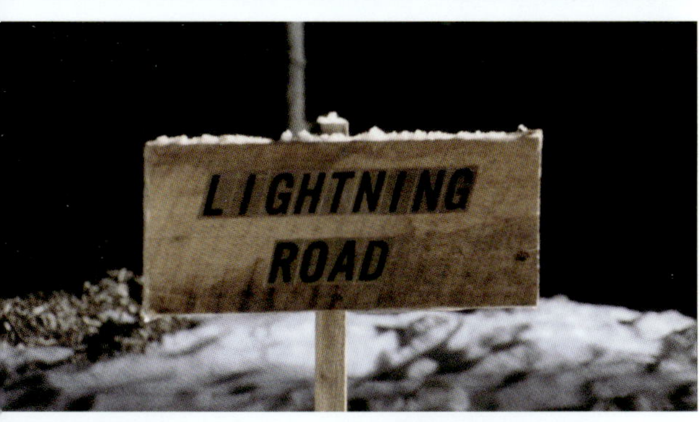

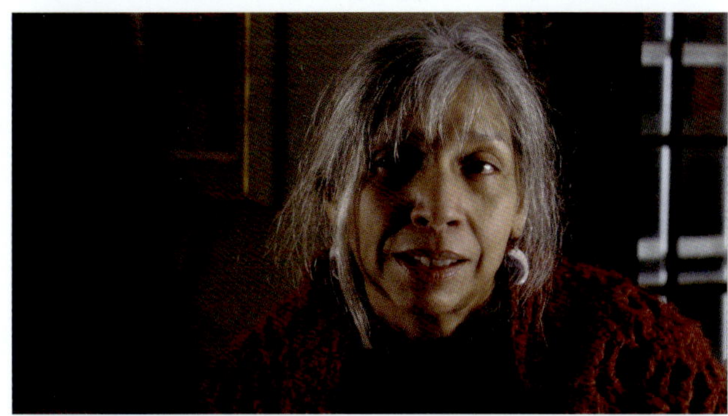
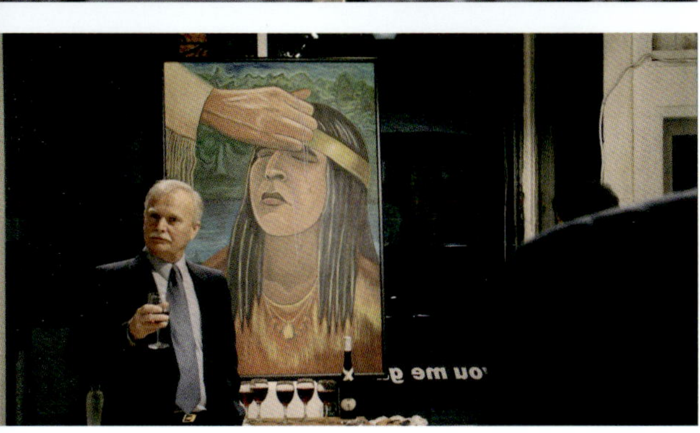
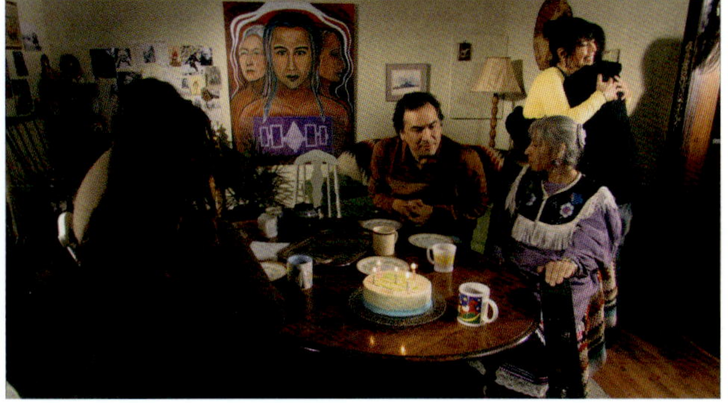

Stills from **Kissed by Lightning**, 2009

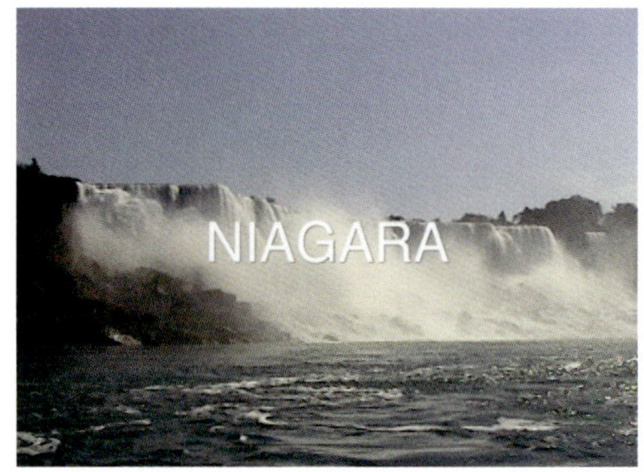

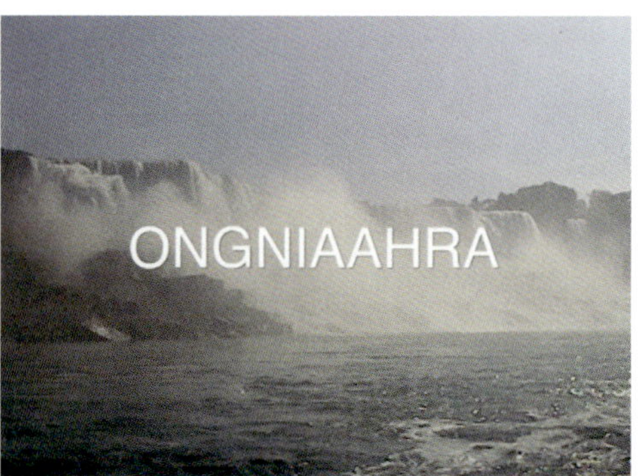

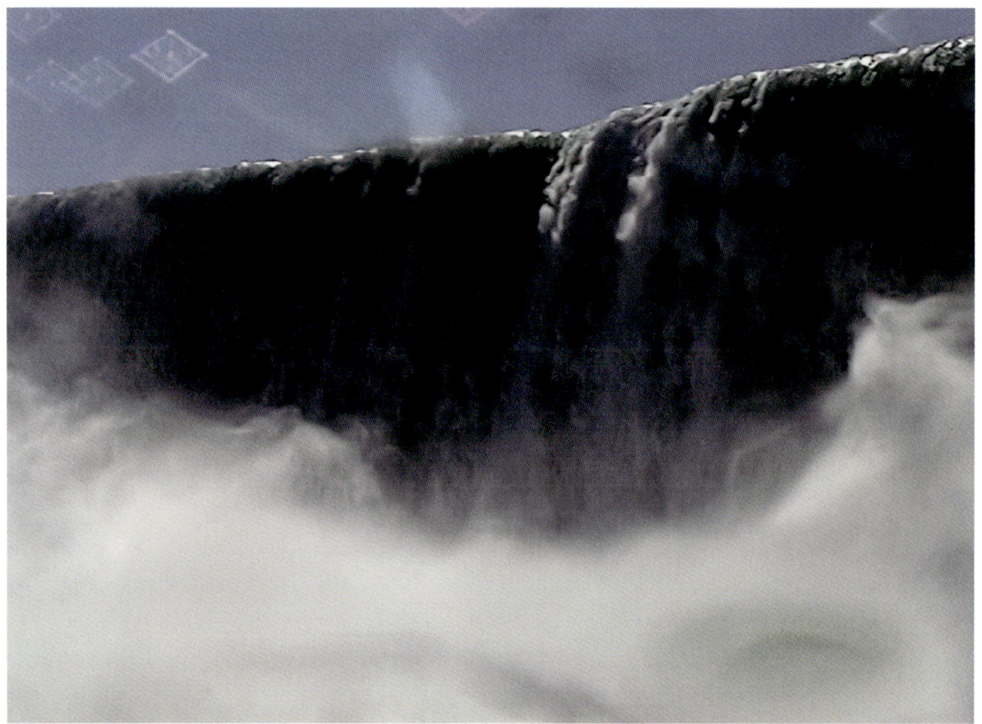
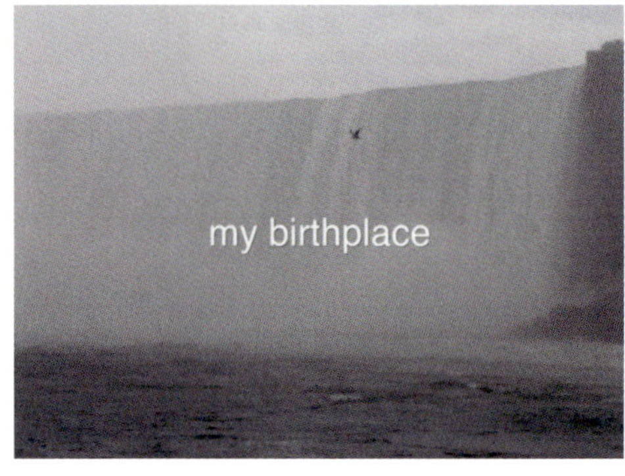

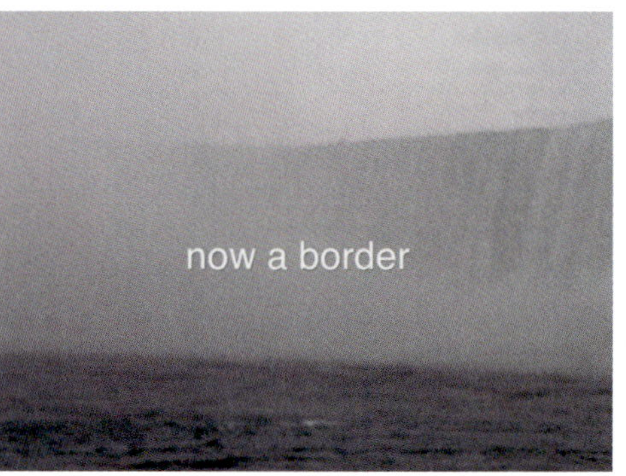

   Stills from **Niagara**, 2015

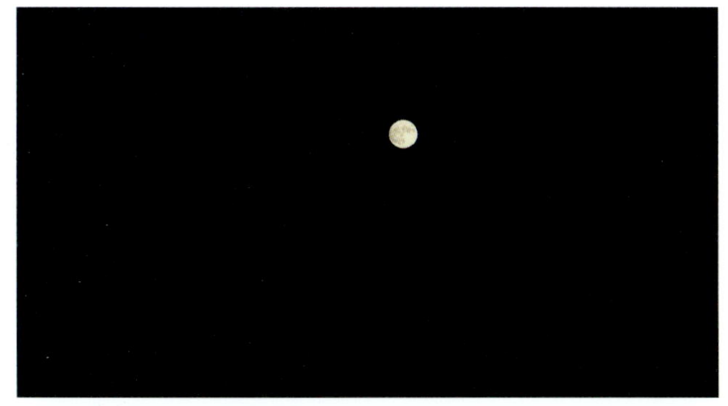
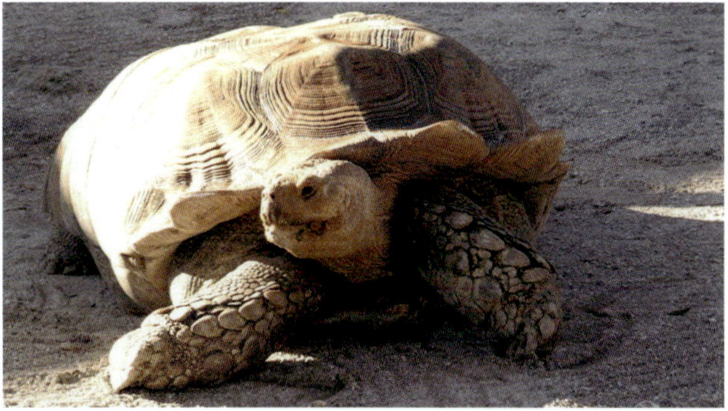
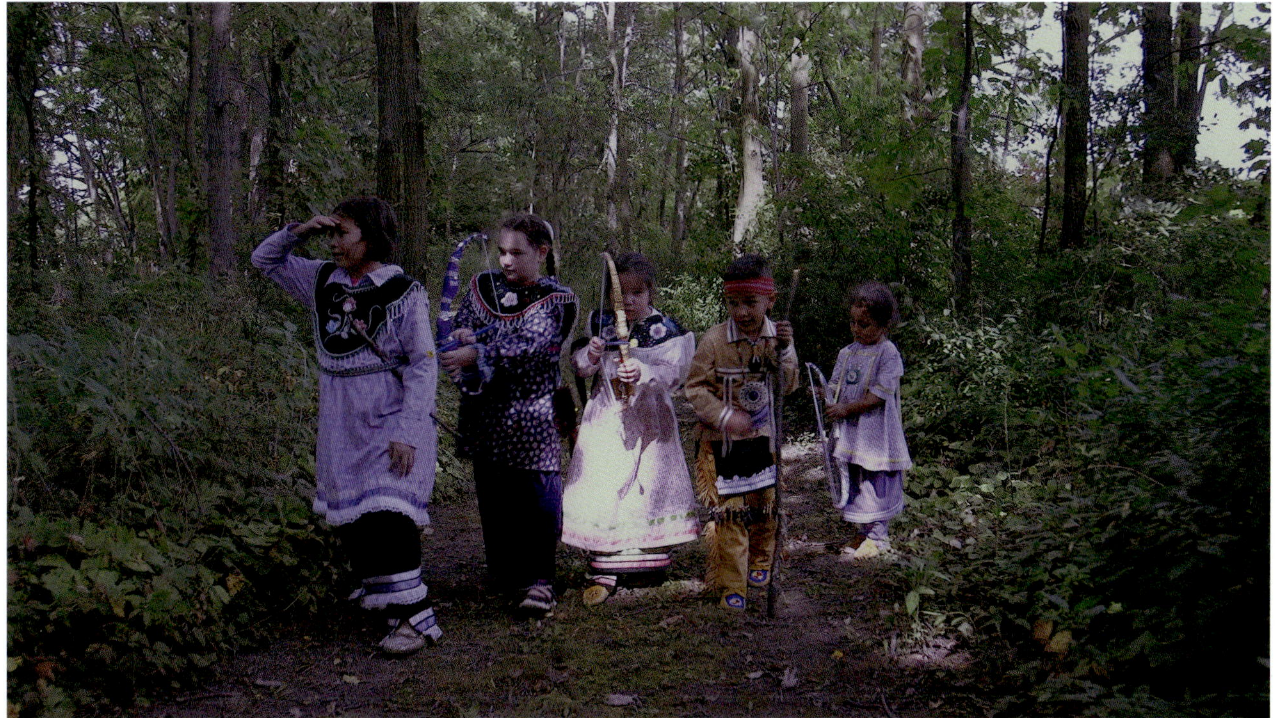
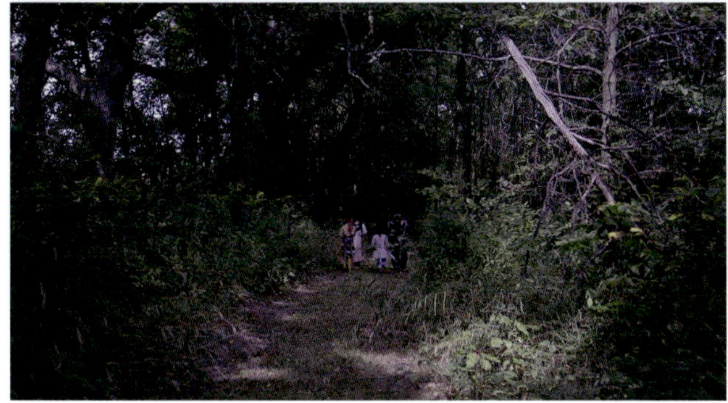
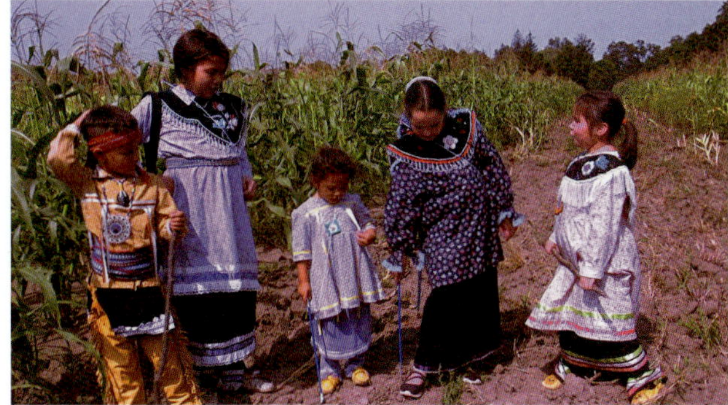

Stills from **My Heart is in the Forest**, 2017

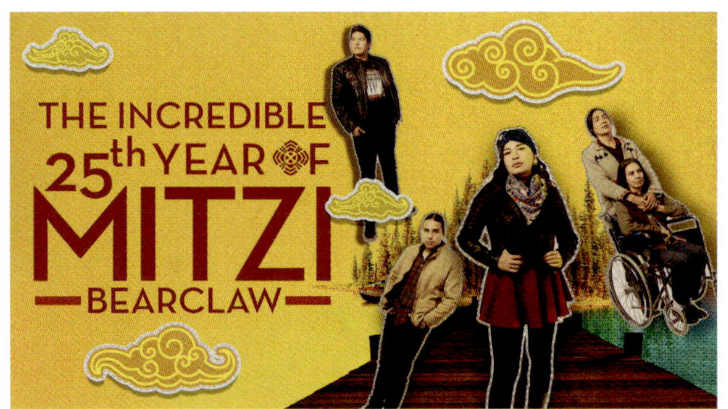
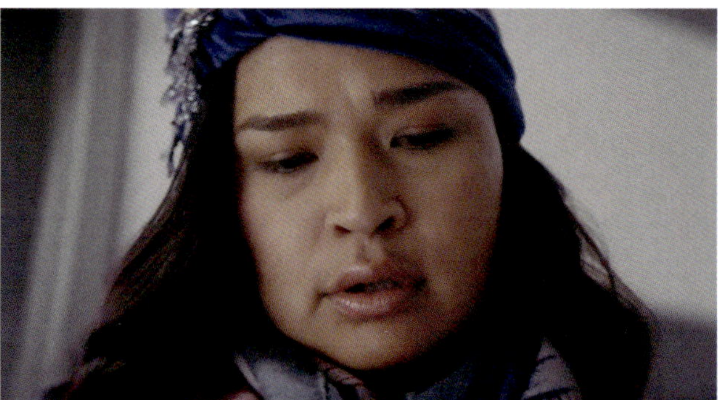
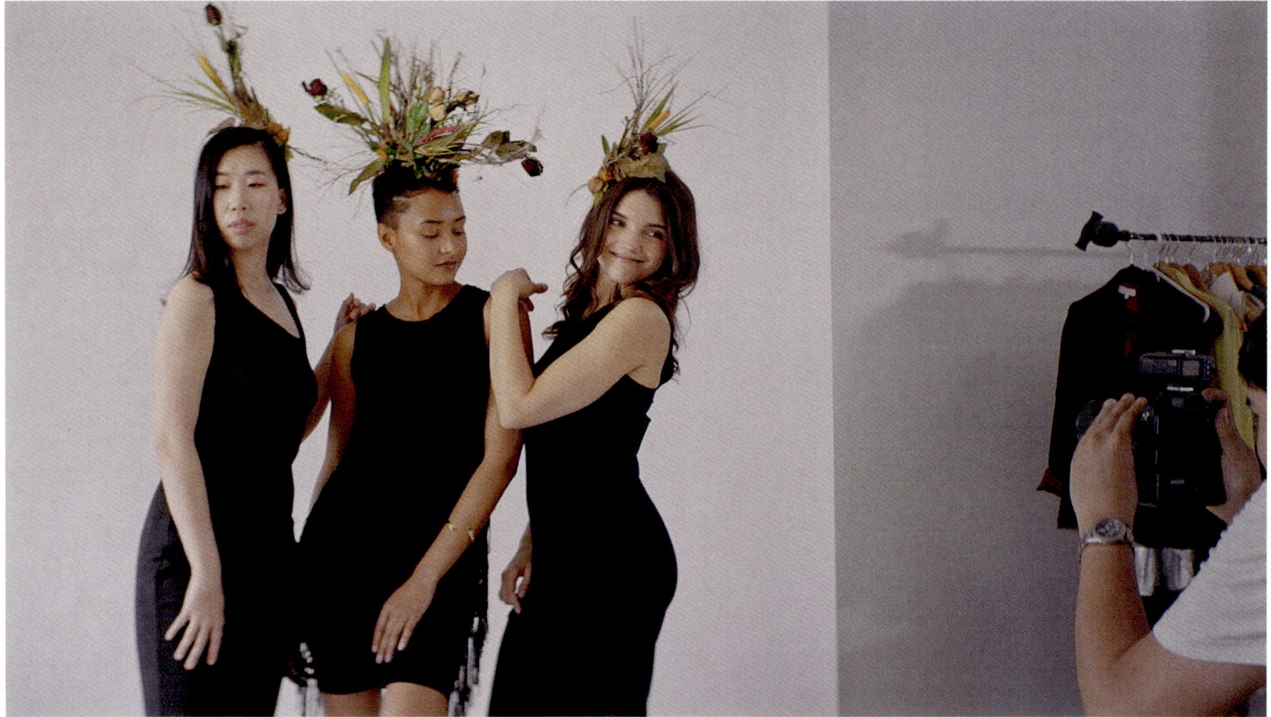
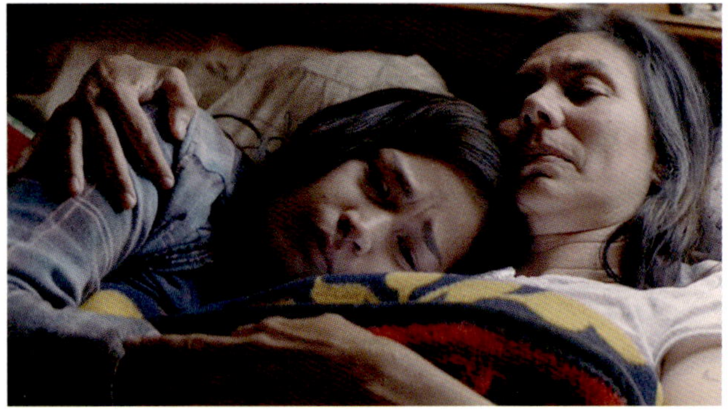
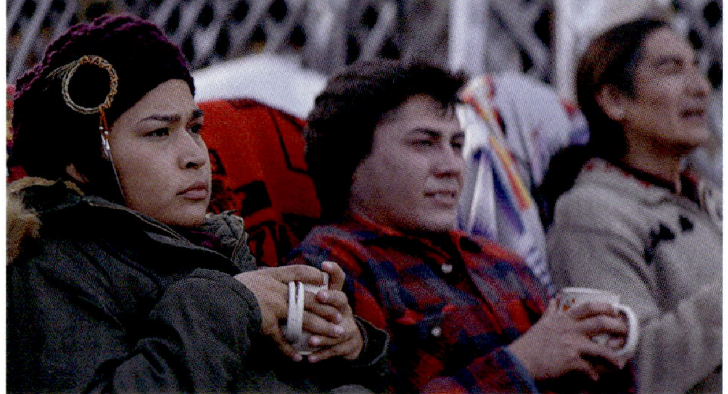

Poster and stills from **The Incredible 25th Year of Mitzi Bearclaw**, 2019

AN INCREDIBLY SHORT INTERVIEW WITH SHELLEY NIRO

HULLEAH J. TSINHNAHJINNIE

HULLEAH J. TSINHNAHJINNIE: I was thinking about your latest feature film, *The Incredible 25th Year of Mitzi Bearclaw* (2019, p. 132), having attended the premiere screening at the Art Gallery of Ontario on February 22, 2019, approximately a year and two months before the global lockdown in response to COVID-19. I mention the lockdown because of the effect it had on distribution of the film. The screening was packed and the film was well-received. Actors, musicians, artists, producers, relatives, and fans were in the audience. It was beautiful to witness such a strong show of love and support. How would you describe the film?

SHELLEY NIRO: *Mitzi* is a pan-Indian story. It's meant to cover most Native reserves and more or less talk about issues that we are aware of. Above all, it's about community and how we have to hang in there, making love the strongest emotion as opposed to making hate the most felt.

HJT: That makes me consider the multitude of Indigenous filmmakers, and how we seem to be able to categorize the majority of Native feature films as Sad, Sadistic, or Revelation Reservation Brutal. Then there are your films which reflect a unique authorship. They are ethereal, combining fantasy, comedy, and love with an ever-present dose of colonial reality, which is very Niroesque. It seemed that symbolism was represented from multiple worlds, including those that intersect with the Native world. Though when I reviewed articles about *Mitzi*, it seemed that a lot of the writers did not delve into the heavy symbolism you placed within the characters, such as the Four Horsemen of the Apocalypse, or Faith, Hope, and Charity. What is your reaction?

SN: I don't think [the reviewers] want to pass that border. They don't want to think of [the film] in those terms. When I brought those characters into the story, it was convenient for me to put them in there, because everything that has gone wrong with Native Nations is grounded in the Bible teachings. The Muskrats symbolize the Four Horsemen: Pestilence (Black Muskrat), War (Simone Muskrat), Famine, and Death. Another Muskrat represents Liquor and the extraction of resources from the land, which is represented within this context, bringing death.

HJT: And there are the ethereal characters representing Faith, Hope, and Charity, which are usually associated with the ultimate virtues of the ideal Christian. The actors portraying them are Mitzi's family: her dad, Charley B., and her mom....

SN: It was also convenient to give those characteristics of Faith, Hope, and Charity to Mitzi's family. Charley B. represents Charity and in the end he dies, he is the sacrifice. Those virtues existed before contact, and Charity is the reason why the colonists survived. If it were not for the Charity given to them when they were starving, they would have perished.

HJT: That's heavy. I was also wondering about the surreal influences in your films. Is there a source for them?

SN: Every time I make a film I think of Akira Kurosawa's *Dreams* (1990). Every time I watch those little stories it is a joy and I think that if you can create little stories within a bigger story and have fun, then umbrella them into the bigger story. So that's what I was thinking about when making *Mitzi.* The scene in the spaceship, I wanted it to be nightmarish, but fun to watch.

HJT: Okay, that's how the alter-Native dream-scape evolved. I noticed when Mitzi put her hand up to her head she would enter the Native dreamscape, where Faith, Hope, and Charity would materialize. I also noticed that there were a lot of dreamcatchers and a bicycle. What is the symbolism behind the objects?

SN: The camera needed an entry to the dreamscape. Mitzi's hand to her head was a signifier. As for the dreamcatchers, that's what happens when you have a non-Native art department. The dreamcatchers are static. It's a low-budget symptom. I would have liked them to be floating and to have movement. The bike is just a bike.

HJT: Lol. I thought you had a dreamcatcher fetish or something. So, do you create a lot of the art for your films?

SN: I suppose my films are a work in progress. They usually take years to write and produce. I think while I am in the process of making a film. I also think about the look I want and the objects that I want in the film, and how the placement of them will have an impact. I am starting to realize that you can't expect people to know exactly what you want. So, I go ahead and make the paintings, make the hats, make what I think I can while I am waiting for the show to begin.

I just want to add that the non-Native art department worked hard into the night to create the scenarios. So I can't totally put the blame on them for missing cues that I thought were pretty straightforward. It made me realize that I have to keep my eye on my own interpretation of how [things] get translated from the script.

HJT: Following the screening at the Art Gallery of Ontario, there was a Q&A session. You and the actors were up on stage and one of the questions from Wanda Nanibush, the host, was about the concern for the environment that threads through the film. You responded that it was important to address current environmental issues, especially that of water. Would you mind elaborating.

SN: The environment is the last thing we have, especially when you live on a reserve. When you see kids with sores covering their bodies, and wonder why they are like that, and when the quick answer on the evening news is "because they aren't washed appropriately," it really makes me wonder how journalists can blame the parents for this health disaster. It seems too convenient to put the blame on poor Native people. These reserves are also close to diamond mines and other corporations that put arsenic into the ground, killing the water that gets back to the Native communities, affecting the fish, the wildlife, and the babies.

HJT: The final scenes in the film are of the Bearclaw family getting ready to move to the city so they can be with family for Mitzi's mother, Annabelle Bearclaw's, final days. As the camera pulls away, ascending back into space, Mitzi holds the handles of the wheelchair in which her mother is sitting. Would you like to make a final statement on *Mitzi*?

SN: Making a film for the Native population is a coveted privilege. I truly enjoy making a story and then having it translated for the screen for audiences, young and old, to watch, and to make them laugh and cry. At the end of the day, we want to be together doing these things.

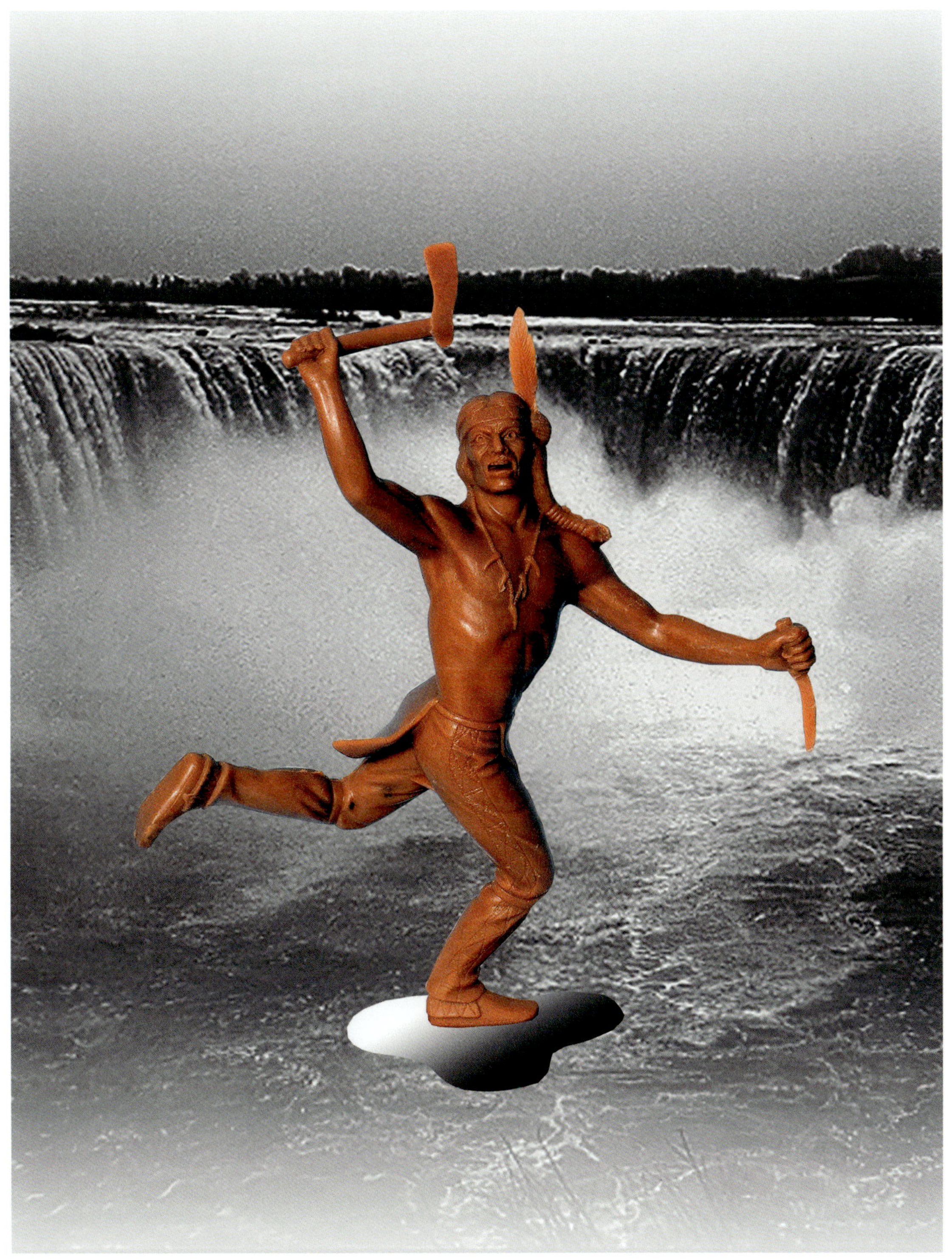

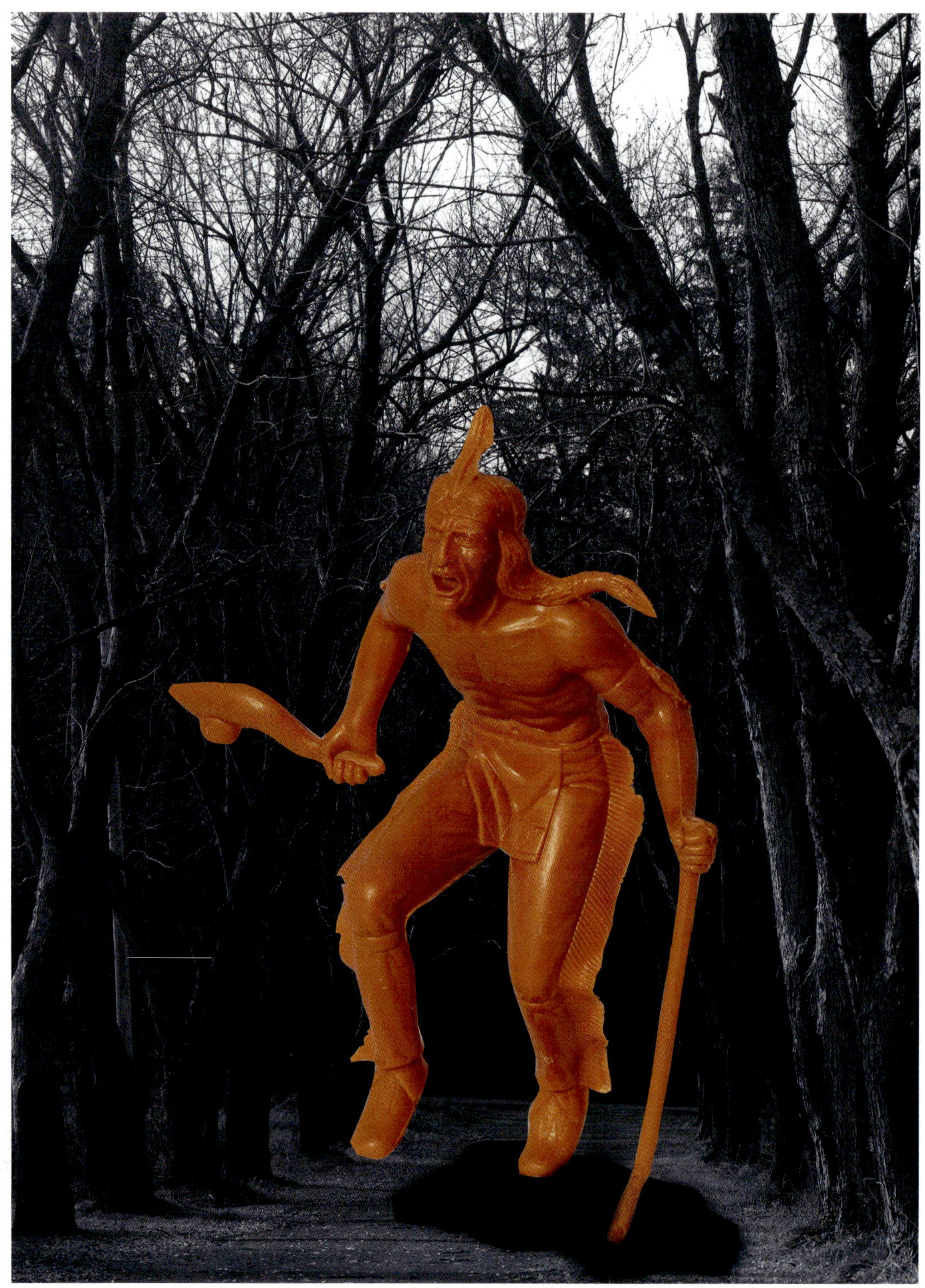

 The Dimpled One

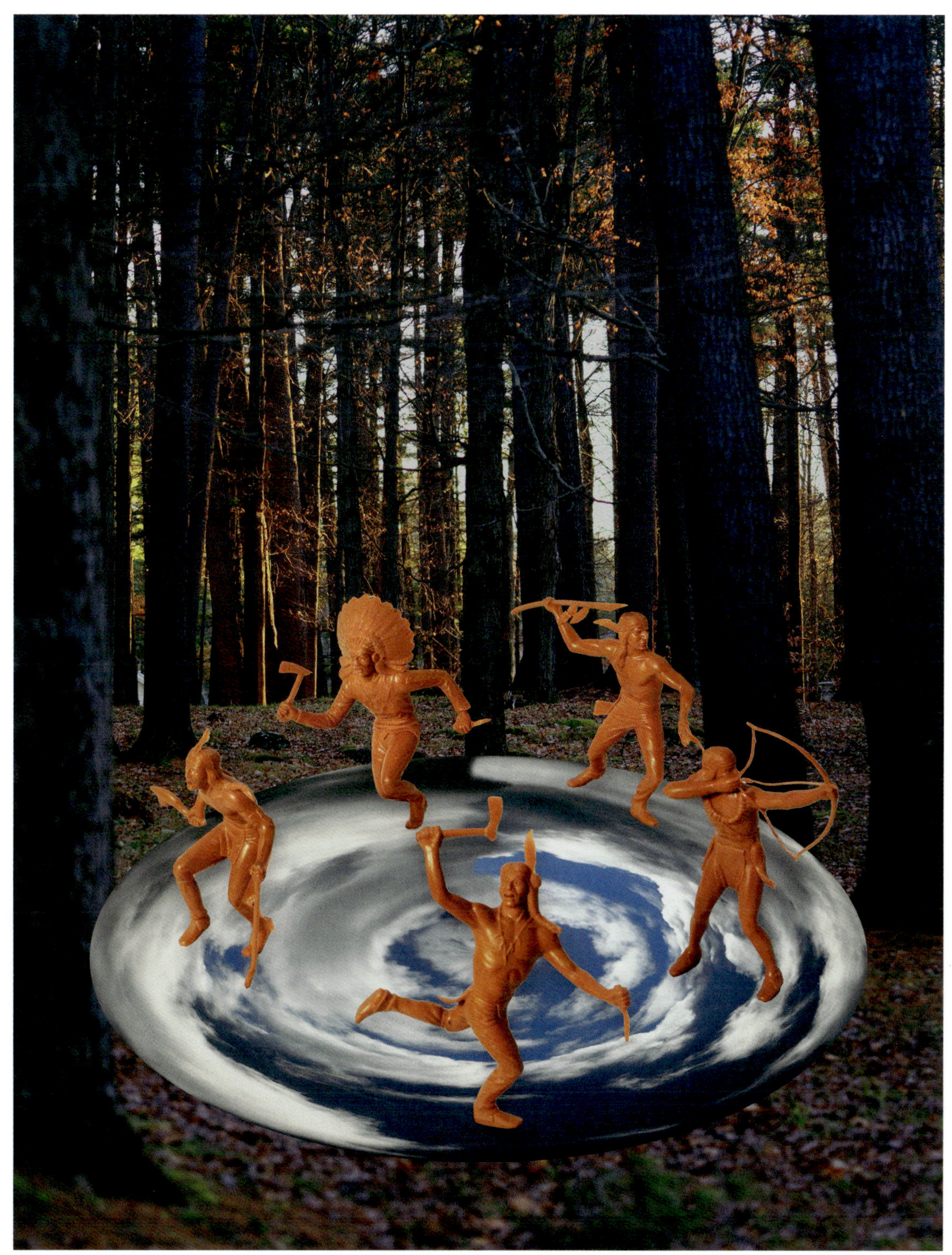

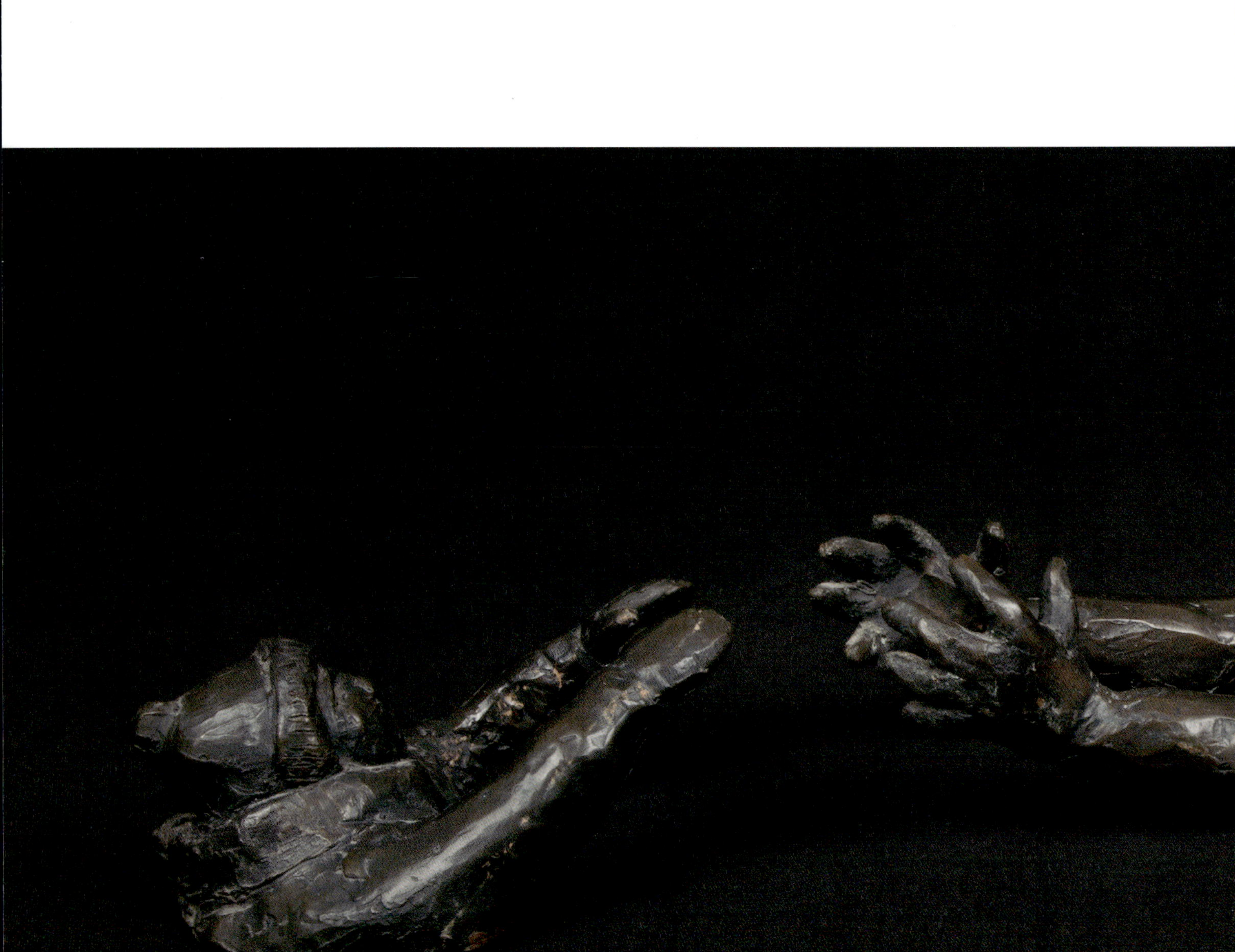

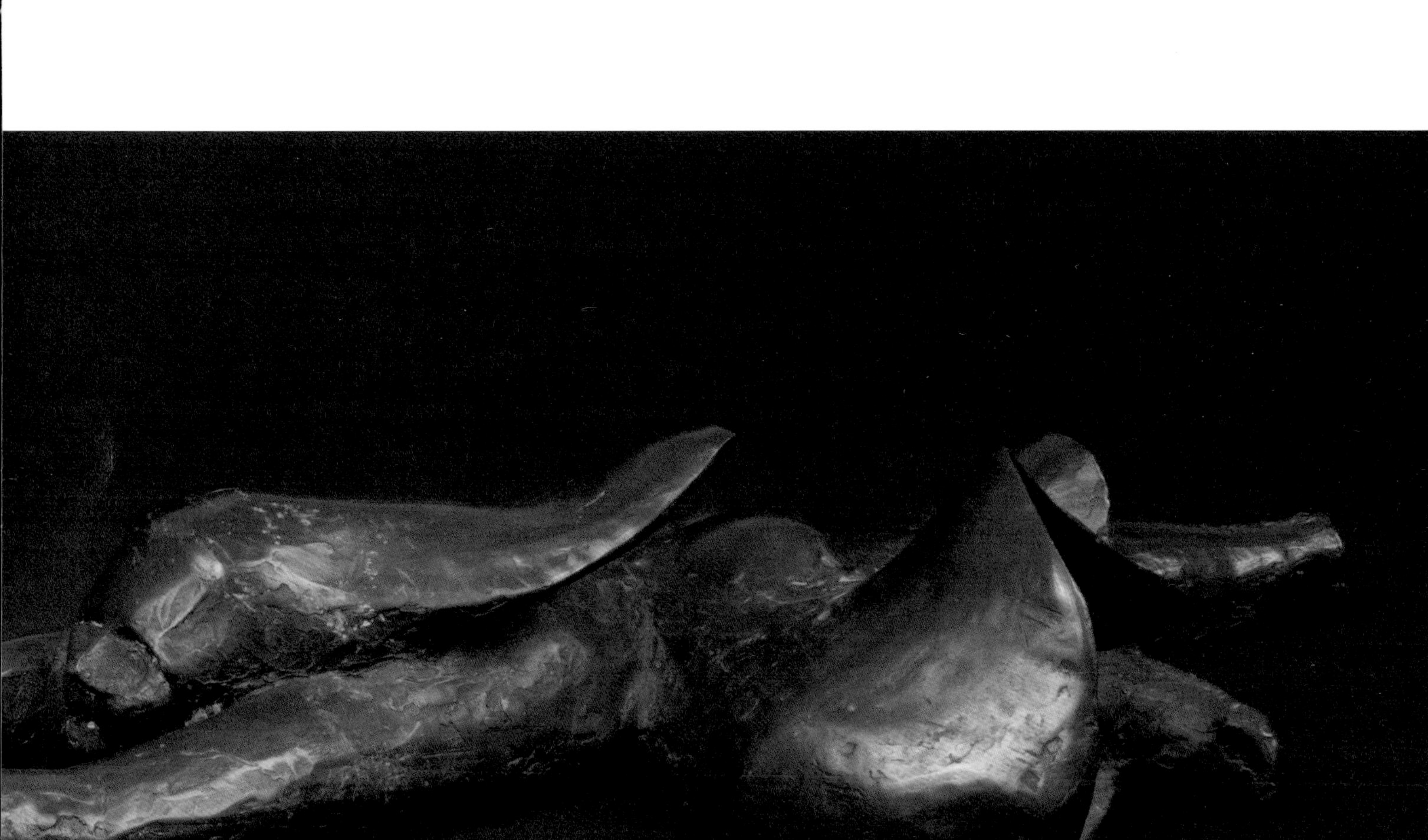

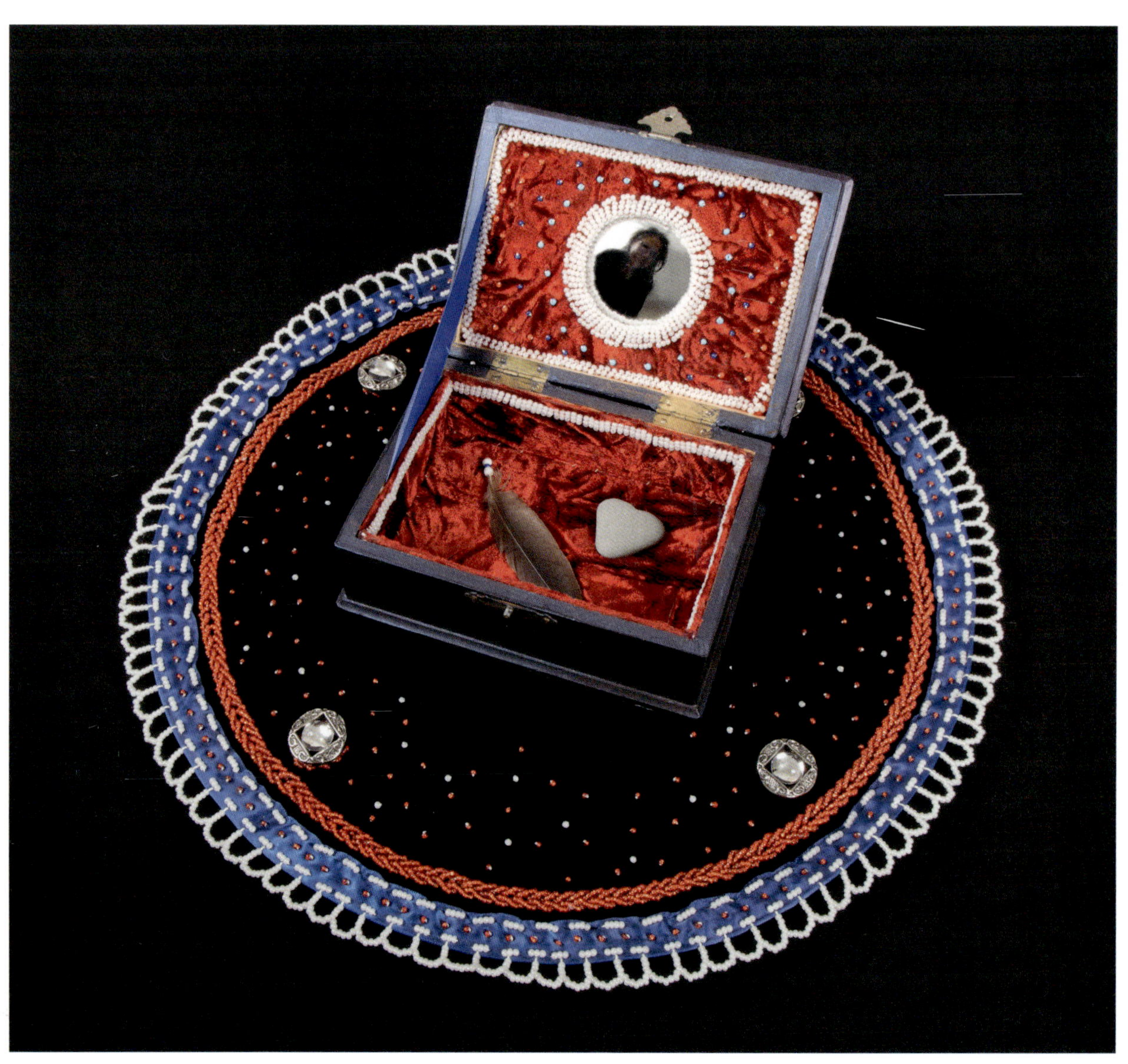

  Here, 1994

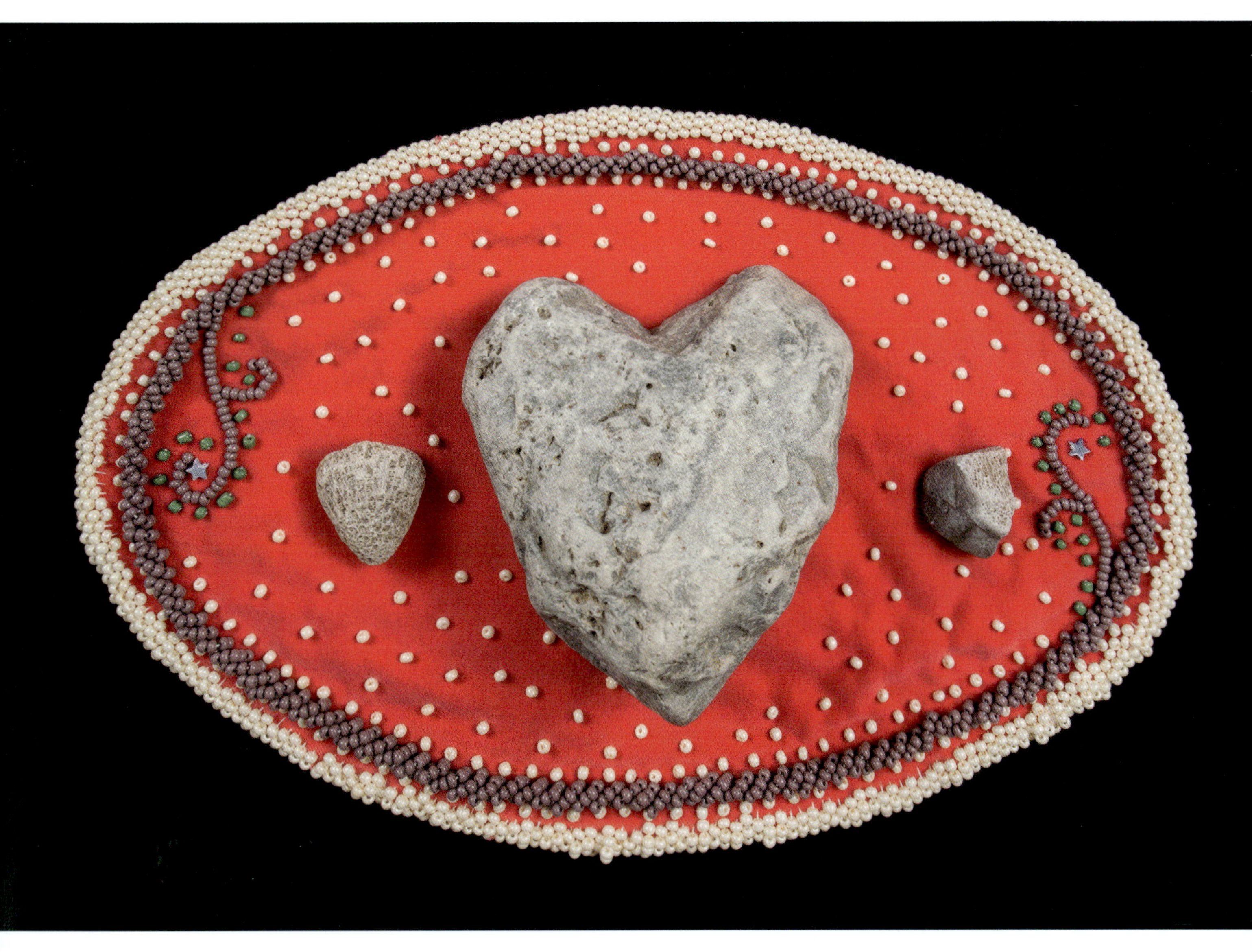

My Stone Cold Heart Needs a Bed Too, 2018   141

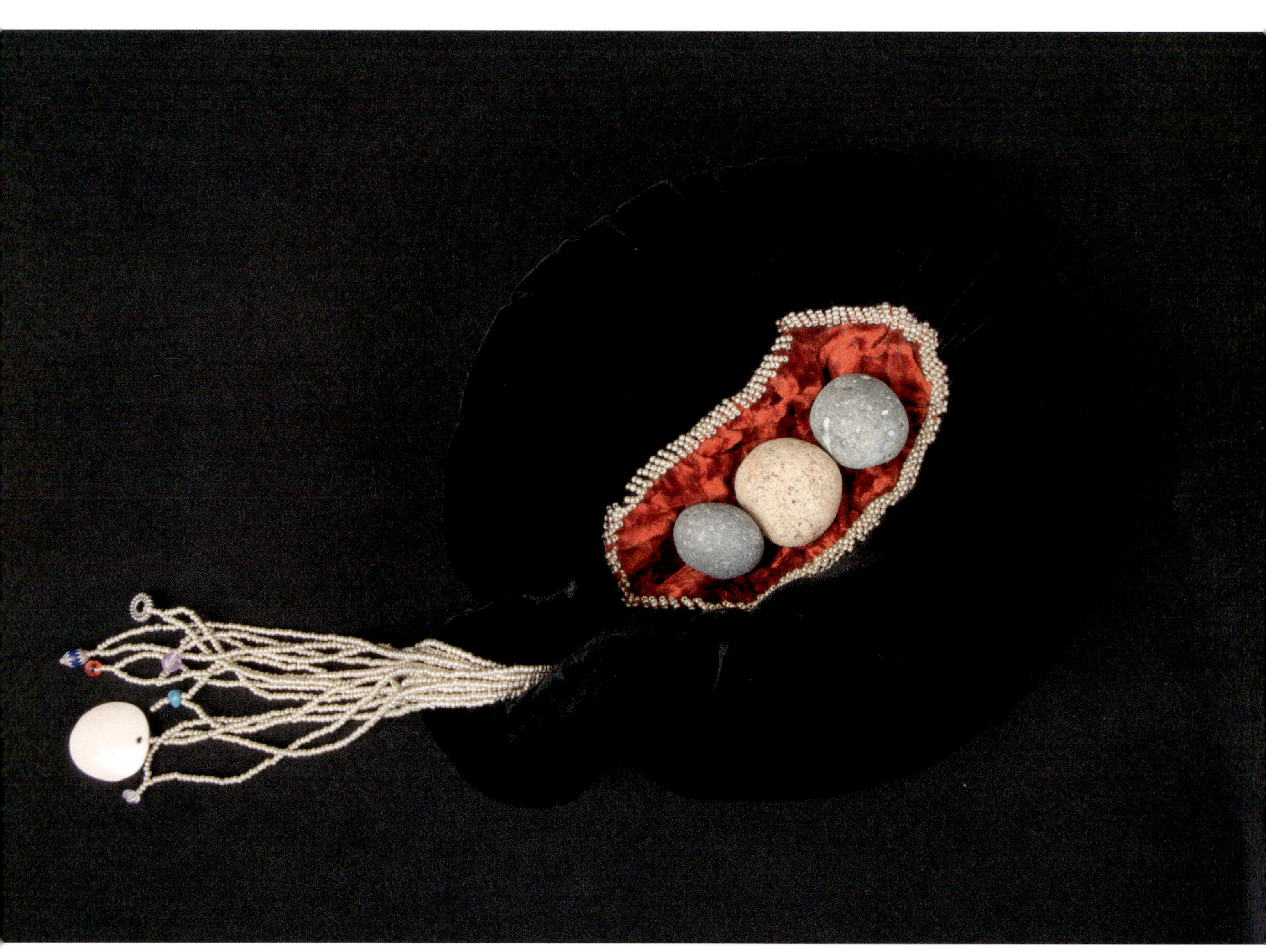

   I Sat on the River Bank and Waited For Signs of Life, 1999

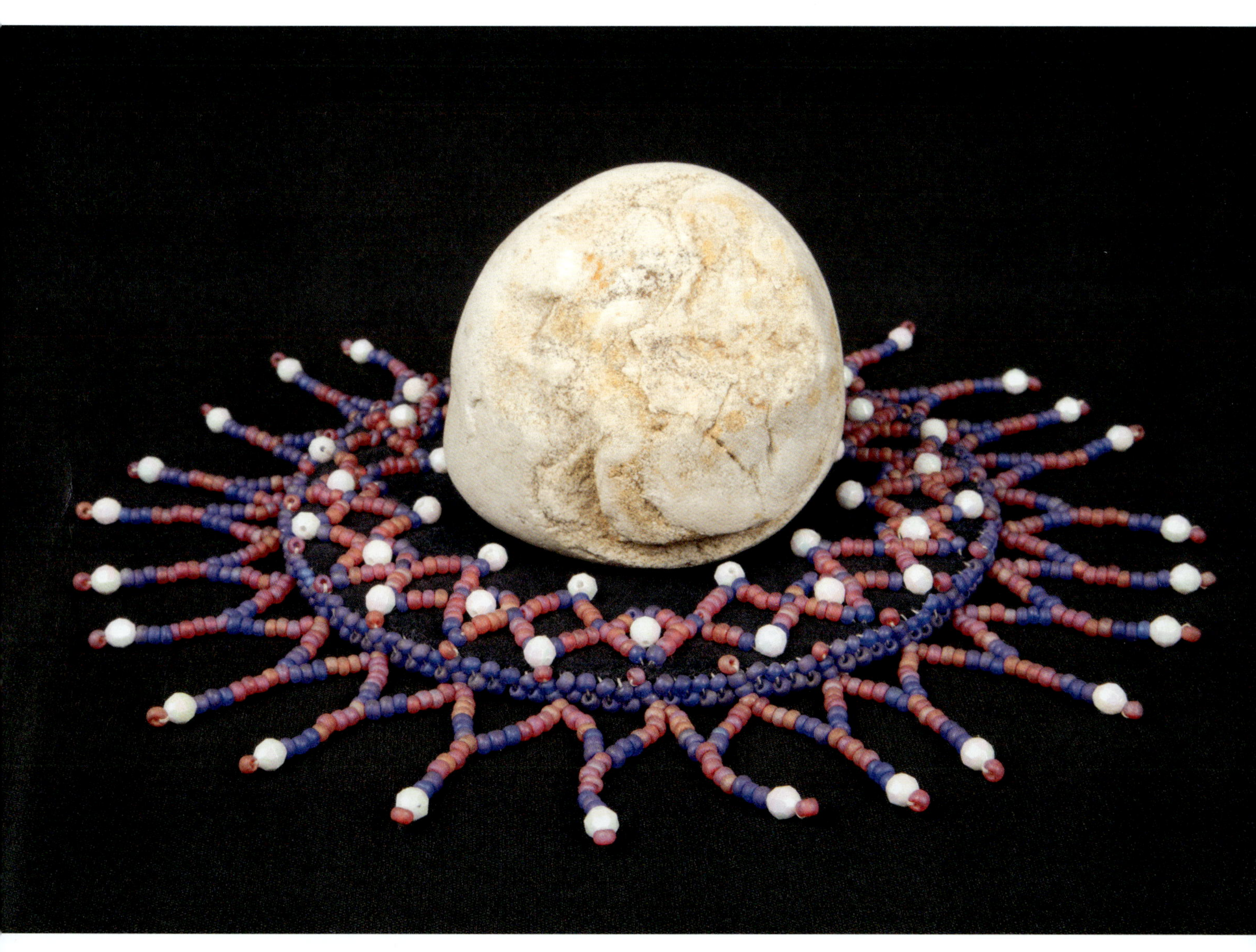

One Day in March, 1999

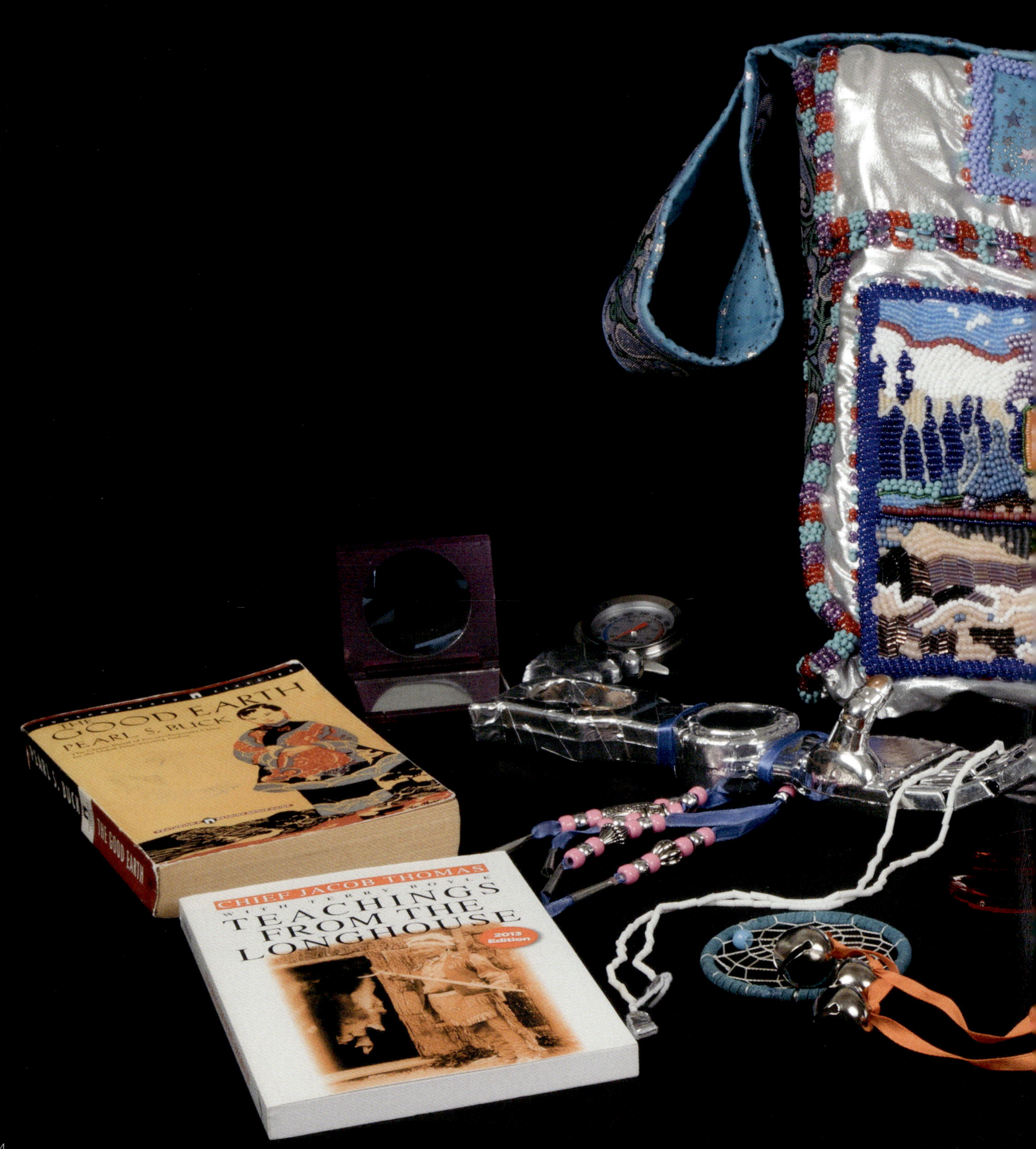

THE GOOD EARTH
PEARL S. BUCK
THE GOOD EARTH
CHIEF JACOB THOMAS
TEACHINGS
FROM THE
LONGHOUSE
2013
Edition

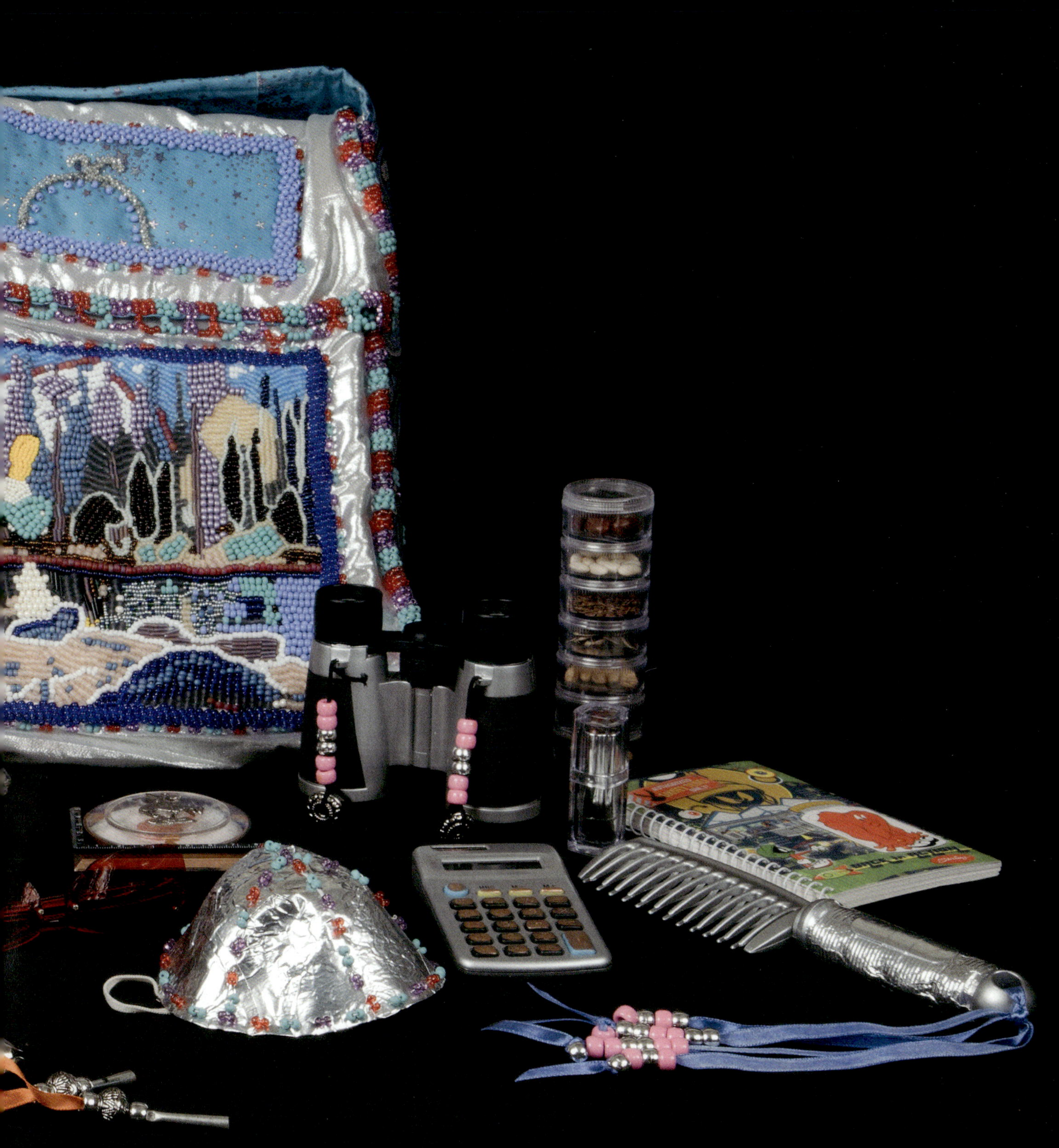

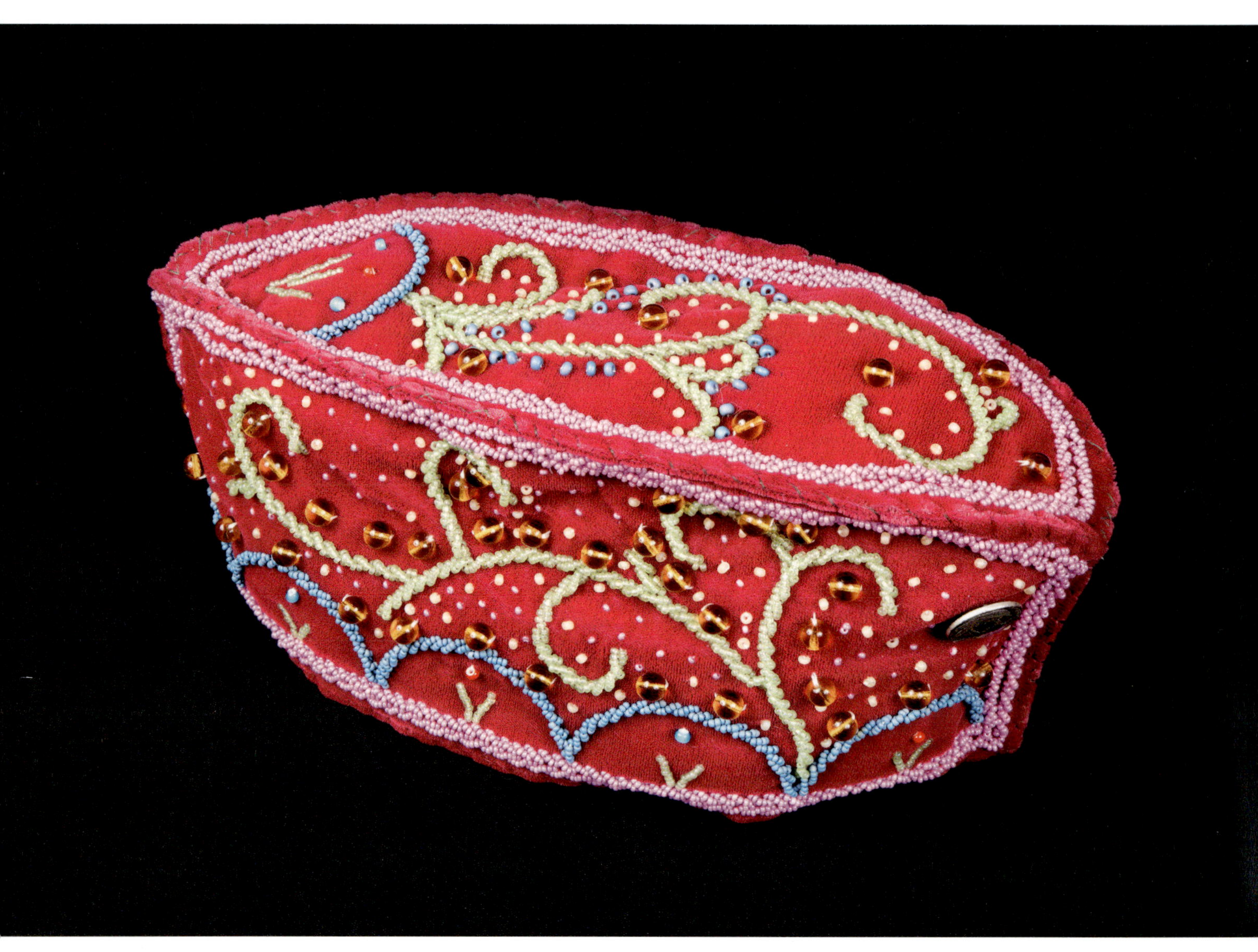

     Forest Thoughts, 2015

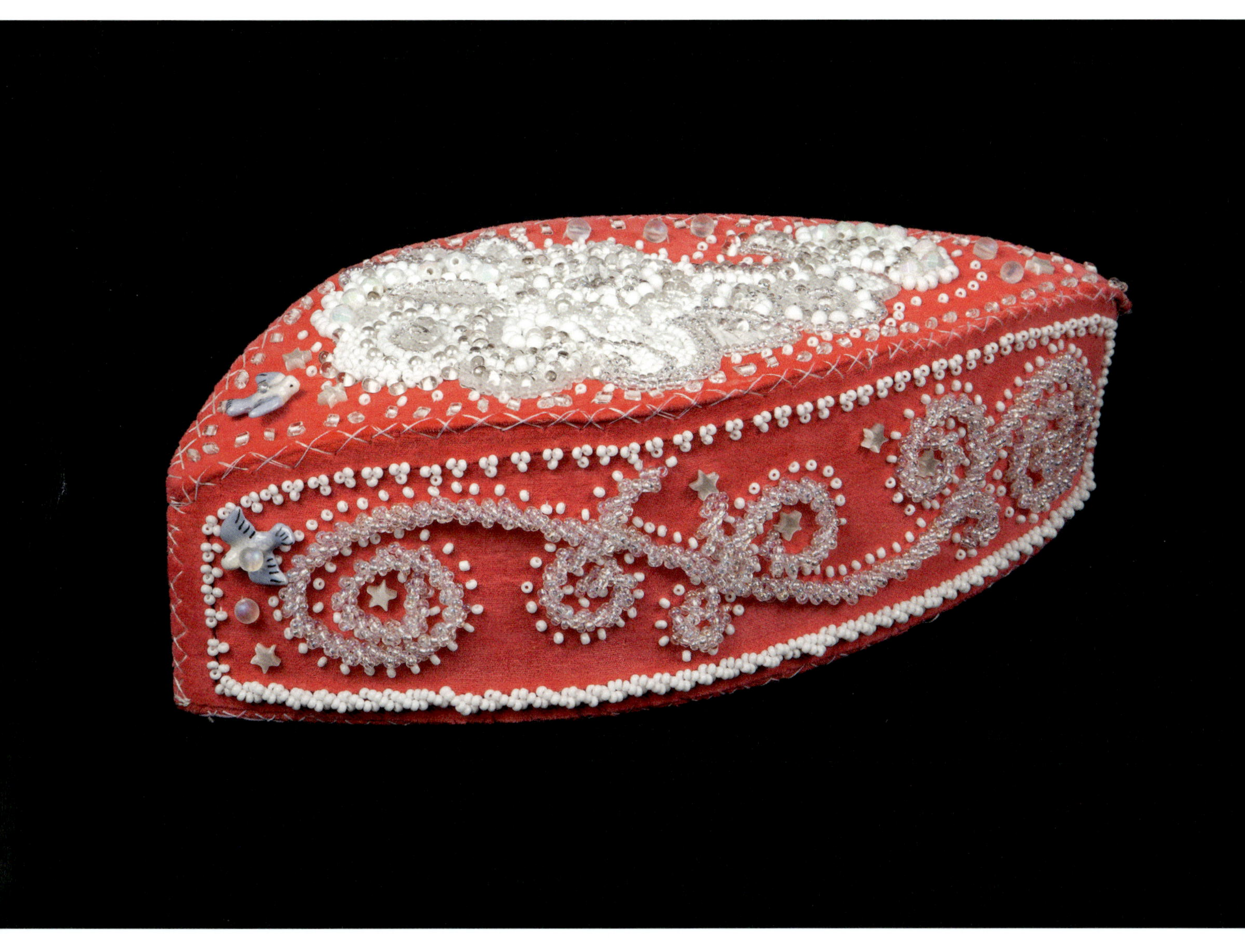

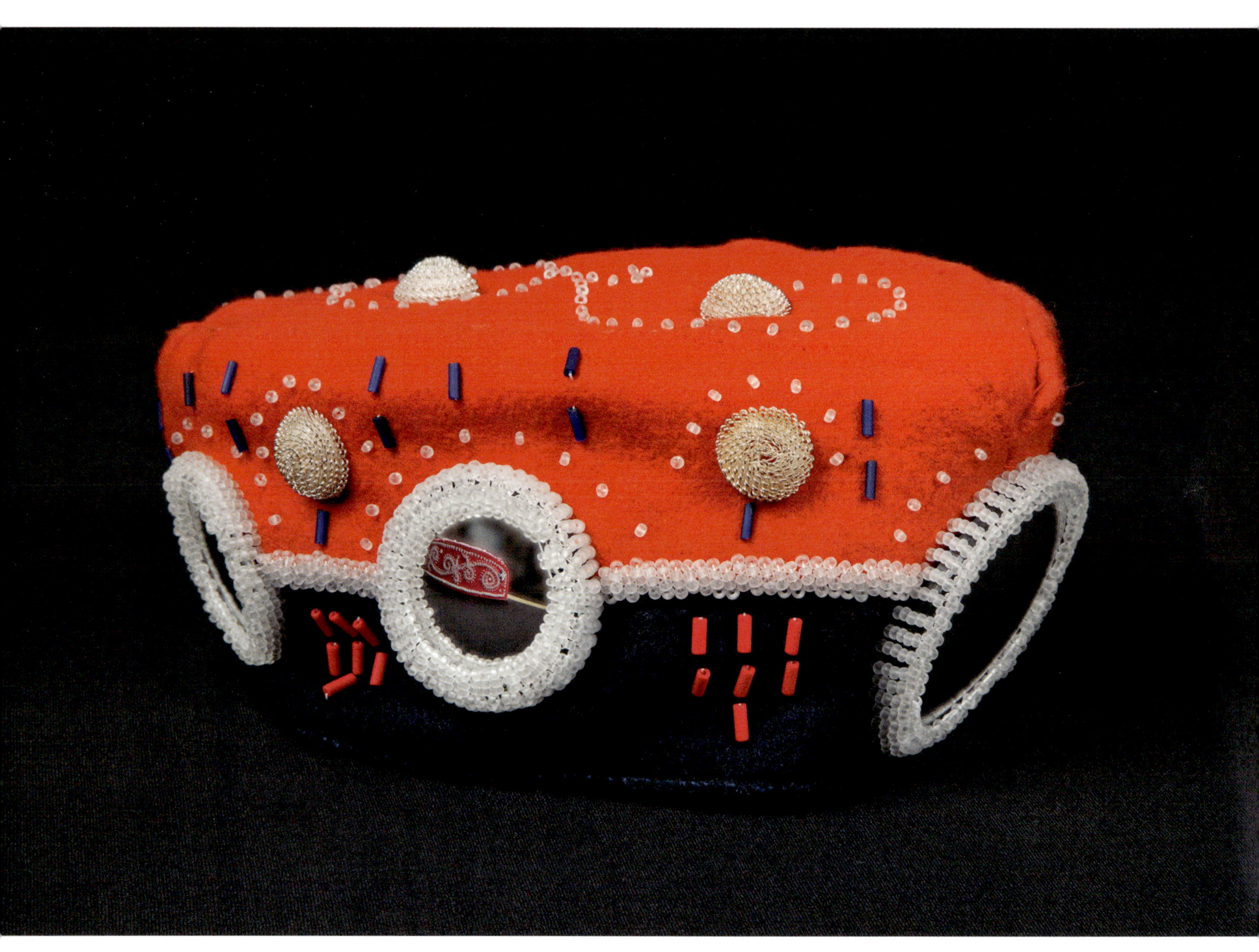

  Keeping Evil Away, 2015

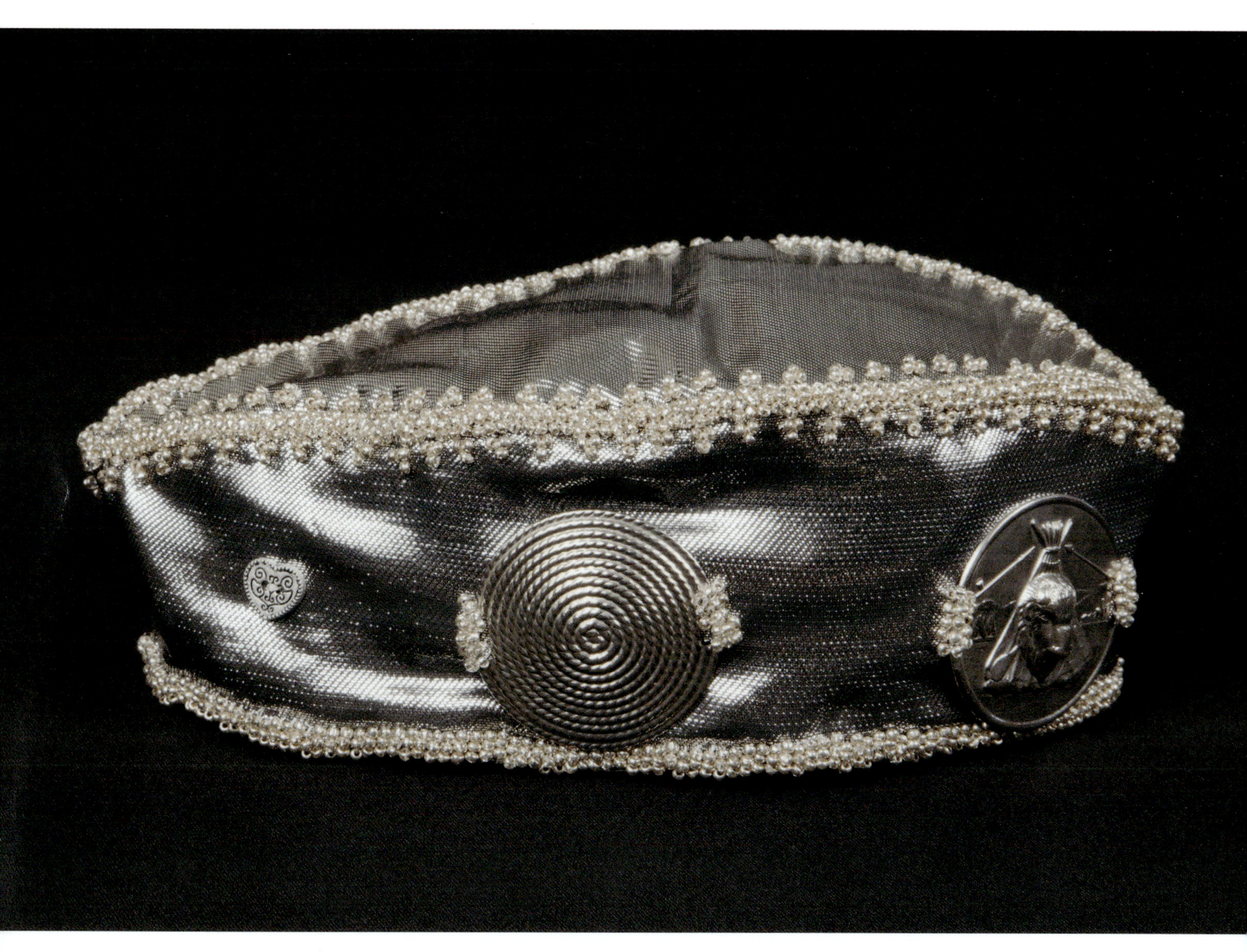

Silver Streams, 2015   149

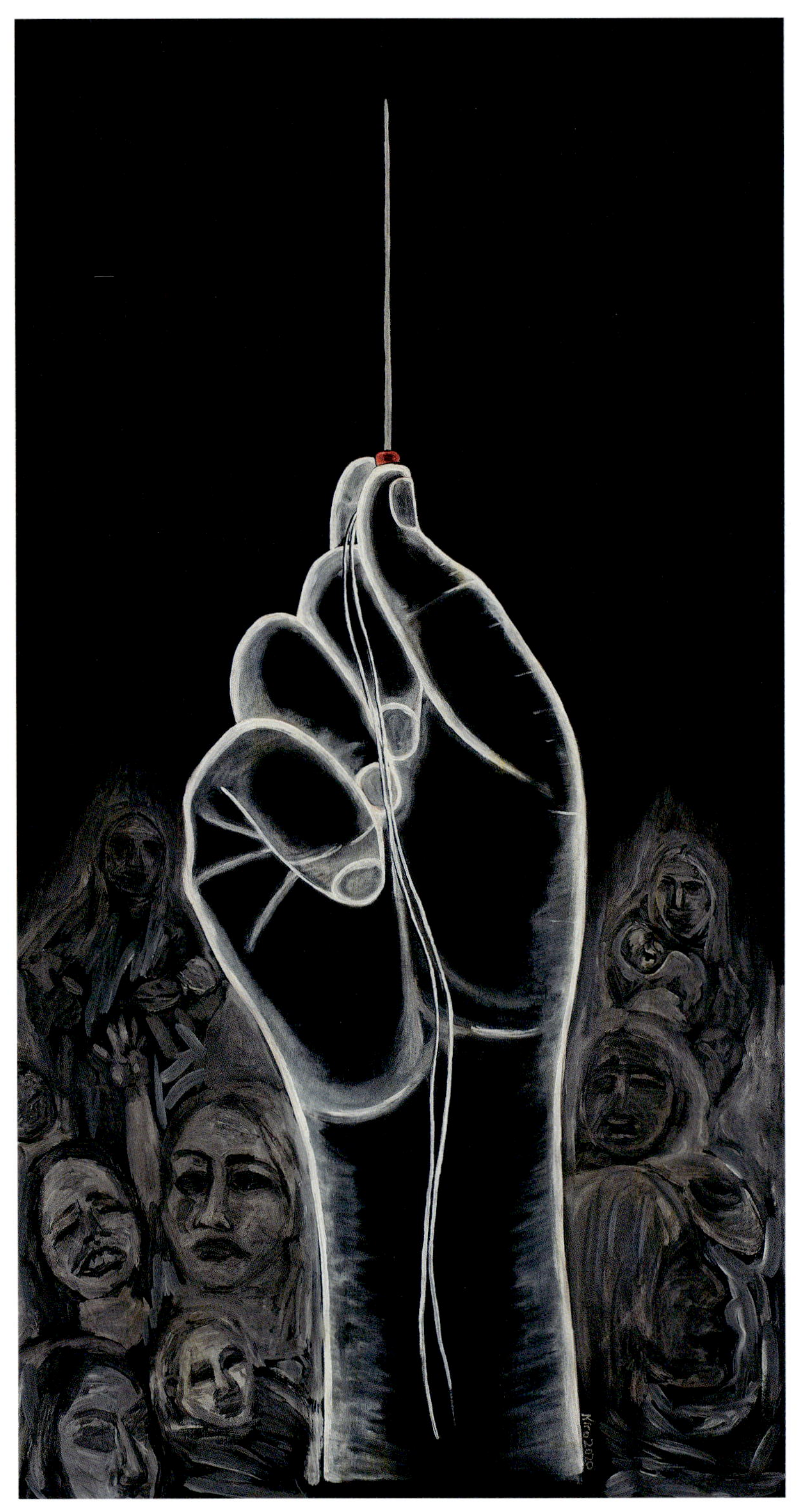

150   **The Weapon**, 2021

AN ARTIST THAT USES BEADS

ADRIANA GRECI GREEN

Beadwork is supposed to represent stars from the sky and when you look at a starry night you can really see how people would be affected by that and how they would want to put those stars into something they would be wearing. I totally relate to that.

I guess I'm a beadworker because I use beads. But there's people who really do it. I'm an artist that uses beads.[1]

Beadwork is a constant feature of Shelley Niro's work. Beaded Celestial Tree designs and curved motifs, along with wampum, are the most frequent manifestations of this presence. These elements appear as photographic works, like the Celestial Tree and Sky Dome in *Flying Woman #8* (1994, p. 109) and images of wampum belts that frame series such as *Ghosts, Girls, Grandmas* (2004, pp. 156–161); as formations of small holes, neatly drilled in mats, which she first started doing with *This Land Is Mime Land* (1992, pp. 266–277); and as evocative details painted in oil on canvas, as in *Waitress* (1987, p. 112) and *Oh My Aching Breaking Beading Heart* (2014). Their presence signals ancestral Onkwehón:we[2] connections to Creation, to Sky Woman, to cosmological geographies, to a deep sense of rootedness to place, to the holding of memory.

My focus here, however, is on works in which Niro presents beadwork in three dimensions. Beadwork links her practice broadly within historic Haudenosaunee artistic efforts, as seen in the cloth frames that envelop her mother and daughters in warm, loving embrace in *Time Travels Through Us* (1999, p. 23), in *Chiquita* (2002, p. 25), and in *My Girls* (2002, p. 24). The description of these frames simply as "mixed media" does not convey how carefully the cloth, glass beads, and sequins have been put together. The way Niro added lace-like edge beadwork along the ribbon trim and curved the tendrils of linework in open-space reference the small hexagonal bags that Haudenosaunee women in the 1830s so richly and inventively embroidered with beads, and channels those older artists' aesthetic sensibilities.

Many of Niro's sculptural works feature beadwork as a coequal, if not primary, material and expressive element. Her experience with beadwork is different from how she engages with the other media: "You can just sit down and make something, you don't have to have any special technology to do that, it's just sitting there doing the same action over and over and over again, doing something you are familiar with and knowing that if you stick with it you will get some kind of presence at the end of your production, but if you get half way through and put it away nothing will ever come of it, so it's just like therapy." Making beadwork is often a social activity shared with family and friends, an affective dimension that is also important to Niro. The realization that what are now historic designs would have been new and innovative at the time of their inception has freed her to develop her own interpretations of traditional ornamentation. Raised beadwork, a Haudenosaunee art form that emerged most famously as decoration for whimsies made for sale at Niagara Falls in the second half of the nineteenth century, allows designs to be built up with structure and depth, so Niro is particularly drawn to it as a sculptural medium in and of itself. She seems to especially favour embroidering strands of the puffy, raised edging composed on the diagonal that looks like twisted cord, as well as the doubled-up version that resembles tire tracks, or a braid.

Throughout the 1990s, Niro made several works featuring rocks encased within or placed atop bases of beaded cloth, like small meditations on the materiality of her world. They connect to her formative years learning basic beading techniques, a time when her parents made crafts to sell at fairs and powwows and there were always materials around the house to encourage her creativity. She often accompanied her father to the river to look for rocks that he'd use to make his specialty item, a gruesome-looking war tomahawk. Picking up rocks has stayed with her, but Niro seems to have a need to create protective and nurturing environments for these special stone beings.

In *I Sat on the River Bank and Waited for Signs of Life* (1999, p. 142) three smooth rocks are nested in a round, black-velvet form within a red cavity edged with shiny metal beads, as if they were deposited inside a geode with crystal encrustations. *Homage to the Old Ones* (1995) acknowledges the lakes, rivers, seas, and mountains from whence four carefully assembled groupings of rocks originated, and these places are referenced in elegantly beaded inscriptions. *Urging On The New* (1994) features pedestals draped in blue velvet that lift up rocks as a metaphor for the emergence of new ideas, and gem-like glass beads dignify this act of sustenance. In *One Day in March* (1999, p. 143) the contemplative title contrasts with the pulsating rhythm of netted beadwork that juts out from under a large round rock. The small, heart-shaped stone in the open box at the centre of *Here* (1994, p. 140) speaks to the geologic time it took for the stone to assume that shape, while the beadwork on the mat, with its concentric rings of raised bead braiding, beaded ribbon, and a looped edge like a halo that extends to the beyond, makes the grouping appear as if it is suspended in a starry galaxy.

Hats are a sculptural form that Niro first experimented with in *Thinking Caps* (1999, pp. 90–94) and that she keeps coming back to. Her millinery explorations include the aviator caps of that work and the one featured in *M: Stories of Women* (2011, pp. 79–89) and *Raven's World* (2015, p. 97), as well as a more recent series of hats inspired by the well-known historic Haudenosaunee beaded glengarry caps.[3] Niro's playful glengarries connect with the fanciful beadwork designs in her photographic works (including the drilled mats), and demonstrate her personal take on Haudenosaunee beadwork designs, especially the Celestial Tree and Sky Dome and the

curved linework seen on historic clothing and regalia. The bright colours and curves of *Forest Thoughts* (2015, p. 146) and the visually complex floral motif and spiraling tendrils of *Thinking of Sunshine* (2015, p. 147), embroidered with chalky and clear white beads, distill Haudenosaunee aesthetics even though there is nothing like them in the historical canon. The metallic *Silver Streams* (2015, p. 149) and *Keeping Evil Away* (2015, p. 148), with mirrors set into cloth by means of a deep, beaded edging, are classic Niro futuristic hats and as such connected in sentiment to the earlier aviator caps.

I close with *1779* (2017, pp. 153–155). Notwithstanding its visual ebullience, this work sharply evokes the Revolutionary violence, displacement, and exile that occurred at the place now known as Niagara Falls, events that Niro references repeatedly in other works. It is poignant that the impact of this elegy is achieved with a distinctively Haudenosaunee type of beadwork, albeit in Niro's style—the fateful date is beaded in eighteenth-century script, and the curvy flourishes flanking it are her version of Celestial Tree designs. Niro is explicit in her artist statement that the gold stiletto boots featured in this work incarnate the crassness that has taken over this place, in effect a continuation of cross-border imperial attempts to neuter the sacred power of Ongniaahra. The beading on the vamps of the boots makes them look like a Las Vegas theatre marquee with blue and white light bulbs and bright lights flashing "Niagara" and "Falls." Carefully threaded beads convey the awesomeness of the falls and capture the effect of the fast, white waters, and our eyes follow the bubbles as they precipitate over the edge. It is perhaps ironic, but fanciful, boot-shaped beaded whimsies were very popular Haudenosaunee souvenirs of this place—*1779* acknowledges this more recent touristic overlay while probing for deeper memories. Niro's sentiments flow by means of beadwork to assert Onkwehón:we history and cultural knowledge.

NOTES

1. All quotes Shelley Niro interview with the author, Fall 2021.

2. *Onkwehón:we* is a Mohawk term that signifies "the original people" and which is also used in reference to Haudenosaunee.

3. This series of four glengarry hats were exhibited in "Shelley Niro: Women, Land, River," guest curated by Lori Beavis at the Art Gallery of Peterborough in 2019.

1779 (detail), 2017. Photograph by Joseph Hartman >

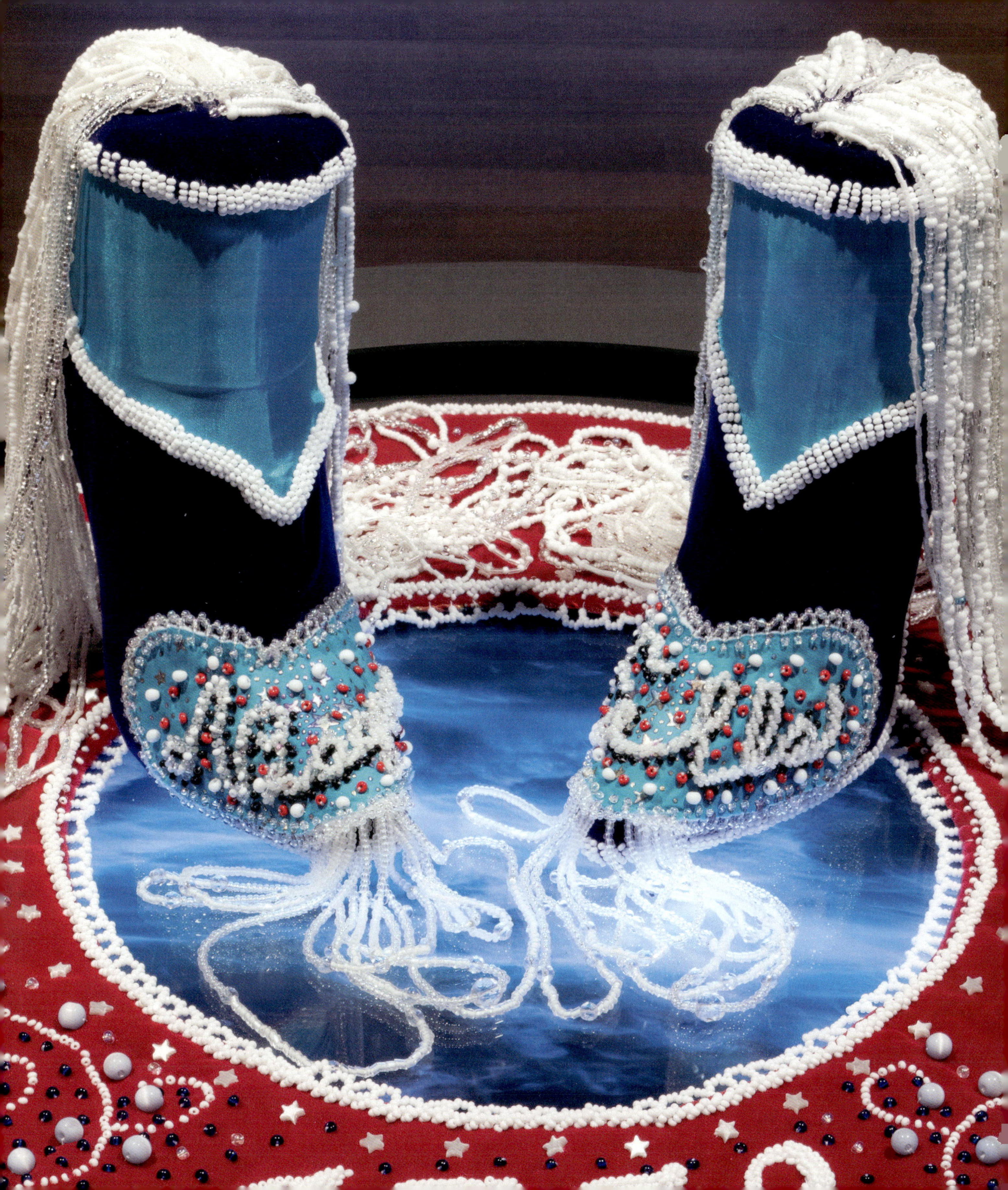

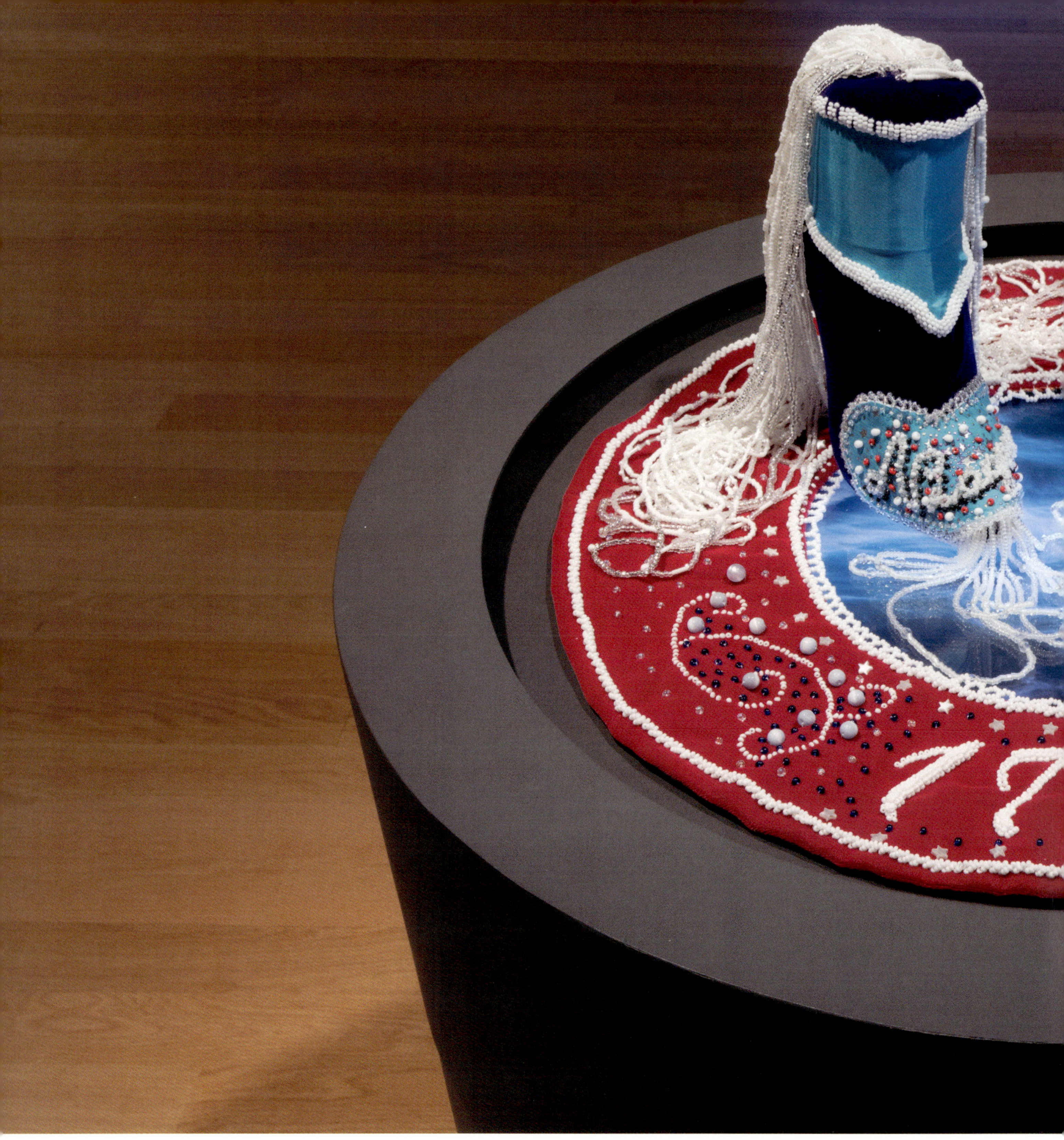

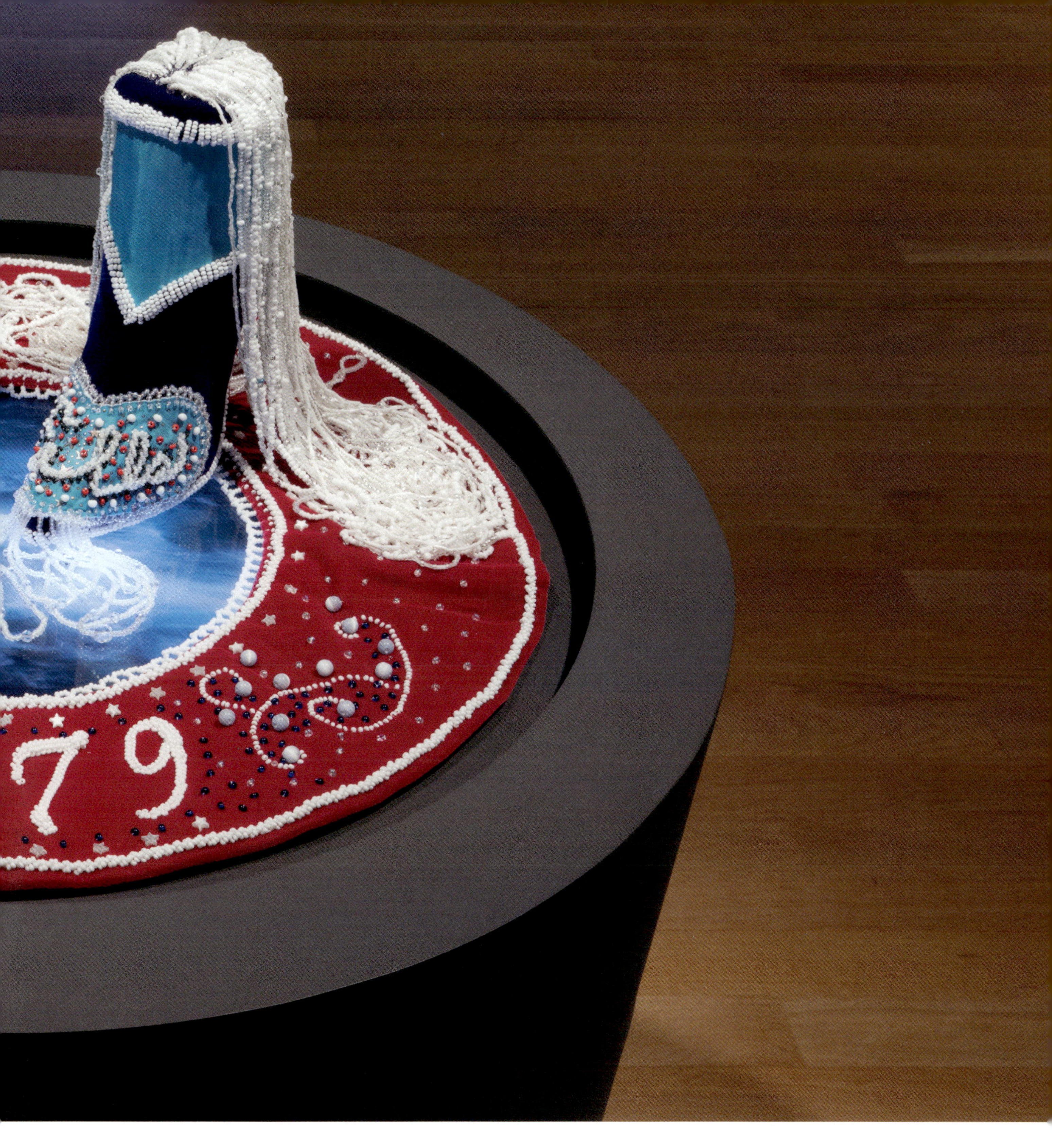

Installation view of **1779**, 2017
Art Gallery of Hamilton, 2017
Photograph by Joseph Hartman

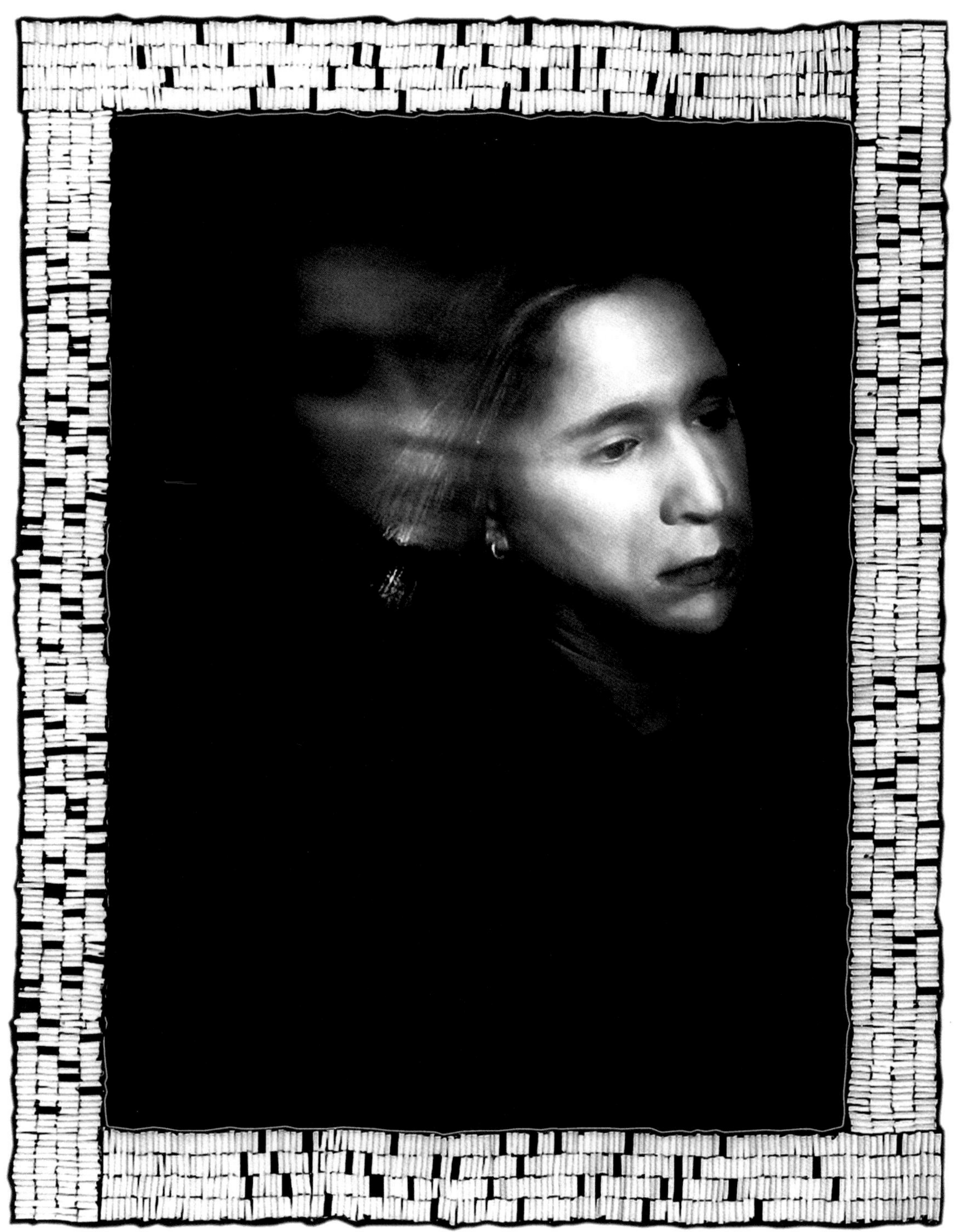

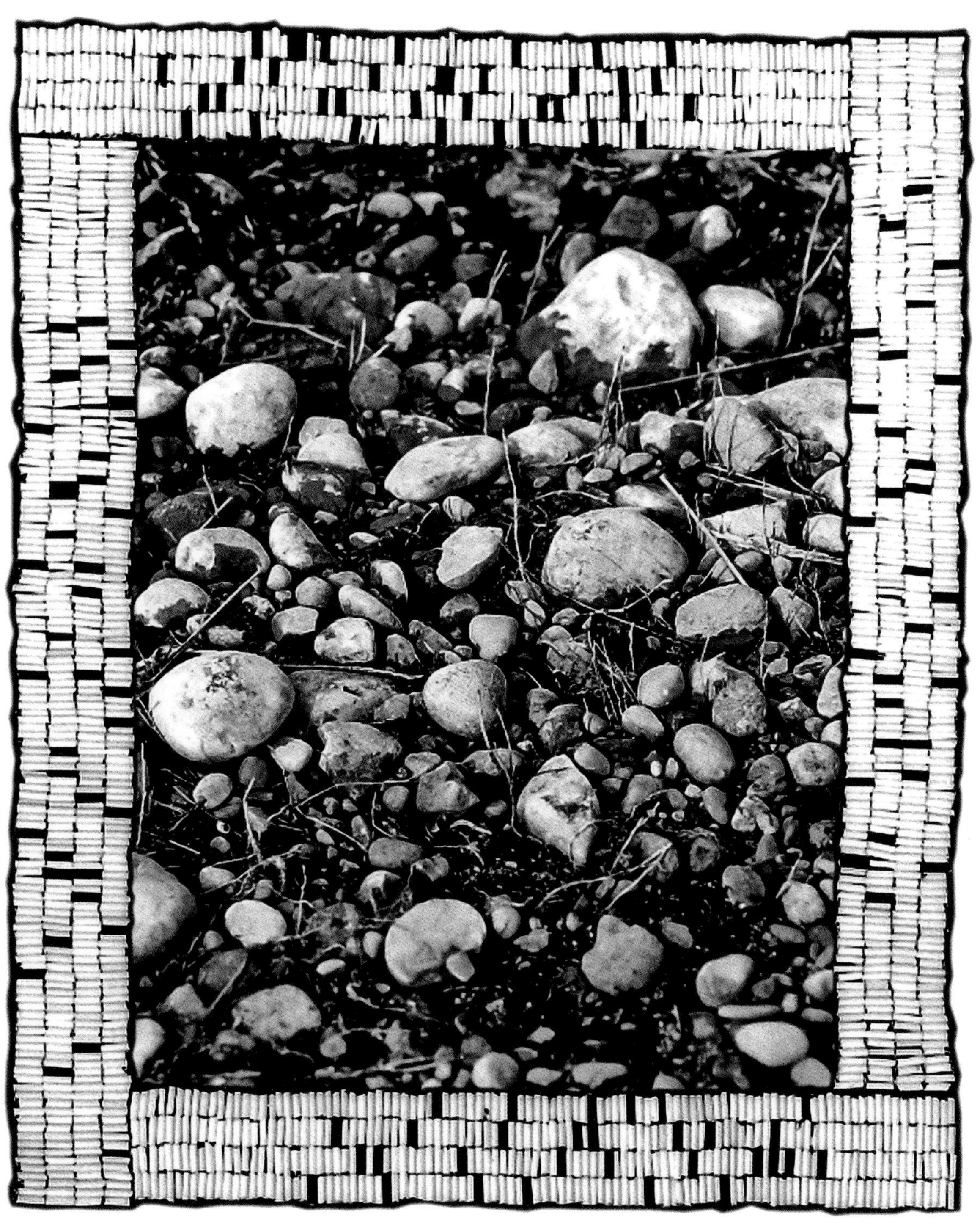

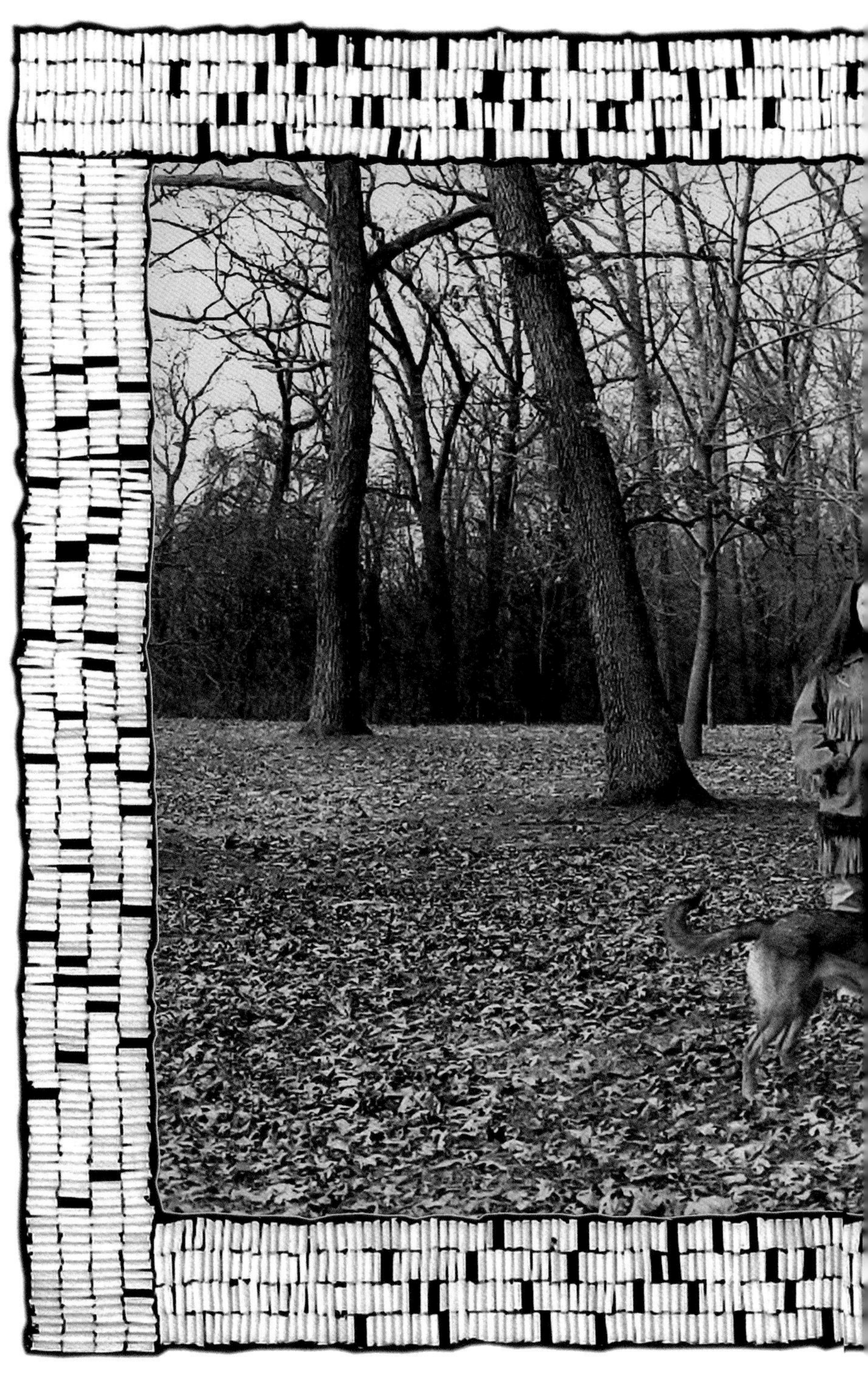

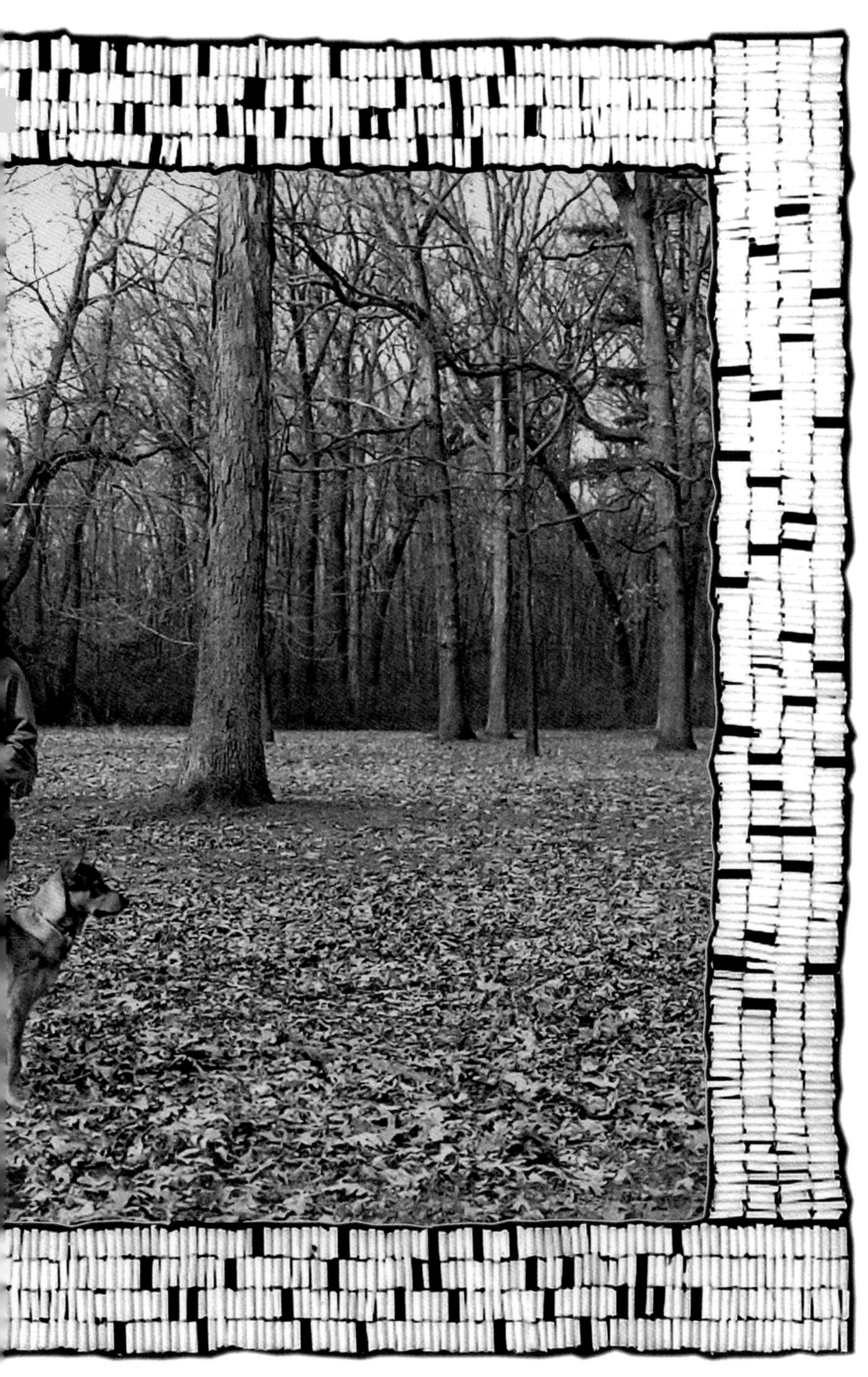

Ghosts, Girls, Grandmas (detail), 2004   159

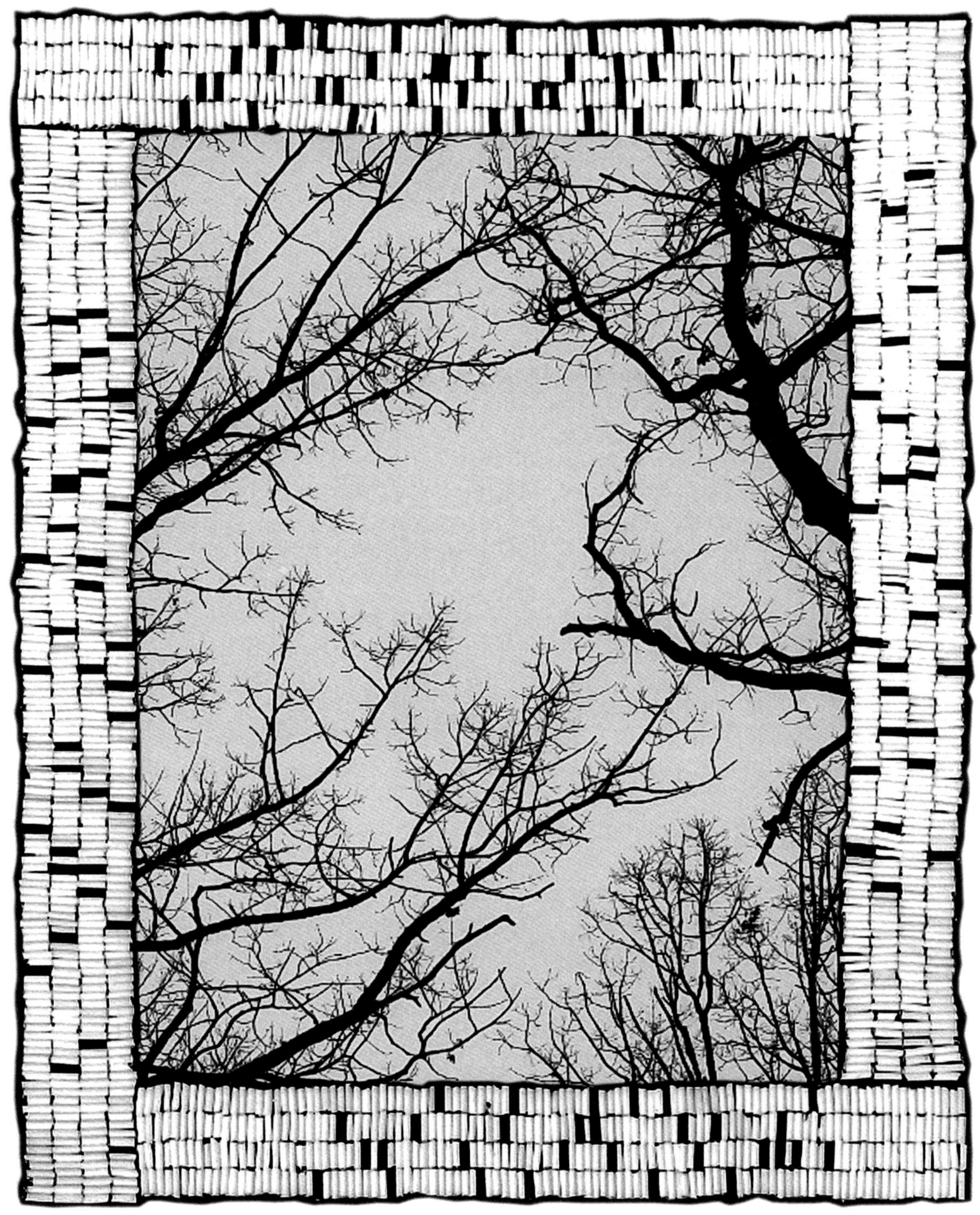

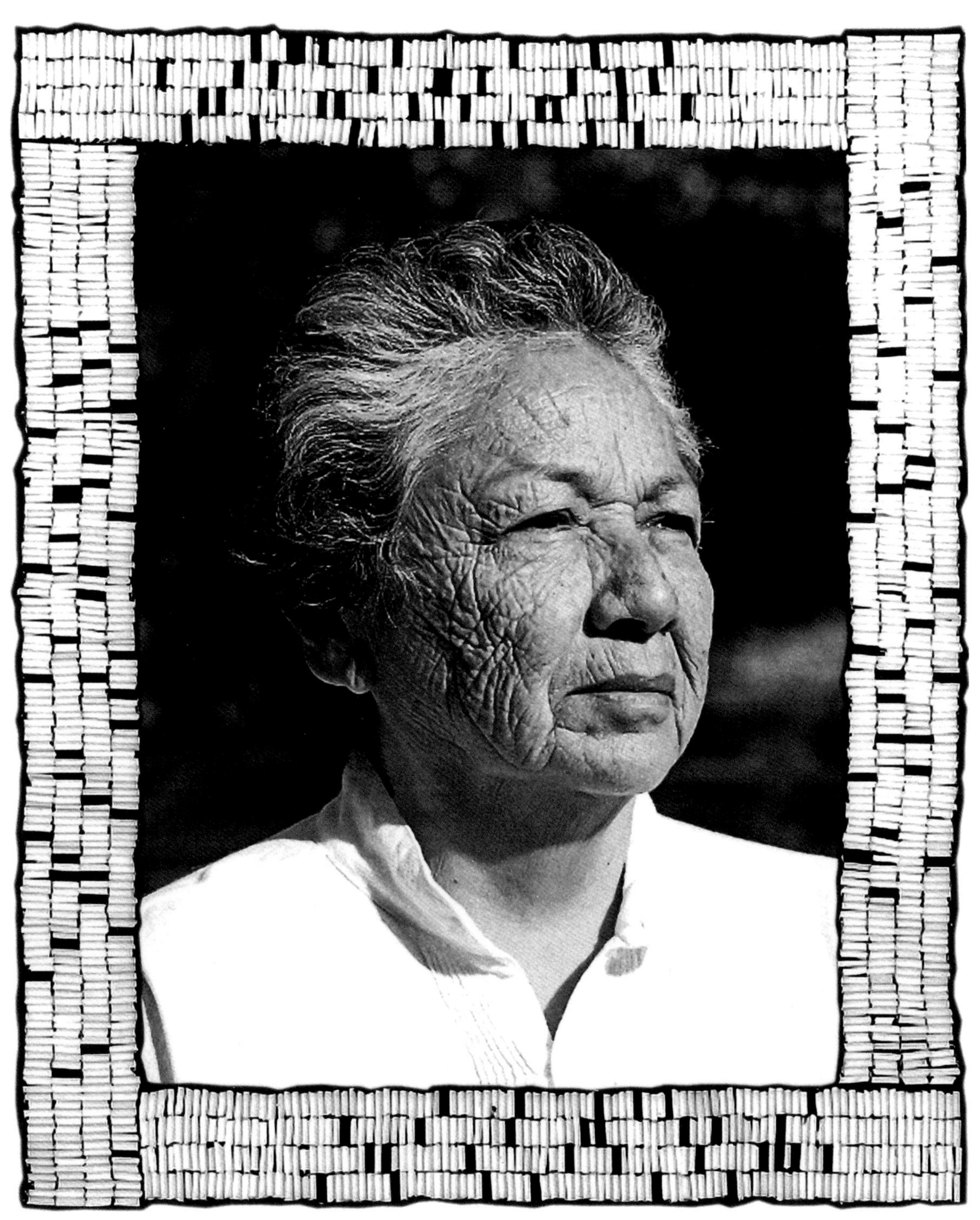

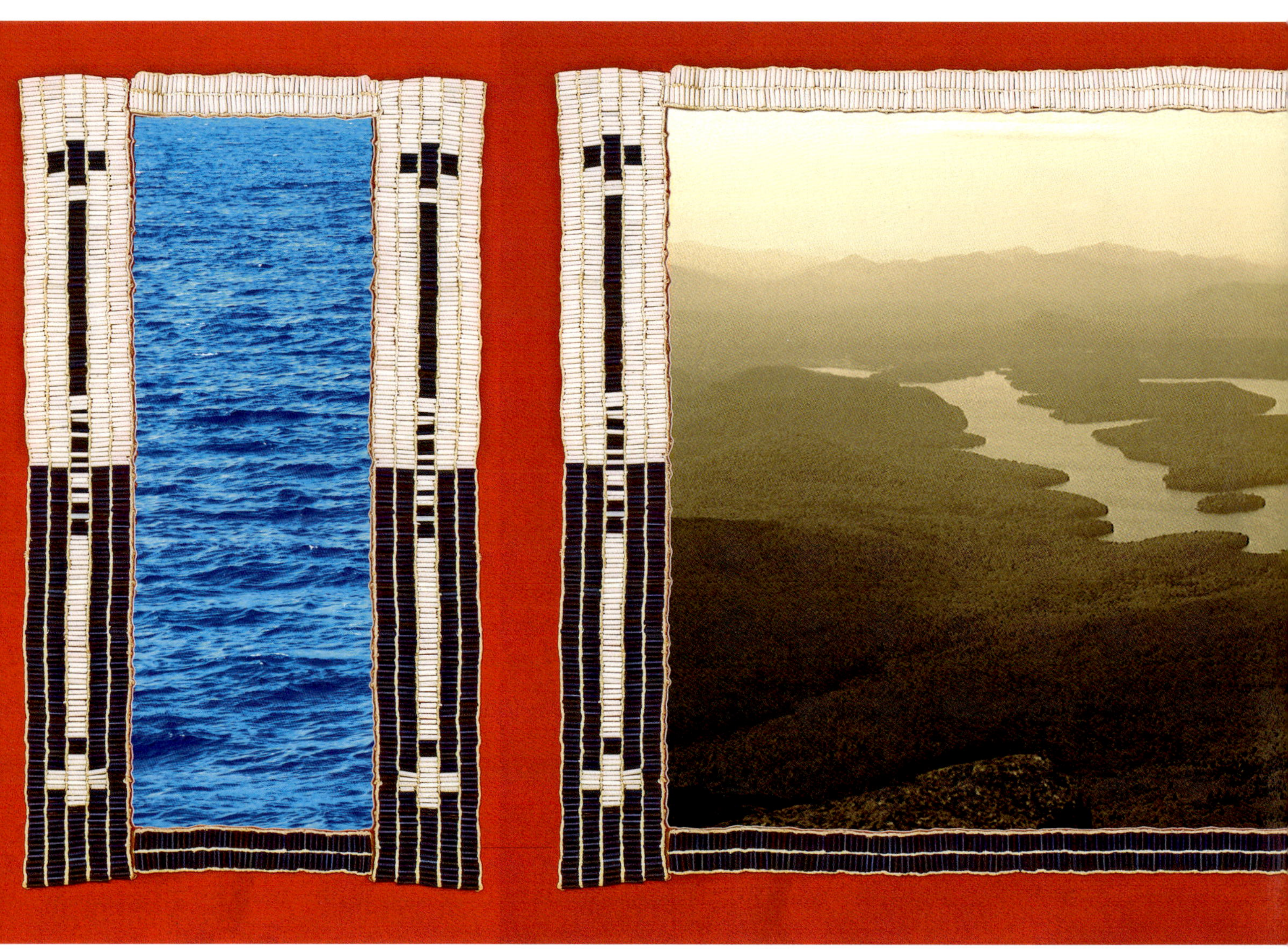

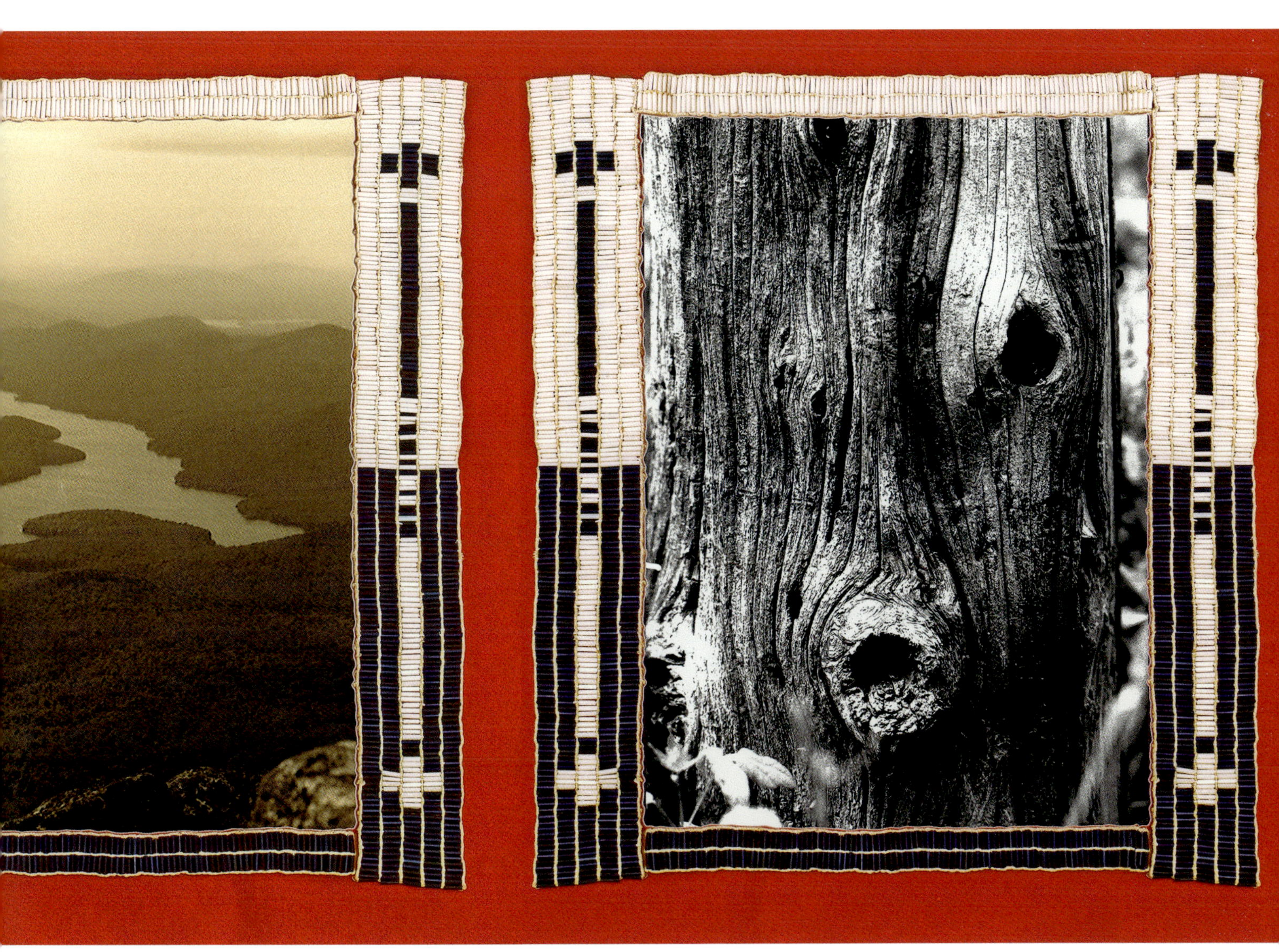

La Pieta (details), 2007

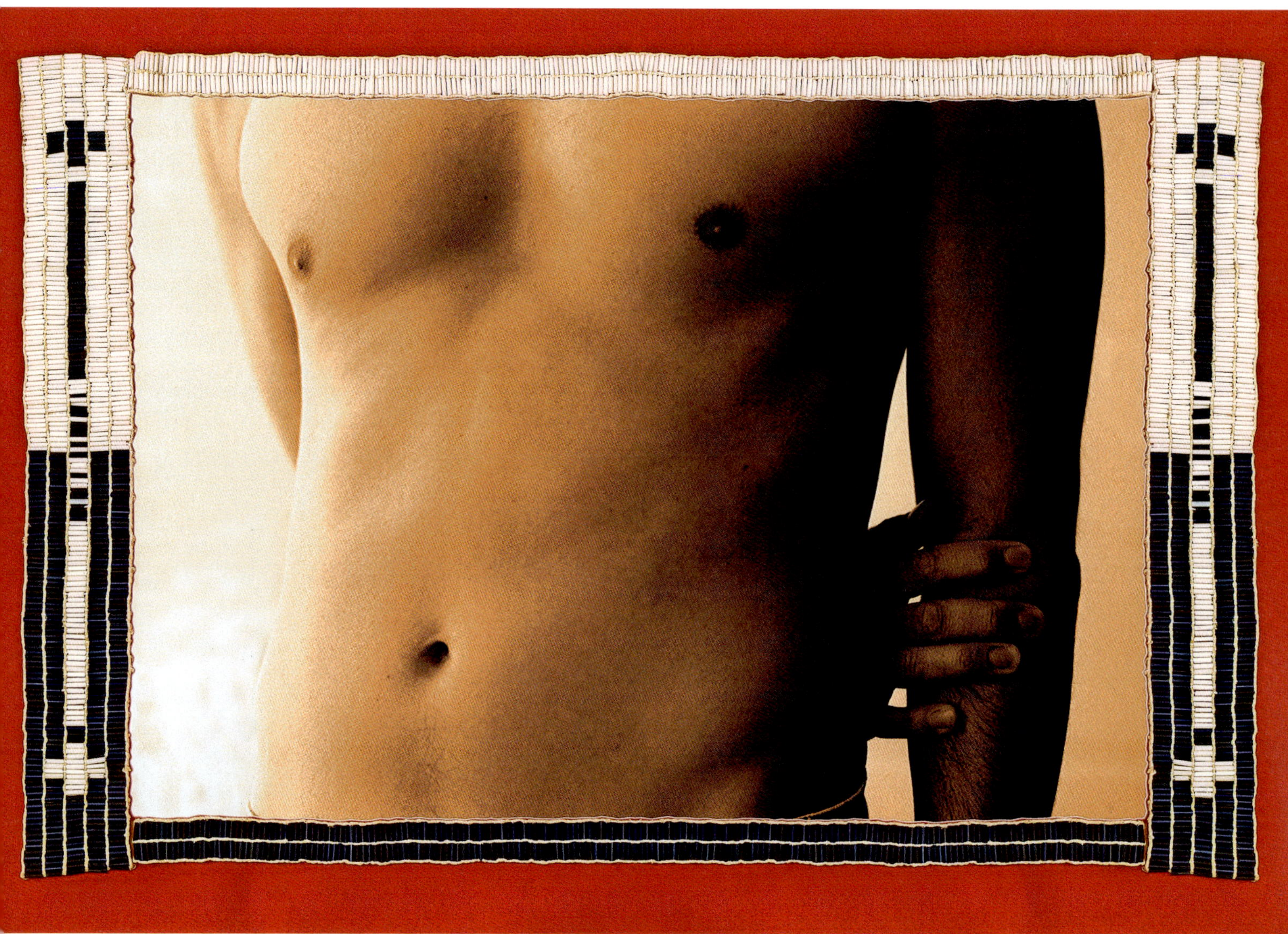

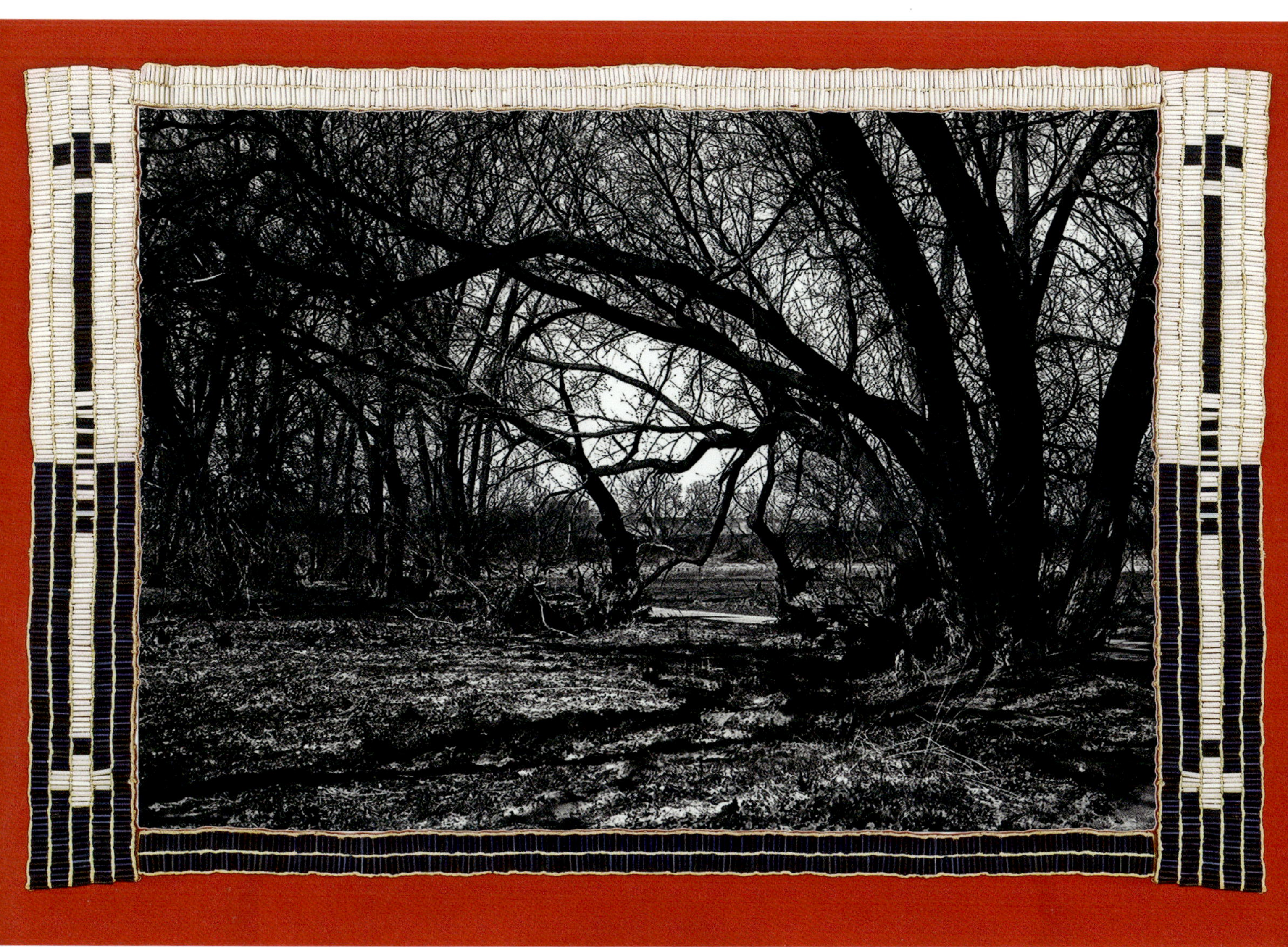

La Pieta (details), 2007

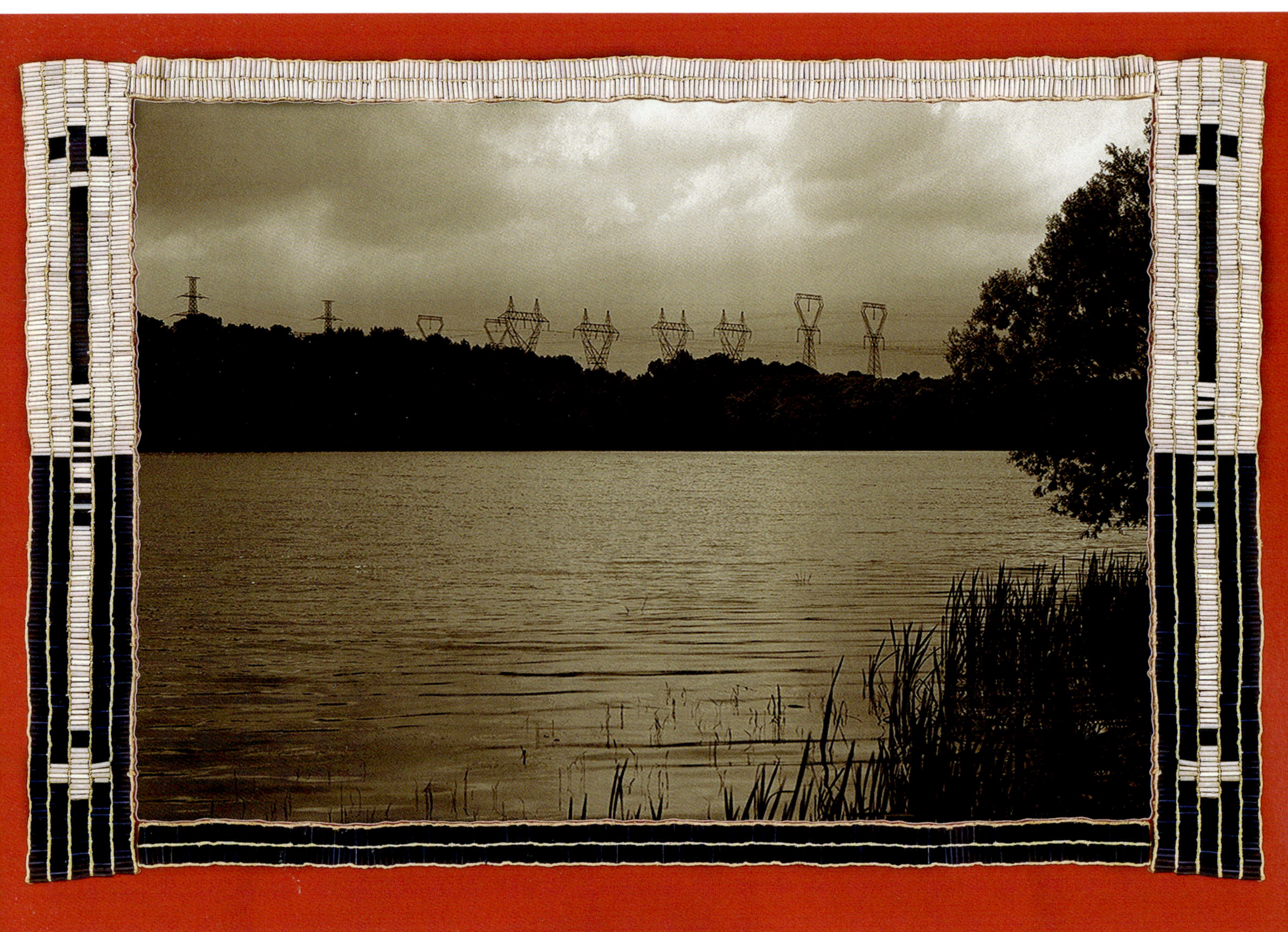

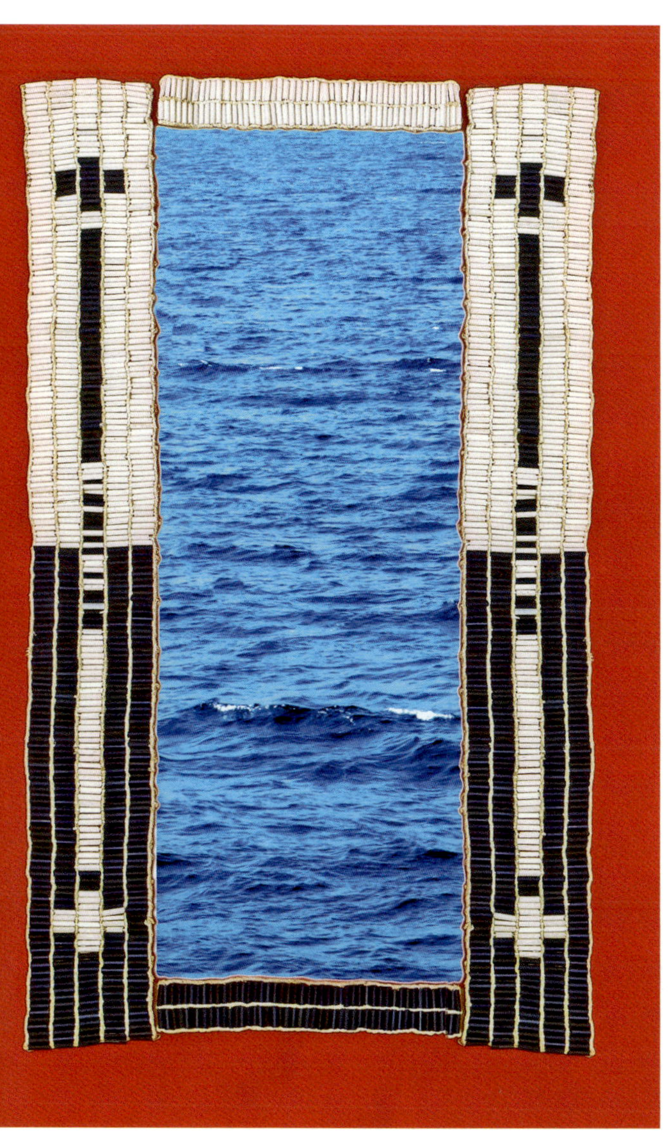

La Pieta (details), 2007   167

Tradition matters; but it is a matter to be worked upon, to mobilize meanings, to subvert and play with the present, to remind us of who we are, to suggest to us where we are going.[1]

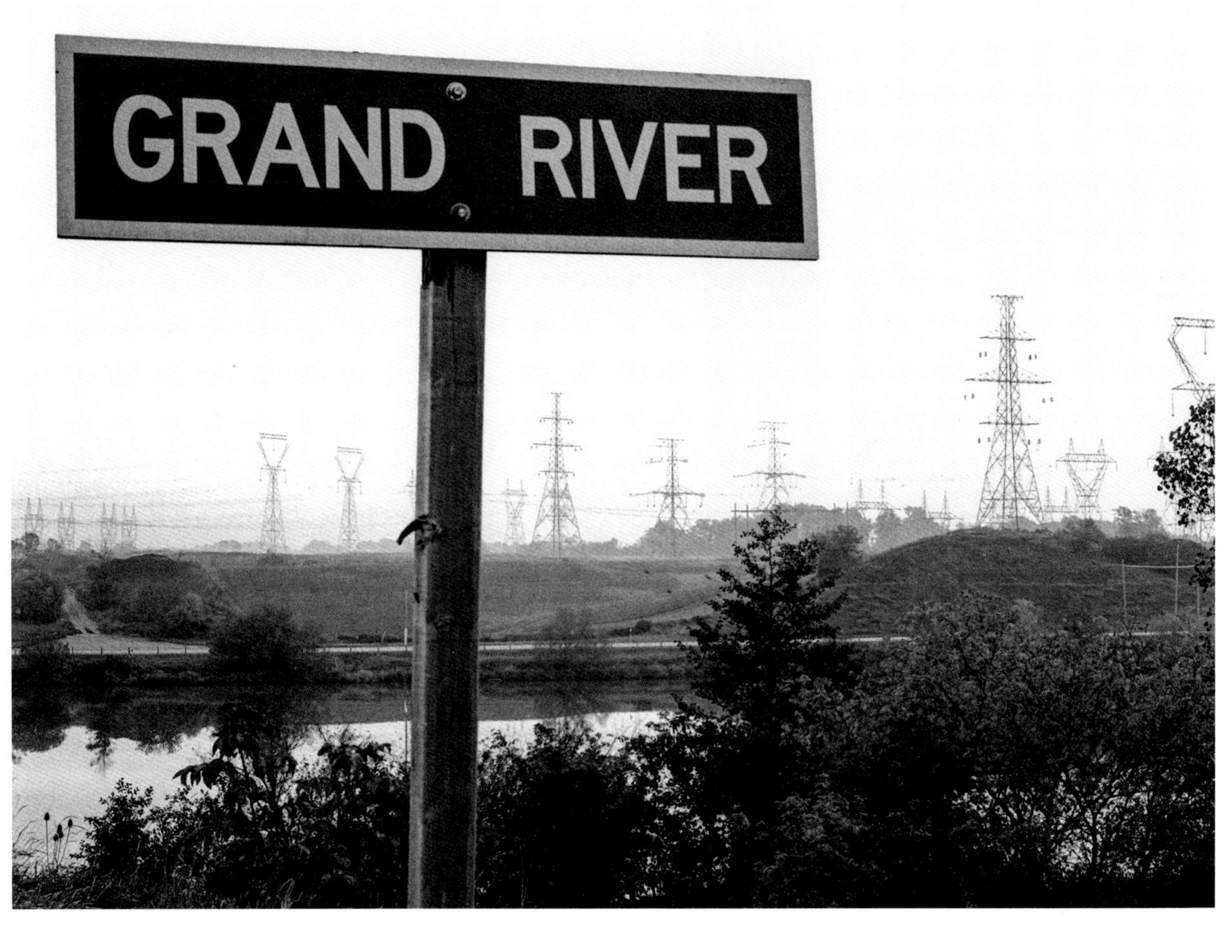

 Grand River from the series **Battlefields of My Ancestors**, 2015

SHELLEY NIRO MATTERS

GREG HILL

As an artist and curator, I come to Shelley Niro's work with awe and wonder at what she does, and the choices she makes in all matters, both aesthetic and in terms of medium, setting, content, intent, colour, light, scale, etc. Her decisions and thought processes intrigue, challenge and confound my ready assumptions and interpretations.

I first met Shelley in 1993, when I was sent as the delegate for Artcite Inc. in Windsor, Ontario, to attend the annual general meeting of ANNPAC, the national association of artist-run centres at the time.[2] As an act of remediation, all artist-run centres had to send a delegate who was a visible minority or First Nations person to the AGM in Calgary.[3]

There were several First Nations artists invited to the AGM to give presentations on their work and one of those artists was Shelley. As a young student with a special interest in what Rotinonhsyonni (Iroquoian) artists were doing, I knew of Shelley's work and her presence in exhibitions and catalogues of the time. I viewed her as a successful and famous First Nations artist and I was honoured and a little intimidated to meet her. She instantly put me at ease with her warm and welcoming demeanour. She was supportive and encouraging, modelling care and openness which has had a lasting impact on me. I felt a connection on the level of values and principles and ideas and an invaluable sense of community at a time when I was developing a political awareness in the turmoil of the aftereffects of the Kanesatake Resistance.[4] This led to my inclusion of her as one of the artists I wanted to be in dialogue with for my master's thesis.[5]

The interview that I conducted with her then, in 1995, and those with the other artists I wrote about, David Kanatawakhon Maracle, Patricia Deadman, and Jeff Thomas, were important moments of community building and affirmation and an opportunity for sounding out—and hearing back—ideas about identity, culture, and politics from Rotinonhsyonni perspectives. It revealed a view, a process, and an aesthetic that Shelley and all of the artists were engaged in with their art.

Iroquois art is a dynamic amalgamation of culture, tradition, and exchange reinforced and informed by ancient, fundamental philosophies and principals that continue to be embraced today. An Iroquois aesthetic is inflected with varying social, political, and cultural sensibilities and actively engages issues of identity, community, and place.[6]

I continue to be fascinated by how Shelley Niro sees the world as framed by her Rotinonhsyonni gaze. It is a perspective that finds expression in all aspects of her work, sometimes literally, sometimes metaphorically, and sometimes expanding into the philosophical. Of course, a Rotinonhsyonni lens is not the only one she uses. She has been viewed as a woman, feminist, activist, provocateur, humourist, traditionalist, and futurist. All of these categories and more can justly be applied, but they must all submit to Niro's own fashioning of the definitions. This in itself may in fact be one of the most defining characteristics of the artist Shelley Niro—her resolute assuredness in her entitlement to define herself, for herself, is a fundamental value of both her Rotinonhsyonniness and her art.

Niro shares with us by telling stories. She proliferates multiple narratives through her multidisciplinary output, often creating compound storylines within individual works. A dense substrate of history, culture, and philosophy are woven into and throughout an installation, a photograph, a photo series, a film. Her stories are derived from those told to her by her father, who absorbed them from his parents, and so on, such as the memories of the Traditional Territories of the Kanyen'kehaka in what is today called the Mohawk Valley. In an interview with curator Lori Beavis, Niro muses about the spirits of the Ancestors and how they must feel being there still when there are not many Rotinonhsyonni People anymore. Holding the memories of this place from her great-grandmother, as passed down to her from her father, and then being there in person, she realized how beautiful it was, and how this beauty stood in contrast to the emotions of people being forced out for fear of being killed.[7]

One scene in her film *Kissed by Lightning* (2009, pp. 128–129) serves as a coming together of past and present, a modern-day retelling of the Peacemaker narrative. In it, the characters Mavis and Bud are driving to New York—through traditional Rotinonhsyonni territory—to deliver Mavis' paintings to an exhibition. Throughout the film, there have been references to the Peacemaker, the origins of the Rotinonhsyonni Confederacy, ceremony, and the Ancestors. While Bud peers out at the landscape passing by, he muses: "When our feet touch the earth our souls mix with the souls of our ancestors."[8] Niro weaves together Rotinonhsyonni culture, history, and the present to reveal past trauma and knowledge that are embedded in the land and permeate the psyche of those so attuned.

These memory narratives sleep and blossom through time, emerging as they are required, as they are summoned, and as they are reimagined, providing a cultural foundation for Niro's personal artistic explorations. These stories are also the grand narratives of a People, the origin chronicles that are the realm of Sky Woman, the Peacemaker, Jigonsaseh, and Hiawatha, principal characters in Rotinonhsyonni world-making and the foundation for the artist's imaginative retellings. Niro brings millennia of oral history together with the present and offers it to us in her creative alchemy of image, object, text, and sign.

As a Rotinonhsyonni person coming to her work, there is much to behold. Signs, symbols, colours, locations, people, and context are all in some way recognizable. The familiarity is welcoming. When there is something beyond my understanding, I am left yearning to know.

For the most part, Niro's work is a decipherable code, as it is composed of long-held and agreed upon ideas made manifest in symbolic representations. These can be designs, objects, materials, and processes, all interwoven into something such as a wampum belt or a beaded object. These representations are then reproduced within, or become a component of, one of Shelley's installations, such as *Thinking Caps* (1999, pp. 90–94), a work that honours and illuminates four stages in a Kanyen'kehaka woman's life.

Thinking Caps consists of four framed photographic assemblages installed on a wall with four wooden tables in front of them, on which four beaded "thinking caps" are mounted. Each of the groupings, made up of a framed photo, table, and cap, represents a successive stage of life and the development of creativity and imagination in the mind of a young Kanyen'kehaka person as they pass from young girl to teenager to woman and finally to elderly woman.

The main images are photographs of Rotinonhsyonni beadwork overlaid with text in English and Kanyen'keha (Mohawk language) and bordered with "snapshot" photographs of hands in the process of doing beadwork. The beadworkers that served as models are aged from nine to sixty-nine years old. Text is used on each panel and starts with birth, "I am born – kena:kere," moving to more complex thoughts, "I dream – kateshens," to a sense of self and one's place within community, "I am a member of the Turtle Clan – keniahten," and finally, the maturity of the elderly woman is represented like poetry "aweriahsa' – heart – atonhets – soul – konnhe' – life." The selection of text and images works together with the beaded "thinking caps" to communicate the idea of passing through these stages of life and the cognitive and relational aspects of this development.

Niro's Haudenosaunee-rooted interpretations or reinterpretations destabilize colonial monotheism and mythologies imposed upon Indigenous Peoples and reconstitute the criticality of seeing through a different lens grounded to place and politic.[9]

Within the many symbols and references that Niro employs that are specific to Rotinonhsyonni culture, I am particularly attuned to her use of the *tekeni teyohate*[10] or two-row wampum belt. This belt is simple in design and complex in meaning.[11] During my research and learning about the belt and its applications, I interviewed Shelley to find those instances of Rotinonhsyonni-ness that formed or influenced her thinking and ideas, considering, in particular, how the *tekeni teyohate* could be considered foundational to the sovereignty of self.

"I always try to go back to the very basic lesson of Iroquois independence," she told me, "which is 'you start with yourself.'"[12]

In the photograph *Treaties* from the series *Borders* (2008, pp. 224–231), the *tekeni teyohate* features prominently, spanning the full width of the wide-format image. It hovers above the central image of two arms coming together, one from each side, to join with clasped hands. Below is a mirrored and repeated landscape, the shoreline of the Grand River. A solarizing effect transforms it into a ghostly apparition of the land.

The reference to the two-row wampum belt is direct, but the ideas of sovereignty are eroded by the other images in this composite. The clasped hands are indicative of an agreement, but the bond is weak.[13] The Grand River is the central land reference of the agreement to compensate the Rotinonhsyonni for lost territories after they had sided with the British during the American War of Independence. This agreement was never fully respected or upheld, and today more than ninety percent of these lands are no longer in Rotinonhsyonni care or control.

In Niro's *Parallel Worlds of Women and Warriors* (2010, pp. 232–233), she places an abstracted image of a two-row wampum belt between two stereoscopes of women she wants to honour. One is Jigonsaseh, the first person to accept the Peacemaker's message and the reason women were given such an important role in the Rotinonhsyonni Confederacy. She is the symbol of the Clan Mothers and their power.[14] The other is Mademoiselle Marcelle Semmer,[15] a French woman who risked her life aiding soldiers during WWI. The two women come together here quite by chance—Niro was inspired to juxtapose them after finding the stereoscope of Mlle Semmer in an antique store.[16]

"There is a link between the two images," she has written of this work. "That link is a two-row image that has been abstracted. It looks more like a clam than a wampum belt. I wanted to create a feeling of time traveling and become aware of that journey."[17] Niro's use of the two-row transcends time and culture. She brings these two women together across time and space, in stereo, with the symbol of the two-row as a reinforcement of their sovereign strength. It is a view that is only possible from her personal perspective as a Rotinonhsyonni woman.

As with the two-row, Niro uses other images of wampum in a variety of ways, sometimes as a framing device which bears meaning. In the series of seven photographs entitled *La Pieta* (2007, pp. 162–167), for example, the wampum belt she creates represents two sides of a conflict, with black beads for bad, and white beads for good. The cross symbol is a reference to directions—the horizontal nature of land and the vertical, upwards direction to the sky. The symmetry achieves a balance that enhances and informs how we interpret the images.

In another series of photographs using wampum as a framing device, the woven wampum beads evoke a code unknown to the viewer, and unknowable. In *Ghosts* from the series, *Ghosts, Girls, Grandmas* (2004, pp. 156–161), the patterns of wampum beads appear randomly assembled. "I didn't want the wampum to represent anything specific," Niro wrote. "I wanted to make the photo look like it was surrounded with the energy of wampum. So it was free form wampum…. Even talking about the work takes away some of the mystery in the photos…."[18]

In contrast, Niro's use of a small wampum belt in *Sense of Touch* in the series *The Essential Sensuality of Ceremony* (2002, pp. 71–75) is an invocation of ceremony, specifically that of condolence. Niro's sacred and secular references make connections to culture and community in a responsible manner, but she also retains the right to interpretation. "It just sort of triggers a lot of, I won't say emotion because it's not," she has said. "I think it's something else other than emotion. It's almost like you're trying to trigger an historical memory. You're really trying to…make links with the past, and trying to do it in such a way that it's not a commodity, because l don't want to commodify those designs to make it so obvious that it's Iroquois, that people think 'This is good stuff, cause look how Iroquois it is.'"[19]

Quite apart from direct cultural references, a recurring image that Shelley uses resonates with me in a personal way. My father is from Six Nations reserve and while this makes me a Status member of an "Indian Band" located there, I never lived there. I was born in the town of Fort Erie, Ontario. The reserve and my home are about a forty-five-minute drive apart. Despite the distance, I am connected by family and, I recently realized, by water. The Grand River—the entire length of which is the geographic centre of Six Nations Grand River Territory—empties into Lake Erie,[20] which flows into and becomes the Niagara[21] River at the site of the town. The river then continues on to Niagara Falls and through the Niagara Gorge (carved out by the cascading water over many millennia) until it empties into Lake Ontario.[22] This water that flows from Six Nations to Niagara Falls is the same water that I consumed all my young life while I lived in Fort Erie. It is part of me. I swam in it, fished in it, floated on it, picnicked along its shores, and cycled along it to the falls and back more than a hundred times.

This same water is used to generate the electricity that flows through the transmission lines of the hydro towers that Shelley shows us in many of her works.[23] They appear in *Power at the Edge* (2004, p. 177), in the individual images *Caledonia* (2015, p. 181), *Grand River* (2006, p. 168), and *The Cohoes* (2015, p. 184) that are part of the series *Battlefields of My Ancestors* (2015, pp. 168, 181–195), in photograph #6 in the series *La Pieta* (2007, pp. 162–167), in *Treaties* (pp. 226–227) from the series *Borders*, and in *The Shirt* (2003, pp. 196–207).[24] These literal, figurative and metaphorical connections are powerful. For Niro, the "power" that the hydro towers represent is not the electricity passing through the wires. They refer, rather, to who has the power to extract energy from the water and then sell it to others to make a profit. She sees the towers as "signs of power, using up resources."[25]

Niro's work operates on many different levels. Multiple facets are accessible, depending on the knowledges brought to it, and it is approachable in a variety of ways. Humour, critique of stereotypes, history, and culture are all presented from her subjective position as a

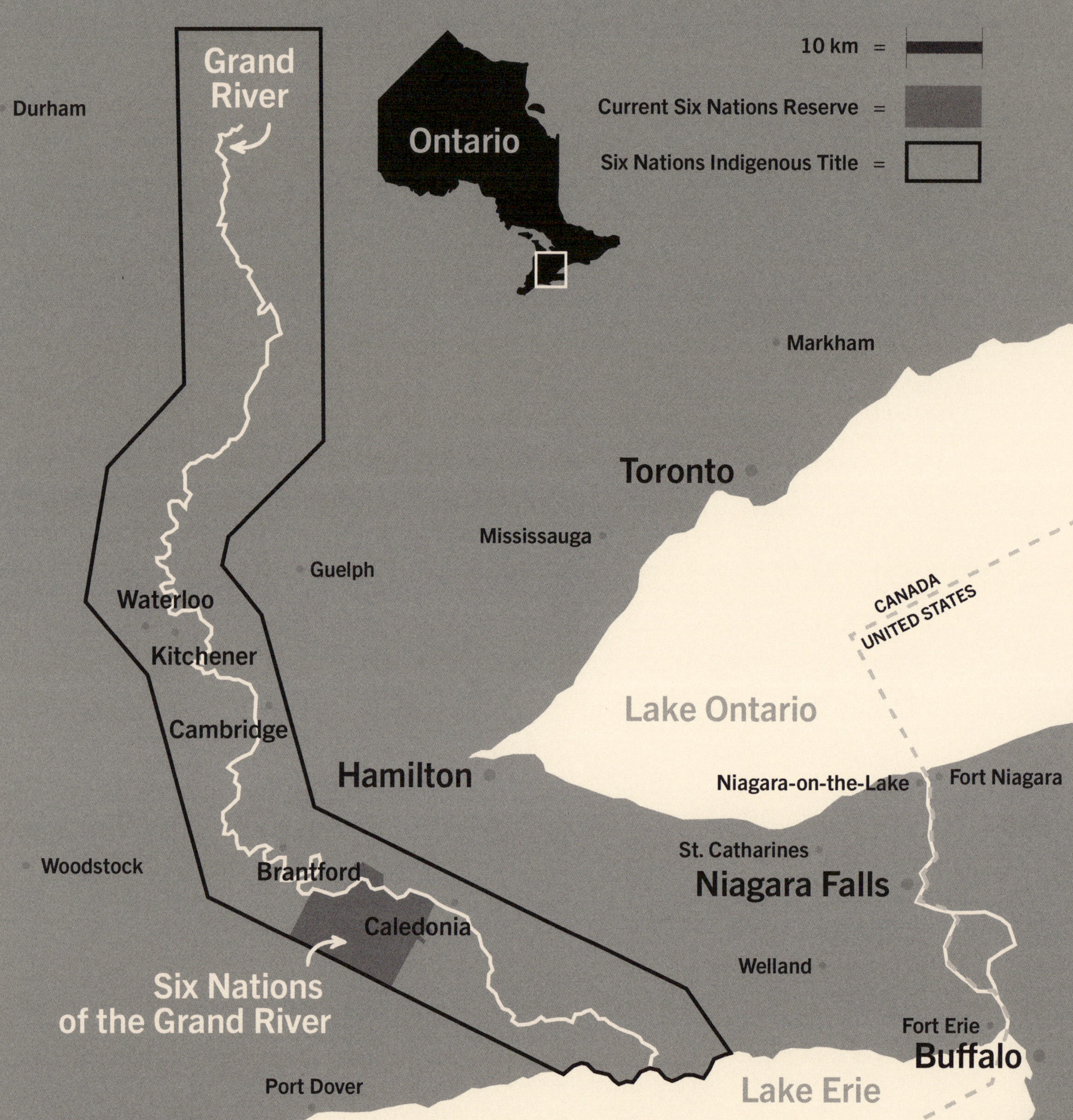

This map delineates the boundaries of the Haldimand Tract, a strip of land on both sides of the Grand River that was granted to the Six Nations Confederacy in 1784 in recognition of lands lost for their alliance with the British during the American Revolution. The tract is central to restitution of Indigenous Title for Six Nations of the Grand River Territory.

Rotinonhsyonni woman. Her work reflects her firm but gentle take on potentially incendiary issues, but she also tells her truth and, by extension, the truths of many Indigenous Peoples, women, and settlers, as we are all implicated in the complex exchange that is the shared history of Turtle Island since those early contact days. Shelly Niro matters because she is able to translate her tactile sense of experience into images that seep into our senses and become embedded in our body memory.

I have been an artist for as long as I can remember. My work is the result of emotion and personal interpretation. It hinges on a taste, feel, or smell of events.[26]

NOTES

1. Audra Simpson, "Art for Our Sake: Contemporary Iroquois Art in the Collection of the Indian Art Centre," (unpublished manuscript), quoted in Ryan Rice, "Oh So Iroquois," *Kwah Í:ken Tsi Iroquois/Oh So Iroquois/ Tellement Iroquois* (Ottawa: Ottawa Art Gallery/Aboriginal Curatorial Collective, 2008), 64.

2. Edwin Janzen, "Fifteen Years Later," Artist-Run Centres and Collectives Conference, accessed January 30, 2022, https://www.arca.art/en/featured/arcas-15th-anniversary/.

3. "At the 1992 conference of ANNPAC, the issue of diversity in the arts was brought to the fore by Minquon Panchayat, a coalition of First Nations and visible minority writers and artists. The coalition felt excluded by the contemporary definition of community, and sought to draw attention to the issue while also becoming a part of the community." "The New Gallery," Wikipedia, last modified August 20, 2022, 17:29, https://en.wikipedia.org/wiki/The_New_Gallery.

4. Also known as the Oka Crisis, which took place in Kanesatake from July 11 to September 26, 1990.

5. Greg Hill, "Re-investing the Kahswenta: Rotinonhsyonni Identities Today" (master's thesis, Carleton University, 1998), https://curve.carleton.ca/815e19f9-394e-4fcd-b0e3-821cfe5c8d9b.

6. Rice, "Oh So Iroquois," 58.

7. "Shelley Niro: woman, land, river - Artist Talk," interview by Lori Beavis, Art Gallery of Peterborough, February 20, 2019, video, 52:37, https://www.youtube.com/watch?v=BA2QHSxFNng.

8. Quoted in Madeline Lennon, *Shelley Niro: Seeing Through Memory* (London, ON: Blue Medium Press, 2014), 65–66.

9. Ryan Rice, "Taiakio'tenhátie / Freefall: The Photography of Shelley Niro," in *Shelley Niro* (Göttingen: Steidl Verlag, 2018), 80.

10. It was pointed out to me by knowledge holder and wampum scholar Rick Hill that the term *Kahswenta* which is often used in reference to the two-row wampum belt is actually a general word for wampum strung in a belt as opposed to the more specific *tekeni teyohate* describing the two rows of the two-row wampum belt.

11. Considered a symbol of sovereignty. To co-exist peacefully; one row representing Onkwehónwe, the other representing newcomers travelling together down a river in parallel, respecting the individual lifeways of each other.

12. Hill, "Re-investing the Kahswenta," 203.

13. This is evident especially in comparison to the gripped arms of the photograph entitled *Unity* (pp. 228–229). In wampum belt designs, the use of metaphors such as lines joining figures, joined hands, and linked arms can indicate the strength of bonds or relationships between figures/peoples/individuals.

14. See *Parallel Worlds of Women and Warriors* (pp. 232–233). A version of her story is in the text below the stereoscoped image of Jigonsaseh.

15. Two soldiers stand on either side of Mlle Semmer, a young woman from Eclusiers, a village on the Somme. She was honored with the Cross of the Legion of Honor and the War Cross for putting herself at risk to aid the French war effort. See "Keystone View Company Ruined Village of Eclusiers, France. M'lle Semmer Decorated for Heroic Actions under Fire," The Gilder Lehrman Institute of American History, accessed February 8, 2022, https://www.gilderlehrman.org/collection/glc09584086.

16. "Artist Talk: Shelley Niro," Ryerson Image Centre, June 5, 2020, video, 1:04:59, https://www.youtube.com/watch?v=wWfnKgb80eo. See also Niro's unpublished artist statement.

17. Artist statement for *Parallel Worlds of Women and Warriors*.

18. Lennon, *Shelley Niro*, 134.

19. Hill, "Re-investing the Kahswenta," 192–193.

20. The lake was named after the Erie Peoples, the Onkwehónwe, who were inhabitants of the south shore until the mid-seventeenth century. See "Lake Erie," Wikipedia, last modified October 11, 2022, 15:38, https://en.wikipedia.org/wiki/Lake_Erie.

21. While the meaning is disputed, this word is generally accepted to be Rotinonhsyonni in origin. (See "Niagara," Wiktionary, last modified September 1, 2022, 16:35, https://en.wiktionary.org/wiki/Niagara.

22. David Kanatawakhon Maracle, who is also a linguist and language teacher, once told me that the word Ontario came from *Skanyatariyo*, meaning "handsome lake" (which is also the name of a nineteenth century Seneca spiritual leader). According to Wikipedia, the name Ontario is derived from the Huron word *Ontarí'io*, which means "great lake." The Onkwehónwe place names—the remnants of a history overwritten by settlement and dominating historical narratives—are further connections to these lands that persist as markers of presence and absence. See "Lake Ontario," Wikipedia, last modified October 12, 2022, 06:02, https://en.wikipedia.org/wiki/Lake_Ontario.

23. With the access to the satellite imaging we enjoy from our desktops, it is possible to trace the route of the transmission lines from Niagara Falls all the way to the point at which they cross the Grand River near Caledonia, Ontario. Transmission lines cross the Grand River in multiple places but the largest set cross at the Caledonia Bypass. I was able to follow these lines all the way back to Niagara Falls, and they traverse dozens of farms and developments. The lines first go north along the Grand River then to a distribution station at Brant, continuing east, south of Hamilton, along Sinkhole Creek, north of Woodburn, south of Grimsby, to Lincoln, Gibson, crossing Fifteen Mile Creek, through Short Hills Provincial Park, across the Welland Canal, and finally to the Sir Adam Beck Generating Stations at Queenston Heights on the Niagara Gorge. Incidentally, this is directly in line to the Tuscarora Reservoir which feeds the power station on the American side of the river that was created by flooding 550 acres of the Tuscarora Reserve.

24. Hydro towers also appear in additional works such as *Grand River Treaties* (2009), a series that includes variations of earlier photographs.

25. Lennon, *Shelley Niro*, 126.

26. Shelley Niro, "An Essential Personal Journey Through Iroquois Myths, Legends, Icons and History" (master's thesis, University of Western Ontario, 1999), preface.

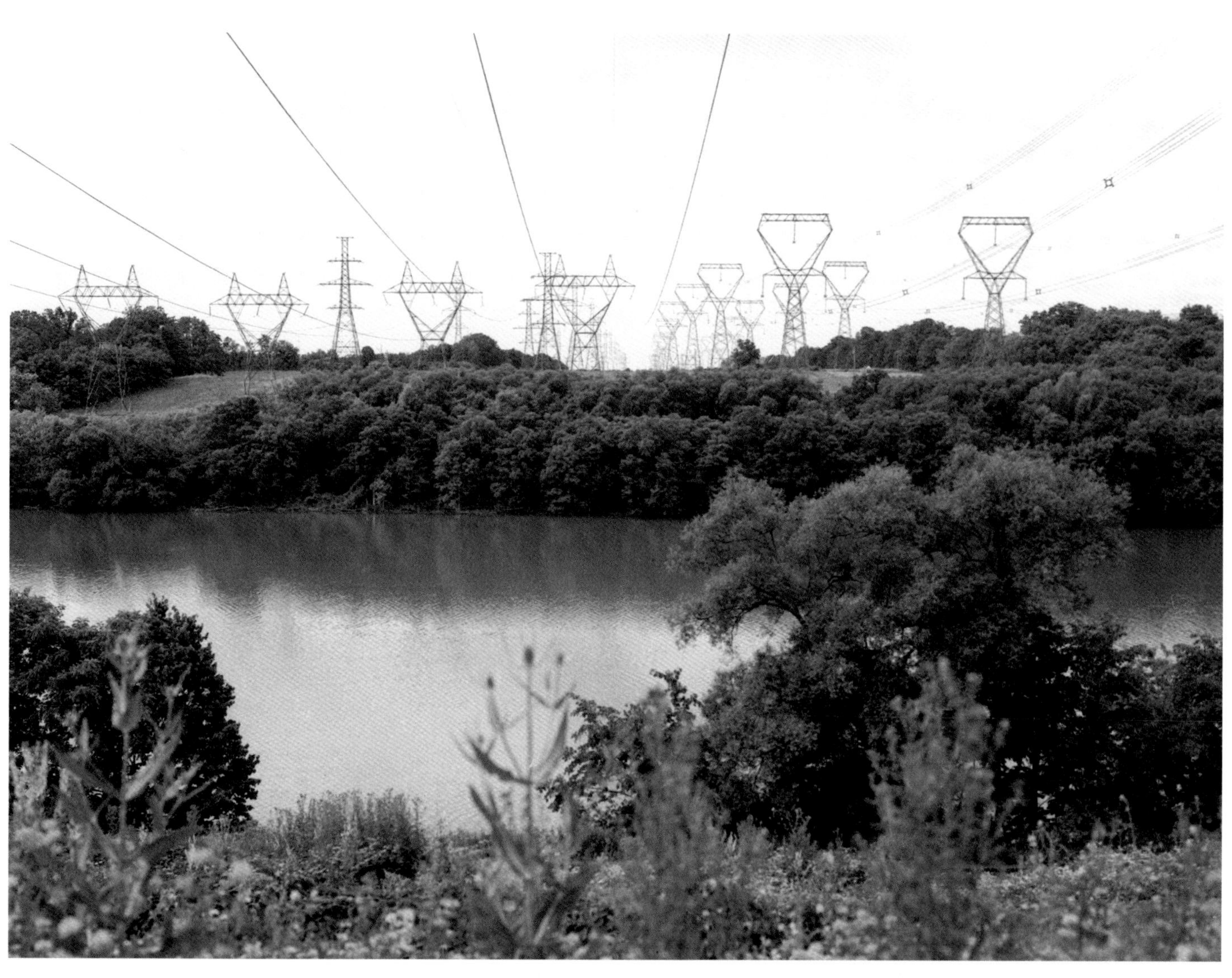

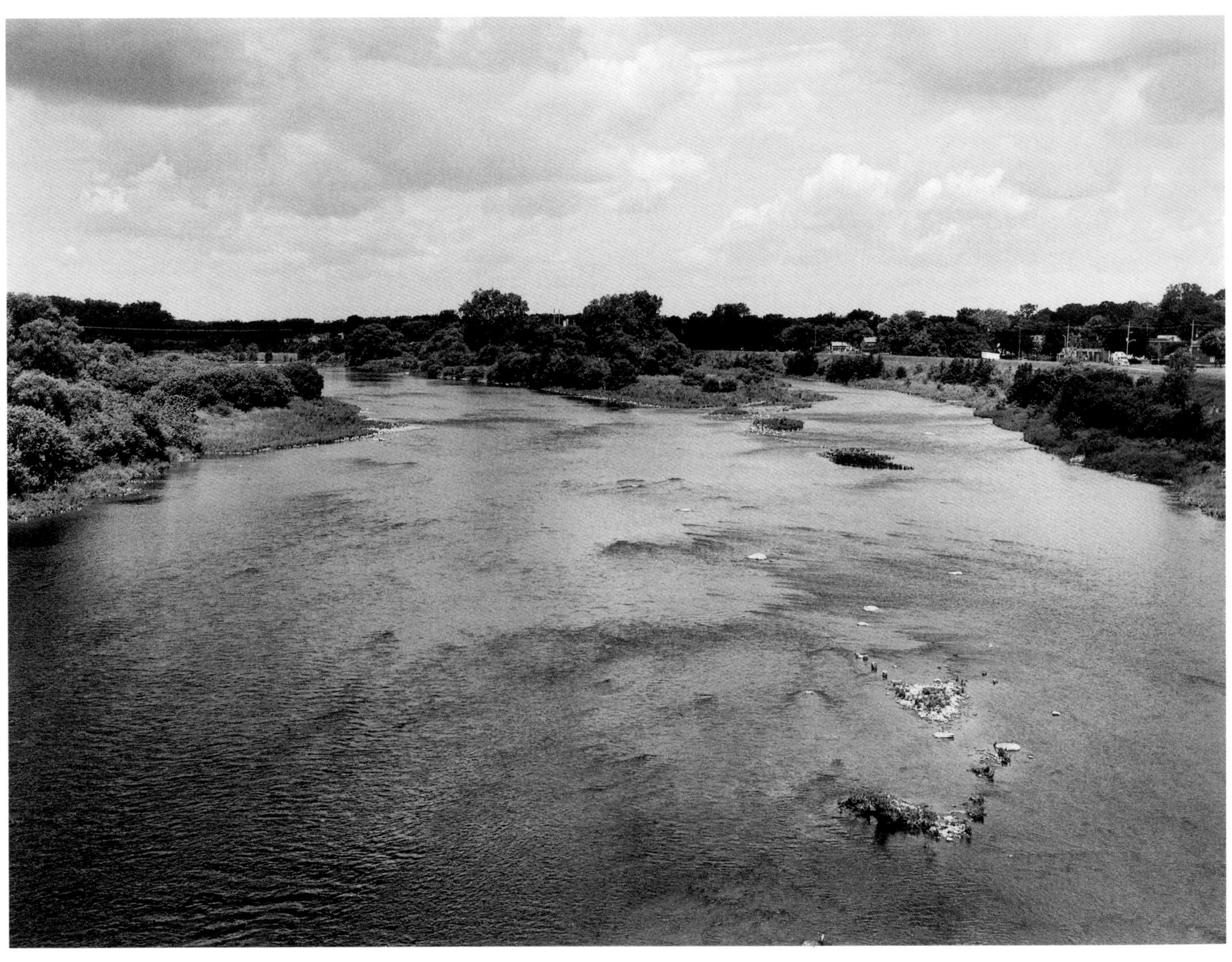

    Brant's Crossing

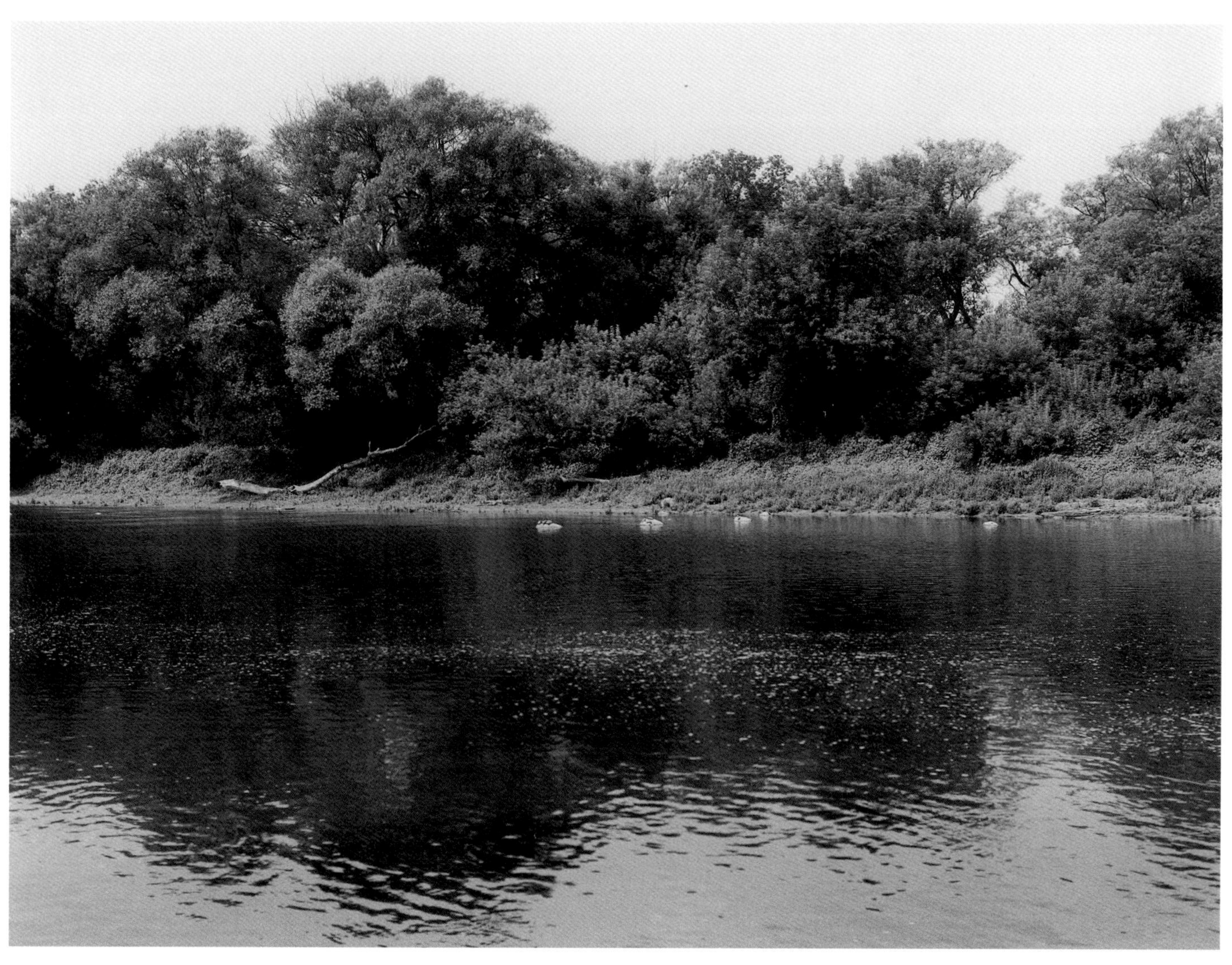

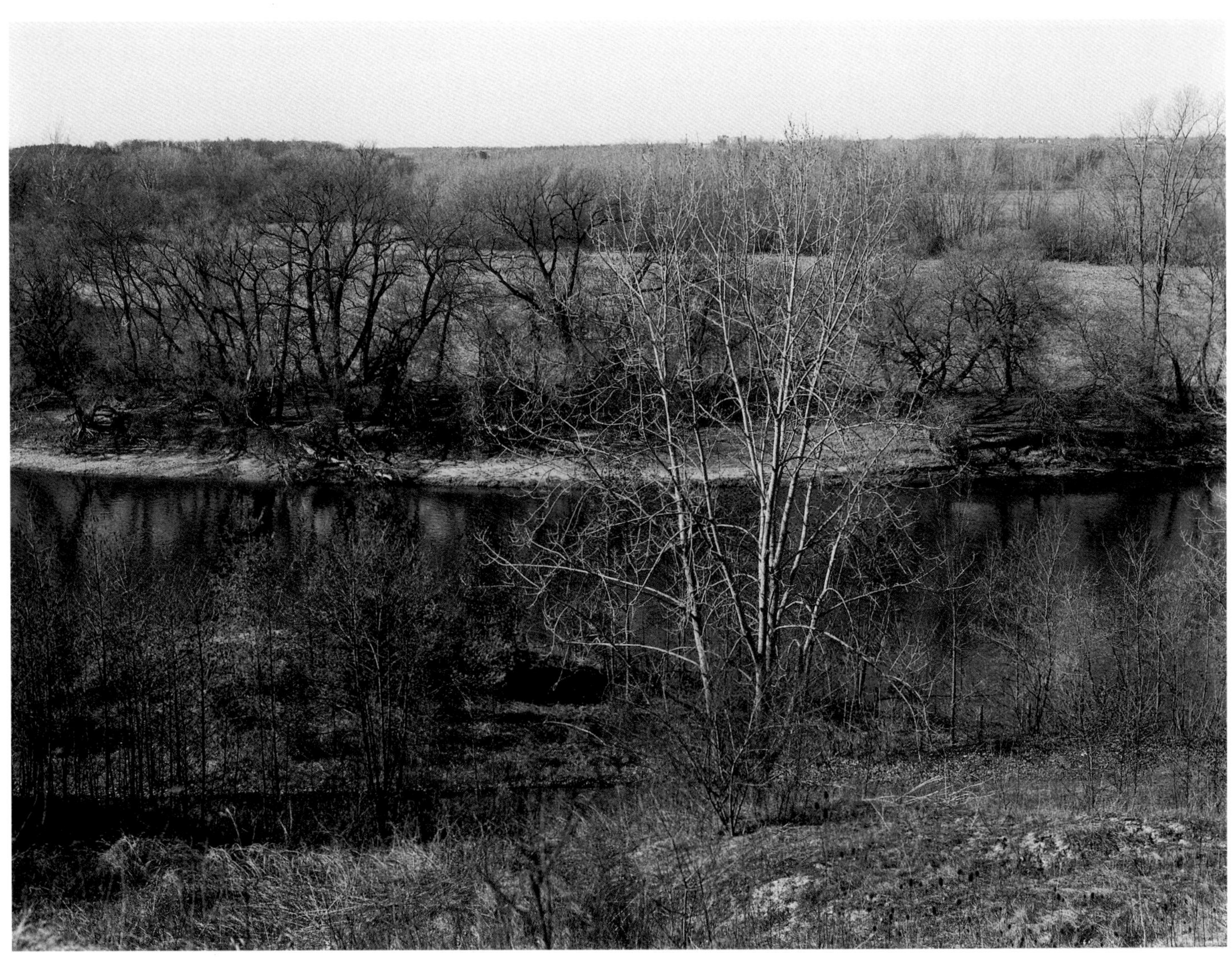

  Tutelo

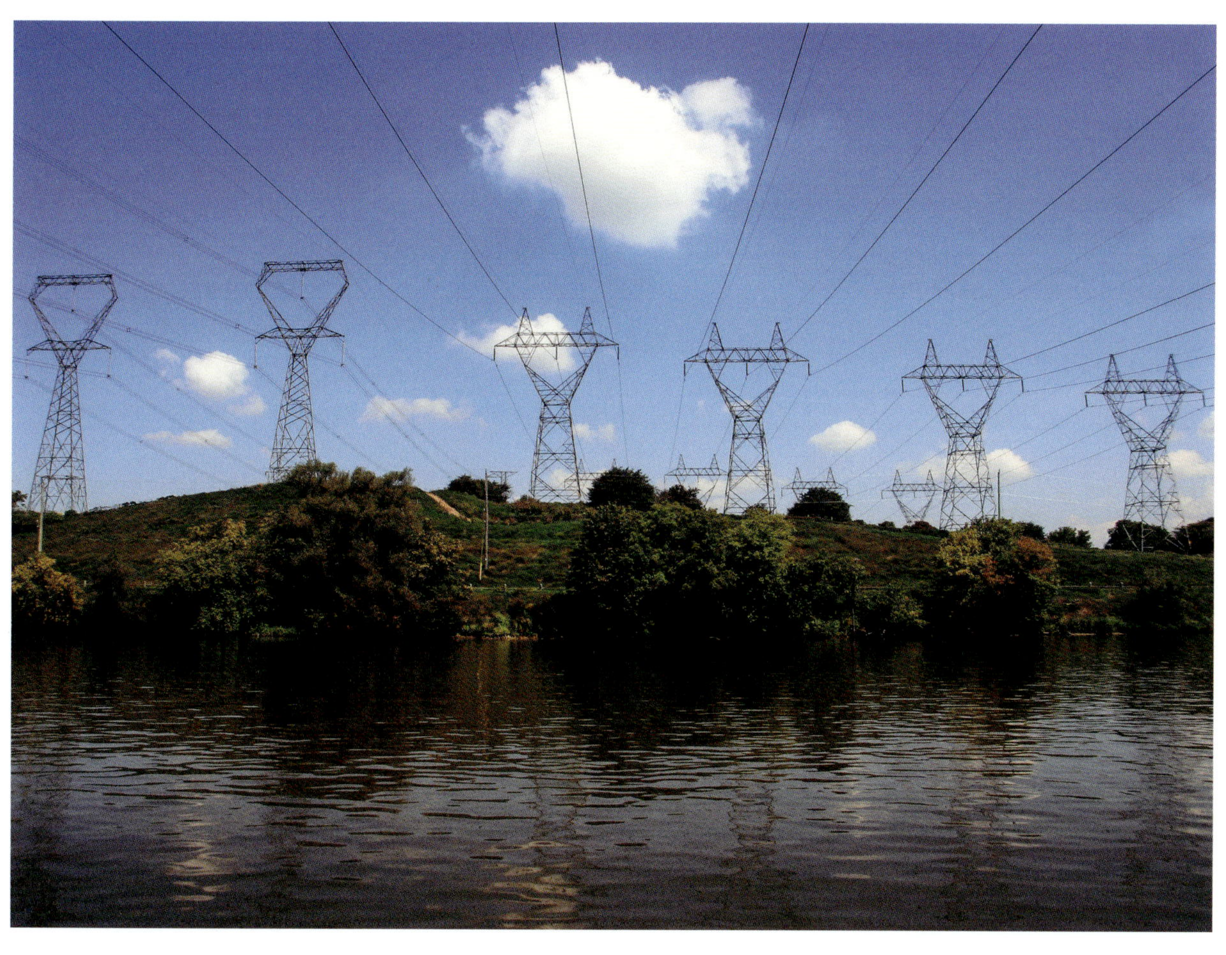

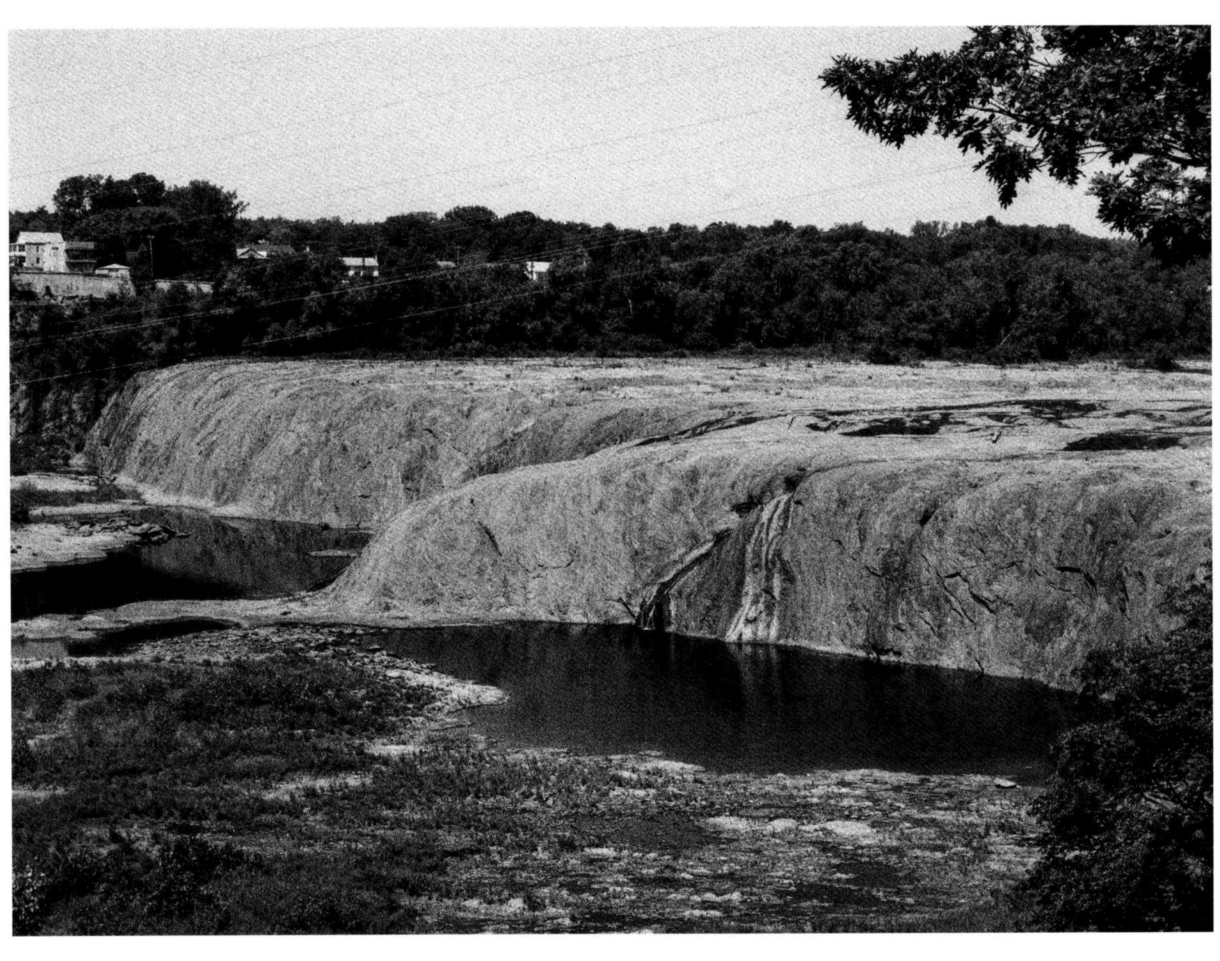

     Where the Mohawk Meets the Hudson

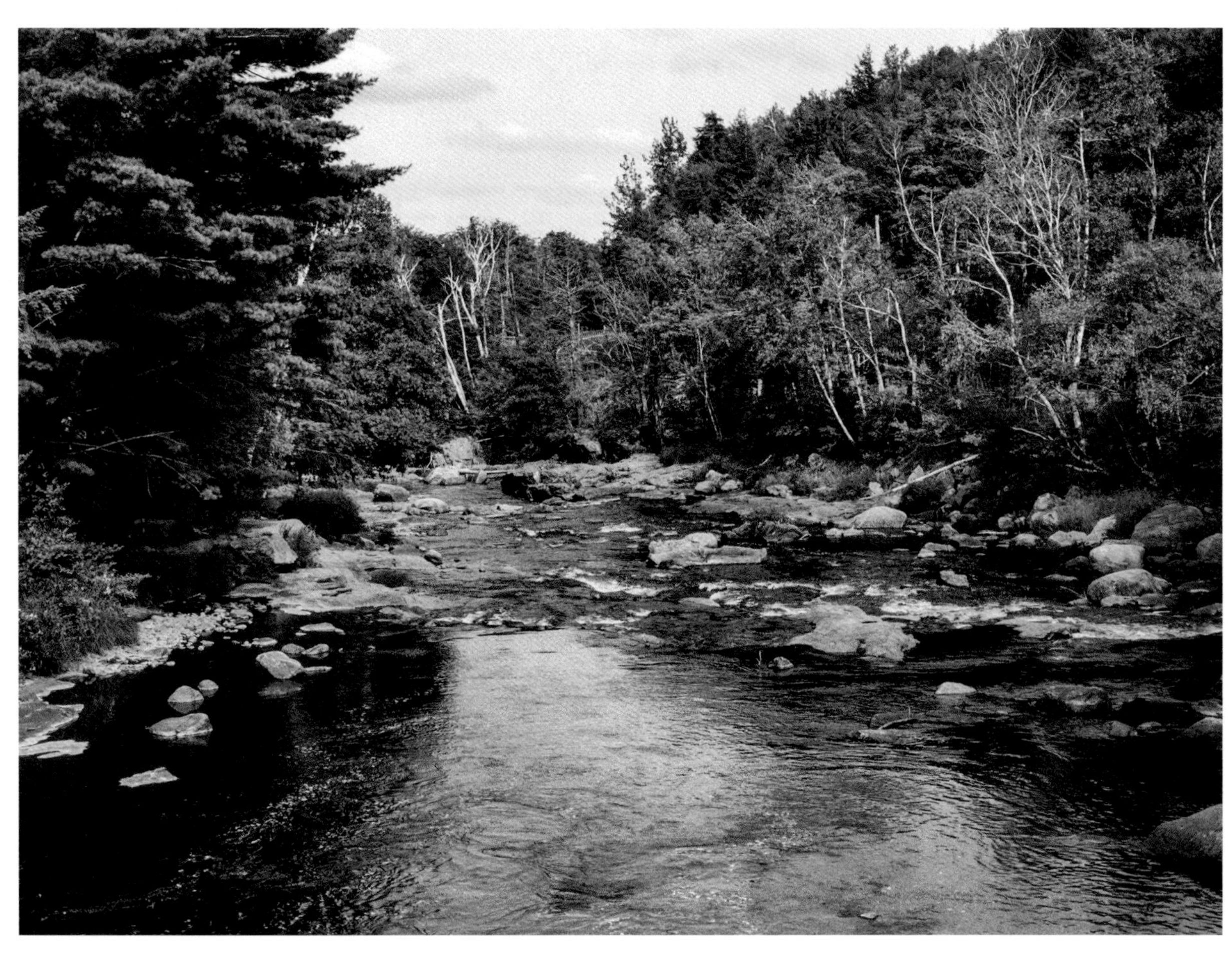

Mohawk River   183

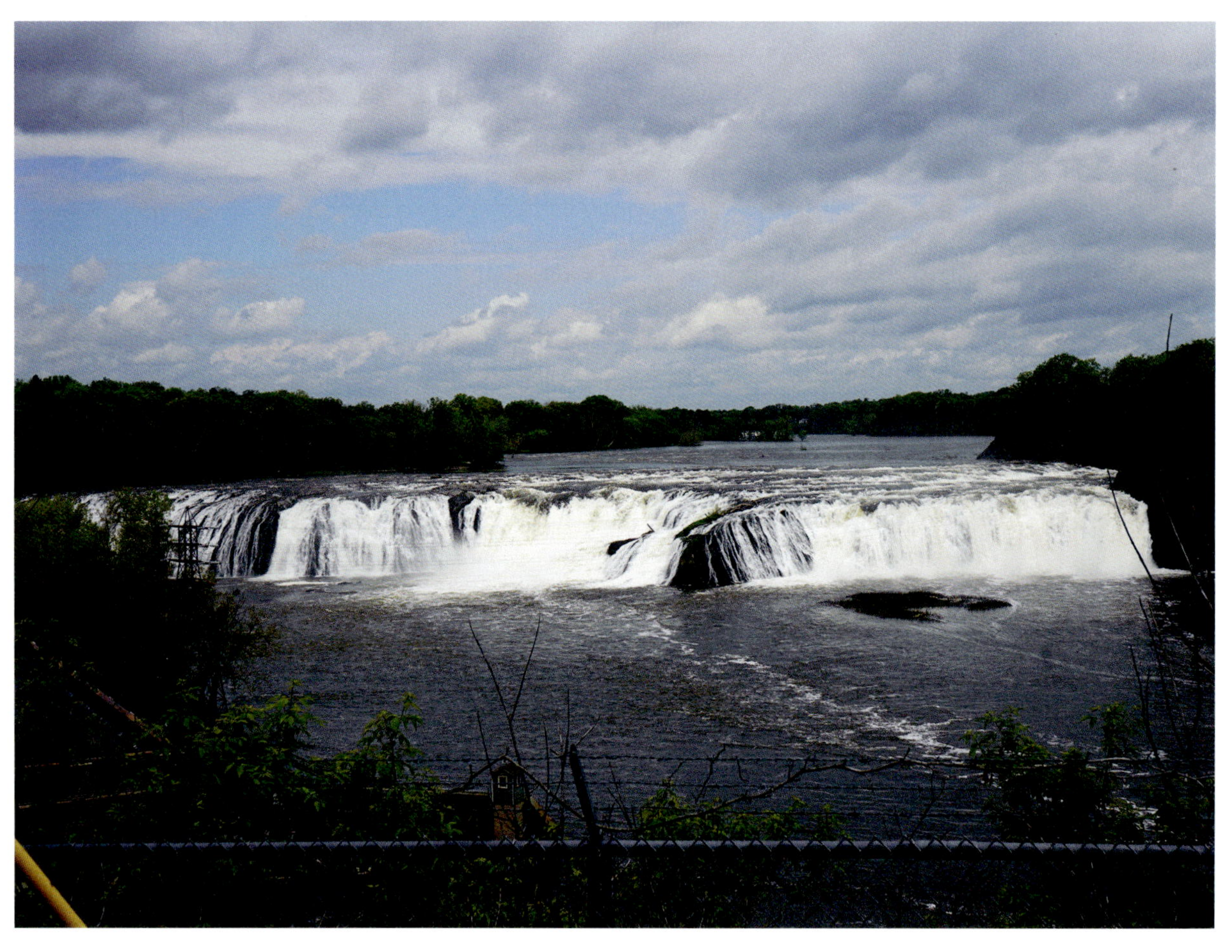

    The Cohoes

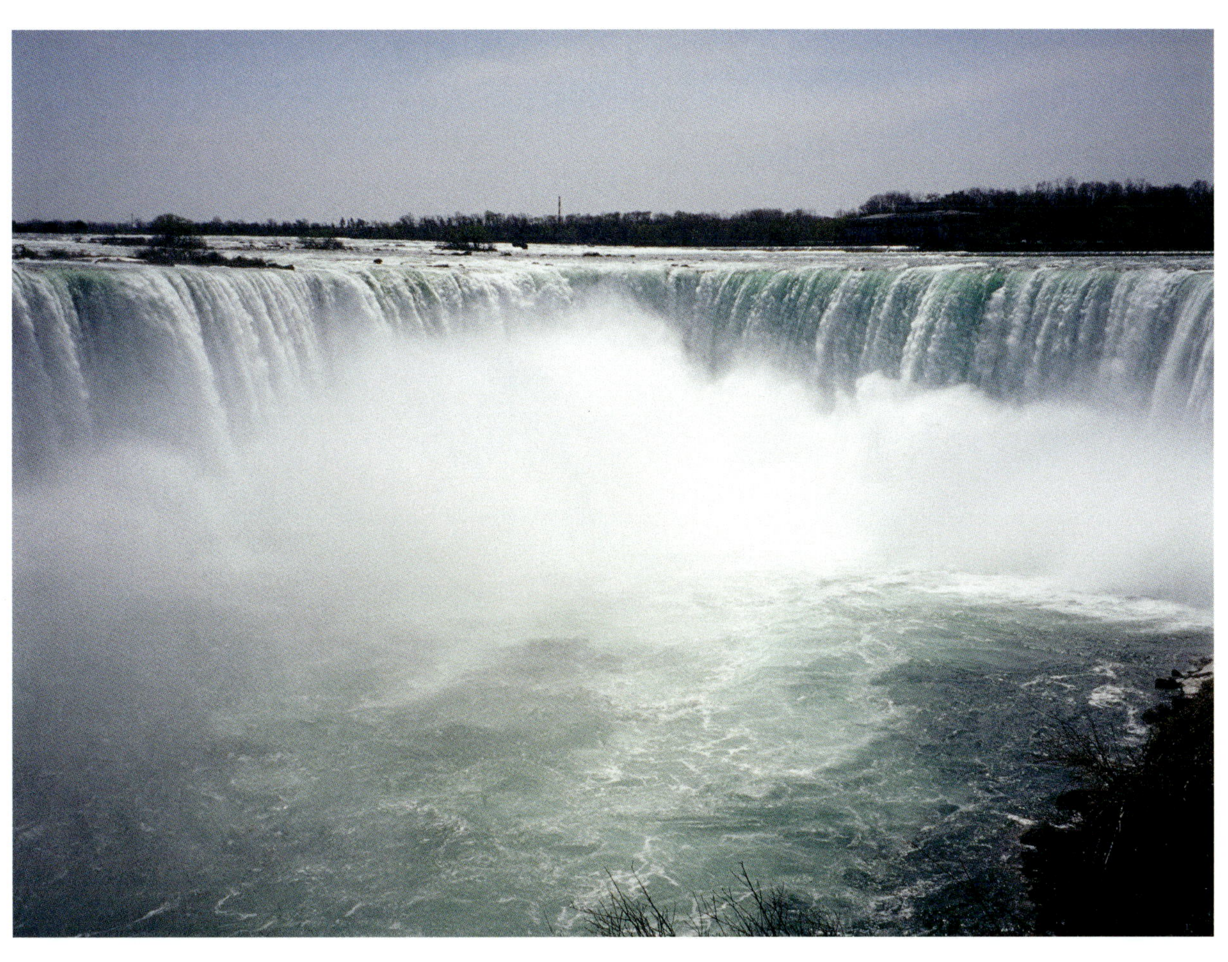

Niagara Falls 185

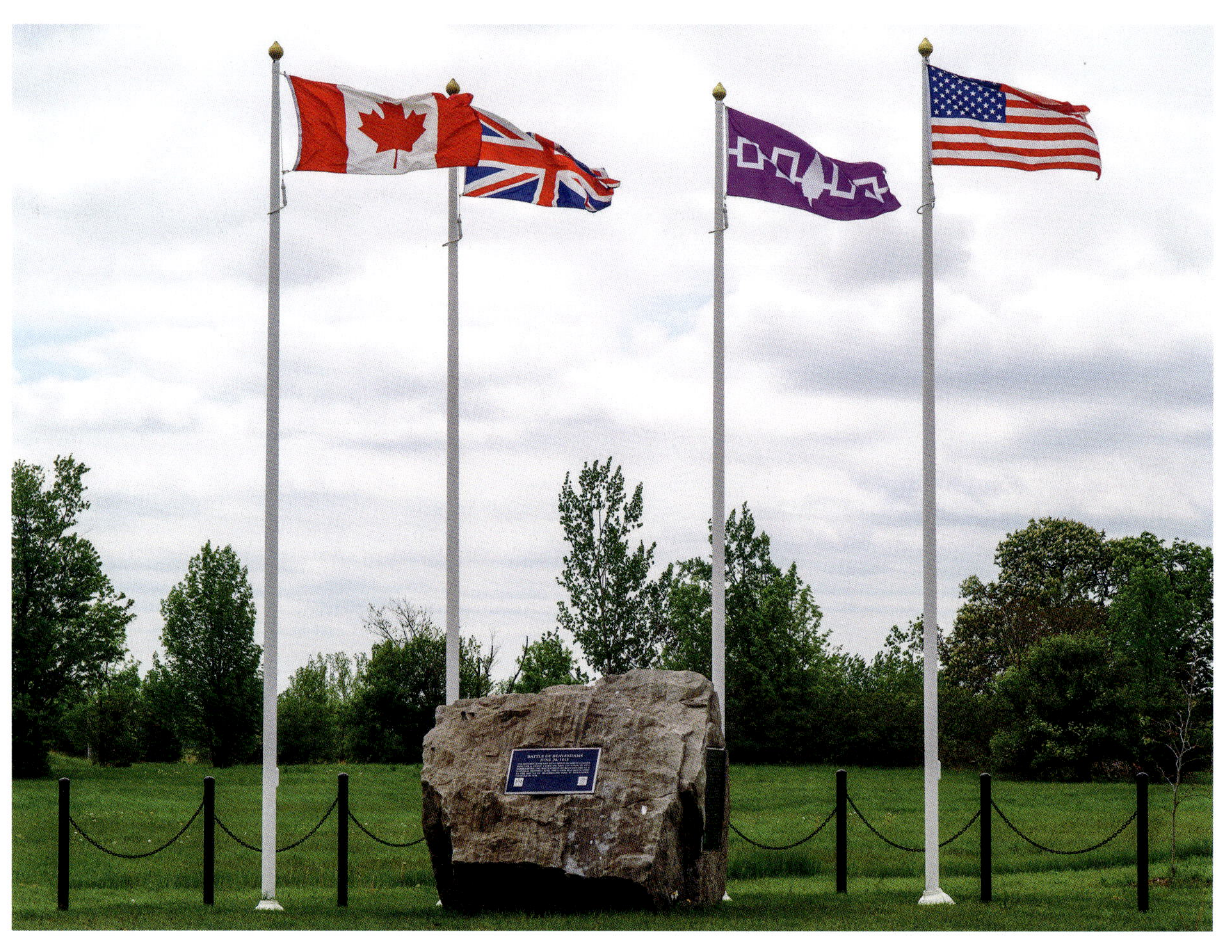

  Battle at Beaver Dam Site

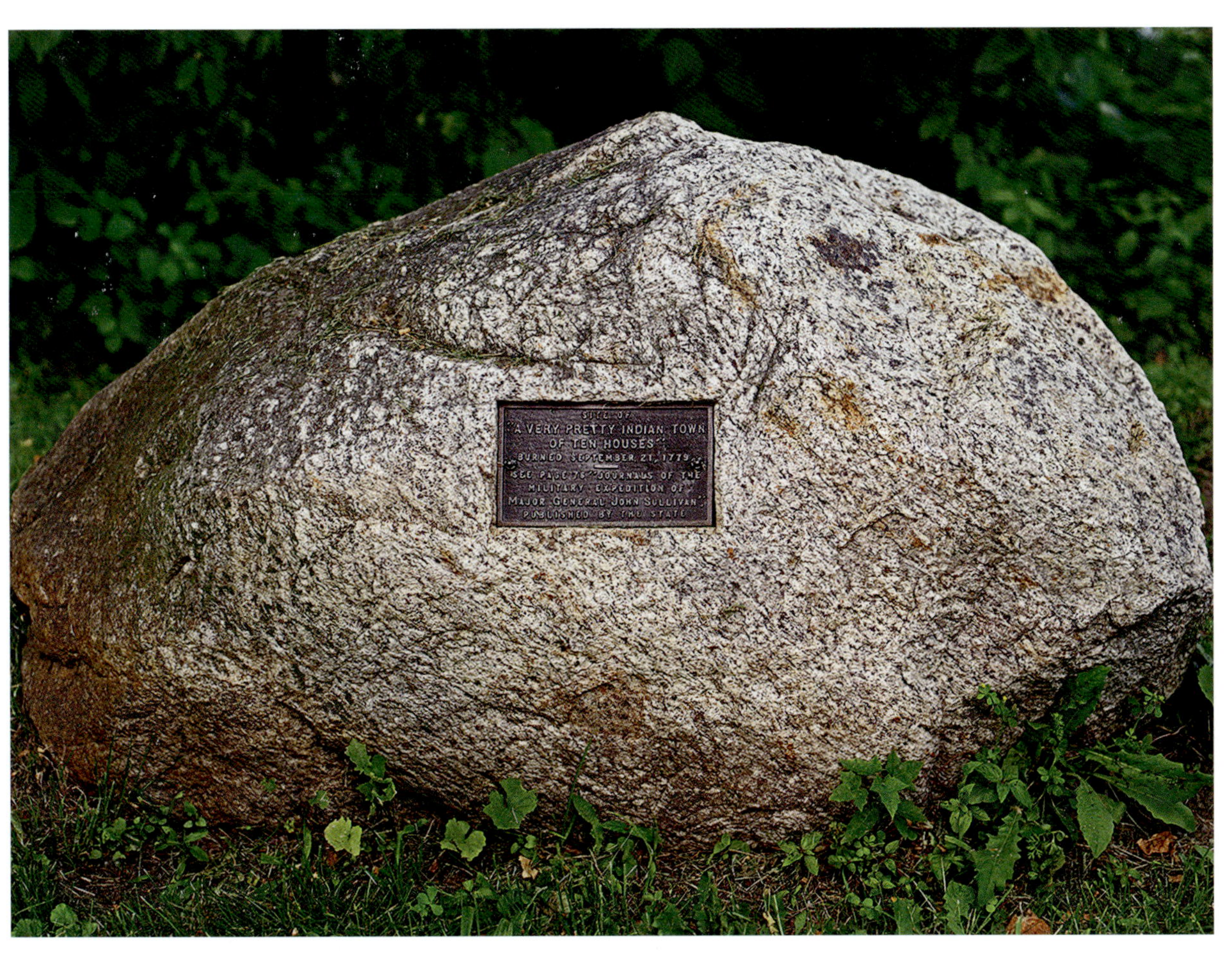

SITE OF
"A VERY PRETTY INDIAN TOWN
OF TEN HOUSES"
BURNED SEPTEMBER 21, 1779
SEE PAGE 76 "JOURNALS OF THE
MILITARY EXPEDITION OF
MAJOR GENERAL JOHN SULLIVAN"
PUBLISHED BY THE STATE

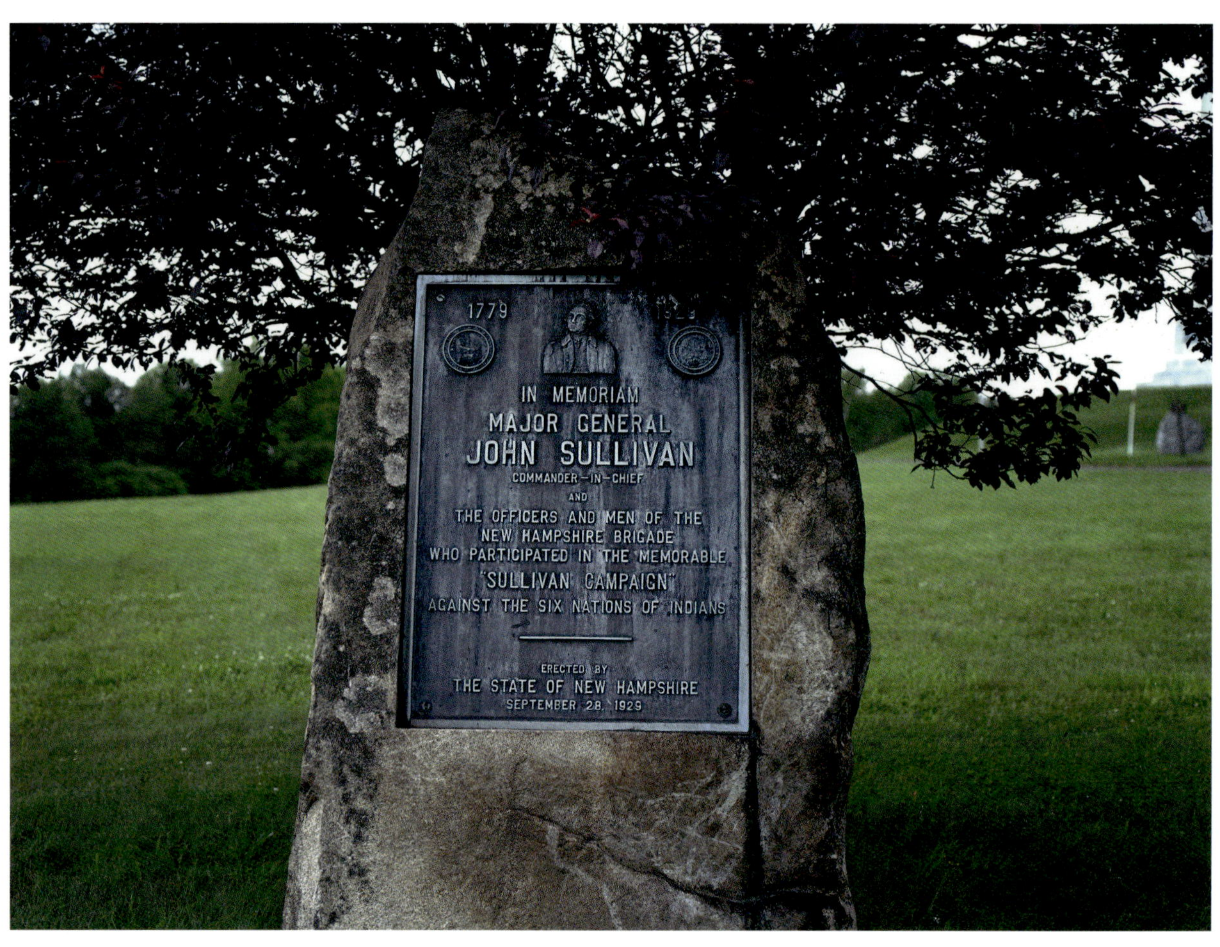

  Against the Six Nations

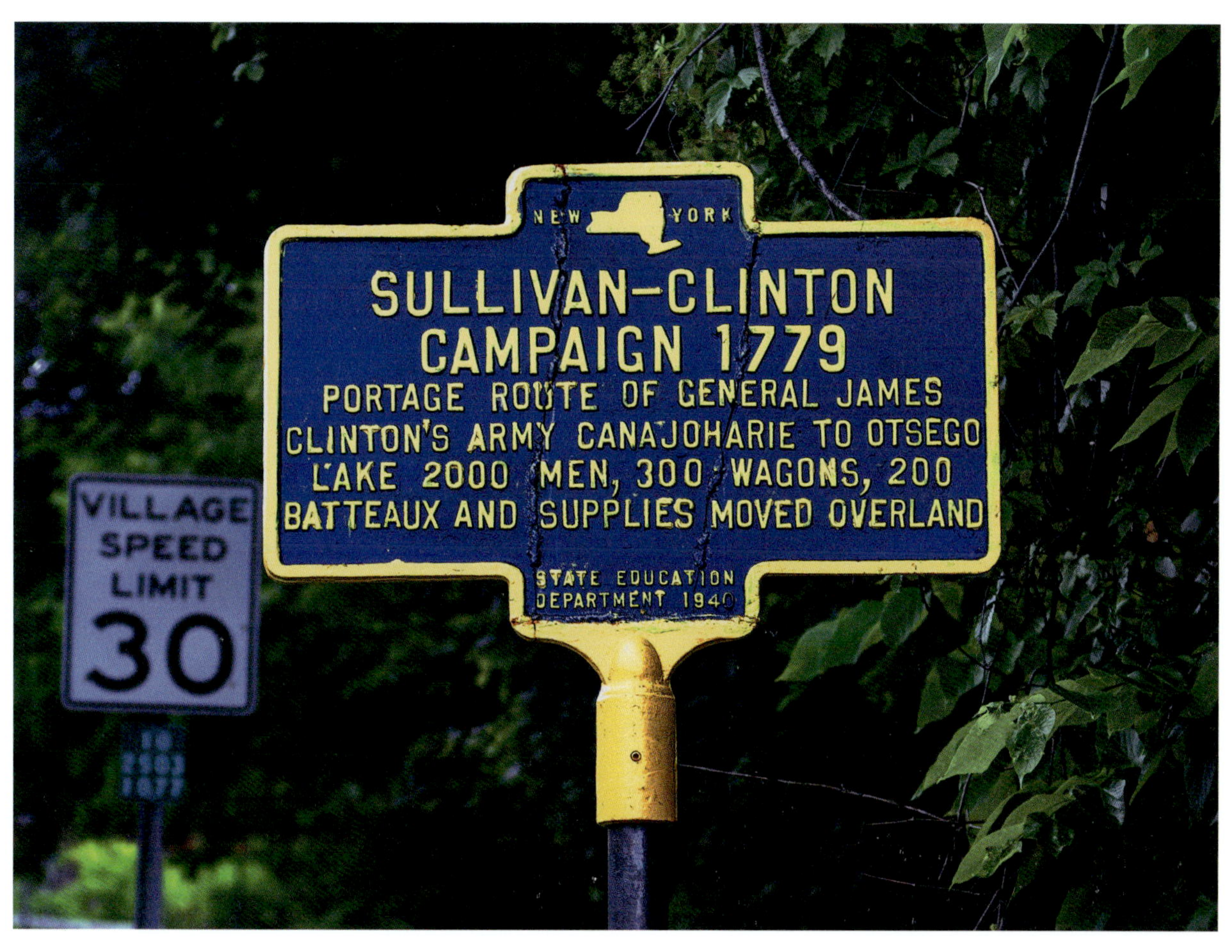

NEW YORK
SULLIVAN–CLINTON
CAMPAIGN 1779
PORTAGE ROUTE OF GENERAL JAMES
CLINTON'S ARMY CANAJOHARIE TO OTSEGO
LAKE 2000 MEN, 300 WAGONS, 200
BATTEAUX AND SUPPLIES MOVED OVERLAND
STATE EDUCATION
DEPARTMENT 1940
VILLAGE
SPEED
LIMIT
30

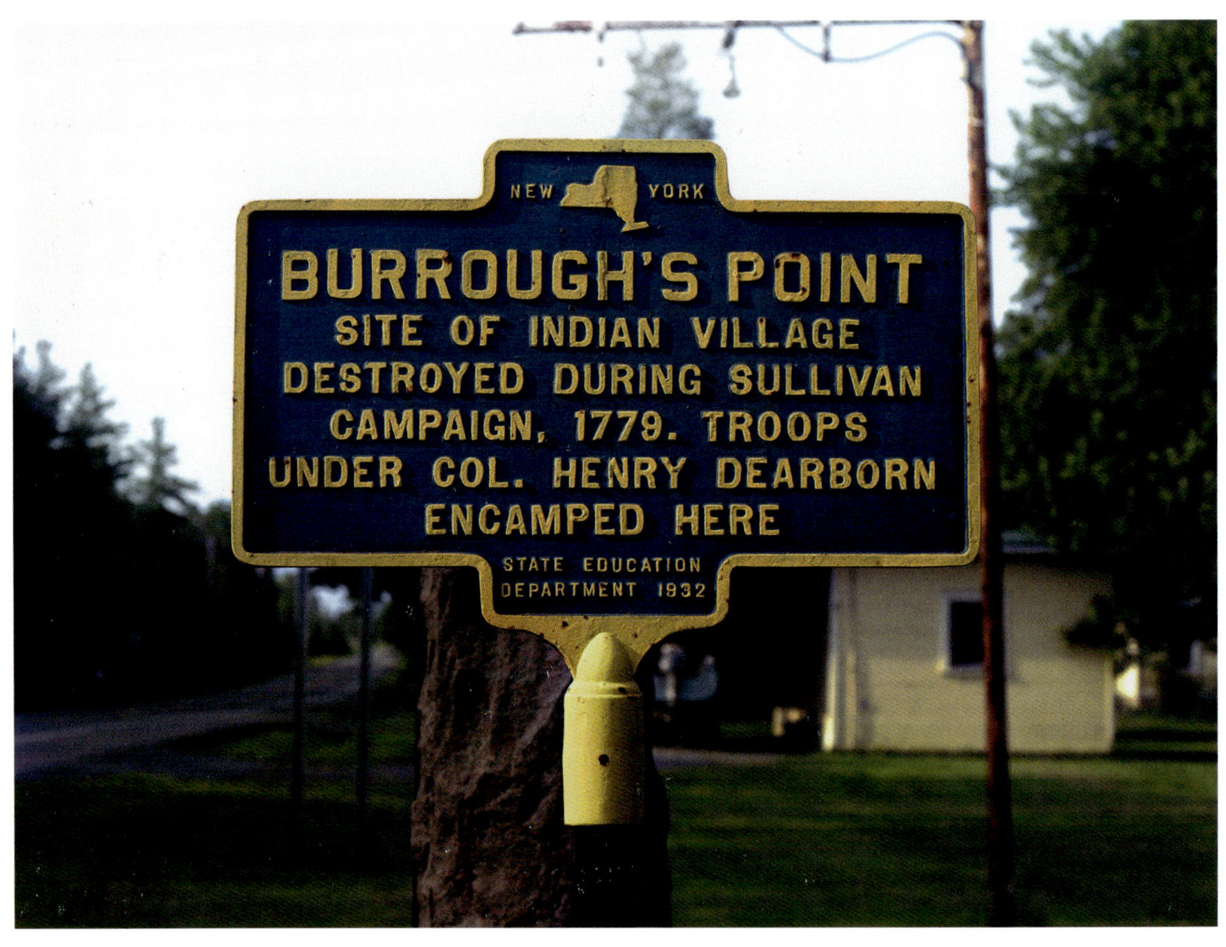

NEW YORK
BURROUGH'S POINT
SITE OF INDIAN VILLAGE
DESTROYED DURING SULLIVAN
CAMPAIGN, 1779. TROOPS
UNDER COL. HENRY DEARBORN
ENCAMPED HERE
STATE EDUCATION
DEPARTMENT 1932

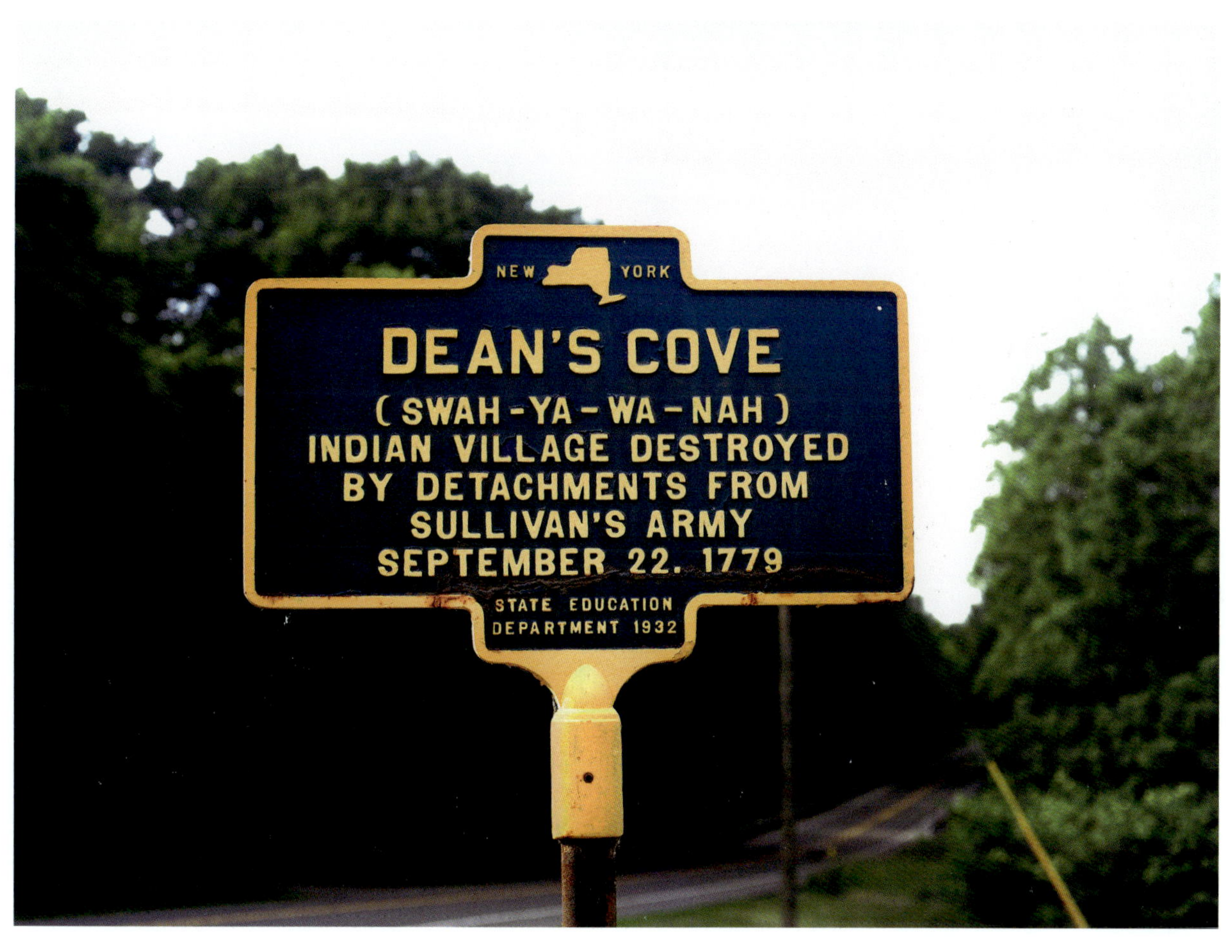

NEW YORK
DEAN'S COVE
(SWAH – YA – WA – NAH)
INDIAN VILLAGE DESTROYED
BY DETACHMENTS FROM
SULLIVAN'S ARMY
SEPTEMBER 22. 1779
STATE EDUCATION
DEPARTMENT 1932

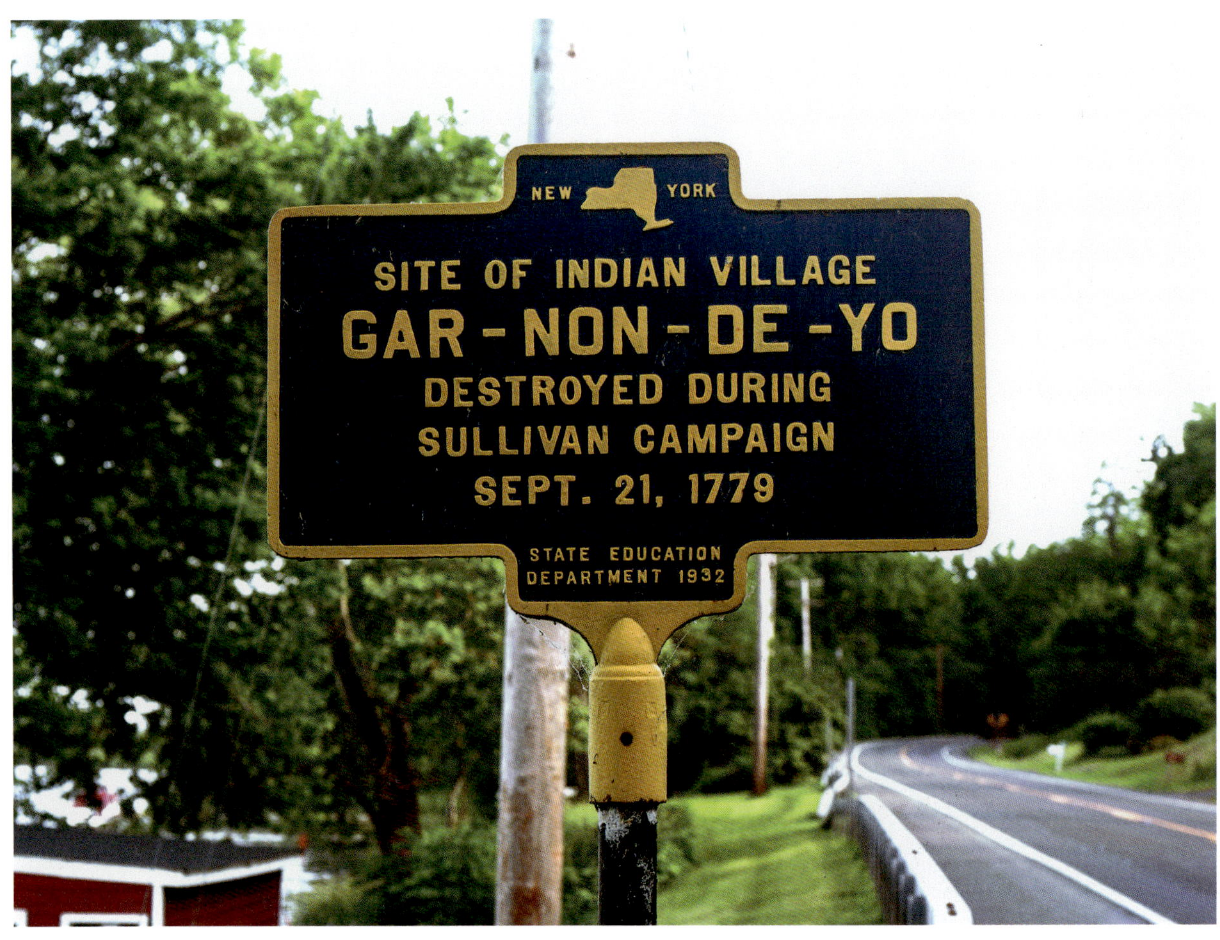
NEW YORK
SITE OF INDIAN VILLAGE
GAR - NON - DE - YO
DESTROYED DURING
SULLIVAN CAMPAIGN
SEPT. 21, 1779
STATE EDUCATION
DEPARTMENT 1932

Gar-Non-De-Yo

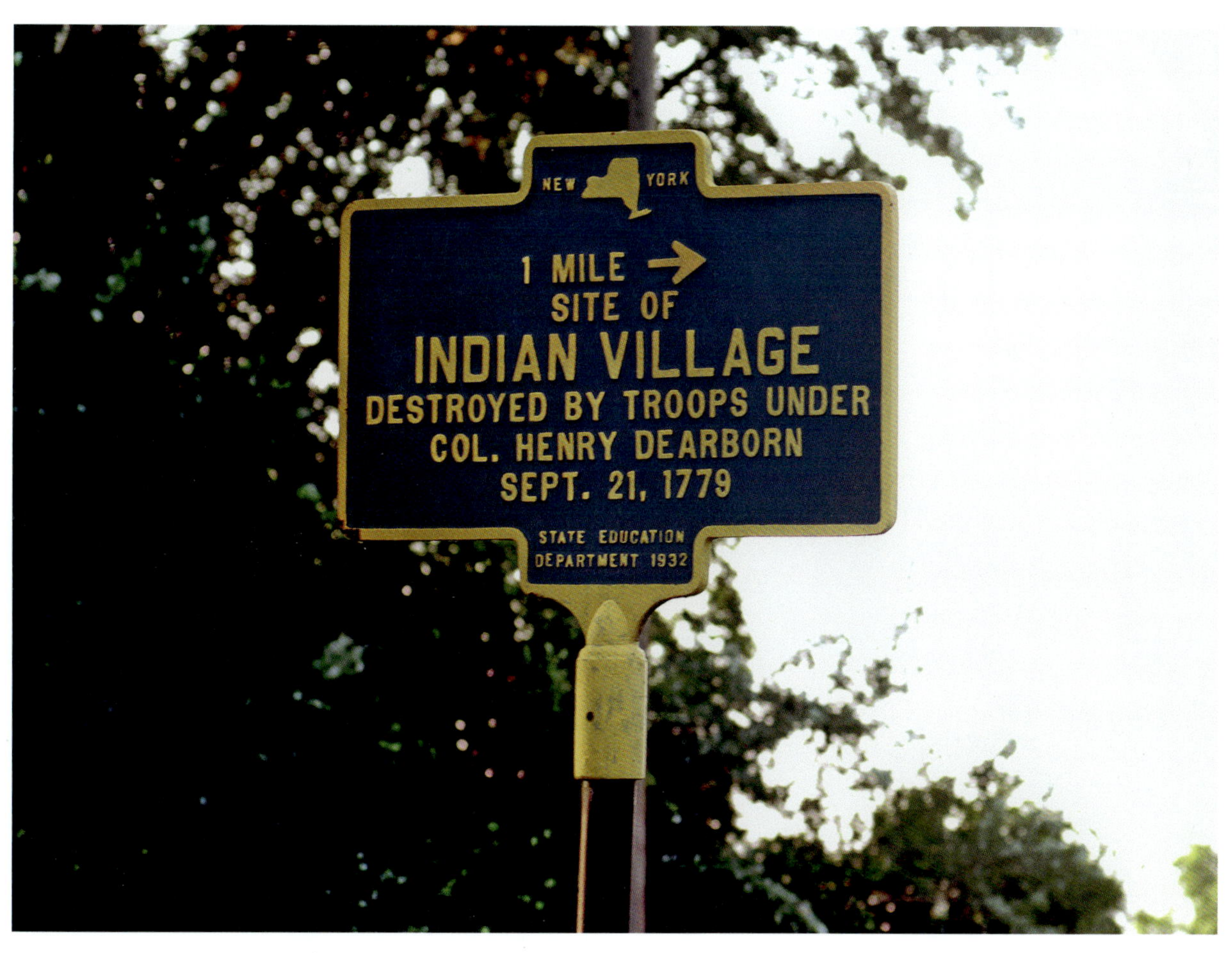
NEW YORK
1 MILE →
SITE OF
INDIAN VILLAGE
DESTROYED BY TROOPS UNDER
COL. HENRY DEARBORN
SEPT. 21, 1779
STATE EDUCATION
DEPARTMENT 1932

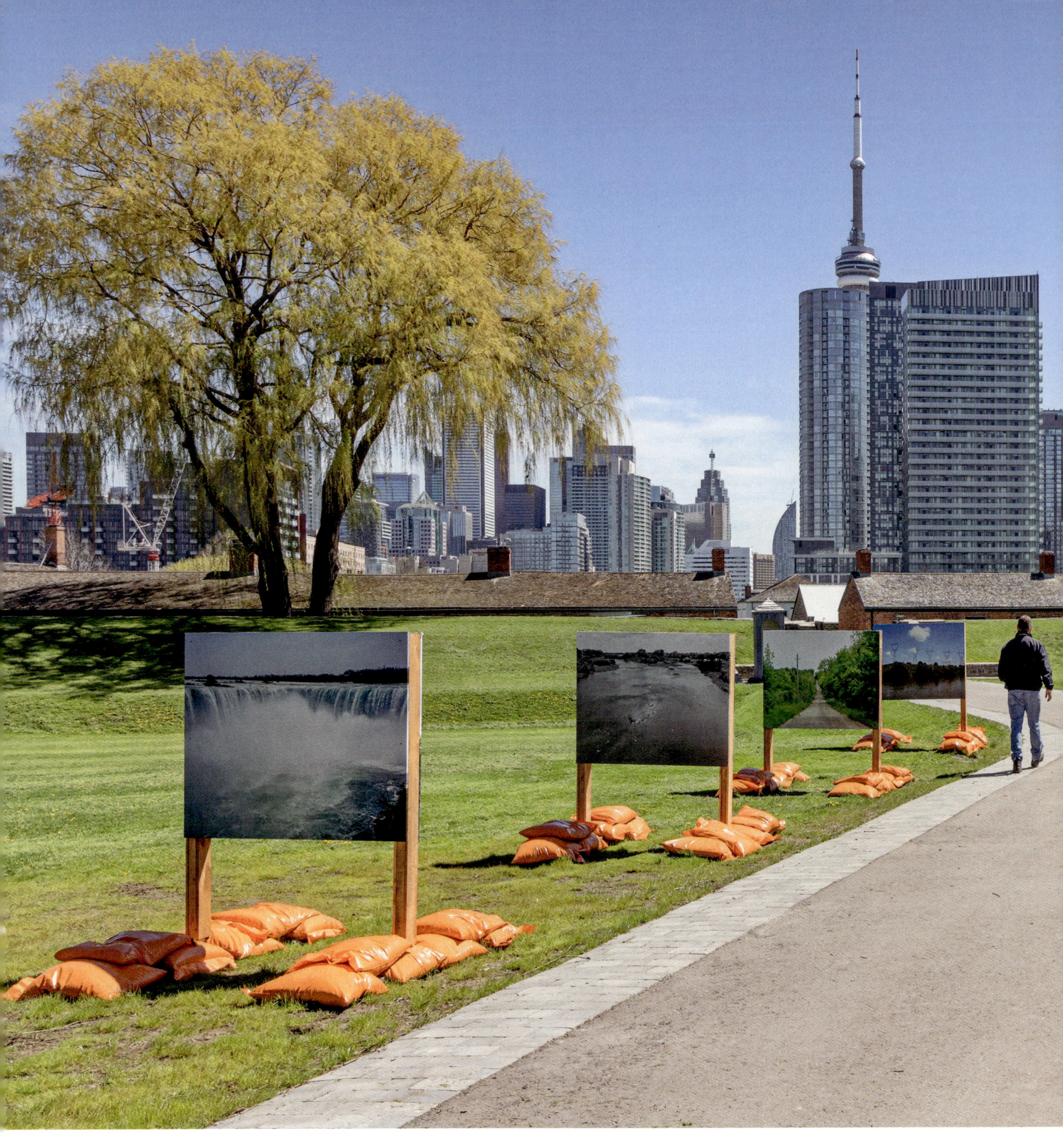

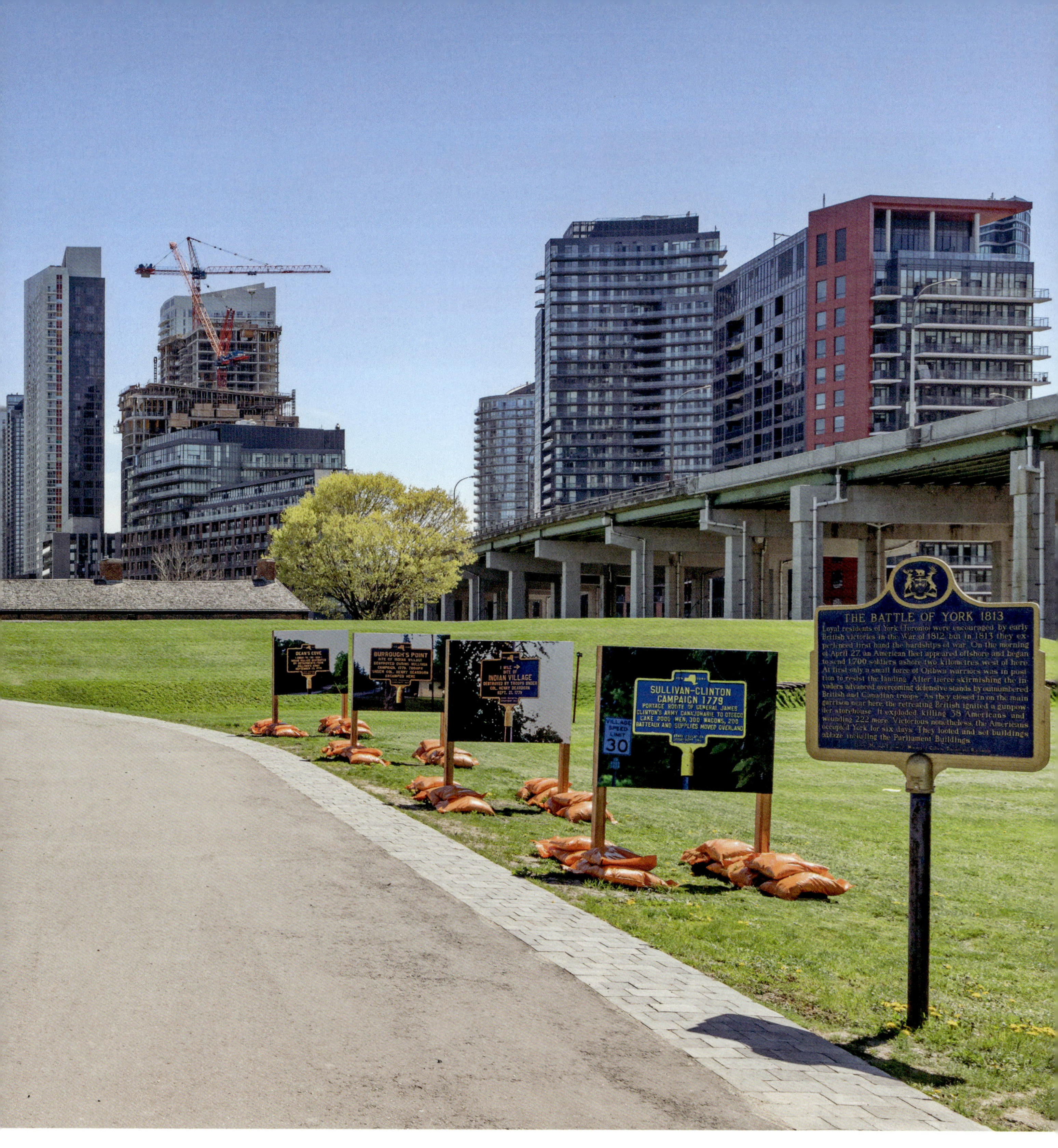

Installation view of **Battlefields of My Ancestors** (2015), Old Fort York, Toronto, 2017
Photograph by Toni Hafkenscheid / Courtesy Scotiabank CONTACT Photography Festival

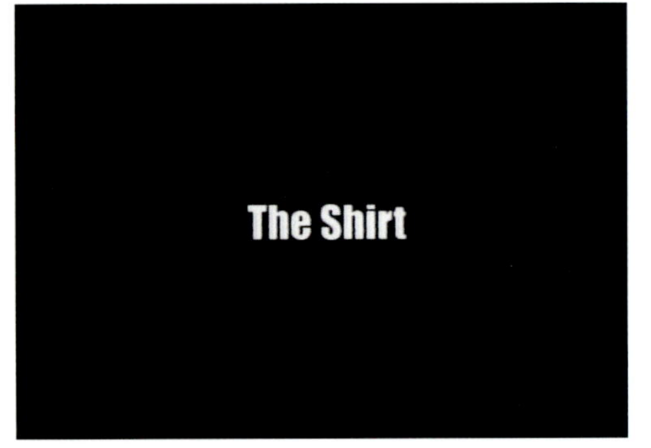

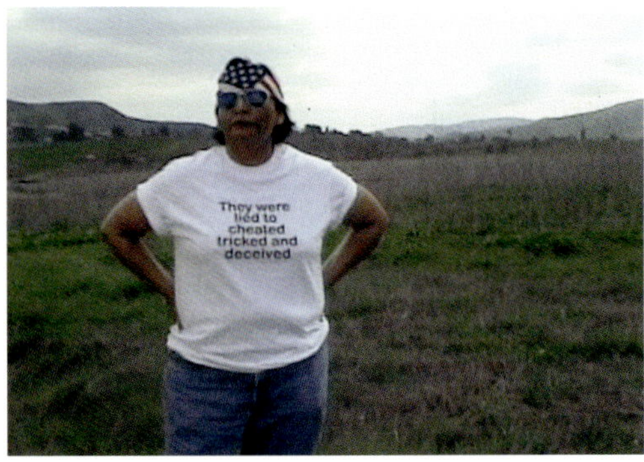

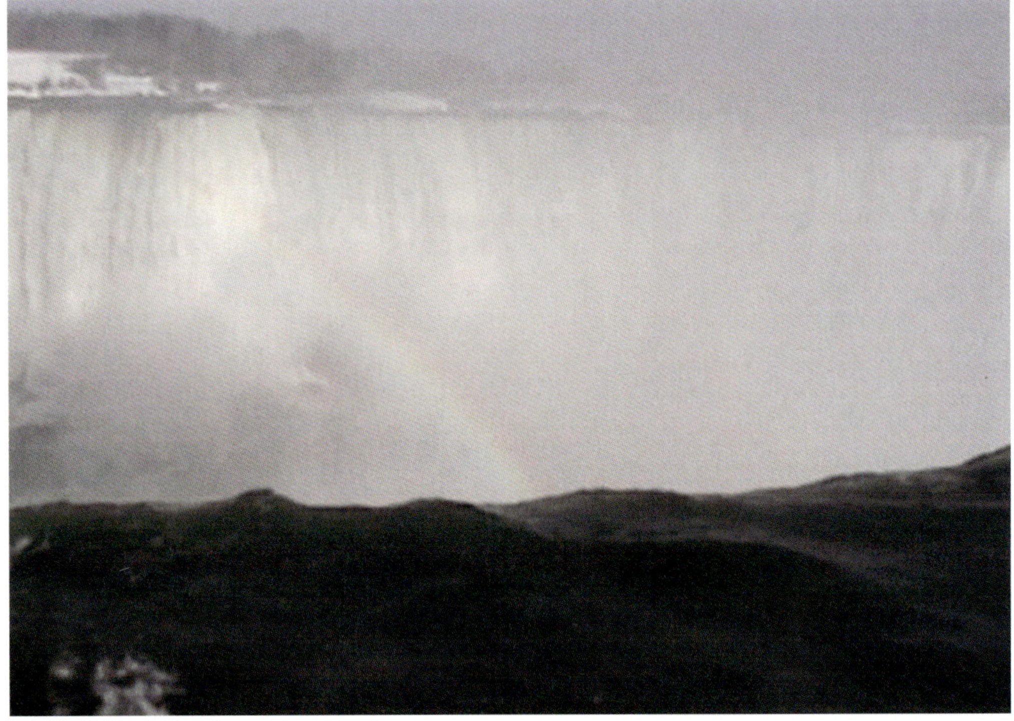

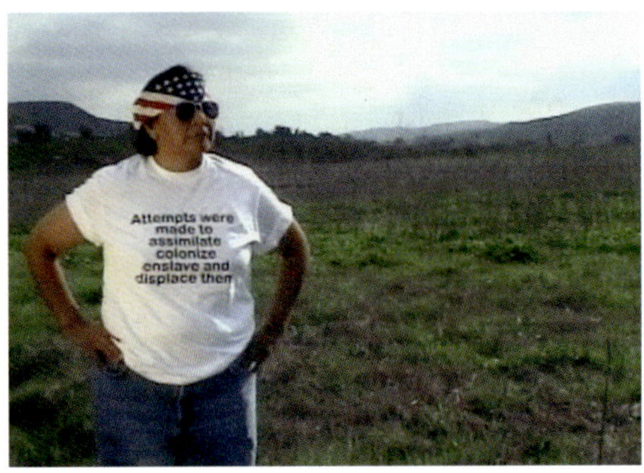

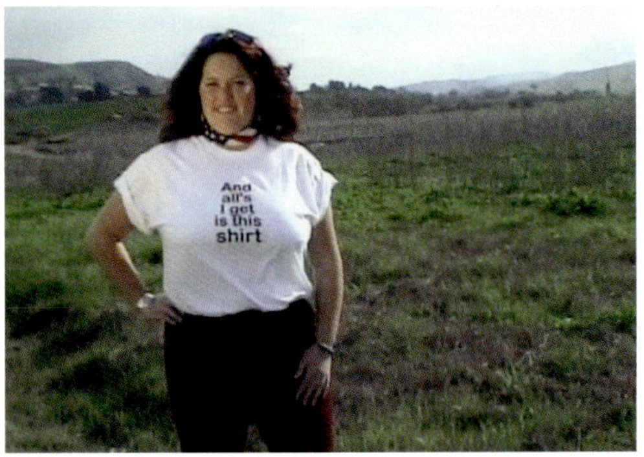

 Stills from **The Shirt**, 2003

The Shirt, 2003 >

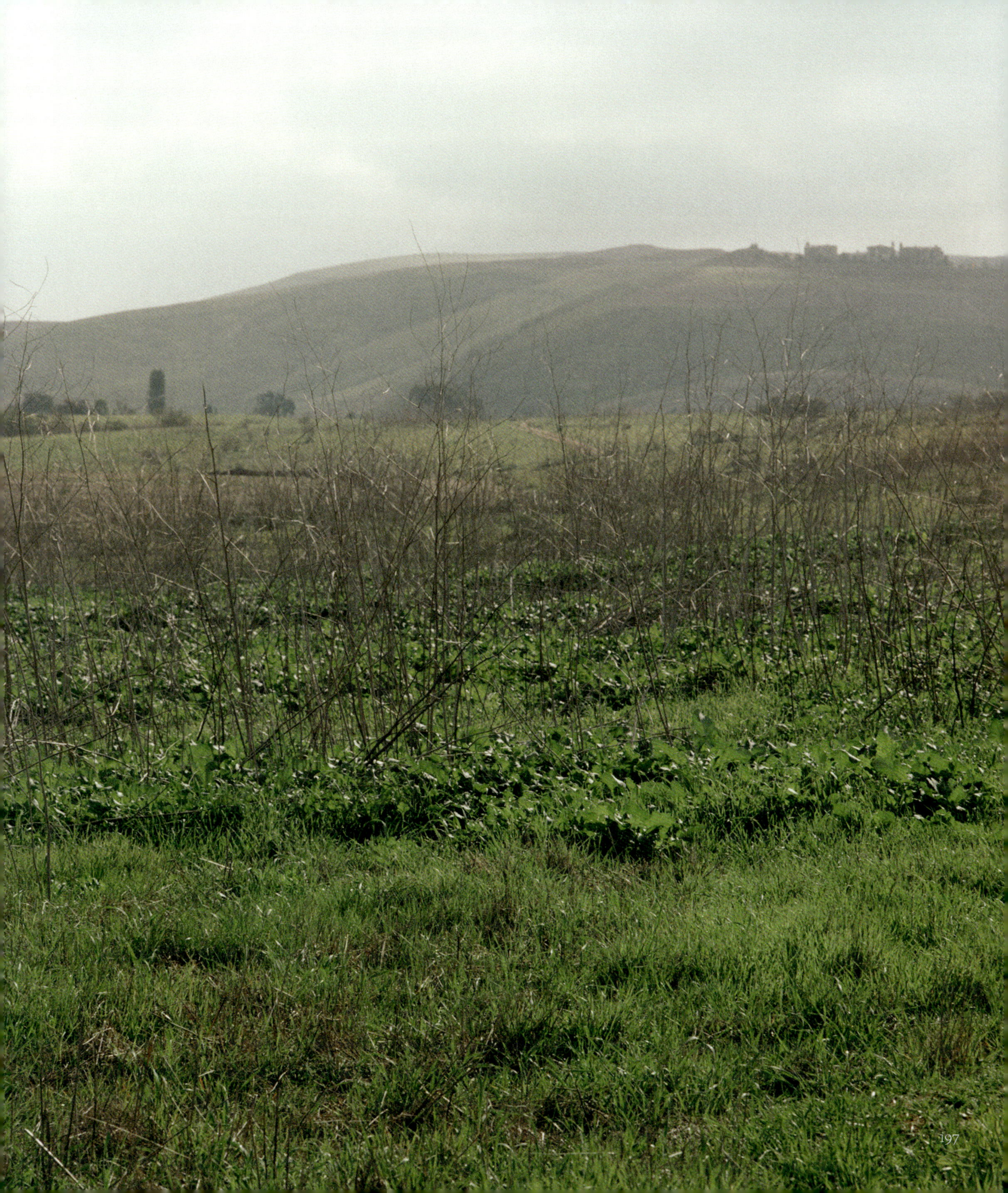

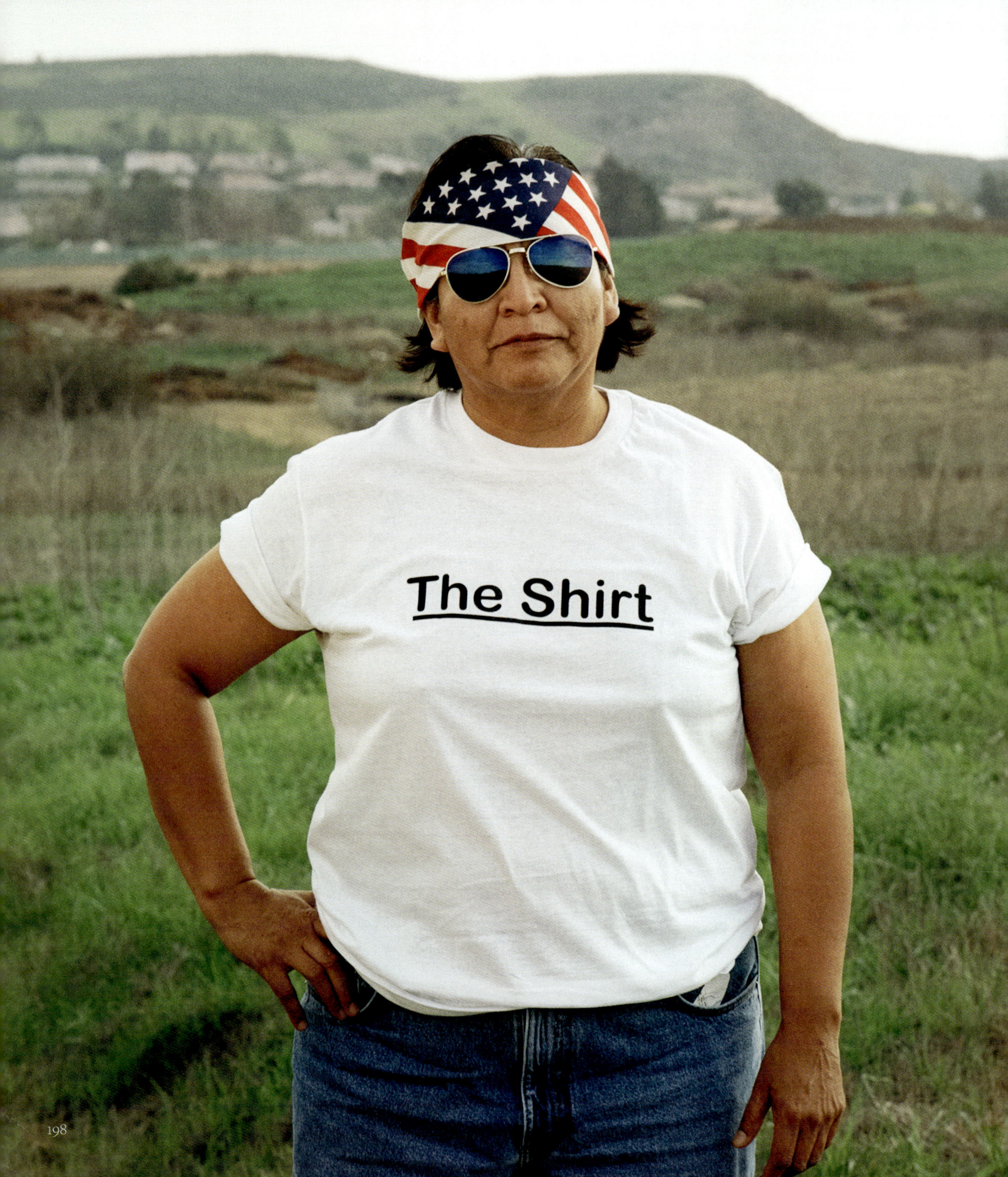

The Shirt

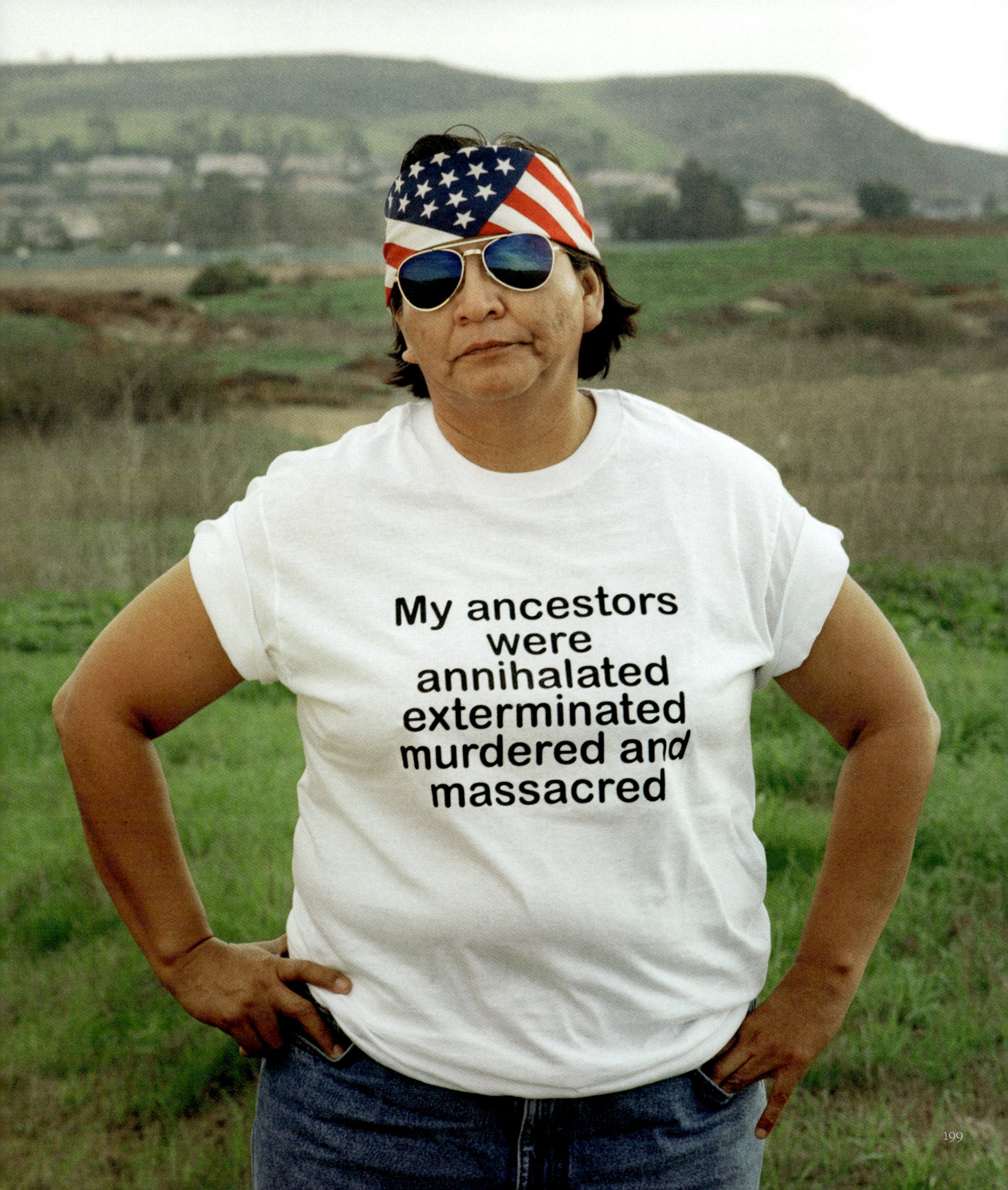

My ancestors
were
annihalated
exterminated
murdered and
massacred

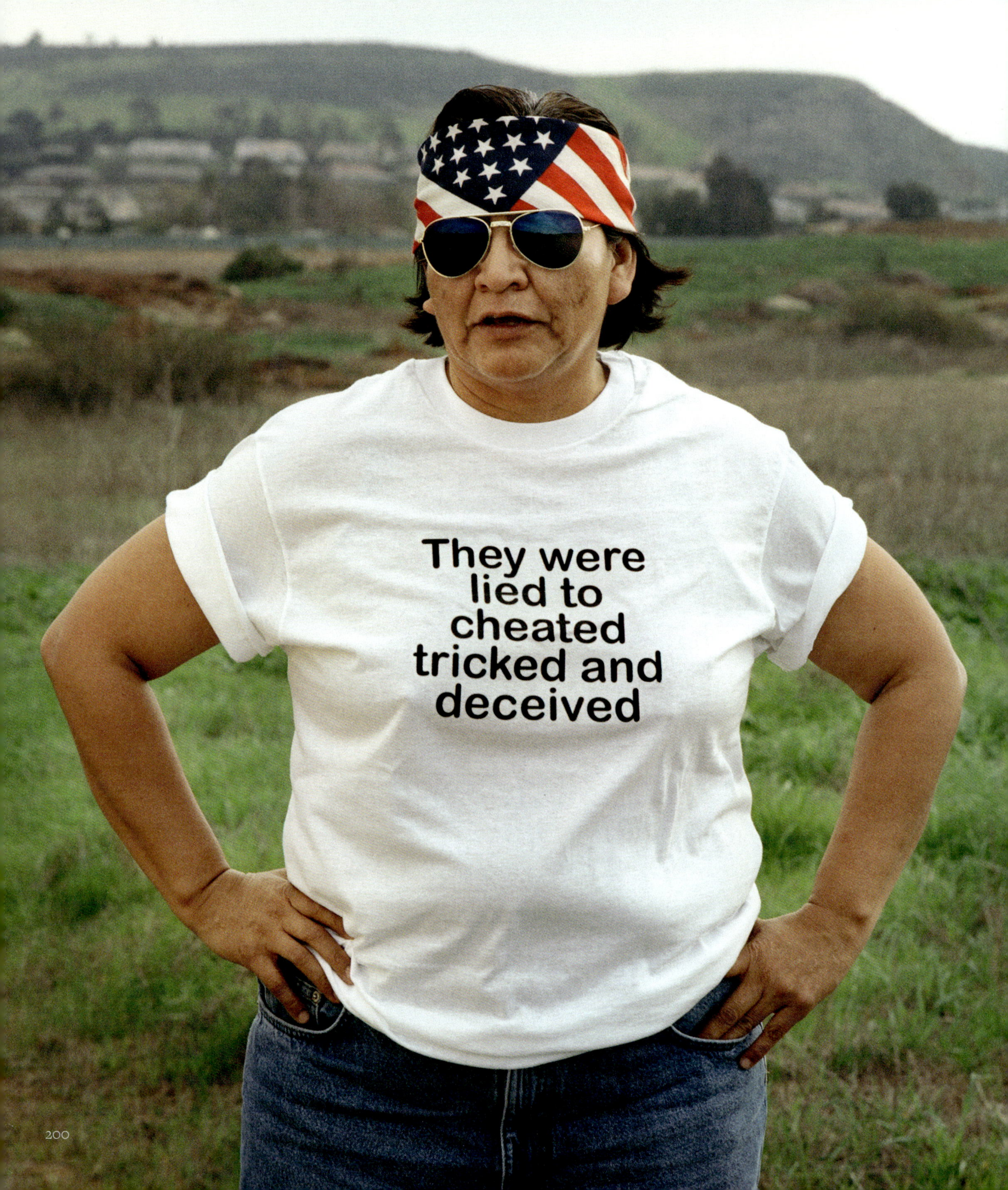
They were
lied to
cheated
tricked and
deceived

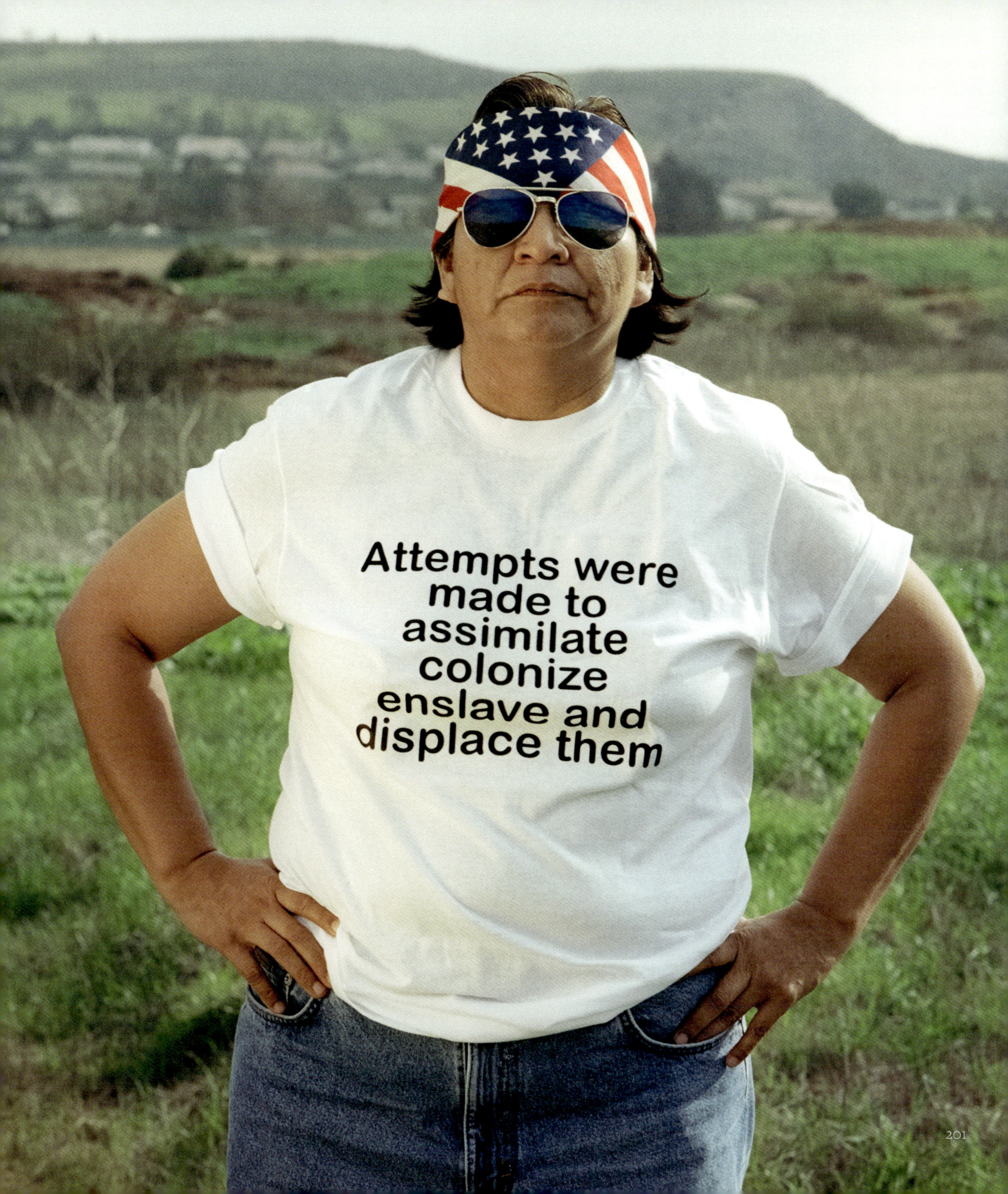
Attempts were
made to
assimilate
colonize
enslave and
displace them

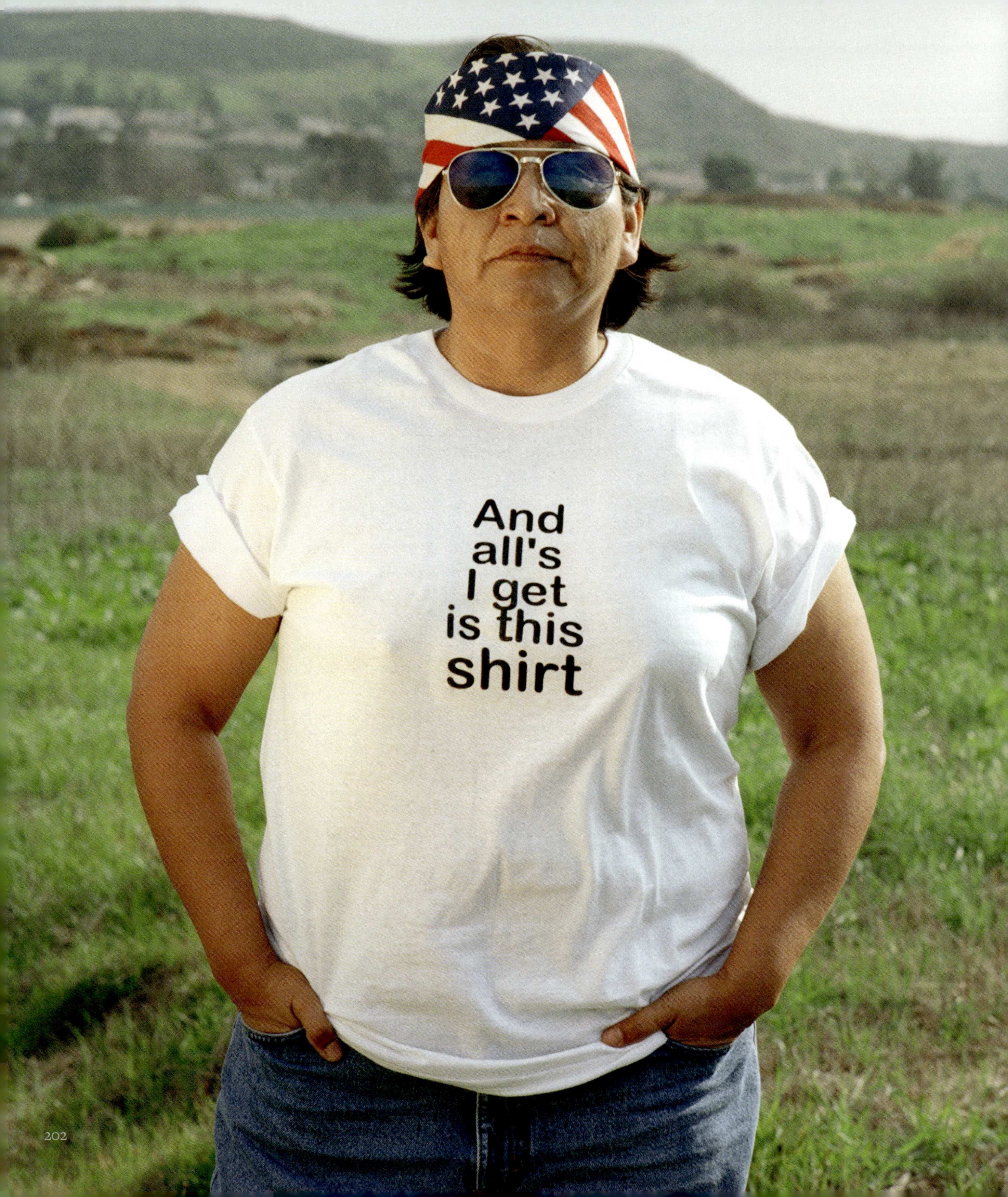
And
all's
I get
is this
shirt

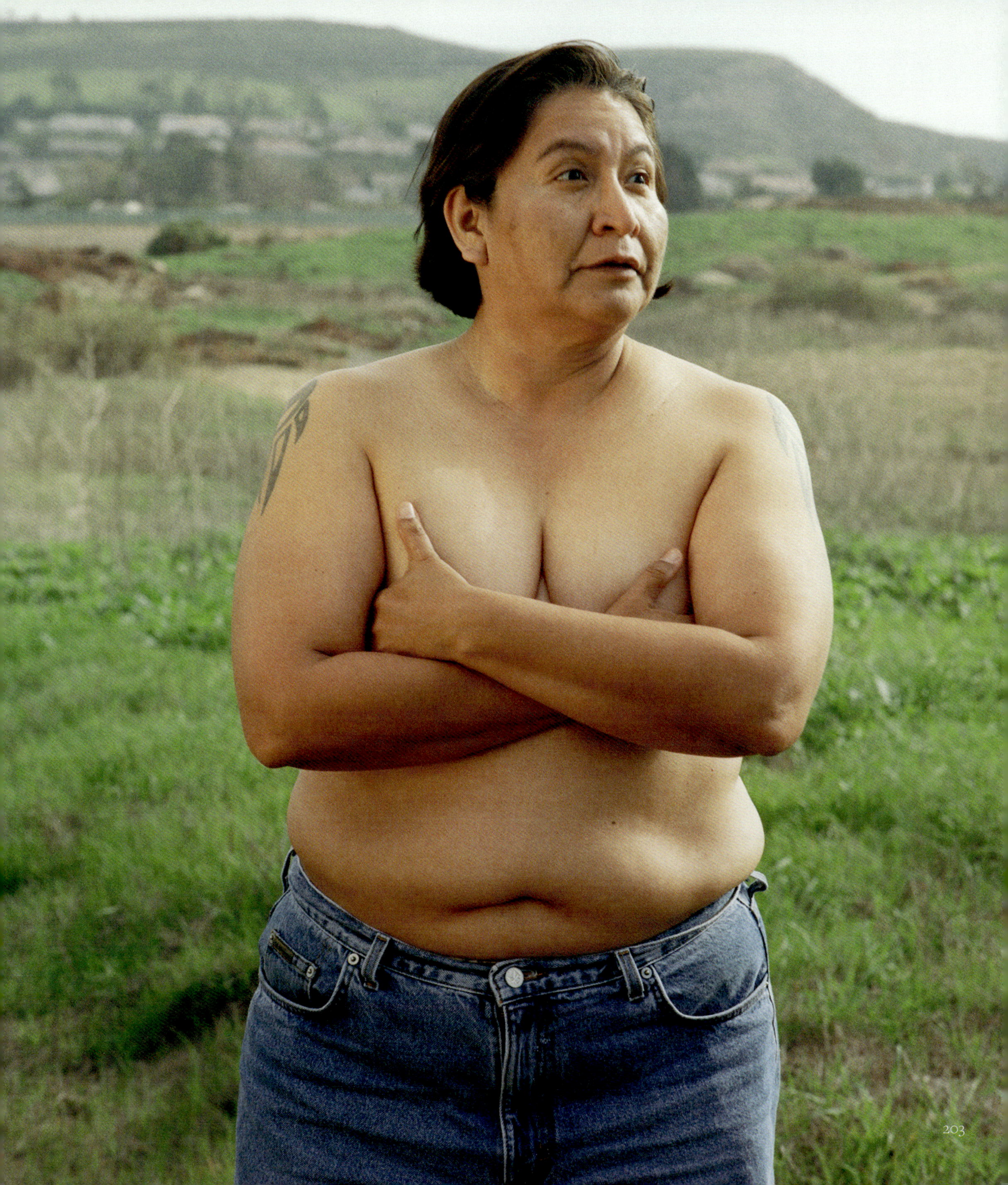

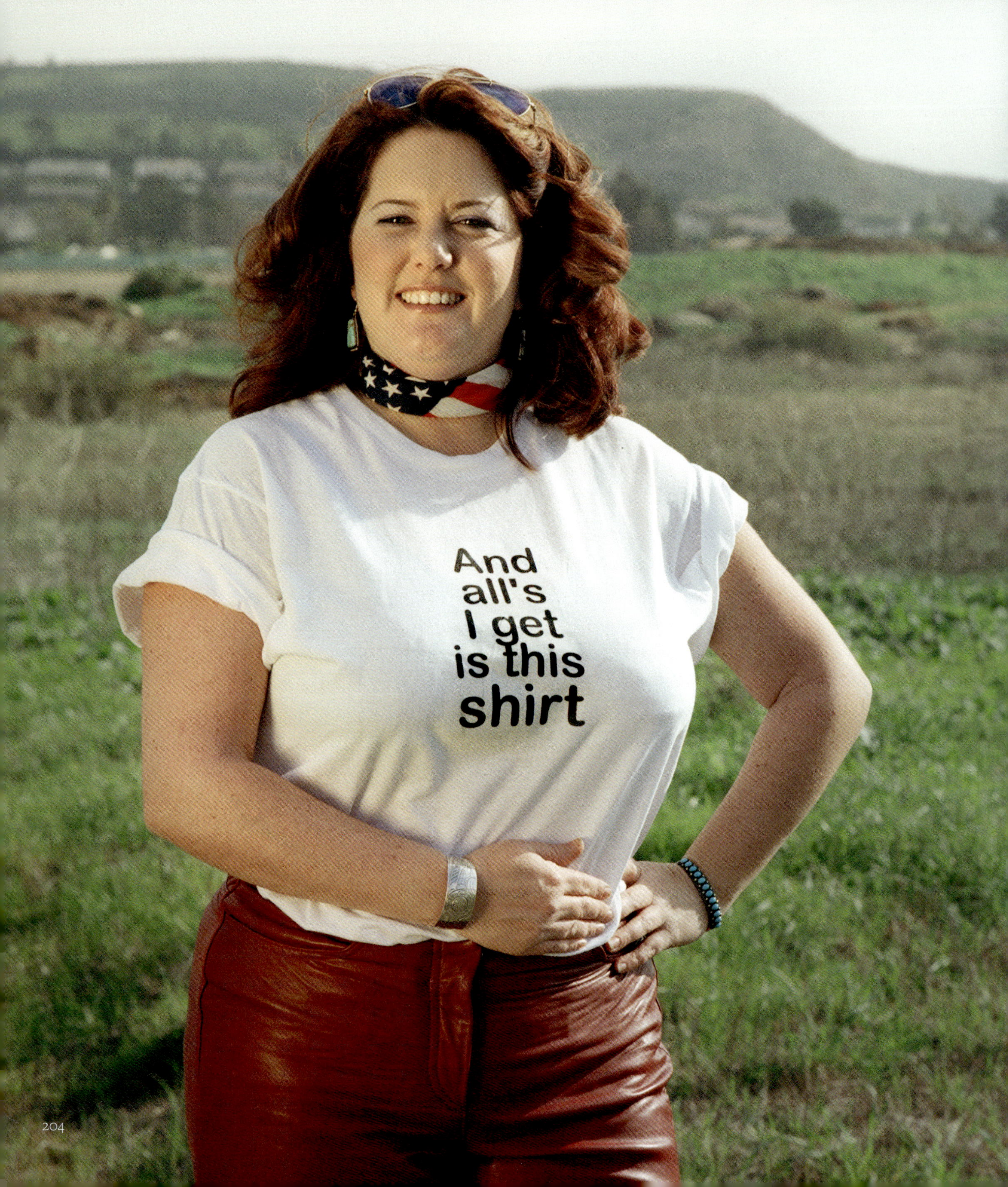
And
all's
I get
is this
shirt

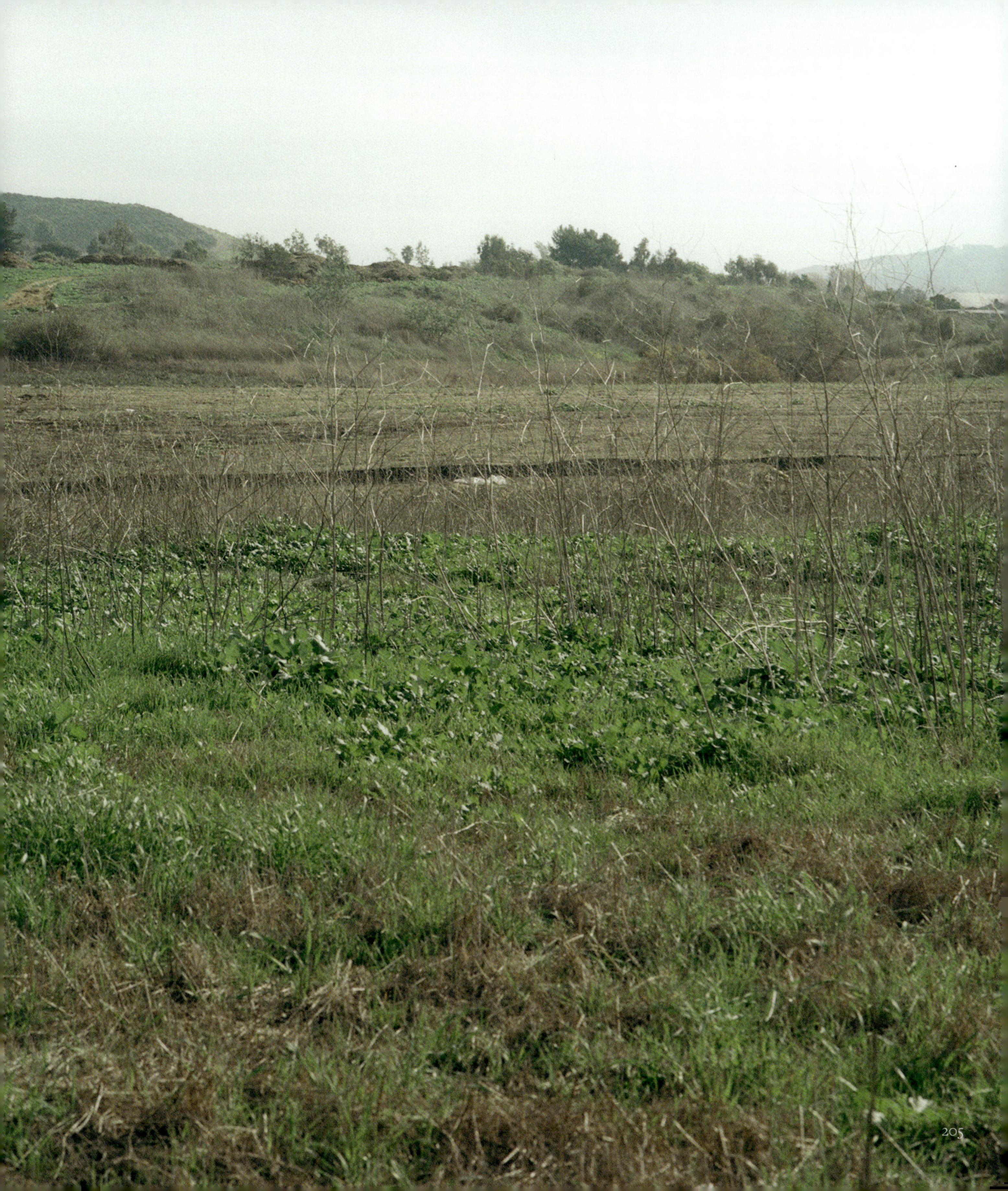

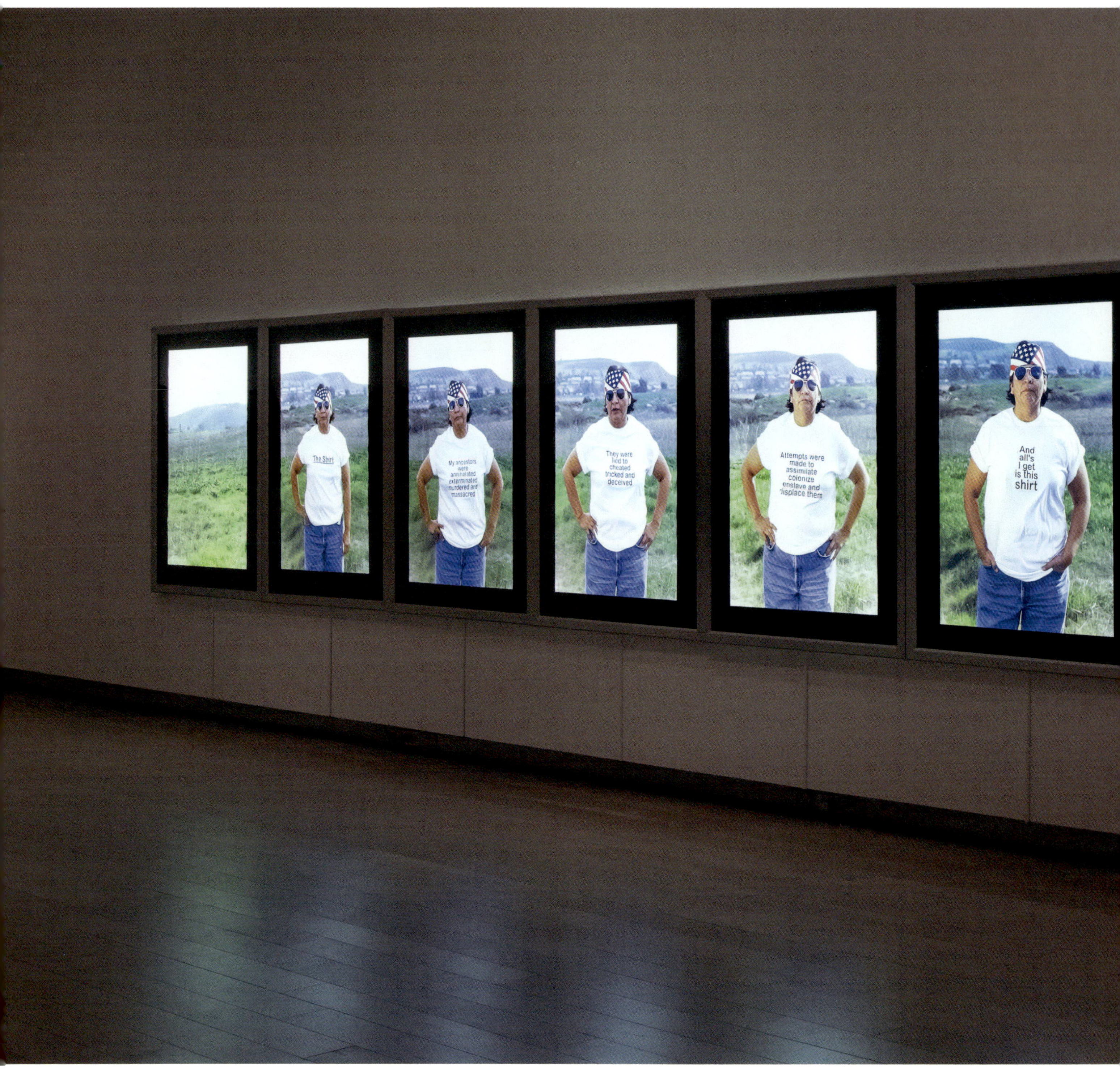
The Shirt
My ancestors were annihilated exterminated murdered and massacred
They were lied to cheated tricked and deceived
Attempts were made to assimilate colonize enslave and displace them
And all's I get is this shirt

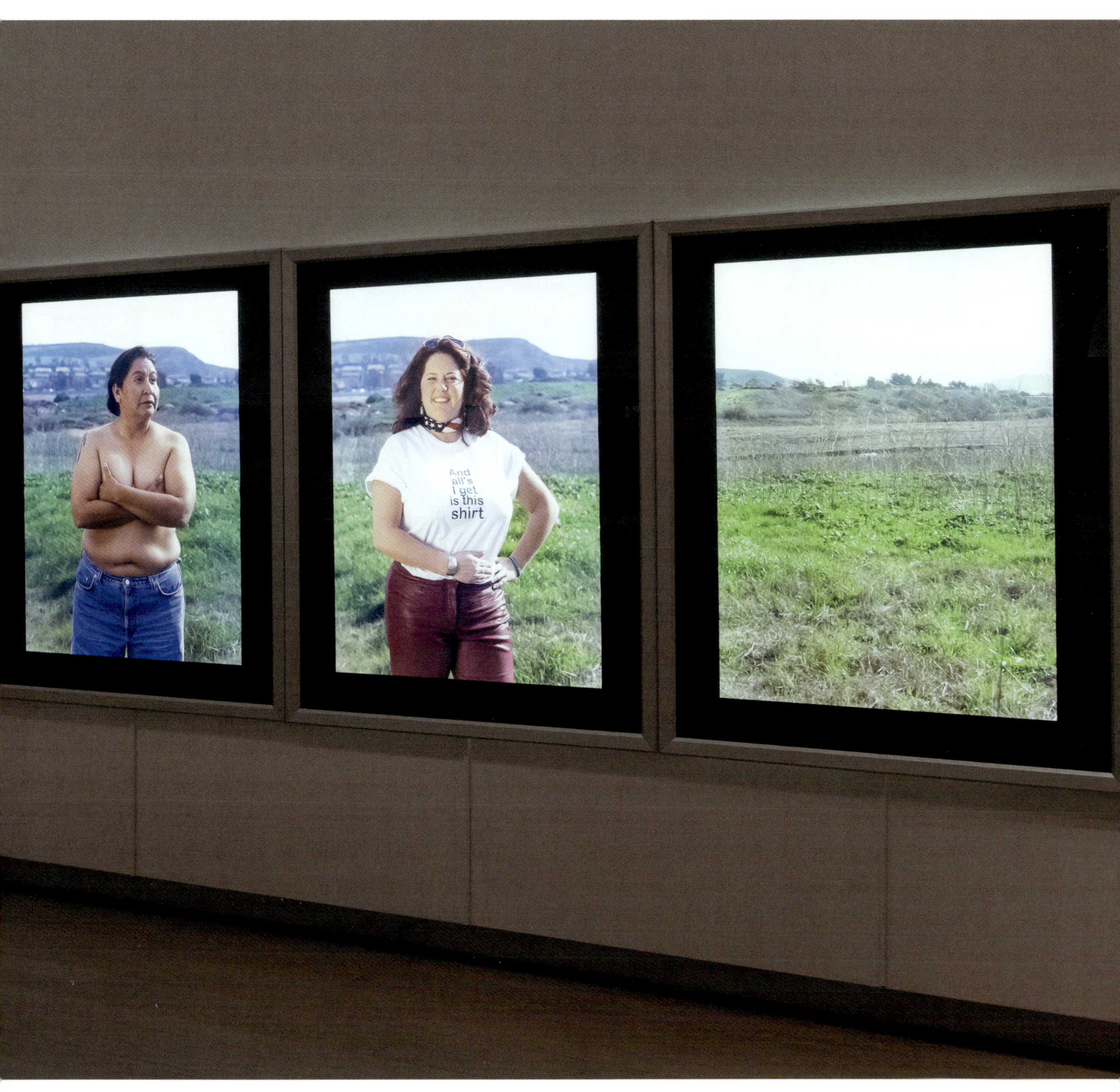

Installation view of **The Shirt**, 2003
Shelley Niro: Scotiabank Photography Award at The Image Centre, Toronto Metropolitan University, 2018
Photograph by Larissa Issler

207

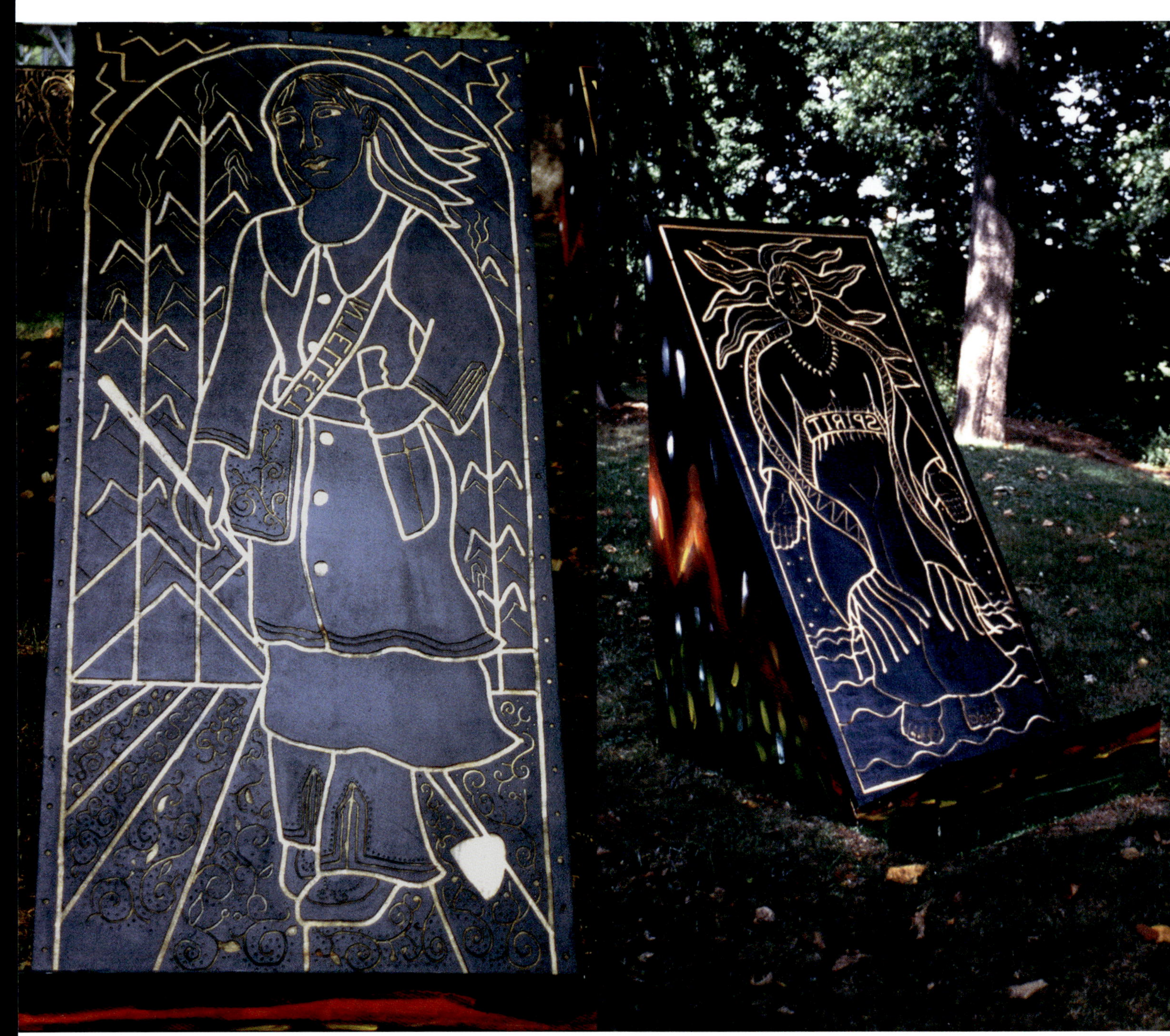

Woodcuts for the printing of **Resting With Warriors**, 2001
Rodman Hall Art Centre, Brock University, St. Catharines

RESTING WITH WARRIORS

SALLY FRATER

Patience and trust are essential for preparing to listen to stories. Listening involves more than just using the auditory sense. We must visualize the characters and their actions. We must let out emotions surface. As the Elders say, it is important to listen with "three ears: two on the sides of our head and the one that is in our heart."

—JO-ANN ARCHIBALD | Q'UM Q'UM XIIEM, *INDIGENOUS STORYWORK*[1]

In 2001, Shelley Niro was invited by curator Terry Graf to create a work for the grounds of Rodman Hall Art Centre at Brock University. The result was *Resting With Warriors* (p. 208; 211), a site-specific work that was (indirectly) informed by the history of the region. Niro recalls visiting the area of Queenston Heights as a child during school trips. The artist and her classmates were gathered around a statue of General Brock and told about the Haudenosaunee soldiers who had helped the British defeat the Americans in the battle for control of the region during the War of 1812. While there is a monument to Brock that commemorates his role in securing a victory for England, there is no memorial that acknowledges the contributions of the Haudenosaunee in the war. In reflecting on the recounting of the battle, Niro came to the realization that there were no women present in these stories. Not only did they fail to appear in the descriptions of the feats of Brock and the British and Haudenosaunee men who accompanied him in battle, there also seemed to be no accounts detailing the actions of the Haudenosaunee women who remained behind and continued to maintain both family and community life during the war.

Resting With Warriors (2001; p. 212-213) addressed the gendered (and racialized) gap in the historical narratives that were constructed around the War of 1812 and consists of a series of four sets of woodcuts in either red, blue, black, or brown ink pulled from life-sized woodblocks carved by the artist. Each print features a large-scale monochromatic rendering of a woman whose presence embodies and personifies one of four traits: Intellect, Spirit, Emotion, and Strength. In Niro's purview, these are the characteristics that would have been necessary for the women to maintain their families and communities: intellectual knowledge would be critical for the women charged with performing agrarian labour; spirit would be needed for grounding and guidance in the tasks at hand; emotion would assist in sensitizing the leaders to their environments and the (emotional) needs of those around them; and physical strength would be critical in realizing all of the aforementioned responsibilities. Each figure looms large before the viewer and is grounded in the elements of nature. The personification of Intellect appears before a background of corn, with swirling embroidered patterns at her feet. The personification of Spirit floats above waves of water, with a starlit sky behind her. The personification of Emotion shields her eyes with her right hand while holding a bag of tobacco in the other, with strawberry plants encircling her feet. The personification of Strength hoists a tomahawk in her left hand while a quiver of arrows hangs from her right shoulder. There are a number of visual cues within the prints that make reference to elements of Indigenous aesthetic culture, such as the representations of embroidery on the bag that Intellect carries or the embroidered floral motifs on the tunic worn by the figure of Strength. The tobacco pouch and strawberry leaves harken back to the figure and story of Sky Woman, the pregnant woman who fell through the sky to land on a turtle's back and who built, with animal helpers, what would eventually become Turtle Island (i.e.,... North America or the world).

As a creationist legend, the story of Sky Woman is a woman-centred narrative that posits the origins of the earth as stemming from a chance occurrence (Sky Woman falling through a hole that formed when a tree was uprooted). A woman-led effort also saw her working alongside animals to create the world. This is a direct contradiction to Judeo-Christian origin stories which posit that the world was created by an all-knowing, all-seeing male god who single-handedly created the world and was punitive towards its inhabitants, punishing those who did not display complete subservience by subjecting them to banishment, pestilence, and flooding. Similar to the story of Sky Woman, one can imagine the four women in *Resting With Warriors*, all of whom embody different traits, working in tandem to protect and nurture their community.[2] Collectively, the woodcuts present imagery that communicates several lessons to us as viewers: the necessity of communal effort in the practice of care; the importance of reverence for and sensitivity to the natural world; how that which appears to be intuitive is often embedded within reason and knowledge, and the ways in which cultural practice and values (can) sustain us.

Niro underscores this latter point in a number of ways. In connecting the figures in the *Resting With Warriors* woodcuts to the figure of the Sky Woman origin tale, the artist reminds us that matrilineal leadership has been a constant in Indigenous societies, specifically in Haudenosaunee culture. It is telling that the strawberry plant appears in both the Sky Woman story and the Emotion woodcut print, as the strawberry fruit represents "the heart and carries good medicine and origin stories." The narrative options that Niro presents us with differ greatly from the impressions that we are left with from tales of Brock and his battles, from which we are likely to conjure up the violent sounds of war and all of the visuals that accompany it. Instead, in *Resting With Warriors*, we are presented with images that show us that there are other ways of existing that can also propel us forward. Resolute in their quiet determination, the warriors convey that we can move forward in love while simultaneously opening up multiple spaces for imagining.

NOTES

1. Jo-ann Archibald, *Indigenous Storywork: Educating the Heart, Mind, and Spirit* (Vancouver: UBC Press, 2008), 8.
2. This notion of support is further emphasized when one considers the source of the title *Resting With Warriors*. Niro carved "life sized" woodblocks for the original commission at Rodman Hall Art Centre, which were later used to pull prints. The woodblocks were placed on the grounds and installed at forty-five degree angles. The artist's intent was that visitors would be able to lean or "rest" against the blocks of wood. This method of installing not only provided viewers with another way to directly connect with the work, it also accentuated the values of care and safekeeping that permeate it.

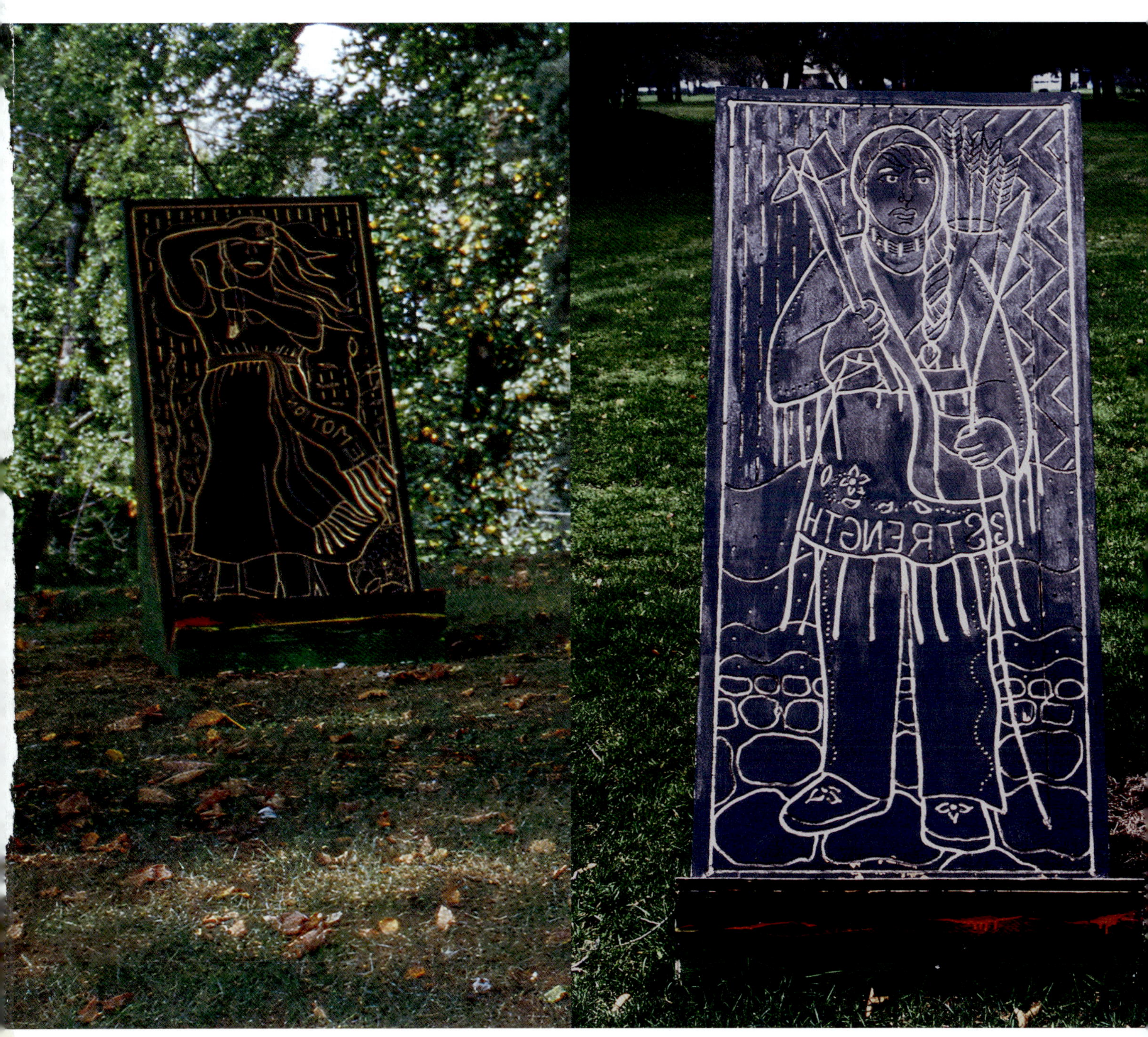

Woodcuts for the printing of **Resting With Warriors**, 2001
Rodman Hall Art Centre, Brock University, St. Catharines

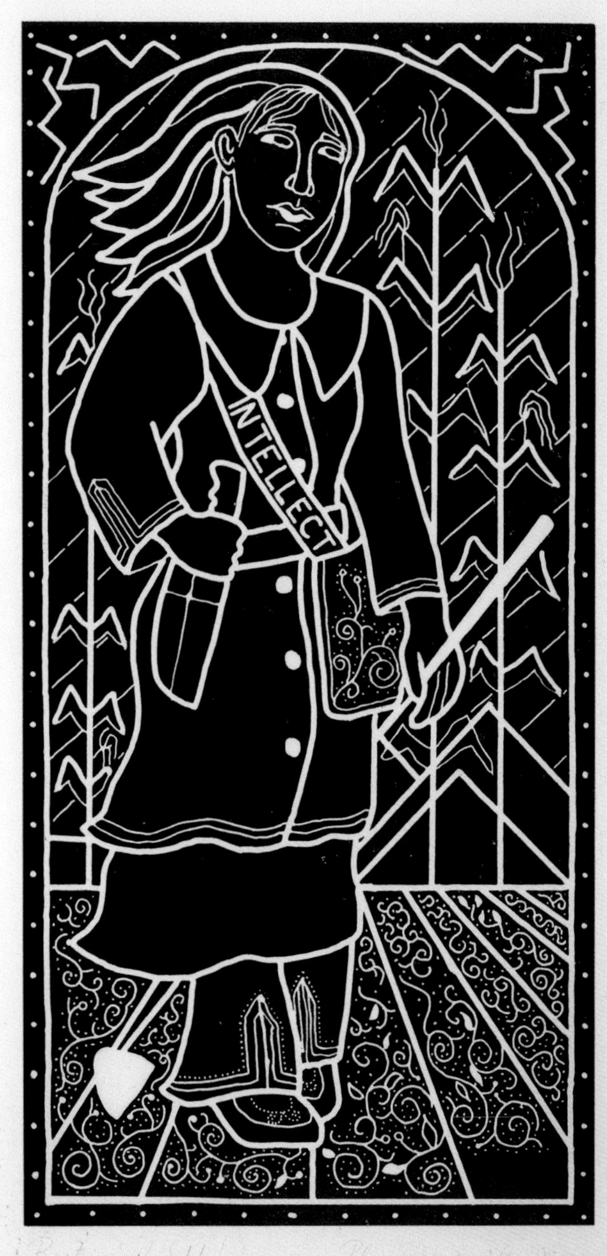
INTELLECT

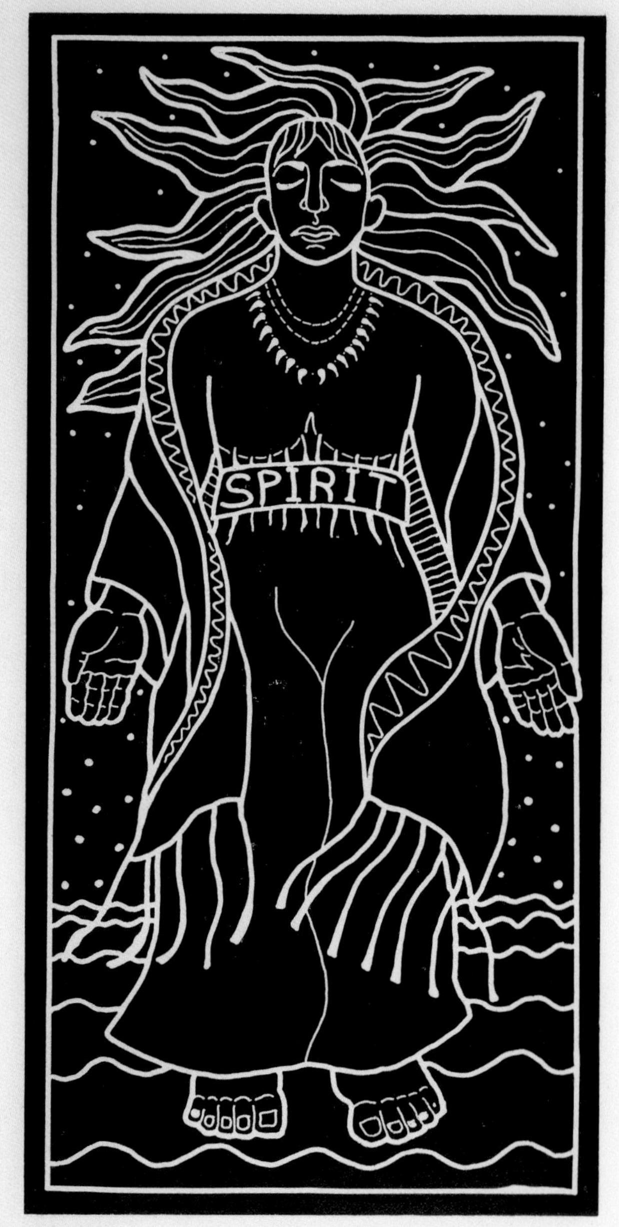
SPIRIT

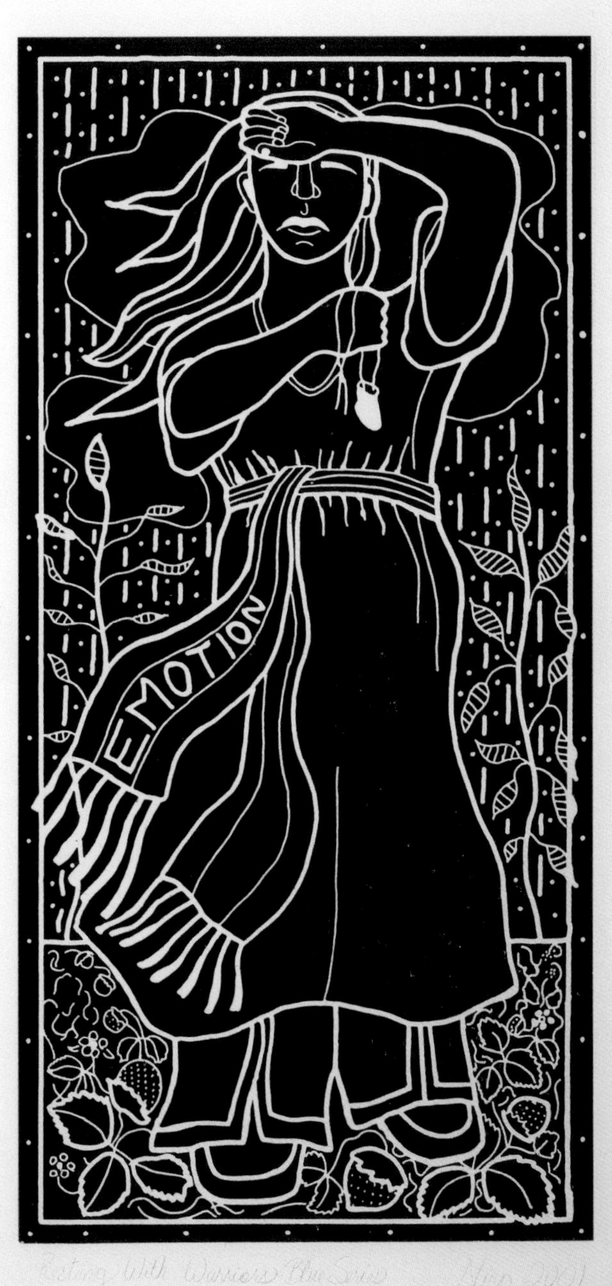

EMOTION

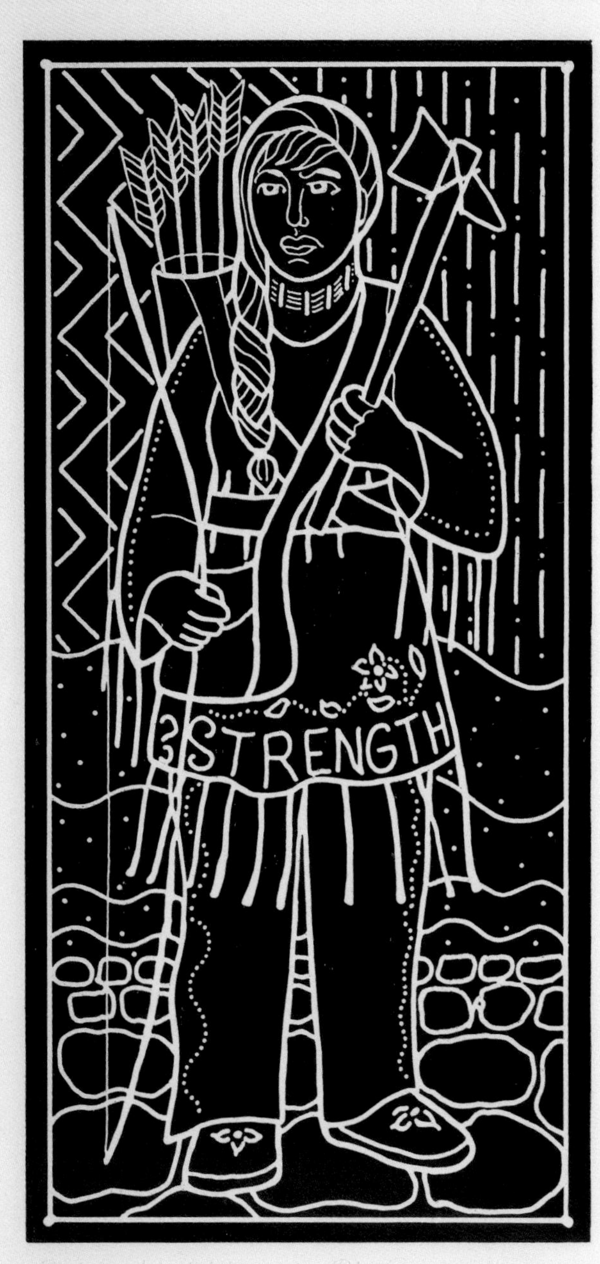

STRENGTH

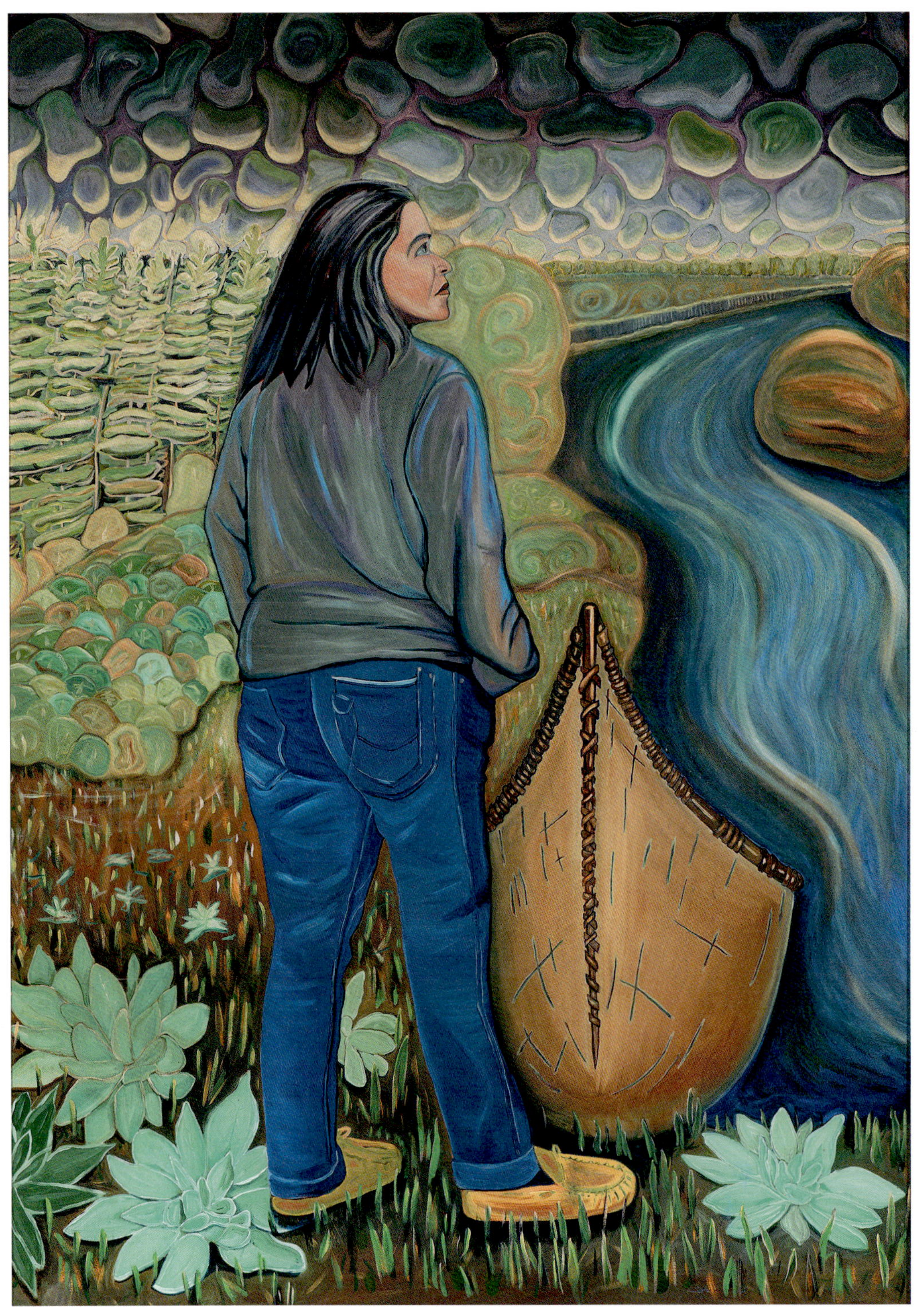

  Wishing a River, 2013

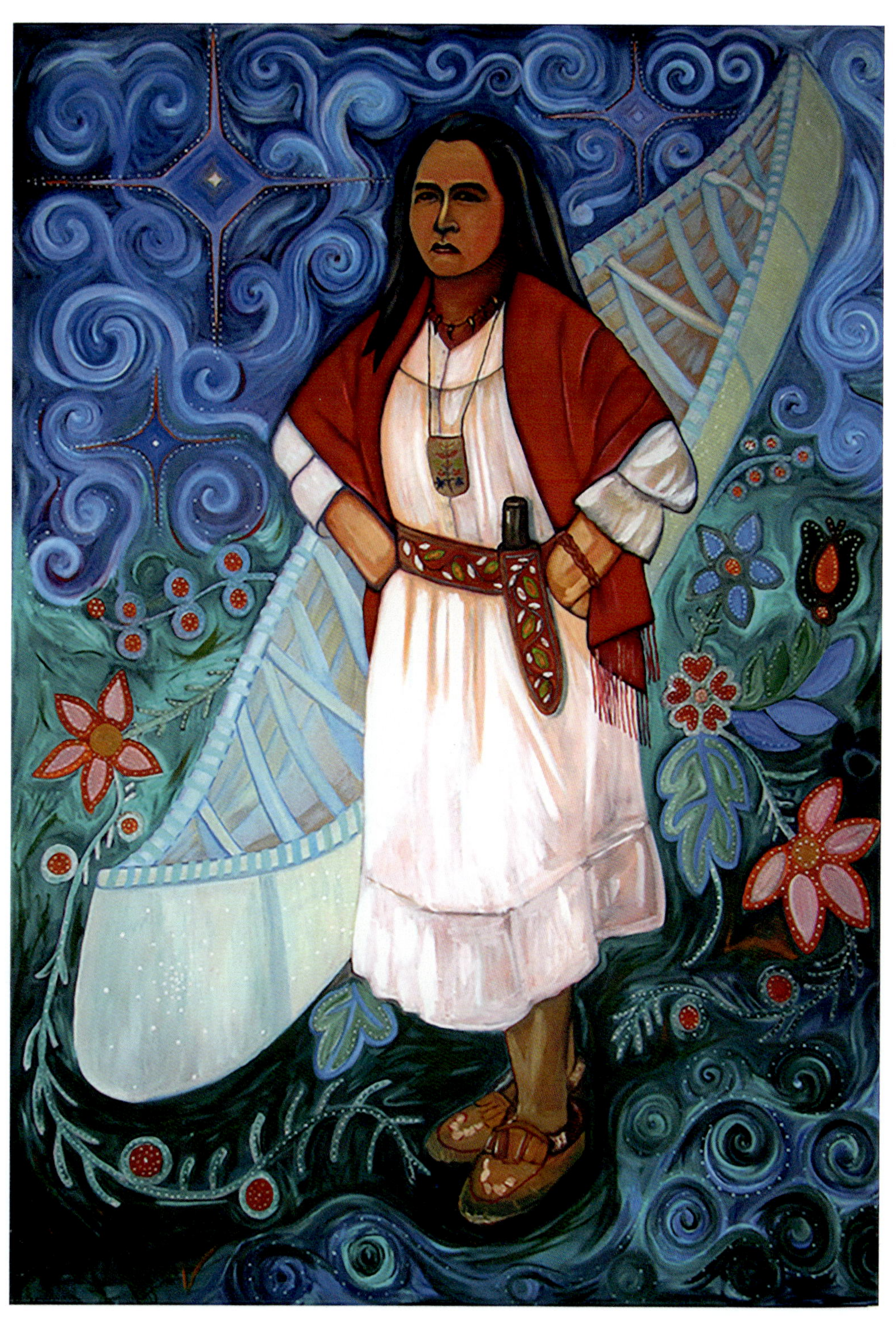

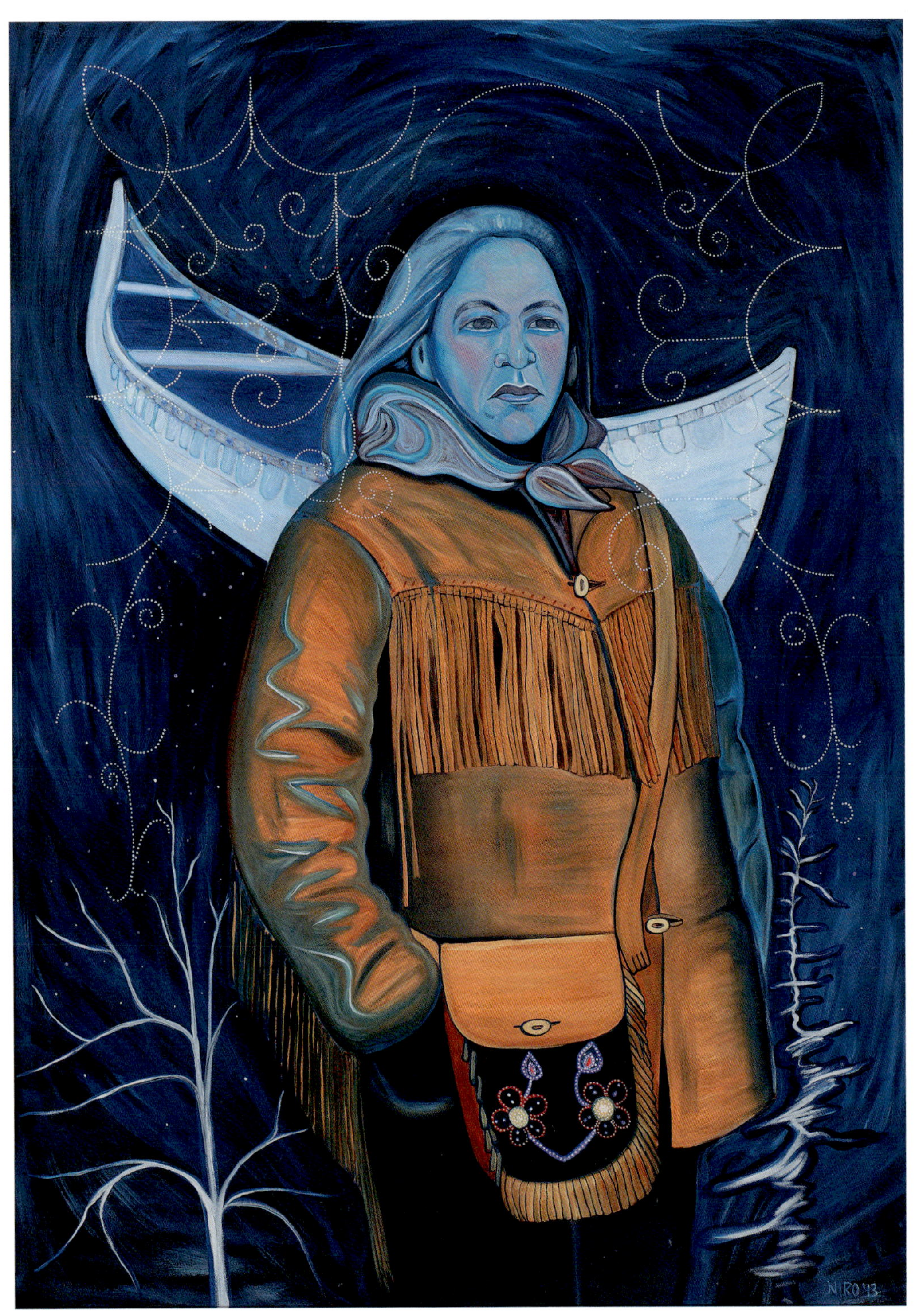

  Continuing the Journey, 2014

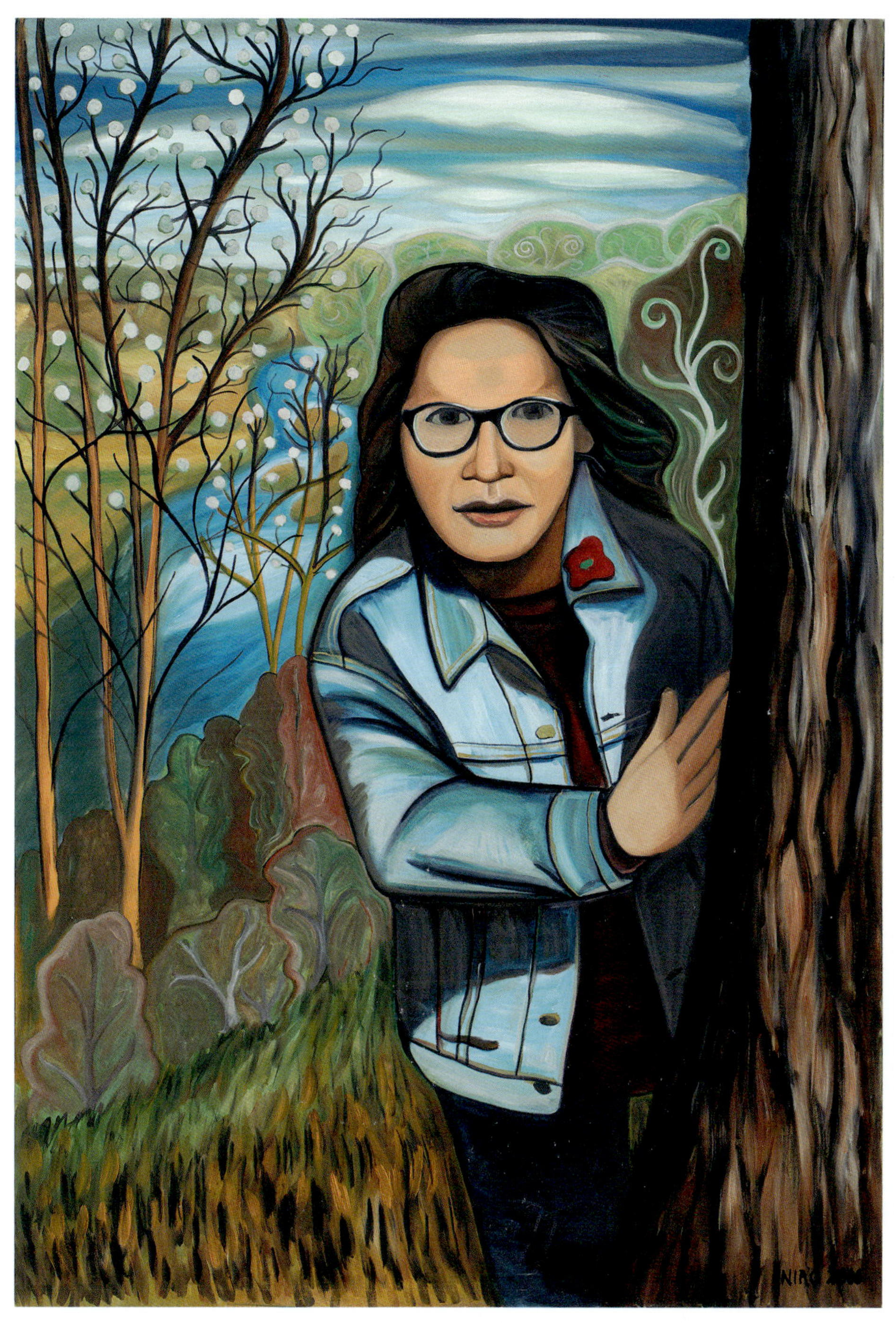

Seeing With My Memory, 2000   217

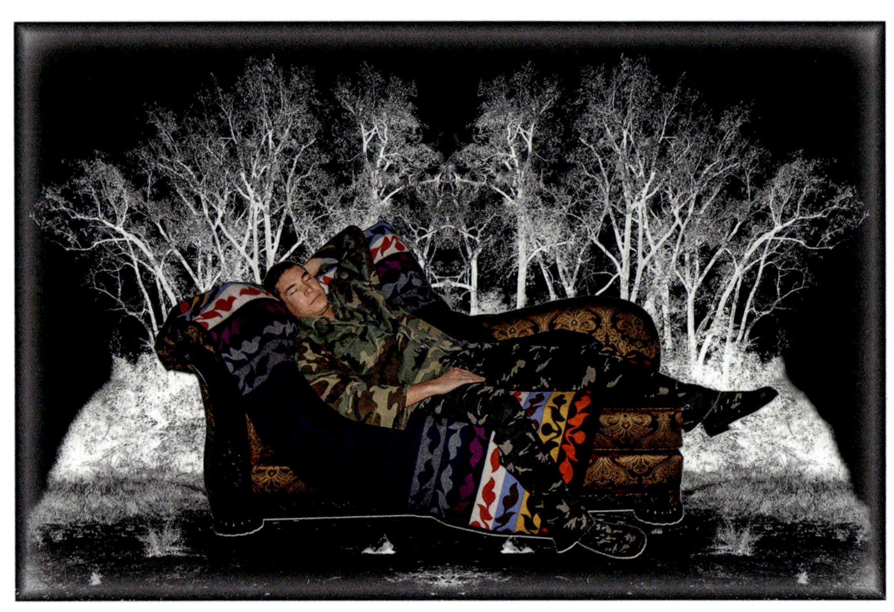

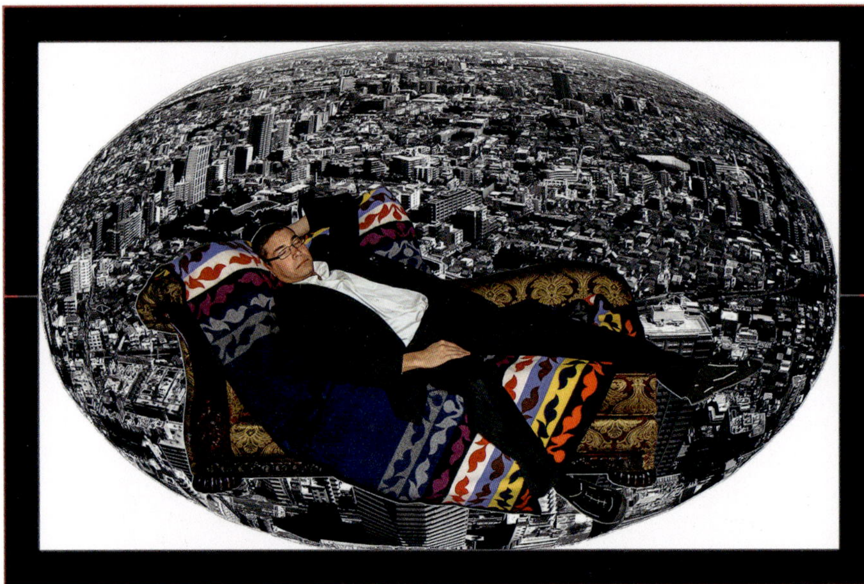

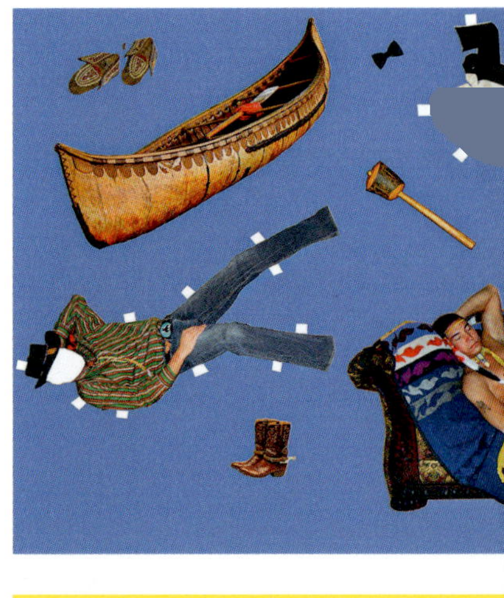

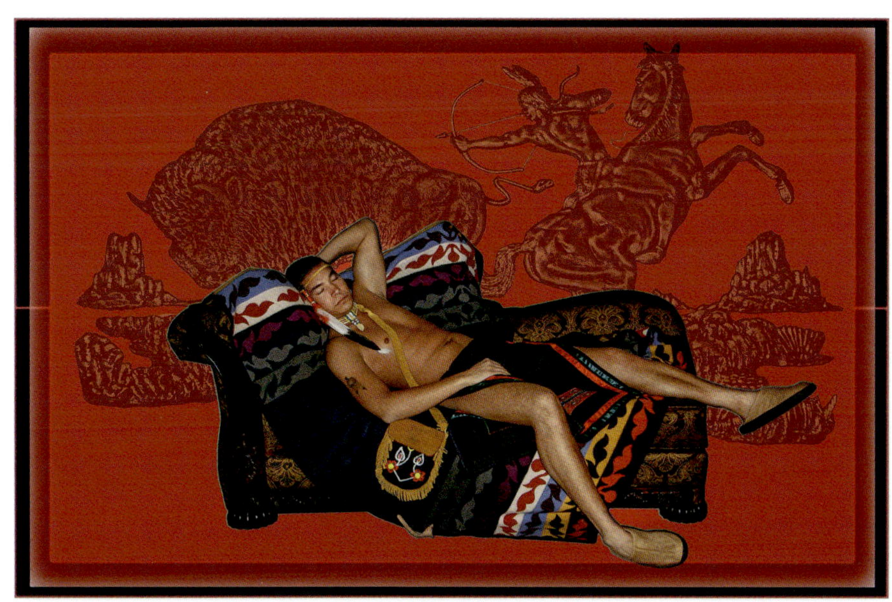

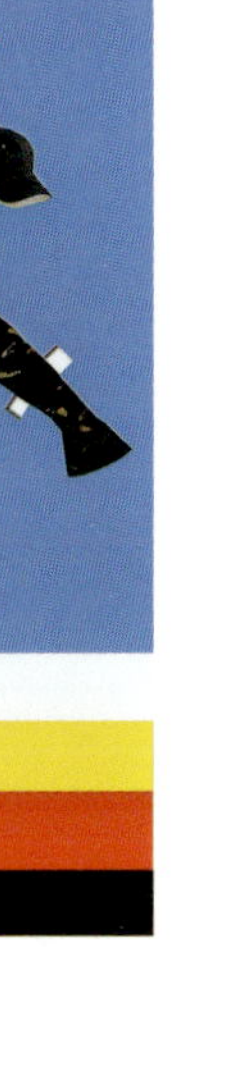

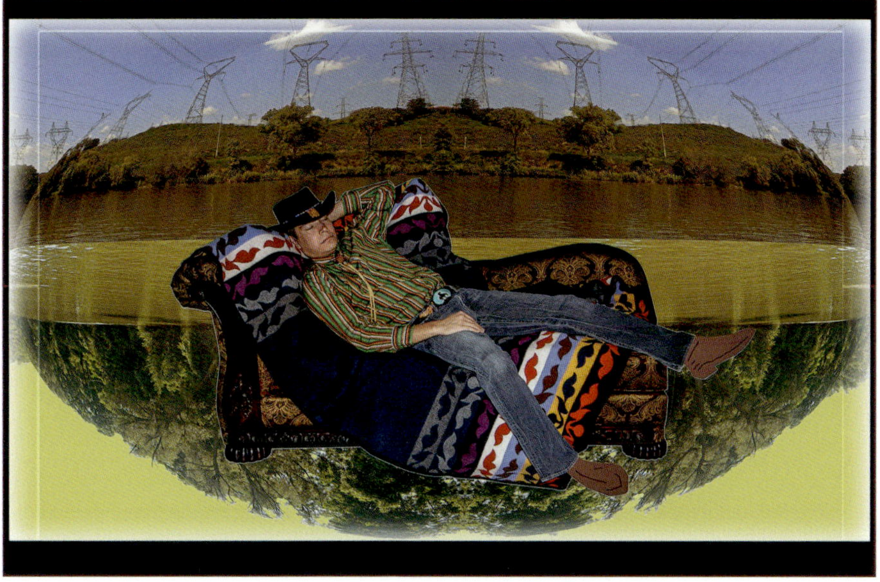

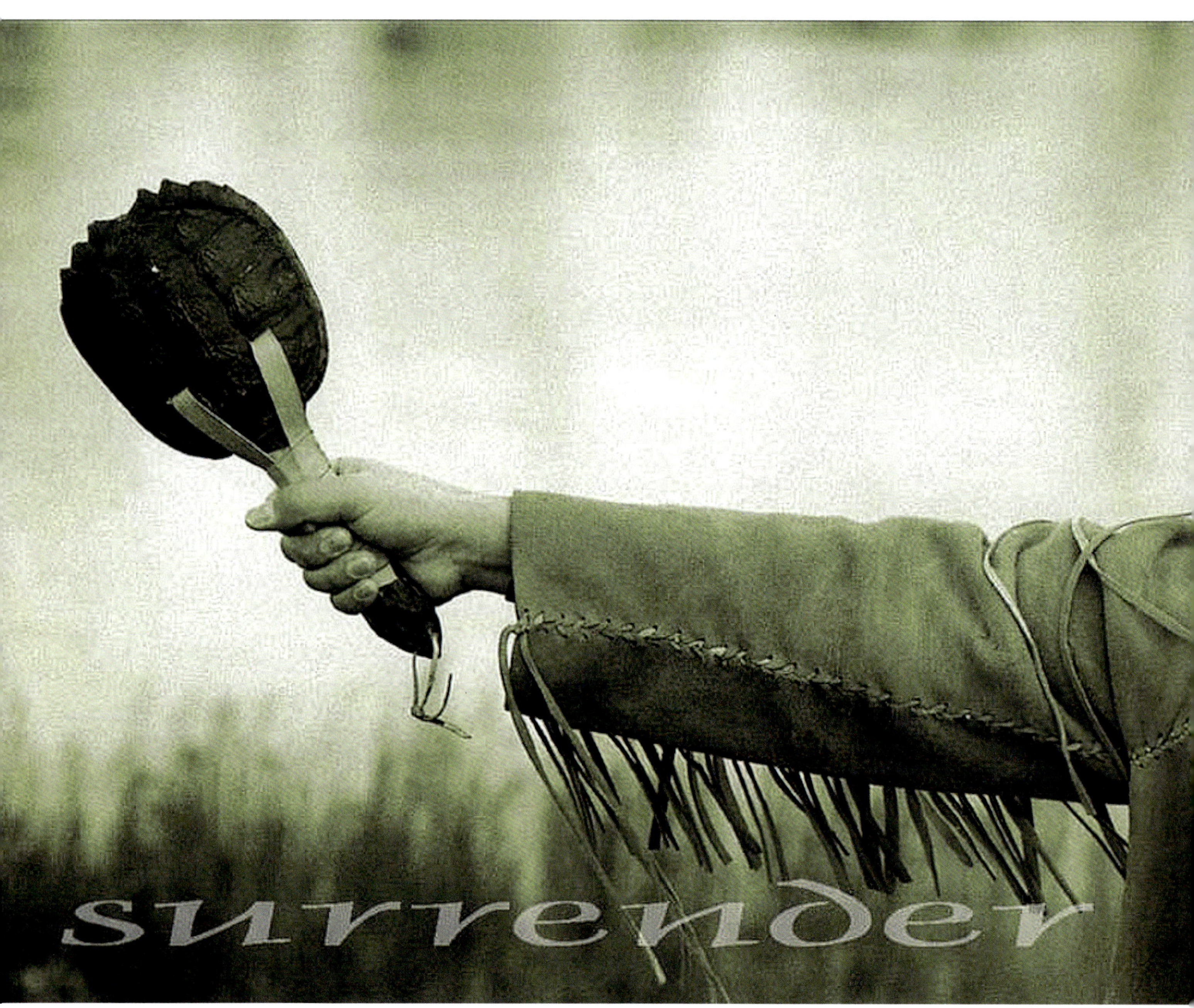
surrender

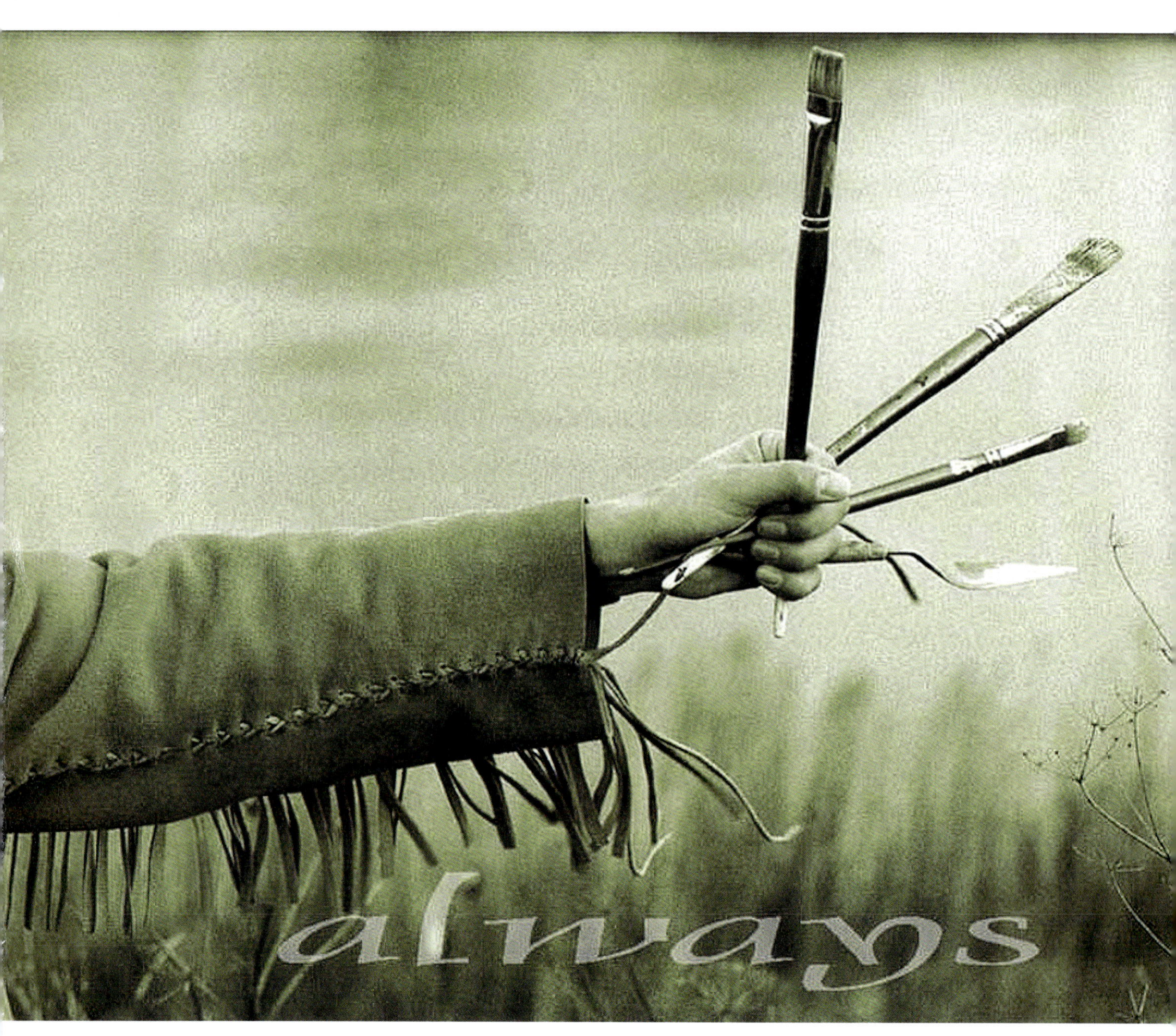

Surrender Nothing Always, 2004

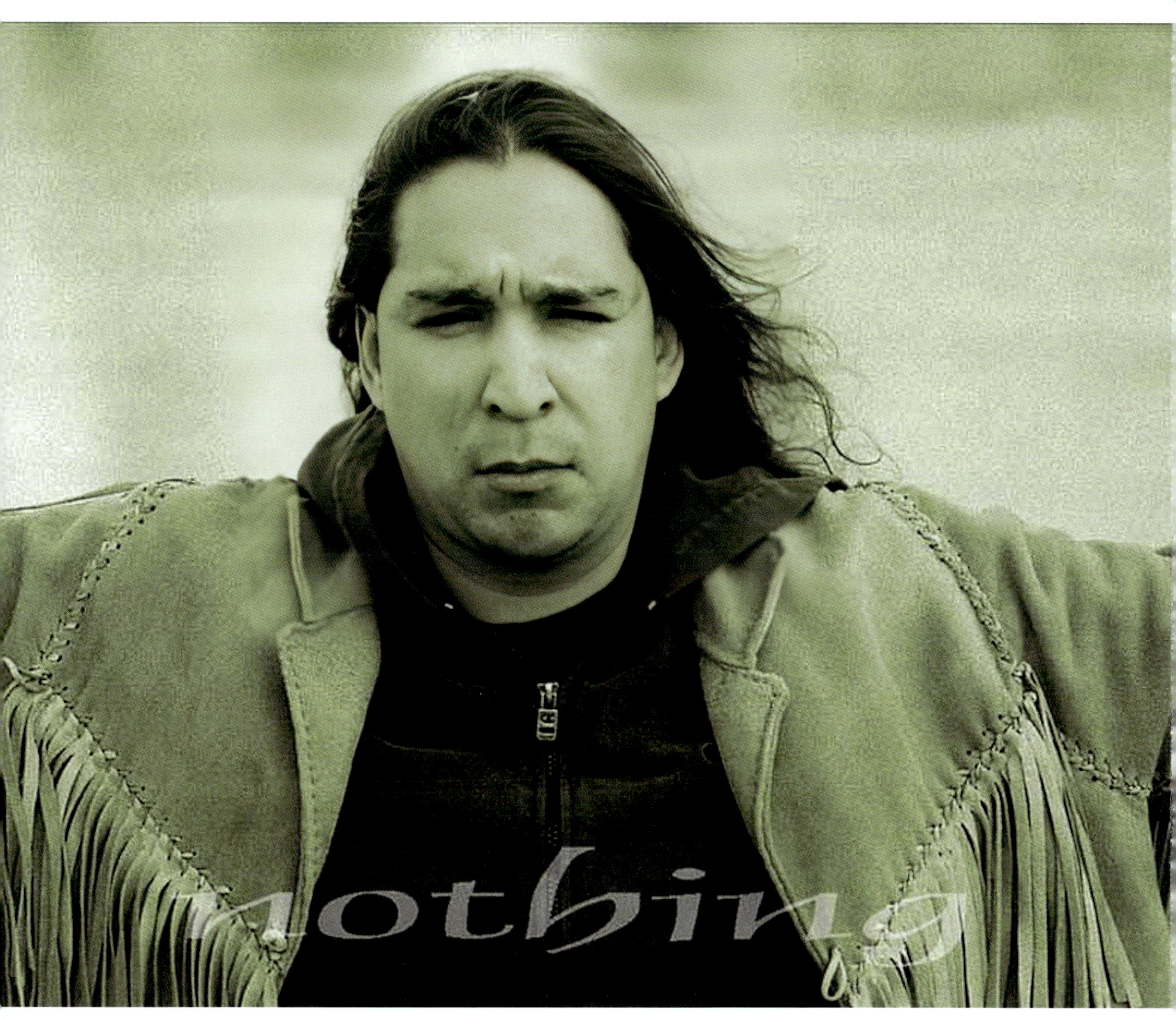
nothing

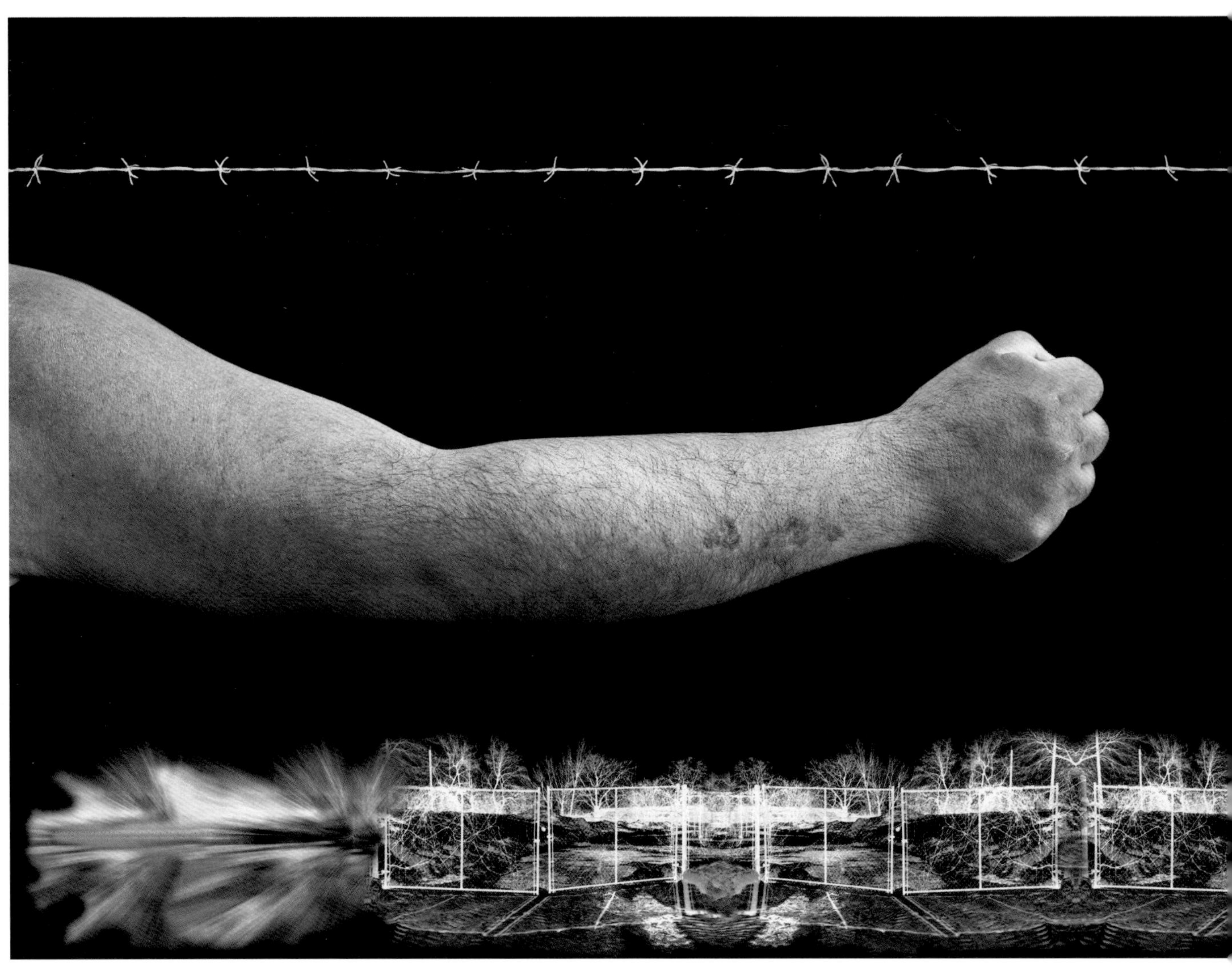

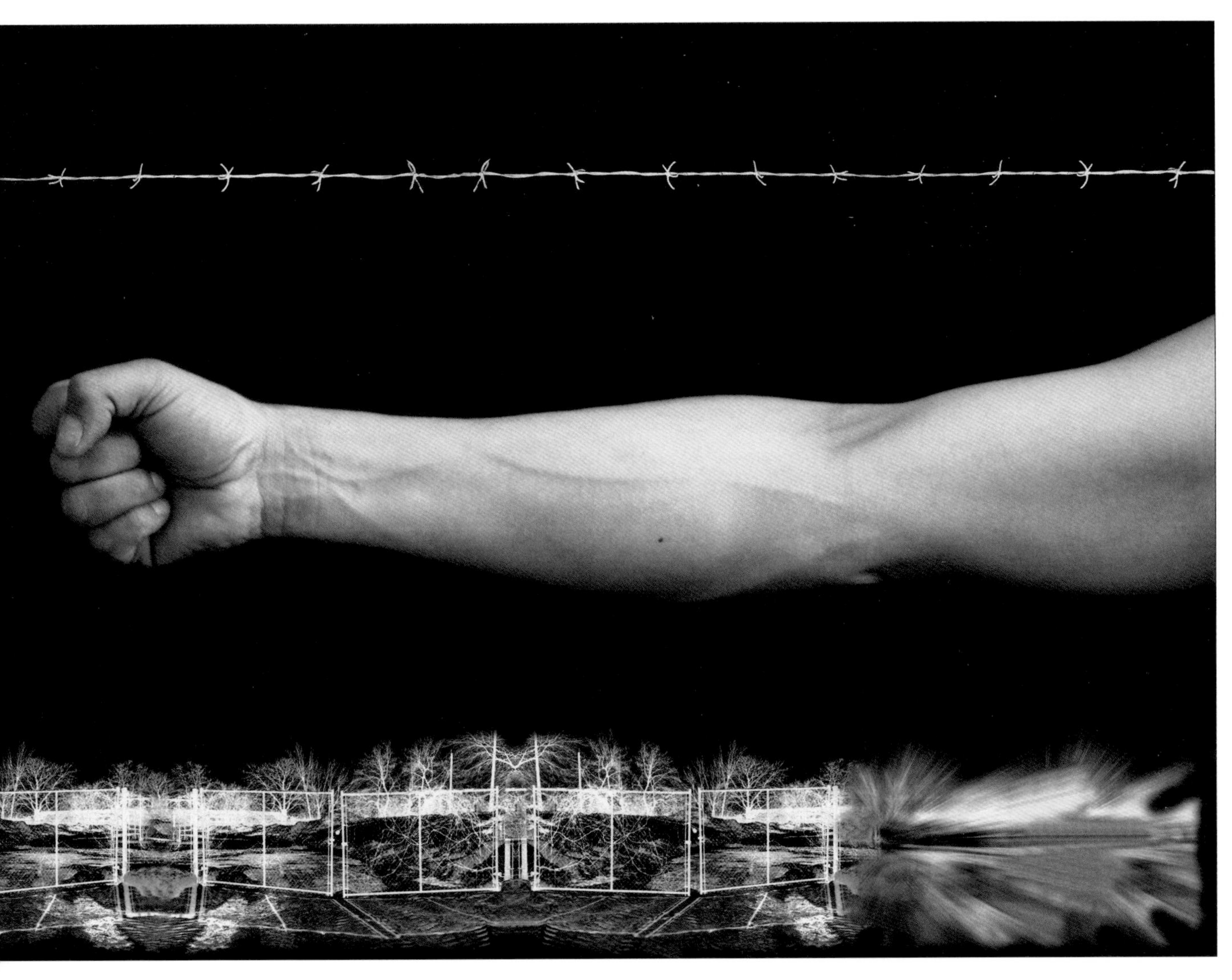

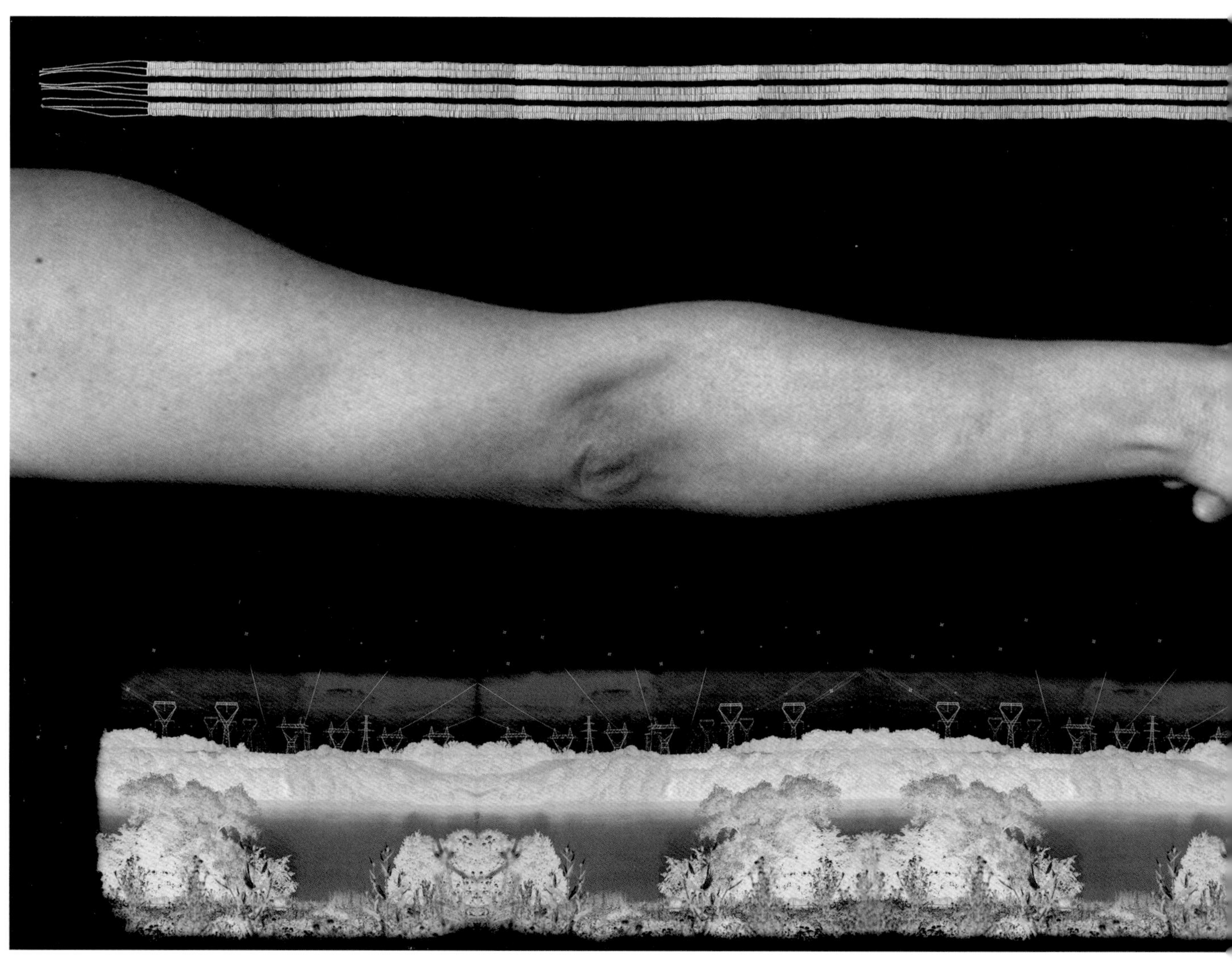

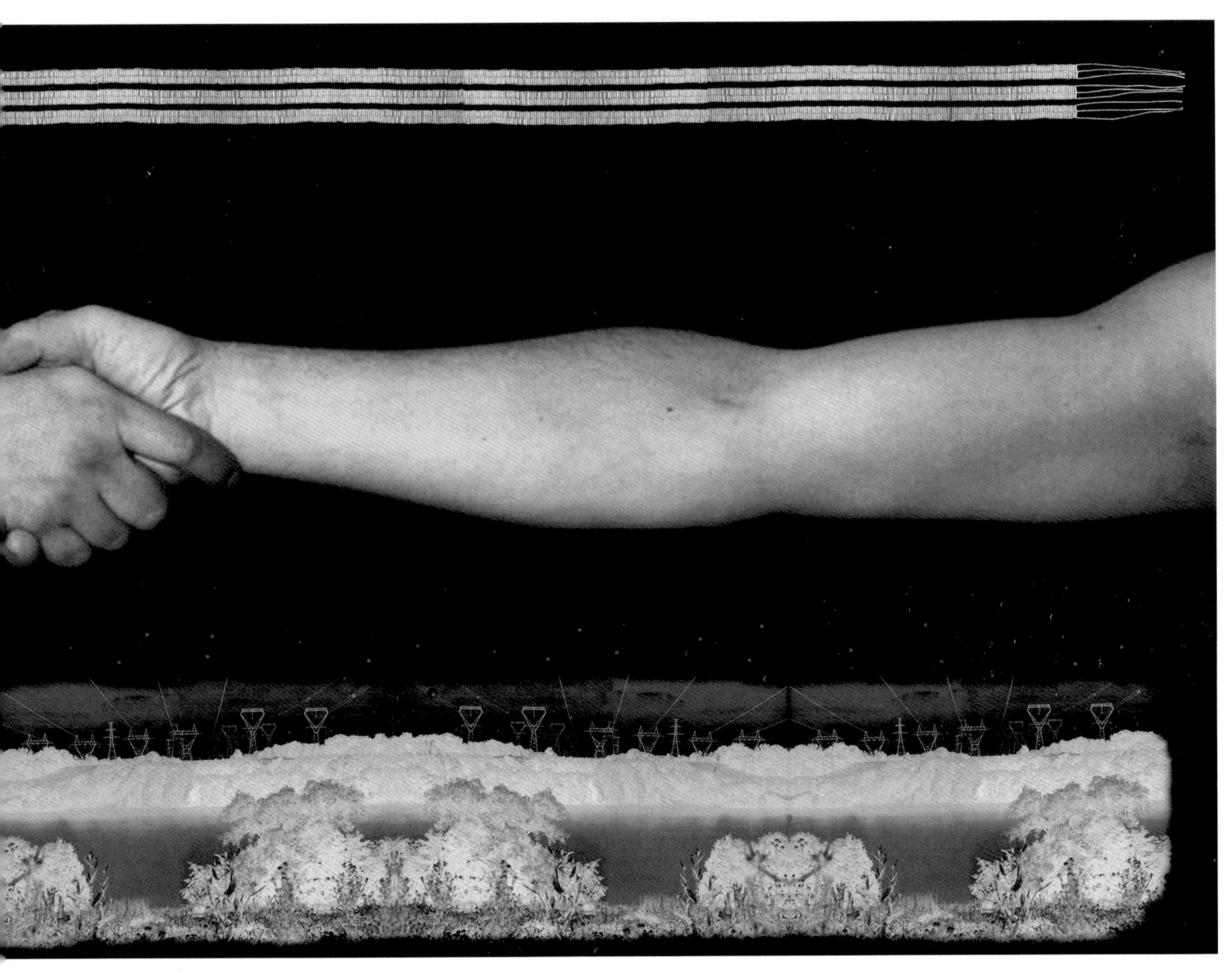

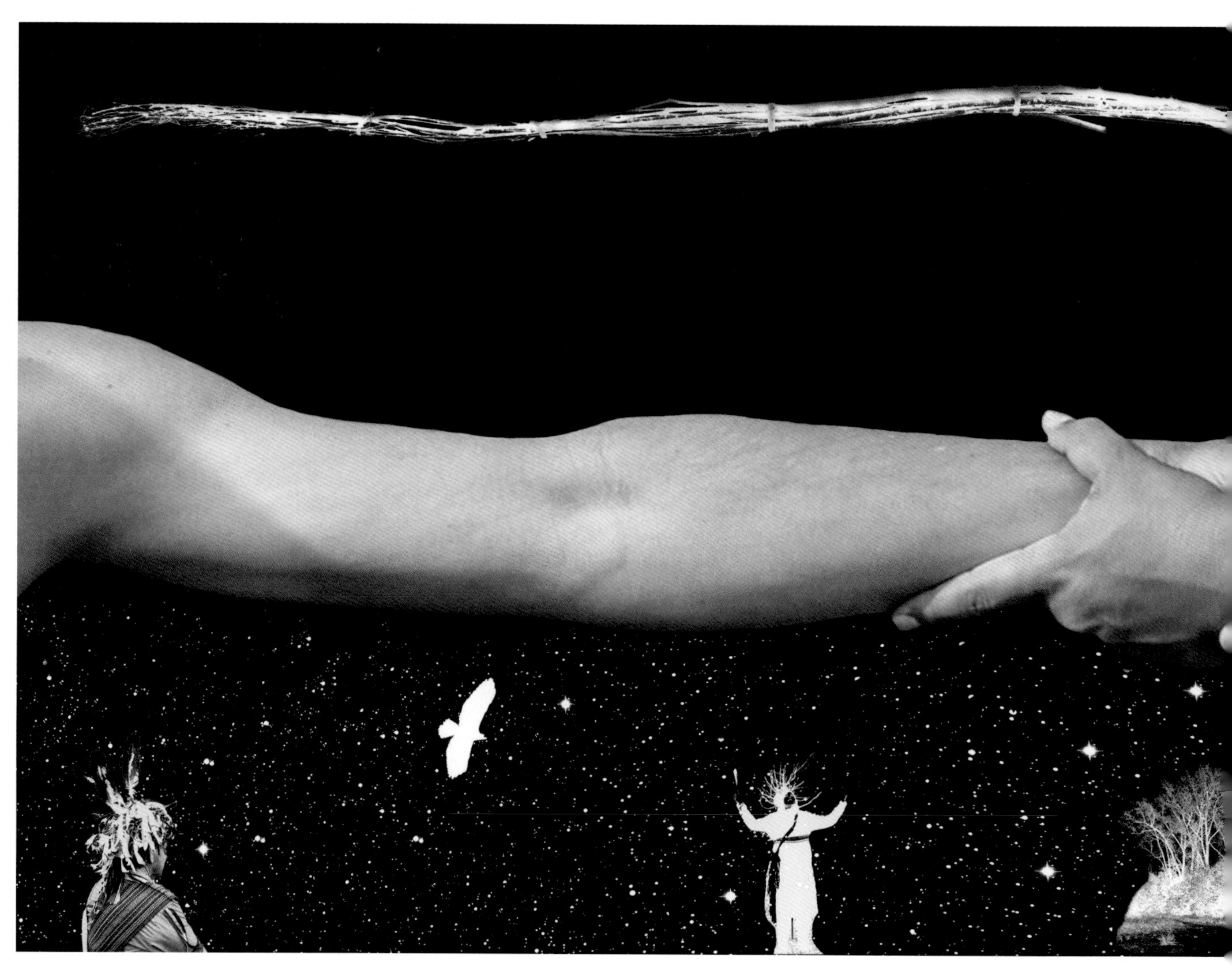

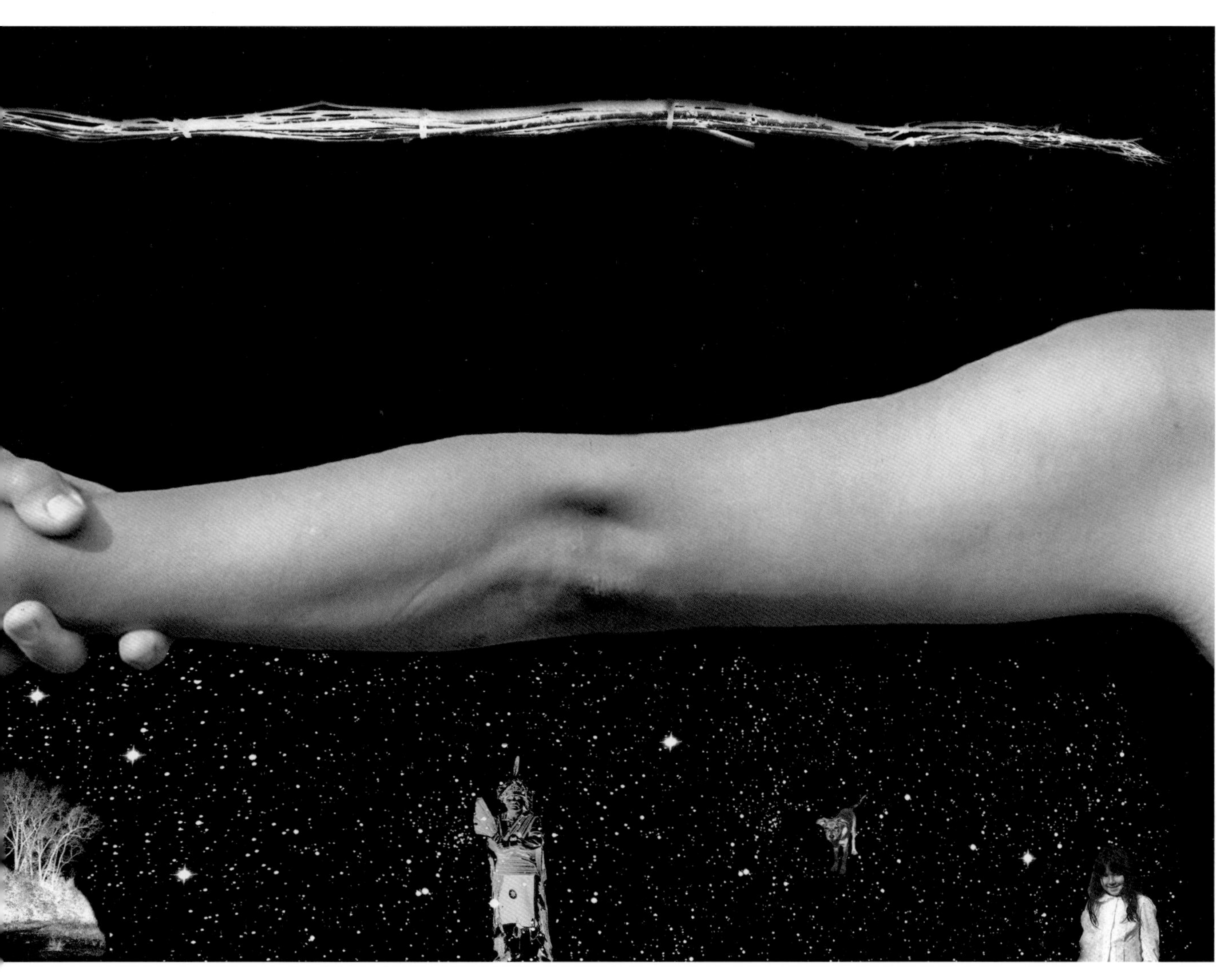

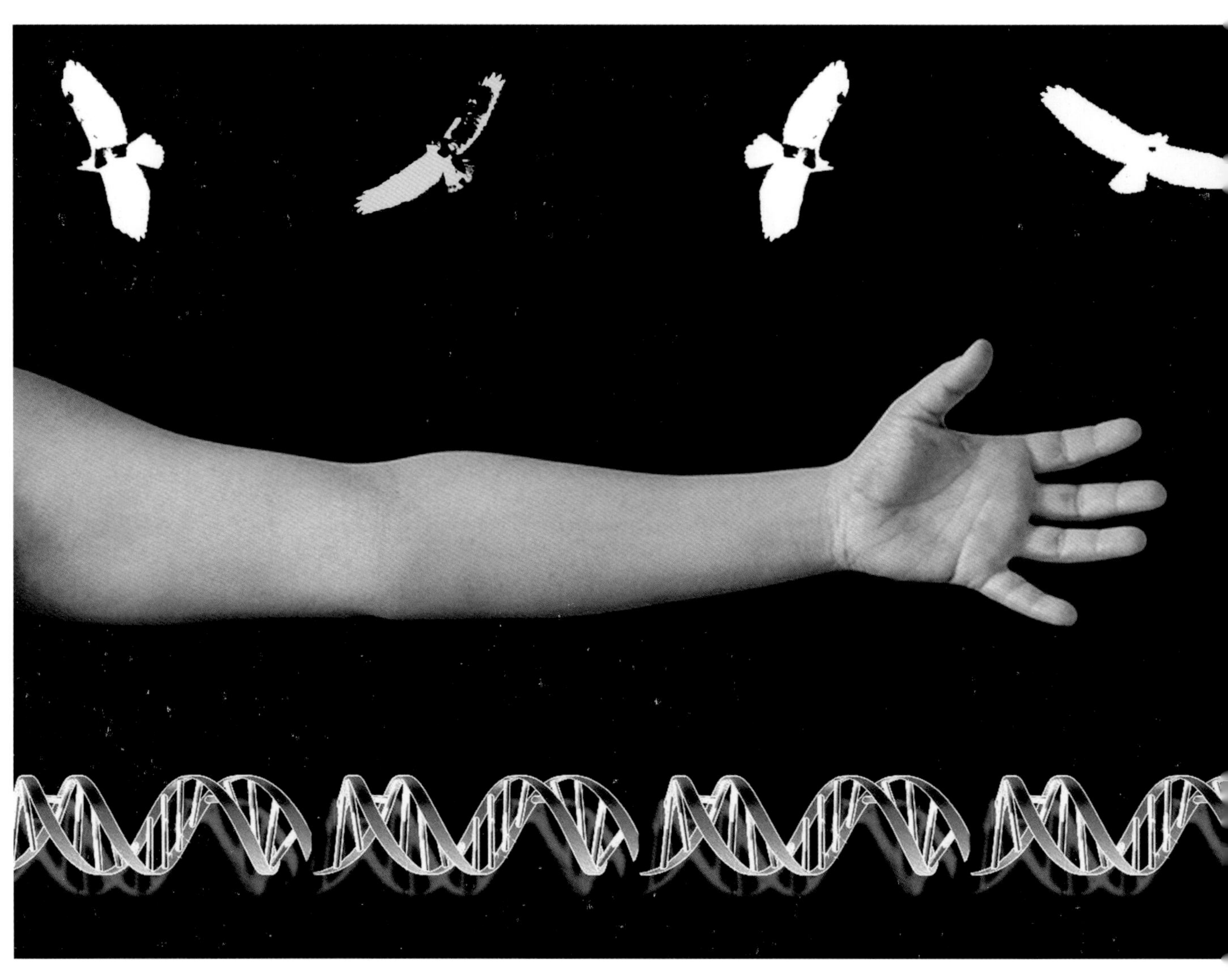

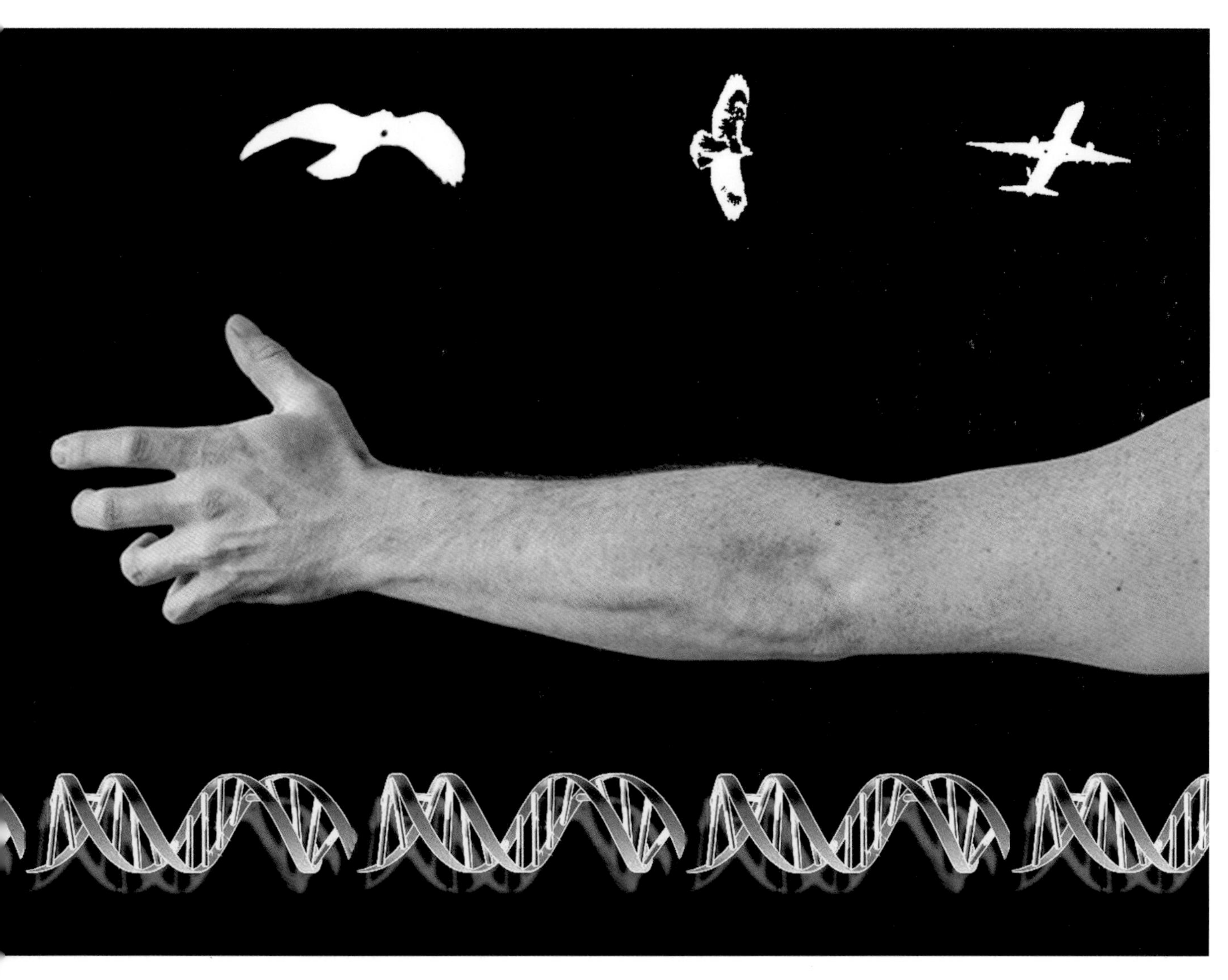

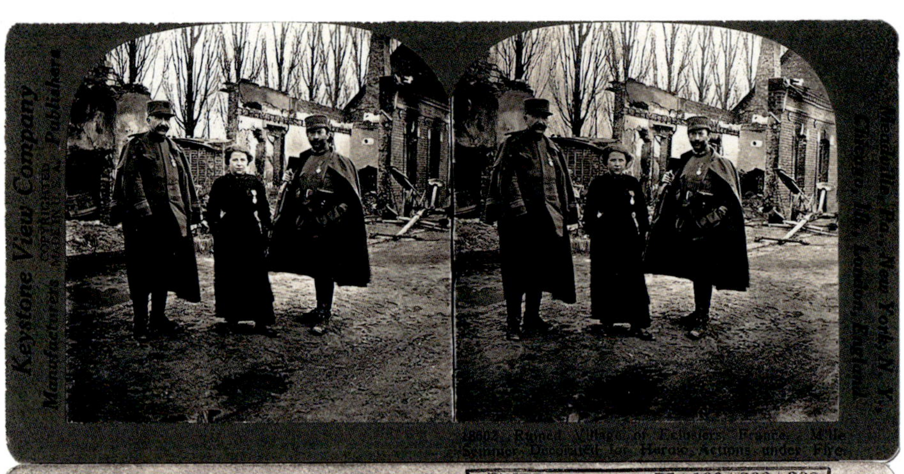

18602

M'LLE. SEMMER DECORATED FOR HEROIC ACTIONS UNDER FIRE

SERIES		75	100	200	300
POSITION					86

In the great hall of the Sorbonne at Paris, where France honors the great poets, scientists and philosophers of the world, there was recently acclaimed the name of Mlle. Marcelle Semmer, a young heroine of the war, who had already won the Cross of the Legion of Honor and the War Cross, before receiving the greatest honor in the power of France to give.

At the outbreak of the war, Mlle. Semmer was an orphan girl living in the little village of Eclusiers, near Frise on the Somme. After the Allies were defeated at Charleroi, the French tried to make a stand at the Somme, but were obliged to retreat across a canal near Mlle. Semmer's home. When the French had passed over the canal, the young girl raised the drawbridge, and for fear the pursuing Germans would compel her to give up the key, without which it could not be lowered again, she threw it into the canal. This held up the Germans for 24 hours. During the occupation of the village by the Germans, Mlle. Semmer concealed a number of French soldiers and aided them to escape, in which act she was finally caught by the Germans and sentenced to be shot. Just as she was placed before the firing squad, the French began to cannonade the village and in the confusion she escaped.

For more than a year she remained in her native village, helping the French soldiers wherever possible. As she knew the locality so well, she sometimes acted as a guide through the marshes, and much of the time she was caring for the wounded. At last, her health broke down and she was persuaded to go to Paris where she entered a school for nurses in order that she might better aid the wounded soldiers.

Copyright by The Keystone View Company

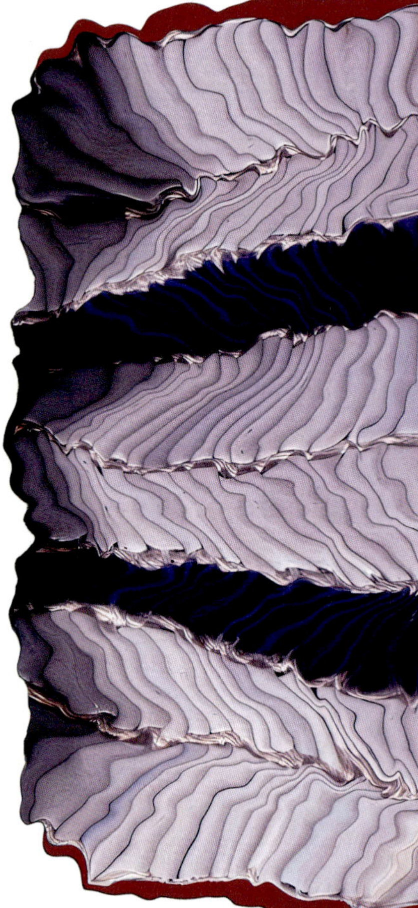

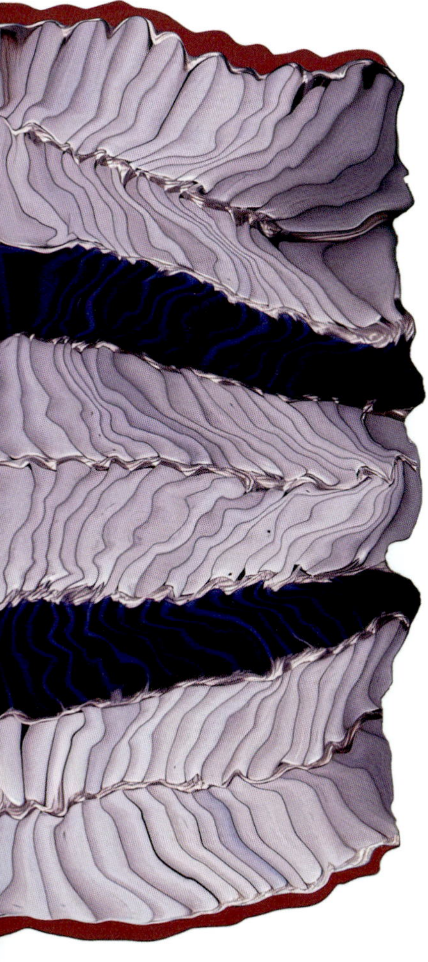

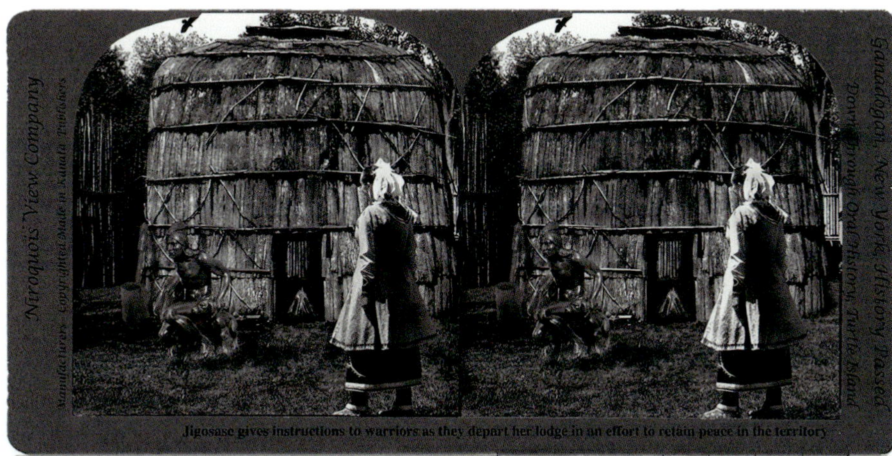

0000

SERIES		00	000	000	000
POSITION		0		00	

JIGOSASE PREPARES WARRIORS AND WARNS THEM AGAINST DANGER

Before recorded history in Haudenosaunee Territory lived a Seneca woman who was considered evil. It was known to others she would poison hunters and travelers as they passed through her area. She witnessed change in a man we now know as Tatadaho after meeting the Great Prophet known as the Peacemaker. He(the cannibal) was a horrible person who lost all humanity within himself. He scared everyone away. When he started to live the good life, he was seen as an intellectual and had great power to reason.

Jigosase realizes that she was not doing good and understood she too can change. She begins by helping warriors by providing rest and food for their journey.

Jigosase has had much influence on the people around her. After the League of Nations is formed she is given the role of choosing the chief within the Iroquois Confederacy. She was the first woman who carried this position and is now known as the Mother of All Nations.

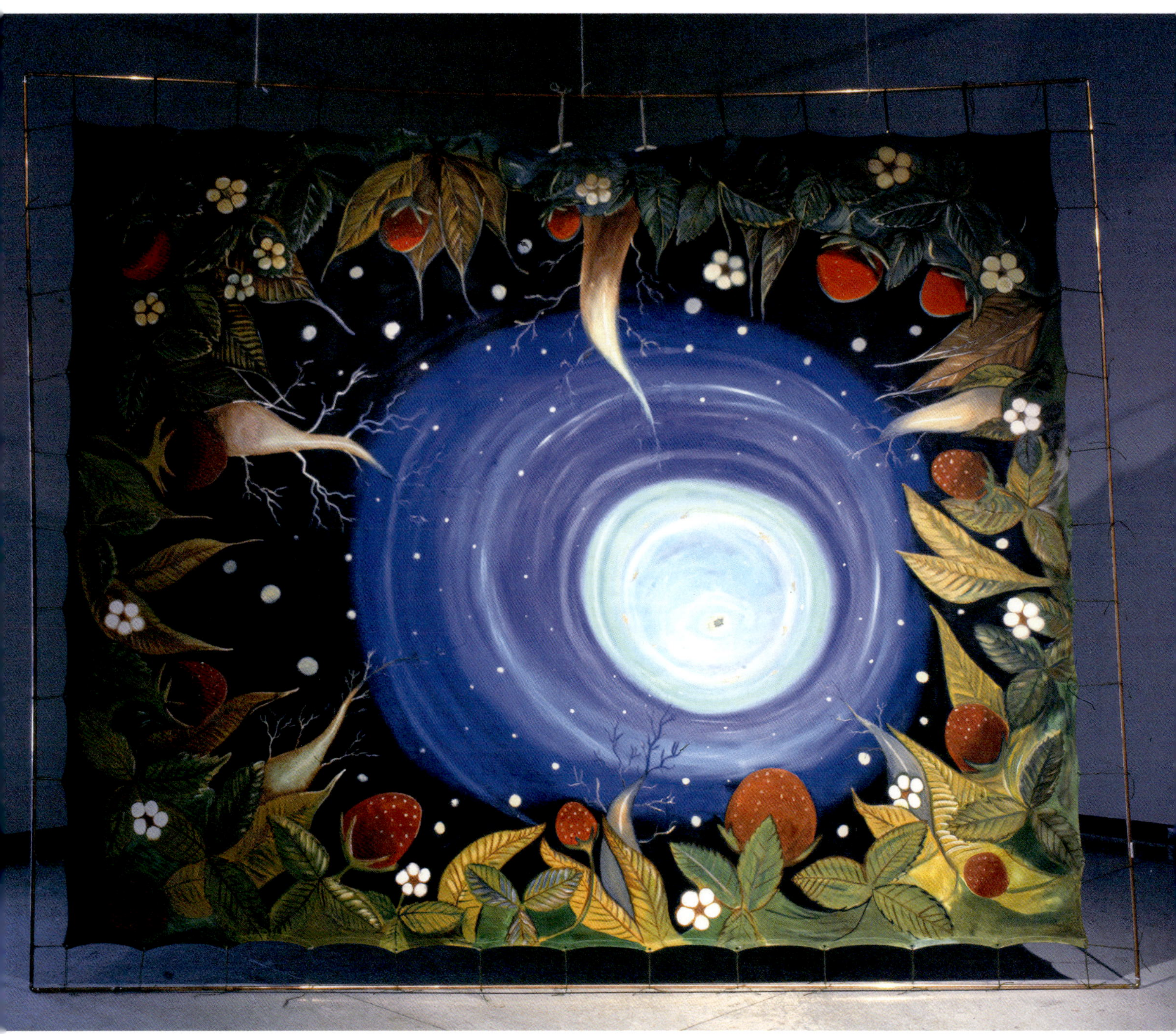

 Skyworld

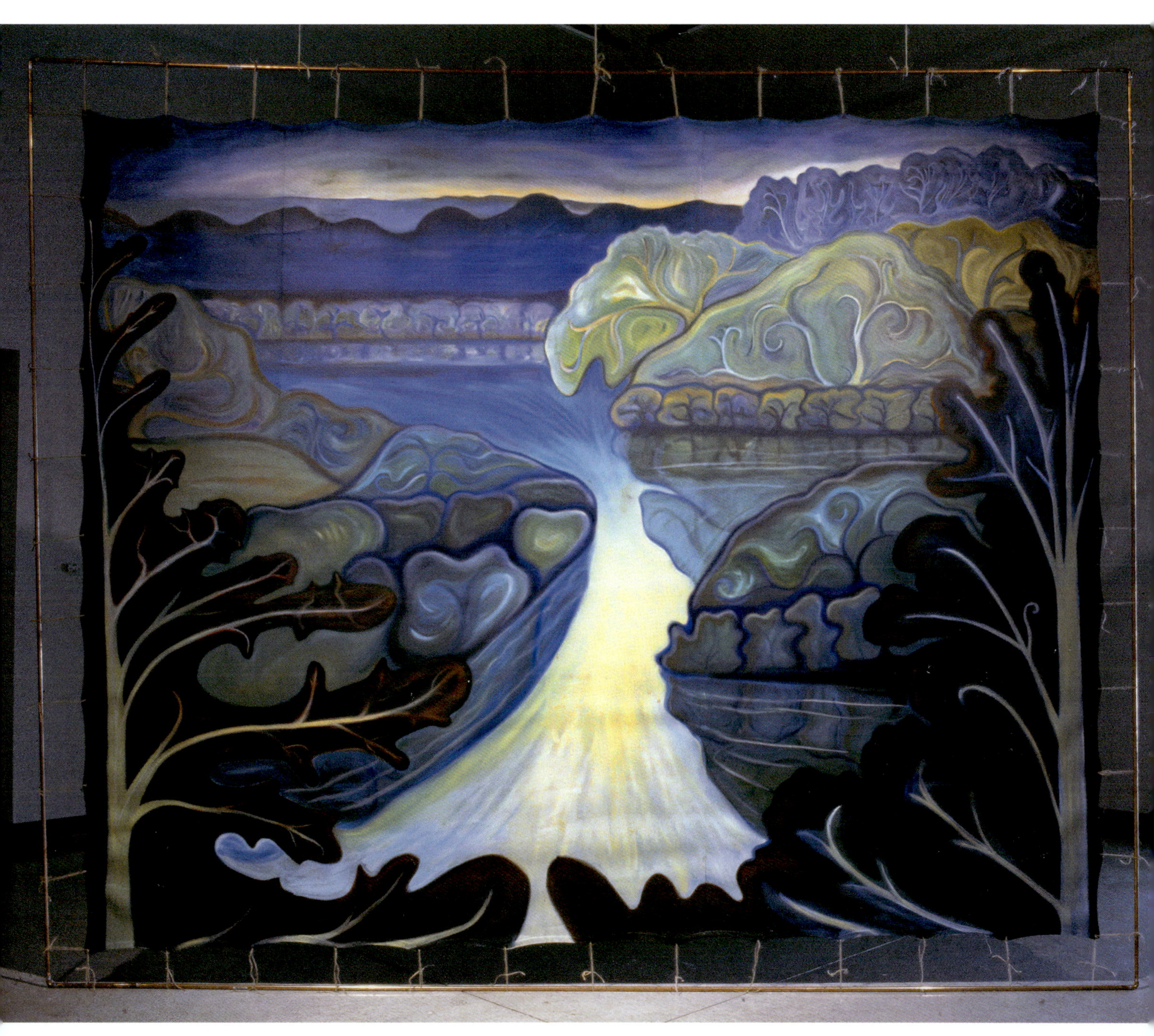

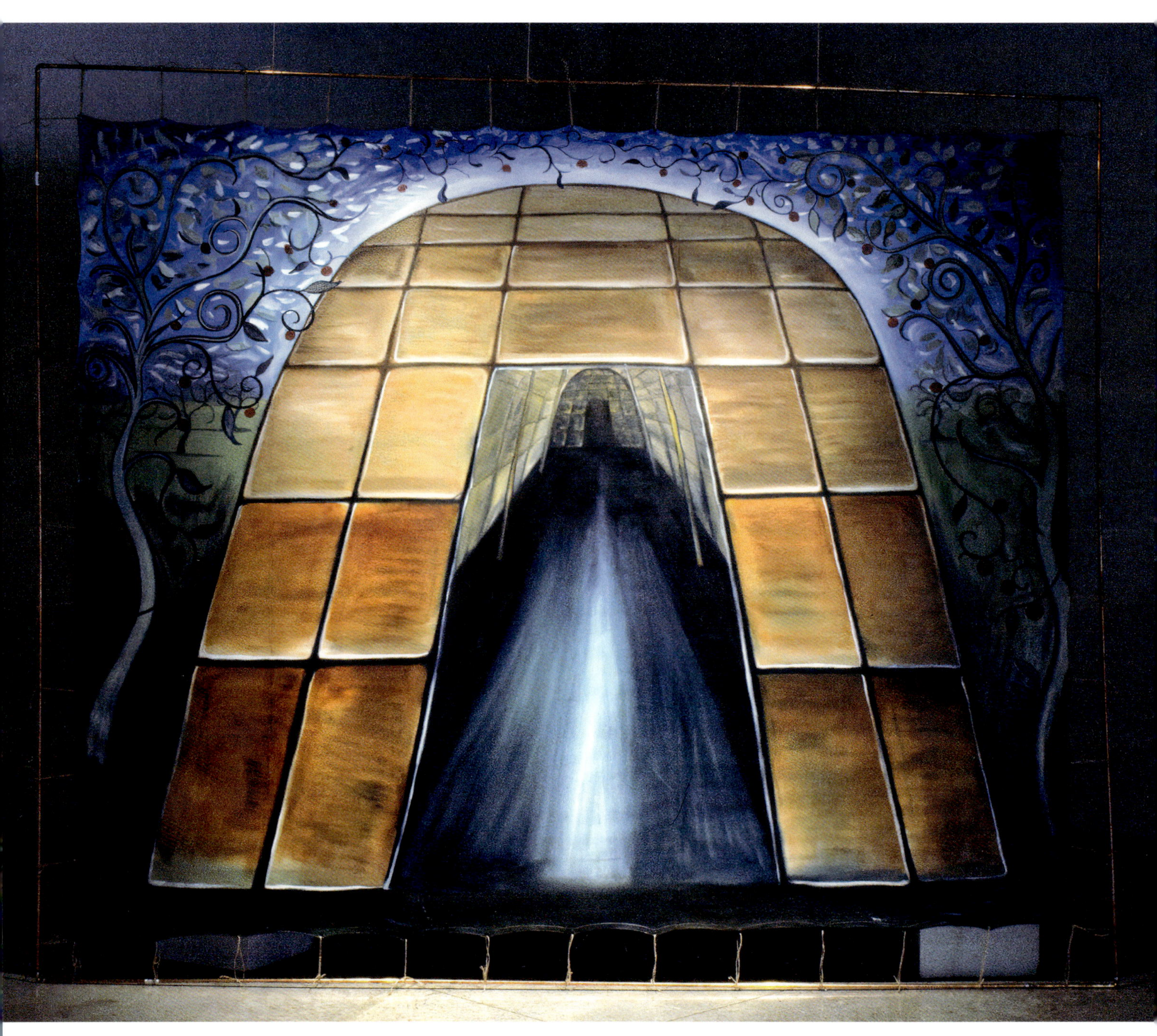

 A Place Like Mindedness

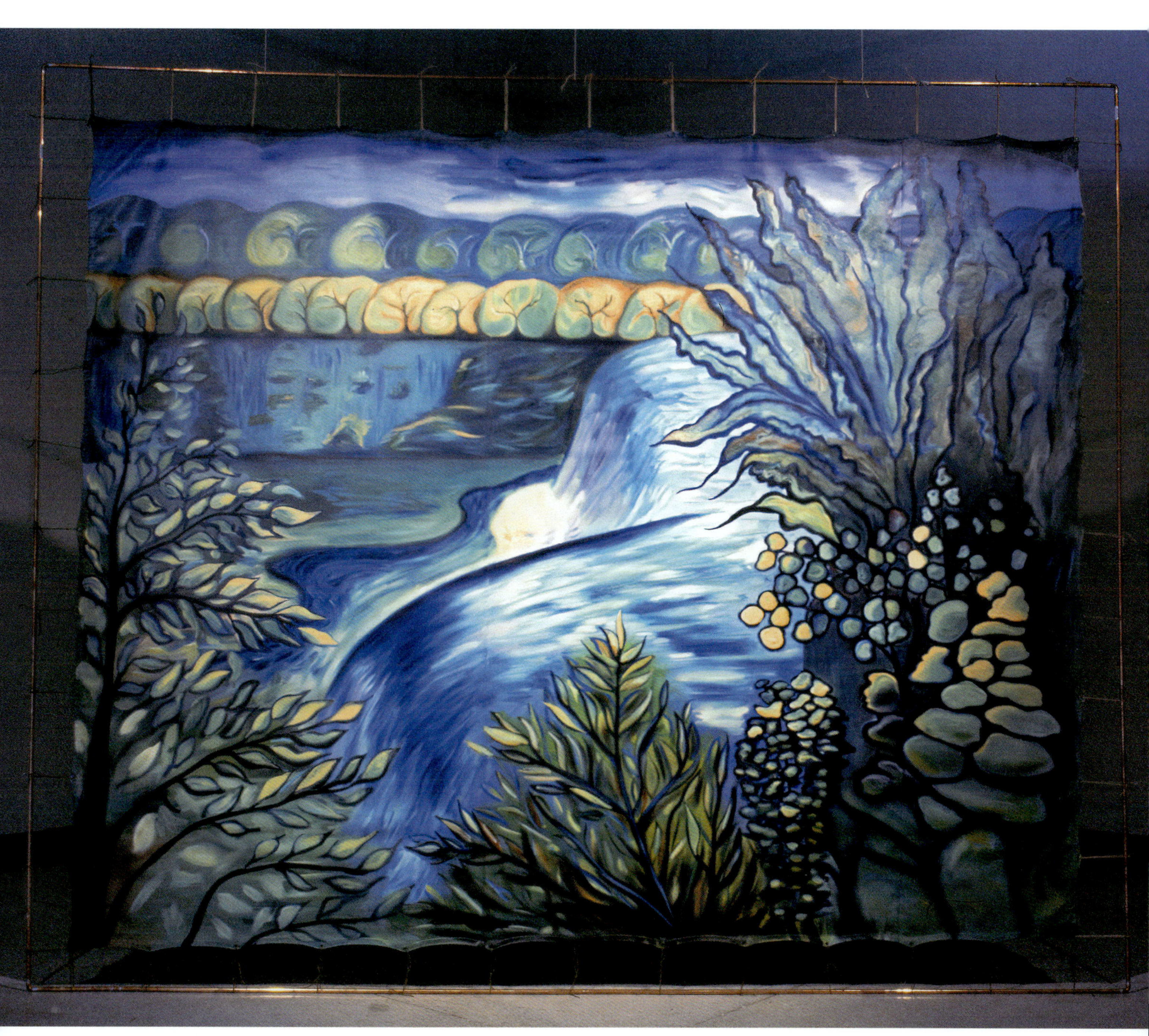

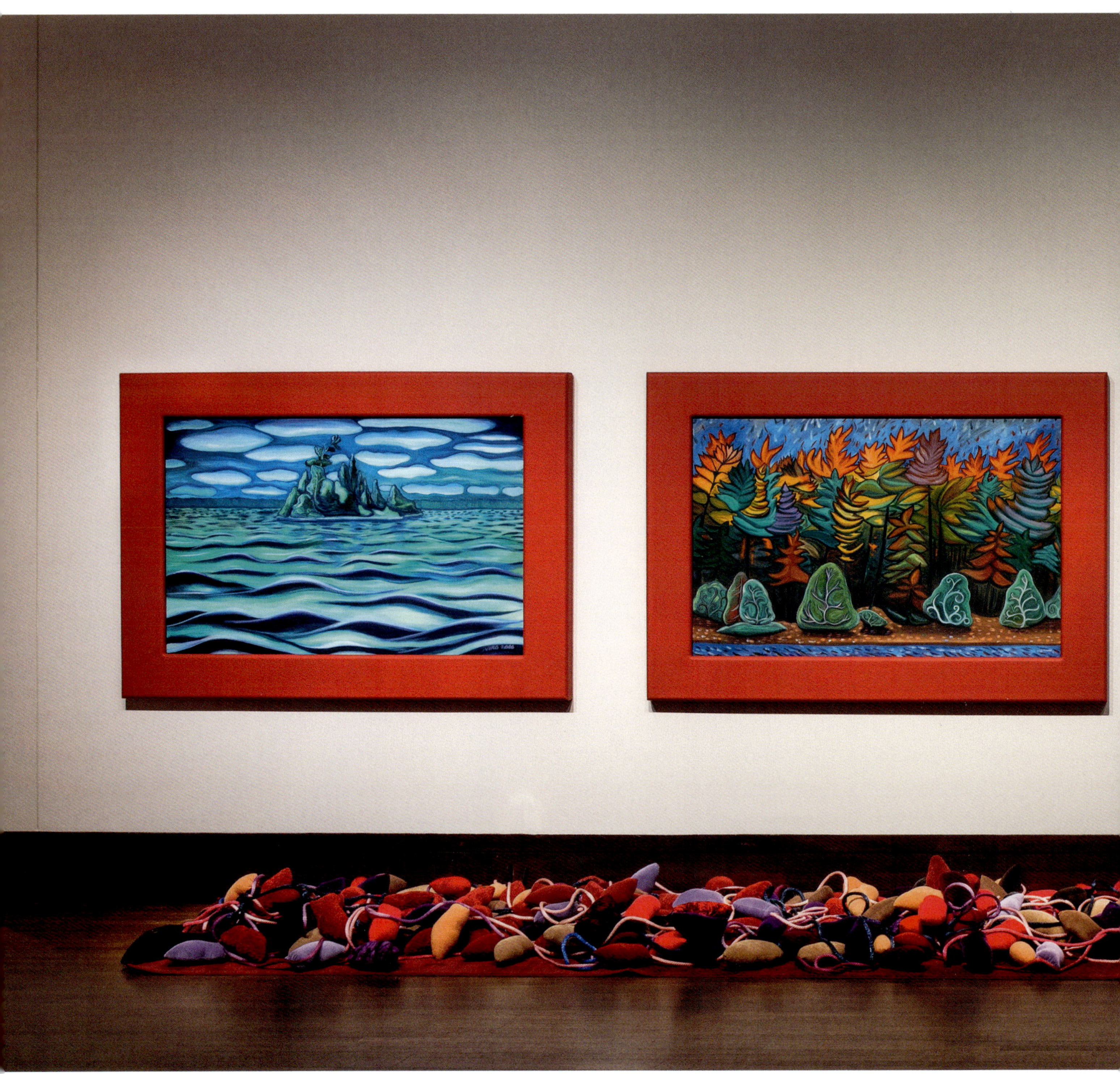

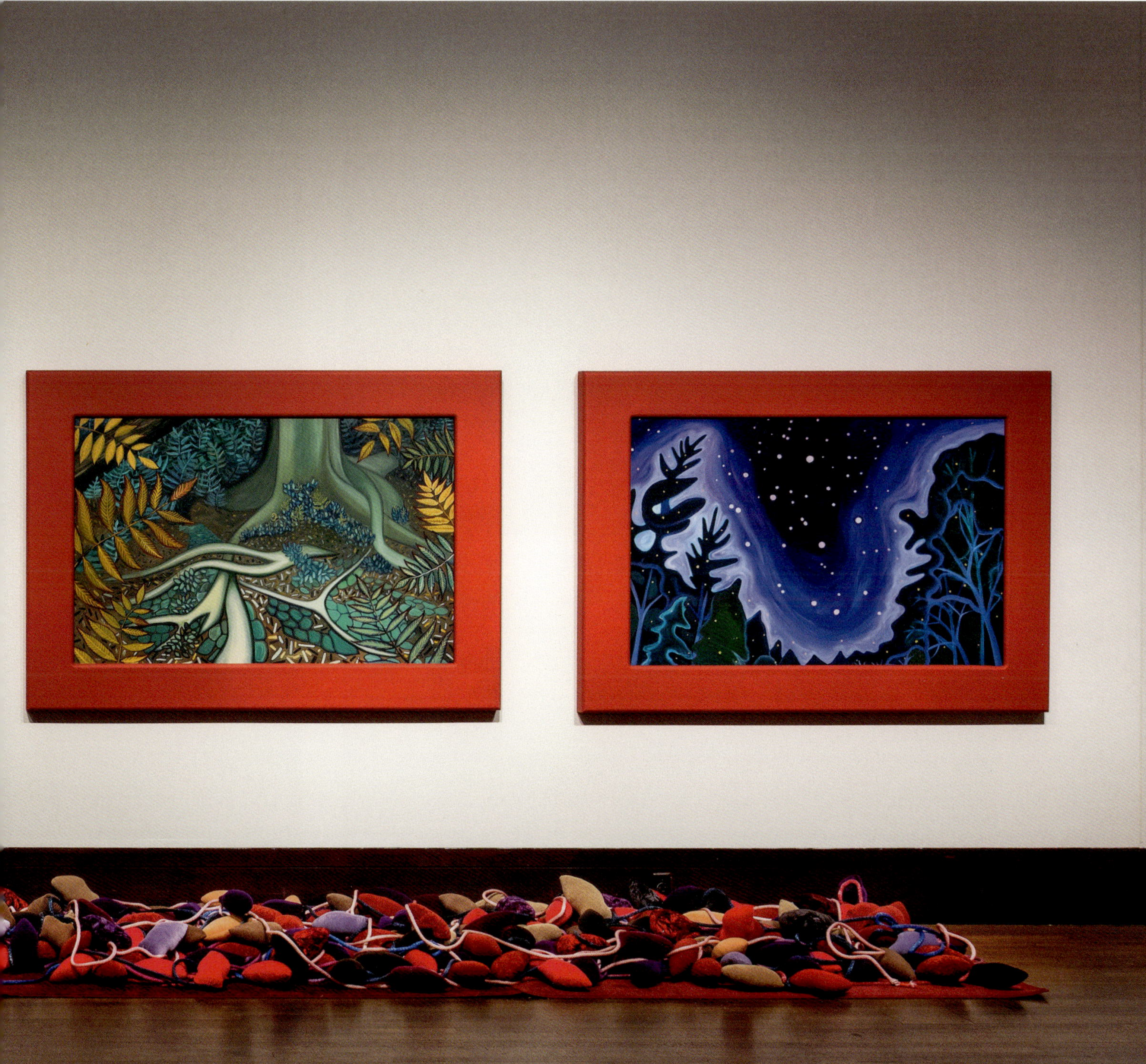

Installation view of **Unbury My Heart**, 2000–2001
Eiteljorg Museum of American Indians and Western Art, Indianapolis, IN

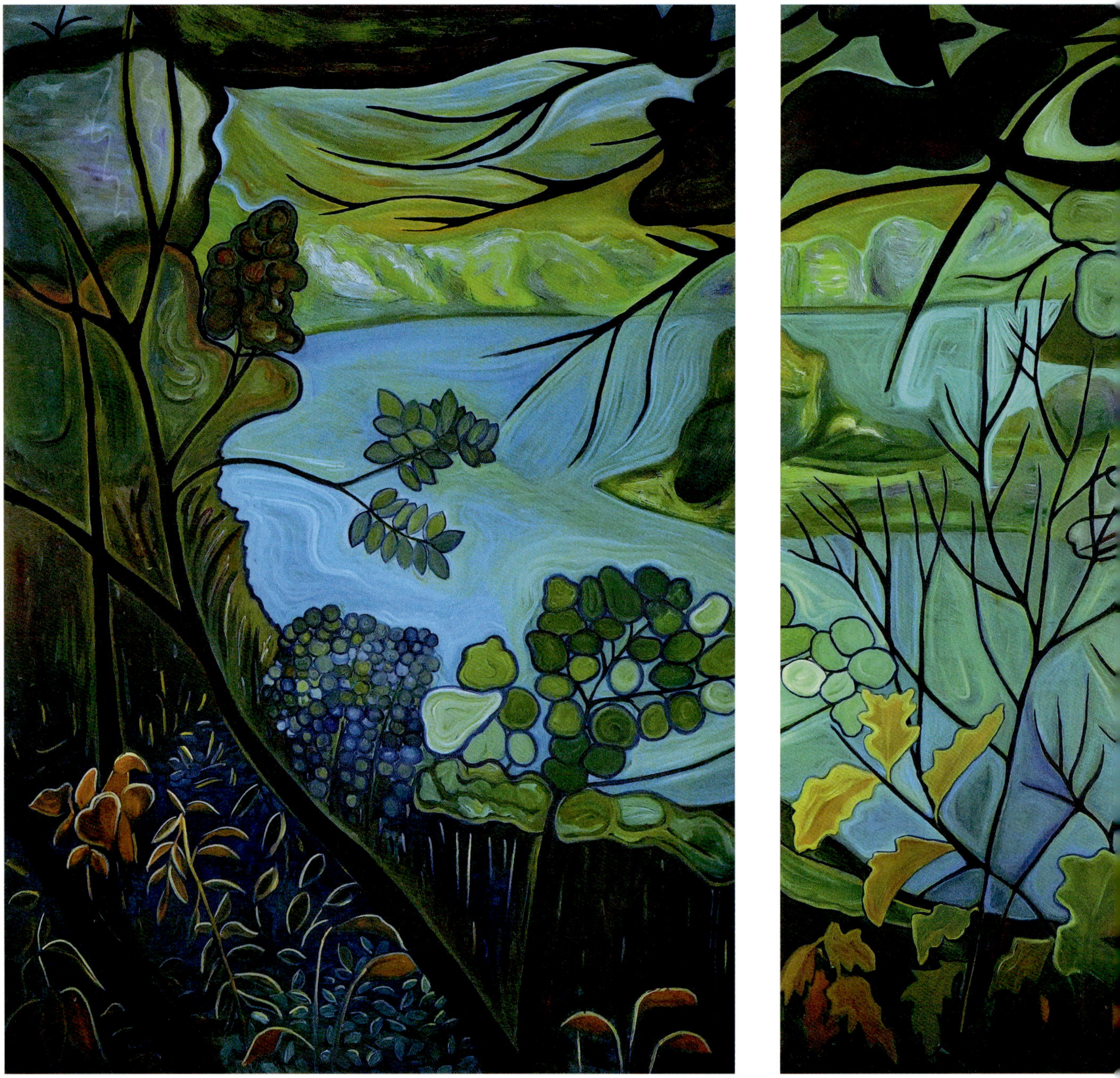

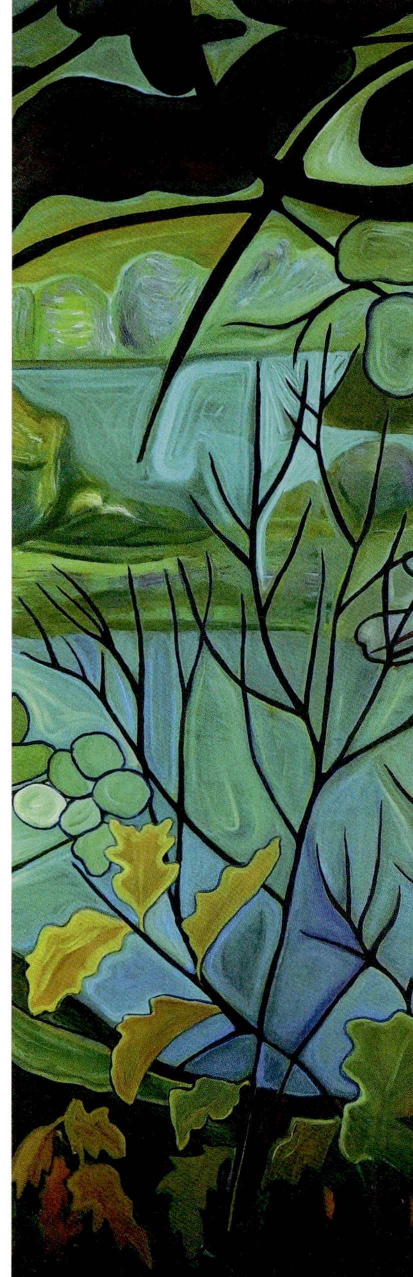

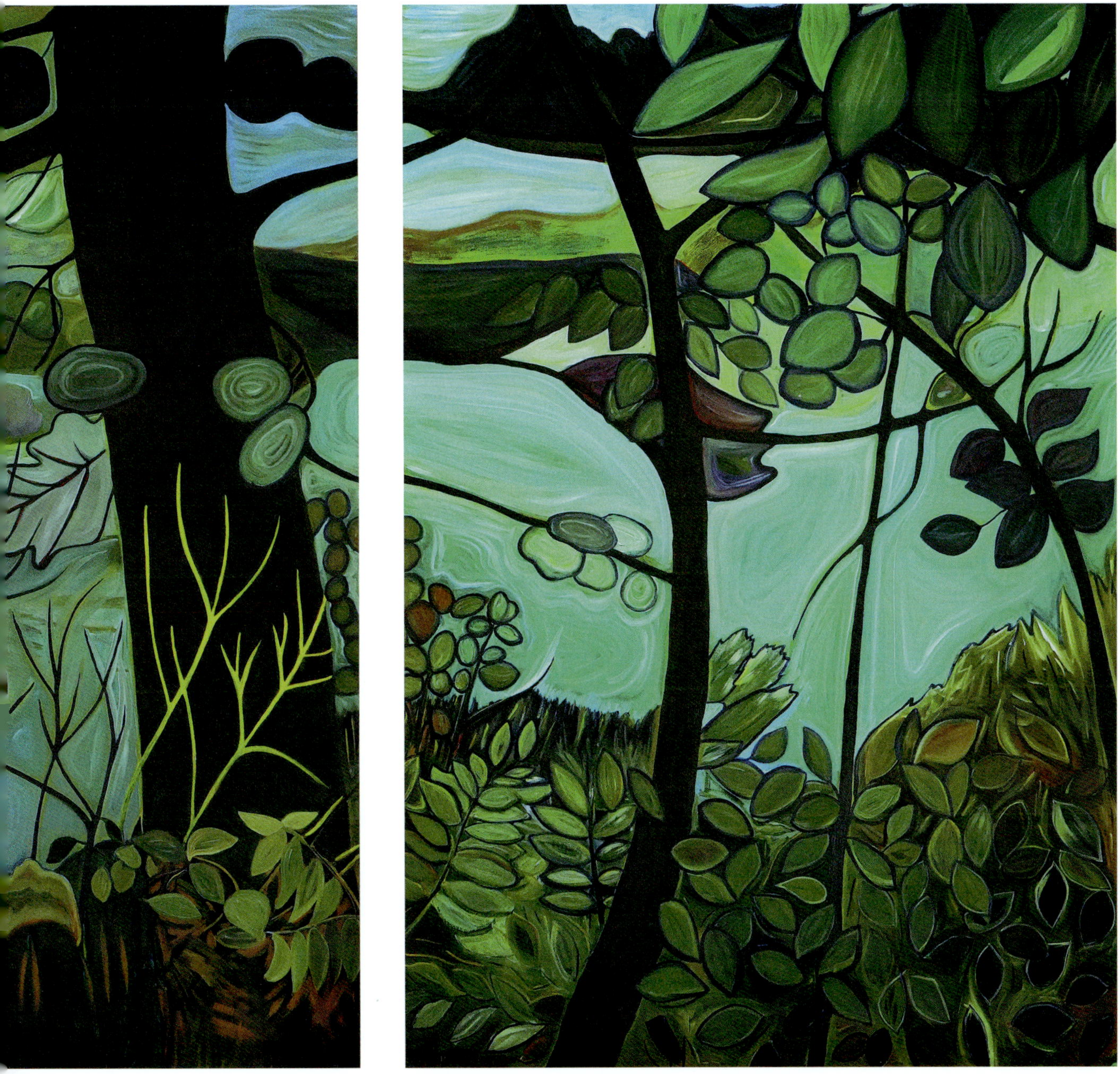

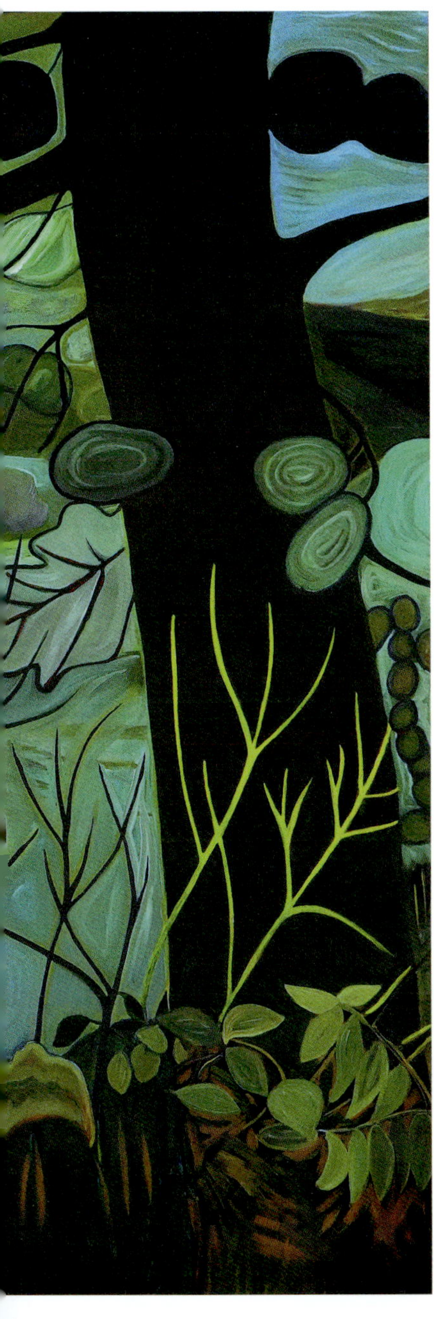

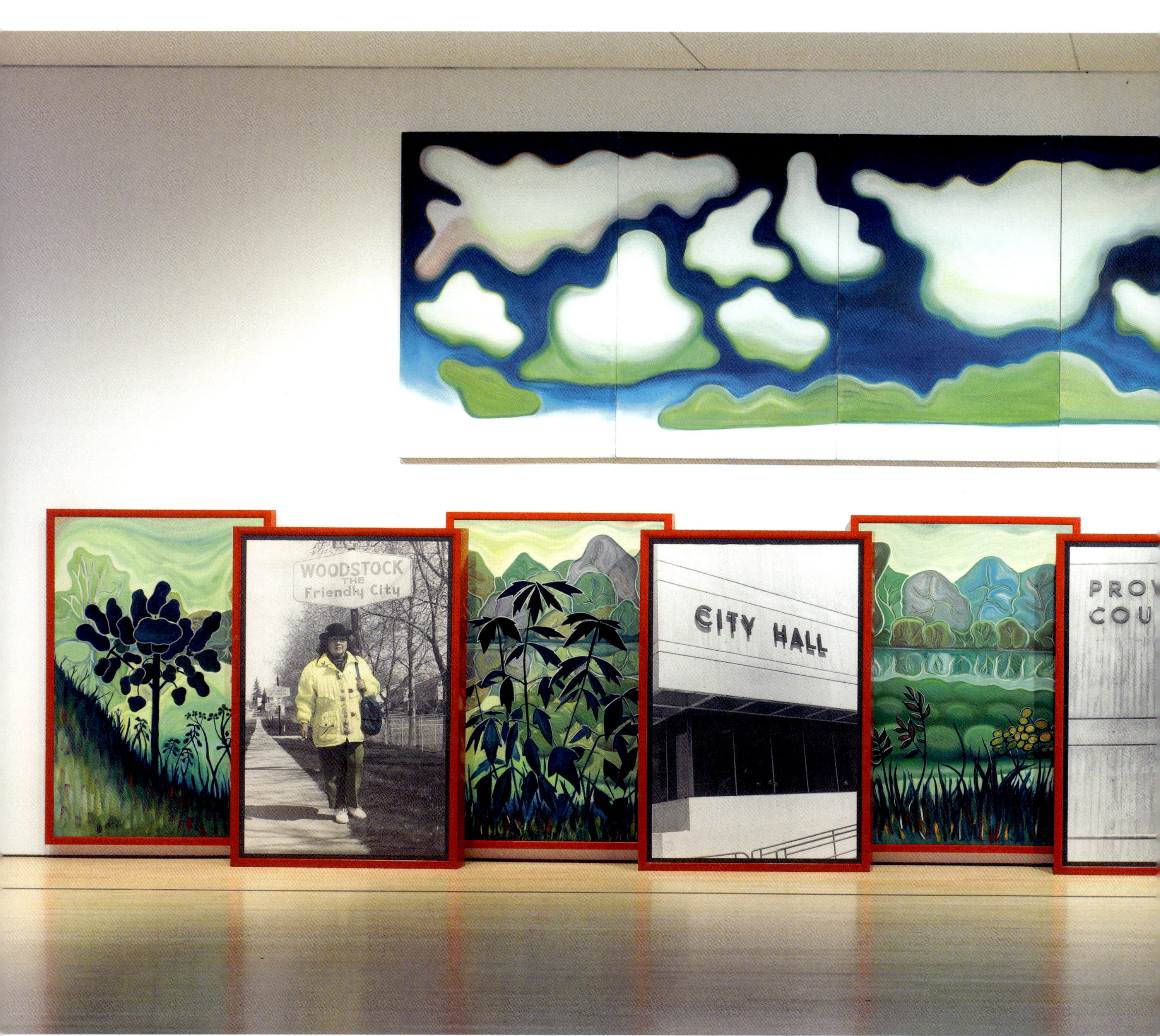

WOODSTOCK
THE
Friendly City
CITY HALL
PROV
COU

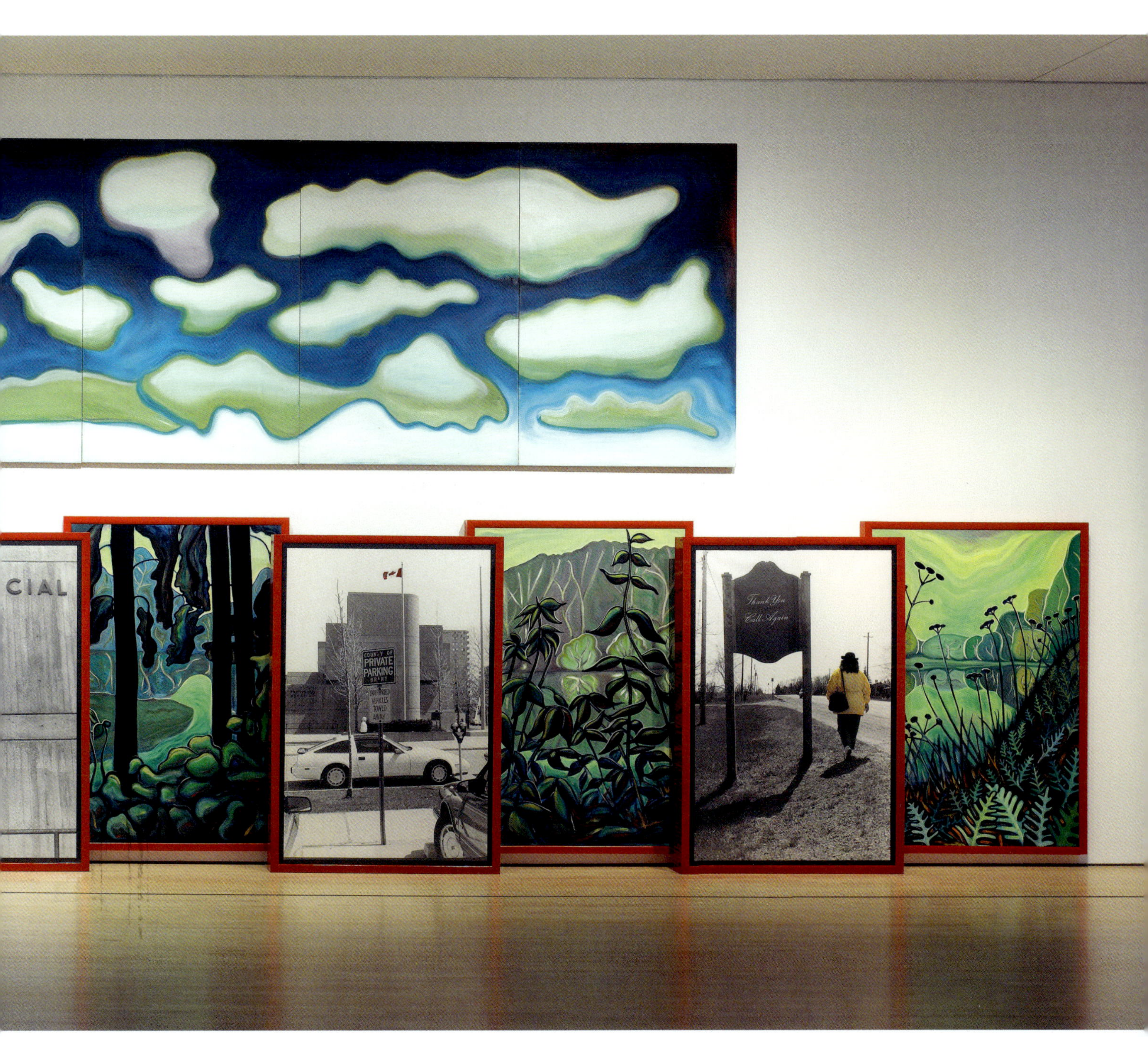

Installation view of **Passing Through**, 1993
National Gallery of Canada, Ottawa
Photograph courtesy the National Gallery of Canada

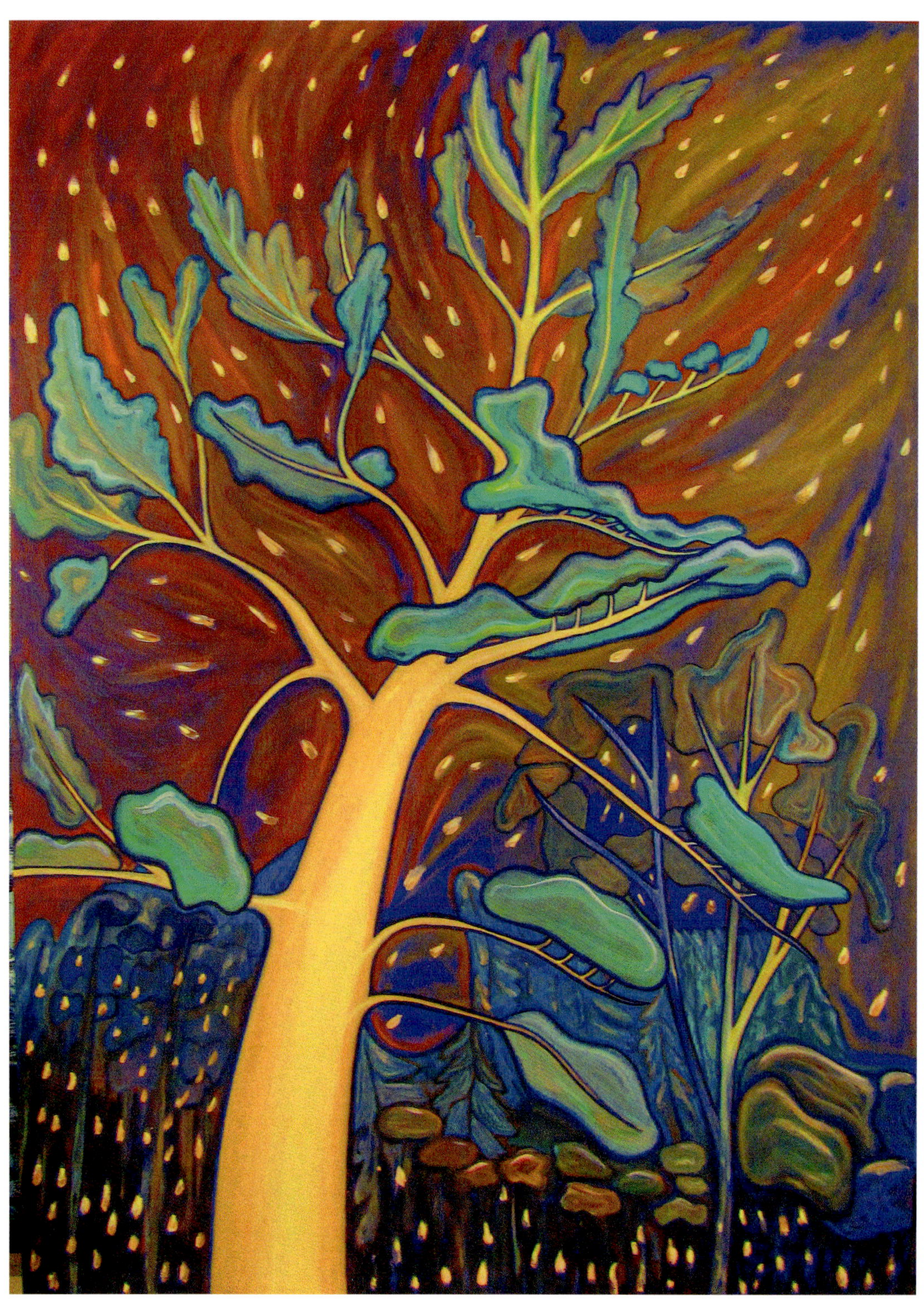

244   Indian Winter, 2015

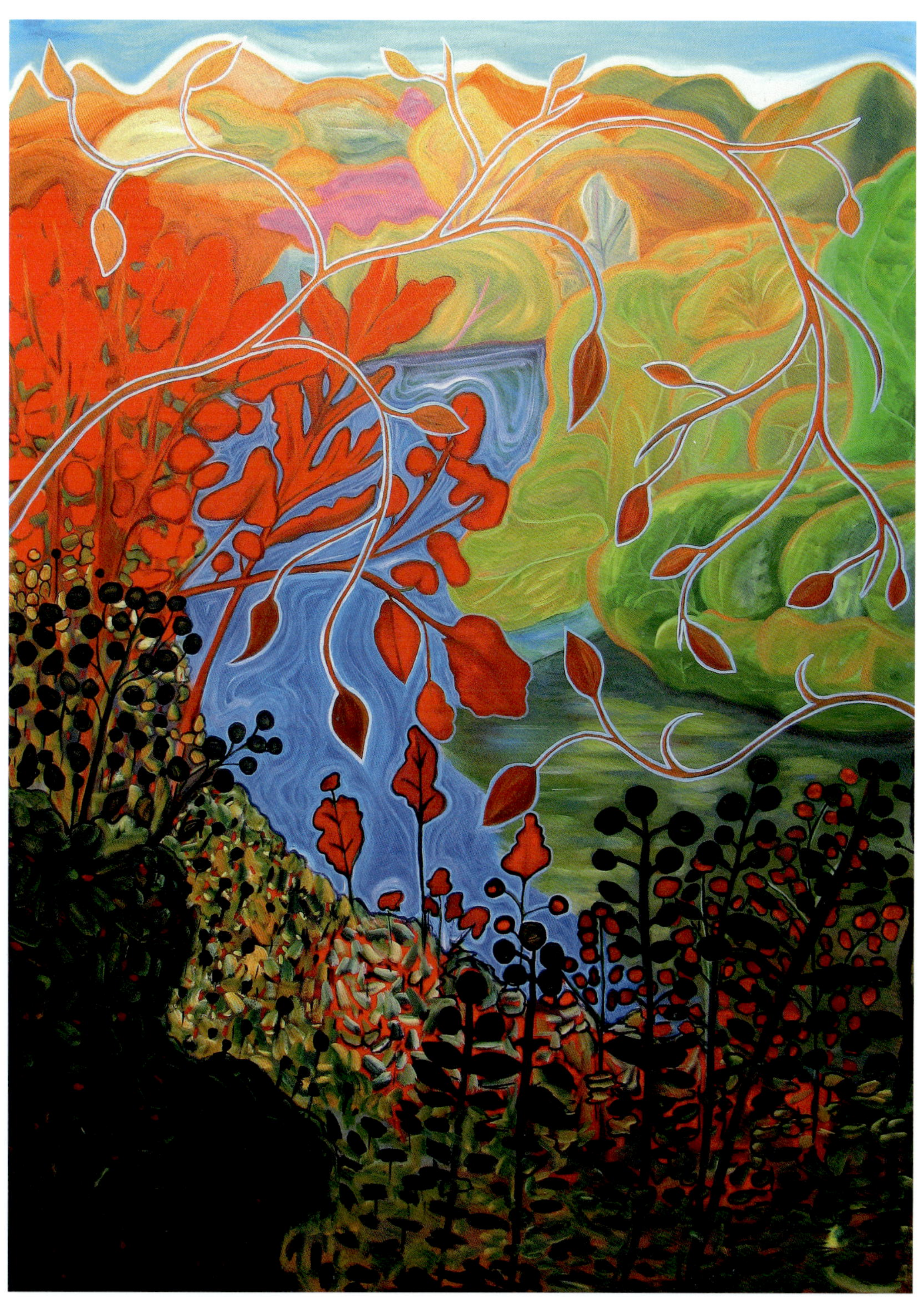

Indian Summer, 2015

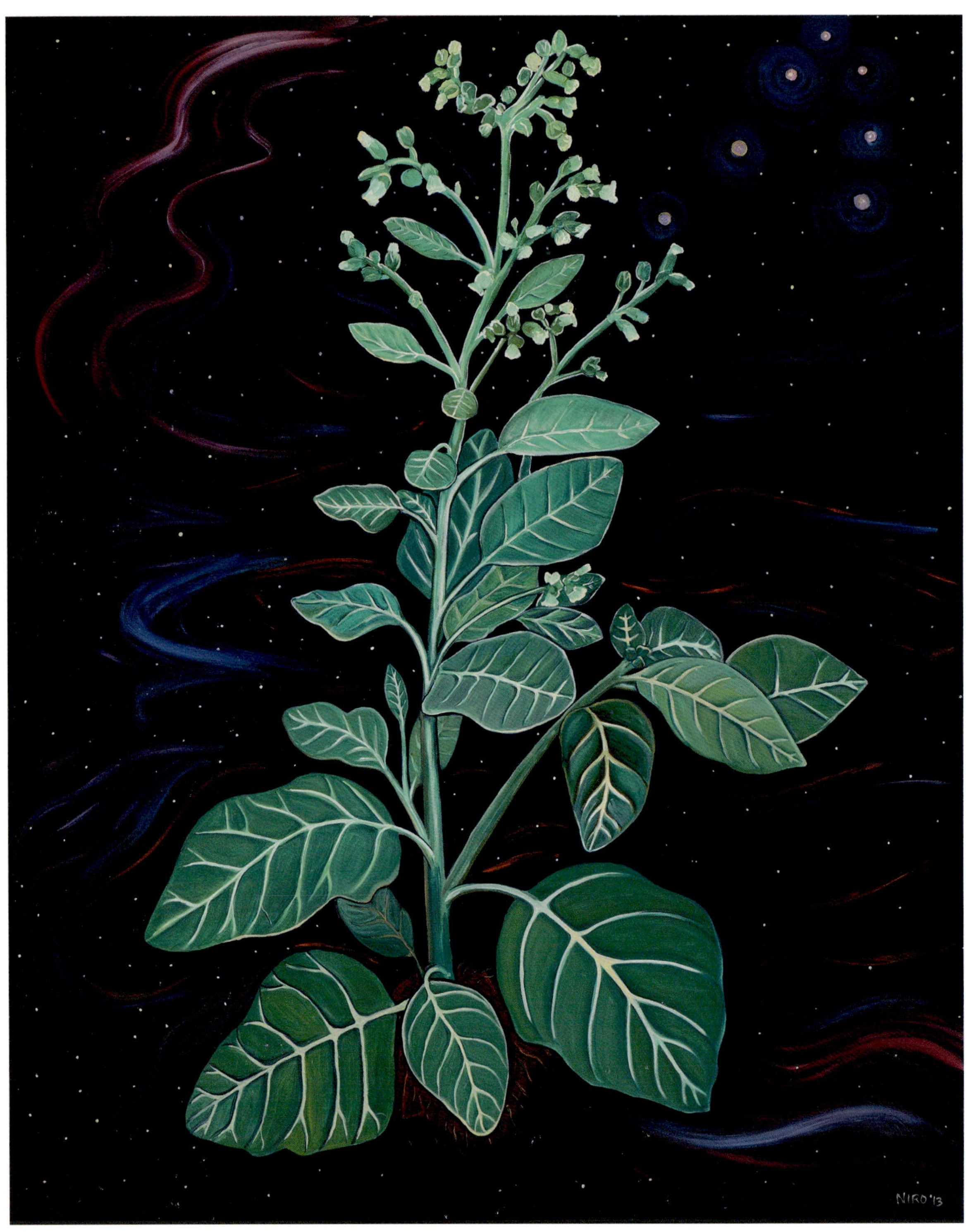

246   **Day One**, 2013

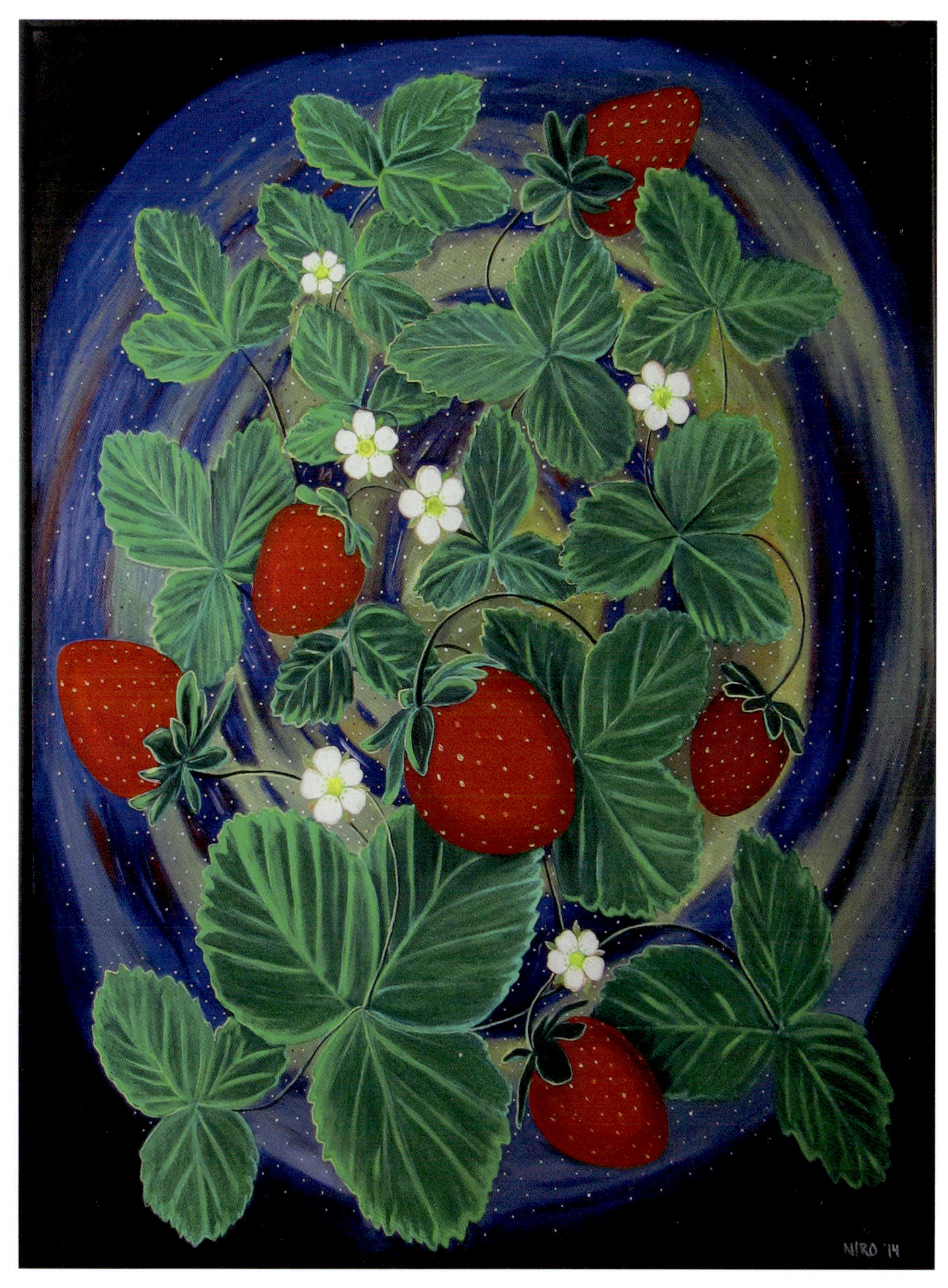

Day One Too, 2014   247

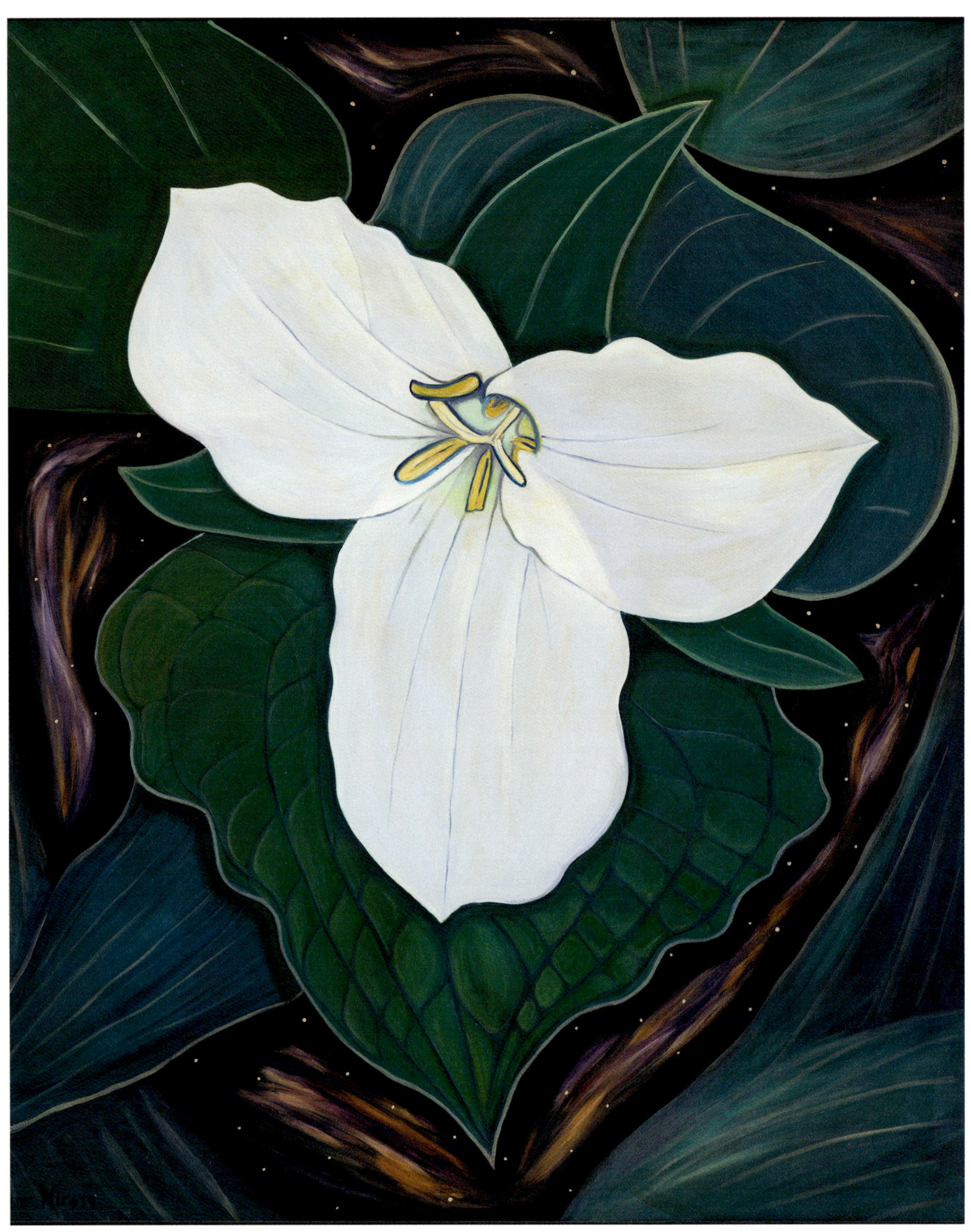

  A Trillion Years Ago, 2015

SHELLEY NIRO
LENSES

DAVID W. PENNEY

This exhibition celebrates Shelley Niro's long career of intense artmaking: paintings, prints, photographs, films, and multi-media installations, often in combinations that defy conventional terms for artistic media. The work stems from who Niro is, and she herself is quick to point out the centrality of identity as a source of inspiration. In this age of acknowledged intersectionality, Niro's audiences are confronted with many overlapping identities: woman; modern Canadian; Kanyen'kehá:ka (Mohawk), more specifically, Kanyen'kehá:ka, who grew up on the Six Nations reserve but now lives in nearby Brantford, Ontario; Turtle Clan Kanyen'kehá:ka from her mother's adoptive family, but also Bay of Quinte Kanyen'kehá:ka on her father's side; daughter; sister; mother; aunt; wife; artist; poet; songwriter; and filmmaking *auteur*, just to scratch the surface. Her work teems with these intertwined identities as well as others she invents. It is deliberative, accessible, and often humourous. But it is not programmatic or explanatory. It draws equally from popular culture (most often linked to that of her generation), memory, experience, history, and more timeless Haudenosaunnee cultural knowledge. And while it can inspire spontaneous chuckles of connection, many of her references elude firm signification. Comprehension of broader historical, personal, and cultural contexts deepens and enriches the experience of it. I am reminded of a statement by Tuscarora artist Jolene Rickard, "I have had to learn all the specifics of other cultures in order to move freely about the world. I want other people to take the responsibility to learn my symbols and thoughts."[1]

MEMORY / MEMORY MAKES HOME OUT OF PLACE

Shelley Doxtater Niro was born in 1954 in the town of Niagara Falls, New York, where she lived until the age of five. It is where her face was pulled up from the earth, to borrow a Kanyen'kéha expression.[2] Niro's short film *Niagara* (2015, p. 130) begins by claiming the falls, *Ongniaahra*. She spells out the Kanyen'kéha word both orthographically and phonically while her camera scans the crest of the falls from below. We see great curtains of water descending in sunlight.

Niro's father George Oliver Doxtater worked construction in Niagara Falls, as an iron worker. The postwar city was a boom town and had been for more than a century. From the moment they found the falls, the French, English, and later the Americans valued them for their strategic and economic potential. The French started constructing fortifications at the mouth of the Niagara River, well below the falls, as early as 1678. The British besieged and took the French fort there in 1759. In 1764, more than 2,000 interested parties, representing twenty-four Indigenous Nations, convened at British Fort Niagara in the wake of Pontiac's War to confirm Britain's 1763 Proclamation Line, the British attempt to stem the flood of settler immigrants into Indigenous Territories west of the colonies. The resultant Treaty of Niagara ceded from the Seneca a four-mile strip around the falls for a portage road and rights to the fort and accommodated a military occupation.[3]

After the American Revolution, the settlements that would become the City of Niagara Falls began expanding along the American side of the river. From the early nineteenth century onward, tourism and industry powered the growth of the site, which first became the town of Manchester and was later incorporated as the City of Niagara Falls in 1892. Hydro-electric power fuelled massive industrial development in the early twentieth century, particularly electrothermic (silicon carbide abrasives) and electrochemical manufacturing (chlorine, phosphorous, and others), both processes that produced enormous quantities of toxic waste. In 1956, when Niro was a toddler, a rock fall destroyed the principal power station of the Niagara Power Company, ushering in a new age of hydro-electric expansion under the New York Power Authority.[4] Their plans included seizure, through eminent domain, of a substantial portion of the nearby reservation of the Tuscarora, the sixth of the Six Nations of the Haudenosaunee Confederacy. The Tuscarora had purchased the land from the Seneca after the American Revolution and the Americans tolerated the reservation in thanks for Tuscarora support during the war. By 1960, when Doxtater had taken his family back to the Six Nations reserve in Ontario, the Tuscarora had lost their legal battle to retain that portion of their lands, with the Supreme Court ruling that "we must hold that Congress, by the broad general terms of...the Federal Power Act, has authorized the Federal Power Commission's licensees to take lands owned by Indians."[5] It was one more episode in the long and constant drumbeat of Haudenosaunee dispossession.

For the Kanyen'kehá:ka in particular, dispossession began arguably when the Dutch negotiated with Kanyen'kehá:ka Chiefs to establish the town of Schenectady on flats adjacent to the Mohawk River in 1662. The Kanyen'kehá:ka signatories of the deed may have indulged the request in the interest of burnishing relations with their Dutch trading partners, and also because the site was prone to flooding—the first year's plantings were destroyed when the river overflowed its banks.[6] The Kanyen'kehá:ka forged far closer relations with the British, who seized the Dutch colony three years later. But thereafter the Mohawk Valley became a battle ground for the intermittent, intercolonial conflicts between the British and the French colony to the north. The French landed a crippling blow when they invaded and destroyed three populous Kanyen'kehá:ka towns, carrying away women and children, during

King William's War (1689–1697).[7] During subsequent intercolonial wars—Queen Anne's War (1702–1713), King George's War (1744–1748), and the so-called French and Indian War (1754–1763)—Kanyen'kehá:ka paid the price for their British alliance with warrior's blood and attacks on their homes. The Kanyen'kehá:ka also contended with massive immigration occupying their territories during those years with settler towns established at Schoharie (1713), German Flats (1723) and the Cherry Valley (1740s), among several others. The pulse of dispossession quickened during the years leading up to the American Revolution with the British immigrant population surging to more than 40,000 in the Mohawk Valley by 1775.[8] Dispossessed Kanyen'kehá:ka scattered north to join their relations among the St. Lawrence communities, west to the Onondaga and Cayuga, or south to the multi-Nation communities near the New York and Pennsylvania border.

The immigrant towns supported the rebellion, for the most part, while the Kanyen'kehá:ka, along with Onondaga, Cayuga, and Seneca to the west, fought for the Crown. After the failed attempt of a combined British and Haudenosaunee effort in 1777 to take Fort Stanwix, the rebels' stronghold in central New York, the conflict devolved into town burning and indiscriminate killing over the summer of 1778. The next year saw George Washington, then Commander-in-Chief of the Continental Army, initiate an effort to eliminate any Haudenosaunee threat to the rebellion by ordering the destruction of the Confederacy. During the early fall of 1779, Washington's army, under the leadership of Generals John Sullivan and James Clinton, destroyed nearly fifty Haudenosaunee towns throughout what is now New York state. Thousands of refugees fled to Fort Niagara, seeking British protection.[9]

Niro's multi-media sculpture *1779* (2017, pp. 153–155)—more like a kiosk really—commemorates those events, insisting on remembering, on memory. "This is a memoriam to the people who didn't make it. And it serves as a memoriam to those who did," she wrote.[10] Boots with stiletto heels that Niro bought at a Value Village store and beaded, stand upon a short column. (These boots are made for walking?) Their gold-plated heels suggested to her the crass commercialism of modern Niagara Falls tourism. The words, "Niagara Falls," beaded on the vamps, mimic generations of beadwork made by her community for tourists at Niagara Falls. Flexing ancestral skills of beadwork technique, Niro shows us the falls with drapery of white beaded fringe and tangles like whirlpools. Below the boots, a video plays on a small monitor positioned horizontally, like a river. We see the rushing water and whirlpools of the lower Niagara River, its mesmerizing turbulence in restless motion.

For the some 5,000 refugees encamped around Fort Niagara in 1779, exile from their homes imposed a state of fluid, rootless, and disorienting liminality. With the Treaty of Paris concluding the war in 1783, Britain surrendered its role as ally and protector of the Six Nations. Instead, they offered lands in Canada at the Bay of Quinte and Grand River in compensation (although arguably the Confederacy already possessed these lands).[11] Confirmation of the Haldimand Tract on the Grand River, named for the Governor of Quebec who proffered the deal, "Six Miles Deep from each Side of the River beginning at Lake Erie & extending in that proportion to the Head of Said River," waited until the fall of 1784. Hunger and hardship marked the migrations from Niagara. The swift, overpowering turbulence of war carried the Niagara refugees to their new homes.[12]

Niro recalls how often her father spoke about the beauty of the Mohawk Valley, although he never visited. He remembered the words of his grandmother, although, given the generational span, she had been too young to live there: memories of the place had been told from one generation to the next. In a suite of photographs entitled *Battlefields of My Ancestors* (2015, pp. 168, 181–195), Niro visualizes these memories with majestic views of the Adirondacks, the Mohawk River, and other homeland places. The work is punctuated by images of historic markers documenting burned towns and concludes with an image of the Grand River. It is a visual travelogue of memory.

Another suite of images, a set of seven giclee prints bordered in red, offer a more nuanced approach to this history. Titled *La Pieta* (2007, pp. 162–167), the work draws a metaphor for grieving mothers from Michelangelo's well-known marble sculpture. Niro arranged the seven images in sequence, framing each one with red, for the blood of war, and wampum belts figured with cosmological symbols of earth and sky. In the centre image, titled *Hearing Trees Fall* (p. 164), a young male torso, sensuous and vulnerable, suggests Michelangelo's depiction of the supine body of Christ on his mother's lap. Men bring their communities to war, Niro argues, and they pay with their fragile bodies and the grief of their relations and loved ones. The other images, arranged symmetrically on either side, shift to metaphors of land and place. The black-and-white images *Sorrow* (p. 163) and *Tomorrow* (p. 165) show an old, weathered tree trunk and a bleak, wintery landscape. *An Infinite View* (pp. 162–163) and *On the Edge of Tomorrow* (p. 166), printed in warmer sepia tones, present, on one hand, a vast airborne view of central New York's lake country and, on the other, high-voltage electrical towers clustered along the edge of the Six Nations reserve. Images of cleansing and purifying sky-blue water, stressing the larger cosmological context for this very human history of suffering and grief, bookend the ensemble on either side.

But the exodus to the Grand River didn't resolve much. The deed to the Six Nations reserve, prepared in 1783 by the Lt. Governor of Upper Canada, John Graves Simcoe, lopped off the upper headwaters land, a full third of the Haldimand Tract. The Six Nations Council pursued the "headwaters claim" with the Crown government for years afterwards, until Lord Henry Bathurst, British Secretary of State for War and the Colonies, ruled in 1821 that Haldimand had simply made a mistake in geography. Six Nations continues to press this claim today. Then there were the immigrant squatters. They occupied lands throughout the Haldimand Tract, becoming so numerous and belligerent in the region around the major ford on the Grand River that the Six Nations Council felt compelled, in 1829, to surrender the land, now the City of Brantford, bordering the present Six Nations reserve, and lost more land thereafter to the burgeoning settler town.[13] Many Six Nations citizens remember that Council Chiefs cursed a portion of the unceded townsite during the early nineteenth century, a memory made more widespread by the writings of Kanyen'kehá:ka historian and Clan Mother, Alma Greene.[14] Niro agrees that Brantford, where she now lives, has failed to thrive. Through theft, coercion, fraud, illegal occupation, and miscalculated accommodation, the Six Nations reserve has today been reduced to only a small fraction of the original Haldimand Tract. Six Nations government and citizens continue to contest this long history of relentless dispossession.

This unceasing pressure, the injustice, the "lamp-lighting" about the facts, it all takes a long, pan-generational toll. In a suite of captioned photographs, titled *In Her Lifetime* (1992/2018, pp. 278–283) and arranged like a train of thought, Niro shows us her younger sister Deborah ("Bunny") Doxtater musing about the pleasures and frustrations of her daily life. She leans into the camera, her expression holding us, remembering that, as the title of the work declares, "Native Issues Would Never be Resolved in her Lifetime" (1992, pp. 278–283).

Another photographic series, *For Fearless and Other Indians* (1998/2022, pp. 295–301), presents the Statute of Liberty with typewritten captions. Niro recalls being a child growing up on the Six Nations reserve and reading a particular Li'l Abner comic featuring the character "Fearless Fostick." He'd been stabbed in the heart with a big knife and survived, yet the knife "couldn't be removed for fear of death." He lived his life thereafter with "the big handle getting in the way of everything." Claiming her metaphor, Niro concluded, "I now carry the blade for Fearless and other Indians."

Like the knife blade precariously embedded in Fostick's chest, the burden can have consequences. Returning now to her short film *Niagara*, after introducing the Kanyen'kéha word and approaching the falls from the river below, the camera lingers on falling water and rising mist while the soundtrack thunders with the roar of descending water. Niro then offers a poem-like text that scrolls over the imagery. The camera operator's thumb periodically wipes the fogged lens, reminding us of the act of Haudenosaunee condolence, the wiping away of tears.

The last time I saw her
She told me of a dream she had
about her grandmother

She looked happy
talking about it

As she left the restaurant
she waved through the window
I waved back

She was always in jail then
She told me she cried
calling for me
A boy she knew
Recognized her voice
Asking Is that you?

When she told me this
she laughed
remembering

surprised　　　　　　　　　　　　*ongniaahra*

someone knew　　　　　　　　　*a mohawk word*

who she was　　　　　　　　　　*my birthplace*

　　　　　　　　　　　　　　　　now a border

　　　　　　　　　　　　　　　　dividing

The Great Law, inspired by the teachings of the Peacemaker, built the Haudenosaunee Confederacy on a foundation of kinship relations, more specifically, the matrilineal Clans that make up each of the Six Nations of the Confederacy. The Clan is the extended family of a maternal lineage; one is born into their mother's Clan. The first Council of the Chiefs, when coming together to form the Confederacy, recognized nine Clans, unevenly distributed among the first five Nations (the rafters of the Confederacy longhouse were later extended to include the Tuscarora, the sixth Nation) and designated fifty titles drawn from the nine Clans of the five Nations that would serve the Confederacy as Council Chiefs. The fifty titles, or proper names, would descend through the generations, to be bestowed upon honorable men by Clan Mothers, women selected by their female peers within the Clan. Clan Mothers also had the power to depose their Chiefs should they judge their efforts insufficient.[15] By this means, the structure of maternal family became the foundation of government. In an idealized sense, an individual is nurtured within this web of relations of living peers, lineages of ancestors, and obligations to descendants. One's identity and relations to others are determined to a significant degree by such ties of kinship.

Seneca scholar and activist John Mohawk contrasts this notion of the extended family with the "nuclear family," the latter a consequence of modernity, or the "industrial revolution," as he puts it. The extended family provides for the means of sustenance, reproduction, or replenishment of its members, education, and socialization, a judicial function of judgment for proper behavior, and spiritual direction or psychological support. When the nuclear family is reduced to simply parents and their children, Mohawk argues, most of these functions become alienated from the family and are taken up by institutions of the state and commerce. For Haudenosaunee, this meant wage labor, residential schools, state control of Reserve funds, the intervention of social welfare agencies, and relentless missionizing. Mohawk saw the repair of kinship ties and the restoration of their traditional functions as key to the survival of the Confederacy and its citizens into the future.[16]

Niro's lineages experienced these kinds of disruption firsthand. Niro's mother, Chiquita June Doxtater, was born "out of wedlock," to use Niro's expression, at a residential school in northern Ontario and was adopted and raised at Six Nations by Belva Ferguson. Niro's Turtle Clan identity stems from her adoptive grandmother. Niro's father, George Oliver Doxtater, a Wolf Clan Kanyen'kehá:ka, came from the Bay of Quinte. Niro's family has come to learn that his biological father was Moses Monture, a Delaware from Six Nations. The Bay of Quinte, or Tyendinaga, had been established in 1784 by Kanyen'kehá:ka war captain John Desorontyon, who had faithfully supported the British cause during the American Revolution by staging raids from Lachine near Montreal. His Kanyen'kehá:ka followers came largely from towns on the Mohawk river in the vicinity of Scholarie Creek.[17] They are, perhaps, the source of pan-generational memory of the Mohawk Valley recounted by Niro's father. When asked what her father had to say about his lineage, however, Niro replied simply, "he came from a very dysfunctional family."[18]

Some of Niro's work reasserts a sense of lineage and an ancestral past, providing roots to the present and future. Sometime during the early 1990s, Niro's mother gave her a box of glass negatives of photographs depicting family members, among them an image of her paternal grandmother. Her image takes centre place in the large triptych *Ceremonies* (1992, pp. 68–69). Niro's great-grandmother wears a floral print and stands in front of a leafy bower, her hand resting on the back of a wooden chair. Her image is flanked by two equally scaled photographs of Niro's nieces, Meryl to the left and Crystal to the right, both daughters of Niro's younger sister, Beverly. They are dressed in floral prints as well, and the images are colourfully hand-tinted. They stand next to modern, vinyl-covered chairs mimicking their great-great-grandmother's pose. A hand-written text runs along the bottom of all three images and positions Niro's father, George Oliver Doxtater, as the intermediary between this span of generations. "They [his granddaughters] came with him to pow wows, fairs, and ceremonies," the text begins. "He walked with her [his grandmother] down long dusty roads, through winter storms, and to church." Niro then positions herself as documentarian, fixing the moment with topical references to popular culture and technologies of the day. "I took these photos [of Meryl and Crystal] on a cold October day", the text continues. "After we bought a Bryan Adams tape, ate Laura Secord ice cream and rented a video." Niro threads these memories along a continuum of five generations.

For Niro, evidently, family tends to close upon a circle of immediate relations: parents, siblings, and children. Her family's sociability often revolved around the cultural practice of craft production and beadwork (see Adriana Greci Green's essay on pp. 151–152). For many Indigenous families, the vicissitudes of the cash economy were often tempered by making crafts for sale, which was a cottage industry for all family members. Niro laughs when she recalls her father's replica tomahawks, painted with blood-red nail polish and draped with horsehair "scalps," that he made and sold to tourists at Niagara Falls. But the habit of making things and the sociability of doing something with your hands in the intimate company of others became a salient and desirable characteristic of family life, one that Niro celebrates in her multi-media work, *Chiquita, Bunny, Stella* (1995, pp. 66–67). With a format that she developed for several ambitious works that followed, Niro combined photographic images with objects, in this instance, images of making combined with things made. Their heads bowed in concentration, Niro's mother Chiquita assembles a feather fan, her sister Bunny makes a corn husk doll, and her younger daughter Stella Michelle stitches a beaded bag.

They are framed by the materiality of their creations—images of feathers, corn husks, and Haudenosaunee beadwork patterns. The results of their efforts sit on pedestals in front of the images. The three generations of relations situate Niro in the centre of her family circle, the work itself the evidence of her own contribution to their combined creative efforts.

In her work *Time Travels Through Us* (1999, p. 23), beadwork becomes a kind of metaphor for familial intimacy, like a protective maternal embrace. A photograph groups Niro's mother, Chiquita, with Niro's two daughters, Stella Michelle and (Anastasia) Naoga. Chiquita holds a bird's nest with two eggs inside, a symbol, according to Niro, of femininity and promises of the future. Naoga holds a turtle, a symbol of our world's foundation from which all else grew. All three are enclosed within a frame of Niro's beadwork on a subtle calico fabric. Here again, Niro situates herself in the centre of a matrilineal triad of mother, self, and daughters, stressing maternal generational ties and eliding, for the moment, their fragility and the forces that mothers struggle to protect against.

ACTORS / MIME LAND

In 1987, Niro created a large, rather unusual painting titled *Waitress* (1987, p. 112). At the time, Niro thought of herself primarily as a painter. Instead of her customary portraits though, *Waitress* enacts a scene, a snapshot of a narrative. A waitress, a white apron tied around her waist, holds a tray of plated food above her shoulder and looks downward as she fumbles a glass of red wine. The red liquid is suspended mid-air as it descends toward the lap of an appropriately alarmed white lady who looks wide-eyed, not at the impending spill, but evidently in outrage at the disengaged waitress. Somehow, however, our sympathies lie with the waitress. More bizarrely, a broadly grinning white couple dances behind the waitress and patron in front of a wall of grotesque faces immersed in flames. What is going on? Something is happening. There is a story here.

Waitress is an early example of a pictorial allegory developed through narrative. It is an artistic strategy that Niro often pursued thereafter, casting herself or others as actors playing out a role or character. This interest would later lead to the creation of short and feature-length films and videos. The waitress in the painting is a self-portrait. Niro re-inhabits a role she experienced while working as a waitress in a Chinese restaurant in Brantford, close to the Six Nations reserve. The incident Niro references in the painting, she recalled, was sparked by a patron complaining that she was not Chinese.[19] The situation is redolent of many issues: the subordination of workers in the service economy; the desire among the powerful for "authentic" experiences of ethnic others; and the general sense of entitlement and obliviousness of the privileged classes. Is the wine spilled accidently on purpose? Is the "accident" an act of political resistance?

But this small encounter, this incidental skirmish between the over- and under-privileged, is set within a much broader political and cosmological context. The Canadian Prime Minister at the time, Brian Mulroney, and his wife, Mila, dance in the background, and his First Nations policies are the subject of Niro's critique. In 1985, Mulroney had convened a two-day constitutional conference on "aboriginal rights," where he complained about government "intrusion" into the daily life of Canadian citizens, asserting that, "the most regulated, controlled and intruded upon in Canada are the aboriginal peoples." His advocacy for "self-government," critics recognized, was a thinly veiled call for the reduction of long-standing Crown obligations to Canada's Indigenous Peoples and the return to assimilationist policies. The objective of Indigenous Peoples becoming "important contributors to the national economy" meant simply more policy emphasis on a wage economy, like Niro's job as a waitress.[20] And, of course, the larger environment for this everybody-for-themselves policy, in which Mulroney dances and Niro waits tables, broadens to encompass long-standing injustices and continuing pressure on Indigenous Peoples' land and sovereignty. In Niro's painting, a wall of *ga:go:sah*, powerful healing spirits among the Haudenosaunee, observes the scene in judgment while symbols of the Haudenosaunee Sky Dome and Celestial Tree on the dance floor, referencing the origins of Turtle Island, summon the foundational perspectives of First Nations. The dancing Mulroneys and the restaurant's outraged patron, in contrast, flagrantly insist upon their own primacy.

For Niro's generation of First Nation citizens, the late twentieth century proffered hard choices. Social and economic policies in Canada promised jobs and advocated self-reliance, but undermined the sovereignty of remaining homelands and ties to traditional extended family, language, and culture. In her photographic series *This Land is Mime Land* (1992, pp. 266–277), Niro impersonates archetypal identities of an enveloping popular culture that First Nations citizens, particularly youth, had been enticed to embrace, a culture that was in contrast with the Indigenous knowledge they were pressured to abandon. The work consists of eight triptychs. Each triptych includes a self-portrait of Niro wearing the same shapeless, androgenous clothing—a blank slate perhaps. Her pose and gestures, however, suggest a quizzical inner life and she appears to interact with the other two images. The second image in each triptych features family photographs, either old or new. The third photograph is another self-portrait, but Niro is now dressed in rented or fabricated costumes, and inhabits her characters through the use of staging, gestures, and make-up. She tries on different personas and we are left to judge the fit. They include: Santa Claus (who wouldn't want to be Santa Claus?); Marilyn Monroe and Elvis Presley, dead cultural icons who have grown to mythic stature as a result of their tragic demise (all too fitting but hardly satisfying); a mute actor and a one-eyed trapeze artist (which could feel right, in a twisted kind of way); a judge (why not? but not likely); and a false idol of Liberty for settler immigrants (WTF?). The family photographs that accompany Niro's self-portraits stand witness, perhaps representing resistance or vulnerability, particularly when they depict children. Or they may more simply represent forbearance of the ironies summoned by Niro's allegorical characters. The overall message seems to be that the culture of the conquerors offers little, and much of it is toxic, despite its promises. Niro critiques this culture with her gaudy and seductive self-representations.

In the early spring of 1990, Kanyen'kehá:ka in the community of Kanesatake, near Montreal, blocked plans to expand a golf course on their unceded land by setting up barricades, beginning a summer-long confrontation that pit the Kanyen'kehá:ka community against provincial police and eventually the Canadian military.[21] The dispute raised concerns internationally and Niro, watching from a distance, felt compelled to respond. She enlisted her three sisters as collaborators and set off for Victoria Park in downtown Brantford to create a series of photographs in front of the memorial to the Kanyen'kehá:ka founder of the Six Nations community, Joseph Brant. In *Standing on Guard for Thee* (1991/1996, p. 45) Niro's three sisters stand in a close semi-circle at the base of the memorial, leaning back, faces lifted, smiling, dressed in denim jackets, sunglasses, and red shoes. Their appearance contrasts with the archaic, essentialist dress of the bronze Indians visible on the memorial with their feathers and fringed jackets. As a trio, they evoke something a little more otherworldly. They are not quite the three graces, nor the three witches of Macbeth. They may be more like three punkish fairy godmothers or a women's Greek chorus. Niro calls them "matriarchal clowns."[22] They are three sisters from Six Nations, somebody's aunties. Their apparition cheerily revives the mordant monument, refreshing neglected histories and half-forgotten memories.

Niro developed *Red Heels Hard* (1991, pp. 46–53) from the same shoot. It is comprised of six photographs with text arranged in a choreographed sequence within a handmade mat. Niro plays with metaphors drawn from the old Judy Garland movie, "The Wizard of Oz." The trio cavort and dance with exaggerated music hall gestures in front of the memorial and each photo is inscribed with a line cadenced like the lyric of a song about the "late great chief J.B." Niro enhanced the red of their ruby slippers and colored the underlying pavement as a yellow brick road. "Carried in his jeweled bag and blown into the wind…we grew as Maples, Oaks & Pines along the banks of the Grand," the text reads. Brant had brought them to Oz, so to speak, but no matter how "hard" they click their "red heels," there would be no return to the Mohawk Valley, no return to the past. The trio promise, "this is where we will stay forever." Implied but not acknowledged in this song and dance is the climactic moment in the popular movie when the man behind the curtain is revealed. Brant, like the lost doctor from Kansas, had all too human failings. The legality of Brant's insistence on selling portions of the Haldimand Tract and his gifts of land to non-Indigenous allies remains in dispute and his controversial acts are the source of ongoing Indigenous Title issues.[23] The three sisters from Six Nations seem to apply some corrective perspective on Brant, their feminine and broadly teasing humor offering a pointedly matriarchal counter to ambitious war captains and the grim outcomes of their judgments and actions. "And for thee we stand guard," they conclude, forever watchful against the threat of well-intentioned wrongheadedness, and ready to protect what remains.

MATRIARCHY / THE IROQUOIS IS A HIGHLY DEVELOPED MATRIARCHAL SOCIETY

Early American feminists of the mid-nineteenth century took great interest in the traditional roles and rights of Haudenosaunee women. Activist Matilda Joslyn Gage, for example, wrote extensively about the Haudenosaunee in her advocacy for what she called a "matriarchate" or "mother-rule."[24] The writings of early feminists highlight how much Haudenosaunee women stood to lose under an enveloping settler patriarchy and its assimilationist policies: they would become property of their husbands, lose rights to their children and land, and forfeit any formal role in government. The Council of Hereditary Chiefs appointed by Clan Mothers persists at Six Nations, but the Indian Act of 1924 in Canada imposed an elected council for Six Nations, which meant that the Canadian provincial and federal governments no longer recognized the Council of Chiefs, who also lost the right to administer their funds.[25] Up until 1984, under the Indian Act, Six Nations women who married non-Indigenous spouses lost their status, meaning that they and their children lost First Nations citizenship, contradicting Haudenosaunee rules of matriarchal descent.[26] Some recent Indigenous critics view non-Indigenous feminism with suspicion due to a perception of complicity with settler colonialism. More specifically, they question the disavowal of traditional family roles for women and feminism's objection to "anatomy as destiny." In contrast, some Indigenous feminists privilege "motherwork" and women as the foundations and guardians of family and societal health and well-being. "Native women's motherwork," writes Lisa Udel, "in its range and variety, is one form of…activism, an approach that emphasizes Native traditions of "responsibilities" as distinguished from Western feminism's notions of 'rights.'"[27]

For Niro, women's proprietary relations to land and society can be traced back to the origins of our shared world as recounted in the Haudenosaunee stories of Sky Woman, the subject of several of Niro's projects. According to these stories, Sky Woman was raised and lived in the Sky World. Pregnant, she fell through a hole created by an uprooted tree. She descended through a featureless darkness for an indeterminate span of time until a universe began to form around her. Birds found her eventually and guided her down to the back of a turtle swimming in a limitless sea. The birds set her down on what would become our earth, where she bore the first terrestrial child, a daughter.[28] Niro tends to focus on that episode of free fall, that liminal state in which Sky Woman is pregnant and her future is unknown. Her ambitious sculptural installation, *Sky Woman* (2001, p. 76), for the Canadian Museum of Civilization (now the Canadian Museum of History) illustrates the story with a three-dimensional column of liminal space where Sky Woman descends headfirst, birds and celestial bodies around her, all sculpted in foam and suspended between the sky above and the turtle's watery world below.

More recently, in 2011, Niro returned to the theme of Sky Woman in a series of ten oversized photographic prints entitled *M: The Stories of Women* (2011, pp. 79–89). Five prints visualize the Sky Woman story: *Beginnings*; *Ancestors*; *Legacy*; *Finding Her Helpers*; and *Memories of Flight*. *Legacy* features an image of young Sky Woman, modeled after Niro's eldest daughter Naoga, who wears a hand-embroidered aviator's cap. Niro positions her between two landscapes. One is inverted to face the terrestrial world below, blossoming with power windmills, a hopeful sign, in Niro's thinking, of a more responsible future. The windmills echo a superimposed image of a beadwork pattern, sampled from a dance legging made by one of Niro's sisters, included in the composition showing the Sky Dome and the Celestial Tree of the ancestral Sky World. Naoga appears as Sky Woman again in *Finding Her Helpers* (p. 79). She is supine in flight, in high-heeled boots, with birds hovering around her, and is clearly pregnant (with

Niro's granddaughter Raven). In *Beginnings* (pp. 88–89), Naoga, in her aviator's cap, offers a sidelong look accompanied by that same beadwork pattern of Sky Dome and Celestial Tree, framed above and below by graphic spirals of genetic DNA. At the base of the Sky Dome we see an XXXX pattern, suggesting female chromosomes. All women, Niro claims, possess a genetic connection reaching back through lineages of women to Sky Woman and her daughter.

But of course, the story of Sky Woman is not that simple. Her daughter became pregnant with twin boys. They argued in the womb about who would emerge first into the world. Sapling (also called "Sky Holder" in English), who was to be first, was born the natural way, but Flint, jealous of his brother, forced his way out through his mother's armpit, killing her. The two males then worked to expand their grandmother's world, but at cross purposes. Sapling strove to make a land of comfort and plenty for all. Flint undid his twin's work and filled the world with hard, craggy, and sterile places. As a result, the earth offers human beings both bounties and challenges. The story genders this all too familiar dual nature as male, the twin potentialities of Sky Woman's grandsons. When projected into the social world, the dual nature of men veers between destructive ferocity and tempering wisdom and compassion.[29] Women, as modeled by the traditional role of Clan Mothers, guard and privilege familial responsibilities to community, the obligations of relations, nourishment, and protection and safety, sometimes in resistance to unmitigated male nature.

Women predominate in Niro's imagery, inhabiting heroic Sky Woman and matriarchal themes. Niro also playfully addresses the issue of male potential in a series of five photographs called *Sleeping Warrior* (2012, pp. 218–219). Her original concept for the work was far more critical, but she softened over the years before making it. The series shows a muscular and attractive man who sleeps on a couch and dreams of different possibilities. Titles for each scene describe his dreams. He dreams of "fighting no more" dressed in camo gear and comforted by a blanket. He dreams of "life in the sky" wearing a business suit and suspended over a city crowded with skyscrapers. He dreams of "pastures and power" with a cowboy hat beneath high power lines and their towers. And he dreams of "hunting" in feathers and a breechcloth with touristic images of a Plains Indian on horseback hunting buffalo behind him. Considering him from the vantage point of Indigenous women, Niro, the artist, urges only that he choose carefully, and the fifth print offers paper doll clothes to choose from.

YOU ARE HERE TO LIVE YOUR LIFE

Shelley Niro's first film, *It Starts With a Whisper* (1993, pp. 30, 115), produced in collaboration with Toronto filmmaker Anna Gronau, touches upon all these contextual frameworks, tropes, or "lenses"—of memory, relations, allegorical story-telling, and the matriarchal family. Niro develops the story within the film by referencing a Haudenosaunee narrative, a ritual structure of transition, or "crossing,"[30] with a particular emphasis on young adulthood tied to the story of Sky Woman's journey to create a new world and a new future. The film begins with a whispered recitation describing the welcoming yet threatening world left by Sky Woman's grandsons Sapling and Flint:

Whispering waters
Earth of bounty
Breath of air
Fire that warms

Raging torrents
Parched and starving land
Cyclones sting
Flames that burn

The film tells the story of young woman, Shauna, who wanders through a verdant spring by the Grand River at Tutelo Heights (in present-day Brantford), the former home of a now absent people. Hearing the sound of frogs peeping and a gentle wind in the trees her mind is filled with voices. "Voices of the past calling you. Voices of the present urge you on. Voices of the dead tell you their sorrow." She is troubled by "tears that won't come, peace that won't come." Names of Nations parade through her thoughts: the names of those who survive, or who have just barely survived, and those, like her ancestral Tutelo, now gone. Shauna's age, her uncertainty about her future, and the way in which she seeks her way, link the character to Niro's concept of a young, pregnant Sky Woman journeying between worlds, unsure and fearful of what lies ahead.

In downtown Toronto, Shauna walks with an oversized briefcase, in business clothes, to meet her aunties, who mysteriously materialize in a worn-out car. They are played, in the film, by Niro's sisters, Bets, Bev, and Bunny, who are billed in the credits as "aunties" and "matriarchal clowns." They all drive together to Niagara Falls where they will stay in a honeymoon hotel room won in a bingo game. The sisters amuse themselves on the way with laughter, making fun of Shauna's clothes, trying on her high heels, and offering her tea and pickles to eat. Serious and interrupted from her reading, Shauna bursts out, "all you do is laugh and eat!" The scene points to the corporeal and spiritual priorities of traditional Matriarchy: food and laughter. What is more important, fundamental, and necessary, Niro seems to ask, than nourishment of the body and psyche?

Later, at night, Shauna walks alone by the falls, the names of Nations still ringing in her ears. Elijah Harper appears, as if in a vision, wearing an eagle feather headdress. (Elijah Harper was the Oji-Cree member of the Manitoba Assembly, from Red Sucker Lake community, who famously forced negotiation for inclusion of First Nations Treaty Rights as part of Canada's Constitution Act by filibuster of its ratification in 1990, an eagle feather in his hand.) Shauna confides in Harper after his triumph, telling him of her worries, the pain of her knowledge, the incessant voices she hears, and the troubling thoughts that she fears might cause her heart and her head to "blow up." "Shauna, whatever you do, don't blow up," says Harper, reassuring her of her good heart and his confidence that it will guide her in the right direction. "Stop feeling guilty about your existence," he says. "You are here to live your life." By referencing Harper's decisive leadership, and giving him compassionate and modest words, Niro models male action and responsibility.

Shauna later rejoins her aunties in the gaudy honeymoon suite. Together they vamp through a choreographed song and dance, performing a saxophone-led, country-twang ballad of self-affirmation with a kiss-off to an abusive and controlling boyfriend, a thinly disguised metaphor for what we might call patriarchal settler colonialism. The performance is so broad, so fun, so funny. With Esther Williams synchronized swim choreography on a heart shaped bed in evening gowns, and her sister Bets' exit concluding with a rose in her teeth, the song and dance number insists on the healing power of art and laughter.

I am Pretty. I am Pretty.
I am pretty mad at you.
Don't come in here. Don't call me dear.
I am pretty mad at you

You said I was crazy. Too damned lazy.
And you took me away from my kind.
You made me speak gibberish instead of my language
But you can't control my mind

I am surviving. I am thriving.
I am doing fine without you.
Our affair was a crime. I won't waste no more time.
I'm doing fine without you.

On the New Year's Eve of the quincentennial, now that her "helpers" have flocked around her, broadening her "circle," Shauna and her aunties celebrate the survival of Sky Woman's descendants through the preceding five centuries. The "500 year itch," to borrow a title from one of Niro's later works. They greet the new half-millennia hopeful to remake a renewed world. Fireworks above the falls sketch out Sky Woman's world, a Celestial Tree growing from the back of the terrestrial turtle. Niro dedicated the film to "Native Women around the world."

NOTES

1. Gerald McMaster, ed., *Reservation X: The Power of Place in Aboriginal Contemporary Art* (Hull, QC: Canadian Museum of Civilization, 1998), 128.

2. Jeanette Rodriguez, *A Clan Mother's Call: Reconstructing Haudenosaunee Cultural Memory* (Albany, NY: SUNY Press, 2017), 53.

3. Six Nations Legacy Consortium, "1764 Treaty of Fort Niagara Wampum Belts," July 15, 2014, http://www.canadiancrown.com/uploads/3/8/4/1/3841927/treaty_of_fort_niagara_wampum_belts.pdf.

4. Francis R. Kowsky and Martin Wachadlo, *Historic Preservation Industrial Reconnaissance Survey* (Niagara Falls, NY: City of Niagara Falls, 2007), https://irma.nps.gov/DataStore/DownloadFile/582126.

5. Federal Power Commission v. Tuscarora Indian Nation; Power Authority of State of New York v. Tuscarora Indian Nation, 362 U.S. 99, 80 S.Ct. 543, 4 L.Ed.2d 584 (1960), https://www.law.cornell.edu/supremecourt/text/362/99.

6. Jonathan Pearson, *A History of the Schenectady Patent in the Dutch and English Times* (Albany, NY: J. Munsell's Sons, Printers, 1883), 9–11, http://www.schenectadyhistory.org/resources/patent/index.html.

7. Dean R. Snow, Charles T. Gehring, and William A. Starna, eds., *In Mohwak Country: Early Narratives of a Native People* (Syracuse, NY: Syracuse University Press, 1996), 222–237.

8. Nelson Greene, ed., *History of the Mohawk Valley: Gateway to the West 1614–1925* (Chicago: The S.J. Clarke Publishing Company, 1925), chapters 29–35, 51, http://www.schenectadyhistory.org/resources/mvgw/contents.html.

9. Barbara Graymount, *The Iroquois in the American Revolution* (Syracuse, NY: Syracuse University Press, 1975), 104–222.

10. Shelley Niro, "Statement for the Art Gallery of Hamilton," accessed November 3, 2022, http://shelleyniro.ca/statement-for-art-gallery-of-hamilton/.

11. Susan M. Hill, *The Clay We Are Made Of: Haudenosaunee Land Tenure on the Grand River* (Winnipeg: University of Manitoba Press, 2017), 103–110.

12. Hill, 135–148.

13. Hill, 148–182.

14. Alma Greene, *Forbidden Voice: Reflections of a Mohawk Indian* (London: Hamlyn Publishing Group, 1971).

15. For a Clan Mother's perspective, see Rodriguez, *A Clan Mother's Call*, 37–47. See also, Elisabeth Tooker, "The League of the Iroquois: Its History, Politics, and Ritual," in *Handbook of North American Indians, Volume 15, Northeast*, ed. Bruce G. Trigger (Washington, DC: Smithsonian Institution, 1978), 418–441.

16. .José Barreiro, ed., *Thinking in Indian: A John Mohawk Reader* (Wheat Ridge, CO: Fulcrum Publishing, 2010), 118–129.

17. Hill, *The Clay We Are Made Of*, 137.

18. Shelley Niro, interview with the author, September 30, 2021.

19. Ibid.

20. Tony Hall, "Self-Government or Self-Delusion?: Brian Mulroney and Aboriginal Rights," *The Canadian Journal of Native Studies* 6, no. 1 (1986): 78, 77–89, https://cjns.brandonu.ca/wp-content/uploads/6-1-hall.pdf.

21. Loreen Pindera and Laurene Jardin, "78 days of unrest and an unresolved land claim hundreds of years in the making," CBC News, July 11, 2020, https://www.cbc.ca/news/canada/montreal/oka-crisis-timeline-summer-1990-1.5631229.

22. See closing credits for the film *It Starts With a Whisper* and discussion below.

23. Hill, *The Clay We Are Made Of*, 166–167.

24. Sally Roesch Wagner, *Sisters in Spirit: Haudenosaunee (Iroquois) Influence on Early American Feminists* (Summertown, TN: Native Voices, 2001), 28.

25. Hill, *The Clay We Are Made Of*, 234–236. See also, Susan M. Hill, "Conducting Haudenosaunee Historical Research from Home: In the Shadow of the Six Nations-Caledonia Reclamation," *American Indian Quarterly* 33, no. 4 (Fall 2009): 479–498.

26. Mary C. Hurley and Tonina Simeone, "Legislative Summary of Bill C-3: Gender Equity in Indian Registration Act," publication number 40-3-C3-E, November 15, 2010, https://lop.parl.ca/staticfiles/PublicWebsite/Home/ResearchPublications/LegislativeSummaries/PDF/40-3/40-3-c3-e.pdf.

27. Lisa J. Udel, "Revision and Resistance: The Politics of Native Women's Motherwork," *Frontiers: A Journal of Womens Studies* 22, no. 2 (2001): 42–62.

28. For Iakoiane Wakerahkats:the's discussion of Sky Woman, see Rodriguez, *A Clan Mother's Call*, 21–35. Niro's compact version can be found at https://www.historymuseum.ca/cmc/exhibitions/aborig/fp/fpz2f22e.html. See also, Hill, *The Clay We Are Made Of*, 16–24. For a discussion of the literature of the Haudenosaunee, see Hill, *The Clay We Are Made Of*, 56–59. The key source in English is J.N.B. Hewitt, *Iroquoian Cosmology* (Washington, DC: Government Printing House, 1904), https://archive.org/details/iroquoiancosmolooohewi/mode/2up.

29. For sources of the origin stories, see the resources in note 28. For interpretations of the significance of twins, see Rodriguez, *A Clan Mother's Call*, 30–33, and Horatio Hale, "Huron Folk-Lore. I. Cosmogenic Myths. The Good and Evil Minds.," *The Journal of American Folk-Lore* 1, no. 3 (October-December 1888): 177–183, https://www.jstor.org/stable/pdf/534233.pdf?refreqid=excelsior%3A2b9c1dd2198afcb7d738d07b13fcddb4https://www.jstor.org/stable/pdf/534233.pdf?refreqid=excelsior%3A2b9c1dd2198afcb7d738d07b13fcddb4. Clan Mother Kakerahkats:teh objects, appropriately, to the Christian interpretation of their nature as "good and evil."

30. "Crossing" refers to Haudenosaunee "cross over ceremonies" or ceremonies marking transition of an individual through different stages of life. See Rodriguez, *A Clan Mother's Call*, 49–80.

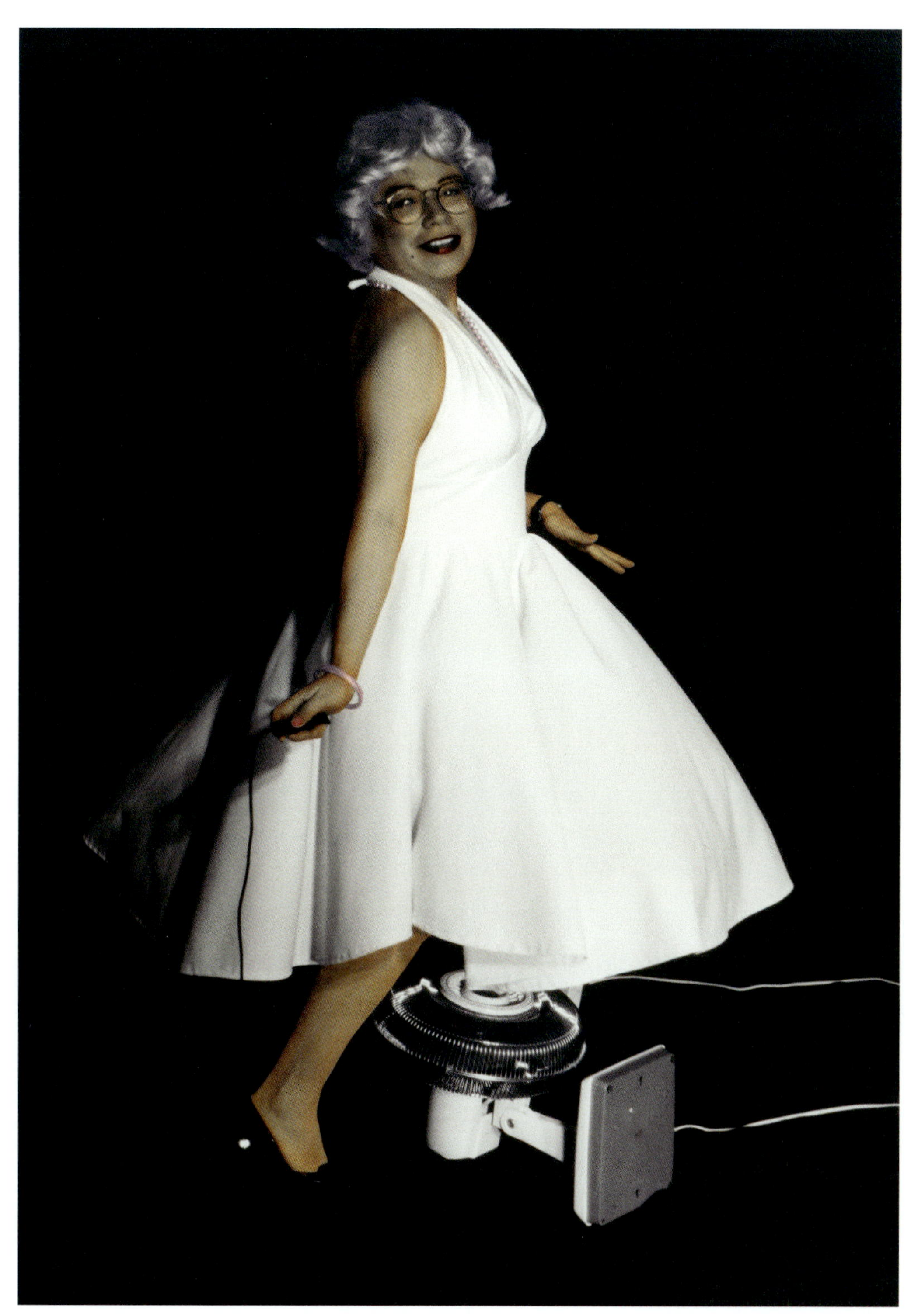

265

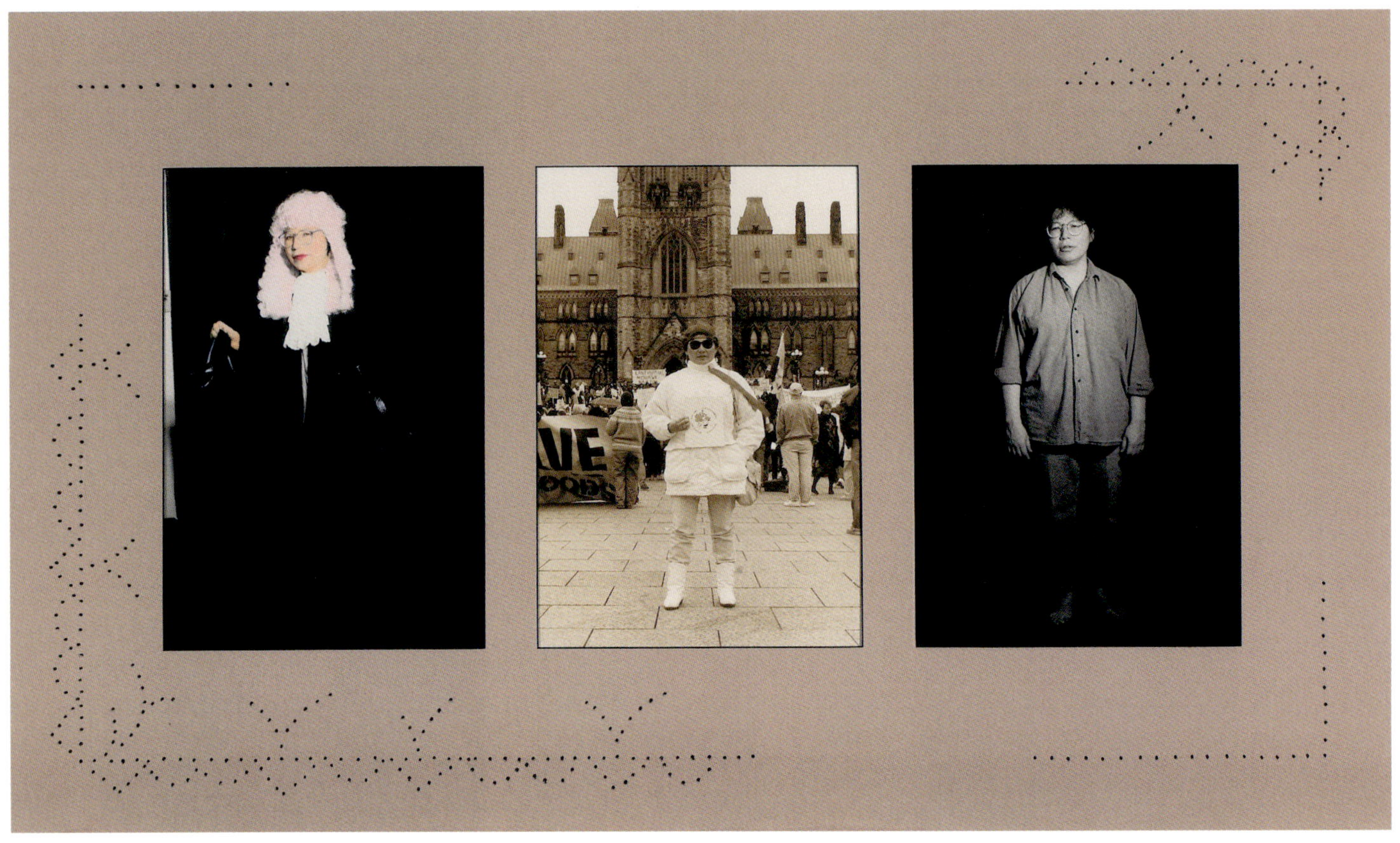

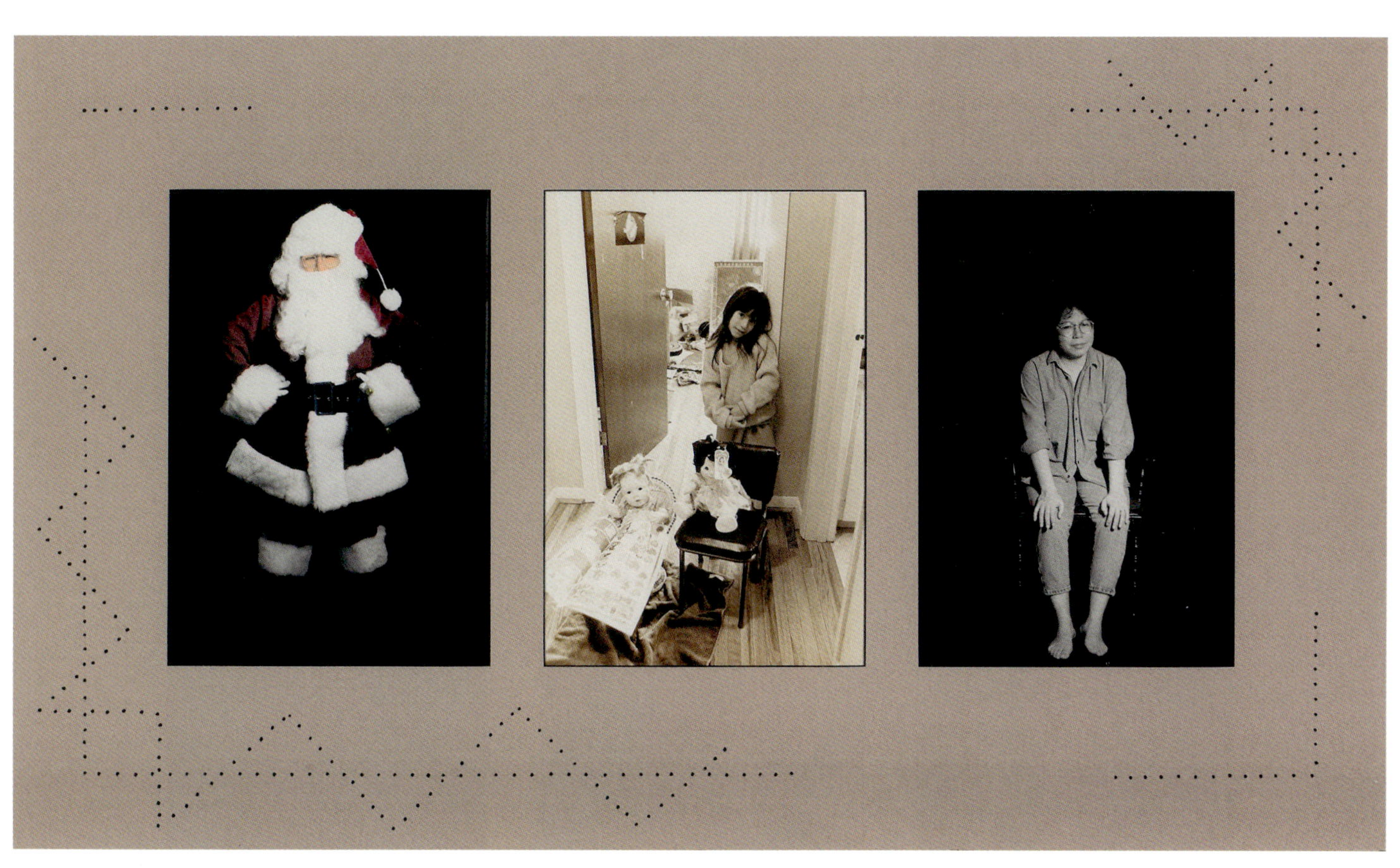

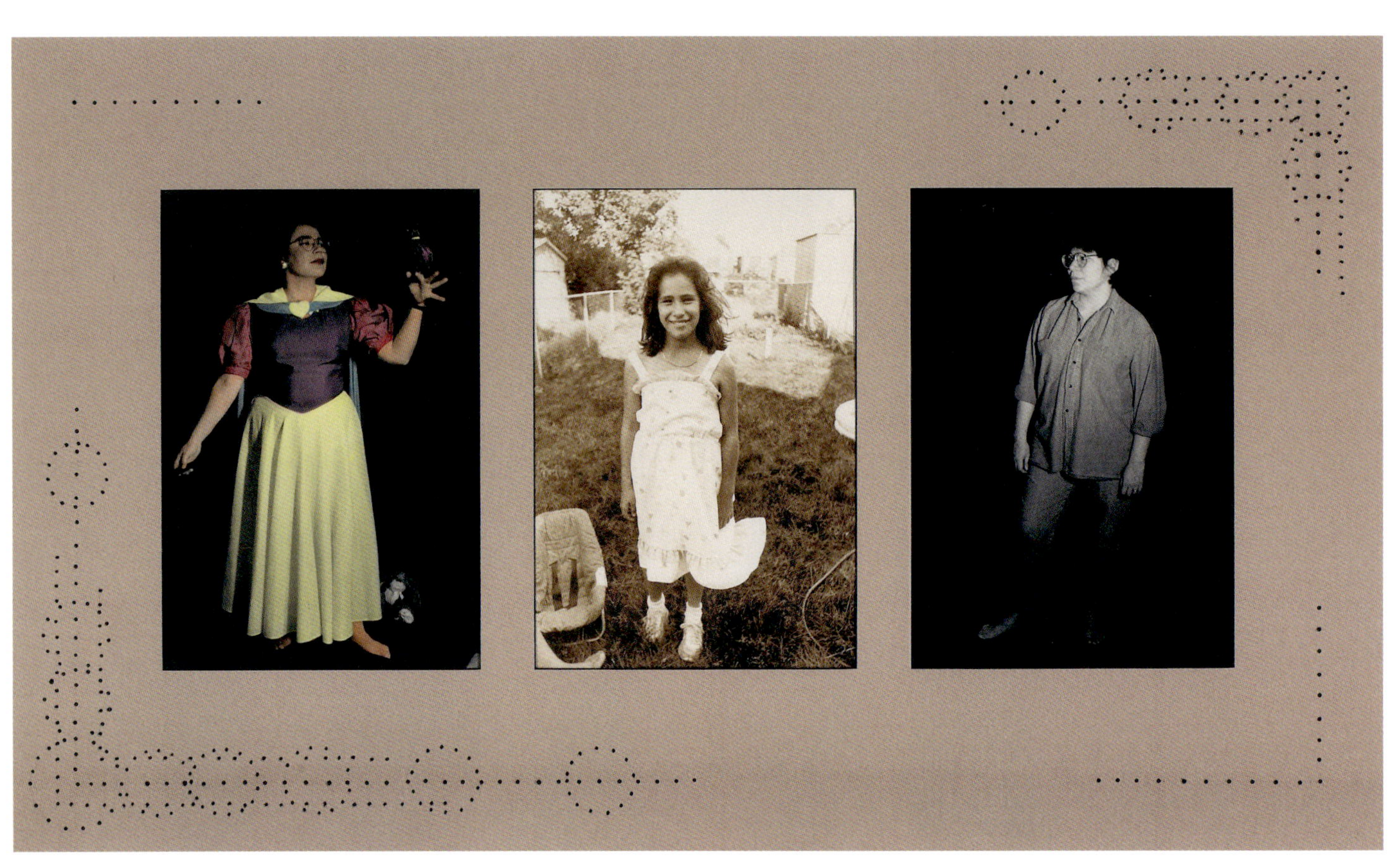

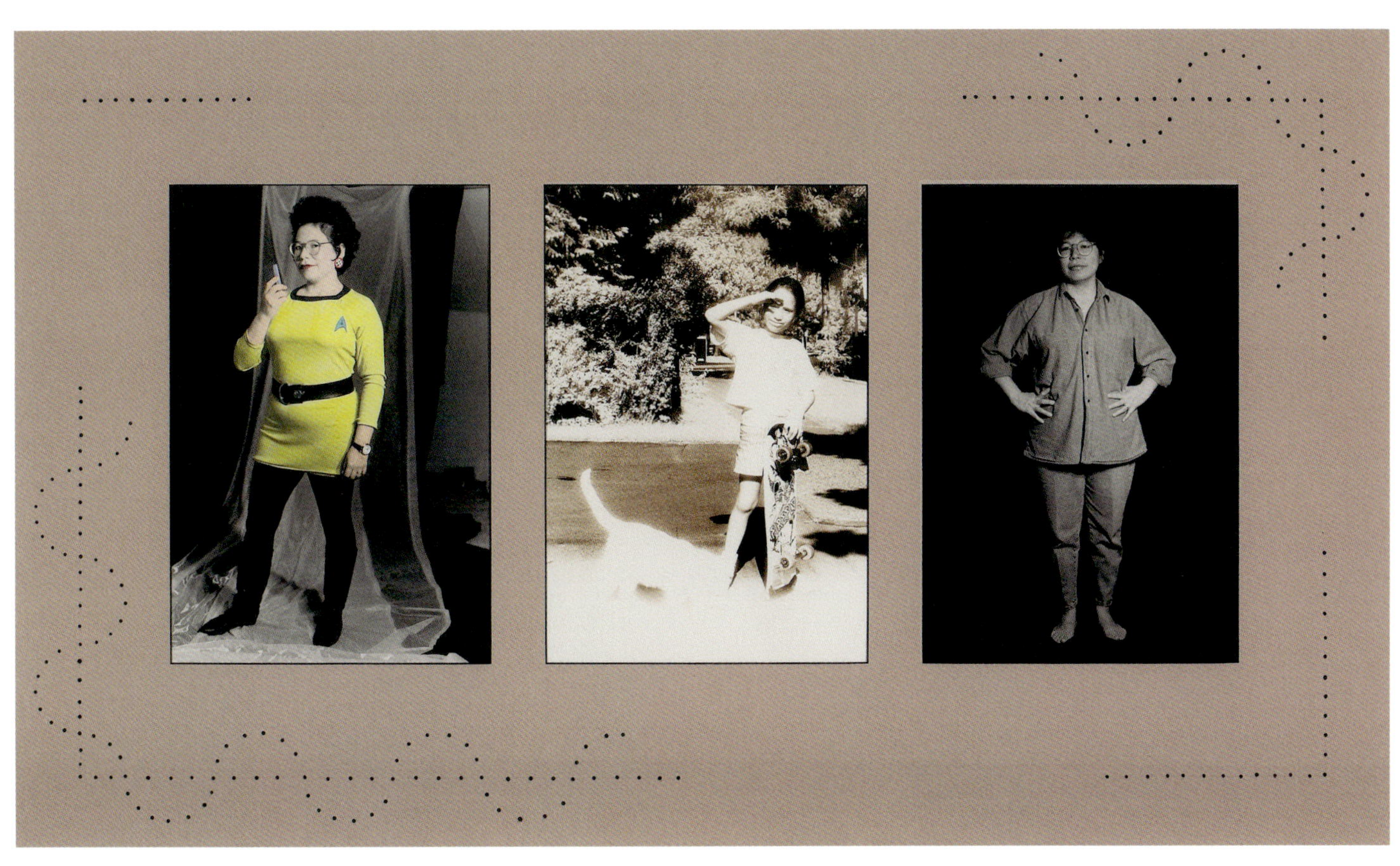

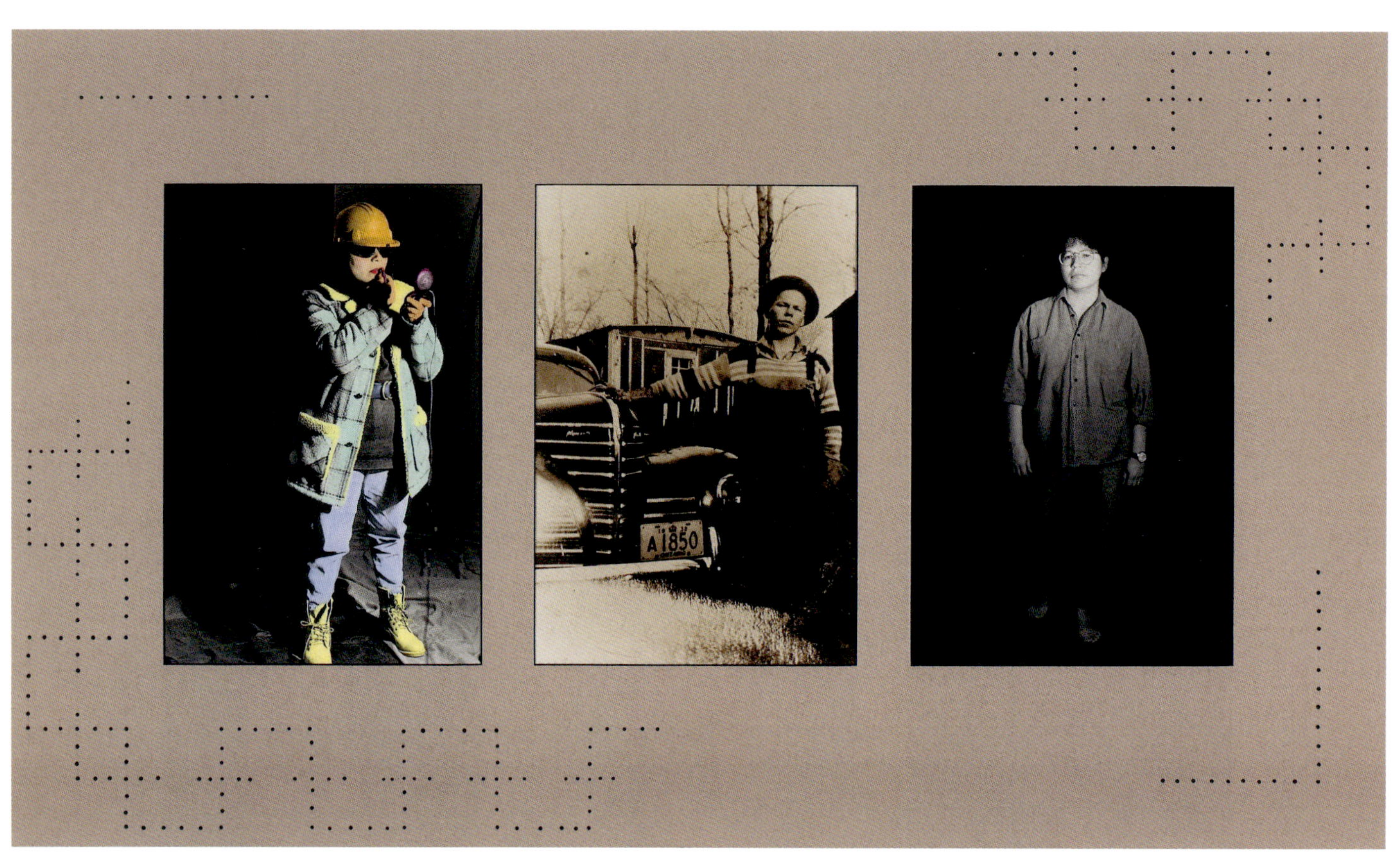

A 1850

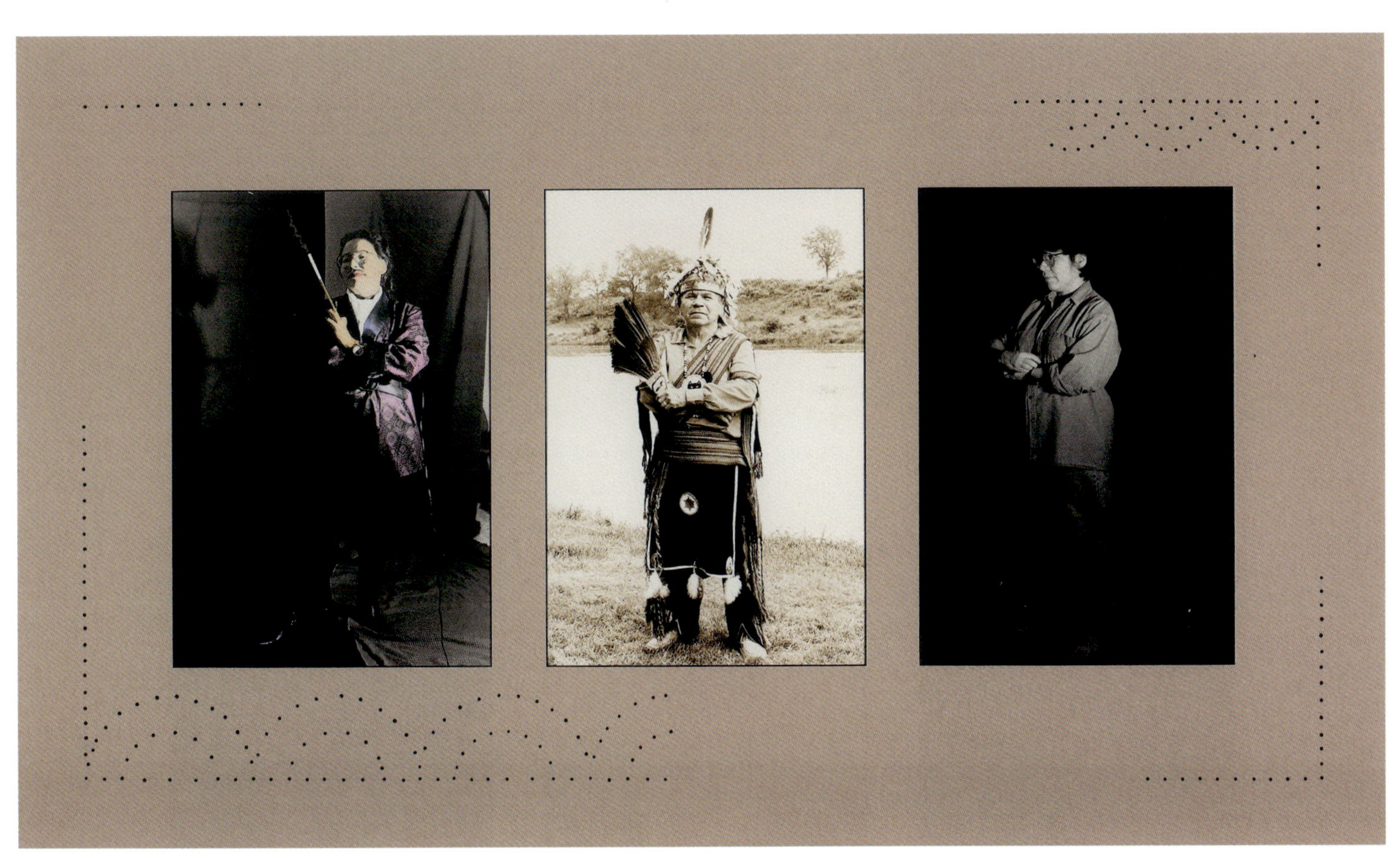

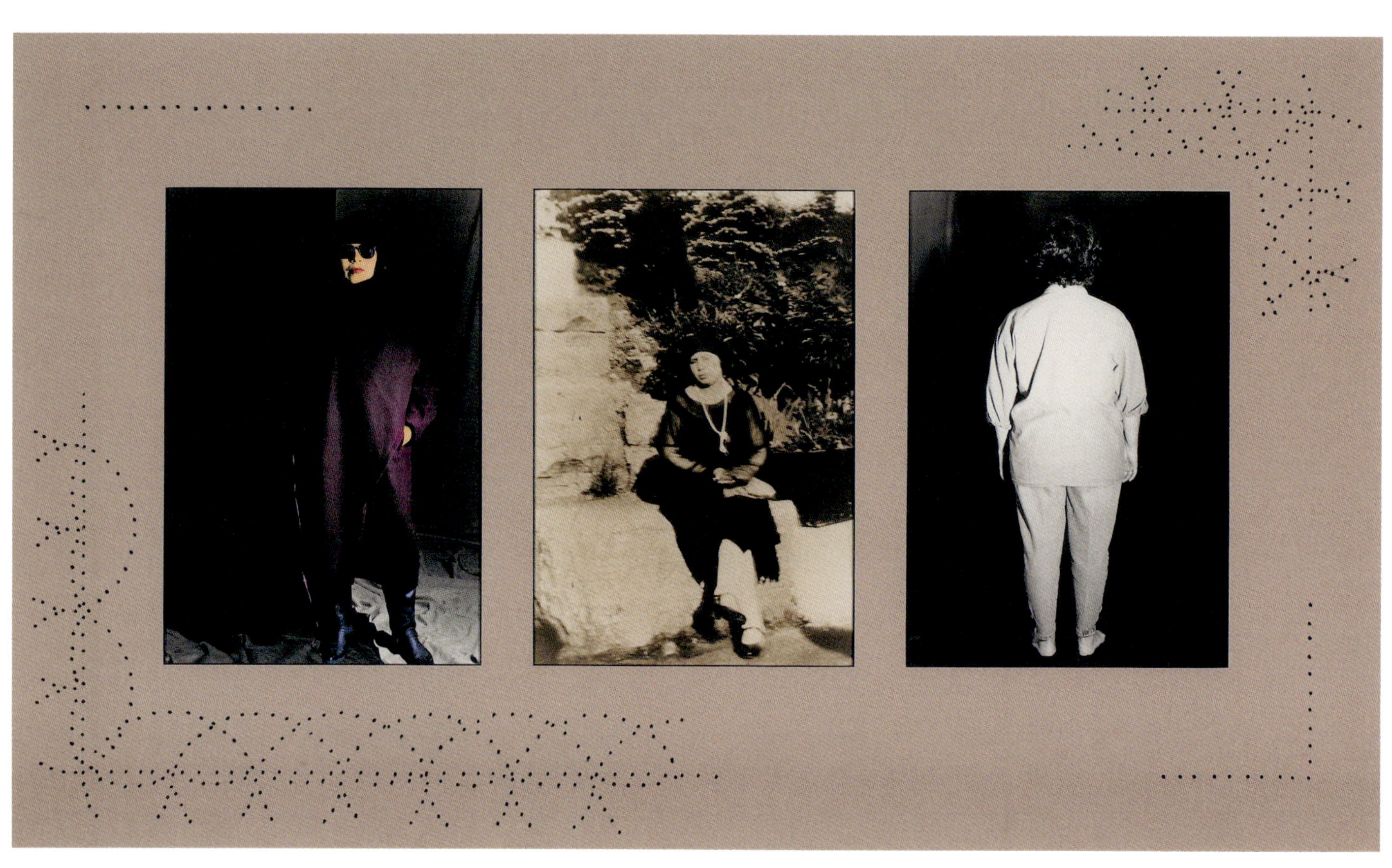

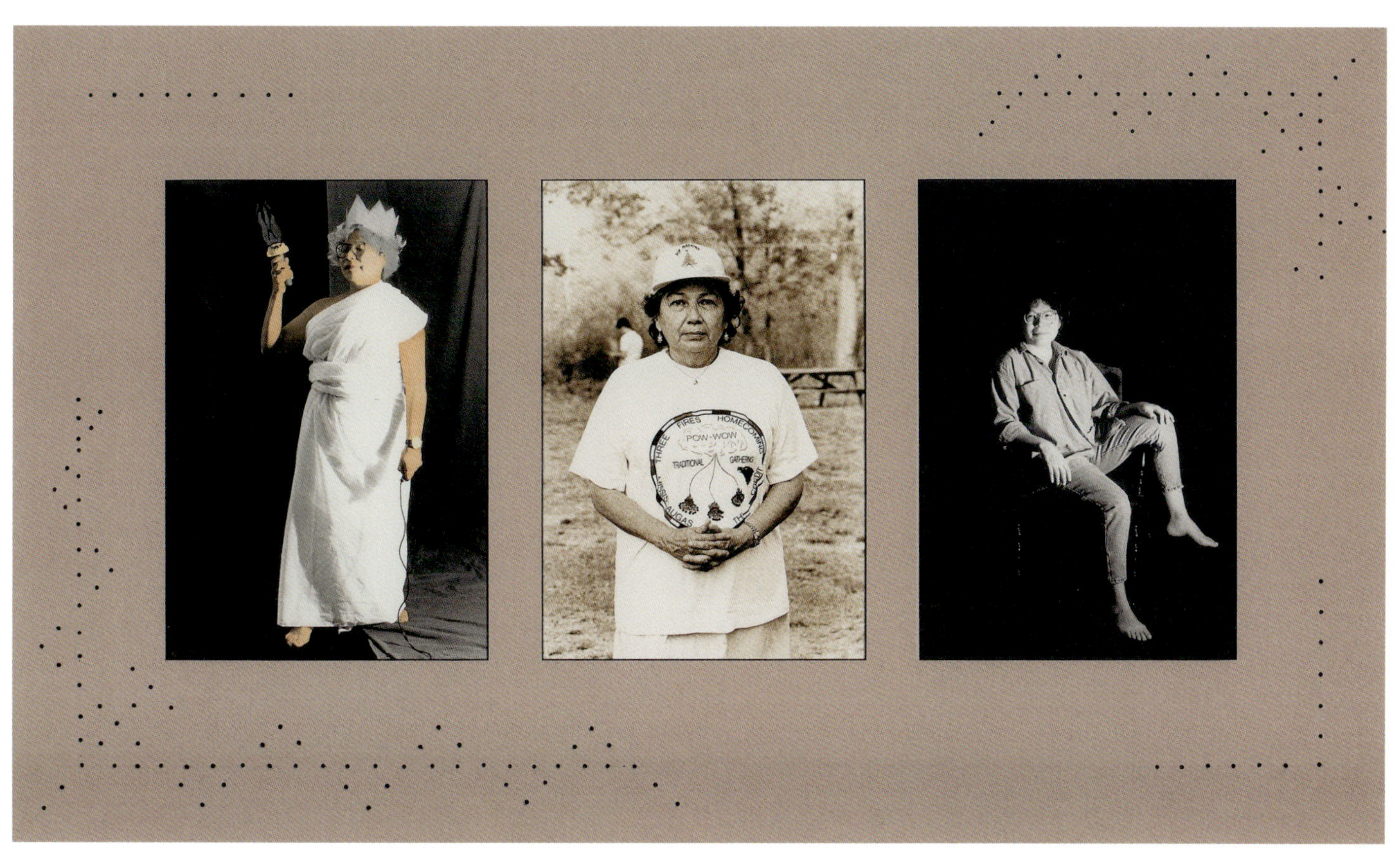

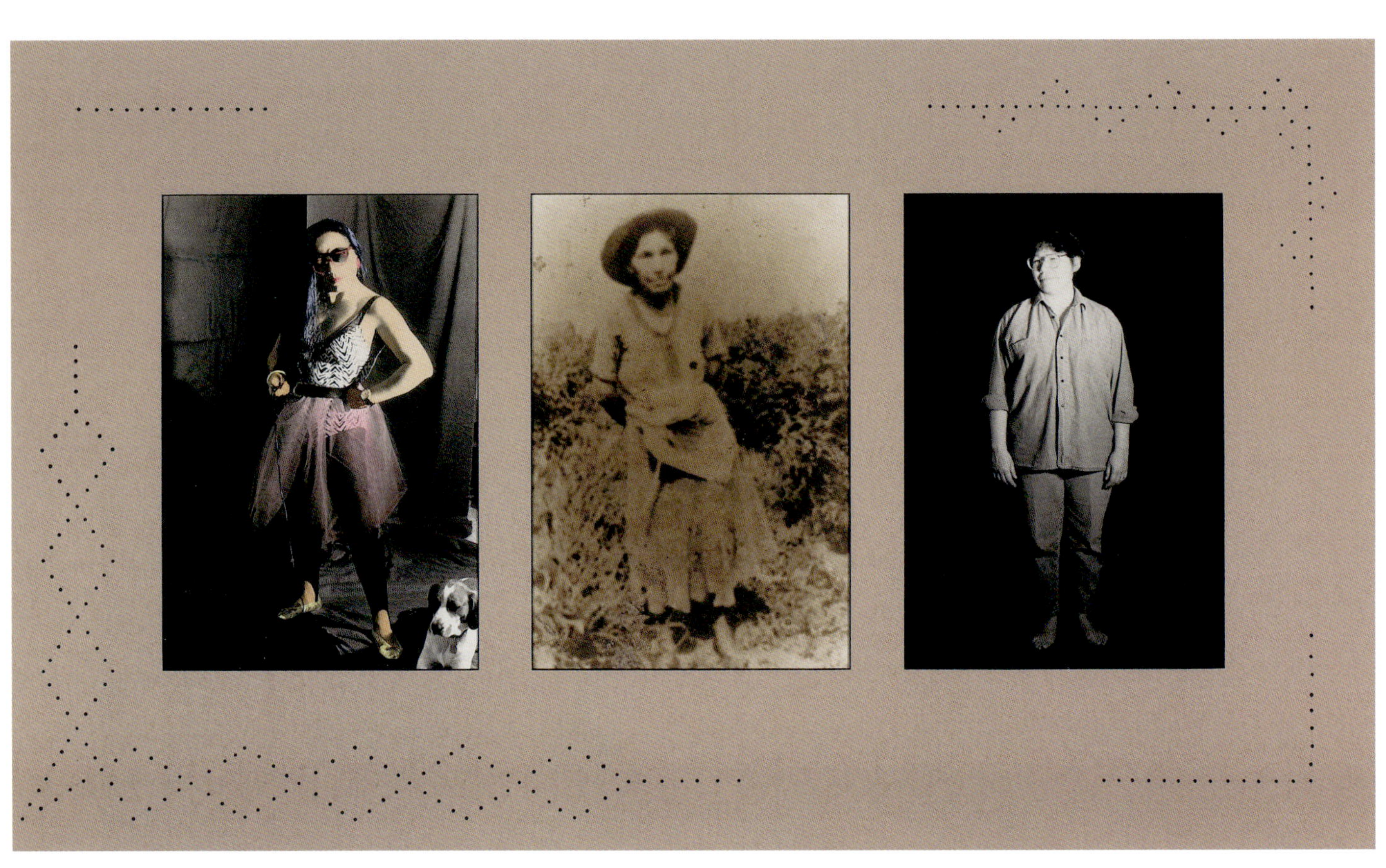

 Survivor

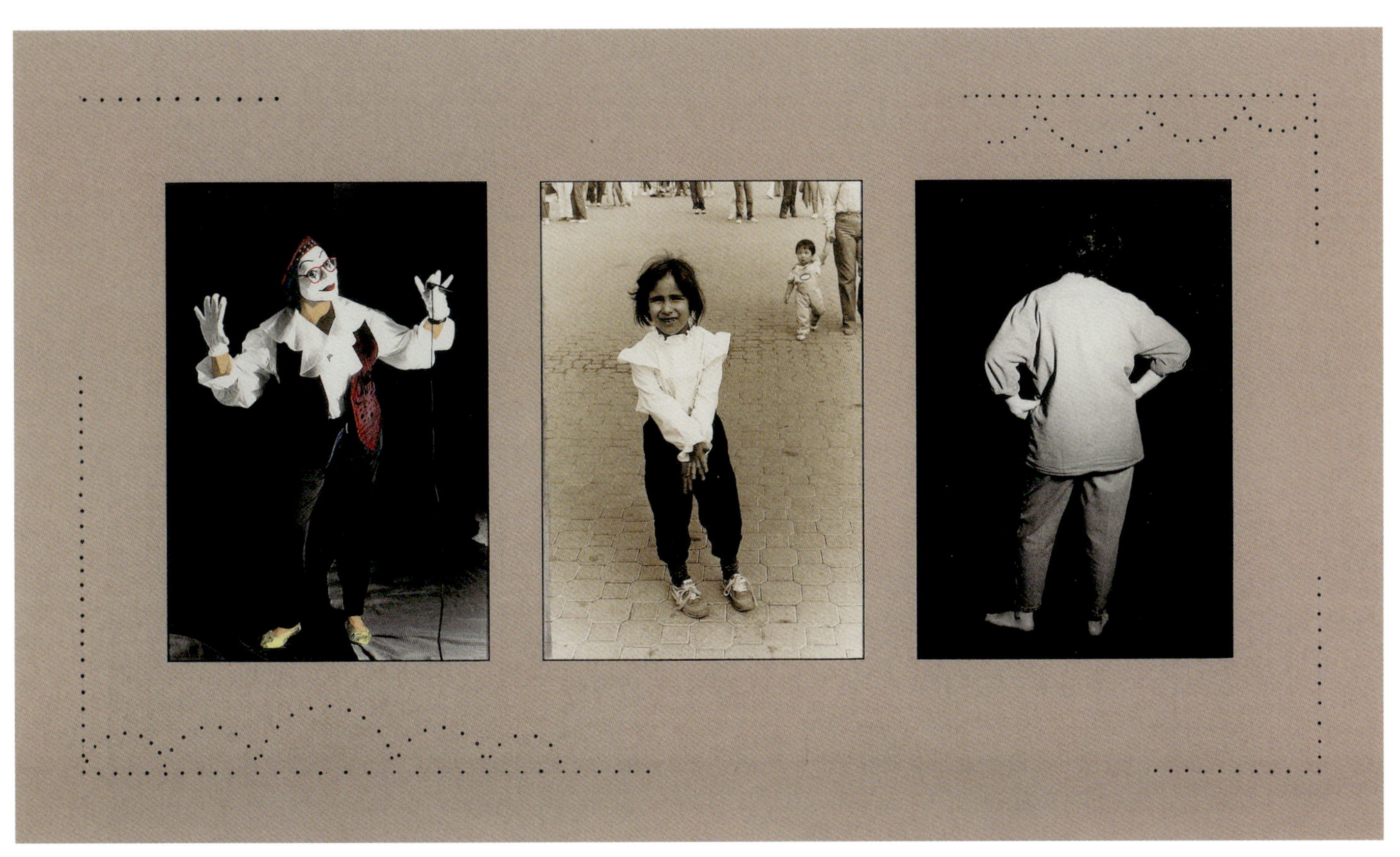

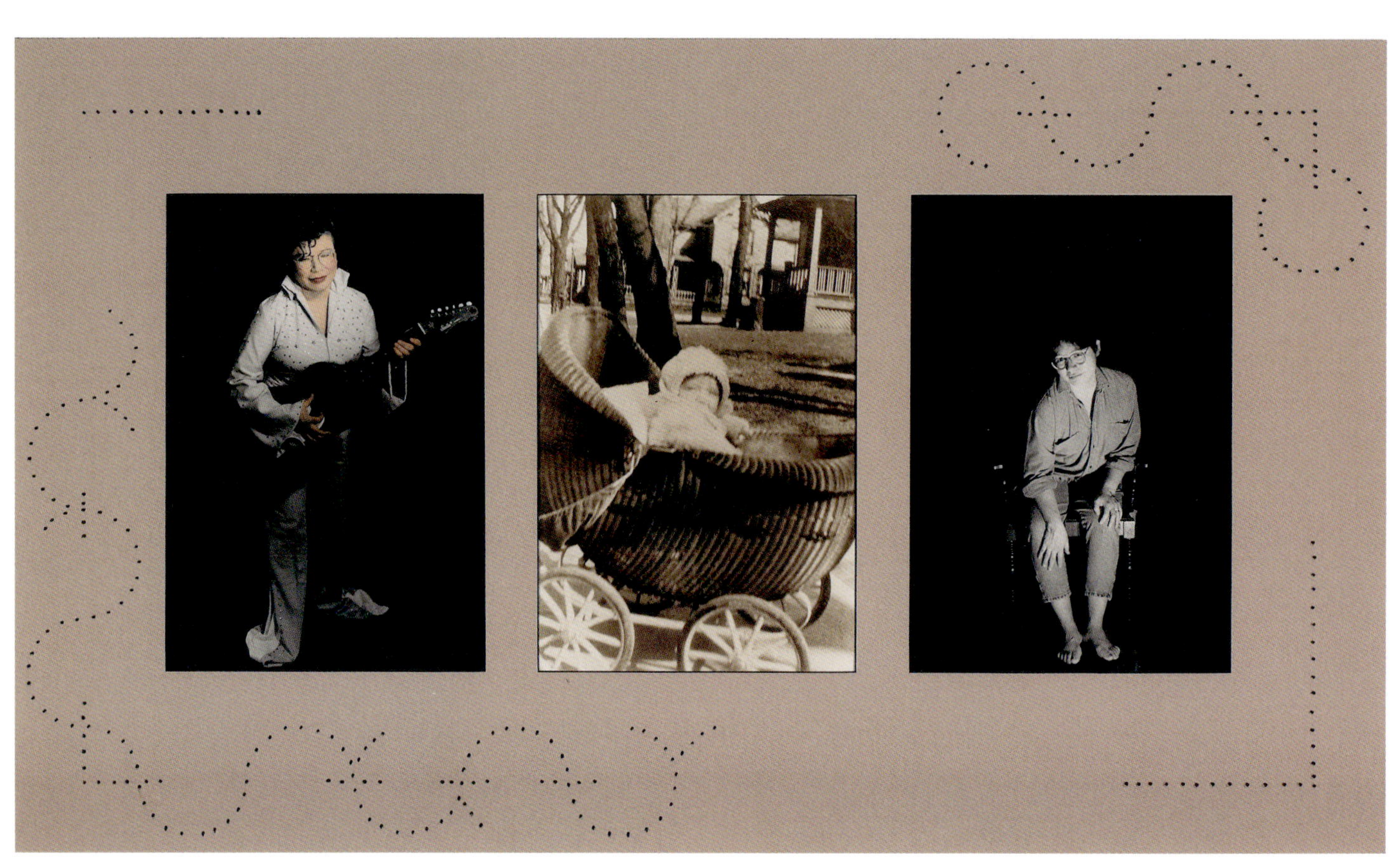

     Love Me Tender

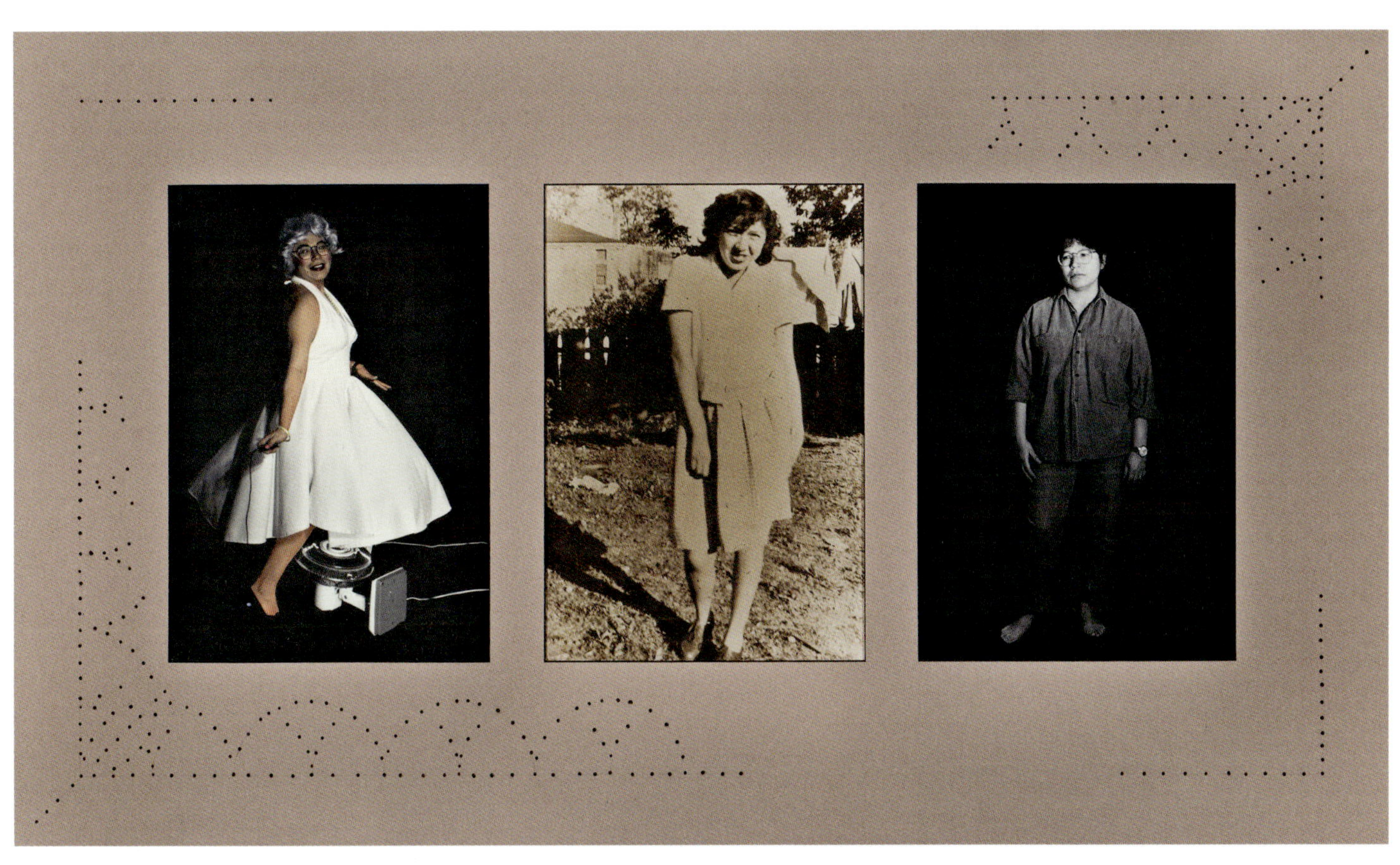

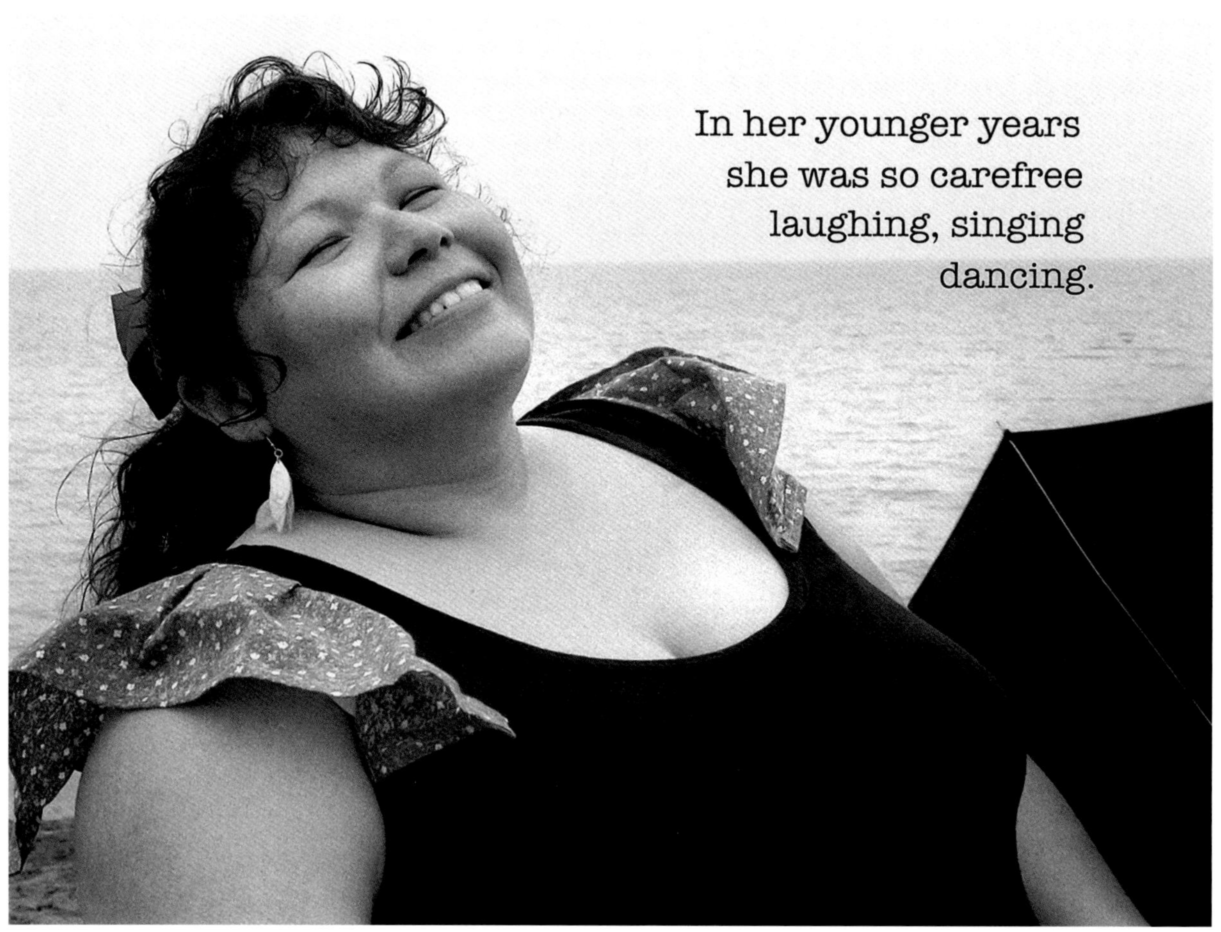
In her younger years
she was so carefree
laughing, singing
dancing.

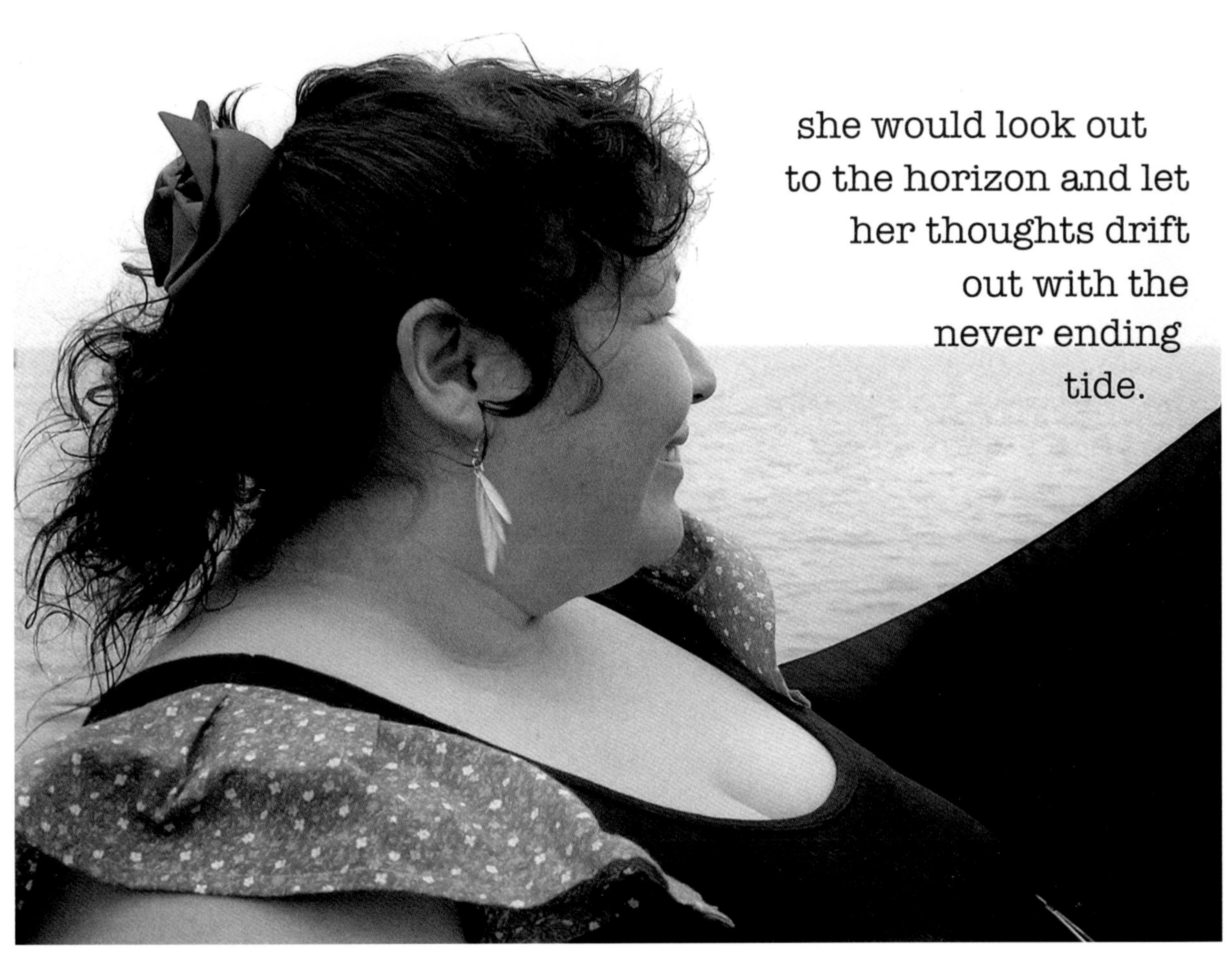
she would look out
to the horizon and let
her thoughts drift
out with the
never ending
tide.

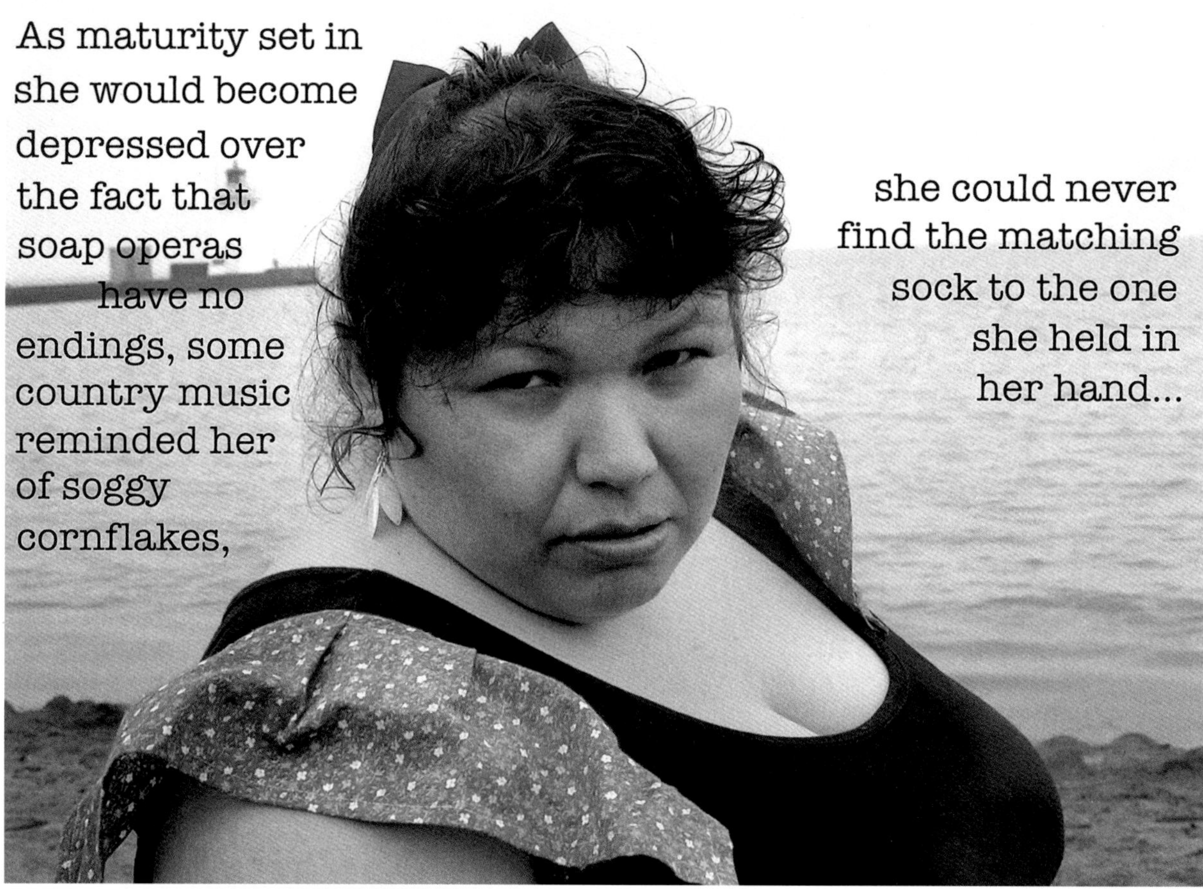

As maturity set in she would become depressed over the fact that soap operas have no endings, some country music reminded her of soggy cornflakes,
she could never find the matching sock to the one she held in her hand...

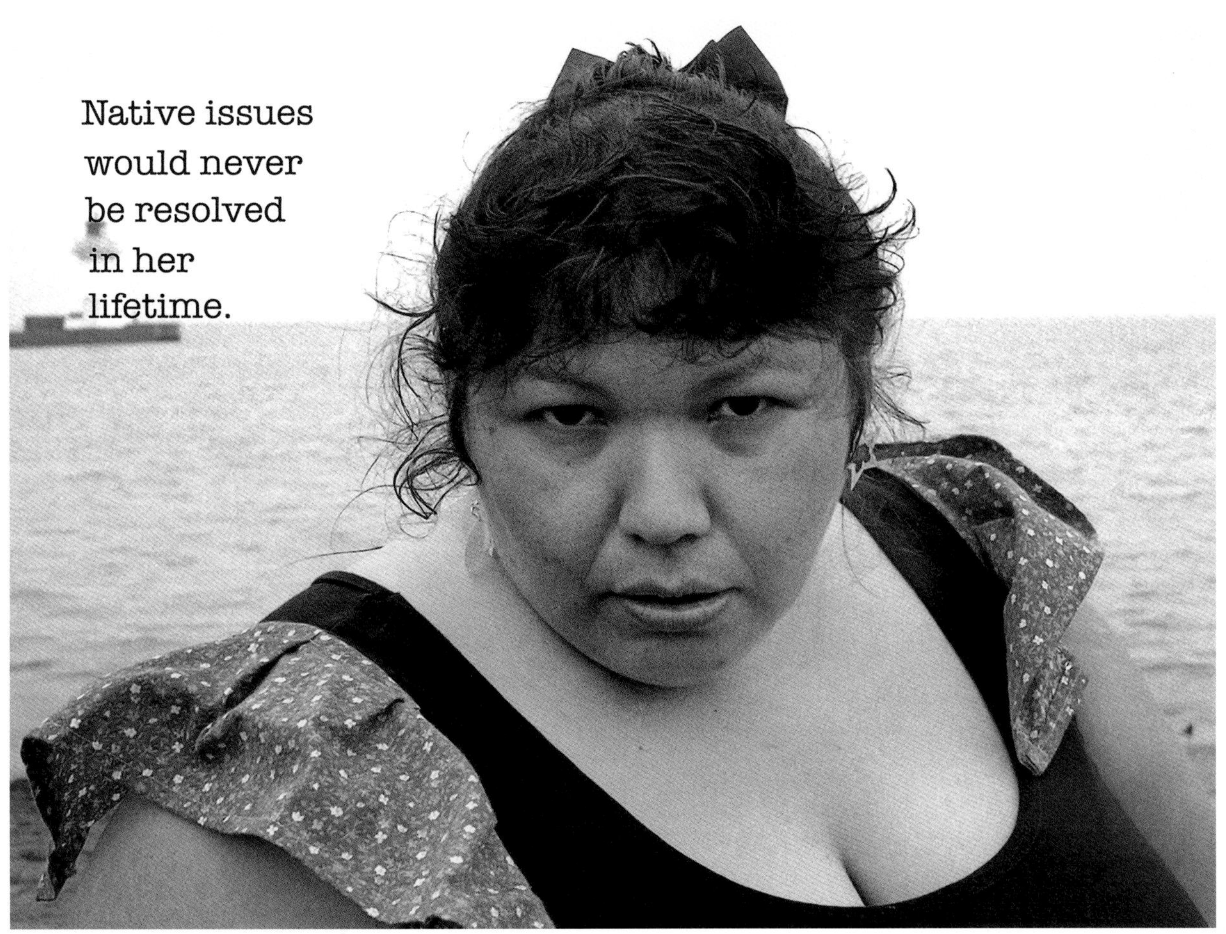
Native issues
would never
be resolved
in her
lifetime.

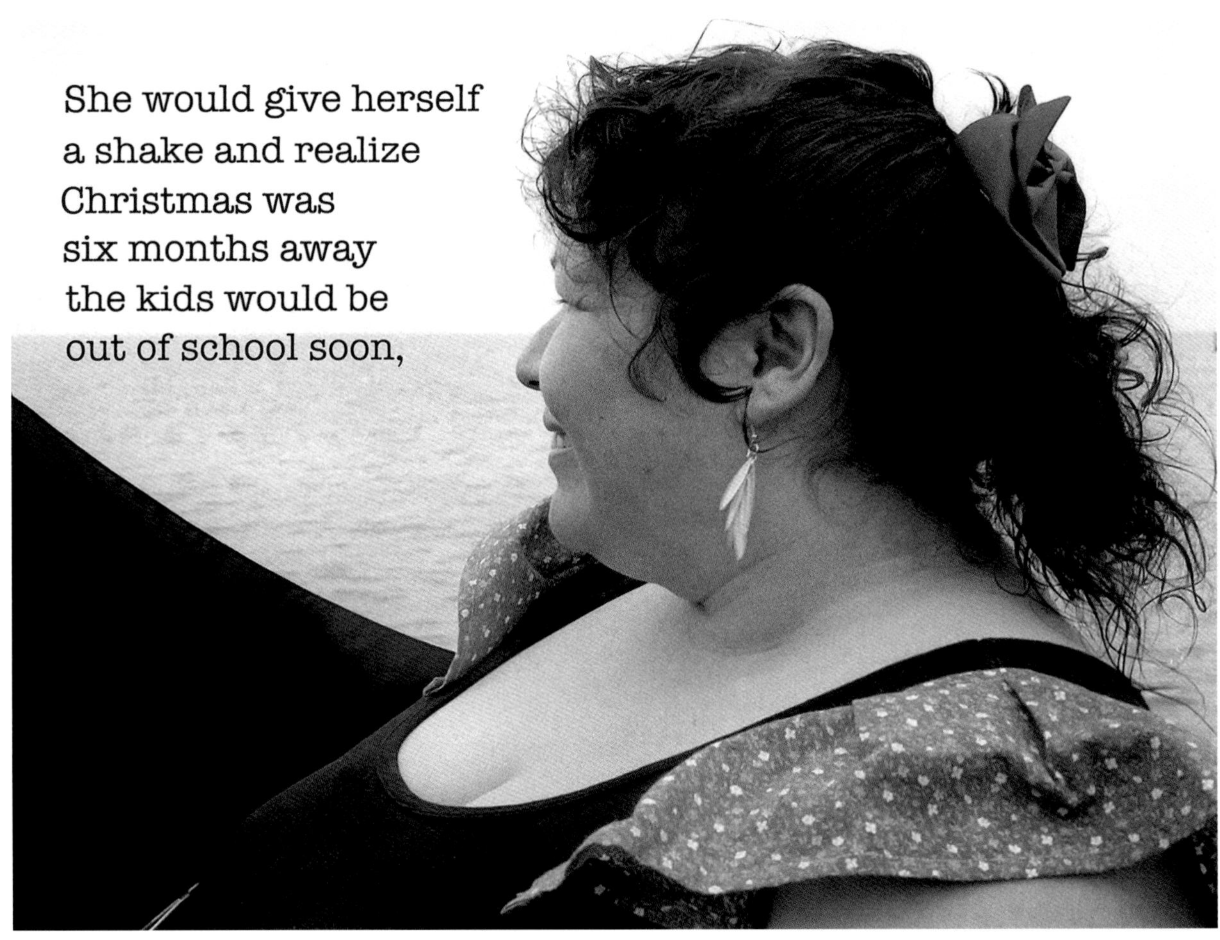

She would give herself
a shake and realize
Christmas was
six months away
the kids would be
out of school soon,

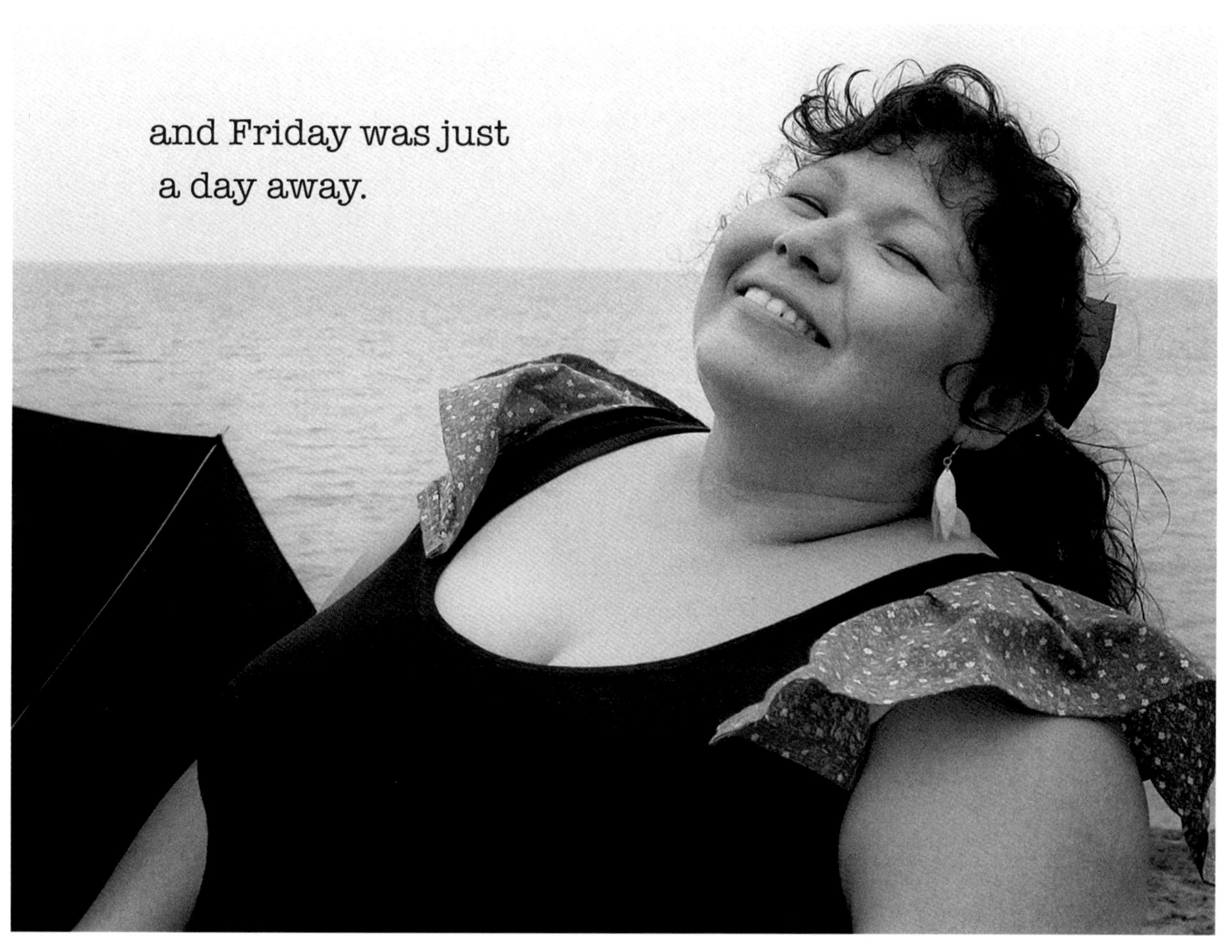

and Friday was just
a day away.

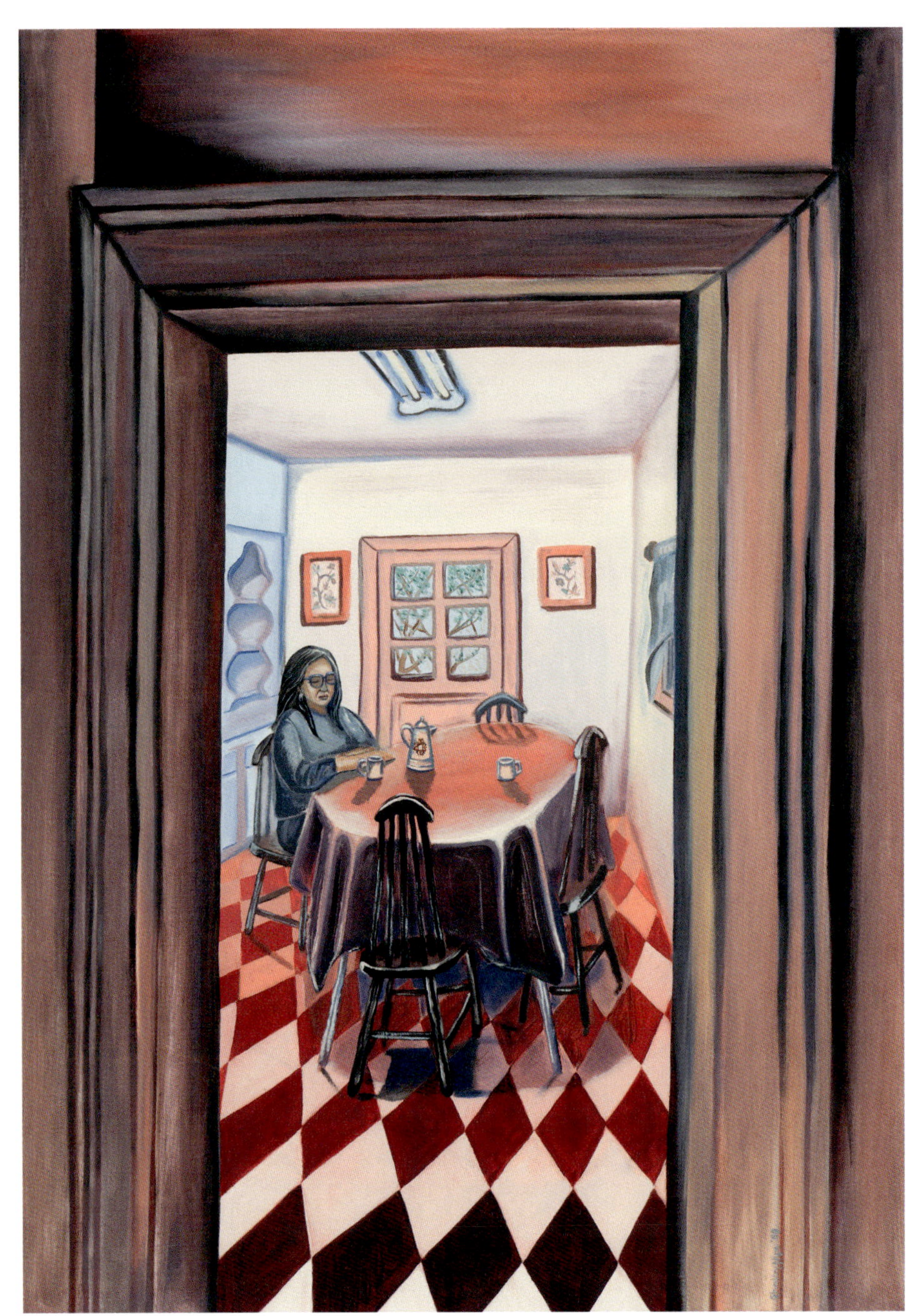

284   **10:30 am**, 1990

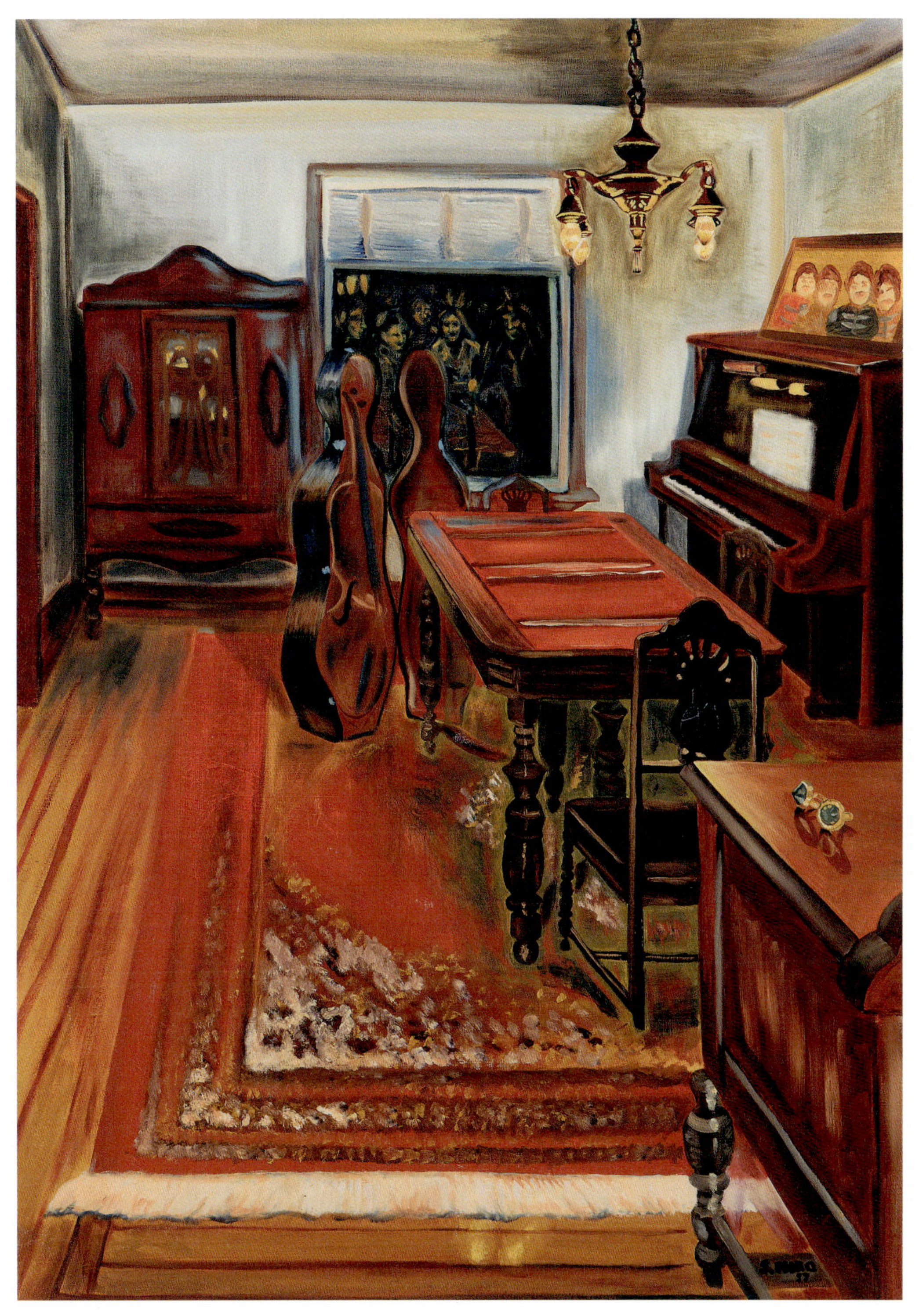

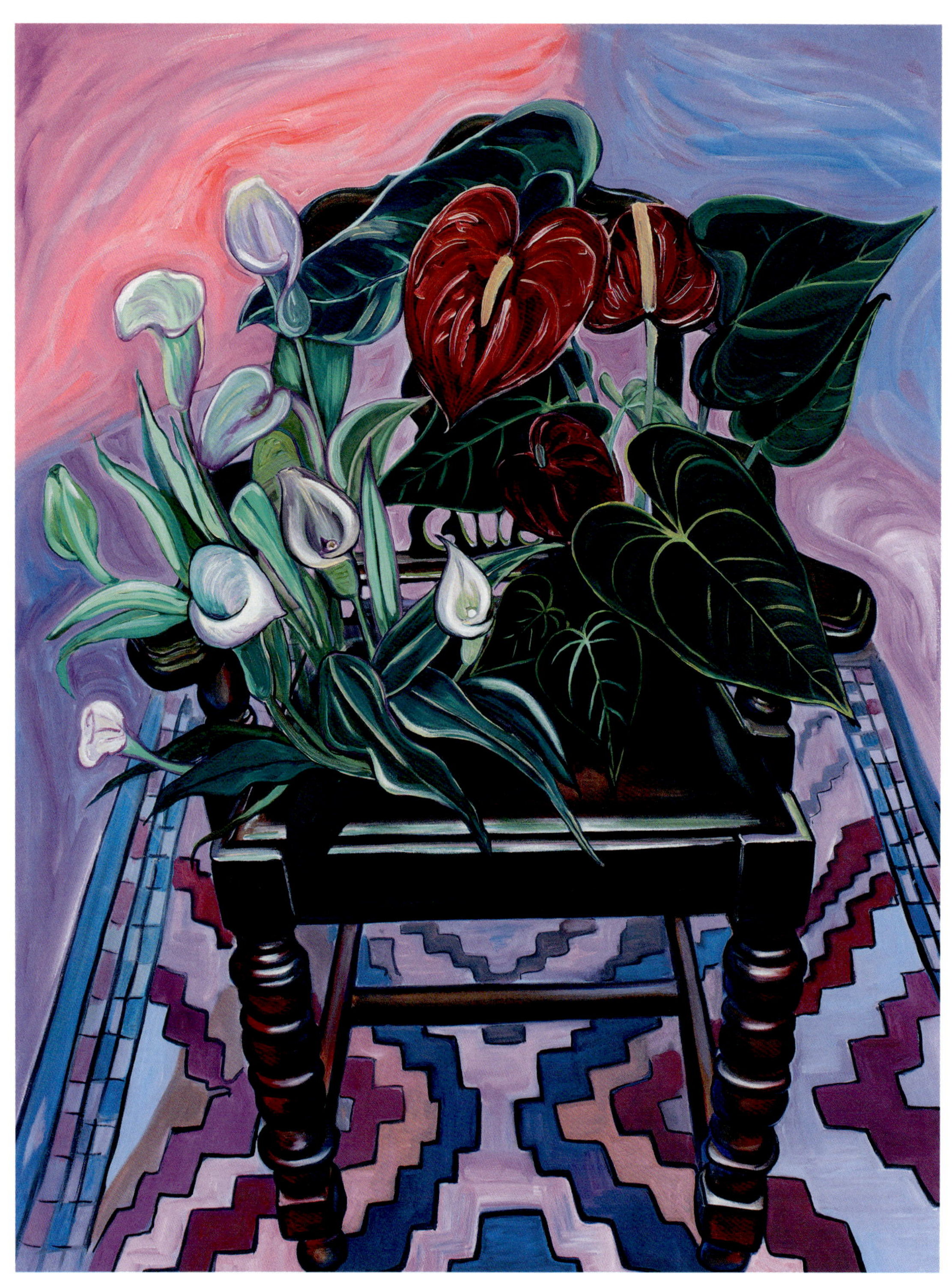

286   **Abundance**, 2013

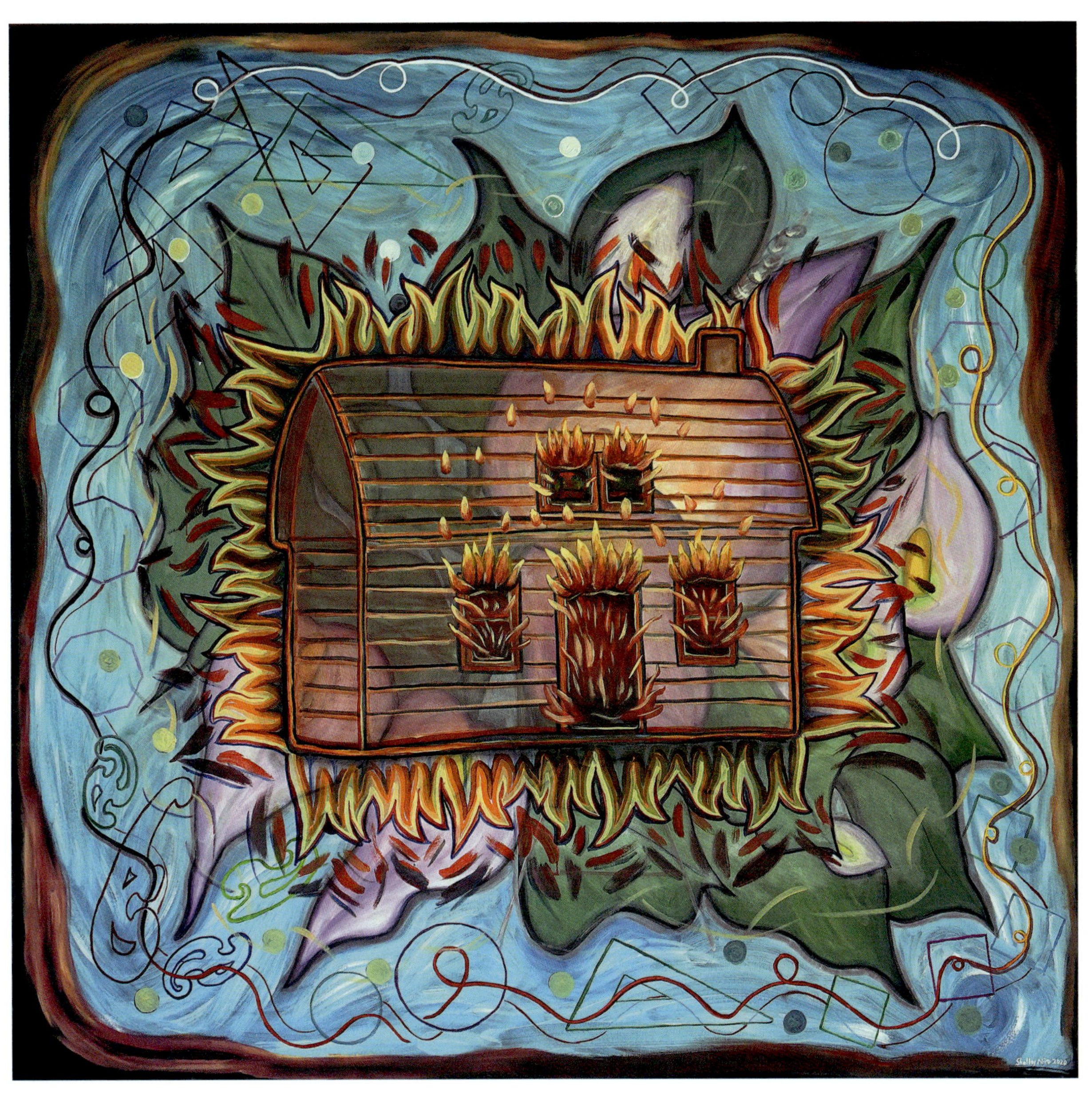

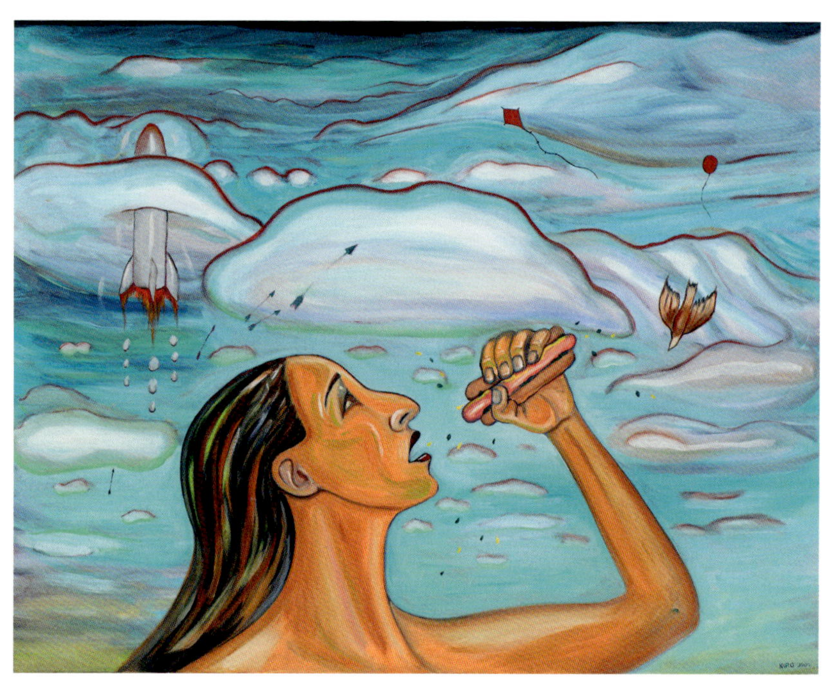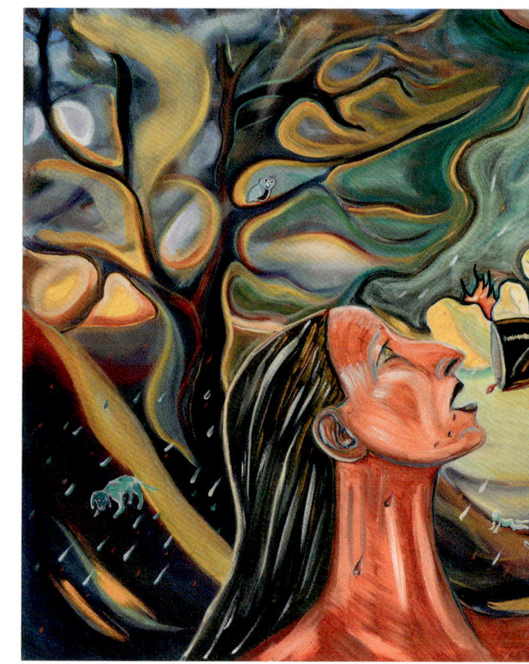

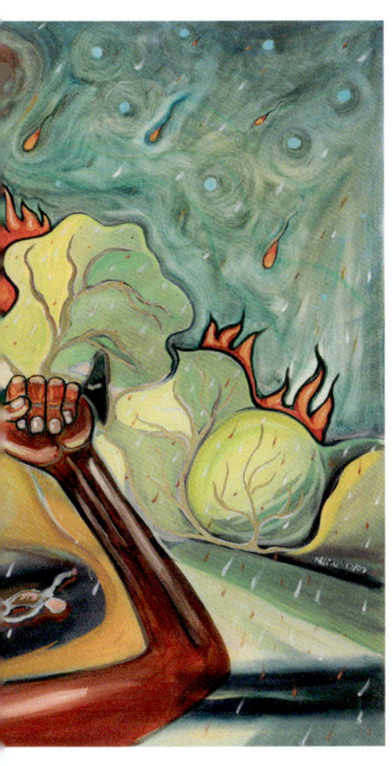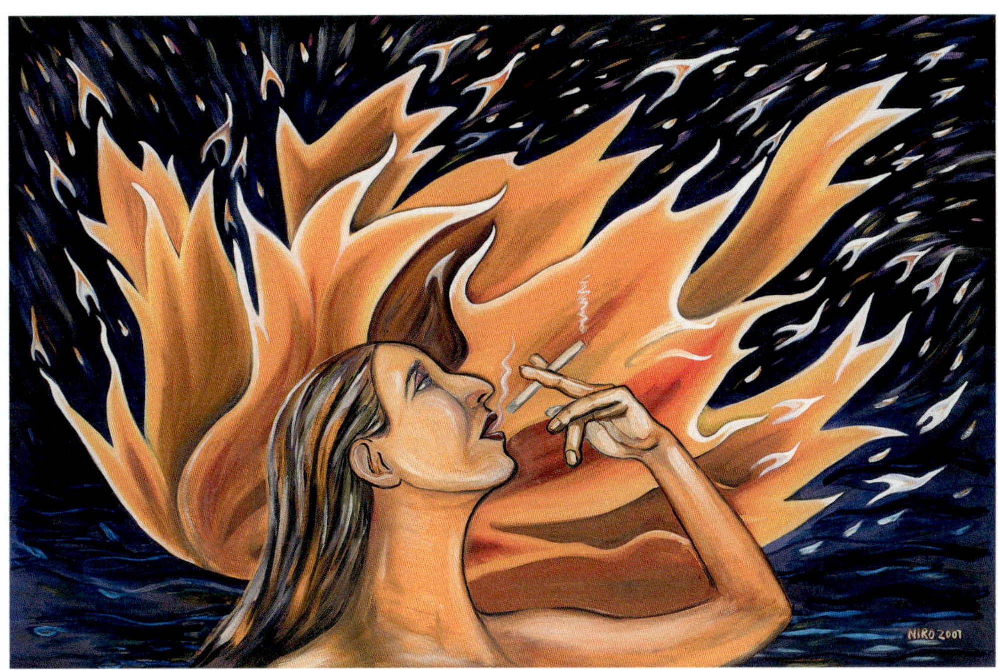

Eating / Drinking / Smoking, 2007   289

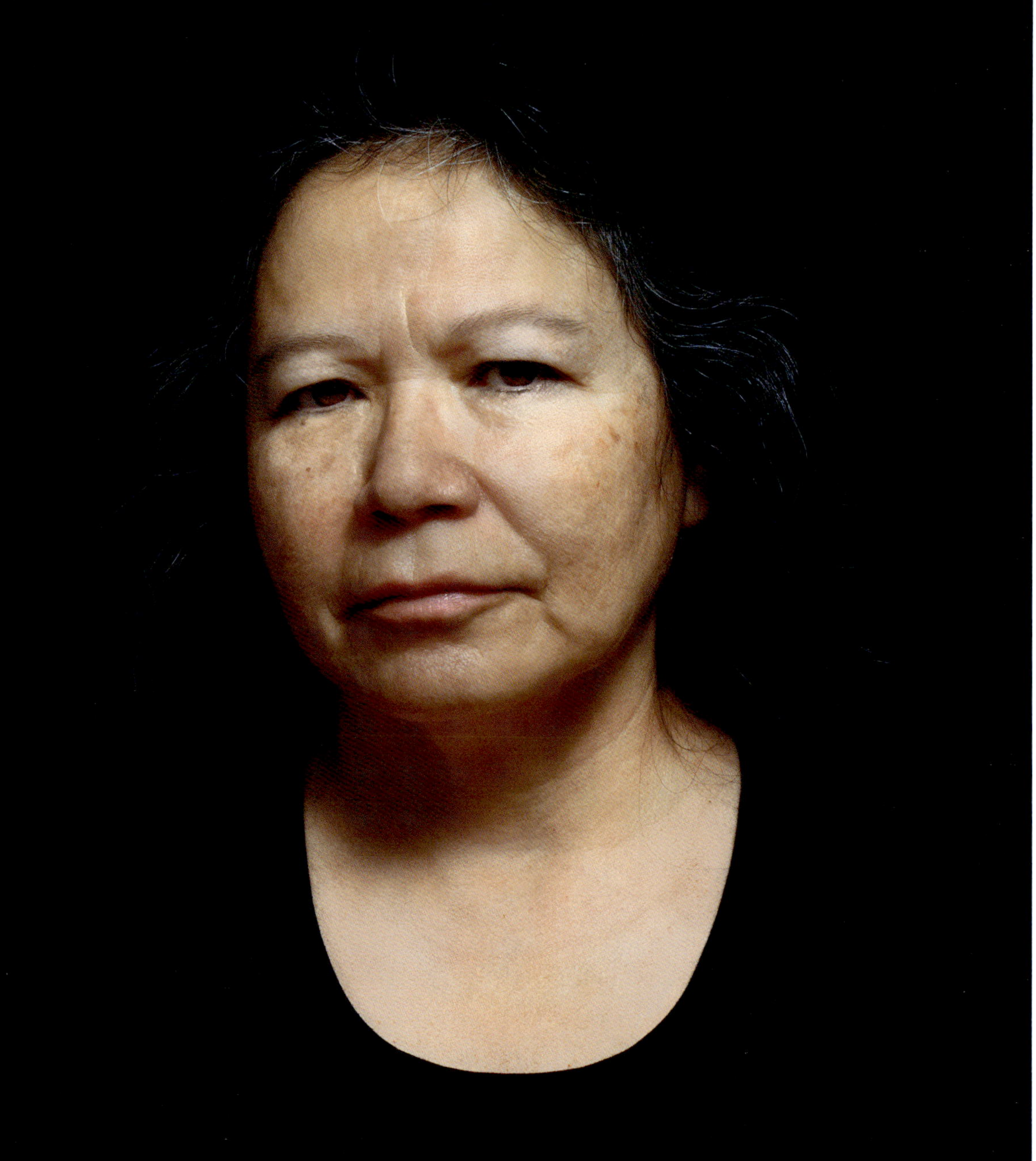

< Abnormally Aboriginal, 2014/2017

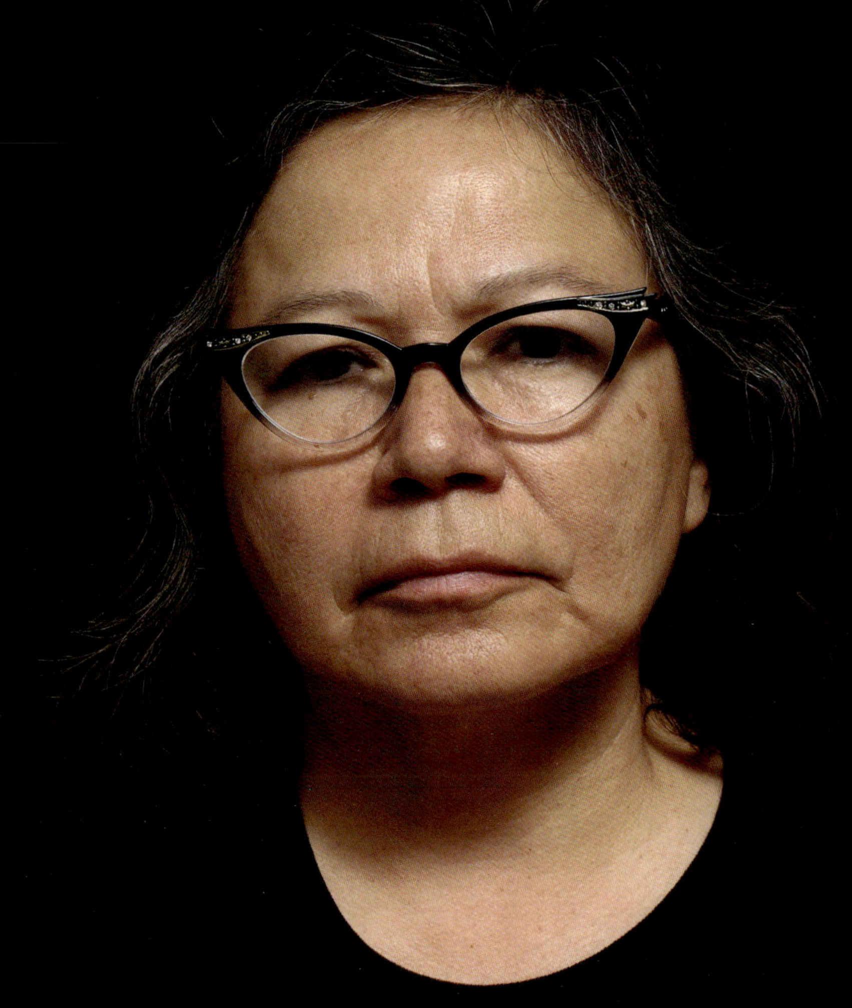
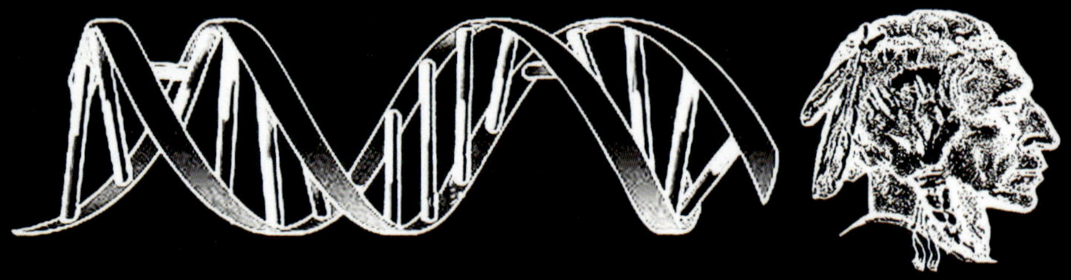

abnormally
aboriginal

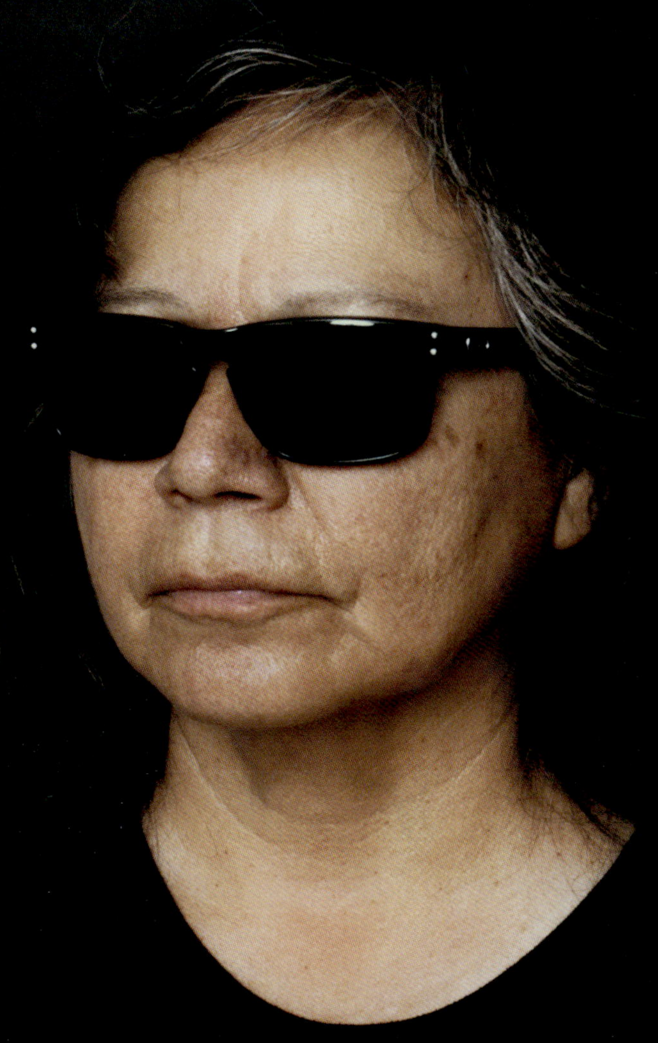
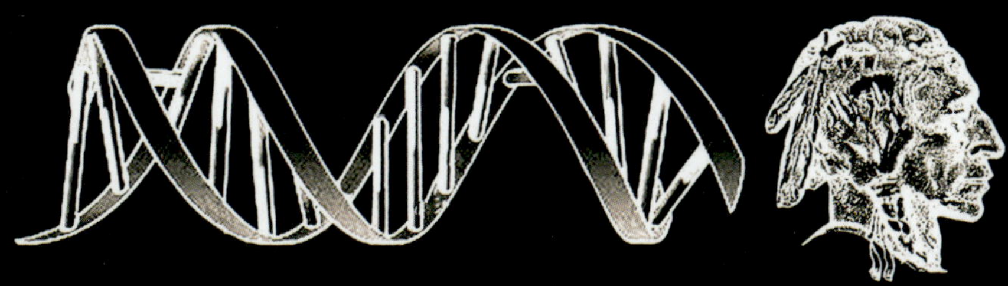

normal
original

For Fearless and Other Indians, 1998/2022 >

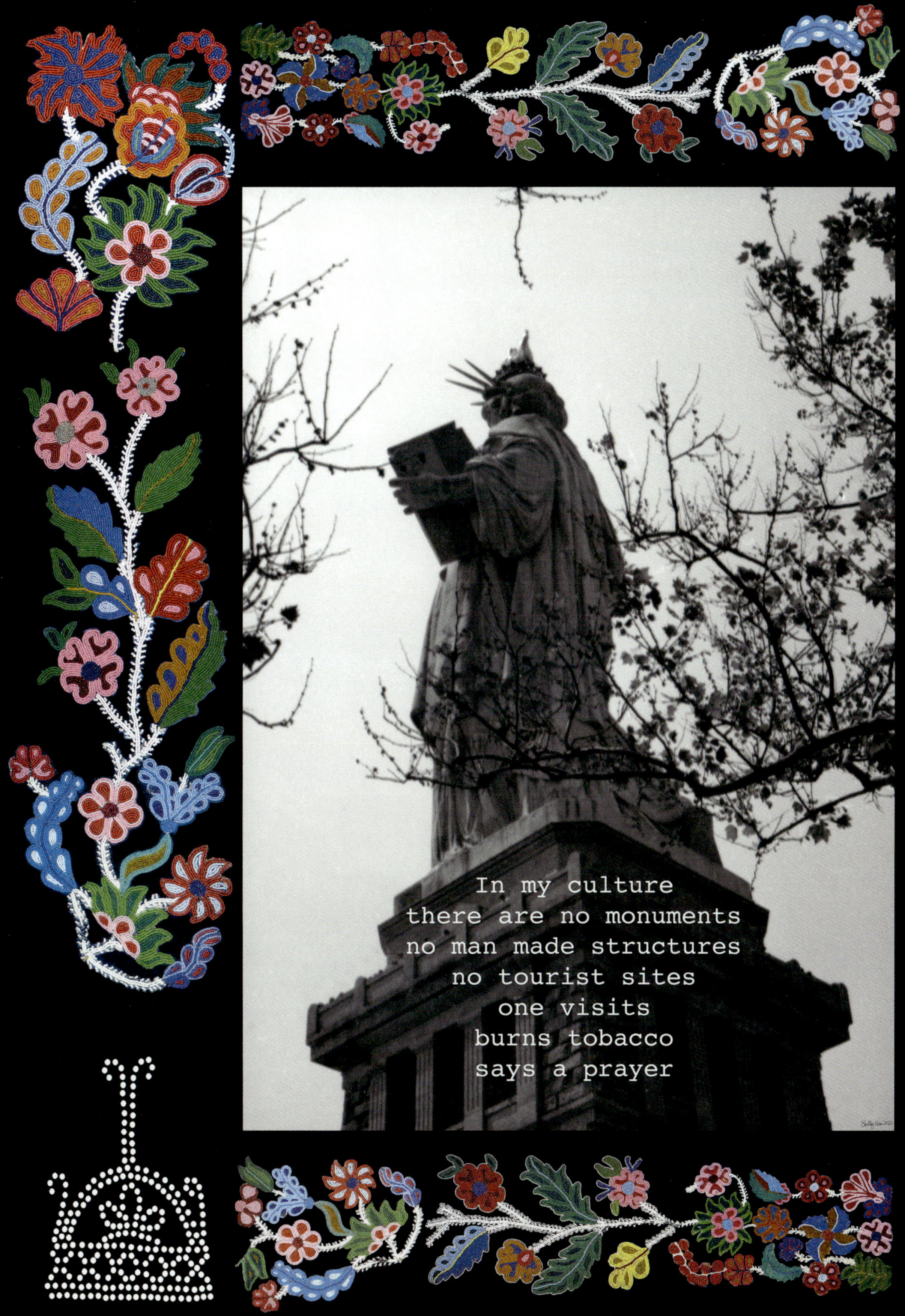

In my culture
there are no monuments
no man made structures
no tourist sites
one visits
burns tobacco
says a prayer

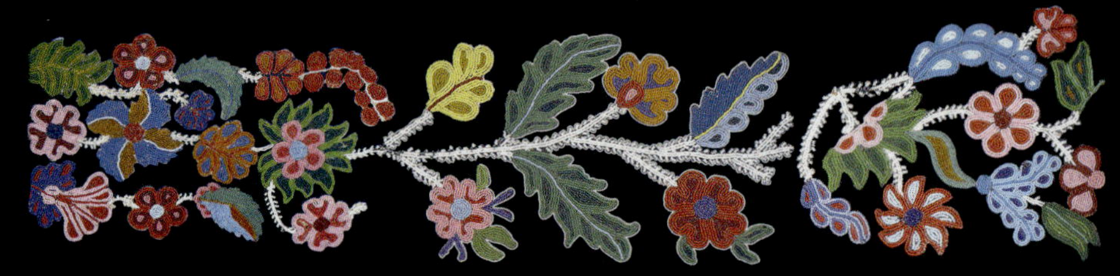

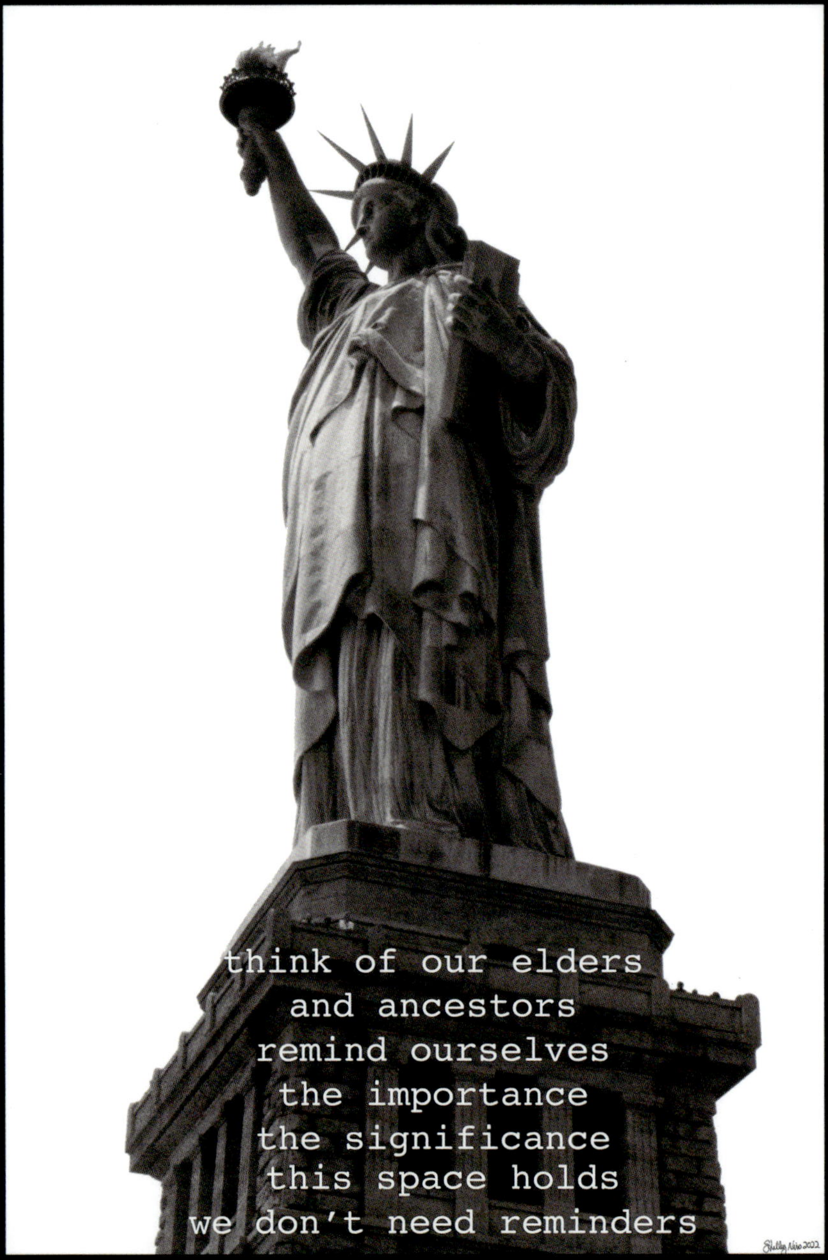

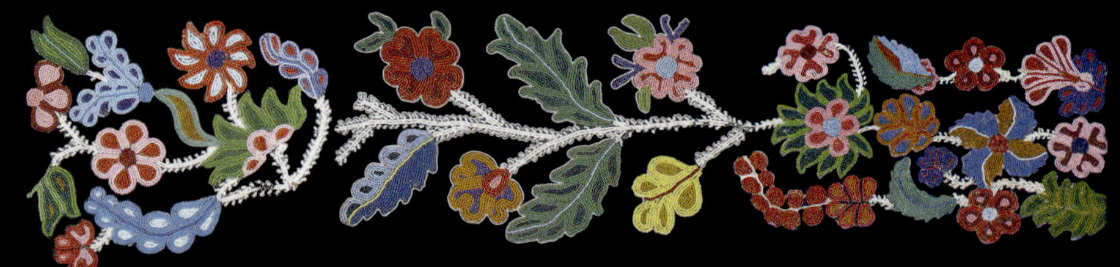

think of our elders
and ancestors
remind ourselves
the importance
the significance
this space holds
we don't need reminders

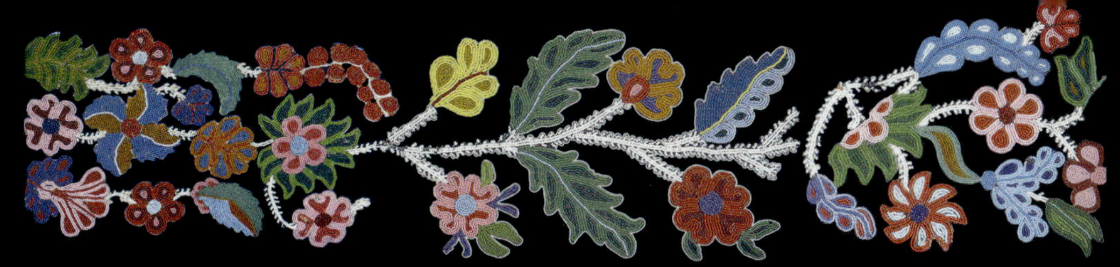

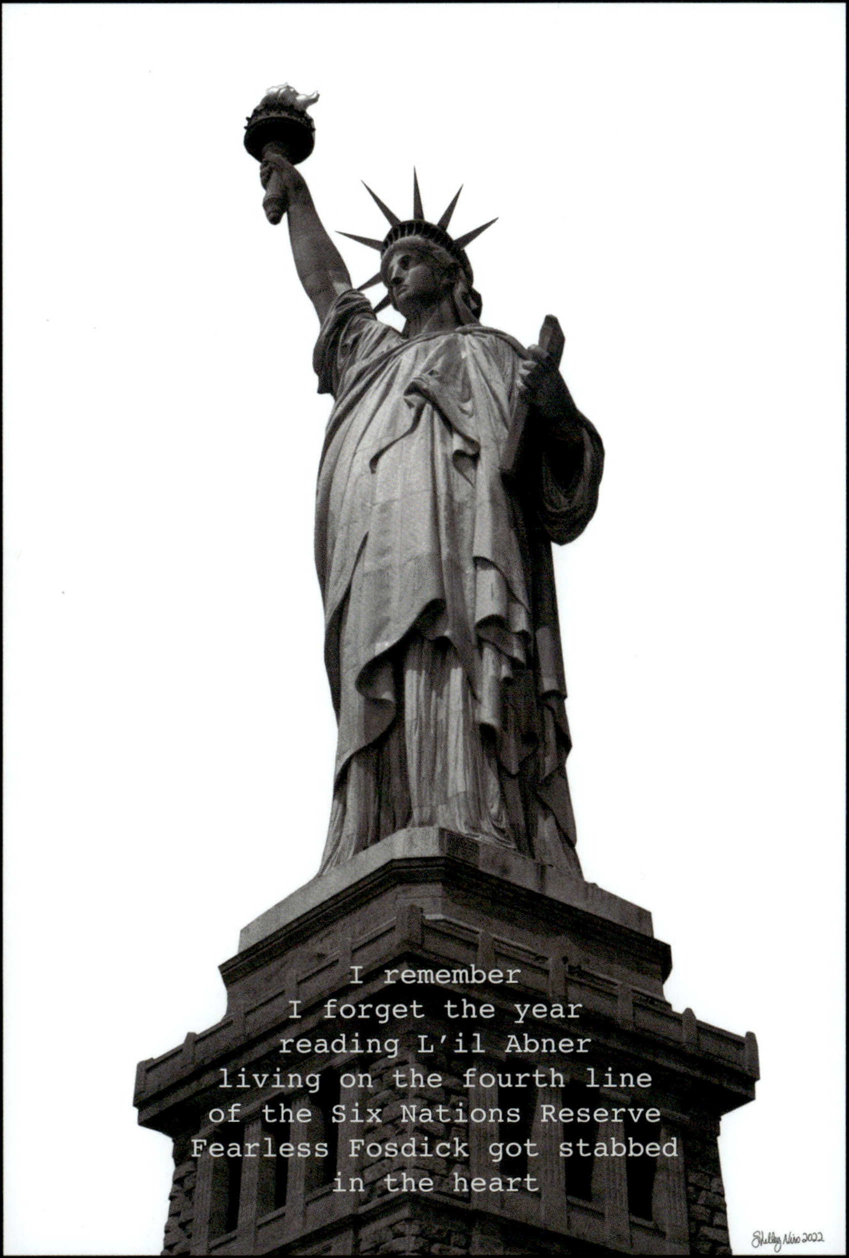

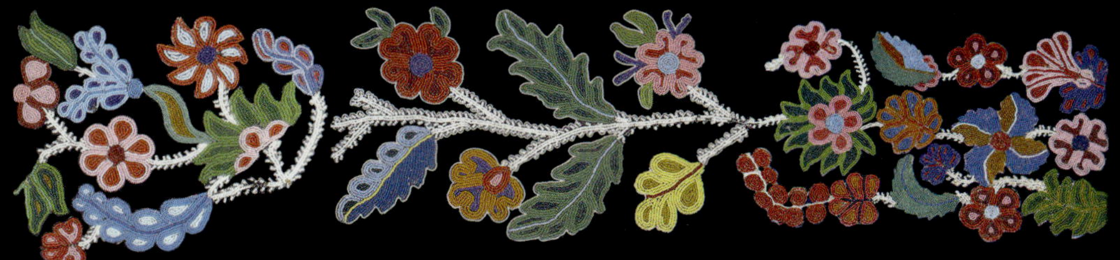

I remember
I forget the year
reading L'il Abner
living on the fourth line
of the Six Nations Reserve
Fearless Fosdick got stabbed
in the heart

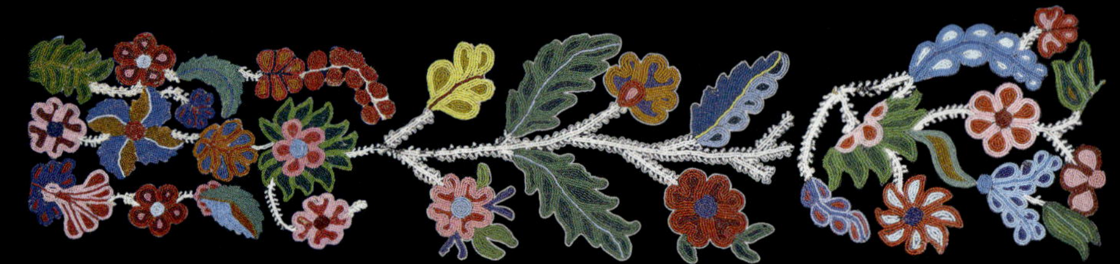

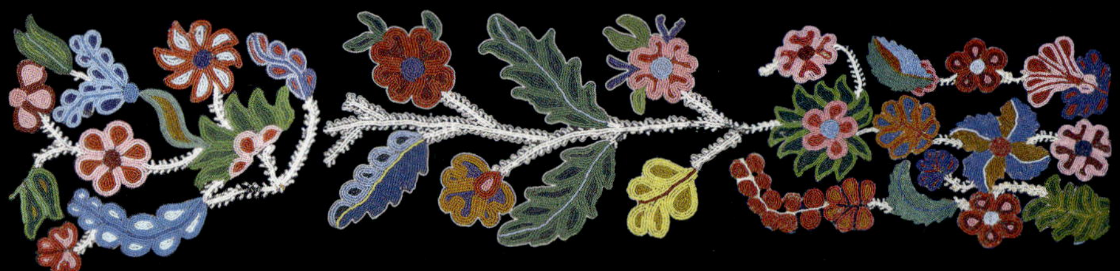

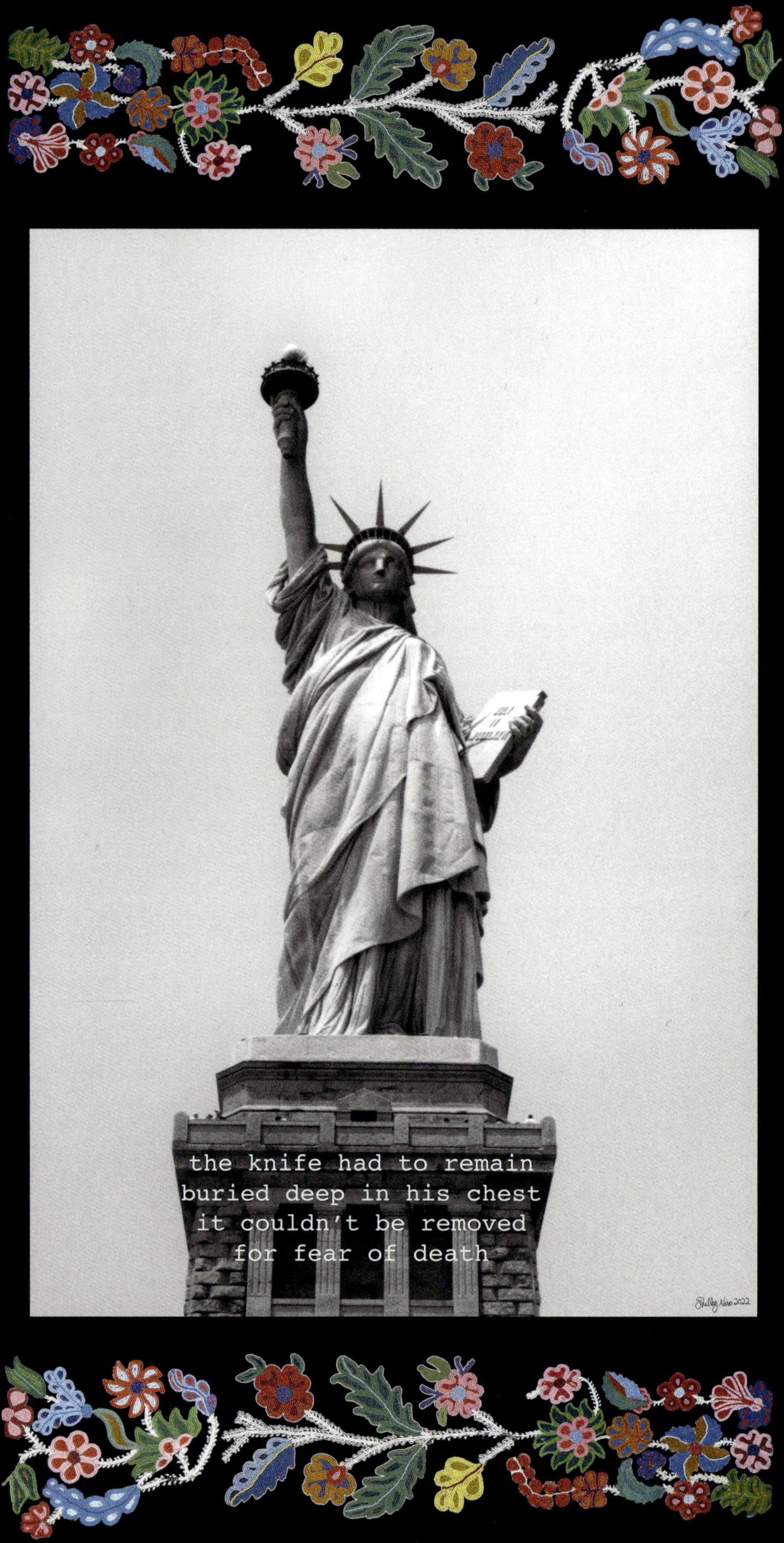

the knife had to remain
buried deep in his chest
it couldn't be removed
for fear of death

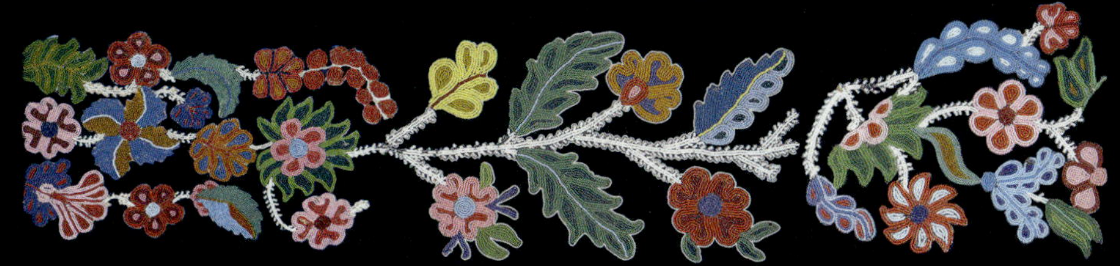

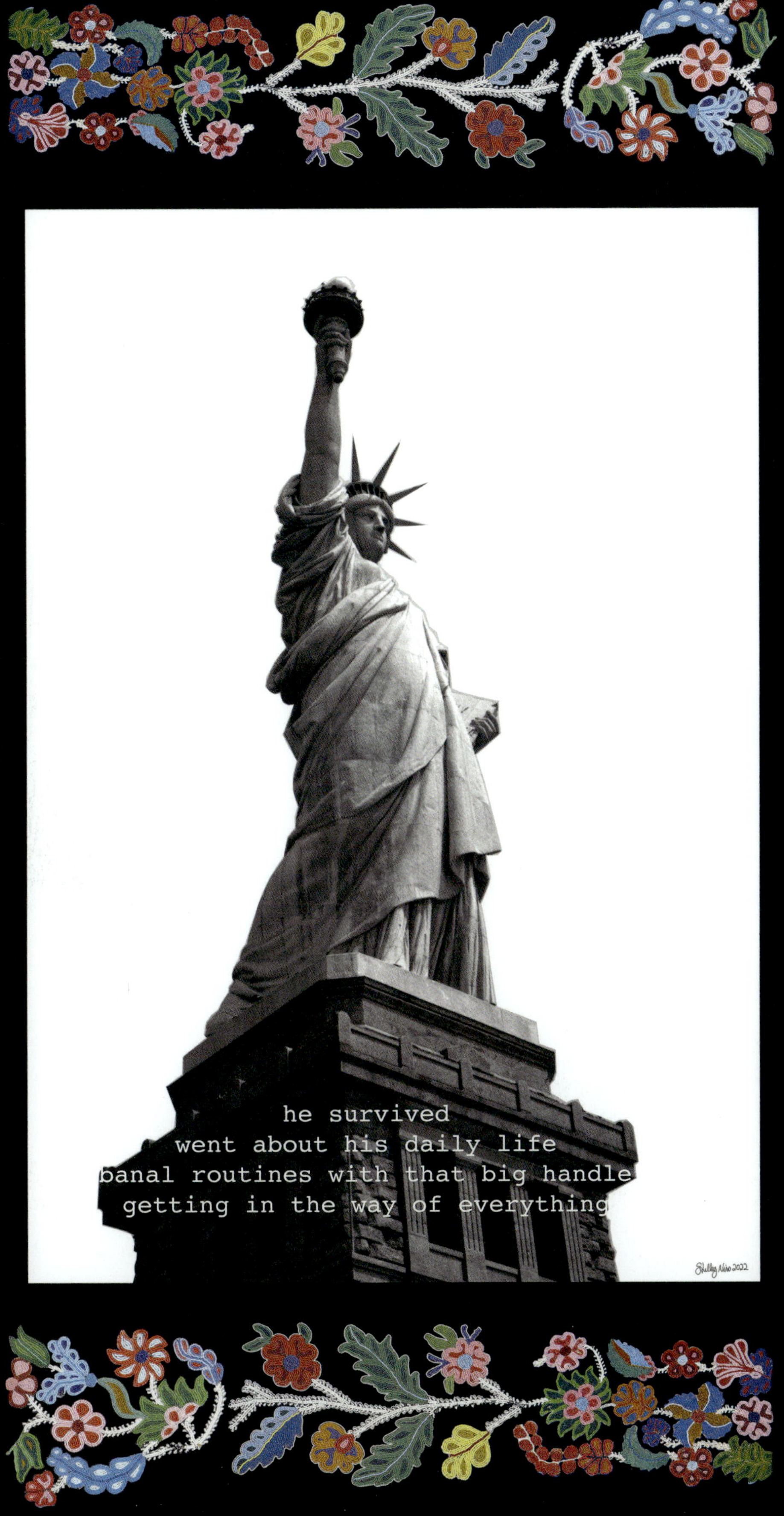

he survived
went about his daily life
banal routines with that big handle
getting in the way of everything

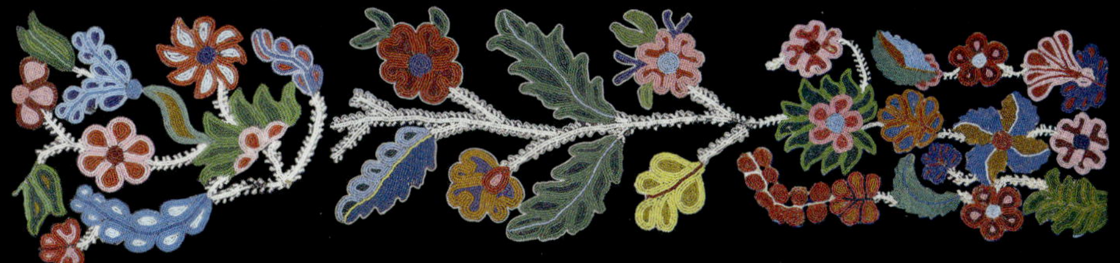

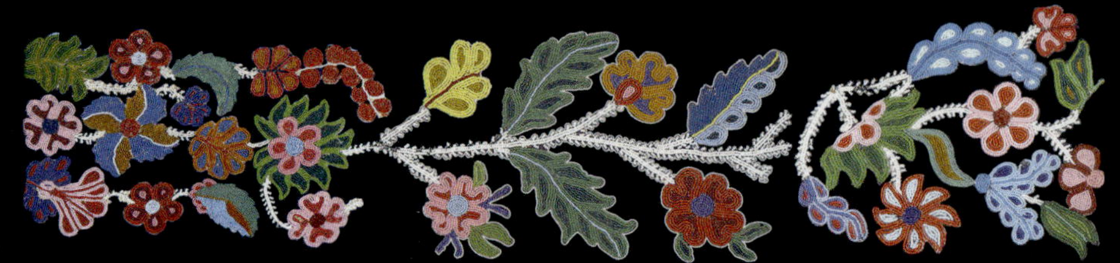

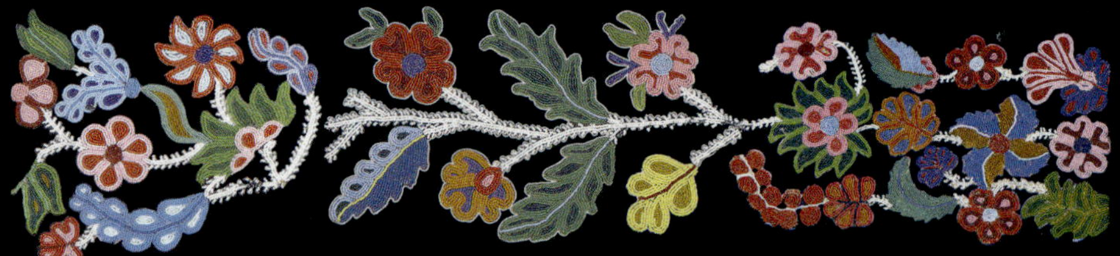

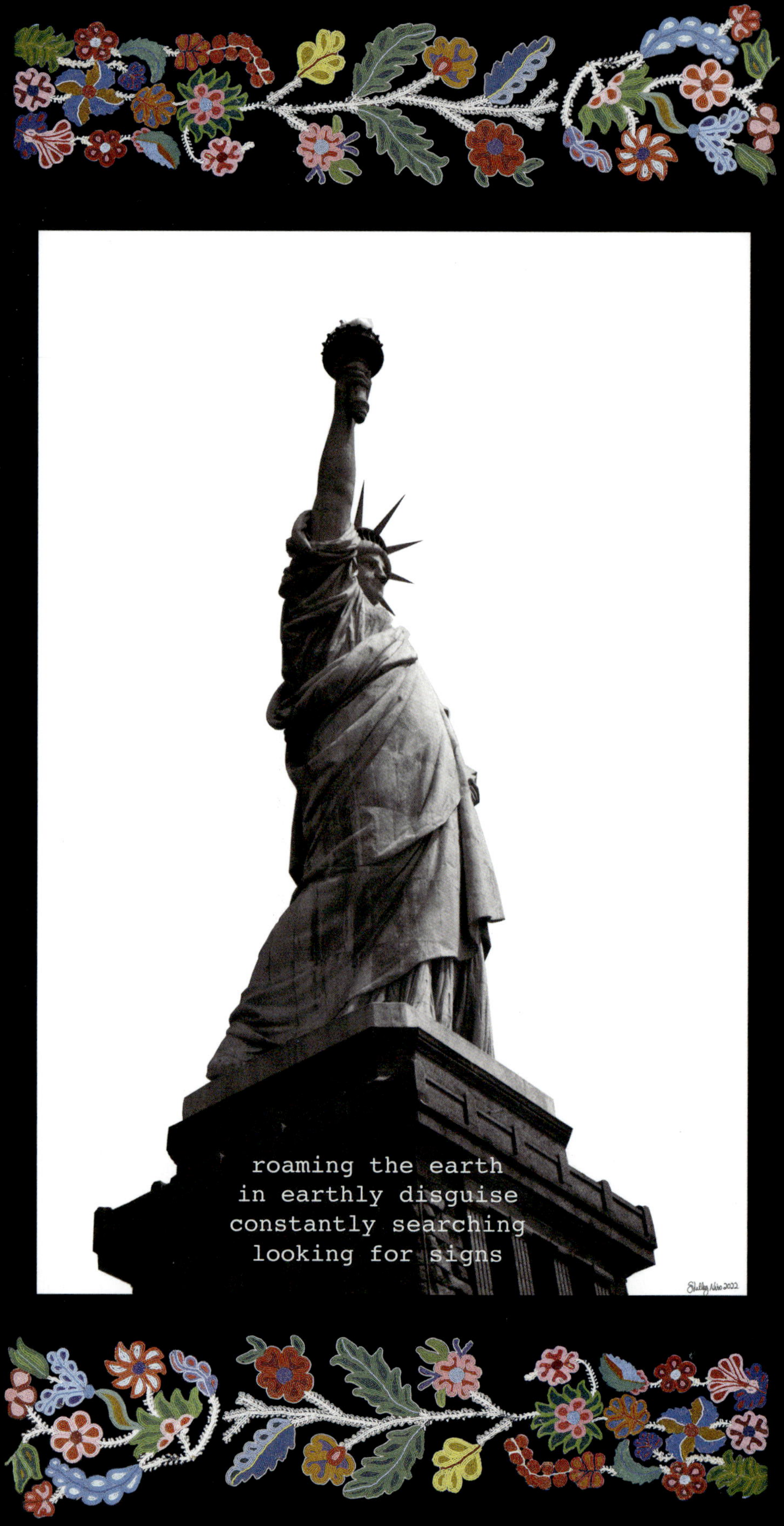

roaming the earth
in earthly disguise
constantly searching
looking for signs

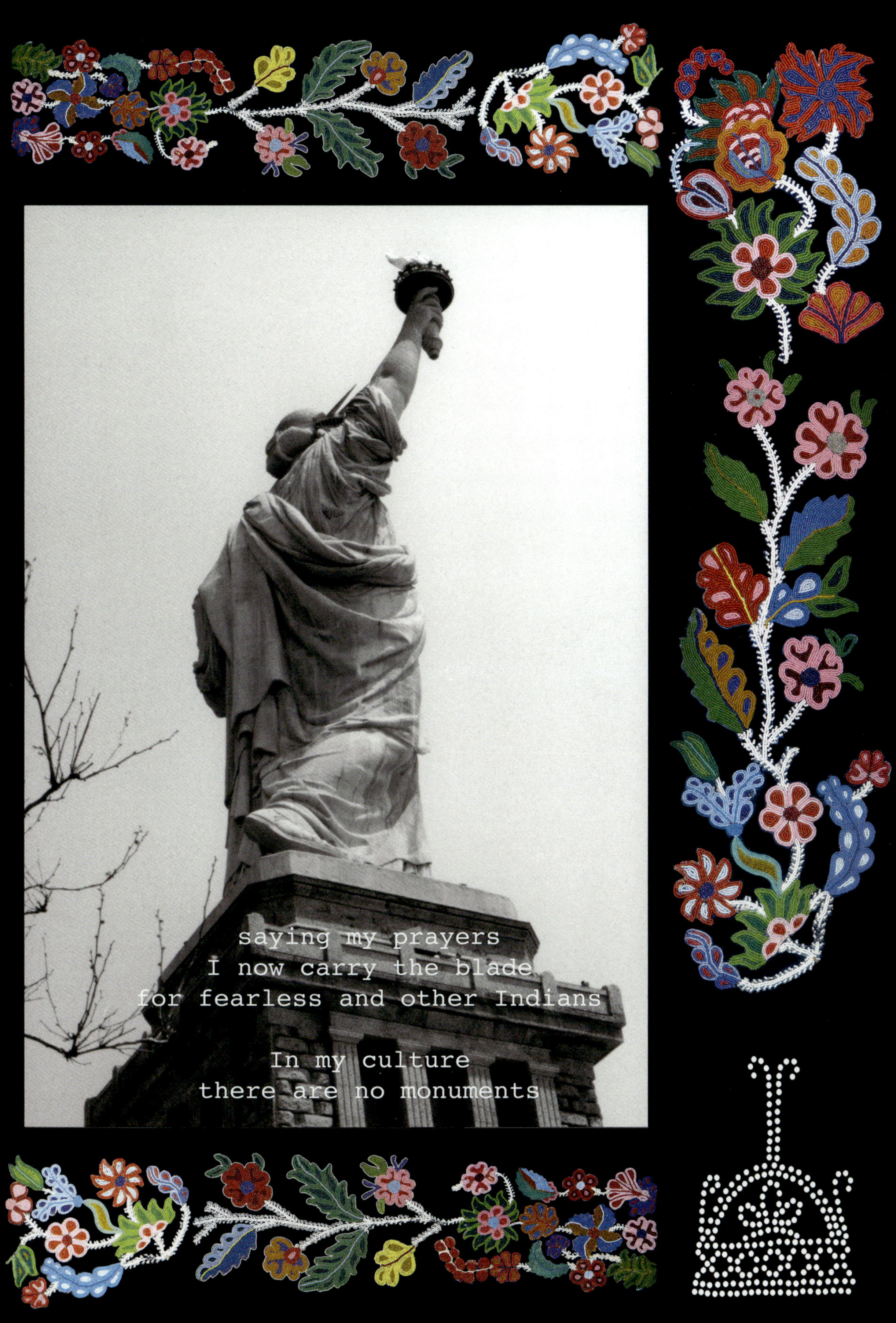
saying my prayers
I now carry the blade
for fearless and other Indians

In my culture
there are no monuments

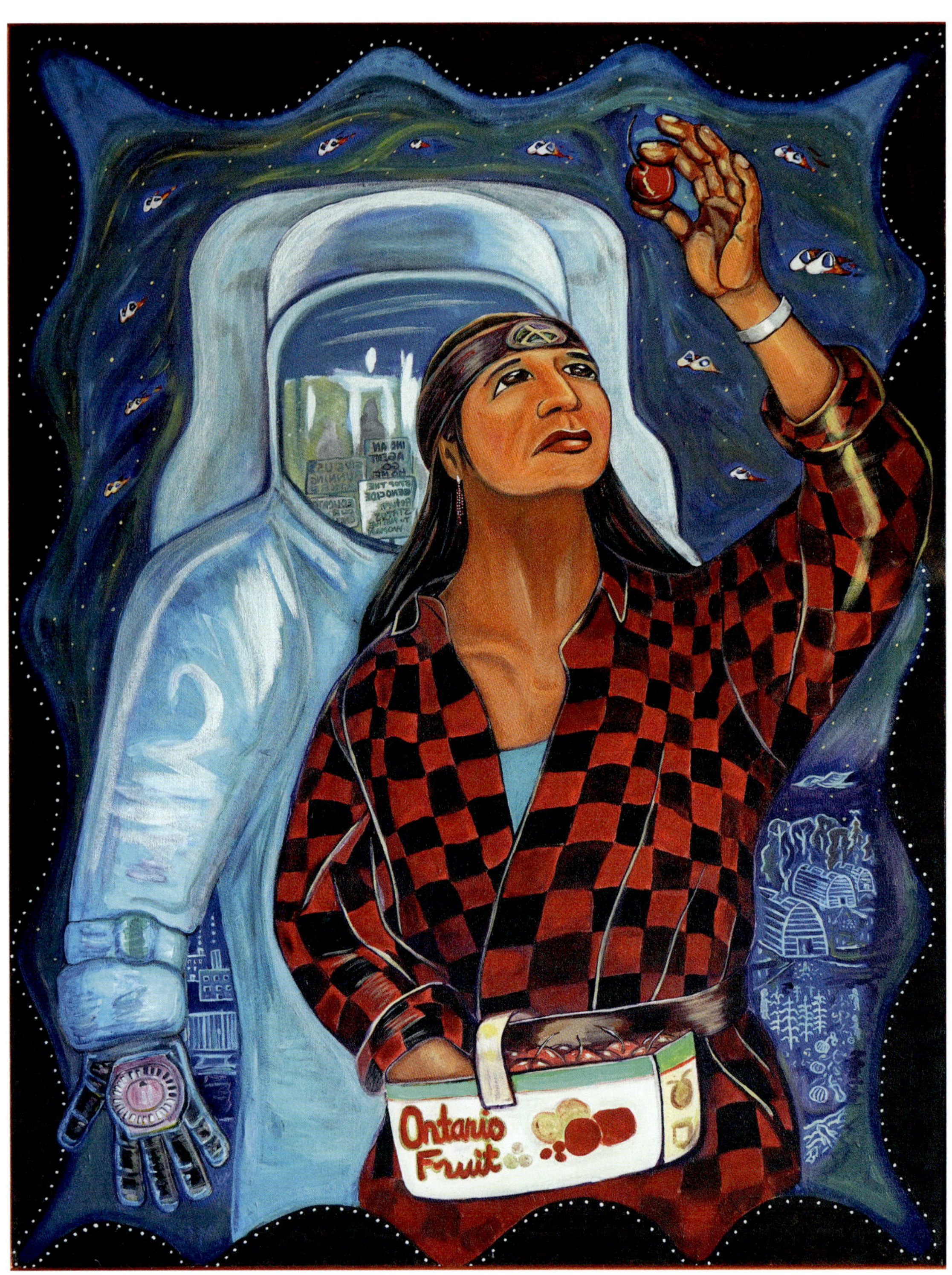

Cherry Picker, 2007

cover, p. 3
**Pandemic Moon (Post-Industrial /
Pre-Colonized)**, 2023
Duratrans in circular lightbox
36 × 36 × 4 inches / 91.4 × 91.4 × 10 cm
Edition of six
Co-published with Barr Gilmore, MORE
(or less) Editions, Algonquin Highlands, ON

p. 6
Sisters, 1982 / 1987
Gelatin silver print
10 × 6 ⅞ inches / 25.5 × 17.5 cm
Indigenous Art Collection,
Crown-Indigenous Relations and
Northern Affairs Canada

p. 9
Cousins, 1982 / 1987
Gelatin silver print
7 × 10 inches / 18.5 × 25.5 cm
Indigenous Art Collection,
Crown-Indigenous Relations and
Northern Affairs Canada

p. 10
Crystal, 1987
Gelatin silver print
9 × 6 ½ inches / 24 × 16.5 cm
Indigenous Art Collection,
Crown-Indigenous Relations and
Northern Affairs Canada

p. 13
The Moon and Me and A Celestial Tree,
2010 / reprinted 2022
Colour inkjet print on metallic paper
23 ½ × 17 inches / 59.5 × 43 cm
Collection of the artist

pp. 14–15
Black Whole, 2021
Oil on canvas
59 × 90 ⅝ inches / 149.9 × 230.2 cm
Collection of the artist

pp. 16–17
**The Iroquois is a Highly Developed
Matriarchal Society**, 1989
Three hand-tinted, sepia-toned
photographs in drilled black matboard
21 × 38 inches / 54 × 95.3 cm
Indigenous Art Collection,
Crown-Indigenous Relations and
Northern Affairs Canada

p. 18
Bush Kids, 1982
Hand-tinted gelatin silver print in drilled
black matboard
16 × 20 inches / 40.6 × 50.8 cm
Collection of the artist

p. 19
Grandma and Cousins, 1982
Hand-tinted gelatin silver print
8 × 10 inches / 20.3 × 25.4 cm
Collection of the artist

pp. 20–21
The Rebel, 1982 / 1987
Hand-tinted gelatin silver print
8 × 10 inches / 20.3 × 25.4 cm
Canadian Museum of History, Gatineau, QC
(III-I-1694)

p. 23
Time Travels Through Us, 1999
Gelatin silver print, cotton and beaded mat
work, silver painted wood frame
37 × 33 inches / 94 × 83.8 cm
CMCP Collection, National Gallery of
Canada, Ottawa, ON

p. 24
My Girls, 2002
Cyanotype, cotton, satin and beaded mat
work, metallic/gilttery purple painted frame
33 × 25 inches / 83.8 × 63.5 cm
Collection of the artist

p. 25
Chiquita, 2002
Cyanotype, velvet and beaded mat work,
metallic/glittery violet painted frame
33 × 25 inches / 83.8 × 63.5 cm
Collection of the artist

pp. 26–27
Chiquita I, II, III, 2021
Archival inkjet prints
40 × 40 inches / 101.6 × 101.6 cm each
Collection of the artist

pp. 30, 115
It Starts With a Whisper, 1993
(with Anna Gronau)
Digital video, colour, sound, 27:29 minutes
National Gallery of Canada, Ottawa, ON

p. 45
Standing on Guard for Thee, 1991 / 1996
Hand-tinted gelatin silver print
14 × 11 inches / 35.6 × 27.9 cm
Library and Archives Canada, Ottawa, ON
(a195401)

pp. 46–53
Red Heels Hard, 1991
Six hand-tinted gelatin silver prints in hand-
drilled black matboard
14 × 62 inches / 35.6 × 157.4 cm
Indigenous Art Collection,
Crown-Indigenous Relations and
Northern Affairs Canada

pp. 54–55
Mohawks in Beehives, 1991 /
reprinted 2022
Hand-tinted gelatin silver print
8 × 10 inches / 20.3 × 25.4 cm
Collection of the artist

pp. 56–57
Queen Bees, 1991
Hand-tinted gelatin silver print
8 × 10 inches / 20.3 × 25.4 cm
Library and Archives Canada, Ottawa, ON
(e010767996)

p. 58
Spring Fever, 1991
Three hand-tinted gelatin silver prints in
hand-drilled black matboard
26 ½ × 14 ¾ inches / 67.3 × 37.5 cm
Collection of the artist

p. 59
Mohawk Sitting on a Cloud, 1991
Three hand-tinted gelatin silver prints in
hand-drilled black matboard
21 ¼ × 37 ½ inches / 54 × 95 cm
Collection of the artist

p. 60
I Enjoy Being a Mohawk Girl, 1991
Three hand-tinted gelatin silver prints in
hand-drilled black matboard
36 × 15 ½ inches / 91.4 × 39.4 cm
Collection of the artist

p. 61
**Portrait of the Artist, Sitting with a Killer,
Surrounded by French Curves**, 1991 /
reprinted 2022
Hand-tinted gelatin silver print in hand-
drilled black matboard
11 × 14 inches / 28 × 36 cm
Collection of the artist

pp. 62–63
Mohawks in Beehives II, 1991
Three hand-tinted gelatin silver prints
17 ⅛ × 25 ⅞ inches / 43.5 × 65.7 cm
Collection of the artist

pp. 64–65
Are You My Sister?, 1994
Fourteen gelatin silver prints in hand-drilled
matboard
40 × 252 inches / 101.6 × 640 cm
Agnes Etherington Art Centre, Queen's
University, Kingston, ON
Purchased with the support of the Canada
Council's Acquistion Assistance Program

pp. 66–67
Chiquita, Bunny, Stella, 1995
Installation including three framed gelatin
silver prints on fibre-based paper with three
vitrines containing a feather fan, a cornhusk
doll, and a beaded bag
Dimensions variable
Collection of the Thunder Bay
Art Gallery, purchased with the support
of the Canada Council for the Arts
Acquisition Assistance Program, 1996

pp. 68–69
Ceremonies, 1992
Three hand-tinted gelatin silver prints
45 × 36 inches / 114.3 × 91.4 cm each
Indigenous Art Collection,
Crown-Indigenous Relations and
Northern Affairs Canada

p. 70
Haudenosaunee Senses, 2001
Colour lithograph on paper
24 × 40 inches / 61 × 101.6 cm
Collection of the artist

pp. 71–75
The Essential Sensuality of Ceremony,
2002
Series of five black-and-white prints on
fibre-based archival paper
Sense of Smell
Sense of Sound
Sense of Touch
Sense of Sight
Sense of Taste
40 × 30 inches / 101.6 × 76.6 cm each
Library and Archives Canada, Ottawa, ON

p. 76
Sky Woman, 2001
Installation including: foam, fiberglass
resin, oil paint, canvas and metal
Dimensions variable
Canadian Museum of History, Gatineau, QC

pp. 79–89
M: Stories of Women, 2011
Series of ten colour inkjet prints
Finding Her Helpers
Ancestors
Legacy
Memories of Flight
Land of Opportunity
Many Horizons
Routes
Blanket
Bagging It
55 × 35 inches / 139.7 × 88.9 cm
Beginnings
35 × 55 inches / 88.9 × 139.7 cm
Edition of two
Collection of the artist; and the
National Museum of the American Indian,
New York, NY/Washington, DC
(27/0643)

pp. 90–94
Thinking Caps, 1999
Sculpture, mixed-media installation
Dimensions variable
National Gallery of Canada, Ottawa, ON

p. 97
Raven's World, 2015
Oil on canvas
80 × 56 inches / 203.2 × 142.3 cm
Art Gallery of Hamilton, Hamilton, ON
purchased in part through the
support of the Elizabeth L. Gordon
Art Program, a program of the
Gordon Foundation and
administered by the Ontario Arts
Foundation, and the Permanent
Collection Fund, 2021

pp. 144–145
**Preparing the Runner for the 23rd
Millenium**, 2005
Beads, cloth, found objects, photograph
Dimensions variable
Collection of the artist

p. 146
Forest Thoughts, 2015
Beaded velvet hat
3 × 5 × 11 inches / 7.6 × 12.7 × 27.9 cm
Collection of the artist

p. 147
Thinking of Sunshine, 2015
Beaded velvet hat
3 × 5 × 9 inches / 7.6 × 12.7 × 22.9 cm
Collection of the artist

p. 148
Keeping Evil Away, 2015
Beaded wool with mirrors hat
4 × 6 × 10 inches / 10.2 × 15.2 × 25.4 cm
Collection of the artist

p. 149
Silver Streams, 2015
Beaded velvet hat with silver material and
belt buckles
4 × 5 × 9 inches / 10.2 × 12.7 × 22.9 cm
Collection of the artist

p. 150
The Weapon, 2021
Oil on canvas
61 × 31 inches / 154.9 × 78.7 cm
Collection of the artist

pp. 153–155
1779, 2017
Mixed media sculpture with video, beaded
velvet, and stiletto heels
50 × 30 ¼ × 30 ¼ inches /
127 × 77 × 77 cm
Art Gallery of Hamilton, Hamilton, ON
Gift of the Women's Art Association of
Hamilton, 2018

pp. 156–161
Ghosts, Girls, Grandmas, 2004
Series of five black-and-white prints on
fibre-based archival paper
41 × 31 inches / 104.1 × 78.7 cm; and
41 × 60 inches / 104.1 × 152.4 cm
Collection of Library and Archives Canada,
Ottawa, ON

pp. 162–167
La Pieta, 2007
Series of seven colour/black-and-white
prints on beaded red cloth
Passage
Infinite View
Sorrow
Hearing Trees Fall
Tomorrow
On The Edge of Awakening
Passage #2
40 × 28 inches / 101.6 × 71.1 cm (two
panels); 40 × 60 inches / 101.6 × 152.4 cm
(four panels); and 50 × 28 inches / 127 ×
71.1 cm (one panel)
National Museum of the American Indian,
New York, NY / Washington, DC
(26/7463)

pp. 168, 181–195
Battlefields of My Ancestors, 2015
Series of black-and-white/colour inkjet
prints on archival paper,
Included in this publication are the
following prints:
Grand River
Caledonia
Where the Mohawk Meets the Hudson
Mohawk River
The Cohoes
Niagara Falls
Battle at Beaver Dam Site
Ten Pretty Little Indian Houses
Against the Six Nations
Sullivan–Clinton Campaign
Burrough's Point
Dean's Cove
Gar-Non-De-Yo
Site of Indian Village

17 × 22 inches / 43.2 × 55.9 cm each
Collection of the artist

pp. 177–180
Scenes from the Grand River, 2004
Series of four gelatin silver prints on fibre-
based archival paper
Power at the Edge
Brant's Crossing
Returning to Life
Tutelo
44 ½ × 54 ½ inches / 113 × 138.4 cm each
CMCP Collection, National Gallery of
Canada, Ottawa, ON

p. 196
The Shirt, 2003
Digital video, colour, sound, 5:55 minutes
National Gallery of Canada, Ottawa, ON

pp. 197–207
The Shirt, 2003
Series of nine Duratrans in lightboxes
54 ⅜ × 43 ⅜ × 4 ¾ inches /
138 × 110 × 12 cm
Art Gallery of Ontario, Toronto, ON
Purchased with assistance from the
Estate of P.J. Glasser, 2016

pp. 208, 211–213
Resting With Warriors, 2001
Series of four woodcut prints on wove paper
81 ½ × 41 ¾ inches / 207.5 × 106 cm
Edition of four in four different ink colours
(red, blue, black, and brown)
Art Gallery of Hamilton, Hamilton, ON
Purchased through the Permanent
Collection Fund, 2016; and
National Gallery of Canada, Ottawa, ON

p. 214
Wishing a River, 2013
Oil on canvas
80 × 56 inches / 203.2 × 142.3 cm
Collection of the artist

p. 215
Travelling Through, 2013
Oil on canvas
80 × 56 inches / 203.2 × 142.3 cm
Collection of the artist

p. 216
Continuing the Journey, 2014
Oil on canvas
80 × 56 inches / 203.2 × 142.3 cm
Collection of the artist

p. 217
Seeing With My Memory, 2000
Oil on canvas
50 × 40 inches / 127 × 101.6 cm
Collection of the artist

pp. 218–219
Sleeping Warrior, 2012
Series of five colour prints
Warrior Dreams of Fighting No More
Warrior Dreams of Life in the Sky
Dressing Warrior
Warrior Dreams of Hunting
Warrior Dreams of Pastures and Power
50 ⅜ × 70 ⅜ inches / 128 × 178.8 cm each
Collection of the artist

pp. 220–222
Surrender Nothing Always, 2004
Colour inkjet print on canvas; and colour
inkjet print on paper mounted to aluminum
24 × 144 inches / 61 × 365.8 cm each
Edition of two
New York State Museum, Albany, NY

pp. 224–231
Borders, 2008
Series of four black-and-white inkjet prints
Borders
Treaties
Unity
Boundless
40 × 120 inches / 101.6 × 304.8 cm each
Collection of the artist

pp. 232–233
Parallel Worlds of Women and Warriors,
2010
Colour inkjet prints, triptych
36 × 36 inches / 91.4 × 91.4 cm each
Collection of the artist

pp. 234–237
Passages, 1996–1997
Oil on canvas, four panels
Skyworld
The Cohoes
A Place Like Mindedness
Grand River
144 × 168 inches / 365.8 × 426.7 cm each
Collection of the artist

pp. 238–239
Unbury My Heart, 2000–2001
Installation including a series of four
paintings, four carpets with five hundred
fabric, felt, synthetic velvet and satin hearts
sewed to twelve dyed nylon ropes
88 × 360 × 48 inches /
223.5 × 914.4 × 121.9 cm
Eiteljorg Museum of American Indians and
Western Art, Indianapolis, IN, 2001.4.1 A-T

pp. 240–241
The Grand Behind Glenhyrst, 2021
Oil on canvas, triptych
72 × 48 inches / 182.9 × 121.9 cm each
Collection of the artist

pp. 242–243
Passing Through, 1993
Installation including a series of five hand-
tinted gelatin silver prints and seven oil on
canvas paintings
161 ½ × 496 ½ × 13 inches /
410 × 1261 × 33 cm installed
National Gallery of Canada, Ottawa, ON

p. 244
Indian Winter, 2015
Oil on canvas
80 × 56 inches / 203.2 × 142.2 cm
Collection of the artist

p. 245
Indian Summer, 2015
Oil on canvas
80 × 56 inches / 203.2 × 142.2 cm
Collection of the artist

p. 246
Day One, 2013
Oil on canvas
61 ⅝ × 49 ½ inches / 156.5 × 125.7 cm
Collection of the artist

p. 247
Day One Too, 2014
Oil on canvas
60 × 50 inches / 152.4 × 127 cm each
Centre for Wise Practices in Indigenous
Health at Women's College Hospital,
Toronto, ON

p. 248
A Trillion Years Ago, 2015
Oil on canvas
61 ½ × 49 ½ inches / 156.2 × 125.7 cm
Collection of the artist

p. 265
500 Year Itch, 1992
Gelatin silver print heightened with applied
colour, mounted on masonite
73 ⅜ × 49 ⅜ × 2 inches /
186.3 × 125.3 × 5 cm
National Gallery of Canada, Ottawa, ON
Gift of Victoria Henry, Ottawa, 2003

pp. 266–277
This Land is Mime Land, 1992
Series of twelve triptychs, each with three
hand-tinted and toned gelatin silver prints
in hand-drilled matboard
Judge Me Not
Santa is a Dene
The Warning of Snow
Final Frontier
Mohawk Worker
Always a Gentleman
Camouflaged
North American Welcome

Survivor
This Land is Mime Land
Love Me Tender
Five Hundred Year Itch
22 × 37 inches / 56 × 94 cm each
CMCP Collection, National Gallery of
Canada, Ottawa, ON; Gift of Sandra
Jackson, Bramalea, ON, 1995

pp. 278–283
In Her Lifetime, 1992/2018
Series of six black-and-white digital prints
40 × 60 inches / 101.6 × 152.4 cm each
Collection of the artist

p. 284
10:30 am, 1990
Oil on canvas
38 ¾ × 26 ½ inches / 98.4 × 67.3 cm
Collection of the artist

p. 285
The Guest, 1987
Oil on canvas
48 × 33 ¾ inches / 121.9 × 85.7 cm
Collection of the artist

p. 286
Abundance, 2013
Oil on canvas
50 × 38 inches / 127 × 96.5 cm
Collection of the artist

p. 287
The Architect, 2021
Oil on canvas
60 × 60 inches / 152.4 × 152.4 cm
Collection of the artist

pp. 288–289
Eating, 2007
Oil on canvas
41 ¾ × 42 inches / 106 × 106.7 cm
Collection of the artist

Drinking, 2007
Oil on canvas
41 ¾ × 55 ⅝ inches / 106 × 141.3 cm
Collection of the artist

Smoking, 2007
Oil on canvas
41 ¾ × 61 ⅝ inches / 106 × 156.5 cm
Collection of the artist

pp. 290–292
Abnormally Aboriginal, 2014–2017
Colour inkjet prints on canvas, triptych
54 × 34 inches / 137.2 × 86.4 cm each
Collection of the artist

pp. 295–301
For Fearless and Other Indians,
1998/2022
Series of seven colour inkjet prints
48 × 280 inches / 121.9 × 711.2 cm overall
Collection of the artist

p. 302
Cherry Picker, 2007
Acrylic on canvas
51 × 39 inches / 129.5 × 99 cm
Collection of the artist

p. 317
The Last Moon, 1999
Oil on canvas
50 × 60 ⅞ inches / 127 × 154.6 cm
Collection of the artist

FILM/VIDEOGRAPHY

Café Daughter, 2022
Feature film, colour, sound, ~120 minutes

Tekahionwake, Pauline, 2021
Digital video, colour, sound, 19:38 minutes

**The Incredible 25th Year of
Mitzi Bearclaw**, 2019
Feature film, colour, sound, 96 minutes

My Heart is in the Forest, 2017
Film, colour, sound, 7 minutes

Niagara, 2015
Digital video, colour, sound, 5 minutes

Robert's Paintings, 2011
Digital video, colour, 52 minutes

Kissed By Lightning, 2009
Feature film, colour, sound, 89 minutes

Hunger, 2008
Digital video, colour, sound, 6:03 minutes

The Flying Head, 2008
Digital video, black-and-white, 3 minutes

rechargin', 2007
Digital video, colour, sound, 2:49 minutes

Tree, 2006
Digital video, black-and-white, sound,
5 minutes

Suite: INDIAN, 2005
Digital video, colour, sound, 57 minutes

The Shirt, 2003
Digital video, colour, sound, 5:55 minutes

Sky Woman With Us, 2002
Digital video, colour, sound, 7 minutes

Pelarosa, 2001
Digital video, 10 minutes

Honey Moccasin, 1998
Digital video, colour, sound, 49 minutes

Overweight With Crooked Teeth, 1997
Digital video, colour, sound, 5 minutes

It Starts With A Whisper, 1993
Digital video, colour, sound, 27:29 minutes

    Please note that not all artworks listed are included at every venue of the exhibition tour.

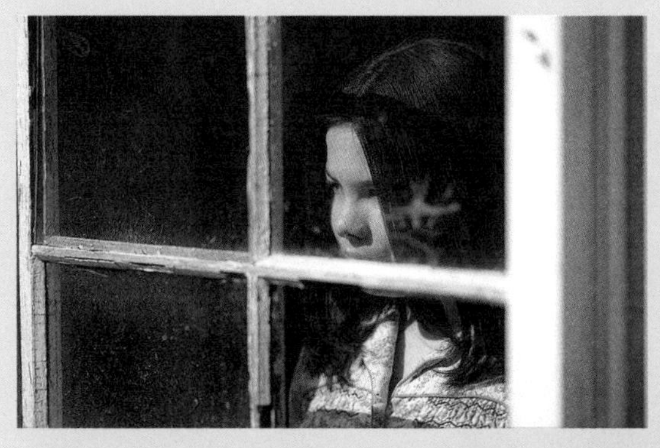
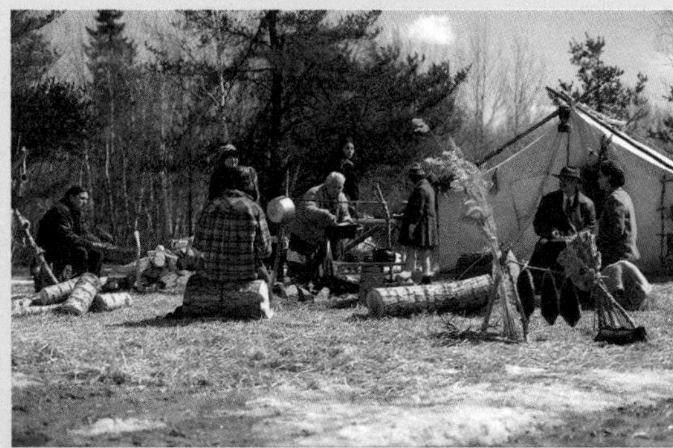
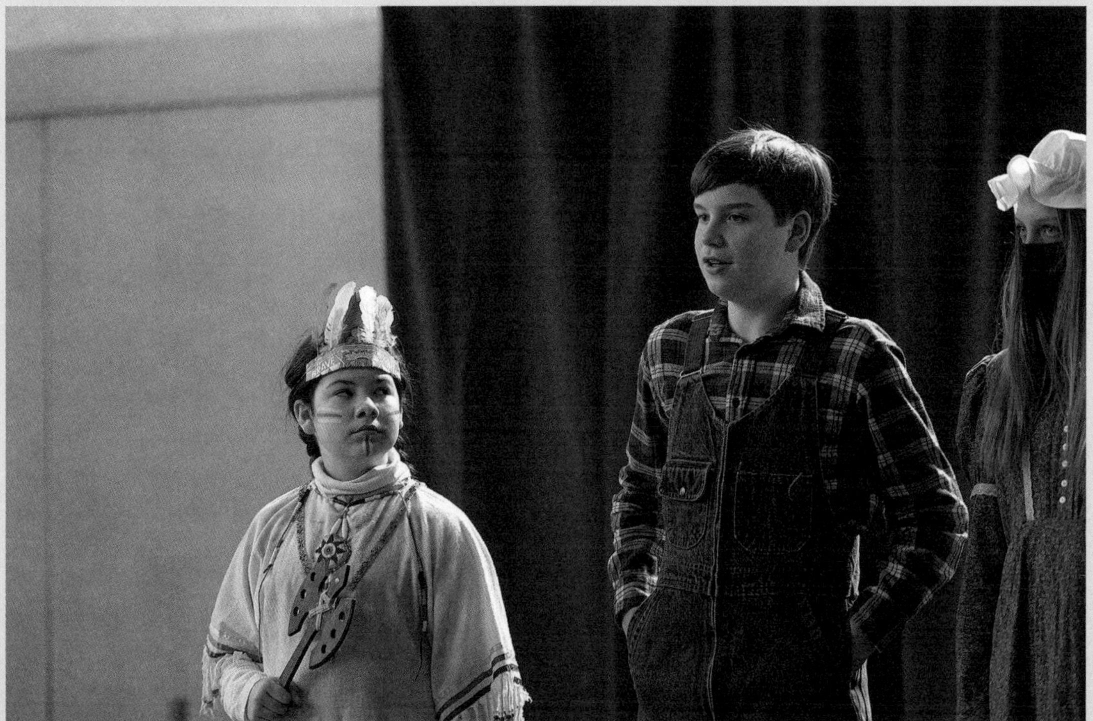
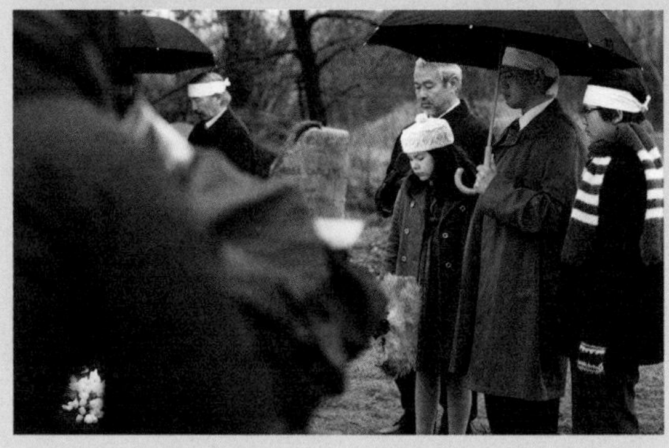
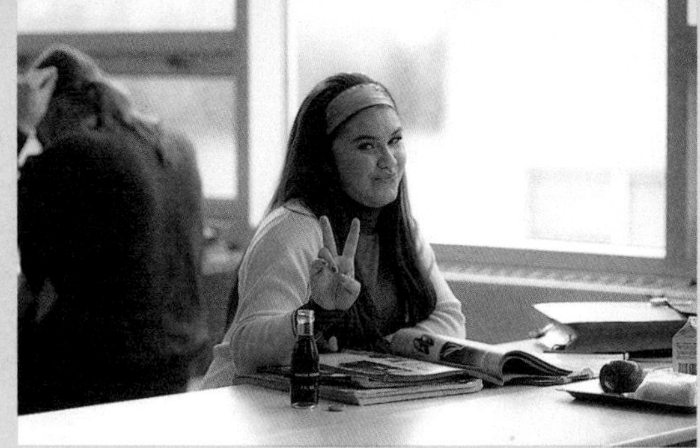

EXHIBITION & CURATOR ACKNOWLEDGEMENTS

MELISSA BENNETT • GREG HILL • DAVID W. PENNEY

This catalogue and exhibition would not have been possible without the generous assistance and cooperation of all of our lenders. We thank our colleagues from across Canada and in the United States, including at the Smithsonian's National Museum of the American Indian (whose collaborators are thanked in the Foreword). We are grateful to Dr. Sasha Suda, Isabelle Corriveau, Virginie Denis, Clément Lormand, Anne Tessier, Lela Radisevic, Jasmine Inglis, and Raven Amiro at the National Gallery of Canada. Thanks also to Stephen Jost, Wanda Nanibush, Donna Austria, Alexandra Cousins, and Jim Shedden at the Art Gallery of Ontario; Allison Evans at the Eiteljorg Museum; Kevin Sakolinsky at the Indigenous Art Centre, Crown-Indigenous Relations and Northern Affairs; Johanna Smith and Megan Lafrenière at Library and Archives Canada; Sharon Godwin and Meaghan Eley at Thunder Bay Art Gallery; Dustin Lawrence and Wanda vanderStoop at Vtape; Lauren Seager, Dr. Lisa Richardson, and Selena Mills at Women's College Hospital; and to Ryan Rice for early conversations.

The curators are grateful for support received during the research and writing stages. Melissa Bennett extends her thanks to editor Chris Hampton and to Alana Traficante for early collaborations, to Melissa Neil for her detailed management of the exhibition and publication, to Shelley Falconer for her vision and ambitions for the Art Gallery of Hamilton, and to Tobi Bruce for initiating the project at AGH and for her immense support and commitment to this undertaking. David W. Penney is grateful to his wife Adriana Greci Green, Curator for the Fralin Museum of Art, University of Virginia, who introduced him to Shelley and Celestino Niro. Greg Hill is thankful for the support, love, and critical insights of his life partner, actor, singer, and playwright Émilie Monnet. The curators are indebted to Barr Gilmore for his collaborative design work, expressing Niro's works and their many written interpretations effectively and creatively through these pages, to Laurel Saint Pierre for her dedicated editing, and to Bryne McLaughlin for his close copy edit.

Our collective thanks goes to Shelley Niro for entrusting us to gather these interpretations of her work, for her support and guidance throughout the research and development of this project, and for having us in her and Chel's home, where we were always warmly welcomed.

Major support for this project is provided by the Canada Council for the Arts and the Terra Foundation for American Art.

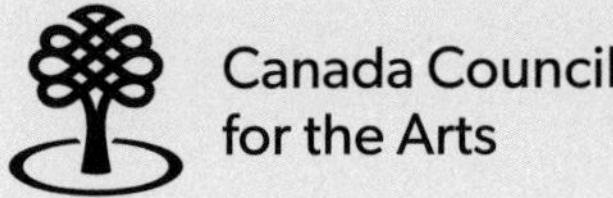

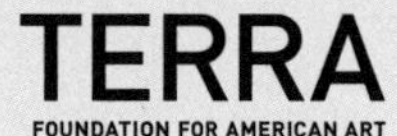

ARTIST ACKNOWLEDGEMENTS

SHELLEY NIRO

In a land when time began, I have great attachment to stories told to me through teachers, parents, knowledge keepers, and cultural sharers. Seeds were planted and from these seeds I developed my own stories and imagined versions of myth and legend. I have tried to push the boundaries of these cultural and familial foundations, remaining true to the intent and at the same time cultivating my own environment for intrigue and the unknown.

I acknowledge Ayonwatha:Hiawatha (He Combs the Hair) and Tekanawite: Rasken:nonhawi (The Peacemaker) as the Creators of signs and symbols that we use and celebrate in our work today. We, Rotinohnshionikon, are children of the Iroquois, Haudenosaunee, and Six Nations of the Grand River. We are Onkwehonwesohna, the "Real Human Beings."

Matoaka / Rebecca / Pocahontus, Tatanka Iyotake / Sitting Bull, and Joseph Brant / Thayendanegea are a few of the many historical figures who have created a path for me to follow. As I continue, I am constantly surprised by the openings, new understanding, and comprehension these directions lead me to.

There are many who have helped me in that search for a path to tread down. Here are a few of them: Tom Hill, Patricia Hiemstra, Sylvia Thelan, Zdenak Konicek, Ken Chubb, Shirley Barrie, Norman Denver, Carolyn Vesely, Sheila Butler, Madeline Lennon, Victoria Henry, Elizabeth Weatherford, and Andrew Smith.

And friends who have it made it a fun adventure: Hulleah J. Tsinhnahjinnie, Amos Adetuyi, Floyd Kane, ElizaBeth Hill, Samuel Thomas, Daniel David Moses, Louise Noguchi, Rosalie Favell, Wanda Nanibush, and Darlene Naponse, to name just a few.

I have a brother and three sisters—Michael, Bunny, Beverley, and Betts (Doxtater)—who are artists in their own fields. Their constant creativity invites me to remain true in the quest for innovation and thoughtfulness. My parents George and June Doxtater were hard-working, sacrificing their own talents and artistry to make ends meet.

Barr Gilmore makes the working environment a continuous joy. I thank him for his keen eye and dedication to detail. I want to thank the editor Laurel Saint Pierre and Lucas Elke at Type A for making this book as excellent as possible.

I am forever grateful to the Art Gallery of Hamilton—namely, Melissa Bennett, Tobi Bruce, Melissa Neil, Shelley Falconer, Christine Braun, Greg Dawe, Paula Esteves Mauro, and Bo Shin.

And to David W. Penney and Jennifer Lynn Wood at the National Museum of the American Indian, and Greg Hill, Audain Chair and Senior Curator of Indigenous Art at the National Gallery of Canada.

Big thanks to the essay writers and contributors for *Shelley Niro: 500 Year Itch*.

I know I cannot include every one in this condensed testimony, however. I am so grateful for the galleries, art centres, and all who have supported and exhibited my work throughout the years. I also thank the Canada Council for the Arts, the Ontario Arts Council, and the Indigenous Curatorial Collective for supporting my work throughout the years.

Most of all, I thank my family, my husband Celestino, my daughters Naoga and Stella and my granddaughter Raven, whom I've had to leave at different times to pursue knowledge in the making of art.

Nya Weh.

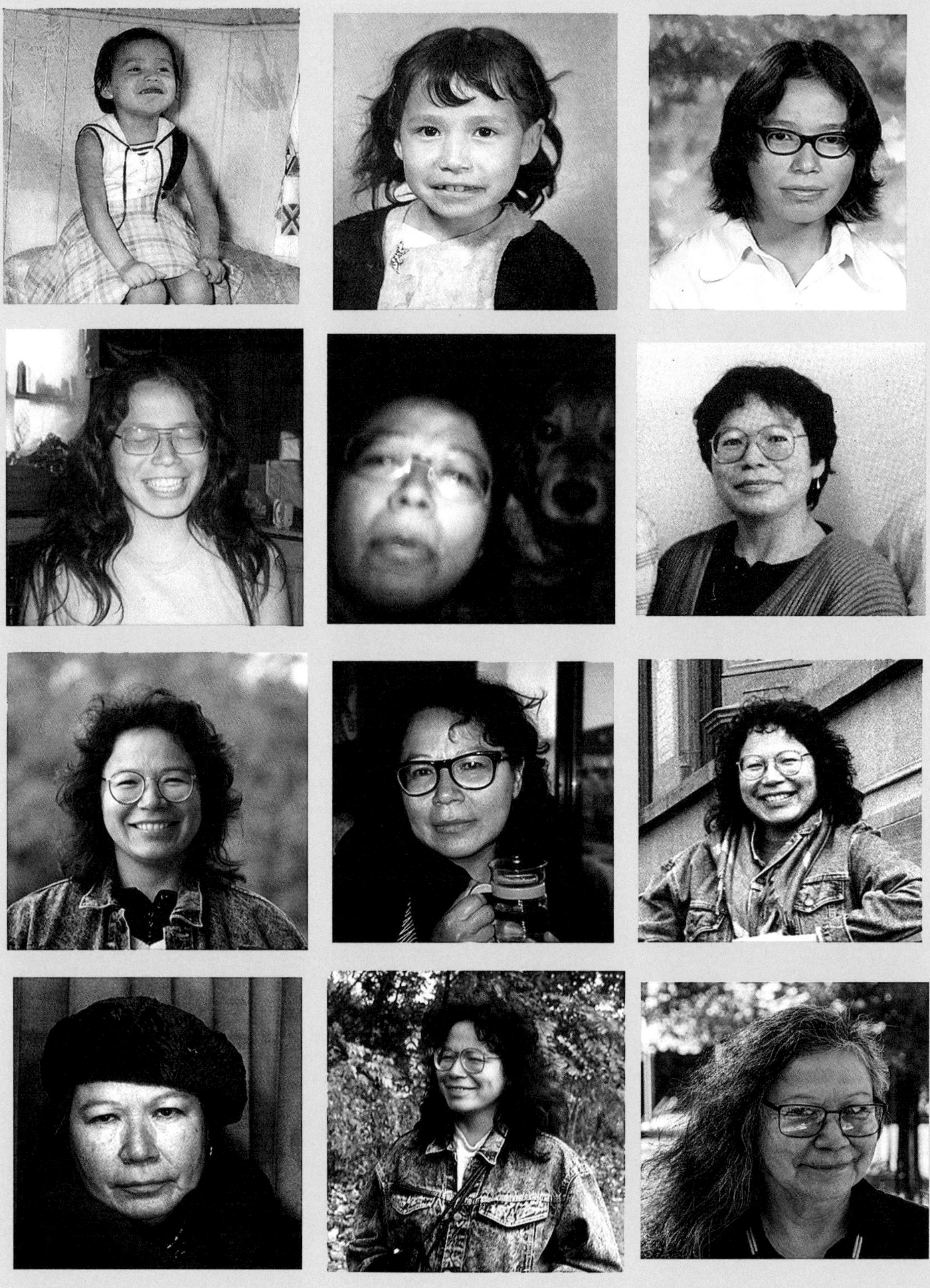

SHELLEY NIRO

Shelley Niro is a Bay of Quinte Mohawk (Kanyen'kehaka) and member of the Six Nations of the Grand River, Turtle Clan.

Niro attended a graphic arts course at Durham College in Oshawa, concentrating on photography, drawing, and art history. Years later, she went to the Ontario College of Art in Toronto, where she graduated with Honours. In 2019, she received an honorary doctorate from the Ontario College of Art and Design University.

Shelley was the inaugural recipient of the Aboriginal Arts Award, presented through the Ontario Arts Council in 2012. In 2017, Niro received the Governor General's Award in Visual and Media Arts from the Canada Council for the Arts, the Scotiabank Photography Award, and the Hnatyshyn Foundation Reveal Award. She is an honorary Elder in the Indigenous Curatorial Collective. In 2019, Niro received the Paul de Hueck and Norman Walford Career Achievement Award from the Ontario Arts Foundation.

Niro has recently completed film production on *Café Daughter.* Her film work has received support from Telefilm Canada, the Indigenous Screen Office, Ontario Creates and the Northern Ontario Film Office.

Recent exhibitions of Niro's work include: *Shelley Niro: woman, land, river* (2019, Art Gallery of Peterborough, Ontario); *Something Cold and Hard Like Winter* (2020, Robert Langen Art Gallery, Waterloo, Ontario); *A Good Long Look* (2021, Art Gallery of Southwestern Manitoba, Brandon, and Dunlop Art Gallery, Regina, Saskatchewan); *Greater New York* (2021/2022, MoMA PS1, New York); and *Boundless* (2022/2023, Art Gallery of Windsor, Ontario).

Melissa Bennett is Curator of Contemporary Art at the Art Gallery of Hamilton. She received a MA in Art History and Graduate Diploma in Curatorial Studies at York University, and a BFA in Photography at the Nova Scotia College of Art and Design University. She has held previous positions at Gallery 44 Centre for Contemporary Photography, Toronto; Stephen Bulger Gallery, Toronto; and the Canadian Museum of Contemporary Photography, Ottawa. Her current and recent projects include a major solo exhibition of the works of Duane Linklater, Michèle Pearson Clarke, Nathan Eugene Carson, and Kareem Anthony Ferreira with his father Roger Ferreira. She has been a writer and editor for many exhibition catalogues.

Greg Hill is the National Gallery of Canada's inaugural Audain Chair and Senior Curator of Indigenous Art, an artist, and a Kanyen'kehaka member of the Six Nations of the Grand River Territory. Throughout his career, Hill has been dedicated to expanding the collection, display, and recognition of Indigenous art. He has curated several important retrospective exhibitions for senior Indigenous artists in Canada, as well as a series of contemporary international Indigenous art exhibitions. Hill has led the establishment of a world-leading collection of major works at the NGC, by many of the most significant contemporary Indigenous artists of our time.

David W. Penney was appointed as the first Associate Director of the newly organized Museum Scholarship Group at the National Museum of the American Indian (NMAI) in 2011, after a long career at the Detroit Institute of Arts, which included being Chief Curator and then Vice President of Exhibitions and Collections Strategies. His exhibitions of note include: *Kay WalkingStick: An American Artist*, with co-curator Kathleen Ash-Milby, at the NMAI (2015/2016); *Indigenous Beauty: Masterworks of American Indian Art from the Diker Collection* for the American Federation of Arts (2015/2016); *Before and After the Horizon: Anishinaabe Artists of the Great Lakes*, with co-curator Gerald McMaster, at the Art Gallery of Ontario (2014); *The American Indian: Art and Culture Between Myth and Reality* for De Nieuwe Kerk Amsterdam (2012/2013); and *Art of the American Indian Frontier: The Collecting of Chandler and Pohrt* and *Ancient Art of the American Woodland Indians* at the National Gallery of Art, Washington, DC (1992–1993 and 1985). His publications include the exhibition catalogue for *Before and After the Horizon: Anishanaabe Artists of the Great Lakes* (2013), and "Native American Art: Pre-contact" for the *Oxford Bibliographies for Art History and Native North American Art*.

AUTHOR BIOGRAPHIES

Lori Beavis is Executive Director of Centre d'art daphne, the first Indigenous artist-run centre in Tiohtià:ke / Mooniyang / Montreal. Beavis is an independent curator, art educator, and art historian. Identifying as being of Michi Saagiig (Mississauga Anishinaabe) and Irish-Welsh descent, she is a citizen of Hiawatha First Nation at Rice Lake, Ontario. Her curatorial work, art practice and research articulates narrative and memory in the context of family and cultural history, and reflects on cultural identity, art education, and self-representation.

Sally Frater holds an Honours BA in Studio Art from the University of Guelph and an MA in Contemporary Art from the University of Manchester, Sotheby's Institute of Art. As the daughter of immigrants from the Caribbean, she is interested curatorially in decolonization, space and place, Black and Caribbean diasporas, photography, art of the everyday, and issues of equity and representation in museological spaces. She is currently the Curator of Contemporary Art at the Art Gallery of Guelph and co-director of Artistic Programs at Emerging Curators Institute.

Adriana Greci Green, PhD, is curator of Indigenous Arts of the Americas at the Fralin Museum of Art at the University of Virginia, where she endeavors to reconnect artworks in the collection with their communities of origin and to uncover the Indigenous histories and experiences they reflect. Research interests include Anishinaabe quill art and basket production in the context of transcultural interactions and multigenerational struggles to retain access to the land base and assert Treaty Rights; the material expressions of sovereignty and treaties; and the contexts in which material culture, art, dress, and cultural performance are produced and circulated.

Bryce Kanbara is a visual artist/curator and proprietor of you me gallery in Hamilton. He was a founding member and first administrator of Hamilton Artists Inc. and has held curatorial positions at Burlington Art Centre, Art Gallery of Hamilton, Glenhyrst Art Gallery of Brant, and Art Gallery at the Japanese Canadian Cultural Centre, Toronto. He was Executive Director of the Toronto Chapter, National Association of Japanese Canadians; Visual Arts, Crafts & Design Officer at the Ontario Arts Council; Member of the Governing Council, Hamilton Centre for Civic Inclusion; and Co-chair of the Board of Directors, Workers Arts & Heritage Centre, Hamilton.

Madeline Lennon is a Professor Emerita of Visual Arts at Western University, in London, Ontario. Her fields of expertise are women artists in the modern and contemporary periods, and Renaissance and Baroque art history. She has curated a number of exhibitions and contributed articles and catalogue essays to a variety of publications, including art websites.

Nancy Marie Mithlo (Chiricahua Apache) is a professor of Gender Studies and core faculty with the American Indian Studies Interdepartmental program at the University of California, Los Angeles. Mithlo's curatorial work has resulted in nine exhibitions at the Venice Biennale. A life-long educator, Mithlo has taught at the University of New Mexico, the Institute of American Indian Arts, the Santa Fe Community College, Smith College, California Institute of the Arts, Occidental College, and the University of Wisconsin-Madison. Her book *Knowing Native Arts* was published by the University of Nebraska Press in 2020.

Hulleah J. Tsinhnahjinnie was born into the Bear Clan of the Taskigi (Seminole) Nation and for the Tsi'naajínii Clan of the Diné (Navajo) Nation. She was adopted into Keet Gooshi Hit (Killer Whale Fin House) and the Laxsgiik (Eagle Clan) of Metlakatla. Tsinhnahjinnie is a Professor in the Native American Studies Department and Director of the C.N. Gorman Museum at University of California Davis.

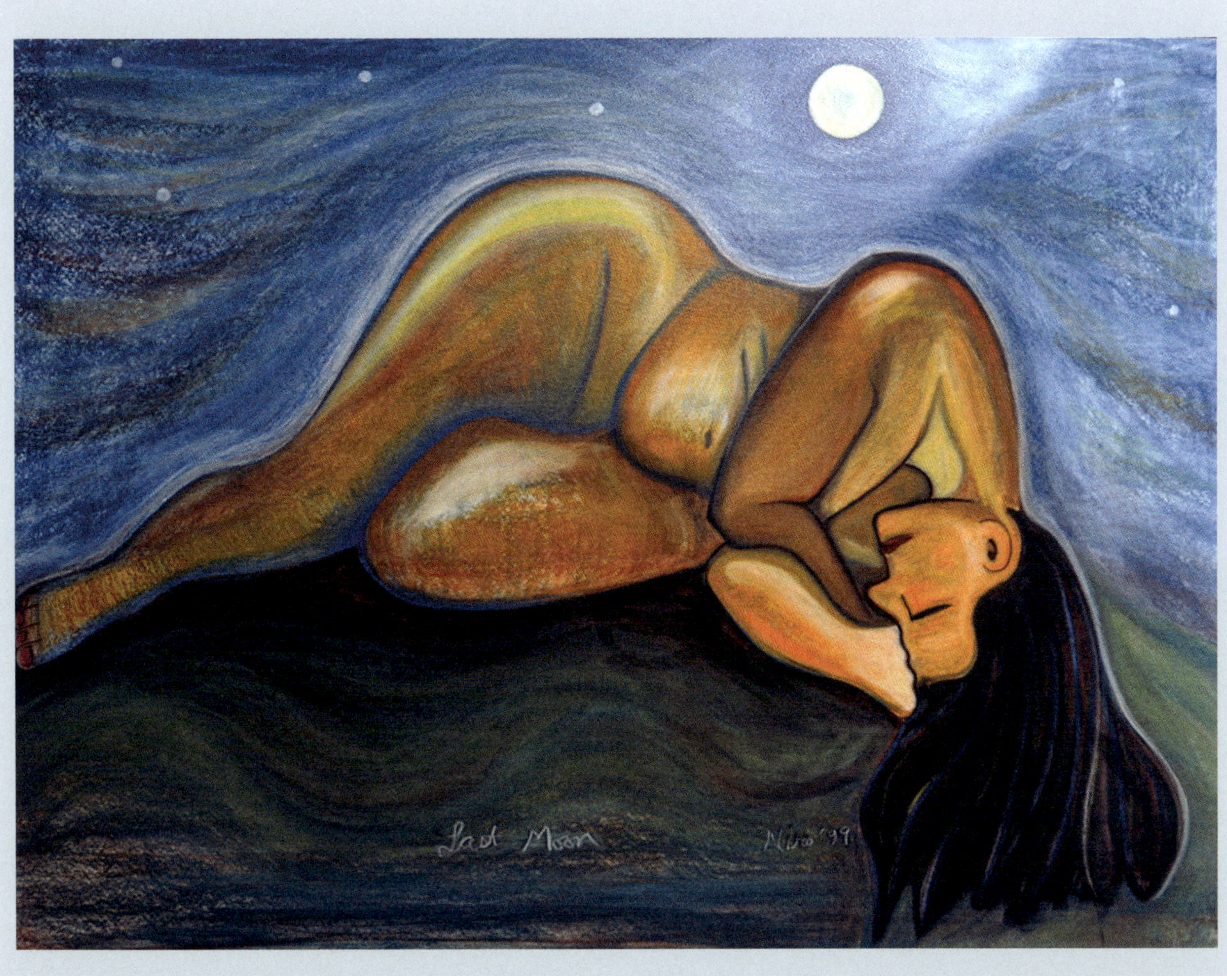

The Last Moon, 1999

First edition published in 2023 on the occasion of the travelling exhibition *Shelley Niro: 500 Year Itch*

Book design by Barr Gilmore
Edited by Laurel Saint Pierre
Copy edited and proofread by Bryne McLaughlin
Publication coordinated by Melissa Neil,
Special Projects Coordinator, Exhibitions & Publications,
Art Gallery of Hamilton
Digital colour work by Gas Company Inc., Toronto
Production and printing by Type A Print, Toronto

Cover image: Shelley Niro, *Pandemic Moon (Post-Industrial / Pre-Colonized)*, 2023

ISBN 978-1-897407-35-6
Printed in Belgium

Library and Archives Canada Cataloguing in Publication
Shelley Niro, 1954–
Shelley Niro: 500 Year Itch
Contributing authors: Melissa Bennett; Greg Hill;
David W. Penney [et al.]

Shelley Niro: 500 Year Itch is organized and circulated by the Art Gallery of Hamilton with the Smithsonian's National Museum of the American Indian (NMAI) and with curatorial support from the National Gallery of Canada, and is curated by Melissa Bennett (Art Gallery of Hamilton), Greg Hill (National Gallery of Canada), and Dr. David W. Penney (National Museum of the American Indian).

Smithsonian's National Museum of the American Indian
1 Bowling Green, New York, NY 10004
AmericanIndian.si.edu
May 27 to December 31, 2023

Art Gallery of Hamilton
123 King Street West, Hamilton, ON L8P 4S8
artgalleryofhamilton.com
February 10 to May 26, 2024

National Gallery of Canada
380 Sussex Drive, Ottawa, ON K1N 9N4
gallery.ca
June 14 to August 18, 2024

Vancouver Art Gallery
750 Hornby St, Vancouver, BC V6Z 2H7
vanartgallery.bc.ca
September 21, 2024 to February 2, 2025

Remai Modern
102 Spadina Crescent East, Saskatoon, SK S7K 0L3
remaimodern.org
Winter 2025

All photography by Shelley Niro, unless otherwise noted: Lawrence Cook (pp. 6, 9–10, 16–17, 20–21, 46–53, and 68–69); Robert McNair (pp. 14–15, 18–19, 58, 62–63, 97, 99, 118, 138–149, 246, 248, 284–286, 214, 216–217, and 288–289); Larissa Issler (pp. 66–67, 206–207); National Gallery of Canada (pp. 90–94, 212–213, and 242–243); Vtape (pp. 115–116, 119–121, and 125–130); Joseph Hartman (pp. 153–155); and Toni Hafkenfsheid (pp. 194–195).

The terminology in this volume was edited using *Elements of Indigenous Style* (2018) by Gregory Younging, except where Indigenous authors requested otherwise.